19/7/68

THE AMERICAN LEGAL SYSTEM

Also by Lewis Mayers

The Federal Service

The Law of Business Contracts

Introduction to the Law of Business Corporations

Shall We Amend the Fifth Amendment?

The Machinery of Justice

THE

AMERICAN

LEGAL

Revised
Edition # SYSTEM

THE ADMINISTRATION OF JUSTICE IN THE

UNITED STATES BY JUDICIAL, ADMINISTRATIVE,

MILITARY, AND ARBITRAL TRIBUNALS

By Lewis Mayers

HARPER & ROW, PUBLISHERS

NEW YORK, EVANSTON, AND LONDON

FIRST EDITION

LIBRARY OF CONGRESS CATALOG CARD NUMBER: 63-17711

D-O

Contents

Preface to the Revised Edition   vii

Preface to the First Edition   ix

Acknowledgments   xi

INTRODUCTION   1

PART I. THE COURTS   3

1. The Dual Judicial Power—National and State   4
2. Criminal Proceedings: Basic Aspects   11
3. Criminal Proceedings: Investigation   42
4. Criminal Proceedings: Prosecution   76
5. Civil Proceedings: Objectives   151
6. Civil Proceedings: Jurisdiction   184
7. Civil Proceedings: Procedure   225
8. The Courts as a Check on Executive Action   289
9. The Courts as a Check on Investigation   306
10. The Courts as a Check on Legislation   313
11. The Courts as Molders of the Law   338
12. Court Organization and the Administration of Justice   367
13. The Personnel of the Courts: Judges, Jurors, and Lawyers   379

PART II. ADMINISTRATIVE TRIBUNALS AND THEIR
SUPERVISION BY THE COURTS   417

14. Enforcement Proceedings   422

15. Proceedings Against Private Parties Other Than Enforcement
Proceedings   464
16. Permissions and Grants   477
17. The Adjudication of Private Disputes   489
18. The Personnel of Administrative Tribunals   499

PART III. MILITARY TRIBUNALS AND THEIR
CONTROL BY THE COURTS   507

19. Courts-Martial: Proceedings Against Members of the Armed
Forces   508
20. Military Tribunals Exercising Jurisdiction Over Civilians in
Domestic Territory   533
21. Tribunals for Offenses Against the Laws of War   538
22. Tribunals Constituted by Military Government in Occupied
Territory   545

PART IV. VOLUNTARY ABRITRATION TRIBUNALS AND
THEIR CONTROL BY THE COURTS   549

Appendix A. Selected References   563
Appendix B. Bibliography   568
Appendix C. Selected Provisions of the Constitution of the
United States of America   574
Index of Cases   577
General Index   582

Preface to the Revised Edition

In the first edition of this volume it was said that American justice is in ferment—that the scene is changing before our eyes. The developments of the past decade have amply vindicated that assertion, rendering many of the details, and in a number of instances extensive passages, of the original volume no longer accurate.

The rapid pace of change in the organization of state judicial systems and in judicial selection methods, for example, has called for much revision, as have also the growth of post-conviction procedures, the imposition of new judicial checks on legislative inquiries, and the emergence of novel problems in connection with the formulation and enforcement of federal court mandates. But perhaps the most extensive revisions have been those called for by the far-reaching decisions of the U.S. Supreme Court during the past few years, imposing new restrictions on state procedures in law-enforcement and in criminal prosecution.

The revision has by no means been confined to changes in content necessitated by these new developments. The entire text has been re-examined, resulting in extensive changes in arrangement and in treatment. An attempt has been made to take note of the most significant titles among the unprecedented outpouring of writings on the administration of justice—academic, judicial, legislative, and professional—that has marked the past decade.

Entering upon an exposition of our then comparatively pastoral legal system a century and a quarter ago, de Tocqueville lamented that "ordinary readers will complain that I am tedious, lawyers that I am too concise." This perennial dilemma was sufficiently acute when the original edition of this volume was prepared. The intervening decade has of course rendered it still more intractable.

November 1, 1963   **L.M.**

Preface to the First Edition

Despite the keen interest in American institutions observable abroad, foreign knowledge of our legal system is still fragmentary. In the presence of what a leading British jurist has declared to be "such a multiplicity both of laws and of jurisdictions as has seldom existed in a single civilized community," even the well-equipped foreign observer is understandably perplexed.

Indeed even the informed American, familiar with the other aspects of our polity, and seeking to form a clear picture of our legal institutions, faces a baffling task. Of special works and learned papers on one or another phase, perhaps as found in a single state, there is a bewildering profusion, continually expanding at an increasing, to some an alarming, rate. But even the systematic student—if not indeed the experienced lawyer seeking ready clarification of some aspect not made familiar to him by his own experience—may well be dismayed by this embarrassment of riches. Nowhere is there to be found, between two covers, a systematic account of our legal institutions—as distinguished from our law—in all their varied aspects. This lack the present volume purposes to supply.

The account is not restricted to an exposition of the current situation. The historical roots of the chief legal institutions of today are also traced. And, too, current proposals for reform, to which the author has made bold in some cases to add proposals of his own, have been given attention.

The volume is not confined to the field occupied by the courts. The vast area of adjudication by administrative tribunals is reviewed at some length, as is also adjudication by voluntary arbitral tribunals, and by the several types of military tribunals, including the special types brought into existence by war and occupation. In short, wherever under American law a tribunal may sit in judgment on the legal rights of those before it, the functioning of that tribunal, and its relation to the total structure, are set forth, resulting, it is hoped, in an integrated account of the entire fabric of American justice.

The task of reducing to a completely accurate summary statement the manifold complexities of a legal system compounded of forty-eight local systems harnessed in parallel with a pervasive national sysetm is obviously fraught with difficulties. To the extent that they may not have been completely overcome, the author would bespeak the indulgence so disarmingly invoked by Blackstone two centuries ago: "And if in some points he is still mistaken, the candid and judicious reader will make due allowance for a search so new, so extensive and so laborious."

LEWIS MAYERS

April 1, 1954

Acknowledgments

In those fields of legal procedure in which my own experience has been little or none I have been fortunate in obtaining the invaluable assistance of specialists. The chapters on criminal justice were reviewed in manuscript by Professor George H. Dession, Lines Professor of Law, Yale University; those on administrative justice by Professor Bernard Schwartz, Professor of Law, New York University; the chapter on courts-martial by Colonel F. W. Schweikhardt, USAF, Staff Judge Advocate, Continental Air Command, United States Air Force; and the section on arbitration by Mr. J. Noble Braden, executive vice-president of the American Arbitration Association, and by Dr. Martin Domke, international vice-president of that association. To all these gentlemen I am under the deepest obligation for their generosity. It is perhaps needless to add that, in these as in other portions of the volume, where opinions are expressed, the responsibility is solely my own.

Over the extended period during which this manuscript and its mimeographed predecessors (in use as a text at The City College of New York) have been in preparation, I have had help at innumerable points of detail from those who have served as Fellow in Law at that institution, particularly from Messrs. Allen Landowne, Algernon Miller, and Martin Gallin, all now of the New York bar, and, more recently and more especially, Mr. Isaac Ciechanowicz of the editorial staff of the *Annual Survey of American Law.*

April 1, 1954   L.M.

I am greatly indebted to Professor Robert B. McKay, Associate Dean of the School of Law of New York University, who as reviewer examined the first edition with a thoroughness above and beyond the call of duty, and gave me the benefit of his comments and criticisms.

November 1, 1963   L.M.

THE AMERICAN LEGAL SYSTEM

INTRODUCTION

The area of government with which this volume concerns itself is wanting in any accepted name—hence the ambiguous one, the "legal system."

In evaluating the legal institutions of a country, attention is often focused to a disproportionate extent on the rules of law in force there, to the neglect of the machinery and personnel by which those rules are applied. Clearly, rules of law, whether expressed in legislative enactments or in the recorded opinions of the courts, merely set forth guide lines and directives for the tribunals which will today decide particular cases. In a sense, these writings merely expound what the rules of law have been in the past, and what they ought to be in the future; what the rule is in the immediate present in any particular case is the rule applied, whether correctly or incorrectly, by the tribunal deciding that case. However sound and well-articulated may be the legislative or judicial formulations of the rules that ought to be applied and enforced in particular cases, they avail the citizen little unless they are expeditiously, expertly, and impartially applied and enforced. Hence, the true significance of our body of laws can be appraised only in the light thrown by an understanding of the way in which our tribunals operate.

Our concern is thus with every variety of proceeding by which a tribunal of whatever description, armed with the power of the state, adjudicates legal rights. Proceedings in which a private party is pitted against the state, whether as plaintiff or defendant, and in which private parties are pitted against each other occupy almost the entire field of such adjudication, but not quite the whole. Where the individual or the collectivity contemplating a course of action risks governmental interference unless permission or dispensation is first obtained, the process by which such permission or dispensation is granted or denied is also, in its largest sense, an adjudication; and with this machinery too we are concerned.

Finally, we are concerned with a large and increasingly important field

1

of governmental action in which no possibility of adverse action against the individual is involved. On the contrary, the petitioner is here seeking something from the government, whether a subsidy payment, an unemployment insurance benefit, an allotment of quarters in a housing project, a position, a loan, a contract, a patent, a land grant—the list is long and grows ever longer. Though not commonly so classified, the process by which the application for such a benefit is granted or denied may also be one of adjudication, and as such within our purview.

As we survey the vast array of agencies engaged in adjudication as thus conceived, we find several distinct types of tribunal. Dominating the scene are, of course, the courts, a complex and multiplex hierarchy. Side by side with the courts looms a bewildering profusion of executive agencies, federal, state, and local, which also engage in adjudication on a vast scale. Still another large area of adjudication is occupied by voluntary arbitration tribunals, functioning in many cases under authority of law and empowered to make awards enforceable by the courts. Finally, we observe a far-flung system of criminal justice, and occasionally of civil justice also, administered by military tribunals.

This vast complex of agencies, deriving power from half a hundred or more separate sources yet all integrated more or less fully by a common ancestry, a common tradition, and a common constitution, is no static institution. Self-criticism is the theme of much of the current literature of American justice. More than many other parts of our institutional apparatus it is in ferment and change. Hence the impossibility of a wholly accurate picture. The scene is changing before our eyes.

Pre-empting as they do the major categories of adjudication, and exercising also in varying degree a control over all tribunals of other kinds, the courts occupy a central and dominant place in this complex of tribunals; and it is to them that attention must first be given.

PART I   THE COURTS

Our courts play a dual role. They function chiefly as self-contained tribunals, dealing with legal proceedings which are initiated as well as terminated within their framework. On the other hand, many of them function also as supervisors of the other types of tribunal—administrative, military, and arbitral—for which our laws provide. Part I deals with their self-contained operations only. Their role in the supervision of other tribunals is discussed in the subsequent sections dealing with those tribunals.

Except for a few federally controlled areas, our court structure is everywhere dual. In each of the fifty states, there functions a self-sufficient state system of courts. Side by side with these courts there sit, in each of the states, one or more federal courts, functioning for the most part in complete isolation from the state courts (yet on occasion interlocked with them in complex fashion) and responding, through a system of intermediate appellate courts, to the Supreme Court of the United States.

But that court is not only the supreme appellate court of the federal court structure: to it come also, for final disposition, appeals from the courts of the fifty states—only in those relatively few cases, however, in which there is involved a "federal" question. Thus the Supreme Court, unique among the courts of the land, brings together strands from all the diverse parts of our judicial web.

At innumerable points in the daily operation of our legal machinery the dual character of our court structure is of importance. A grasp of the chief features of the dual system is thus central to our subject.

1

The Dual Judicial Power—National and State

1. THE JUDICIAL STRUCTURE UNDER THE ARTICLES OF CONFEDERATION. 2. THE ALLOCATION OF JUDICIAL POWER BY THE CONSTITUTION. 3. THE JUDICIARY ACT OF 1789. 4. THE CONSTITUTION AND THE JUDICIAL POWER OF THE STATES.

The court structure of the British colonies in eighteenth century America was that of a virtually autonomous court system in each colony (subject to a very limited appellate review in London), together with a few admiralty courts, based on selected Atlantic ports, responsible directly to the Crown, and not connected in any way with the colonial governments.

The repudiation of royal authority by legislatures of thirteen of the colonies was accompanied by the destruction of all British control of the courts in those colonies and the disappearance of the jurisdiction of the admiralty courts there. For several years, the courts of the former colonies, each now a separate sovereign state, were the exclusive organs of judicial power, the courts of each state being completely autonomous.

1. THE JUDICIAL STRUCTURE UNDER THE ARTICLES OF CONFEDERATION

The adoption of the Articles of Confederation (which, though submitted to the states in 1777, did not secure ratification till 1781) marked the genesis of a federal judicial power, albeit an extremely feeble one. "The United States in Congress assembled" were to have "the sole and exclusive right and power of . . . appointing courts for the trial of piracies and felonies committed on the high seas and establishing courts for receiving and determining finally appeals in all cases of captures"; and the Congress itself was to act as "the last resort on appeal in all disputes and differences . . . be-

4

tween two or more states concerning boundary jurisdiction or any other cause whatsoever." Similar jurisdiction was given to the Confederation in "all controversies concerning the private right of soil claimed under different grants of two or more states."

Of the judicial powers thus vested in the Confederation, only that relative to prize cases was exercised to any considerable extent. Even prior to the adoption of the Articles, the Continental Congress, acting on a suggestion from General Washington, had assumed appellate jurisdiction over the decisions of the state courts in prize cases, though such jurisdiction could, in the nature of the case, be effective only with the permission of the state concerned. When in 1779 the Articles had secured the assent of all but one state, the Congress established a regular court, the "Court of Appeals in Cases of Capture." A total of 109 cases was decided by the Congress and this court, which survived until superseded by the new federal courts under the Constitution.

The jurisdiction over controversies between states was also exercised in one case, Pennsylvania v. Connecticut, a dispute regarding jurisdiction over certain western lands. A number of other disputes between states were however settled before trial.[1]

2. THE ALLOCATION OF JUDICIAL POWER BY THE CONSTITUTION

The initiation, on April 30, 1789, of the new national government under the Constitution effected a profound change in the position of the thirteen states. They ceased to be sovereignties and subjected themselves to the superior power of the national constitution and the national government; for the constitution which they had adopted proclaimed that "this constitution, and the laws of the United States which shall be made in pursuance thereof; and all treaties made, or which shall be made, under the authority of the United States, shall be the supreme law of the land; and the judges in every state shall be bound thereby, any thing in the constitution or laws of any state to the contrary notwithstanding."

From the standpoint of our subject, the basic feature of the new frame of government was the provision (in Article III) creating "the judicial power of the United States." This newly created judicial power, it was provided, was to "extend to" certain enumerated classes of cases only.[2]

[1] For an account of the judicial powers exercised under the Confederation see 131 U.S. (Appendix) xix.

[2] These cases are, to follow the sequence of the enumeration in the Constitution, the following:

1. "all cases, in law and equity, arising under this Constitution, the laws of the United States, and treaties made, or which shall be made, under their authority."
2 "all cases affecting ambassadors, other public ministers and consuls."
3. "all cases of admiralty and maritime jurisdiction."
4. "controversies to which the United States shall be a party."

The classes of cases to which the Constitution ordained that the new federal judicial power should "extend" were, on the one hand, cases dealing with certain subjects—e.g., "cases of admiralty and maritime jurisdiction"—and on the other, cases between certain parties—e.g., "controversies between citizens of different states." Some of the classes of case enumerated, such as "cases arising under this Constitution," had had no existence before the adoption of the Constitution. Others, such as both the admiralty cases and those between citizens of different states, already mentioned, were cases which the state courts were regularly adjudicating.

It is essential to understand that the enumeration in the Constitution of these classes of cases as falling within "the judicial power of the United States" did not, as is so often supposed by persons not familiar with the matter, automatically place those cases within the jurisdiction of the federal courts thereafter to be created by Congress. To what extent a case falling within "the judicial power of the United States" may actually be within the jurisdiction of a federal court depends upon the statute governing that court.[3]

That the federal courts depend for their jurisdiction not upon the Constitution but upon Congress follows necessarily from the fact that the courts are created by Congress and not by the Constitution. Indeed, even the Supreme Court is in fact a creation of Congress, not of the Constitution. The Constitution, it is true, commands that the federal judicial power shall be vested in part in "one supreme court" and it designates "the Chief Justice," presumably meaning the chief justice of that court, as the presiding officer of the Senate when engaged in the trial of the President on an impeachment. But it does not fix the number of judges of the court; until this was fixed by act of Congress (as it was by the Judiciary Act of 1789, since when

---

5. "controversies between two or more states."

6. "[controversies] between a state and citizens of another state" (which, as construed by the Eleventh Amendment, means a controversy in which a state institutes a proceeding against a citizen of another state, but not the reverse).

7. "[controversies] between citizens of different states." (Such a case is commonly referred to as a "diversity of citizenship" case, a term which embraces also a controversy between a citizen and an alien.)

8. "[controversies] between citizens of the same state claiming lands under grants of different states."

9. "[controversies] between a state, or the citizens thereof, and foreign states, citizens or subjects" (which, as construed by the Eleventh Amendment, embraces a controversy in which a state institutes a proceeding against a citizen or subject of a foreign state, but not the reverse).

[3] To this statement there is only one exception: cases to which a state is a party, and cases involving ambassadors, other public ministers, and consuls *must* be within the jurisdiction of at least one federal court—the Supreme Court of the United States. For, alone among the federal courts, that court has its original jurisdiction—but not its incomparably more significant appellate jurisdiction—fixed by the Constitution itself.

it has been modified from time to time by several subsequent acts) the court could not exist.

As to the inferior federal courts, their creation is left by the Constitution wholly to Congress, without even a moral mandate for their creation, such as exists in the case of the Supreme Court.

Because the first article of the Constitution is devoted to the legislative power, the second to the executive, and the third to the judicial, the impression is likely to arise that the three corresponding departments of our national government are coordinate and parallel, a notion unfortunately encouraged by many elementary textbooks. It needs but slight reflection, however, to perceive that the legislature and the executive are brought into existence by the Constitution itself, while the judiciary is not, and can indeed have no existence until Congress and the President have acted. This fact is central to an understanding of the federal judicial power.

3. THE JUDICIARY ACT OF 1789

The provision in the new Constitution for a new body of legislation, in force throughout the states, did not itself necessarily require the provision of a new set of courts. Conceivably, the administration of the federal laws might have been left in the first instance to the state courts, with only a power of review in a federal appellate court; and indeed Congress has occasionally, in creating new statutory rights, provided that action to enforce such rights may be brought in state as well as federal courts. The investment of the state courts with all original jurisdiction in federal cases was, in fact, strongly urged by several members of the Constitutional Convention and of some of the ratifying conventions of the states, who opposed vigorously the proposal to give Congress the power to create inferior federal courts. Such, indeed, was the plan adopted on the formation of the German Empire eighty years later. Such is the system in force in Canada and in Australia.

That alternative was not, however, seriously considered by the first Congress, which, within the first six months of its existence, enacted the celebrated Judiciary Act of 1789.[4] This act created not only the "one supreme court" commanded by the Constitution but a system of inferior federal courts—a system which remains one of the distinctive features of our governmental structure.

Upon these inferior federal courts Congress, in that act, conferred original jurisdiction over most but not all of the classes of cases enumerated in the Constitution as falling within "the judicial power of the United States." With respect to several important classes of cases in which it gave

[4] Act of Sept. 24, 1789, 1 Stat. 73.

them jurisdiction, however, it did not include all cases in that class in such jurisdiction. Thus, controversies "between citizens of different states" were to be cognizable in the federal courts only if the amount in controversy exceeded a certain figure; and that provision (with the figure increased) remains in force to this day. At no time in our history has the plaintiff in such a case enjoyed the right to bring the case in a federal court if the amount in controversy fell below the statutory minimum. The like is true of any "diversity of citizenship" case, however important, which is by its nature incapable of being characterized as having any given "amount in controversy." Such cases remain, as before the Constitution, exclusively within the jurisdiction of the state courts.

So too with respect to a case traditionally within the jurisdiction of the state courts, but to which "the judicial power of the United States" now extended because there might be involved in the case a provision of the Constitution or of a federal statute or treaty, making it in consequence a case "arising under this Constitution, the laws of the United States, and treaties."[5] The Judiciary Act gave the inferior federal courts no jurisdiction of such a case. It was to be decided, as before the Constitution, by the state courts; but power was conferred on the Supreme Court to review the state court decisions, in certain cases only, with respect solely to the federal question involved.

The refusal of the first Congress in these instances thus to place within the jurisdiction of the inferior courts all the possible cases falling within the "judicial power of the United States" illustrates unmistakably the proposition, obviously of fundamental importance, that these federal courts, receiving their very existence from Congress, have only such jurisdiction as Congress chooses to give them.

Moreover, even as to the cases which it did place within the jurisdiction of the federal courts, the first Congress did not in all cases make such jurisdiction exclusive.

In cases of diversity of citizenship, for example, even where the amount in controversy exceeded the prescribed minimum, and was thus cognizable in the federal courts, the plaintiff was still permitted to institute his action if he so preferred in the state courts, as formerly, the defendant in turn being then permitted, in certain circumstances, to have the case removed, if he so preferred, to the federal court. Thus was made plain the further view entertained by the first Congress, and never since questioned, that Congress was not required, on vesting the federal courts with jurisdiction over a given class of cases, to withdraw from the state courts the jurisdiction they had previously had of that class of cases. It could confer jurisdiction, in such cases, on the federal courts *concurrently* with the state courts.

But, as the Judiciary Act of 1789 also made clear, Congress equally

[5] See p. 185.

had the power, on conferring on the federal courts jurisdiction over a class of cases hitherto cognizable in the state courts, to withdraw completely from those courts all further jurisdiction of such cases, vesting such jurisdiction exclusively in the federal courts. This it did, for example, with respect to "all cases of admiralty and maritime jurisdiction."

Finally, to the extent that it permitted a state court to retain initial jurisdiction of a case within the federal judicial power, Congress could provide for the withdrawal of such jurisdiction at any stage of the case prior to its adjudication, and the transfer of the case to the jurisdiction of a federal court.

The Judiciary Act of 1789 thus disclosed at the outset all the varied alternatives from among which Congress could choose in designing the pattern of jurisdiction of the federal courts, and of the relation of their jurisdiction to that of the state courts, in cases to which "the judicial power of the United States shall extend." The basic pattern thus established by Congress in 1789 has persisted, despite important changes, to our own day.

4. THE CONSTITUTION AND THE JUDICIAL POWER OF THE STATES

The transfer of some of the existing jurisdiction of the state courts to federal courts and the review of certain of their decisions by those courts were thus clearly envisaged by the Constitution. As we have seen, these results promptly ensued upon the establishment of the new government. But the Constitution contained a provision which in still another direction imposed an important limitation on the judicial power of the state. This was the provision (Article IV, Section 1) requiring that "full faith and credit shall be given in each state to the public acts, records and judicial proceedings of every other state." This provision, which will be more fully considered at a later point, required every state court to give recognition and enforcement to the judgments of the courts of every other state; to apply in certain cases the laws of a sister state rather than its own; and even to exercise jurisdiction, in deference to the law of a sister state, in certain cases in which it would have refused to act were only the law of its own state involved.[6]

Eighty years later the Fourteenth Amendment added a momentous prohibition on the states—that no state shall "deprive any person of life, liberty, or property, without due process of law." The chief importance of this provision has been in its imposition of restrictions on the states when acting within unquestioned fields of state power; but in the field of state judicial power it has acted as a further limitation. Even though a case is clearly outside the ambit of federal judicial power, and thus prima facie within the judicial power of the states, it may nevertheless, under the

[6] See p. 244.

"due process" provision just cited, be beyond the judicial power of a particular state. The important consequences of this withdrawal from a state of the power it formerly enjoyed, to confer on its courts jurisdiction of any case clearly within state as opposed to federal judicial power, will in due course become evident.[7]

[7] See pp. 205 ff.

2

Criminal Proceedings: Basic Aspects

1. CONSTITUTIONAL FRAMEWORK OF CRIMINAL PROCEDURE. 2. CRIMINAL JUSTICE AND THE FEDERAL SYSTEM. 3. PETTY OFFENSES, MISDEMEANORS, AND FELONIES. 4. CONVICTION ON PLEA OF GUILTY VS. CONVICTION AFTER TRIAL. 5. THE RIGHT TO COUNSEL. 6. THE DEFENDANT'S EXEMPTION FROM QUESTIONING. 7. THE WITNESS'S PRIVILEGE AGAINST SELF-INCRIMINATION. 8. EXCLUSION OF EVIDENCE IMPROPERLY OBTAINED. 9. THE CRIMINAL CONTEMPT PROCEEDING.

It would hardly be accurate to describe the criminal proceeding as one for the punishment of crime; for it is also employed for the punishment of some offenses not regarded as crimes in the ordinary meaning of the term. Our system of criminal justice, developed to deal with crimes of violence, and at a later stage with crimes against the security of the state, has in more recent times been increasingly employed to deal with commercial crimes, and, departing still further from its original uses, with offenses against regulatory laws—offenses which are not inherently antisocial, and in some of which, indeed, criminal intent is not a necessary element. Despite these enlargements of the function of the criminal proceeding, its procedural pattern has remained substantially unaffected.[1]

In the main, however—and this fact should ever be kept in mind in appraising our machinery of criminal justice—the crimes (as distinguished from petty offenses and infractions of regulatory statutes) which concern

[1] The criminal conviction of a corporation, which can be punished only by inflicting financial injury on the often unknowing stockholders, is of course itself a complete departure from the basic concept of criminal justice. Moreover, in at least one field of federal criminal prosecution—under the antitrust laws—despite the principle repeatedly asserted and often applied that a criminal statute must be sufficiently definite to apprise a potential violator of the criminality of his contemplated conduct, the unlawful conduct is defined by the statutes only in language so broad and vague that even the constant guidance of experienced counsel may not avail to insure against a court's subsequently declaring particular acts to be violative of the statute.

11

our courts and law enforcement agencies are typically clear-cut infractions of elementary rules of social order for the protection of the person and of property, crimes against property constituting the majority.[2]

A criminal act quite commonly, in addition to being a breach of public order, inflicts injury on a private party. Under our system of justice however (unlike that of some Continental countries and, indeed, unlike our own in its primitive days),[3] the proceeding for the punishment of crime may not be used for the simultaneous redress of the private wrong, although the evidence required for either purpose is the same.[4] An entirely separate and independent civil proceeding must be instituted by the person or persons injured by the criminal act.[5] If the defendant in that proceeding has already been found guilty of the offense involved, that finding may not, except in a few cases specially singled out by statute, be regarded in the civil proceeding as having established, even prima facie, the defendant's responsibility for the injurious act, and may not indeed ordinarily be introduced in evidence.[6] Proposals aimed at correcting this duplication of proceedings, itself the result of history rather than of design, have received little attention.

1. CONSTITUTIONAL FRAMEWORK OF CRIMINAL PROCEDURE

The administration of criminal justice presents two distinct and quite different faces. On the one hand, we look to it, far more than to our civil justice, for the safety of life and property and the preservation of public order. On the other hand, it is through the processes of criminal prosecution

[2] For the thesis that the predominance of such crimes in the offenses reaching the criminal courts is to be accounted for by the fact that most crimes of a more sophisticated character either escape detection or are not brought to the attention of the authorities by the victims (often corporations rather than individuals) see Sutherland, White Collar Crime (1949).

[3] Hilkey, Legal Development in Colonial Massachusetts, 1630–1686, 142 (1910).

[4] An illegal act may also entail, in addition to criminal and civil liability, the loss of a license; but this can in many cases be effected only by a third proceeding (usually before an administrative tribunal).

[5] Occasionally, however, a statute punishing a crime provides as an additional penalty the imposition of a fine proportioned to the injury inflicted on the victim, the fine to be collected in the usual way, and then turned over to the victim. See for example N. Y. Penal Law, Sec. 1302, regarding misappropriation of property by a fiduciary or officer.

[6] An important statutory exception to this rule is the provision of the federal antitrust laws making a criminal conviction under those laws prima facie evidence against the defendant in a civil suit (for an injunction or for triple damages) subsequently brought against him by a private party, based on the same violations of the statute. 15 U.S. Code, Sec. 16(a). Occasionally, a state court has declared that in exceptional cases the traditional rule may be departed from to the extent of admitting the criminal conviction to be introduced in evidence, without, however, giving it the effect of prima facie proof accorded it in the federal statute just cited. See, for example, Mineo v. Eureka Security Fire Insurance Co., 125 A.2d 612 (Superior Court of Pennsylvania, 1956).

more than through any other agency of government that oppression and deprivation of personal freedom may be inflicted upon the individual by a hostile officialdom. Our criminal procedure reflects this inescapable dilemma.

Viewed in another aspect, the problem is that of devising a procedure whose mesh is strong and fine enough to hold the professional criminal, yet flexible and loose enough to allow the innocent (and in certain cases, even the unfortunate, casual lawbreaker) to free himself from its toils. That the problem is a difficult if not an insoluble one is manifest.

Although there is a copious body of rules, both traditional and statutory, designed to protect the individual against unfairness and oppression at the hands of law-enforcement officers or courts, that protection rests basically on constitutional provisions. Hence, in advance of an examination of particular features of our criminal procedure, it is essential to understand the constitutional framework within which that procedure operates. That framework varies as between federal and state criminal justice.

In federal criminal proceedings, the constitutional position is simple. From the beginning there have been the prohibitions against unreasonable searches and seizures, double jeopardy, and compulsory self-incrimination; the requirements of grand jury indictment and of trial by a jury of the district; the right of confrontation of witnesses and of the assistance of counsel; and the prohibition of excessive bail, of excessive fines, and of cruel and unusual punishments.[7] The specific application of these provisions has been established by a long series of pronouncements by the Supreme Court. In the last two decades the Court has had the further opportunity to express its views through its power, conferred by Congress, to make rules for the conduct of all federal criminal proceedings.

The constitutional framework of state criminal proceedings is more complex, and can best be understood in the light of its historical development. During the century and a half of the colonial regime, criminal justice was almost solely the affair of the individual colony. Nevertheless, certain basic English statutes applied to all the colonies; and in serious cases the possibility did exist of a check by the Privy Council, acting on appeal. For almost a century following the Revolution, however, no corresponding national check existed. Except for the prohibition against state ex post facto laws, the Constitution embodied no restriction on the criminal procedures of the state. Nor (contrary to what is so often popularly assumed) did the Bill of Rights—i.e., the ten amendments to the Constitution adopted in 1791—add any restriction whatever on the states; it applied

[7] The provision for jury trial is found in the Constitution as originally adopted. The remaining provisions are found in the Fourth, Fifth, Sixth, and Eighth amendments to the Constitution. These amendments became effective on December 15, 1791. At that time, the federal courts, authorized by Congress in September 1789, had been operating only a short time.

only to the newly created federal government. In the field of criminal justice each state remained undisputed sovereign.

This sovereignty of the state continued unimpaired until 1868, when a provision was added to the Constitution which was in due course to subject the entire criminal procedure of the states (and indeed their civil procedure and much of their substantive law as well) to the supervision of the Supreme Court. The Fourteenth Amendment, adopted in that year, contained among other provisions, the injunction that "no state shall deprive any person of life, liberty or property without due process of law, or deny to any person within its jurisdiction the equal protection of the laws."

The phrase "equal protection of the laws" was novel; but the phrase "due process of law"—far the more important in the event—was a familiar one. It had been employed in an English statute as early as the fourteenth century, apparently in the same sense as the phrase "the law of the land," which had been employed in Magna Carta in the previous century; and the two phrases recur in subsequent English statutes and in colonial statutes and documents. Neither phrase appears in the Constitution as originally adopted, but the requirement of "due process of law" as to federal action was added to the Constitution in 1791 (in the Fifth Amendment). Precisely what was in the mind of the draftsmen, or what was understood to be the significance of the phrase by the Congress which proposed it or by the state legislatures which ratified the amendment embodying it, is impossible to discover; there is no contemporay discussion that has come down to us.[8] Certain it is however that half a century later, when Joseph Story, a justice of the Supreme Court and one of America's great jurists, published his commentary on the Constitution, destined to become a classic, the phrase was considered of so little significance that he devoted only a few lines to its discussion, treating it indeed as auxiliary to the prohibition against compelling one to be a witness against himself in a criminal case.[9]

Meanwhile, a similar requirement (employing in every case the phrase "law of the land") had been embodied in most of the eleven state constitutions adopted during the Revolution; in the decades that followed, the same requirement, usually in the phrase "due process of law" was incorporated in the new constitutions of perhaps all the states created during that period. When, therefore, the corresponding language was embodied in the Fourteenth Amendment, its effect was apparently simply to reinforce

[8] It has been pointed out that the phrase had sometimes been used in England and the colonies as the equivalent of indictment and trial in the usual course, i.e., by grand jury and petit jury, respectively. Inasmuch as both those procedural features were specifically guaranteed by other provisions of the Amendments added to the Constitution in 1791, it would seem that the phrase was intended to have a broader meaning.

[9] Commentaries on the Constitution of the United States, 660 (1833).

by federal authority a principle already in force throughout the states; the federal power was to be invoked because the Negro, newly emancipated, could not safely be remitted for "due process of law" solely to a state officialdom dominated by his late masters.

Up to that time, the phrase, now five centuries old, and made familiar by the usage of three-quarters of a century in the federal Constitution and later in state constitutions, had as applied to criminal prosecution simply meant that each person was entitled to have the established legal procedure followed in his case. The phrase did not import that the procedure was fair or rational; for it had come into use at a time when trial by ordeal and by combat still prevailed, and had grown old during a period when the most crucial essentials of a fair procedure—the right of the accused to be informed in advance of the accusation against him, to confront his accusers, to have the assistance of counsel—had not yet been firmly established. At the time this phrase was incorporated in the Constitution as a limitation on federal proceedings, the accused was still denied the elementary right to testify on his own behalf; yet no one thought of suggesting that "due process of law" required that he should be given that right, nor was that suggestion made during the decades that followed. Indeed, when the Fourteenth Amendment was adopted, that right was still denied him in almost every state.

It is not surprising therefore that the inclusion in the Fourteenth Amendment of the requirement that the states afford "due process of law" attracted but little attention; far less indeed than did the provisions contained in the same amendment for extending citizenship to the Negro and for reducing the congressional representation of any state which disfranchised him. Yet, the incorporation in the Constitution of this seemingly subsidiary restriction upon the states laid the foundation for the development of that supervisory power of the federal courts, and particularly of the Supreme Court, over all the operations of state government, which has revolutionized our federal system. Here we are concerned, however, with only one phase of that revolutionary process—that related to criminal procedure. In that field the process may be said to have begun in 1884, when the Court was asked to declare it to be a denial of due process of law for a state to put one on trial for a felony on an information filed by the prosecutor, without indictment by a grand jury. The Court rejected this contention,[10] as it did other contentions made in a steadily growing stream of criminal cases in the next half century. As late as 1915 the Court declared that "it is perfectly well settled that a criminal prosecution in the courts of a State . . . conducted according to the settled course of judicial

---

[10] Hurtado v. California, 110 U.S. 516. As early as 1881, however, the conviction of a Negro had been set aside as a denial of "the equal protection of the laws" because Negroes had been excluded from service on the grand jury which indicted him. Neal v. Delaware, 103 U.S. 370.

proceedings as established by the law of the State . . . is 'due process' in the constitutional sense."[11]

It was not indeed until 1927 that a state court conviction was for the first time set aside on the ground that the unfairness of the procedure employed rendered the conviction void for want of due process.[12] In recent decades there has been a marked increase in the number of state convictions carried to the Court, and a substantial number of them have been set aside by it. In addition, the lower federal courts, under a greatly expanded power accorded them by the Court in habeas corpus proceedings,[13] have also set aside numerous state convictions.

At particular points in our review of criminal procedure we shall consider the requirements which the Supreme Court has said are demanded by the concept of "due process." Here it is sufficient to point out that the Fourteenth Amendment, the Supreme Court has repeatedly held, does not impose upon the states the necessity of incorporating in their criminal procedure all the features protective of the accused which the Constitution (and particularly the Fourth, Fifth, Sixth, and Eighth Amendments) makes mandatory in federal criminal proceedings. Thus it does not, in state proceedings, as already noted, require indictment by grand jury, nor does it apparently protect the accused against compulsory self-incrimination.[14] But what it does require is not so easily stated, for Congress has never exercised its power in this field, and the Supreme Court has of necessity confined its pronouncements (not in all cases consistent with its previous holdings) to questions raised in the particular cases which state criminal defendants have happened to bring before it.

When, some three decades ago, the Court entered upon its historic task of setting up, as implicit in the constitutional requirement of "due process," minimum standards of fairness in state criminal procedure, it declared that what is required is only that that procedure shall not violate a "principle of justice so rooted in the tradition and conscience of our people as to be ranked as fundamental."[15] As late as 1943 the Court de-

---

[11] Frank v. Mangum, 237 U.S. 309, 326.

[12] Tumey v. Ohio, 273 U.S. 510 (1927).

[13] See pp. 136 ff.

[14] This has never, however, been expressly held by the Supreme Court. The view that a state may compel the accused to testify, and that such compulsion would not be a denial of due process (a view expressed in incidental discussion even in some opinions of the Court) is based on the Court's refusal to disturb the conviction in Twining v. New Jersey, 211 U.S. 78 (1908) and in Adamson v. California, 322 U.S. 46 (1947). But in neither of those cases was the accused compelled to take the stand; his failure to take the stand voluntarily in his own defense was, under the law of the state, a circumstance which the jury might take into consideration in passing on his guilt, and the judge had so instructed the jury. Several of the present members of the Court have made clear that they would regard not merely compulsion upon the accused to take the stand, but compulsion even on a witness to answer despite a plea of self-incrimination, as a denial of due process.

[15] Snyder v. Massachusetts, 291 U.S. 97, 105 (1934).

clared that all that was required of the state procedure was that it "must be consistent with the fundamental principles of liberty and justice which lie at the base of our civil and political institutions."[16] But in more recent years the Court has imposed on the states novel requirements which can hardly be regarded as "rooted in tradition" or as "fundamental," if the test is to be whether they are to be found in the institutions of the other countries in which the Anglo-American legal tradition prevails. Thus in one recent case the Court imposed upon the states a far-reaching rule respecting the admissibility of evidence in criminal proceedings on the desirability of which the state courts and legislatures have long been sharply divided, which was non-existent in this country half a century ago, which does not obtain in any other country in which the Anglo-American legal tradition prevails, and the absence of which can hardly be said to deprive the criminal defendant of "life" or "liberty" "without due process of law."[17] Indeed, it is notable that that constitutional phrase, supposedly the sole warrant for the Court's action, is sometimes completely absent from opinions delivered by members of the Court in this field.

The criminal procedure of each state thus operates within a twofold constitutional framework—composed on the one hand of the specific limitations contained in the state constitution (as to which there is in certain respects not a little variance among the states) and on the other hand, of the overriding federal requirement of "due process of law" as interpreted from time to time (not always predictably), as cases come before it, by the Supreme Court of the United States.

[16] Buchalter v. New York, 319 U.S. 427, 429. The best exposition of the doctrine in these broad terms is found in Palko v. Connecticut, 302 U.S. 319 (1937). It has been condemned by Justice Black of the Supreme Court as assuming "that this Court is endowed by the Constitution with boundless power under 'natural law' periodically to expand and contract constitutional standards to conform to the Court's conception of what at a particular time constitutes 'civilized decency' and 'fundamental liberty and justice.'" Adamson v. California, 332 U.S. 46, 69 (1947). Despite this plea for self-restraint on the part of the Court, Justice Black has joined in several decisions placing restrictions on the criminal procedure of the states based not, as Justice Black contends they should be, on the provisions of the Bill of Rights, but only on the concept of "fundamental justice" (e.g., Griffin v. Illinois, 351 U.S. 12 [1956], requiring the state to furnish the indigent defendant desiring to appeal his conviction with a copy of the trial record, etc., at public expense). Should a majority of the Court ever adopt Justice Black's (and more recently, apparently, also Justice Brennan's) view that the Fourteenth Amendment automatically makes the first ten amendments to the Constitution applicable to the states, the states which now seldom or never impanel grand juries (the practice in some of them long antedating the Fourteenth Amendment), would be compelled to institute grand jury indictment for felonies; all pending felony prosecutions in those states not founded on grand jury indictments would have to be dismissed, and a foundation would exist for the demand on the part of all persons now imprisoned on felony convictions that their convictions be reversed!

[17] Mapp v. Ohio, 367 U.S. 643 (1961).

Congressional regulation of state criminal justice

The Fourteenth Amendment, in addition to furnishing the basis for federal judicial supervision of state criminal procedure, expressly empowers Congress "to enforce, by appropriate legislation, the provisions" of the Amendment. This grant of power would seemingly enable Congress to prescribe minimum standards in state criminal procedure, having the protection of the defendant as their objective. But Congress has taken no action whatever in this field. It has been content to leave the formulation of such standards to the courts—essentially to the Supreme Court—to be achieved piecemeal, ad hoc, as cases presenting alleged abuses of state criminal justice have happened to come before them. The resulting uncertainties and confusions will appear at various subsequent points. The enactment by Congress of a code of minimum standards of state criminal procedure would, it is believed, effect a major improvement in the administration of criminal justice in a number of the states; and it is in the state courts that criminal justice is chiefly administered.

2. CRIMINAL JUSTICE AND THE FEDERAL SYSTEM

Needless to say, the federal structure of American government is the source of various complexities in criminal justice not found in countries with a unitary government. These chiefly concern, on the one hand, the allocation, as between the state and the nation, of power to punish particular acts; and, on the other, the power of the national government to exercise control over the criminal justice of the states, whether by legislation or court action.

Jurisdiction of offenses

The states have of course power to punish all offenses against their statutes committed within their borders (except in such enclaves within the state on which Congress has under the Constitution the power "to exercise exclusive legislation"); while the national government has power to punish (1) offenses committed anywhere in the United States against the federal statutes of general application, (2) offenses against special statutes applicable to the District of Columbia or to the federal enclaves within the several states,[18] and (3) offenses of "piracy and felonies com-

---

[18] Congress is empowered by the Constitution (Art. I, Sec. 8) "to exercise exclusive legislation in all cases whatsoever" not only over the district to be the seat of government but also "over all places purchased by the consent of the legislature of the state in which the same shall be for the erection of forts, magazines, arsenals, dockyards, and other needful buildings." Federal property is not thus subject to the federal power of exclusive legislation unless purchased "by the consent of the legis-

mitted on the high seas, and offenses against the law of nations."[19]

✻ The assumption by the Constitution of power in the national government to punish offenses committed on the high seas is in accord with the established international practice that a sovereign nation may punish certain crimes committed on the high seas, whether by one of its own nationals or by one of another country, should the vessel on which the offense was committed put into its ports with the offender aboard. It is the practice of sovereign nations to assume also to punish acts which, though committed outside their borders, were intended to and did produce detrimental effects within their borders. Thus, a federal statute makes punishable correspondence by a citizen of the United States, "wherever he may be," with any foreign government in relation to a dispute between that government and the United States.[20] Some of our states have similarly assumed to punish acts or omissions committed beyond their borders; and the Supreme Court has declined to say that such an assumption of jurisdiction is necessarily beyond the power of the state.[21] Thus, one who sends into another state an infernal machine, designed to and which does kill the intended recipient there, may, if the statutes of the state in which the fatal explosion took place so provide, be there constitutionally prosecuted for the homicide, even though he has never set foot in that state. It is perhaps unnecessary to point out that what is here under discussion is the constitutional power of the state to prosecute the offender once it has

---

lature of the state." State laws giving such consent have in a number of instances contained reservations and exceptions, making it uncertain whether the particular area purchased is subject to state or to federal legislation. As to places subject to exclusive federal legislation, Congress has not enacted a federal criminal code but has provided instead, in the Assimilative Crimes Act of 1948, that persons who commit within a federal enclave an act not punishable under federal law, but punishable under the law of the state in which the enclave is situated shall be guilty of a federal offense (18 U.S. Code, Sec. 13). The constitutionality of this statute (which applies also to land "reserved or acquired" by the United States) was upheld in United States v. Sharpnack, 355 U.S. 286 (1958).

[19] In addition, there is found on the Indian reservations a compound of federal, tribal, and state criminal jurisdiction. Certain offenses anciently cognizable by tribal tribunals remain so, except to the extent that such jurisdiction may have been specifically extinguished by federal statute. As to crimes not traditionally so cognizable, the federal courts have jurisdiction both of federal offenses proper and of offenses punishable by the federal courts under the Assimilative Crimes Act, referred to in the preceding note. (Courts of Indian Offenses, created by the Department of the Interior, have jurisdiction to punish infractions of reservation regulations). In 1953 Congress empowered any state in which a reservation is situated to exercise criminal jurisdiction over it if the state so elects. (18 U.S. Code, Sec. 1162).

[20] 18 U.S. Code, Sec. 953.

[21] Thus, the high court of North Carolina upheld the conviction in that state of a resident of Virginia (arrested while on a visit to North Carolina) for failing, while residing in Virginia, to provide support for his illegitimate child, then residing with its mother in North Carolina. State v. Tickle, 77 S.E.2d 632 (1953). The United States Supreme Court refused to review. 346 U.S. 938 (1954).

succeeded in finding him in, or procuring his removal to, its own territory. The questions involved in procuring such removal will be considered at a subsequent point.

Moreover, a state may constitutionally exercise jurisdiction to punish acts committed by its own citizens in places outside the territory of any sovereign—that is, on the high seas. The state retains such jurisdiction at least to the extent that it may make such conduct outside the state punishable should the citizen return to the state. Such at least would seem to be the result of a case decided by the Supreme Court in 1941. In that case, the Court upheld the constitutionality of a Florida statute prohibiting citizens of the state from using diving equipment in taking sponges in certain sponge beds located in the high seas beyond the territorial limits of the state.[22] It is not clear whether the reasoning of the Court would be equally applicable to the attempt by a state to punish one of its own citizens for an act committed in another state, and having no intended consequences within its own borders.

Since federal law extends throughout the territory of every state, a single act may violate both state and federal law. Every state, for example, has a statute punishing robbery; and the federal statutes punish the robbery of a national bank. Such a robbery thus violates both the federal statute and the statute of the state in which the robbery occurs. Both state and federal governments may independently prosecute, convict, and punish the robber; and his conviction on the charge brought against him by the state government will not preclude his subsequent prosecution and conviction by the federal government, despite the provision in the Constitution that no man shall in the federal courts twice be put in jeopardy of life or limb.[23] Whether his conviction in the federal courts will preclude a subsequent state prosecution for the same act will depend upon the construction given by the courts of the state to the corresponding double jeopardy provision in the state constitution. It will not be precluded by the prohibition of the Fourteenth Amendment of denial by a state of "due process of law."[24]

Though the power of Congress to create criminal offenses is limited (except in areas under exclusive federal control) to those few fields to which the Constitution confines the national legislative power, its power to regulate interstate and foreign commerce has been extensively used to supplement the power of the states in dealing with offenses exclusively within state cognizance, such as kidnapping, gambling, the white slave trade, etc. Moreover, the commerce power has been employed in statutes designed to hamper the flight of suspects, defendants, or witnesses from the state in which an offense against state law has been committed. The power

[22] Skiriotes v. Florida, 313 U.S. 69 (1941).
[23] Abbate v. United States, 359 U.S. 187 (1959).
[24] Barkus v. Illinois, 359 U.S. 121 (1959).

of Congress to levy taxes on any species of property or any occupation has also been employed to supplement state criminal statutes, as in connection with gambling and the trade in narcotics.

Federal criminal prosecutions in the state courts

All crimes created by federal statute (and there can be no crimes against the United States except those created by statute)[25] are prosecuted exclusively in the federal courts. In the early days of the federal judicial system, Congress assumed to vest in the state courts, concurrently with the federal courts, jurisdiction of the prosecution of certain crimes created by federal statute.[26] The constitutional question presented, whether Congress may vest jurisdiction to try such crimes in such state courts as might be authorized by the law of the state creating them to entertain such prosecutions, has never been squarely passed upon by the Supreme Court —perhaps because, despite the early statutes referred to, such state court prosecutions were in fact rather rare; but the answer would seem to be in the affirmative.

The question may at this time be regarded as academic however, since the statutes now provide for the prosecution of federal criminal offenses exclusively in the federal courts. However, as recently as the period during which the prohibition amendment to the Constitution was in force (1919–1933), there was discussion in responsible quarters of the practicability of shifting to the state courts a portion of the tremendous burden of criminal prosecutions which the federal prohibition statutes had imposed on the federal courts.

Intervention of federal courts in state criminal proceedings

The "supremacy clause" of the Constitution (in Article VI) declares that federal law, whether embodied in the Constitution itself, or in federal statutes or treaties, "shall be the supreme law of the land." The same clause provides that "the judges in every state shall be bound" by this supreme federal law "any thing in the constitution or laws of any state to the contrary notwithstanding." Should it be claimed that the state courts in a criminal proceeding have nevertheless failed to observe the federal law,

---

[25] In the decade following the adoption of the Constitution it was indeed contended by some, including a few federal judges, that the federal government could punish offenses against it in the absence of any statute, such offenses being "crimes at common law"—a reference to the fact that in the development of the English legal system the courts had indeed entertained prosecutions of offenses not defined by statute, a practice which was carried over to the colonies, and which in theory at least still continues to be recognized in some of our states. It was definitely decided in 1816, however, that the Constitution did not admit of federal "crimes at common law." See 1 Warren, The Supreme Court in United States History, 433–442 (rev. ed., 1935).

[26] See Warren, Federal Criminal Laws and State Courts, 38 Harv. Law Rev. 545 (1925).

the defendant may, under federal statutes, invoke the aid of the federal courts. This aid may, under the statutes, be extended in various ways in various classes of cases: by enjoining the state authorities from continuing with a prosecution; by ordering them to release a person held in custody and awaiting trial; by ordering a removal of the prosecution to the federal court; and, far most important, by reversing a conviction and either ordering the prosecution terminated or authorizing a new trial in the state court.

In addition, in certain cases, though no disregard of federal law by the state is alleged, the federal interest involved in the case, owing to the defendant's being a federal officer or an officer of a foreign country, may under the statutes authorize the intervention of the federal courts.

The circumstances under which these varied forms of federal intervention may be invoked are discussed at subsequent points in connection with the particular stages of the criminal proceeding at which they occur.

3. PETTY OFFENSES, MISDEMEANORS, AND FELONIES

Not all punishable offenses are crimes. There is a category of petty offenses to which the term crime is not commonly applied, even though the procedure for trying and punishing them resembles that used in connection with crimes. The dividing line between such petty offenses,[27] tried under a summary procedure, and those minor violations of law which are classified as crimes and are tried by the more formal procedure used for more serious crimes, is not a clear-cut one, like so many other aspects of our legal system, the product of history rather than of strict logic. It is the severity of the punishment prescribed, rather than the inherent nature of the offense, which governs. Hence the line of division is by no means a uniform one. In any particular legal jurisdiction, it is ordinarily perfectly clear; but to make a statement accurately defining the line of division between the two categories of offenses the country over is impossible.

An approximate generalization is, however, practicable. Unimportant traffic violations, vagrancy, disorderly conduct, public intoxication, and the like are everywhere treated as petty offenses and are prosecuted under a

[27] The term "petty offense," though in common use, is unknown to the statutes of most of the state. Our legal nomenclature is wanting in this report, when contrasted with the very definite classification of offenses as contraventions, delicts, and crimes, found in some Continental countries. In the federal statute a petty offense is defined as one the penalty for which does not exceed imprisonment for six months or a fine of $500 or both. However, the federal statute (18 U.S. Code, Sec. 1) classifies a petty offense as merely one category of misdemeanor, whereas under state statues an offense classified as a petty offense is in most states below the grade of misdemeanor. The only significance of this federal classification of some misdemeanors as petty offenses apparently is that misdemeanors so classified, when committed in a federal enclave, may with the consent of the accused be tried, without jury, by a United States commissioner (see p. 52, note 20). 18 U.S. Code, secs. 3401–3402.

summary, non-jury procedure. Where the traffic violation, the breach of public order, or the infraction of a regulatory statute is of a more serious nature, it is usually treated as a crime, and is prosecuted in the same manner as are offenses against person or property. As to minor violations of regulatory statutes and ordinances, much diversity is found.

Criminal offenses or crimes (as distinguished from petty offenses) are classified in our law according to their gravity as either misdemeanors or felonies.[28] (Treason has in some classifications been treated as a separate category, but in modern American law it may be regarded as embraced in the category of felonies). This distinction is one which appears at various points in our criminal procedure. Upon this distinction may depend whether the accused may be arrested without a warrant; whether he may be brought to trial by the public prosecutor acting alone, or only after accusation by a grand jury; whether he is entitled to trial by jury; whether his conviction may entail loss of the right to vote or to hold public office, or, in the case of an alien, the right to remain in the United States. A grasp of the nature of the distinction is thus of prime importance.

The distinction is an ancient one in the English law; it is based on the punishment that may be imposed. Originally, a felony was any crime punishable by forfeiture of lands or goods or both (with or without capital punishment added); any other offense was a misdemeanor. Today, with the punishment of forfeiture of estate no longer known to our law, the distinguishing punishment which makes an offense a felony is, in virtually all the states, either the death penalty or imprisonment in a state prison. Since in many states, all sentences of imprisonment for more than a year involve imprisonment in the state prison, imprisonment for more than a year is also often treated as the distinguishing punishment for felony; and the federal statutes define a felony as an offense "which may be punished by death or imprisonment for a term exceeding one year."

4. CONVICTION ON PLEA OF GUILTY VS. CONVICTION AFTER TRIAL

Since the objective of a criminal proceeding is to procure the conviction of the defendant, the most satisfactory proceeding, from the standpoint of the law-enforcement authorities, is one in which the conviction results from a plea of guilty by the defendant. This plea obviates the trial otherwise necessary, and precludes the possibility of a reversal of the conviction on appeal, a possibility always present in a conviction after trial.

In every state, and in the federal courts as well, the majority of con-

[28] In some states an intermediate category of "high misdemeanor" is found, embracing some offenses which in most states would be classified as felonies.

victions—in some states the overwhelming majority—result from the defendant's plea of guilty.[29]

This does not mean that the majority of those arrested on criminal charges plead guilty. A mere arrest on such a charge does not compel the person arrested to plead to the charge at all. It is only after a more formal charge has been lodged against him, in the manner prescribed by law, that he is required either to plead guilty or to stand trial. As the reader is doubtless aware, and as will be brought out in subsequent pages, in a considerable proportion of the cases in which an arrest is made on the complaint of the police or the prosecutor the charge is dismissed at the preliminary hearing, or is dropped by the authorities, and no formal accusation is ever made. The cases in which the defendant is required to decide whether to plead guilty or to stand trial thus represent a selection by the prosecuting authorities of those cases in which the likelihood of a plea of guilty is good.

In view of the preponderant proportion of convictions resulting from guilty pleas, the relatively minor part played in our criminal justice by the courtroom trial is apparent. The drama of the criminal trial tends to create the impression, among those not familiar with the law-enforcement process, that the trial is the central feature of the process, and that it is the chief preoccupation of prosecutors and defense attorneys, and the chief activity of the judge. In fact, in the disposition of cases in which formal accusation has been lodged, the principal business of the prosecutor and of the defense attorney is negotiation, both as to the gravity of the offense to which the defendant will plead guilty (there being ordinarily a substantial range of alternatives here) and as to the prosecutor's recommendation with respect to sentence; and what chiefly occupies the judge is consideration as to whether he shall approve pleas of guilty to offenses less than those charged (or to only a portion of the several counts charged) and shall accept the prosecutor's recommendations for sentence.

Where the accused pleads guilty to the crime as charged, the reason presumably is that the evidence is so strong against him that he has no hope of escaping conviction. But he hopes, by saving the time of the court and prosecutor (and perhaps, incidentally, keeping from the court the more unsavory details of his crime), he may earn leniency in sentence; and he may have received assurances from the prosecutor that, to the extent that the court will be guided by the recommendations of the prosecutor, it will be so.[30]

---

[29] Of the 28,511 defendants convicted in the federal courts in the year ended June 30, 1962, only 3,872, or less than 14 per cent, were convicted after trial. The remainder pleaded guilty or nolo contendere. 1962 Report, Administrative Office of the U.S. Courts, 234.

[30] Some have pointed out that not all those who plead guilty at this stage are in fact guilty, at least of the crime charged. A defendant who has been unable to furnish bail has been in custody since his arrest, and thus continually subject to official

In a great proportion of the felony cases, however, the plea of guilty is made to a lesser crime than that charged in the indictment or information —either to a lower degree of the same felony, carrying a lesser penalty, or to a related misdemeanor. Such a plea will be accepted by the court only on the recommendation of the prosecutor, and will therefore be made by the defendant only in pursuance of a previous arrangement with the prosecutor. Manifestly, the power thus vested in the prosecutor is an enormous one; and it has been truly said that in the great numbers of cases in which he exercises it, he, rather than the court or the jury, administers the criminal law.

The virtually uncontrolled power thus exercised by the prosecutor may of course be, and unquestionably often has been, abused in favor of criminals possessed of political connections and doubtless, though far more rarely, in favor of criminals able to cause the prosecutor or one of his assistants to be bribed. Consequently, the control of the prosecutor's office, as much or more than control of the police, has often been the prize chiefly sought by those urban political machines which have been closely allied with, if not dominated by, the underworld. The remedy would seem to lie not in curbing the discretion of the responsible prosecutor, but in removing the office from political selection and in subjecting the local state prosecutor to some form of state-wide supervision cognate to that exercised over the local federal prosecutor by the Attorney General of the United States—matters to be discussed in subsequent pages.

The extent to which the authorities are successful in obtaining pleas of guilty depends of course chiefly on their success in having obtained evidence, whether admissions made by the accused or independent proof, which, in the event of a trial, is likely to insure a conviction. Effective prosecution of crime thus depends chiefly upon effectiveness in investigation. Hence, the importance of the limitations which the law places on the agencies responsible for the investigation of crime with respect to their power to interrogate suspects and witnesses, to search for physical evidence, and to eavesdrop, and on the admissibility at the trial of evidence obtained by these activities—limitations shortly to be examined.

In recent years, with the increasing availability of collateral attack on criminal convictions by postconviction proceedings, there have been a number of cases in which a convict sentenced on his plea of guilty has, perhaps after the lapse of years, asserted that his plea was made under a mistaken understanding of the penalty that could be imposed, perhaps induced by misrepresentations of the prosecutor; or because of threats or false promises of leniency; or because the defendant, unrepresented by counsel, was not aware of possible defenses which might be interposed on

---

pressure to induce him to plead guilty. The provision of counsel at or immediately after the preliminary hearing is particularly required for defendants in this category.

his behalf should he plead not guilty and stand trial. These developments have led to a new emphasis, in the administration of criminal justice, both on the need of the accused for counsel in connection with his plea, and the necessity for careful inquiry by the court, before accepting a plea of guilty, as to the understanding of the defendant as to the nature of the plea and its consequences, and as to the circumstances impelling him to make that plea instead of standing trial.[31]

5. THE RIGHT TO COUNSEL

The constitutional and statutory safeguards which protect the person accused of crime, most of which are relevant only to particular steps in a criminal prosecution, will be referred to at subsequent points. At this point note should, however, be taken of one pervasive constitutional right of the accused which may come into question at any stage of the proceeding— the right to have the assistance of counsel.

In seventeenth century England, a person accused of felony had no right to be represented by counsel at his trial. During the eighteenth century this rule was, however, greatly relaxed by the English courts. As with other features of English procedure, there appears to have been much variation in the colonies as to the extent to which they followed the English practice. In general, the right to counsel in felony cases appears to have been less rigorously restricted than in England; and by the time of the Revolution all restrictions on the right to counsel had apparently disappeared. Nevertheless, memories remained of judicial oppression of prisoners unrepresented by counsel; and a provision guaranteeing the right of counsel was included in no less than seven of the eleven original state constitutions. A corresponding provision, applicable to federal prosecutions, was included in the bill of rights added to the federal Constitution directly after its adoption. Similar provisions were adopted by the states subsequently created; and today all but one state has such a constitutional provision. That state—Virginia— has long had a similar statutory provision.

At the outset, it is necessary to take note of a basic distinction—the distinction between the defendant's right, on the one hand, to employ counsel and, on the other, the right to have counsel furnished him if he has not the means to employ counsel himself. For clarity, each of these two matters, often confused in discussions of this theme, may best be considered separately.

[31] The Rules of Criminal Procedure for the federal courts provide (Rule 11) that "the court. . . . shall not accept the plea [of guilty] without first determining that the plea is made voluntarily with understanding of the nature of the charge." The rule does not, however, specifically require that the nature or magnitude of the possible penalty be stated to the defendant.

Right to employ counsel

In order that he may exercise his right to employ counsel, a person under arrest must be informed of that right and must be afforded an opportunity to communicate with prospective counsel or with persons who may obtain counsel for him. There is undoubtedly room for improvement in the statutes of some states with respect to the obligation of the court to inform the defendant at all proper stages of the proceeding, if unrepresented, of his right to employ counsel, and to afford him a reasonable opportunity to do so. Nevertheless, it is doubtless correct to say that seldom is a person who has the resources to employ counsel denied the opportunity to do so. Such a person is normally aware of his right to do so even if not expressly so informed by the court.

Needless to say, however, in those cases, shortly to be mentioned, in which the person arrested before formal accusation is unlawfully held in custody instead of being promptly brought before a magistrate for preliminary examination, he is with equal disregard of the law denied opportunity to communicate with prospective counsel or with persons who may obtain counsel for him. Moreover, cases have undoubtedly occurred in which in the courts of some states ignorant defendants, who if given proper information and opportunity might have succeeded in procuring counsel, have been hustled before an unfriendly bench and a plea of guilty extracted in unseemly haste. Such a denial by a state court of the right to the assistance of counsel is not only a violation of the express provisions of the state constitution; it constitutes also a denial of the due process of law guaranteed by the federal Constitution; and a conviction thus obtained will be set aside by the Supreme Court. Equally repugnant to state constitutional guarantees and the federal due process guarantee is the forcing of a defendant to trail without affording him a reasonable opportunity for consultation with the counsel who is to represent him, or without affording counsel, on undertaking to represent the defendant, a reasonable opportunity to acquaint himself with the case and to prepare his defense.

On the whole, however, it may be said that the denial, to a defendant possessed of the means to employ counsel, of the opportunity to do so, and to procure adequate representation, constitutes a quite minor problem in American criminal justice. Of far more importance—indeed of an importance equaled by few others—is the problem of providing counsel for the defendant who is financially unable to employ counsel.

Right to have counsel furnished

The historical setting of the provision of the Constitution that "in all [federal] criminal prosecutions, the accused shall enjoy the right . . . to have the assistance of counsel for his defense" has already been reviewed.

In the light of this setting, it is clear that the provision was intended by its framers merely to insure that the counsel employed by the accused would be permitted to conduct the defense; the notion of any obligation on the part of the community to furnish counsel was still in the future. It is not surprising therefore that the doctrine now in force, that in all federal prosecutions an indigent defendant has a constitutional right to have counsel furnished him, is not one of long standing, but was on the contrary definitely promulgated by the Supreme Court only a quarter of a century ago.[32] A tradition had nevertheless for many decades prevailed in federal prosecutions in favor of furnishing the indigent accused with counsel. This tradition was crystallized in the federal criminal procedure rules promulgated by the Supreme Court in 1946, in the inclusive provision that: "If the defendant appears in court without counsel, the court shall advise him of his right to counsel and assign counsel to represent him at every stage of the proceeding unless he elected to proceed without counsel or is able to obtain counsel." Lack of funds for payment of assigned counsel has limited the usefulness of this provision, and legislation to insure that in each district competent counsel will be available to the indigent defendant has long been pending in Congress. Only with the enactment of satisfactory legislation of this character, and the routine annual appropriation of sufficient funds to make the legislation effective in practice, will the indigent's needs in the federal courts everywhere be met.[33]

In state proceedings, the provision of counsel for the indigent defendant rested until 1932 exclusively in state cognizance. In that year, in the famous Scottsboro case,[34] the Supreme Court initiated a series of rulings holding that the due process clause of the Fourteenth Amendment obligates the states to furnish trial counsel to the indigent defendant in certain cases— rulings which, ever wider in their application, culminated in the landmark Gideon case of 1963,[35] sweeping away all the limitations previously announced, and declaring that trial counsel must be provided in every case.

The Scottsboro case was a capital one, and from it and several subsequent capital cases the rule had become clear that the state must furnish counsel to the indigent defendant in every capital case. As to non-capital cases, however, the situation for three decades remained confused; the Court declined to lay down any definite criteria by which the state court could determine when it must furnish counsel to the defendant, despite the absence of any state statute requiring it to do so. During these decades, some thirty-five cases raising the question came before the Court. Yet all that emerged from those cases as a guide to the state courts was that "each case depends

---

[32] Johnson v. Zerbst, 304 U.S. 458 (1938).

[33] For an account of the present provision in the federal courts, in the absence of legislation, see Representation of Indigent Criminal Defendants in the Federal District Courts, 76, Harv. Law Rev. 579 (1962).

[34] Powell v. Alabama, 287 U.S. 45 (1932).

[35] Gideon v. Wainwright, 372 U.S. 335 (1963).

on its own facts," some of the relevant factors being the gravity of the crime, the complicated nature of the offense charged, and the age and education of the defendant. The uncertain state of the law during this long period furnishes a striking demonstration of the unsatisfactory character of the process by which, in the delineation of the rights of the accused—a matter so eminently susceptible of precise definition—the determination of the extent of the federal guarantee was left to piecemeal ex post facto improvisation by the Court, indulged in from time to time as relevant cases happened to come before it. Once the Court had announced that, to insure fairness to the defendant in a state criminal proceeding, state criminal procedure was by virtue of the Fourteenth Amendment subject to federal regulation, the situation plainly called for action by Congress, which has power, under that amendment, to enforce its provisions "by appropriate legislation." A precise definition by Congress thirty years ago, or at any time since, of the conditions under which a state may not carry on a prosecution against one unrepresented by counsel because of indigence would have avoided a vast amount of uncertainty and contention and would have insured the provision of counsel to thousands of unrepresented indigent defendants whose cases never reached the Supreme Court.

There is still ample need for congressional action. The Gideon case, arising out of the failure to provide counsel at a felony trial, does not make clear whether its reasoning applies also to prosecutions for misdemeanors, not to speak of petty offenses. Whether counsel must in all cases be provided at the preliminary examination or when the defendant's plea is taken, as well as at the trial, is also still uncertain.

A number of the states have thus been confronted with the necessity of making provision overnight for furnishing counsel to indigent defendants on a scale far greater than their own statutes or practices have hitherto required. Such statutes and practices have varied not a little from state to state. In all, counsel has been furnished in capital cases. In only about three-quarters of the states, however, it is furnished in cases of non-capital felony; and in only about half, to any extent in the case of misdemeanors. Moreover, the right to be furnished with counsel, where it has existed, has only rarely been extended to the indigent defendant at his preliminary examination, and equally rarely to the defendant who is being urged by the prosecutor to plead guilty. Where counsel has been furnished, the practice in most states has been for the court to request—or as the phrase is, assign—a local lawyer to act as defense counsel. Normally, the willingness of counsel so assigned to serve is known to the judge, or has been indicated to him in advance. In theory, it is the duty of any lawyer so assigned to accept the assignment; nor is it open to the defendant to object to the court's choice except on grounds such as that the counsel chosen is in fact hostile to the defendant.

The value of statutes of this character depends much on the provision made for compensating the counsel thus furnished the defendant. In a few states, no provision whatever is made for compensation; counsel assigned are expected to act out of a sense of obligation to their calling and to the community. In the remaining states the compensation provided is characteristically so meager as to be little more than a token payment. Manifestly, despite striking exceptions, the service rendered to the indigent defendant under these circumstances is inferior to that commonly rendered by properly compensated counsel privately retained.[36]

So much for the system of assigned counsel. For the rest, the matter is left mainly to philanthropy, whether that of organized legal aid societies, of bar association committees, or of individual members of the bar. The situation on this head is undoubtedly improving, but it is probably still true that in misdemeanor cases a majority of the indigent defendants, and in felony cases a large percentage, lack the assistance of competent counsel.

To correct this deplorable condition there began to be established in various places, something over a quarter of a century ago, the office of public defender—a public official charged with the duty of defending persons charged with crime and unable to retain a lawyer, just as fully as the public prosecutor is charged with the duty of prosecuting them. The principal large cities in which the public defender has long functioned are Chicago and Los Angeles. In Connecticut, a public defender is found in each county. Thus far, however, the office has hardly established itself as a common one.

Reluctance to incur the substantial expense which such an office necessarily entails is doubtless responsible in large measure for the slowness with which the institution of the public defender has spread, even in some of the states whose statutes authorize its establishment by any county that so elects. But there is also a more fundamental factor at work. In all institutional arrangements, there is a tendency for the personnel involved to establish working relationships not contemplated by, and indeed often inconsistent with, the intentions of the designers. It is an indubitable fact that in not a few jurisdictions the judge of the criminal court, far from preserving that judicial aloofness which his office demands, becomes, over the years, a boon companion of the prosecutor, with the result that the disposition of the recommendations which the prosecutor is to present to the court—recommendations to "nol-pros" a charge, to accept a plea of guilty to a lesser charge, to exercise leniency or severity in sentencing—are often determined upon in advance in conference. There is a danger that were

---

[36] In several cases in recent years, state prisoners have sought release through habeas corpus proceedings on the claim that, though furnished with counsel at the trial, the service rendered by such counsel was so incompetent that the petitioner was in effect without the assistance of counsel. In a few cases, both in state and federal courts, this has been held to be a proper ground for ordering a new trial.

the public defender's office to become a routine fixture of our criminal justice, similarly amicable arrangements might in many cases develop between the personnel of that office and of the prosecutor's office.[37]

Though the effectiveness of the public defender offices that now exist appears to vary widely from place to place, the over-all experience is undoubtedly favorable.[38]

Of late years the plan has been gaining favor of permitting the philanthropic legal aid society, which has, despite inadequate financial support, been rendering valuable aid to indigent defendants, to expand its work through public subsidy. In the city of New York this plan has been in apparently successful operation for several years.

An apparently unique plan has for some years been in operation in New Jersey, under which, by rule of court, every indigent defendant is to be furnished with counsel, to be appointed by the court, in rotation except in capital cases, from the list of all the attorneys in the county. Neither the assigned counsel plan nor the legal-aid society plan has ordinarily been able to enlist the services of the abler members of the bar by its appeal to their professional responsibility and to their duty to their professional brethren. This the New Jersey plan does. Moreover, through the operation of this plan, every lawyer, from his entry into practice, is brought into contact with the criminal courts (an experience now confined to but a small portion of the bar). A far wider professional interest in the improvement of our criminal justice should result.[39]

Costliness of defense

Even though counsel be furnished to the accused at the expense of the state or by any of the other agencies mentioned, the problem remains of finding, for the indigent defendant and indeed for the defendant by no means indigent but of limited means, the funds needed for his defense. Omitting completely at this point the consideration of the indigent's inability to finance an appeal should he be convicted, and confining attention to the trial, it is obvious that a proper defense may entail the employment of investigators and of expert witnesses. It may entail the bringing of witnesses from outside the jurisdiction—with consequent payment of their transportation and living expenses, at least in part.

[37] For contrasting views on this point, see Dimock, The Public Defender: A Step Toward a Police State, 42 Amer. Bar Assn. Jour. 219 (1956); and Harrington and Getty, The Public Defender: A Progressive Step Toward Justice, 42 Amer. Bar Assn. Jour. 1139 (1956).

[38] For a survey of the existing situation, see Brownell, Legal Aid in the United States (1951) and its Supplement (1961).

[39] A study of the existing provision for counsel for indigent defendants, far more exhaustive than any previously undertaken, is now in progress under the direction of the American Bar Foundation. Publication of the results in the fall of 1964 is anticipated.

There are found in a few jurisdictions provisions for the payment of some of the cost out of public funds, where the defendant is indigent.[40] But nowhere are these provisions entirely adequate to the needs of the penniless defendant; and nowhere is even the defendant with limited means truly on a parity, in this respect, with the wealthy defendant. The reform of our law in this respect still lies in the future; until radical reform is effected it cannot truly be said that in this field the boast that all are equal before the law has real substance.

6. THE DEFENDANT'S EXEMPTION FROM QUESTIONING

A further right of the defendant which recurs at various stages in the investigation and prosecution of a criminal offense is his right to be exempt from questioning.

At the time of the Revolution it was well established, and had been for nearly a century, that a person accused of crime could not, in the investigatory proceedings preceding the trial, be put under oath to answer any question whatever. This did not mean, however, that the authorities could not question him. When arrested and brought before a magistrate for preliminary examination, he was questioned by the magistrate himself (and sometimes by the law-enforcement officers as well), and though he could not indeed be punished for refusing to answer, his refusals (as well as his answers if any) could be put in evidence against him should he subsequently be brought to trial. This practice was abandoned a little over a century ago in some of our states, and was gradually abandoned in all. Today the person arrested in advance of the filing of a formal accusation against him is brought before a magistrate for the sole purpose of ascertaining whether the authorities can present enough evidence against him to warrant his being continued in custody (or in bail) pending further action by the authorities looking either to the lodging of a formal accusation against him or to his release. At this proceeding he may not be called to the stand by the prosecution; nor may he indeed in many jurisdictions be sworn as a witness on his own behalf, being permitted only, should he wish, to make an unsworn statement.

The protection of the defendant against being compelled to answer

[40] The Rules of Criminal Procedure for the federal courts provide that the expenses of the attorney for an indigent defendant, for travel and subsistence in connection with the taking of a deposition, shall be paid by the government. Rule 15(c). They make no provision for the payment of expenses of investigation necessary for the preparation of the indigent's defense. A federal judge nevertheless ordered the United States marshal "or other appropriate official" to pay to the indigent defendant's court-appointed attorney the funds necessary to enable him to proceed to the scene of the alleged crime and there interview witnesses. There being no funds appropriated for this purpose, the order was not complied with. The court thereupon dismissed the indictment, declaring that the defendant was in effect being deprived of his constitutional right to "the assistance of counsel." United States v. Germany, 216 F. Supp. 54 (1963).

questions, on pain of punishment, in the investigatory proceedings preceding trial was incorporated in some of the early state constitutions, and as to federal prosecutions in the Fifth Amendment to the Constitution, adopted in 1791. It was subsequently incorporated in the constitutions of the new states which entered the union during the first half of the last century.

At that time the constitutional provision had no significance with respect to the questioning of the defendant at his trial; for he was not at that time permitted to take the stand, whether at the instance of the prosecution or at his own request. Beginning in the 1860s, however, the right to take the stand in his own defense was, in one state after another and in the federal courts, extended to him.[41] The constitutional provision was then construed to mean also that he was not to be called to the stand by the prosecution; and, in most states, that his failure to take advantage of his newly conferred right to take the stand in his own defense was not to be taken into consideration in passing on the question of his guilt.

But the accused's constitutional exemption from questioning as a witness operates even before he has in fact been either arrested or accused. When a grand jury is conducting an investigation to determine whether it should return an indictment against one or more persons implicated in activities apparently criminal, if the prosecutor who is presenting the evidence to the grand jury has in mind, as he in most cases does, a particular individual against whom he seeks to have an indictment returned, he may not call that person as a witness before the grand jury. If that person is nevertheless called, gives testimony, and is subsequently indicted, he has a right to have the indictment dismissed by the court (the prosecutor having the right however, to seek a new indictment, returned without the aid of the testimony of the person indicted).

It will be observed that in all the situations just described, the questioning from which the defendant, or prospective defendant, is exempt is in the course of a judicial proceeding (the grand jury investigation, though not presided over by a judge, is carried on under the supervision and at the direction of the court). Questioning in private by police or prosecuting officials is clearly not within the terms of the constitutional guarantee, and is sanctioned by long usage. Nevertheless, there is a discernible tendency on the part of some courts to assimilate such questioning to questioning in a judicial proceeding, at least after the defendant has been indicted, and at least to the extent of requiring that the defendant be permitted if he desires to have counsel present at his questioning—a requirement which, in the case of a sophisticated lawbreaker, would in effect exempt the defendant from questioning.

[41] Georgia alone has failed to extend this right to the defendant, permitting him only to make an unsworn statement at the end of the testimony. If he is represented by counsel, counsel must be permitted to question him to assist him in making his statement clear and complete. So held by the Supreme Court, reversing a conviction where counsel was not so permitted, in Ferguson v. Georgia, 366 U.S. 570 (1961).

7. THE WITNESS'S PRIVILEGE AGAINST SELF-INCRIMINATION

Still another constitutional right which pervades the entire field of criminal justice (and of all civil, administrative, and legislative proceedings as well) is the privilege of a witness to refuse to answer a question put to him on claiming, whether with or without justification, that his answer would tend to incriminate him.

At the time of the Revolution this rule was of comparatively recent origin, and had by no means been well established in the English, not to speak of the colonial, courts. By the early years of the nineteenth century the witness's privilege had become firmly entrenched in American courts. But some decades were to elapse before it began to be regarded as a *constitutional* privilege.

The provisions of the eighteenth century state constitutions regarding self-incrimination were quite clearly limited in their application to the defendant; they had no reference to a mere witness. Some of them, and a number of state constitutions adopted in the first half of the nineteenth century as well, expressly confined the clause against self-incrimination to "the accused." The Fifth Amendment to the Constitution, adopted in 1791, employed, however, a different and novel phraseology. It provided (the application of the provision being limited, as are all the provisions of the Fourth to Eighth amendments, to federal proceedings) that no person "shall be compelled in any criminal case to be a witness against himself"; and this language was copied into several of the nineteenth century state constitutions. For more than a century the question whether the language in the Fifth Amendment was intended to embrace the witness as well as the accused did not arise, at any rate in such form as to come before the Supreme Court. Even if not constitutional, the witness's privilege was recognized by traditional rule, by this time firmly established. Only if Congress should attempt to abridge the privilege would the question of its *constitutional* character arise. Space does not permit a recounting of the course of decisions by which it was finally established, in the present century, that the witness's privilege of refusing to answer on the ground of possible self-incrimination is constitutionally protected in every variety of federal proceeding, civil as well as criminal, administrative and legislative as well as judicial.[42]

The course of decision in the states (even in those in which the consti-

[42] The first case in which the Supreme Court held that the constitutional provision protected one other than the defendant in a criminal proceeding was what the Court characterized as a "quasi-criminal" proceeding (a proceeding by the government to declare forfeited goods attempted to be imported in fraud of the customs) and the person claiming the constitutional privilege, while not a party (the proceeding being in rem), was, the Court said, "the substantial party," being the importer of the goods. Boyd v. United States, 116 U.S. 616 (1886). Six years later, the Court held the witness before a grand jury to be constitutionally protected, a grand jury investigation being a "criminal case" within the meaning of the constitutional provision, and the

tutional provision is still expressly confined to "the accused") has paralleled that of the Supreme Court. In two states, there is no constitutional provision on the point; but the witness's privilege in its full amplitude is recognized by the courts as a traditional or statutory one. Several of the justices now sitting on the Supreme Court clearly hold that the exercise of compulsion on a witness by state courts, to extract from him an answer which he claims would be incriminating, is a denial of due process and is therefore forbidden by the Constitution; but the precise question has never come before the Court.[43]

The witness's right to silence is not absolute. Although there is in theory no way of knowing whether the answer to the question which he refuses to answer would in fact be criminatory, a court has the power, if in its opinion an answer to the question would not be incriminating, to direct the witness to answer and to commit him to custody until he does. The importance of the witness's privilege in permitting him to withhold essential evidence thus depends in chief measure on the latitude allowed the witness by the courts. Until nearly the end of the last century it was everywhere the rule that the witness could be excused from answering only if it was possible that the answer, if given, would furnish an essential link in the chain of proof necessary to convict him of crime. In 1892, however, the Supreme Court declared that the federal witness was protected also against the compulsory disclosure of facts which, while themselves forming no part of the proof of a crime, might assist the prosecutor in finding such proof.[44] A vast new area of exemption from answering was thus opened to the federal witness; and the state courts, though under no obligation, when construing state constitutional provisions, to follow the Supreme Court, have in most cases done so. In recent years the tendency of the Supreme Court has been to uphold the witness's refusal to answer in cases in which the possibility that the answer, if given, would give the slightest assistance to the law-enforcement machinery in a criminal proceeding subsequently instituted against the witness, on any charge what-

---

witness who claimed the constitutional privilege being a potential defendant. Counselman v. Hitchcock, 142 U.S. 547 (1892). It was not till 1922 that the Court held constitutional protection applicable to the witness in every federal civil proceeding. McCarthy v. Arndstein, 266 U.S. 34 (1924). For the view that the Fifth Amendment provision against self-incrimination, and the corresponding provisions of all the state constitutions adopted up to the middle of the last century, and perhaps later, were intended by their framers to protect only the accused, and not the witness, see Mayers, Shall We Amend the Fifth Amendment? 183 ff. (1959). See also 8 Wigmore, Evidence (McNaughton rev. 1961), Sec. 2252.

[43] In Regan v. New York, 349 U.S. 58 (1955), a case arising out of the attempt of a state to punish a witness who refused to answer after having waived his privilege against self-incrimination, Chief Justice Warren was at pains to point out, correctly, that the Supreme Court "has never held that a state, in the absence of an adequate immunity statute, can punish a witness for contempt for refusing to answer self-incriminatory questions" (at p. 65).

[44] Counselman v. Hitchcock, 142 U.S. 547, 564 (1892).

ever, is so remote as to be from any practical standpoint non-existent. The result is that the federal witness may in effect refuse to anwser a question even though he has no fear whatever of incriminating himself, but is intent merely on shielding another, perhaps an associate or relative, if not a confederate. Here again, the state courts have for the most part followed suit. In consequence the witness's privilege is now regarded by some qualified observers as a major obstruction to the investigation of sophisticated crime (such as conspiracies to extort, to defraud, to bribe, or to evade the payment of taxes) and to the conviction of the guilty.

The obstacles which the witness's privilege against self-incrimination places in the way of the investigation of crime by authorized agencies through the examination of witnesses early gave rise to the immunity statute. This statute withdraws from the witness, in certain cases, the right to refuse to answer because of possible self-incrimination and at the same time confers upon him immunity from the consequences of his testimony. Typically these statutes at first merely precluded the reading of the witness's testimony, given under this compulsion, in any subsequent criminal proceedings against him; and such statutes were held by the courts of some of the states to satisfy constitutional prohibitions against compulsory self-incriminating testimony. In 1892, however, the Supreme Court of the United States, in passing on a case arising under a federal statute of this character, declared that the mere prohibition of the reading of the witness's testimony in any subsequent criminal proceeding against him did not afford the witness sufficient protection against self-incrimination. The compulsory statute, to meet the constitutional requirement, "must afford absolute immunity against future prosecutions for the offense to which the question relates,"[45] even though evidence sufficient for conviction should subsequently come into the prosecutor's hands wholly independently. Since that decision, which again the state courts almost without exception have followed, federal and state statutes have tended to be correspondingly broadened[46]—giving rise to the term "immunity bath."

Immunity statutes as found in the states are frequently limited in their terms to grand jury investigations of corruption of public officers or of other types of unlawful conduct involving in their nature participation or guilty knowledge on the part of a number of people; federal statutes are likewise found only in limited areas. There is strong support for extending these statutes, under suitable safeguards, to all grand jury investigations. Only thus, it is urged—by compelling the minor inhabitants of the underworld, under grant of immunity, to incriminate the overlords of crime—can organized crime be destroyed.

[45] Ibid., p. 586.
[46] A complete compilation of such statutes is given in 8 Wigmore, Evidence (McNaughton rev. 1961), Secs. 2281–2282.

8. EXCLUSION OF EVIDENCE IMPROPERLY OBTAINED

In recent years, the doctrine has developed that evidence improperly obtained by the law-enforcement authorities may not be received in a grand jury investigation or at a criminal trial, no matter how relevant or crucial it may be. This doctrine, which is almost entirely the handiwork of the courts, and particularly of the Supreme Court, is of increasing importance. In its origin, it was not regarded, by the minority of courts which at that time honored it, as a means of preventing injustice to the defendant against whom the evidence might be introduced. The rights of the defendant may have been invaded when the evidence was obtained— as when his premises were searched without a search warrant, where one should have and could have been obtained, and incriminating evidence found; but the introduction of the evidence against him at his trial is no more an invasion of his rights than if it had been lawfully obtained. The courts thus justified their adoption of the doctrine not as a measure for the protection of the defendant but as one for the disciplining of the law-enforcement authorities. The Supreme Court, after having, in 1914, declared evidence obtained by unlawful search to be inadmissible in federal criminal trials, for decades refused to apply the same rule to state trials; the rule had been promulgated by it for federal trials, it declared, not as a shield for the defendant but as a means of enforcing on federal law-enforcement officials a due observance of the law.

But in recent years, as we shall see, the original purpose of the doctrine has tended to be disregarded; and the exclusion of evidence improperly obtained to be regarded as demanded by the requirement of due process of law. The far-reaching effect of this change on the administration of criminal justice will appear at several points as we proceed.[47]

Exclusion of certain types of evidence at a criminal trial is of course commonplace. Thus, hearsay evidence or the uncorroborated testimony of an accomplice who has turned state's evidence may be excluded because of unreliability; evidence of a confession made by the defendant may be excluded if it is found to have been extorted from him by coercion, and so on. In all these cases it is the defect inherent in the evidence itself that is responsible for its exclusion. Evidence unlawfully obtained may, however, be free from any defect as evidence; it is only the manner in which it was acquired by the authorities that is defective.

9. THE CRIMINAL CONTEMPT PROCEEDING

The criminal proceeding is not the only form of proceeding by which punishment may be imposed on an offender. There is also the quite different proceeding known as the criminal contempt proceeding.

[47] See pp. 57 ff.

Interference with conduct of judicial proceeding

One who engages in disorderly conduct in a courtroom during the progress of a proceeding, or in disorderly conduct so near the court as to interfere with the orderly conduct of the proceeding is, like one acting in a disorderly manner anywhere, subject to arrest and prosecution in the regular form of proceeding used for the punishment of petty offenses generally. In addition, however, he exposes himself in the alternative to punishment at the hands of the judge in whose presence, or near whose court, the offense—termed "contempt of court"—was committed. Though characterized as a criminal contempt, it is punished not through the conventional criminal proceeding, but through a "contempt proceeding" in which the judge may be at once prosecutor, witness, and tribunal.

But it is not merely disorderly conduct which may be thus punished. Disobedience to any direction given by the judge to a party, attorney, witness, or spectator in connection with the conduct of the proceeding may also ordinarily be punished by the court. How much further this judicial power of punishment for contempt extends must be examined separately in each jurisdiction. In some jurisdictions the courts have treated as criminal contempt of court various acts calculated to impair the administration of justice already condemned by specific criminal statutes, such as false swearing, preventing, delaying, or interfering with the execution of a legal process, or tampering with evidence or witnesses. In other jurisdictions, however, whether by doctrines announced by the courts themselves or by statute, this class of offenses is outside the contempt power. Thus the federal statute, unchanged in this respect since its enactment in 1831,[48] provides that the only act of this character which a federal court may punish as contempt of its authority is misbehavior in its presence or so near thereto as to obstruct the administration of justice.[49] Similar restrictive statutes are found in some but by no means in all of the states.

If the conduct constituting the criminal contempt was committed in the actual presence of the court and was seen or heard by the judge, the judge may, in most jurisdictions, proceed forthwith to impose punishment, without affording to the person declared in contempt any opportunity for contest. Aside from such cases, criminal contempt proceedings follow a procedure very similar to other proceedings, with a hearing on notice, presentation of evidence, opportunity for cross-examination, etc.

In the federal district courts, by a rule promulgated by the Supreme

---

[48] Act of March 2, 1831 (4 Stat. 487). The original Judiciary Act merely provided that "all the said courts of the United States shall have power . . . to punish by fine or imprisonment at the discretion of said courts all contempts of authority in any cause or hearing before the same." (1 Stat. 83.)

[49] 18 U.S. Code, Sec. 401. The "misbehavior of any of its officers in their official transactions" is also declared by this section to be punishable as a contempt.

Court, if "the contempt charged involves disrespect to or criticism of the judge, that judge is disqualified from presiding at the trial or hearing except with the defendant's consent."[50] Such a provision is not usual in state contempt procedures.

In some states, certain forms of disobedience to the judge's directions given in the course of a proceeding—e.g., refusal of a witness to answer a question—are declared to be criminal offenses, punishable through the ordinary forms of criminal prosecution.

Traditionally, the courts possessed complete discretion as to the size of the fine or the length of the term of imprisonment they might impose for a criminal contempt. In many jurisdictions, however, statutory limitations have been imposed.[51]

The constitutionality of the limitations which Congress has imposed on the power of the federal courts to punish for contempt has been upheld by the Supreme Court.[52] From this, the inference is permissible that that power is, like other matters of procedure in the federal courts, subject to congressional regulation.[53] In a few opinions in the state courts, however, the view has been taken that the power to punish is, at least as to the higher trial courts which have traditionally exercised it, an "inherent" one, and is consequently protected against diminution by the legislature by reason of state constitutional provisions calling for the separation of powers. If by the term "inherent" it is intended to assert that every court of general jurisdiction, by the mere fact of its existence, necessarily must possess the power to punish summarily interference with its proceedings, the untenability of the contention can be established without the necessity of resorting to foreign systems in which the power does not exist. Within our own legal system we have administrative tribunals which adjudicate matters of greater consequence than do many courts (e.g., the Federal Trade Commission, which may order the discontinuance of business operations of great magnitude); yet they have no power to punish interference with their proceedings.

The characterization of the power of the courts to punish for contempt as an inherent power can accordingly be accepted only if taken to mean that the power has so long traditionally been possessed by American courts that when a state constitution creates, or authorizes the creation of, a court, what is thereby intended is a court with power to punish sum-

[50] Federal Rules of Criminal Procedure, Rule 42 (b).

[51] In the federal courts, if the act done consists of the willful disobedience of an order or process of the court and constitutes a federal or state criminal offense, the fine payable to the United States may not exceed, if the accused is a natural person, $1,000, and the term of imprisonment may not exceed six months. 18 U.S. Code, Sec. 402.

[52] Ex parte Robinson, 19 Wallace 505 (1874).

[53] See Frankfurter and Landis, Power of Congress over procedure in criminal contempts in inferior federal courts, 37 Harv. Law Rev. 1010 (1924).

marily for contempt; and the legislature may not accordingly impair that power.

The power of punishing for contempt has not traditionally been enjoyed by inferior courts; nor have legislatures, in creating such courts, commonly vested them with this power. (In some cases, however, legislatures have empowered them to impose small fines or commitment to custody for very short periods for disorder in the presence of the court).

Despite the drastic character of the criminal contempt power, its exercise by the courts has not, on the whole, provoked any marked dissatisfaction. It is to be borne in mind that the finding of the court and the sentence imposed by it are subject to review and modification on appeal—a possibility calculated to counsel caution and moderation to a judge sitting in a contempt proceeding.

Following precedents antedating the Revolution, the trial of a criminal contempt charge is characteristically by the court without a jury.[54] Despite the characterization of a contempt as criminal, the proceeding to punish it is not a "criminal prosecution" within the meaning of the constitutional guarantee of jury trial in such prosecutions in the federal courts;[55] and the like is true of corresponding provisions in state constitutions. Congress has, however, provided that in the federal district courts, if the act prosecuted was not committed in the presence of the court (or so near thereto as to obstruct justice) and it also constitutes a criminal offense under any federal or applicable state statute, the defendant may demand trial by jury.[56] There are, however, very few state statutes of this nature.

Contempt by publication

In one field, however, the occasional assumption by a court of the power to punish for criminal contempt has encountered not only public criticism, but constitutional obstacles, with resultant disallowance by appellate courts, and in several notable instances by the Supreme Court, of the penalties imposed. This is the field of public comment on judicial conduct, in which the doctrine has developed, over the past two centuries, that there may be "contempt by publication."

Often mentioned in connection with the matter of allegedly objectionable public criticism of judicial conduct, but quite distinct from it, is the

[54] Holdsworth traces the assumption by the English courts of the power to "punish summarily offences which in the Middle Ages would have been remedied by an indictment" to the beginning of the seventeenth century; but the decision which "forms the basis for the modern law on the subject" was not rendered till 1765. 9 History of English Law 394 (1938).

[55] In re Debs, 158 U.S. 564 (1895). The soundness of this holding (since several times reaffirmed by the Supreme Court) has, however, been questioned. See dissenting opinion of Justice Black in Sacher et al. v. U.S., 343 U.S. 1, 14 (1952). See also dissenting opinions in Fisher v. Pace, 336 U.S. 155 (1949) and in Green v. United States, 356 U.S. 165 (1958).

[56] 18 U.S. Code, Sec. 3691.

public disclosure in connection with a criminal case of alleged information, particularly information in the hands of the police or prosecutor, regarding evidence against a person held as a suspect, or as a defendant already held to answer. The publication of such information may seriously impair the possibility of a fair trial for a person so held, a matter adverted to in a subsequent chapter, in the discussion of criminal prosecution.

Reverting then to the quite distinct matter of criticism of judicial conduct, we find that there have been in our history a number of cases in which the publication (in almost all cases, publication in public prints) of criticism of judicial conduct in a pending case has been treated by the judge so criticized as contempt of court. With the announcement by the Supreme Court, in 1924, that freedom of speech and of the press is protected by the Constitution against unreasonable limitation by the states (such limitation being a denial of "due process of law," prohibited to the states by the Fourteenth Amendment), the extent to which a state may constitutionally go in punishing comment on judicial conduct has become a matter for the Court to define. In several cases which have come before the Court in recent years, it has set aside state court contempt punishments, arising out of public criticism of judicial conduct, as invading freedom of publication, there being in its view no "clear and present danger" that the publication in those cases tended to deflect the judge criticized from the fearless and impartial discharge of his judicial function in a case then pending before him.[57] Whether this is to be the test hereafter, and whether where a jury rather than a judge is the target of criticism a "clear and present danger" would more readily be apprehended, are matters not yet clear. There is a strong body of opinion that the attempt to check intemperate public criticism of judicial conduct by contempt proceedings is unwarranted and in any case ineffective.[58]

Disobedience to order or judgment in civil proceeding

In addition to its employment to punish interference with the conduct of the court, or disobedience to directions given by the court to counsel, witness, juror, or spectator in the course of conducting the proceeding, the criminal contempt proceeding is used for a quite different purpose—to punish past disobedience, by a party to a civil proceeding, of an order, judgment, or decree of the court, issued at the instance of the other party to the litigation and prohibiting or directing the performance of a specified act. The use of the criminal contempt proceeding for this purpose (as well as of the allied proceeding, termed the civil contempt proceeding, used to compel present compliance with the court's order or decree) is discussed in Chapter 7.

[57] See Bridges v. California, 314 U.S. 252 (1941); Pennekamp v. Florida, 328 U.S. 331 (1946); Craig v. Harney, 331 U.S. 367 (1947).
[58] See Note, 59 Yale Law Jour. 534 (1950).

3

Criminal Proceedings: Investigation

1. POLICE AND PROSECUTOR: THEIR INTERRELATION. 2. POLICE AND PROSECUTOR: QUESTIONING OF PERSONS IN CUSTODY. 3. POLICE AND PROSECUTOR: USE OF LAWFUL DETENTION. 4. POLICE AND PROSECUTOR: SEARCHES AND SEIZURES. 5. CORONER'S INQUEST. 6. PRELIMINARY EXAMINATION OF CHARGE AGAINST PERSON ARRESTED. 7. GRAND JURY INVESTIGATION. 8. INVESTIGATION BY ADMINISTRATIVE AGENCIES. 9. INVESTIGATION BY JUDICIAL OFFICER.

Our subject is adjudication; in strictness, investigation—the operations of the vast machinery which, incessantly active, searches out possible violations of law and pursues suspected malefactors—is no part of that subject. In the field of criminal justice the machinery of investigation is, however, so closely integrated with that of adjudication that a clear-cut demarcation would at some points be a purely scholastic one. More compelling still is the fact that the processes of criminal investigation trench so closely upon the rights of the individual that to ignore them in a study of our legal system would be unrealistic.

1. POLICE AND PROSECUTOR: THEIR INTERRELATION

A large part of the personnel of government is continuously engaged in inquiring, by means of routine physical inspections and by examination of records, whether regulatory and tax statutes are being complied with by those subject to them. In the routine conduct of other administrative activities, infractions of law continually come to light. Our concern is not, however, except incidentally, with these routine activities. Rather are we concerned with the procedure for the investigation of particular suspected crimes.

Such investigation is the function not of a single agency but of several, falling into two distinct categories. On the one hand are the police agencies—using that term in its broadest sense—and the public prosecutor. These agencies proceed informally; they have no power to compel the attendance or testimony of witnesses. The second category comprises the coroner, the examining magistrate, the grand jury, and other less important agencies vested with the power to compel the attendance and testimony of witnesses—the subpoena power, as it is termed. These agencies proceed formally, through the interrogation of witnesses. Needless to say, the actual work of investigation of most crimes is accomplished by the police and prosecutor, rather than by the agencies of formal interrogation.

In the category of police and detective forces are embraced not only the diversified types of peace officer found in our states—local, county, and state police, and, in areas lacking such forces, the county sheriff and his deputies—and the detective officers usually found connected with all but the smallest of such organized police forces, but also an extensive federal agency charged with the investigation of federal crimes generally—the Federal Bureau of Investigation. In addition, specialized agencies of detection and investigation exist in the federal government in connection with the postal service, the immigration service, and the divisions of the Treasury responsible for the currency, the internal revenue, the customs, the control of navigation, and the control of the narcotics trade; and cognate specialized agencies of investigation are found in some of the states.

The other chief agency of criminal investigation is the public prosecutor. This officer is found in the states both for the state as a whole (commonly known as the attorney general of the state) and ordinarily for each county or multicounty unit (being variously known as the county, district, or state attorney or prosecutor). Ordinarily the power of the state attorney general to prosecute and, hence, to investigate crimes is extremely limited. It is commonly confined to violations of particular regulatory or taxing statutes. The prosecution of crimes generally is wholly in the hands of the local prosecutors, who, being in nearly all the states elected, are not subordinates of the attorney general of the state. In the federal government, by contrast, the attorney general is in complete charge of all prosecutions, the local federal prosecutor, known as the United States Attorney (found in each of the eighty-seven federal judicial districts into which the country is divided), being a subordinate of the Attorney General.

In the states, in the investigation of a particular crime, the prosecutor may rely entirely on the police, merely accepting the evidence which they turn over to him; he may entirely disregard the police, and any evidence they may have gathered, and make his own investigation; or he may supplement the police investigation by his own, the two investigations perhaps proceeding simultaneously and pursuant to an agreed plan.

State criminal investigation at the local level is thus marked by a striking division of responsibility. The local police and detective forces responsible for the investigation of crime are (barring such detectives as may be directly attached to the prosecutor's office, ordinarily quite inadequate for major investigations) wholly independent of the public prosecutor; nor is there any common authority to which they both respond. Moreover, in the urban areas the police and detective forces are ordinarily organized on a city or village basis, and in the rural areas, if found at all, ordinarily on a state basis; but the prosecutor's office is by contrast based on the county or on a multicounty unit.

Not infrequently, not only is there no coordination between police and prosecutor, but they may be at swords' points, contending for the publicity of a given case, or reflecting in their official behavior some feud raging between the rival political organizations to which the prosecutor and the mayor or other official controlling the police respectively profess allegiance.[1] On the other hand, here, as elsewhere, friendly cooperation, where it exists, may somewhat overcome the weakness of the administrative design.

In the federal machinery for the investigation of crime there is found no such division of responsibility, at least over the major areas of criminal prosecution. Special investigative agencies not under the direct control of the Attorney General of the United States there indeed are, as we have seen. But all these agencies are ultimately responsible to the President, who in turn looks to the Attorney General for law enforcement. In the main, however, responsibility for the detection and investigation of federal crimes of importance rests with the Bureau of Investigation, an agency responsible directly to the Attorney General—the official also responsible for all federal criminal prosecutions. The contrast to the typical state situation is obvious.[2]

In addition to the lack of local integration of investigative agencies in the states, there is an equal lack of state supervision or control over those agencies. This is undoubtedly one of the gravest weaknesses of our state systems of criminal investigation. The lack of state control over the local police and over the sheriffs is in some states virtually total. More recently however state police forces have increasingly supplemented or superseded the local police in difficult criminal investigations; and in a few states the policing of certain cities has been made a state instead of a local function.

State control of the local prosecutor is characteristically equally tenuous. There is provision in some states for his removal by the governor for cause, and in some the authorities may supersede him in a particular case,

---

[1] Occasionally, this division of responsibility may work for good. A corrupt police may find their efforts to protect a wrongdoer thwarted by an upright prosecutor, and vice versa.

[2] Nevertheless, the extent of overlapping of function in the federal law-enforcement agencies has for some time given concern. See Smith, Police Systems in the United States, 178 ff (2nd rev. ed. 1960).

or may initiate a prosecution independently. But these are extreme measures, reserved for extreme cases.[3]

In consequence, in a number of states, a citizen aggrieved by the conduct of the police, the sheriff, or the prosecutor ordinarily has in effect no state agency to which he can complain. Unquestionably, it is this lack of administrative supervision of these officers that has made possible the tendency found among certain of them to refuse observance of the limitations which the law places on their conduct. This has in turn been partly responsible for the increasing attempts by the courts to check police excesses by the sole, but nevertheless dubious, means open to them—the exclusion of evidence unlawfully obtained, a matter discussed in the preceding chapter.

One aspect of the complete decentralization of responsibility for the investigation and prosecution of crime characteristic of our states has received little notice. This is the slenderness of the financial resources available for these purposes in many of our counties. As a result, a crime, though in theory one against the state, may in practice be merely one against the county; and if the county budget does not permit its thorough investigation and persistent prosecution, the perpetrator may escape by default. There is no provision, generally, in our states for assisting the county in these circumstances.

2. POLICE AND PROSECUTOR: QUESTIONING OF PERSONS IN CUSTODY

It is a remarkable feature of our system of criminal investigation that although the police and the prosecutor are the chief agencies of such investigation, they are vested with no power whatever to summon any one before them, or to compel anyone, whether under arrest or not, to answer their questions. The prosecutor may indeed cause a witness to be summoned to appear before a grand jury, there to be compelled to answer (subject of course to his privilege against self-incrimination); but this is a procedure ordinarily much too cumbrous and, except in the larger cities where grand juries are virtually continuously in session, too dilatory for the routine examination of witnesses in the preliminary investigation of a crime against the person or against property.

Despite their lack of the power of compulsory interrogation, the police and detective forces and prosecuting officers exhibit a high degree of effectiveness in obtaining information. Their success is to be explained

[3] The variations, from state to state, in the extent to which the attorney general of the state is empowered to conduct, supervise, or intervene in prosecutions are too numerous to make summary statement practicable. There has over recent decades been a trend toward greater state control of criminal justice, and correspondingly greater powers in the attorney general, but change has been slow. See Stark, Politics and the State Department of Justice, 30 Jour. Crim. Law and Criminology 183 (1939).

largely by the cooperation of persons sincerely desirous of assisting in the preservation of law and order; by information furnished them out of malevolence toward a suspect or by a paid or intimidated standing informer; by the belief (in most cases unfounded)[4] that a legal obligation exists to furnish the authorities with information; and by a fear that, whatever the legal limitations on their powers, the authorities will take reprisal for a failure to give them information, perhaps by illegal detention or even illegal arrest—a fear unfortunately not without some foundation in fact.

Although as just stated the lack of power to compel answers to questions is just as complete in the case of a person in police custody as in the case of one not in custody, the person in custody is manifestly at a great psychological disadvantage, to say the least, in resisting persistent efforts on the part of the police or prosecutor to extract information from him. The questioning of persons in police custody is thus one of the chief instruments of criminal investigation.

There are several possible stages of a criminal proceeding in which the defendant may be in lawful custody, a determinative factor being the gravity of the offense. In petty offenses, the defendant, if arrested at all, rather than summoned, is commonly brought before the court promptly after arrest. In criminal offenses proper, the arrest may have been made only after a formal accusation—commonly termed either an information or an indictment—had been lodged against the person arrested. In this case he must promptly be brought before the trial court to plead, i.e., either to plead guilty or to be held (ordinarily subject to release on bail) to await trial. In neither of the foregoing situations does the defendant's being in custody have much importance from the standpoint of police or prosecutor interrogation. When, however, the arrest is the first action taken, the person arrested being not yet a defendant but only a suspect, as is the case in the overwhelming majority of cases of crimes of violence and crimes against property, the interrogation of the suspect is of prime importance. In such a case the next step is to take the suspect before a magistrate for a hearing (termed the "preliminary examination"), the purpose of which is to determine whether there is sufficient evidence against him to warrant his being held in custody (subject, in almost all cases, to release on bail) pending the decision of the authorities whether to prosecute him. The interval between the arrest of the suspect and his production before the magistrate varies from one place to another, depending on the legal rules there in force and also, in many places, on the degree of disregard of those rules which the police and prosecuting authorities permit themselves.[5]

---

[4] Occasionally, a statute makes the refusal to divulge information concerning crime of a particular category punishable. See, for example, New York Penal Law, Sec. 1250.

[5] In some jurisdictions, a person arrested is, by police department rule rather than by statute, entitled to make one or two telephone calls—a regulation obviously easy for the police to ignore when they deem it desirable. The refusal to permit a

Whatever the interval, the authorities, aware that the suspect may soon be out of their hands, are likely, in cases where the seeming absence of other proof makes it probable that a conviction can be obtained only on the suspect's own admissions, to utilize this period to the fullest for extracting such admissions.[6]

The methods used by the police to compel disclosure of information or confession by the prisoner may range from mere prolonged and repeated questioning to physical brutality or more refined forms of torture, such as keeping the prisoner awake for unendurable periods. To all unlawful practice of this type the term "the third degree" is commonly applied. The extent to which it is resorted to, of course, varies with the traditions and practices of the particular police force involved, as well as with the type of suspect involved and, doubtless to an extent in some parts of the country, with the race of the suspect.

In the nature of the case, an accurate picture of the prevalence and character of the use of the third degree is almost impossible to obtain.[7] The unlawful acts of the police in this field are carried out for the most part with due precaution against the possibility that the suspect may be able to establish a charge of physical violence. Even were he able to establish the facts, he is unlikely to wish to institute an action for damages; and if he does he will encounter the unwillingness of jurymen to return a substantial verdict against a police officer whom they believe to have been engaged in an honest, though perhaps extralegal, attempt to convict a malefactor. Indeed the unformulated recognition, by the man in the street, of the difficulties which the police encounter in dealing with the professional criminal, if they confine themselves to strictly lawful methods, is doubtless responsible for the tolerance with which the use of unlawful methods by the police is so widely regarded. That such methods, once sanctioned, are likely to be used against the innocent as well as the guilty, and as well against the unfortunate citizen who may by chance find himself wrongly suspected by the police as against the professional burglar, is all too casually overlooked.

---

person arrested to communicate with a lawyer has been held by the Supreme Court not to be such a denial of due process of law as to render inadmissible in evidence the admissions obtained from the defendant subsequent to such refusal. Crooker v. California, 357 U.S. 458 (1958).

[6] The questioning of the defendant after indictment, in the short period between his arrest and arraignment, or between his arraignment and release on bail, had been held by the high court of New York to be improper unless his counsel is present; and admissions obtained from him will not be admitted in evidence at his trial. People v. De Biasi, 7 N.Y.2d 544 (1960).

[7] The most recent discussion is that of the U.S. Commission on Civil Rights (Report, 1961, Book 5). For a discussion of the report made in 1931 to the National Commission on Law Enforcement and Observance (entitled "Lawlessness in Law Enforcement")—still occasionally cited as descriptive of present-day conditions—see Waite, 50 Mich. Law Rev. 54 (1931). See also Mueller, Book review, 35 N.Y. U. Law Rev. 379 (1960).

If the magistrate holds (or, as the phrase often is, "binds over") the suspect to await the further action of the authorities, and he is unable to furnish bail (or, in exceptional cases, is denied bail), the conditions of his further custody vary, depending upon the place; and the same is true of a defendant against whom a formal accusation has been lodged, who is awaiting trial and is similarly unable to procure his release on bail. If the official now having custody of the prisoner has complete independence of the police and prosecuting authorities, the chance that third degree methods will be permitted is of course greatly reduced, and indeed in the more highly organized custodial systems of our great cities doubtless largely eliminated. In the rural counties, however, the sheriff, who ordinarily retains custody of the prisoner under these circumstances, is himself responsible for repressing crime and is usually closely allied politically with the county prosecuting official. In this situation a prosecutor in alliance with a sheriff may well subject a prisoner being held to answer or awaiting trial to unlawful inquisition with but little fear of exposure or retribution, unless the prisoner is aided by zealous counsel. The extent to which such things actually occur is, of course, difficult to discover.

The defendant who is confined after the preliminary examination because he cannot obtain bail owing to lack of money remains subject to questioning by police and prosecutor, while the better-situated defendant is not.[8] The defendant is not entitled to have counsel assigned to assist him during this period, should he be unable to afford counsel. Under these circumstances, the doctrine that he may lawfully remain mute when interrogated while in custody is without significance. Experience is commonplace that when in confinement even hardened characters are often unable to maintain silence under persistent questioning. It is obvious that, unless most thoroughgoing measures are enforced to insulate the defendant from police and prosecutor during this period, there is a very clear advantage in favor of the more prosperous defendant, who, at liberty on bail, is immune from questioning.

Quite aside from this aspect of the detention of suspects or defendants unable to furnish bail, there has been in recent years a disposition to question the necessity for the whole concept of bail, venerable though it is, in the case of one of previous good reputation, whose home and employment ties make it unlikely that he would choose the hazardous and almost certainly futile course of becoming a fugitive from justice. An extended and apparently successful trial in the City of New York of the plan of releasing such suspects on their own recognizance[9] (a procedure long familiar to

---

[8] The same is true of the release of the defendant on bail before the completion of the preliminary examination on the hearing being adjourned.

[9] See Ares, Rankin, and Sturz, The Manhattan Bail Project: An Interim Report on the Use of Pretrial Parole, 38 N.Y.U. Law Rev. 67 (1963).

the courts in connection with persons of established reputation and responsibility) perhaps spells the beginning of a far-reaching reform in this matter.

By long-standing doctrine of the criminal law, a confession extorted from the defendant by coercion is to be excluded from evidence at his trial—a doctrine developed by the courts not primarily out of concern for the defendant, but out of distrust of the reliability of admissions thus extracted. The doctrine was however raised to the constitutional level by the Supreme Court some thirty years ago, when it announced that a conviction in a state court after a trial in which there had been introduced a coerced confession is a denial of due process of law, and will be set aside by the Court.[10] In subsequent cases the Court has made clear that the conviction will not stand even though there may have been abundant evidence aside from the confession to support the finding of guilt. The question of whether the confession was in fact voluntary or involuntary is in some states passed upon by the judge, but in most states by the jury; but the Court has taken the position that it is not bound by the finding of the jury on this point, and will itself re-examine the facts as set forth in the record.[11]

The rule that a coerced confession is inadmissible would seem to have little practical effect in curbing third-degree methods in those places in which the use of such methods is resorted to. The fact that he has confessed will ordinarily have a potent effect in inducing the defendant to plead guilty (particularly if the confession of guilt is true, as, despite its unsavory genesis, it in most cases doubtless is), rather than take his chance that at his trial the confession may be excluded from evidence. In any event, the difficulty faced by the defendant in convincing a jury of the truth of his version of what happened in the back room of a police station in the face of the completely contradictory testimony of several police officers, or perhaps a prosecuting official, is obvious.

Moreover, however rigorous the exclusion at the subsequent trial of admissions obtained from the accused by third-degree methods, there is nevertheless another incentive to such methods which remains unaffected—the possibility of obtaining from the person in custody (whom the police or prosecutor may indeed not consider a suspect at all) clues which may enable them to obtain independent evidence sufficient of itself to effect a conviction.[12]

[10] Brown v. Mississippi, 297 U.S. 278 (1936).

[11] For an extreme case of such a re-examination, see Leyra v. Denno, 347 U.S. 556 (1954).

[12] In those courts, however, which have been most disposed to develop exclusionary rules of evidence as a means of discouraging the use by the police of improper methods of obtaining information, there has begun to emerge the doctrine that there will also be excluded from evidence information obtained legally, if obtained only as the result of clues obtained illegally—the "fruit of the poisonous tree."

One is led to the reluctant conclusion that the occasional exclusion of an allegedly coerced confession at the trial, or the occasional reversal of a conviction, for failure of such exclusion, by an appellate court, including the Supreme Court (or by a lower federal court in a habeas corpus proceeding), can have but a peripheral effect on police methods. Only through an upgrading of police personnel and a determined effort of supervisory officers (perhaps aided, as is already the case in a few cities, by a citizen complaint tribunal), and by more effective judicial sanctions against the irresponsible police officer,[13] can this and other abusive police methods be checked in those police forces in which they have taken root.

An interesting development of police interrogation of persons under arrest, unaided by legal authorization, is found in the "line-up"—now a familiar feature of the police routine of our larger cities. Daily, persons arrested on felony charges on the preceding day who have not been liberated on bail are exhibited under a blinding light before assembled detectives, ostensibly that the latter may thereby become acquainted with the features of the professional criminals among the prisoners. Advantage is taken of the occasion, however, to interrogate each prisoner as he appears. Although he is under no obligation to answer, the situation in which he finds himself is so calculated to intimidate that even hardened criminals have been surprised into damaging admissions by this procedure.

In the foregoing, discussion of police procedure in seeking information from persons under arrest has been confined to the mere process of interrogation. The police frequently however subject the prisoner, more or less against his will, to other procedures, such as requiring him to put on or remove apparel, to make footprints, to submit to physical examination, to write a specimen of his handwriting, and so on. When evidence thus obtained has subsequently been introduced against the prisoner, the objection that it violates his constitutional privilege of immunity from self-incrimination has sometimes been raised, and sometimes the procedure has been attacked as an "unreasonable search" and thus unconstitutional on that ground as well. The diverse views of the courts before which these matters have been litigated cannot here be reviewed. On the whole they have refused to reject the evidence thus offered.[14] That such litigation has been possible, however, and that the courts have in some instances refused to receive these helpful forms of evidence illustrate the questionable length to which the privileges of immunity from self-incrimination and search have been carried.

[13] See p. 296.
[14] The subject is fully covered in Inbau, Self-Incrimination: What Can an Accused Person Be Compelled to Do? (1950).

3. POLICE AND PROSECUTOR: USE OF UNLAWFUL DETENTION

As already pointed out, the period between arrest and preliminary examination is the only period in which the suspect will surely be in custody; and it is in any event the most favorable one, psychologically, for extracting admissions from the suspect. Hence, in a case in which a confession by the suspect seems the most promising way of "breaking" the case, there is a strong temptation to prolong this period in the hope of extracting a confession, or if that proves impossible, of obtaining helpful admissions and information. However, in the majority of states, and in the federal courts, the governing statute or rules require that the prisoner be produced before the magistrate without unreasonable delay (the phraseology varies somewhat from state to state)—a requirement the observance of which, in the larger cities where the magistrate sits daily all day (and in a few cities even at night), reduces to a minimum the period during which the prisoner may lawfully be continued in the custody of the police. Under these circumstances the police may unlawfully hold the arrested suspect (particularly if he is a known criminal character) incommunicado for several days, or even longer, before bringing him before a magistrate.[15] For such unlawful detention, the participating officers are everywhere liable civilly, and in some jurisdictions criminally; but these rather remote possibilities of being subsequently called to account have little deterrent effect. More important from a practical standpoint is the question whether, on a showing by the defendant at his trial that his confession was obtained during such a period of illegal detention, the confession will nevertheless be received in evidence against him. In the federal courts, by reason of a doctrine announced by the Supreme Court for the first time in 1943,[16] it will not, even though there is no evidence, and indeed no claim, that the confession was coerced. A trend toward the adoption of the federal rule has in recent years become evident in the observations made by high court judges in several states in their opinions; but thus far the state courts have (except in Michigan) declined to adopt this extreme rule, holding merely that if the defendant claims his confession was coerced, the circumstance that he was under illegal detention when the confession was made is relevant to his claim of coercion. Since the right to a prompt preliminary examination is not a constitutional one, the Supreme Court has thus far declined to declare the

---

[15] A study made in Chicago in 1958 disclosed that, in 25 per cent of the approximately 2,000 arrests examined as samples, the prisoner was detained for over seventeen hours before being brought before the magistrate (the statute requiring that he be so brought "without unnecessary delay"). Amer. Civil Liberties Union, Ill. Div., Secret Detention by the Chicago Police (1958).

[16] McNabb v. United States, 318 U.S. 332 (1943).

federal rule to be part of the "due process of law" mandatory on state courts.[17]

The problem of detention of the prisoner for questioning beyond the time when it would be practicable to bring him before the magistrate for preliminary examination is bound up with the severe restrictions on the right of the police to arrest one whom they suspect, but as to whom they have little if any legally acceptable proof, of complicity in a crime they know to have been committed. As a result of these restrictions, they may arrest a suspect, knowing full well that if no additional proof is obtained it will be fruitless to bring him before the magistrate. They hope to obtain additional proof before it becomes necessary to do so; and they are understandably reluctant to bring him before the magistrate if there seems a likelihood that a somewhat longer detention either will exonerate the suspect, as often indeed happens (in which case they release him without any charge having been placed on any court record), or will, through further questioning of the suspect or otherwise, yield the necessary additional evidence for the preliminary examination. Unless our law is changed to permit limited detention of a suspect (perhaps only with the approval of some higher authority, whether administrative or judicial, than the desk sergeant) without a charge being lodged against him, it seems unlikely that such detention beyond the time at which the suspect can be brought before the magistrate will disappear.

A number of our states do not require that the suspect arrested be produced before the magistrate as promptly as practicable; in a few of these the statutes fix a definite period of lawful detention before such production, apparently because of a recognition that detention for questioning is in some cases justified.[18] Again, even where the statute or rule requires that the prisoner be brought before the magistrate promptly, the actual length of the period available to the police for interrogation may depend on such purely fortuitous circumstances as the time of day or day of the week when the arrest is made, on whether it is made on the day before a legal holiday,[19] on whether the magistrate before whom the suspect is brought is indisposed, and on the distance from the place of arrest to the courthouse.[20] Quite clearly, if protection from police interrogation is thought to be a valuable right of the person arrested, its application should

[17] Gallegos v. Nebraska, 342 U.S. 55 (1951).

[18] See Waite, The Law of Arrest, 24 Texas Law Rev. 279 (1946). See note 23 below.

[19] It is said that the police sometimes designedly delay arresting a suspect until Friday evening, where they have no fear of his decamping, in order to have the entire week end available for questioning him.

[20] In order that there may be a magistrate near at hand before whom a person arrested on a federal charge before information or indictment may be brought for preliminary examination, Congress has provided for a federal officer, termed a

not depend on factors as capricious as these. The whole question is one which has received inadequate sustained study.[21]

In some places, in addition to unlawfully prolonged detention following lawful arrest, there prevails the practice of detention without the pretense of the formality of an arrest. This unlawful course may be adopted by the police either because under the circumstances an arrest would necessarily be followed by the prompt production of the defendant before a magistrate for preliminary examination, followed by his discharge or his release on bail, with consequent destruction of the opportunity for prolonged questioning; or because knowledge of a formal arrest may give warning to the suspect's confederates; or because the suspicions of the police do not justify an arrest, and the arrest itself might open the arresting officer to liability for damages. In such a situation, an arrest, a matter of public record, is readily established; an unlawful detention, without arrest, may be impossible to establish.

It is moreover important to appreciate that under our law of arrest, the power of a peace officer to make an arrest, when acting without a judicial order of arrest (or "warrant")[22] is closely limited. The law on this matter is of ancient lineage, coming down from a period antedating organized police forces, when arrests were generally made by private persons. Under the rules so developed a private person could arrest only for a crime committed in his presence, and if the crime were a misdemeanor only if it constituted a breach of the peace. With the development of specialized police officers, the strict limitations developed by the courts on the power of a private person to make an arrest were imposed on officers as well.

United States Commissioner, found in most cities, vested with power to hold the preliminary examination and to fix bail. Each district court is empowered to appoint as many commissioners as it deems necessary, their compensation being on a fee basis.

[21] The most thorough public exploration of the problem was that made in 1958 before a congressional committee in hearings on a bill to permit "reasonable" delay in bringing the person arrested before a magistrate in the District of Columbia. The bill resulted from public dissatisfaction with a decision of the Supreme Court reversing the conviction of a defendant charged with a brutal crime (and generally believed to be unquestionably guilty), because his confession, which constituted the indispensable evidence against him at his trial, had been obtained from him some hours after his arrest, when he was under detention and was being questioned by the Washington police, a period during which he should have been brought before a magistrate. Mallory v. United States, 354 U.S. 449 (1957). The bill, in various forms, passed both houses, but the Congress came to an end before the differences could be resolved.

[22] In the absence of information or indictment, the warrant may be issued only "upon probable cause, supported by oath or affirmation," made by either a police officer or a private person. The quoted language is found in the Constitution (Fourth Amendment) and is thus specifically applicable only to federal warrants; but recent decisions of the Supreme Court indicate that it regards the requirement as equally applicable to state warrants, as an essential element of due process of law.

But in time some relaxation became necessary. In most states today an officer may arrest for any misdemeanor committed in his presence even if no breach of the peace is involved, and in some he may arrest merely on reasonable suspicion that a misdemeanor has been committed. More important, an officer may arrest for a felony not committed in his presence, if he has reasonable ground for believing the person arrested to have committed the offense; and in not quite half the states the officer is in any case free from liability if the person arrested is subsequently found guilty.

As with other restrictions on police methods, these severe restrictions on the power of the police officer to arrest for offenses not committed in his presence are not infrequently disregarded in practice. Persons who are without much standing in the community are often arrested on suspicion of knowing something about a felony, or of having had "something to do with it"—suspicion far below that "reasonable ground for believing" that the person to be arrested actually committed the felony which the law requires.[23] Similarly, such persons are arrested, unlawfully, by police officers, for misdemeanors not committed in the officer's presence. Finally, in some states, a loophole in the legal theory is furnished, as to the professional criminal class and persons having no settled abode, by the offense of "vagrancy"—a form of offense initially and still for the most part below the grade of misdemeanor, if indeed an offense at all, but one for which arrest is lawful without the necessity for any overt act by the so-called offender.[24] A charge of vagrancy is thus often found the most convenient available pretext for arresting a person suspected of complicity in or knowledge of a crime, where the evidence in hand would hardly justify an arrest based on the crime itself. In a few states the law authorizes the arrest as a "disorderly person" of any one found abroad at night who fails to give a satisfactory account of himself, thus in effect providing, in the guise of arrest, a procedure for detention for questioning.

In characterizing police practice in the matter of arrests as in effect frequently unlawful, there is no thought of suggesting that the purpose of such unlawful practice is invariably sinister. On the contrary it reflects, in

[23] Although in theory a person arrested is to be brought before a magistrate in all cases, in most cities, as already noted, a considerable percentage of those arrested are released by the police without any charge being entered against them. In a painstaking study of police practices in two cities in California (a state whose police practices are rated highly by those in the field) it was found that those so released constituted from 18 to 34 per cent of all those arrested. Barrett, Police Practices and the Law—From Arrest to Release or Charge, 50 Calif. Law Rev. 11 (1962). A bar association committee in Detroit reported that in 1956 45 per cent of all arrests made in that city were "for investigation," no offense being stated to the person arrested at the time of his arrest, and that in 80 per cent of the arrests in this category, the person arrested was released by the police without any charge being made against him.

[24] See Lacey, Vagrancy and Other Crimes of Personal Condition, 66 Harv. Law Rev. 1203 (1953).

many cases, a praiseworthy zeal in the pursuit of the criminal, leading the zealous officer to chafe against, to strain, and occasionally to break the shackles which the law has thrown about his operations. There is a considerable and respectable body of opinion in favor of enlarging the power of the police to arrest without warrant persons suspected of crime. The detailed proposals are beyond the scope of this book.

In the absence of such provision, suspects and even witnesses, not suspected of guilty knowledge, are thus frequently detained, despite the want of legal power, by police and prosecuting authorities. Force is, of course, hardly ever used to enforce such detention; rather is it enforced by the implied threat of arrest on a charge not then specified—an arrest which, as we have seen, would in most cases itself be illegal—should the person detained seek to leave the premises where he is detained or the presence of the officers detaining him.

It has been suggested that a police officer should have power to stop any person who he has reasonable ground to believe has committed (or is about to commit) a crime, and require him to identify himself and to state where he is bound; and that, if not satisfied with the answers given the officer should be empowered to place him under detention for not more than two hours, during which time further questioning and investigation may be had. Such an enactment (assuming it were not declared by the courts to be a denial of due process) would doubtless legalize many of the acts of unlawful detention and some of unlawful arrest now committed by the police; but the prolonged illegal detentions often resorted to by the police in serious cases would doubtless continue.

Moreover it will be noted that the proposal referred to applies only to a person reasonably suspected of having committed or being about to commit a crime. It leaves untouched the impotence of the police or prosecuting authorities to detain one not so suspected.[25]

It is characteristic of proposals to enlarge police powers in this field, that if enacted, their efficacy as reforms would depend chiefly upon whether the police would observe the new, less severe limitations on their power any better than they observe the admittedly too severe limitations that now exist. One may be permitted to doubt whether they would, unless indeed the new powers were as broad as the police idea of what they ought to be— hardly a practical probability. The difficulty is that abuse by the police

[25] In some states, a witness to a crime who refuses to identify himself to an officer at the scene may thus be detained for a brief period. Moreover, in many states, provision exists for the detention of witnesses by judicial order, once a charge is before a magistrate or grand jury. The statute usually provides that a judge may, after an opportunity for hearing, order a material witness to enter into a written undertaking (with such sureties and in such sum as the judge may deem proper) to the effect that he will appear to testify; and in default of such undertaking being furnished, the judge may order him taken into custody.

of their powers with respect to persons detained is extremely difficult to establish. Probably only an independent agency, expressly created to watch the police and check such abuses, would be equal to the task. However, as has already been pointed out, a reduction of the almost complete autonomy enjoyed by local police and prosecuting officials and their subjection to some measure of control and supervision by a state authority would undoubtedly have a most salutary effect in checking abuses in this field.

If an arrest is made unlawfully, the person making the arrest, whether private person or officer, becomes personally liable in damages to the person arrested; and suits of this nature, if not common, are by no means rare. Moreover, an unlawful arrest, even by an officer, is denounced by the statutes of most states as a misdemeanor. More important from a practical standpoint, however, is the effect which the unlawful character of the arrest may have upon the admissibility of evidence obtained in the search made incidental to the arrest, a matter shortly to be considered.

In theory our law provides an immediate remedy against illegal detention, as well as against illegal arrest. Application may be made to a court for an order commanding the officer having custody of the prisoner forthwith to bring him before the court so that the court may inquire into his allegedly illegal detention and, if the detention is found to be indeed illegal, to order his immediate release. The order which thus commands the jailer to produce the prisoner in court is known as a writ of habeas corpus (from the opening words of the ancient writ, meaning, in Latin, "have the body").[26]

The enormous importance of this historic remedy as a protection against arbitrary arrest and detention cannot be overestimated. But, obviously, in the great majority of unwarranted arrests and detentions occurring in the routine police activities of large cities, the person arrested or detained lacks the knowledge and the resources needed to set in motion the machinery of a habeas corpus proceeding before a court of superior jurisdiction (for only such courts are vested with jurisdiction of the proceeding) even should he be permitted, as he often is not, to communicate freely with counsel or friends. Moreover, some delay will necessarily ensue before he is actually produced before the court, with possible further delay while the matter is under consideration by the court. Such delays will in most cases extend well beyond the time at which he would in any event be released by the police or brought before the magistrate for preliminary examination.

Unquestionably, it is the legal impotence of police and prosecutor to

---

[26] Sometimes, in modern practice, the initial order of the court, instead of requiring the jailer to produce his prisoner, merely directs him to set forth by what authority he holds the prisoner. If the papers filed in answer to this direction indicate that a hearing should be held, the jailer is ordered to produce the prisoner at the hearing. Regardless of the procedure followed in this respect, the proceeding is known as a habeas corpus proceeding.

interrogate which causes them to resort to illegal detention and unjustified arrests. It is worth considering whether our procedure should not provide for the compulsory questioning, under proper safeguards, by qualified police officials, or by the prosecutor or his qualified deputies, of persons who do not voluntarily answer questions. If the vesting of such power in the higher police officials or the prosecutor is thought dangerous, a further safeguard could be provided by requiring the interrogation to take place before a qualified judicial officer. Under present constitutional provisions such interrogation would of course be subject to the witness's privilege against self-incrimination.

4. POLICE AND PROSECUTOR: SEARCHES AND SEIZURES

Next to questioning, and in some cases of even greater usefulness in the investigation of crime, is of course the search for physical evidence and its impounding when found. Here we encounter the constitutional prohibition against "unreasonable" searches and seizures and also, indeed, the constitutional privilege against self-incrimination; for despite the use, in the standard constitutional provision against self-incrimination, of the words "witness" or "give evidence," the courts have sometimes cited that privilege also in this connection.

The provision that no "unreasonable" searches or seizures may be made —a provision that for practical purposes may be regarded as controlling only searches made without warrant—is found in the Constitution (in the Fourth Amendment), as a restriction on federal officers, and in virtually all state constitutions. Regardless of the past construction of the prohibtion by state courts, it is now settled by holdings of the Supreme Court that the guarantee contained in the Fourth Amendment is an essential part of due process of law and hence binding on the states, and that in enforcing the guarantee against state officers the same standards are to be employed as have been applied by the Court to federal officers.[27]

Search and seizure incident to arrest

Although a person under arrest has a right to refuse to answer questions, there is one respect in which, despite the broad scope of the privileges against self-incrimination and unreasonable search, he may be compelled to yield incriminating information. The arresting officer may lawfully search the person arrested and take into his own possession anything found which he may deem to be evidence of crime (as well as anything which might be of aid to the prisoner should he attempt to escape). Moreover, the officer is empowered to search the immediate vicinity of the place where the arrest is made and similarly take into his own possession any evidence there found, the basis of this rule being the presumption that objects in

[27] Ker v. California, 374 U.S. 23 (1963).

the immediate vicinity of the person arrested are in his control. If however the arrest is illegal, the search of the prisoner's person and of objects in his immediate control is likewise illegal. Since, as will shortly be noted, objects seized in the course of an illegal search are inadmissible in evidence in our courts, the importance of strict observance by the arresting officer of the limitations on his power to arrest without warrant is obvious. Moreover, even though the arrest be unquestionably a legal one, the claim may be set up by the person arrested that the search was actually made before the arrest had been technically consummated, and was therefore illegal, and its fruits equally inadmissible in evidence. The difficulties of determining, retrospectively, the precise moment of time when the arrest was completed have perplexed some of our high courts; it is hardly to be wondered at that the police officer making the arrest may be equally perplexed.

Inspection and search of premises; seizure of evidence

The obligation to open one's doors to the agents of the state engaged solely in investigation is found in two quite distinct settings. On the one hand is the obligation to admit officials engaged in routine inspection to ascertain whether the laws regulating the structure itself, or the activities currently carried on in it, are being complied with. Contrasted with this is the obligation to admit an officer searching for evidence of crime— such as stolen goods—suspected of being on the premises. The second is of course of much earlier development.

Fairly early in the development of the English law after the Conquest there appears the practice of search of premises by an officer of the law seeking stolen goods, and seizure of the goods if found, the officer acting under authority of a warrant issued by a magistrate, specifying the place to be searched and the goods to be seized. From this practice developed the principle that the subject was not obligated to admit an officer wishing to make such search and seizure unless the officer was armed with a specific warrant of the character described; and that a forcible entry of the premises by an officer not so armed constituted an actionable wrong.

This principle did not, however, enjoy complete obedience. From time to time Parliament by special act authorized the issuance of general warrants, empowering officers to search anywhere for certain classes of contraband—particularly goods smuggled into the country. The application of these acts to the American colonies, and their allegedly oppressive enforcement, created violent opposition in the seaports.[28]

It was against this background that there were included in several of

[28] In the attempt of the Stuarts in the seventeenth century to repress popular criticism, there developed without statutory authority the further practice of the issuance by the government, without any judicial action, of general warrants authorizing the search for and seizure of seditious libels. In the late eighteenth century, however, a struggle against this type of warrant resulted in its virtual abolition.

the state constitutions adopted during the Revolution prohibitions against general warrants; and a like prohibition was included in the series of limitations upon the power of the newly created federal government, embodied in the first ten Amendments, adopted in 1791, the language being that "no warrant [for a search and seizure] shall issue but upon probable cause, supported by oath or affirmation, and particularly describing the place to be searched and the . . . things to be seized." Similar provisions are found in virtually all state constitutions.

To obtain lawful access to premises for purposes of inspection and search of contents, and of seizure of contents believed to constitute evidence of crime, the law-enforcement officer, whether police officer or detective, must accordingly seek authorization from a judicial officer.[29] Such an authorization, known as a "search warrant," may be issued by the judicial officer—usually referred to in this connection as the magistrate—only upon the basis of a sworn statement setting forth the reasons for believing that evidence of crime is to be found on the premises in question.

Such is the constitutional mandate. But what is the citizen's remedy if, despite the constitutional prohibition, the officer does forcibly enter and search his premises and does seize property there found? The injured citizen may indeed sue the officer for damages. He may bring action for the return to him of the property thus unlawfully seized. But as a practical matter these remedies are in most cases ineffectual, nor have the legislatures provided any additional remedies. The executive also has in general shown little disposition to check unlawful searches, which are said to have become virtually routine in the practice of some police departments. It was in this posture of the matter that the Supreme Court, in 1914, announced that objects seized by federal officers in illegal searches would not be received in evidence in the federal courts, making plain that it hoped thereby to discourage such illegal searches.[30] In the succeeding quarter-century an increasing number of high state courts adopted the same exclusionary rule; but the majority of them, unwilling that the criminal should escape merely "because the constable has blundered,"[31] refused to do so, adhering to the traditional principle, still in force in all other English-speaking countries, that the means by which a particular object had been obtained has no bearing on its admissibility in evidence. State legislatures

[29] Because of the ease with which a vehicle or vessel may be removed before a search warrant can be obtained, some courts have ruled that, if an officer has reasonable ground for believing that evidence of crime (chiefly of course smuggled, stolen, or contraband goods) is to be found in a vehicle or vessel, he may lawfully search it without a warrant; such a search (and the possibly resultant seizure) not being "unreasonable." The difficulties that may confront both the officer in applying this rule, and the courts in subsequently passing on the propriety of his action, are obvious. See Brinegar v. United States, 338 U.S. 160 (1949).

[30] Weeks v. United States, 232 U.S. 383 (1914).

[31] Cardozo, J., in People v. Defore, 242 N.Y. 13, 21 (1926).

also generally refused to change the traditional rule. In 1961, however, in the landmark Mapp case,[32] the Supreme Court, overruling its previous holdings to the direct contrary,[33] declared the enforcement of the federal rule by the state courts to be indispensable to due process of law. The federal rule thus became overnight the national rule.

Traditionally, the property sought to be seized by a search conducted under a search warrant was either stolen or contraband articles; and the traditional form of warrant limited the seizure to such articles. If strictly construed, such a warrant did not authorize the seizure of books of account, an invaluable type of evidence in the case of many sophisticated offenses, such as bribery, extortion, and the like. Some courts have in consequence construed the traditional rule to permit the seizure of such items, accepting the assertion of the police or prosecutor, made in the affidavit submitted in support of the application for the warrant, that the books of account were indispensable instrumentalities in the commission of the alleged crime, and not merely evidence thereof. In some states a liberalization of the traditional rule has been effected by statute.

An important exception to the rule that premises may not be searched without a search warrant exists in connection with an arrest made under a warrant of arrest. In executing such a warrant, the officer may lawfully enter on the premises where the person named in the warrant may be (using force to effect an entry if necessary); and, after making the arrest he may, if the premises are owned or occupied by the person arrested, conduct a "limited" search of the immediate premises for evidence of the guilt of such person. The Supreme Court has held that if in the course of such search, he comes upon evidence of a criminal act by the person thus arrested, other than the act charged in the warrant, he may seize such evidence also. At any rate, if he does seize it, it will thereafter be received in evidence in the federal courts, against the person whose premises were searched, in a prosecution for such other crime.[34] The logical inconsistencies involved, whatever the value of the practical results, are self-evident. The precise limitations on the permissible extent and thoroughness of the search of premises by a federal officer whose sole authority for the search is that he has, under a warrant of arrest, made an arrest on the premises, remain to be defined by the Court.[35]

In sharp contrast to the total absence on the part of police or detective forces (and the same is true of federal agents) of a general right of access

[32] Mapp v. Ohio, 367 U.S. 643 (1961).

[33] Wolf v. Colorado, 338 U.S. 25 (1949).

[34] United States v. Rabinowitz, 339 U.S. 56 (1950); cf. Abel v. United States, 367 U.S. 217 (1960).

[35] As already indicated, any limitations placed by the Supreme Court on the permissible extent of the search of premises under a warrant, whether a search warrant or a warrant of arrest, by a federal officer are equally binding on state officers. The states may of course place additional limitations upon their officers.

to premises, is the right of the inspector who demands access in order to examine the premises themselves, or the operations there conducted, to ascertain whether applicable legal regulations are being observed. Laws authorizing such inspections without warrant are of course of long standing; but their constitutionality, as applied to the inspection of a private home, has been brought into question only in recent years, the contention being that they violate the constitutional "right of the people to be secure in their . . . houses . . . against unreasonable searches." The Supreme Court, by a divided bench, has sustained the constitutionality of a local sanitary ordinance of this character.[36]

Listening in on telephone conversations

A final related aspect of the permissible invasion of the privacy of the individual concerns "wire tapping"—i.e., making secret connection to a telephone line to eavesdrop on telephone conversations—by officers of the law. The Supreme Court of the United States, before the matter was regulated by statute, ruled that evidence of such conversations was admissible in federal prosecutions—that wire tapping did not constitute an "unreasonable search and seizure" within the meaning of the Constitution. Subsequently, in 1934, Congress made it unlawful for any person, unless authorized by the sender, to "intercept" any communication by wire or radio, or to "divulge" the contents of a communication so intercepted.[37] The Supreme Court, in pursuance of its view that evidence illegally obtained should not be received in evidence in the federal courts, promptly laid down the rule that evidence obtained by federal officers by wire tapping should not be received in those courts. Inasmuch as the statute does not expressly prohibit the reception of evidence obtained by wire tapping, the state courts in most cases continued to receive it; and many still do. The Supreme Court has refused to set aside a state conviction, based on such evidence, obtained by state officers.[38] Nevertheless, subsequent decisions on related aspects of state wire tapping[39] have given rise to the belief that the Court may declare evidence so obtained by state officers to be inadmissible in state courts. Meanwhile, in several states, wire tapping is expressly authorized by law, the police being required to obtain a court order, analogous to a search warrant, before making the tap.

More recently, some state prosecuting authorities have refrained from

[36] Frank v. Maryland, 359 U.S. 360 (1959).

[37] 47 U.S. Code, Sec. 605. This provision, unlike other provisions of the same section, is not in its terms restricted to interstate and foreign communications. The Supreme Court has construed the provision as applying to intrastate communications. Weiss v. United States, 308 U.S. 321 (1939). The power of Congress to regulate intrastate commerce where necessarily incident to the regulation of interstate commerce is well established.

[38] Schwartz v. Texas, 344 U.S. 199 (1952).

[39] Benanti v. United States, 355 U.S. 96 (1957).

the introduction of wire tap evidence, professing a fear that its introduction might cause a reversal of the ensuing conviction, as being the fruit of an unconstitutional search and seizure under the Supreme Court decision of 1961, banning the use in state prosecutions of evidence obtained by such unlawful search—this despite the fact that the Court, before the enactment of the federal statute forbidding it, had declared that wire tapping does not violate the constitutional prohibition.[40]

Of late a form of eavesdropping somewhat akin to wire tapping has come to be employed by detective forces—electronic devices which enable the user to listen in on conversations at a distance much beyond that possible to the unaided ear.[41] Although eavesdropping, sometimes made possible only through concealment and through techniques not far removed from housebreaking, has long been an accepted detective procedure, the improvement in effectiveness accomplished by the electronic hearing aid has excited libertarian hostility; and in at least one state (New York) the use of such devices by law-enforcement officers, except briefly in emergencies, is prohibited unless authorized by a court order analogous to a search warrant.[42]

It need hardly be said that legislative prohibitions against wire tapping have no inherent effectiveness. The individual whose wire is tapped is extremely unlikely to detect the fact, and even if he does, the identification of the law-enforcement officers responsible, and their prosecution for violation of the statutory prohibition, are equally unlikely. To the statutory prohibition the responsible authority must add a self-denying ordinance. The rule prohibiting the use in evidence of transcripts of telephone conversations thus unlawfully overheard does of course, where that rule is followed, reduce the usefulness of unlawful wire tapping to the detective; but it by no means destroys it. Even though the overheard conversation may not be testified to, its content may furnish the listener with invaluable information; and the evidence secured from the lead thus illegally obtained may, when subsequently introduced at a criminal trial, disclose no trace of its illegal genesis. It is to be suspected that unlawful wire tapping by law-enforcement officers continues on a scale greater than is commonly appreciated.[43]

5. CORONER'S INQUEST

In one field of criminal investigation—that of violent or suspicious deaths—the prosecutor's responsibility is in many states further divided, being shared with an independent county official (usually indeed inde-

[40] Olmstead v. United States, 277 U.S. 438 (1928).

[41] The term "wire tapping" was coined at a time when physical connection with the telephone wire was necessary. It is said that there are now devices which function without this, by mere induction.

[42] Penal Law, Secs. 728–29, enacted in 1957.

[43] See Dash, Schwartz, and Knowlton, The Eavesdroppers (1959).

pendently elected) known as the coroner. The coroner's office, transported to these shores by the English colonists, is today the vestigial remnant of an office once of considerable dignity in the administration of English justice, and embracing a variety of functions. The American coroner of today, however, has ordinarily no function but that of the investigation of accidental and suspicious death;[44] and in that field his function overlaps that of the police and the prosecutor, both often better equipped for such investigation than he. He possesses, however, in some states one advantage over them—he may subpoena witnesses to attend before him at an "inquest." The evidence is taken at the inquest either before the coroner alone or before a jury of six or more who render a verdict (generally taking the form of a finding that the deceased committed suicide or that he met his death at the hands of persons unknown). A coroner's inquest, in contrast to a grand jury session, is open to the public. Questioning of the witnesses may be by either the coroner or the prosecutor. Witnesses are of course entitled to refuse to answer on the ground of possible self-incrimination.

In some states the coroner has the power, on the conclusion of the inquest, to issue a warrant for the arrest of a person found by the inquest to have caused the death, and to conduct, in the same manner as a magistrate, the preliminary examination of the person arrested—a proceeding shortly to be described.

With the obsolescence of its functions, the coroner's office has suffered a corresponding decline in dignity and attractiveness. Even if its continuance could be justified on any rational theory of division of function, the low estate to which the office has almost everywhere fallen in this country and its tendency to form an unsavory connection with political machines would furnish strong grounds for its abolition. But it has, like so many political organs that have outlived their function, shown a great power of survival.[45] In a growing number of states, however, the office has been abolished, either generally or in the larger cities, and the office of medical examiner, a purely technical, nonpolitical office, frequently charged with medical functions additional to the performance of autopsies (but usually without power to hold an inquest), has been created.

6. PRELIMINARY EXAMINATION OF CHARGE AGAINST PERSON ARRESTED

As already noted, if a person is arrested on a criminal charge of such gravity that he cannot be required to stand trial on the mere complaint of the police officer or private party responsible for his arrest, but must first

[44] In some states the coroner may also investigate suspicious fires. In a few states, a special officer known as a fire marshal is vested with subpoena powers for this purpose.

[45] In a few states, however, the office of coroner does not exist. In at least one state, the functions of the office are performed by the justice of the peace.

be formally accused by the proper authorities, he is entitled to a prompt judicial hearing of the charge, to determine whether the evidence against him is sufficient to warrant his being further held in custody (subject to release on bail) pending a determination whether such formal accusation shall be filed. To such a hearing, the term preliminary examination is ordinarily applied; and the judicial officer before whom such preliminary examination is held is termed in this connection, whatever his official judicial title, a magistrate. The preliminary examination is thus in theory not an investigative procedure at all. Its investigative value is purely incidental.

The concept of the preliminary examination as a proceeding solely for the benefit of the person arrested is, as such things go, a comparatively recent arrival on the Anglo-American legal scene. In its origin in the sixteenth century, and in its development for three centuries thereafter, the proceeding before the examining magistrate was an important element in the English system of criminal investigation. The magistrate, regarded as not solely or perhaps even primarily a judicial officer, but also, in the absence of any organized police or detective forces, as the official responsible for the investigation of crime, was empowered in felony cases to interrogate the accused (without however putting him on oath) and to reduce his answers to writing. The record, together with the record of the testimony of the witnesses, was then forwarded to the authorities for use in the subsequent prosecution. No punishment was imposed for the refusal of the accused to answer a question put to him by the magistrate, but at his subsequent trial such refusal (as well as his answers) could be put into evirence against him. This system, carried over to the colonies, persisted in this country till the middle of the last century—in some jurisdictions indeed into the latter decades of the century.[46] The questioning of the accused at the preliminary examination thus continued long after the right of the accused to exemption from being "a witness against himself" or from "giving evidence against himself" had been enshrined in constitutional provisions. Since the questioning was not under oath, he was not a "witness" nor was he giving "evidence."

About the middle of the last century the practice began to develop of requiring the magistrate merely to inform the accused that he might make a statement, not under oath, if he so desired, and that such statement might be used against him. This is the formula (in many states incorporated in statute) still in use today.

Despite the hallowed constitutional position of the privilege against self-incrimination, it is difficult to see why it should be preserved with respect to the preliminary examination of the charge before the magistrate. Indeed the privilege in general has in recent years come increasingly

[46] Cf. Wilson v. United States, 162 U.S. 613 (1896).

under attack.[47] It has become clear that the historical importance attached to the privilege by the courts in their opinions justifying their expansion of it has been greatly overstated. The classical argument of Bentham, now over a century old, that the privilege is devoid of any substantial rational foundation, is generally accepted; and the continuance of the privilege is defended on purely empirical grounds. Thus an authoritative commentator declares that "the strongest consideration in support of the privilege is that it stimulates the police and prosecuting officers to make a more thorough investigation of the facts than they would if they could rely on getting the proof by grilling the prisoner."[48] Presumably, the "grilling" of the prisoner on which the police and prosecutor might thus be encouraged to rely would be his interrogation before the magistrate at the preliminary examination (or subsequently before the grand jury); for he is not now protected by the privilege against self-incrimination from being grilled by police or prosecutor while in their custody. It protects him from questioning by them only when he is before the examining magistrate or the grand jury. (It also protects witnesses before those forums, not indeed from questioning, but from the necessity of answering questions allegedly calling for a self-incriminating answer.)

Putting aside the question of whether there is any important value in the making of an investigation, whether more or less thorough, when the proof can be obtained by "grilling" the prisoner, it is not clear why the police and prosecutor should be denied, in their often baffling task of investigation, the assistance which could be derived from the answers that both the suspect and the witnesses might be compelled to give at the preliminary examination, were the privilege withdrawn. The danger doubtless exists that where the person arrested is without counsel, the magistrate might fail to protect the suspect or the witnesses from being browbeaten and threatened by the prosecutor or police interrogator; but it could be reduced to a minimum by proper provision for furnishing counsel at the preliminary examination to all indigent defendants (a matter discussed at a later point); by a detailed code of procedure governing the examination, any breach of which would make both the magistrate and the interrogator liable to discipline; and by improving the quality of the justices of the peace and police judges who so often in so many areas preside at the

[47] "The immunity from compulsory self-incrimination . . . might be lost, and justice still be done. Indeed, to-day as in the past, there are students of our penal system who look upon the immunity as a mischief rather than a benefit, and who would limit its scope, or destroy it altogether. No doubt there would remain the need to give protection against torture, physical or mental. Justice, however, would not perish if the accused were subject to a duty to respond to orderly inquiry." Cardozo, J., in Palko v. Connecticut, 302 U.S. 319–326 (1937). See, generally, 8 Wigmore, Evidence (McNaughton rev. 1961) Sec. 2251; and Mayers, Shall We Amend the Fifth Amendment? (1959).

[48] McCormick, "Evidence," in 5 Encyc. Soc. Sci. 640 (1932).

preliminary examination, obviously a factor of prime importance in this connection.[49]

The presentation of the evidence at the preliminary examination is occasionally, particularly in misdemeanor cases, in the hands of the private complainant; but in the bulk of cases the police or prosecutor take charge. Ordinarily the purpose, in either case, is to present only enough evidence against the suspect to insure his being held by the magistrate. From a tactical standpoint the presentation of more than this may be regarded by the police or prosecutor as unwise. There is in most jurisdictions neither legal rule nor ethical tradition obliging them to produce at the preliminary examination all the evidence in their possession. On the other hand the preliminary examination furnishes the prosecutor with his first opportunity to compel answers from an uncooperative witness, or from one even friendly to the person arrested.

Moreover, in the case of a witness who has voluntarily given information, the preliminary examination affords the prosecutor an opportunity to elicit the witness's statement under oath in open court, thereby insuring against the witness changing his story at the trial. In this respect the preliminary examination may be regarded as an aid to the prosecutor in establishing a case against the suspect at the subsequent trial, rather than as a procedure for investigation.

To prevent this result, a sophisticated lawbreaker, usually represented by counsel even at the preliminary hearing, frequently "waives examination"—i.e., consents to be held in bail (which he promptly furnishes) for the action of the prosecutor or the grand jury without any witnesses being heard by the magistrate—a procedure the law obviously would not tolerate were the preliminary examination designed to aid in the investigation of the crime.[50] On the other hand, the prisoner, though fully aware that he will be held in bail, may prefer not to waive examination but to require the witnesses against him to be produced, hoping to learn thereby the extent of the information in the hands of the prosecutor. He may then at the close of the testimony adduced by the prosecutor waive the privilege which he enjoys of making a statement and of calling witnesses on his own behalf; for the record which may then be made may, should he later be required to stand trial, arise to plague him.

The defendant's failure to take advantage of the opportunity to make a statement before the magistrate may not be disclosed at his subsequent

[49] It should be noted that the interrogation of the suspect under the conditions suggested would have no resemblance to the interrogation conducted by the French juge d'instruction, often referred to in this connection. That official may indeed occupy a judicial office, and may discharge, in other connections, judicial functions; but when acting as a juge d'instruction he is not, despite his title, a judical officer at all. He is an inquisitor and investigator who is part of the machinery of prosecution.

[50] In a few states, however, the magistrate may, despite the waiver, take the testimony of the prosecution's witnesses.

trial. The possibility of such disclosure would, in the prevailing view, though the question has not been authoritatively adjudicated, place him under such compulsion to make a statement before the magistrate as would be repugnant to the concept of the privilege against compulsory self-incrimination; hence, proposals to permit such disclosure, though strongly urged, have not been adopted. This extreme application of the doctrine has been severely criticized. It is urged that since the suspect is protected by the constitutional guarantee from any legal penalty for declining to make a statement, he should at the least be subjected to the moral compulsion arising from the knowledge that such refusal will be disclosed at his trial.

7. GRAND JURY INVESTIGATION

The grand jury is a body of citizens (the number varying greatly) summoned by the court to inquire into and make accusation of crimes committed in the county (or, in the case of a federal grand jury, in the federal court district).[51] The methods by which the citizens called to serve as grand jurors are selected are substantially the same as those used in the selection of trial jurors, a matter to be discussed subsequently.

Although provision for the impaneling of a grand jury is found in all of our states, in only about half of them does the grand jury function as a regular and indispensable part of the machinery of criminal justice. In the remaining half, the prosecutor has been empowered to make formal accusation of all, or all but the most serious, crimes on his own responsibility. In consequence, the grand jury as an organ of accusation has in those states become largely obsolete and is convened only for special reasons.

As an agency of investigation a body of citizens, sitting as a body and summoning witnesses before them, is obviously a relic of a way of life which has, in most American communities, long since disappeared. The persistent survival of the grand jury under modern conditions is doubtless largely to be explained by its possession of an instrument of investigation not possessed, as we have seen, by the police or the prosecutor—the power (with the aid of the court)[52] to compel the attendance of witnesses, to put them under oath, and to compel answers to questions and the produc-

[51] In England the number could be anything from twelve to twenty-three, and this is still the rule in some states. In others a minimum of sixteen is required, and in still others the maximum size of the jury has been reduced by statute in varying degree, a grand jury of seven being found in one state and of five in another. The tendency is to reduce its size. The term "grand" (meaning merely large) came into use because the number of jurors, originally always twenty-three, was larger than that composing the trial or petit jury, numbering twelve.

[52] If a subpoena issued by the prosecutor in the name of the grand jury is not obeyed, the witness may be cited for contempt of court before the court under whose supervision the grand jury sits. In addition, disobedience may in some jurisdictions be punished by a criminal prosecution.

tion of books and papers and of other objects.[53] These powers make of the grand jury potentially a powerful agency of investigation. Today, however, even in the states where it is regularly convened (and the same is true of the federal grand jury, likewise of necessity regularly convened), the grand jury ordinarily conducts no independent investigation. It merely hears such witnesses as the prosecutor calls before it. The prosecutor, in turn, seldom contents himself with merely producing before the grand jury such witnesses as are available, without having previously questioned them. To allow the facts to develop for the first time in the presence of the grand jury would in most cases be inordinately time consuming. Instead, the prosecutor, unless the witness has already testified fully at the preliminary examination, ordinarily questions him fairly thoroughly in advance of the grand jury sitting, and calls before that body only such witnesses, and elicits only such testimony, as he deems necessary. Where, however, witnesses have proved uncooperative, the grand jury is of course a powerful aid in eliciting information as well as in obtaining under oath the testimony of a witness who might be tempted to disavow the unsworn statements he has already made to the prosecutor.

The subpoena power of the grand jury is necessarily limited to witnesses within the state. By virtue however of reciprocal state legislation—termed "the uniform act to secure the attendance of witnesses from without the state in criminal cases"[54]—the grand jury may, if sitting in any of the forty-five states which have enacted such legislation, procure the attendance of a witness from any of the reciprocating states. In addition, a federal statute enacted in 1946, and broadened in 1961, punishes any interstate movement made to avoid giving testimony in any criminal proceeding in which the offense involved is a felony.[55]

The proceedings of the grand jury are not only private but secret. Disclosure of what has occurred before it, whether by a member of the jury itself, or by any of the officials assisting it (including the prosecutor) is

[53] In compelling the appearance of a witness, the grand jury may also compel him to bring with him any records it may specify. The records remain in the custody of the witness however. They may be marked in evidence but may not be impounded except by order of the court—an exceptional procedure. The grand jury does not therefore furnish a convenient method of searching books and papers minutely for possible bits of evidence—an invaluable procedure in the investigation of certain classes of crime. In many cases, however, the witness, to avoid the loss of time involved in testifying, voluntarily surrenders the books to the prosecutor for examination.

[54] The procedure calls for the issuance of an order by a judge in the county where the desired witness is, directing him to appear in the state in which his testimony is desired, on pain of being in contempt of court; and if the judge deems it necessary, he may even order the witness to be taken into custody by an officer of the requesting state for removal to that state.

[55] 18 U.S. Code, Sec. 1073. See also 28 U.S. Code, Secs. 1783–1784, empowering a federal court to subpoena an American citizen abroad whose testimony in a criminal proceeding is desired by the Attorney General.

punishable; and though a like legal obligation of secrecy is not in most jurisdictions imposed on the witness, he is commonly enjoined to observe secrecy and does so. On the other hand, the place and time of meeting of the grand jury cannot possibly be kept secret. Consequently the identity of the witnesses called before it is invariably a matter of common knowledge—with obvious loss of some, occasionally perhaps much, of the advantage of secrecy.

From time to time, but very rarely, the grand jury, in the investigation of a particular crime, may take the initiative away from the prosecutor, itself insisting that he call before it witnesses he has not seen fit to call, or has even advised against calling. The severe limitations under which a "runaway" grand jury labors, however, are obvious—impaneled as it ordinarily is for only a month (though the statutes may provide for its term being extended by the court), without any funds under its control, and legally incapable, ordinarily, of retaining even unpaid counsel who would act independently of the prosecutor. In those states in which the governor or attorney general possess the requisite power, a grand jury in this situation may induce him to furnish it with special counsel displacing the uncooperative prosecutor.

Although, historically, the grand jury was not regarded as having the power to conduct a general investigation to discover crimes, that power has, in greater or less degree, come to be assumed from time to time by the grand jury in some at least of the states. In some states, a special grand jury for a particular county may be impaneled by the governor to investigate a particular group of alleged infractions of the law, such as an allegedly systematic course of official bribery. This grand jury pursues its investigations wholly independently of the successive monthly regular grand juries. Sometimes there is appointed for its guidance and assistance a special prosecutor, independent of the regular prosecutor of the county. A grand jury of this type is of course particularly serviceable where the regular prosecutor is suspected of being predisposed to leniency or laxness in dealing with some particular type of lawbreaking, or particular group of lawbreakers, by reason, presumably, of an unholy alliance between such lawbreakers and the political machine to which the prosecutor owes his political debts. It has even been suggested that "watchdog" grand juries of this type should be made a regular part of our county governmental machinery.[56]

It is in connection with the grand jury investigation that the privilege against self-incrimination exhibits its chief importance in criminal procedure—an importance greater than it possesses in the preliminary exam-

[56] Where the grand jury is no longer in active use, other agencies with power to compel testimony have characteristically been created for the task of investigating official wrongdoing. Dession and Cohen, The Inquisitorial Functions of Grand Juries. 41 Yale Law Jour. 687 (1932).

ination and much greater than it possesses in the trial.[57] Earlier the question was raised whether there is any valid reason for perpetuating the privilege against self-incrimination in the preliminary examination of a criminal charge against a person under arrest. The question is equally if indeed not more pertinent to the grand jury investigation. It is difficult to see how the power of the grand jury to compel answers from a suspect, or from a person having guilty knowledge, would (as has been urged) cause the police or prosecutor to slacken their efforts to obtain independent evidence. Manifestly, if the witness before the grand jury could not hide behind the privilege, the success of the prosecutor in obtaining damaging admissions from him would depend largely on how much information the prosecutor already had. The notion that a prosecutor seriously intent on results would come before the grand jury without previous thorough investigation, relying solely or chiefly on the chance of extracting self-incriminating admissions from the persons called by him, is at odds with all experience.

In the only Supreme Court opinion in which the rationale of the witness's privilege is set forth (a case dealing with a witness before a grand jury), the Court, speaking of the situation of a suspected person "asked to explain his apparent connection with a crime under investigation," stressed "the ease with which the questions put to him may assume an inquisitorial character, the temptation to beset the witness unduly, to browbeat him if he be timid or reluctant, to push him into a corner, or to entrap him into fatal contradictions."[58] The Court did not indicate whether the witness it had in mind was innocent or guilty. If innocent, the likelihood of his being entrapped into "fatal contradictions" would seem remote. In any event, the potential abuses described could readily be curbed by permitting a witness to be accompanied in the grand jury room by his own counsel—a procedure by no means without precedent—or by cognate measures.[59]

The unqualified power of the grand jury to compel witnesses before it to answer allegedly self-incriminating questions—a power to be effectuated through the commitment of the witness, by order of the court, until he answers—would tremendously increase the effectiveness of the grand jury as an agency of investigation. It is difficult to see how the exercise of such

[57] If the grand jury is of opinion that the belief in the possibility of self-incrimination, advanced by a witness as the reason for his refusal to answer, is feigned, or that even if real it has no legal foundation, the jury may request the court under whose direction its sits to direct the witness to answer, on pain of commitment for contempt of court until he answers (and in some states, at the risk also of criminal prosecution). The propriety of the witness's claim of privilege is then for the court to determine. A cognate procedure obtains in other proceedings in which a witness's right to refuse to answer on grounds of possible self-incrimination is questioned.

[58] Brown v. Walker, 161 U.S. 591, 596 (1896).

[59] A witness is often excused to consult his attorney, present outside the grand jury room for that purpose.

a power could be injurious to the innocent. Indeed, the privilege in its present form is a danger to the innocent; for it permits a hostile witness, or one seeking to shield the real culprit, to withhold testimony and even records which might exonerate an innocent suspect—this on a false plea of possible self-incrimination, a plea whose validity it is in the nature of the case impossible to evaluate.

Mention has already been made of the exemption which the prospective defendant enjoys, not only from answering questions calling for allegedly criminatory answers, but from appearing at all before the grand jury, and of the invalidity, if he is called and testifies, of any indictment that may be returned against him. In consequence, the prosecutor, before calling an implicated witness before the jury, may request him to waive the immunity from indictment which his testimony may confer upon him, and on his declining to do so may excuse him. This procedure is particularly frequent where the witness is a public official whose official acts are under investigation, for the officer is put under obvious pressure to avoid the unsavory inferences raised by his refusal to waive immunity from prosecution.[60]

8. INVESTIGATION BY ADMINISTRATIVE AGENCIES

We have seen that neither in the states nor in the federal structures do the administrative agencies exclusively charged with the investigation of crime—the police, detective, and prosecuting agencies—have the power to compel the attendance or interrogation of witnesses, the production of books or papers, or the giving of access to records in the possession of parties. In sharp contrast to this, not a few administrative agencies charged with the enforcement of particular regulatory statutes are vested with some or all of these powers; and statutes are also found in the states which vest similar powers in a permanent administrative agency, charged with investigating the conduct of official business, or in an agency created ad hoc to investigate a particular situation, often involving possible unlawful conduct. Since in not a few instances these agencies, in the course of their investigations, bring to light evidence of infractions of law constituting criminal offenses, which they turn over to the prosecuting agencies, they may be regarded as being, even though only incidentally, agencies of

[60] In New York is found an interesting provision (necessarily accomplished by constitutional rather than merely statutory amendment) aimed at public officials who refuse to waive their privilege against self-incrimination when interrogated before a grand jury with respect to matters affecting their official conduct. An official so refusing forfeits his office. This provision has been in force for nearly three decades and has seemingly given rise to no abuses or evils. A similar provision is found in Louisiana. It is difficult, however, to understand why the person suspected of bribing a public official is any more entitled to exemption from self-incrimination than is the officer whom he is suspected of bribing.

criminal investigation. An investigation by such an agency has the great advantage over a grand jury investigation that it may be prolonged without inconvenience, and that it need not confine itself, as must a grand jury investigation, to evidence of apparent criminality.[61]

Among agencies charged with the enforcement of regulatory statutes, the federal agencies are of special interest; and among these the Federal Trade Commission enjoys perhaps the widest powers of investigation. That commission is charged, among other things, with proceeding, either on its own motion or on complaint made to it, against persons using unfair methods of competition or unfair or deceptive practices in interstate or foreign commerce, and with investigating the organization, business, conduct, practices, and management of any corporation (with certain exceptions) engaged in such commerce. In carrying out these duties the commission, or its duly authorized agents "shall at all reasonable times have access to, for the purpose of examination, and the right to copy any documentary evidence of any corporation being investigated or proceeded against"; and the statute provides severe punishment, including imprisonment, for any person who "shall wilfully refuse to submit to the commission or to any of its authorized agents, for the purpose of inspection and taking copies, any documentary evidence of such corporation in his possession or within his control." Moreover, this agency is empowered, as are not a few other federal administrative investigating agencies, "to require by subpoena the attendance and testimony of witnesses." Provision is made, in the event of disobedience of its subpoena, not only for invoking the aid of a federal court possessed of the contempt power to compel obedience to the subpoena (as is the case with administrative subpoenas generally), but also for a severe criminal penalty.[62]

The federal tax officials are empowered to compel the attendance and

[61] The power to subpoena records and even to interrogate witnesses exists in some cases for the purpose of determining not merely whether any infraction of the law has been committed, but for the purpose of determining whether the person whose papers are subpoenaed, or the person who (whether personally or through his employees) is required to submit to interrogation, falls within the ambit of the regulatory statute. Perhaps as wide a grant of power as any in this category is that contained in the federal Fair Labor Standards Act (Sec. 11a) which empowers the Administrator "to enter and inspect such places and such records (and make such transcriptions), question such employees and investigate such facts, conditions, practices, or matters as he may deem appropriate to determine whether any person has violated any provisions of this Act *or which may aid in the enforcement of the provisions of this Act*" (italics supplied), a provision which has been expressly held to have the scope indicated. Curiously, though the Federal Trade Commission has for half a century had the power (15 U.S. Code, Secs. 46d, 49) to subpoena records and interrogate witnesses when investigating alleged violations of the antitrust laws (such investigation to be made, however, only upon direction of the President or of Congress), it was only in 1962, and after prolonged effort on its part, that the Department of Justice was empowered to subpoena records (but not to interrogate witnesses) in its investigations of violations of those laws. 15 U.S. Code, Secs. 1311–1314.

[62] 15 U.S. Code, Secs. 49–50.

testimony of taxpayers, and the production of their records. The investment of state tax officials with such powers is not common.

In some states the attorney general is vested with the subpoena power in making investigation of violations of the state antitrust laws, or the state laws regulating the sale of securities, or cognate violations. This power is quite independent of any power he may have to subpoena witnesses on behalf of a grand jury which is conducting an investigation under his guidance.

Among agencies charged with investigation of the conduct of the public business, of particular interest is the temporary commissioner appointed by the governor under authority of statute, to make an examination of a particular public office or project. Statutes empowering the governor to appoint such commissioners, and vesting a commissioner so appointed with power to compel the attendance and testimony of witnesses, are found in several states.

Needless to say, the privilege against self-incrimination has been declared by the courts to extend to witnesses under compulsory interrogation by administrative agencies; and Congress has thought it necessary in connection with the investigations conducted by several of the federal regulatory agencies to grant to witnesses before them immunity from prosecution for any matter in relation to which they have testified.

A valuable instrument of investigation is placed in the hands of some administrative agencies by the requirement that persons subject to regulation maintain prescribed records, and permit agency representatives to inspect such records on the premises where kept. While such records may technically be the private property of the person keeping them, they are not, being records which he is specifically required by law to keep, entitled to the same protection against inspection, and hence compulsory production, as are his purely private records.

The requirement that records be kept, and that they be available for inspection by governmental agents, has long been a familiar one in connection with regulatory statutes, as well as in connection with tax statutes; but the statutes in question were applicable only to particular categories of persons who had elected to engage in the particular business or occupation or to the particular variety of property ownership affected by the statute. The income tax statutes, however, are applicable to all persons receiving income; and they impose an obligation on certain taxpayers at least to keep specified records, and a corresponding obligation, as just noted, to make such records available for inspection.

9. INVESTIGATION BY JUDICIAL OFFICER

In several states—in at least one of the states by provision dating from colonial times—powers of investigation essentially similar to those enjoyed by the grand jury are conferred upon a single officer. It might be thought that this officer would be the public prosecutor. Instead, however, he is in every case a judicial officer (or a deputy appointed by him). In this investigative capacity the judicial officer may, under some of the state statutes in question, be furnished with detectives and other investigative personnel not available to the grand jury, which for investigation in the field must rely on the prosecutor, not under its control. The investigating judicial officer, under these statutes, may subpoena witnesses and examine them under oath, such examination, as in the case of the grand jury, being secret and without the privilege of counsel. The witness summoned before him enjoys, needless to say, the same privilege against self-incrimination as does the witness before the grand jury.

This procedure joins the compulsory power of interrogation enjoyed by the grand jury with the speed, investigative efficiency, and resources of a prosecutor. It is not clear why it has not been more widely adopted.[63] The explanation perhaps lies at least partly in the unwillingness to compromise the judicial character of the judicial office. Even though the judicial officer who conducts the investigation does not preside at the subsequent trial of the persons accused as a result of his investigation, his investigative activities have associated him in the public mind, and perhaps, even though unconsciously, in his own mind, with the prosecution, and to that extent derogated from the complete impartiality of the judicial character which our tradition demands.[64]

From the standpoint of effectiveness, the same results could be secured by vesting the prosecutor with the power of compulsory interrogation under oath; but this has nowhere been done, even though the investment of other administrative investigative officers with such powers, is, as it has been noted, quite common. Of course, were it done, provision would have to be made for the investment of some other official with like power when it is the prosecutor's own conduct that is under investigation.

Like the grand jury, the judicial investigator finds his greatest usefulness in investigations of widespread laxity or corruption in law enforcement—situations in which the public prosecutor is, not infrequently, believed to be unduly friendly to the public officers under fire, if not indeed in league with them.

It is to be noted that in no case is the judicial investigating officer em-

[63] In Connecticut is found an apparently unique provision by which an inquiry may be conducted by three justices of the peace or three grand jurors. See McCarthy v. Clancy, 110 Conn. 482 (1930).

[64] The judicial investigating officer bears superficially a resemblance to the French juge d'instruction—an investigative official independent of the police and prosecutor, having the power of compulsory interrogation. The juge d'instruction also makes field investigations which would be thought inconsistent with the character of a judicial officer in this country. Cf. Note 49 above.

powered to lodge an accusation on which the person named therein must stand trial. His function is merely to transmit to the executive or prosecuting authorities the evidence of criminality he has uncovered. Hence the complete inaccuracy of the term "one-man grand jury" sometimes applied to such a judicial investigator.[65]

The type of investigative proceeding by a judicial officer just described is to be sharply distinguished from the proceeding authorized by the statutes of some states in which the judicial officer presides at an investigative proceeding conducted before him in open court, usually by the public prosecutor, who has in this setting the power to subpoena witnesses in the name of the court. Here the function of the judicial officer is merely that of a presiding officer, with power to rule on the propriety of questions and on the witness's obligation to answer—a power that is exercised similarly by the judge under whose direction the grand jury sits, when asked by the jury to compel a witness to answer.

[65] See Winters, The Michigan One-Man Grand Jury, 28 Jour. Amer. Judicature Soc. 137 (1945).

4

Criminal Proceedings: Prosecution

1. DEVELOPMENT OF CRIMINAL PROCEDURE. 2. ARREST BEFORE FOR-
MAL ACCUSATION: PRELIMINARY EXAMINATION. 3. ARREST: EXTRADI-
TION. 4. ACCUSATION. 5. ARRAIGNMENT. 6. PROCEEDINGS PRELIMI-
NARY TO TRIAL. 7. TRIAL: MODE OF PROOF. 8. TRIAL BY JURY:
INSTITUTIONAL ASPECTS. 9. TRIAL BY JURY: PROCEDURAL ASPECTS.
10. ORDERING NEW TRIAL BECAUSE OF NEWLY DISCOVERED EVIDENCE.
11. SENTENCE. 12. REVIEW ON APPEAL. 13. COLLATERAL ATTACK
ON CONVICTION BY POSTCONVICTION PROCEEDING. 14. FEDERAL RE-
VIEW OF STATE CONVICTION. 15. PARDON AND COMMUTATION OF SEN-
TENCE. 16. PAROLE. 17. INDEMNITY FOR WRONGFUL CONVICTION.
18. PROSECUTION OF PETTY OFFENSES. 19. PROCEEDINGS AGAINST
YOUTHFUL OFFENDERS. 20. IMPEACHMENT PROCEEDINGS.

In surveying, in this and succeeding chapters, the procedure of our
courts, it is essential to keep in mind throughout that there exists no entirely uniform American system of court procedure. There do exist, however, detailed patterns of procedure which recur, with greater or less
fidelity, everywhere in the United States. We shall attempt to trace these
patterns, and occasionally to draw attention to divergencies from the accepted pattern found in one or another of the states or in the federal tribunals, beginning, as already indicated, with criminal proceedings
conducted in the courts. Criminal proceedings conducted before military
tribunals will be considered at a later point.

In entering upon an examination of the procedure in criminal prosecution, it is hardly necessary to emphasize that it is impossible, within the
limits of the present work, to touch upon any but the most salient features of that procedure. Around virtually every procedural step there has
grown up a multifarious collection of legal rules. This body of technicality
is chiefly the result of the unremitting efforts of defendant's counsel,
through the years, to make use of procedural obstacles to conviction or to

obtain the reversal of a conviction, on appeal, on the ground of alleged procedural error. It has been due also to the disposition of our courts, particularly during the period of independent development of American criminal law in the first half of the nineteenth century, to bend over backward to give the accused the full benefit of every possible procedural safeguard. With most of this profuse growth of technicalities, the layman has no concern; indeed, even among lawyers it is familiar learning only to those who deal with it from day to day. We shall confine ourselves to those aspects of criminal procedure most crucial from the dual standpoint of effective law enforcement on the one hand, and on the other, of the protection of the accused from oppression.

However, in thus dismissing from consideration the formidable body of technical doctrine of criminal procedure, it would be misleading to leave the impression, so often entertained by laymen, that it furnishes innumerable loopholes for the escape of the guilty. The trend is distinctly away from that meticulous adherence to strict technicality in criminal cases, even where no real injury to the accused was involved, which formerly obsessed the appellate courts of some of our states. It still survives, even if not in its former vigor, here and there, despite the statutory command to the appellate courts, now found in most jurisdictions, that technical error is to be disregarded where no substantial right of the accused is prejudiced. But even where it is applied most strictly, the importance of technicality in facilitating the escape of a guilty defendant from the clutches of the law is quantitatively very slight. The principal effect of technicality in our criminal procedure is rather to impose upon prosecuting attorneys the necessity of moving carefully and with due regard for the procedural requirements for the protection of the accused.

An exception must, however, be noted with respect to the rules which exclude evidence offered by the prosecution not because of any defect inherent in the evidence itself, but because of the circumstances under which it was obtained—rules the growing importance of which has already been mentioned. The doctrines which determine whether the action of the law-enforcement officers who obtained the evidence was or was not illegal are in some respects quite technical; and the law-enforcement officers who must be guided by them must often act without legal advice. In this crucial field the prosecutor may find technicalities a real obstacle to successful prosecution of the apparently guilty.[1]

---

[1] For the thesis that latter-day developments in criminal procedure have tended to shift the balance in favor of the professional lawbreaker, see, among others, Barrett, Personal Rights, Property Rights and the Fourteenth Amendment, in Kurland (ed.), Supreme Court Review—1960 (1960) and Waite, Judges and the Crime Problem, 54 Mich. Law Rev. 169 (1955). For a contrary view, see Goldstein, The State and the Accused: Balance of Advantage in Criminal Procedure, 69 Yale Law Jour. 1149 (1960).

Discussions of reform in our criminal procedure quite frequently fail to put the problem in its proper perspective. The machinery of criminal justice is obviously but one in a complex of agencies which influence the likelihood of the commission of crime. In a broad view, the schools and churches of the land are among the most important of such agencies. But, confining attention to those agencies whose primary purpose is the prevention and repression of crime, we must take account of the police, the prosecutor, the probation system, the prison, and the parole system, as well as the court. In so far as crime can be prevented or repressed by the state, the prevalence of crime will depend upon the joint operation of all these agencies; and the role of the courts in the process will at best be a secondary one. Even within the limited area of the criminal proceeding itself, the procedure followed by the court is of secondary importance.

1. DEVELOPMENT OF CRIMINAL PROCEDURE

The seventeenth century, the century of the English colonization of America, was in England a century of progress in the administration of the criminal law. The growing independence exhibited in the early years of the century by the courts of law in their contests with the Crown was followed, in 1641, by the abolition of the Court of the Star Chamber, a tribunal closely connected with the Privy Council, exercising a criminal jurisdiction in felonies and treason concurrent with that of the courts of law, under a non-jury inquisitional procedure. The two decades of the Long Parliament and the Commonwealth (1640–1660) were marked by reforms in criminal procedure, looking to the protection of the accused against the combined powers of the court and prosecutor acting, as so often in the criminal prosecutions of that time, in concert to secure a conviction. The quarter century of the Restoration during which Charles II reigned (1660–1685), if marked by no great reforms, witnessed, despite the subservience of the judges in state trials, a strengthening of the tendency toward the protection of the accused. The reversal of this tendency during the brief reign of James II (1685–1689), in connection with the prosecution of heretics and the suppression of the Monmouth rebellion, served only to strengthen the popular demand, on the accession of William and Mary, for a more enlightened criminal justice; and the end of the century saw the popular feeling beginning to be reflected in the courts and in Parliament.

In the founding of the several English colonies in America during this century, the established English criminal procedure, dominated in England by the Court of Kings Bench, was not immediately transplanted. The segregation of the judicial function, and the investment of specialized judges with its exclusive charge, emerged only slowly in our colonies, the governor and his council continuing to exercise judicial power even in criminal cases in some of the colonies until a relatively late date. Gradually, however, forms of criminal procedure substantially on the English model were constructed in the several colonies, and during the eighteenth century underwent the same process of liberalization and of increased consideration for the rights of the accused as was going forward in England.

The incorporation in state and federal constitutions of express provisions for the protection of the accused laid the foundation for the tendency of our courts in the nineteenth century to strain the law, even to the point of technicality, in favor of the accused, a tendency perhaps aided by the growth of popular election of judges. The reduction of criminal procedure to statutory form, a development which began about the middle of the century in New York and proceeded rapidly, while it swept away many of the outworn technicalities of the traditional procedure, opened the way, as codification inevitably does, for the development of new technicalities. By the present century, this tendency appears to have largely run its course; and subsequent development has been in the direction of simplification and of facilitating prosecution. In a number of the states judicial councils, drawn from the legislature, the bench, and the bar contribute to the continuing improvement of procedure, civil as well as criminal.

Perhaps the most significant development in the field of state criminal procedure during the present century has been, however, not its improvement by state action, but its latter-day supervision by the Supreme Court of the United States, acting under the "due process" and "equal protection of the laws" clauses of the Fourteenth Amendment—a development referred to in an earlier chapter.

Congress, in the Judiciary Act of 1789, made no provision as to the procedure in criminal cases in the federal courts. Its development was thus left almost entirely to those courts themselves, or rather to each individual judge of those courts, except as a doctrine binding on all the federal courts might from time to time be announced by the Supreme Court. From the first, the practice of federal courts was one of conformity to state procedure, the federal criminal procedure thus varying from state to state. It was, however, the procedure of the state in 1789, rather than that procedure as it changed from time to time thereafter, that in theory controlled, at least as to the thirteen original states; and only Congress could authorize a change. The steady accession of new states necessitated, in those states, a different theory; but no clear statement of such a theory appears to have been enunciated by the Supreme Court. In the early years of the present century, despite the vast increase in federal criminal prosecutions since 1789, the procedure followed by the courts in such prosecutions remained uncodified and to a certain extent unsettled, though in the main conforming to state practice.

With 1917, however, began a period of statutory regulation of federal criminal procedure, culminating in the acts of 1933 and 1940, which gave the Supreme Court power to prescribe (subject to disallowance by Congress) a uniform procedure in criminal prosecutions for all federal courts. Under the authority thus given rules were promulgated, the process culminating in the Federal Rules of Criminal Procedure of 1946.[2] In addition the Court has increasingly taken it upon itself to lay down, in its decisions, express procedural rulings for the guidance of the federal courts. Through annual conferences of the chief federal judges, presided over by the Chief Justice of the United States, current procedural problems of the courts are presented for solution. For federal procedure there is thus performed, within the body of the federal judiciary itself, much of the function which in Continental countries is the responsibility of a ministry of justice.

2. ARREST BEFORE FORMAL ACCUSATION: PRELIMINARY EXAMINATION

Earlier, the distinction was pointed out between those offenses in which a sworn complaint by a police or other public officer, or by a private citizen, is sufficient to put the person named therein on trial, and those offenses in which a more formal accusation (commonly termed either an information or an indictment, and filed in the former case ordinarily by the public prosecutor and in the latter by the grand jury) is prerequisite to trial.

In the case of the latter class of offenses, the person accused is in many instances not arrested until after the information or indictment has been lodged against him. In perhaps the overwhelming majority of cases, however, his arrest has preceded such formal accusation, having been made by a police officer who allegedly witnessed the offense or who thinks he has reason to believe that the person he arrests has committed an offense, or having been made on the basis of a complaint by the prosecutor or other investigating agency, in some cases on the authority of a warrant of arrest issued by a court at the instance of the law-enforcement authorities.

A person so arrested is, as we have seen, entitled to be promptly brought before a magistrate to determine whether he shall be released or shall be "held to answer"—i.e., held in custody (or in bail) to await the decision as to whether an information or indictment shall be filed against him. That the requirement, found in a number of jurisdictions, that the accused shall be produced before the magistrate for such preliminary examination without unnecessary delay is in fact disregarded by police and prosecuting officials in certain cases has already been pointed out.

[2] These rules are framed in somewhat general terms. They do not constitute a detailed code, such as is found in a number of the states. Much is left to the discretion of the trial judge. In many of the minor matters left unregulated, state practice continues to be followed.

Under the statutes of some states, and under the federal rules, the magistrate conducting a preliminary examination is under a duty to inform the prisoner that he has a right to employ legal counsel. In almost all states he must postpone the hearing, should the prisoner request this, until the prisoner has had an opportunity to obtain counsel. The Supreme Court has declared that the right to "the assistance of counsel" in federal criminal proceedings, given by the Sixth Amendment, entitles the indigent to be furnished with counsel at every stage of the proceeding, a pronouncement which embraces even the preliminary examination. No funds have, however, been appropriated for the purpose, and since the preliminary examination is commonly held not before a judge but before a special part-time federal magistrate known as a commissioner, compliance with the constitutional mandate in that proceeding is far from complete.

In the states, the provision of counsel to the indigent defendant at the preliminary examination is virtually unknown, even in those states which have interpreted the state constitutional guarantee of the assistance of counsel most broadly. The Supreme Court has not yet had occasion to decide, since its recent sweeping extension to defendants in state proceedings of the right to be furnished with trial counsel, how far it is prepared to extend that right to the preliminary examination as well.[8]

The value of the preliminary examination as a protection of the citizen against detention following unwarranted arrest varies greatly from one place to another, depending upon the competence and independence of the magistrate. The question whether the evidence adduced against the arrested suspect is sufficient to warrant holding him pending further action by the prosecutor is one that in some cases calls for legal learning. Nevertheless, it is characteristically entrusted, in the rural areas, to the justice of the peace and, in the cities, to the police courts. In a few of the larger cities, however, the number of arrests on charges of crime, in which preliminary examination is required, is so large that specialized divisions of the police court have been set up exclusively for the purpose of preliminary examination and the related function of fixing bail. Moreover, in some jurisdictions, the preliminary examination of persons arrested for homicide, and perhaps other grave crimes, is held by the judges of the criminal courts proper.

3. ARREST: EXTRADITION

With mobility ever on the increase, the problem of procuring the arrest of one who has fled to another jurisdiction, and his return, is of growing importance.

---

[8] The Court has, however, held that the reception in evidence, at the trial, of an admission of guilt made by the defendant, unrepresented by counsel, at the preliminary hearing, is a denial of due process of law. White v. Maryland, 373 U.S. 274 (1963).

Interstate extradition

A state officer may ordinarily make an arrest only within the state under whose authority he acts. In recent years, however, a number of states have enacted reciprocal statutes permitting an arrest in the state by a peace officer of another state, where he has entered the state in close pursuit of a person in order to arrest him, and continues in such close pursuit. Under such statutes, an arrest may thus be made by a state officer, under the conditions specified, beyond the borders of his state.

In the absence of close pursuit, however, and in any case in a state where he is not thus authorized under a reciprocal statute, the peace officer of another state, even though armed with a warrant of arrest, is powerless to make an arrest under such warrant.[4] Resort must be had to an extradition proceeding in the state in which the person to be arrested is found.

The law of interstate extradition is based upon the constitutional provision that "a person charged in any state with treason, felony, or other crime, who shall flee from justice, and be found in another state, shall, on demand of the executive authority of the state from which he fled, be delivered up, to be removed to the state having jurisdiction of the crime." This is the whole of the constitutional provision. It will be observed that it speaks of a person "found" in another state being "delivered up" by that state; but of course he cannot be delivered up unless he is first arrested. There is no way in which the authorities in the place in which the fugitive is "found" can be compelled to arrest him; and in fact the degree of compliance extended by police forces to requests from other states for the apprehension of fugitives varies considerably from place to place. Some decline to arrest a fugitive charged only with a misdemeanor; and some are unwilling to arrest even one charged with a felony unless he has already been indicted, or an information has been lodged against him.

Assuming the fugitive to have been placed under arrest however, and a demand to have been made by the "executive authority," i.e., the governor, of the state from which he has fled, what is the compulsion on the asylum state to deliver the fugitive to the officer of the demanding state? The quoted constitutional provision, despite its categorical language, provides no sanction for compelling obedience to its command, nor does it empower Congress so to provide. And indeed no effective method has in fact been developed for compelling compliance even in the clearest cases.

This anomalous weakness in our legal system has come about as an incident to the development of the doctrine that the executive head of the government—in the case of a state government, the governor—is immune from the process of the courts. The Constitution does not itself require

[4] In theory he has, however, the same power of arrest, in felony cases, as any private person.

that, when a demand is made on a state for the extradition of a fugitive from justice, the governor of that state shall pass upon the request. So far as the Constitution is concerned, the statutes of the state might provide that such a demand shall be made upon the secretary of state of the state, for example, and that he shall refer it to the chief justice of the highest court of the state. In actual fact, however, the states have uniformly provided that the governor of the state shall pass upon a request for extradition, and that his warrant shall be necessary for the surrender of the fugitive. His refusal to issue the warrant, however unjustified and however violative of the constitutional mandate, has hitherto been thought to be without remedy, because of the traditional immunity of the chief executive, of state as well as nation, from judicial process. In other connections, however, the federal courts have in recent years ignored this tradition; and it is quite within the bounds of possibility that in due time the tradition will be broken in this matter as well.

It would seem that inasmuch as the constitutional duty to deliver up the fugitive is imposed not on the governor of the state of refuge but on the state itself, the refusal of the state, whether expressed by the governor or any other state authority, constitutes an injury to the demanding state for which it may seek redress by a suit against the recalcitrant state. Assuming that the Supreme Court (which alone has original jurisdiction in controversies between states) were to accept jurisdiction and were to find in favor of the demanding state, its order to the asylum state to deliver the fugitive to the officers of the demanding state might well be addressed to the particular official of the defendant state in whose custody the fugitive was. If, however, the recalcitrance of the state of refuge has gone to the point of refusing to arrest the fugitive, or of releasing him after arrest, so that the fugitive is still at liberty, the order of the court could hardly be addressed to any particular officer; and a failure to obey the order could therefore be punished only with difficulty. It is manifest that attempts in this direction to improve the situation confront serious technical obstacles.

However, a development in a quite different direction has in recent years furnished substantial amelioration. In 1934 there was enacted a federal statute making it a federal crime for one to leave a state to avoid criminal prosecution by the state (or custody or confinement after conviction) for any of several major crimes; and in 1961 the statute was broadened to include all felonies.[5] Under this statute a fugitive may be arrested by federal officers in any state where he may be found, and brought back by them to the state from which he fled to answer the federal charge there. Once there, he may of course be surrendered by the federal officers to the state officers.

It should not be thought, by reason of the attention here given to the

[5] 18 U.S. Code, Sec. 1073.

unenforceability of the constitutional mandate, that it is defied with frequency. Nothing could be further from the truth. Interstate extradition, in the ordinary case, is a routine affair. Some states, however, have adopted a policy of extraditing only for felonies.

Not a few of the states provide in their statutes for extradition in cases in which the Constitution does not require it—cases in which the person whose extradition is sought has not in fact "fled from justice" (as the Constitution has it), but is charged in the demanding state with bringing about, while outside the state, a criminal result within the state. The Uniform Criminal Extradition Act, in force in 1963 in forty-five states, provides for the surrender to the demanding state of a person charged in that state with committing, either in the surrendering state or in some other state, an act intentionally resulting in a crime in the demanding state, "when the acts for which extradition is sought would be punishable by the laws of this [the surrendering] state, if the consequences claimed to have resulted therefrom in the demanding state had taken effect in this state."

The process of interstate extradition is initiated by the local prosecutor or police authorities in the place where the crime was committed. They request the governor, on the basis of a sworn complaint charging the fugitive with a crime, to issue a demand on the governor of the asylum state—termed a "requisition"—that the fugitive(who is ordinarily already in custody in the asylum state) be delivered up to an officer of the demanding state to be removed to that state. Upon the presentation of the requisition to the governor of the asylum state, he, after such investigation as he may choose to make, but without any notice to the alleged fugitive, or opportunity for hearing, issues a warrant authorizing his delivery to the agent of the demanding state.

Before delivering him, however, the officer having custody of him is required by the uniform statute, and usually also by the statutory provisions of states not having the uniform statute, to take him before a court of the state having power to issue the writ of habeas corpus, the judge of which is required to inform the fugitive that he has the right to demand and procure legal counsel, and to give him an opportunity to procure such counsel. Should the prisoner then desire to test the legality of the proposed extradition, the court is required to allow a reasonable time within which a habeas corpus proceeding may be initiated. If, as a result of the evidence adduced upon the ensuing hearing, it appears that the prisoner (assuming as is almost invariably the case that he is accused of an act committed within the borders of the demanding state) was not in the demanding state at the time he is alleged to have committed the act there, or that the act which he is charged with having committed is not a crime in the demanding state, or that he has not in fact been properly charged with crime in that state, the judge will release the prisoner, and there is, in some states, no provision for appeal. If, on the other hand, his petition is denied, the prisoner may appeal and may seek a stay pending the determination of such appeal.

Even where the state statute does not expressly provide for the taking of the prisoner before a court prior to his delivery to the officer of the demanding state, he may, as soon as arrested, as may any person arrested, institute habeas corpus proceedings either before a state or a federal court. Application to a federal court is, however, obviously futile unless some federal question is involved; and in the ordinary course, there having as yet been neither trial nor even formal accusation, a federal question is almost impossible to raise.

The constitutional and statutory provisions governing interstate extradition embrace, in addition to persons charged with crime, persons convicted thereof, who have fled while under bail, or who have violated conditions of parole or probation by leaving the state, or who have escaped from confinement. It is indeed in connection with the last mentioned class of cases that there has emerged one of the most striking aspects of the unenforceability of the constitutional mandate for interstate extradition—the contention that, though the language of the constitutional command is unqualified, a state may properly refuse to deliver up a fugitive to another state, if, in the opinion of the authorities (in effect, the governor) of the state of refuge, the penal servitude to which the fugitive would be subjected were he to be surrendered is of a cruel and inhuman character. In several cases the governor of a northern state has refused to surrender a fugitive to a southern state alleged by the fugitive to have a barbarous penal system. However strongly one may condemn the abuses of the penal system in some of our states, one may still feel that there is something rather absurd in the spectacle of the governor or courts of one state sitting in judgment on the penal system of another, and passing sentence thereon by way of refusing to surrender an escaped convict—or presumably (for it could be done with equal logic) one charged with crime in that state, who, if extradited and convicted, would be sentenced to imprisonment in that same penal system.[6]

Extradition from foreign countries

Where the person charged with crime in this country is in a foreign country, his extradition is ordinarily possible only if that country is

[6] Application to the federal courts has on several occasions been made by an escaped state convict apprehended in another state and about to be extradited to the state from which he fled, to order his release on the ground that he had suffered, and if returned would suffer, cruel and unusual punishment and hence would be denied due process of law. On one or two such occasions the release of the fugitive was in fact ordered. In 1952, however, the Supreme Court, one justice dissenting, declared such action by a federal court to be improper. Sweeney v. Woodall, 344 U.S. 86 (1952).

obligated by treaty with the United States to return him. Treaties (which are of course in each case reciprocal in character) now exist with virtually all foreign governments. Their provisions do not, however, cover all offenses, but only those in specified categories; and these categories may differ in the several treaties. Thus, in a well-known case involving the attempt of the United States to procure the return by Great Britain of a fugitive charged with violation of a federal statute penalizing the making of a false statement, a British court decided that the offense in question did not fall within the category of "perjury," the only relevant category covered by the governing treaty between Great Britain and the United States.

In several of the reciprocal extradition treaties which the United States has with foreign countries, express reservation is made by the foreign country of its right to decline to extradite to this country any of its own nationals charged with crime here. These countries fellow the practice, however, of themselves trying and punishing their nationals so charged.

The procedure followed in a foreign country up to the point at which the fugitive is given into the custody of the American officer, state or federal, named in the requisition issued by the President is of course governed by the law of that country. In all countries enjoying a formal system of jurisprudence—and today there are few, even of the more primitive, which do not—there is of course opportunity for the person taken into custody by the authorities of that country to test the legality of his arrest and detention prior to his actual delivery to the custody of the American officer. In the case of a foreign fugitive arrested in the United States, the federal statutes make provision for a hearing.

4. ACCUSATION

The several varieties of formal accusation necessary before one may be required to stand trial on a criminal charge—the sworn complaint, the information, and the indictment—have already been mentioned. The information and the indictment call for further discussion.

The information

In some jurisdictions the term information is applied to the original sworn complaint on which the arrest was made. This complaint, together with a transcript of the testimony of the witnesses who testified at the preliminary examination, is sufficient to bring the defendant to trial for a misdemeanor. In general, however, the term connotes a formal accusation lodged by the public prosecutor; and it is in this sense that the term will here be used.

The extent of the power of the prosecutor to bring a person to trial by filing an information against him varies greatly from state to state. In some states he may do so only after the person to be charged has been arrested, and has been held to answer by the magistrate after preliminary examination; in others, and in the federal courts, he may file the information without there having been any arrest of the person named therein, without prior notice to him, and without there having been any preliminary examination of the charge. In some states, and in the federal courts, he may file only an information charging a misdemeanor.[7] In about half the states, however, he may also file an information charging a felony, some states making an exception of capital or other grave crimes, permitting them to be charged only by a grand jury.

In most of the states in which the prosecutor is empowered to file a felony information, it is required that the person to be charged be first arrested, brought before a magistrate for preliminary examination, and held to answer by the magistrate. If the judge presiding at the examination is of sufficient stature, and the information thereafter lodged is required to conform to the charge on which the examination was held—a matter too technical for discussion here—that requirement may prove a valuable check on the abuse of his power by the prosecutor. There is considerable variation, however, in the extent to which these desiderata are satisfied in the several states.

The indictment

Both accusation by an official—sheriff, constable, or the like—and accusation by a body of the freemen of the vicinage were about equally ancient in England, their origins being traceable to the twelfth century, the period in which began the centralization of royal justice. By the sixteenth century, however, it had apparently become well established that accusation for felonies could be made only by the grand jury.

As with many other English legal institutions, however, this principle was but little regarded in the colonies of the early seventeenth century. It was not until the latter part of the century that the colonial governors and their subordinates began to surrender the power of bringing the subject to trial for felony without the intervention of the grand jury. By the

---

[7] Federal Rules of Criminal Procedure, Rule 7(a). The rule does not use the term misdemeanor. It permits prosecution by information in all crimes not punishable by death or imprisonment for more than a year at hard labor. In a few statutes creating minor offenses in connection with the violation of regulatory statutes, Congress has authorized the prosecutor to file a "statement of complaint" on which the accused may be brought to trial. See for example 33 U.S. Code, Secs. 391 ff. It is not apparent that the result is different from that which would follow from the filing of an information, as provided by the rules.

time of the destruction of the British authority, however, the exclusive use of the grand jury in accusations of felony appears to have been well established in all the colonies.

That it had not, nevertheless, yet come to be universally regarded as a necessary safeguard against official persecution may be inferred from the absence of any specific mention of it in several of the state constitutions adopted after the Revolution. Moreover, the framers of the federal constitution, though they provided for jury trial of federal crimes, omitted any guarantee of grand jury accusation—a guarantee which was, however, added in 1791, together with other provisions protective of the accused.

The provision thus added to the Constitution requires indictment by grand jury before one may be "held to answer for any capital or otherwise infamous crime" against the federal statutes. In defining the term "infamous crime" the Supreme Court has looked not to the nature of the offense but rather to the place and kind of punishment, and in substance has made the term synonymous with the term "felony." In effect, therefore, the constitutional provision protects against federal prosecution for felonies without grand jury accusation; federal misdemeanors may be prosecuted by information.

The federal Constitution contains no mention of grand jury indictment in state prosecutions; nor does its mandate of "due process" in state procedure require grand jury indictment.[8] Such requirement is to be found, if at all, in the provisions of the several state constitutions. These provisions (and the same is true of the statutory provisions found in the ten states without constitutional provision) exhibit a wide diversity—a diversity wider perhaps than is found with respect to any other major feature of our criminal procedure. Half of the states require grand jury action in felony cases, and eleven of these require it even in misdemeanors. In the remaining states, as already indicated, either the constitution itself permits, or the legislature is empowered to permit (and has in every case done so), not only misdemeanors but felonies (except in some states, capital offenses or others of extreme gravity) to be prosecuted either by indictment or information. In these states, prosecution by information has tended to become the rule, and prosecution by indictment the exception, in the prosecution of felonies.

The erosion of the grand jury as an institution has proceeded at a somewhat irregular pace. Although not required in all the original thirteen states by constitutional provision, it did in fact exist in all. Connecticut was the first state to discard it (retaining it only for crimes punishable by death or life imprisonment), and her example was followed by a few others in the first half of the nineteenth century. In Louisiana, with a tradition of Spanish and French procedure, it never gained a strong foothold; and the

[8] Hurtado v. California, 110 U.S. 516 (1884).

like was true of California. The example of this latter state greatly influenced the newer states of the Southwest and of the Rocky Mountain area. In general, it is the newer states that have tended to dispense with the grand jury. It persists chiefly in the eastern states.

It is a rather remarkable circumstance that there should thus have existed in the United States, side by side, over many decades, states in which indictment by grand jury is exceptional—indeed in some cases virtually nonexistent—and states in which indictment for felony is exclusively by grand jury, without any apparent tendency for the latter group of states, about half of the total, to abandon the ancient institution. Despite repeated and seemingly justified criticism of the grand jury system as wasteful, costly, and dilatory, and despite repeated predictions that the institution is on its way to extinction, it exhibits remarkable vitality. In part, its persistence is of course due to the constitutional protection which it enjoys in the federal courts and in many of the states.

The protection supposedly afforded by the requirement of grand jury action, against being compelled to stand trial on an unjustified charge, was no doubt of real substance in earlier centuries, when criminal prosecutions were very often instituted and carried forward by private parties (a procedure which indeed survived in England well into the last century).[9] As a protection against the institution of an unjustified prosecution today, however, its value is in most cases minimal. Ordinarily, the prosecutor who wishes to procure an indictment finds little difficulty in getting the grand jury to vote one (except perhaps in a situation in which community sympathy is so unanimously with the alleged offender that even if indicted he would doubtless be acquitted by the trial jury). As a check on the prosecutor, the grand jury thus much less effective than is the provision, in states where the grand jury has been dispensed with, that the prosecutor cannot bring the accused to trial (by the filing of an information) unless the judicial officer presiding at the preliminary examination has found that there is sufficient evidence to warrant such action.

Even where constitutional provisions guarantee against prosecution except on grand jury indictment, the accused may, under the prevailing view in the states, and in the federal courts (except in capital cases) under express rule of the Supreme Court, waive the benefit of the constitutional provision, and consent to be prosecuted by information. The waiver privilege is of great value to an indigent defendant, held to answer, who is unable to furnish bail. He must, if not permitted to waive indictment, as he still is not in some jurisdictions, undergo imprisonment until the grand

[9] Traces of the right of the injured party to control the prosecution, survivals of colonial procedures, are still found in this country, as in the statutory provisions in some states authorizing the discharge by the magistrate of a person charged with an assault, upon acknowledgment by the injured party that he has received satisfaction.

jury convenes—which may, in sparsely populated countries, mean a delay of months.

5. ARRAIGNMENT

Once in custody, the person named in an information or indictment must promptly be brought before the court in which the information or indictment was filed, there to be arraigned.

Arraignment consists in a formal reading of the substance of the information or indictment to the accused in open court with the inquiry as to how he "pleads"—whether "guilty" or "not guilty."[10]

It is a fact little appreciated that it is at this stage that the great majority of criminal proceedings come to an end. For, as already noted, the great majority of those thus arraigned proceed (either at once or after a requested adjournment) to plead guilty to the offense charged or, with the consent of the prosecutor and the court, to an offense of less gravity; so that it ordinarily remains only to announce the sentence imposed by the court.

If, however, the accused declines to plead guilty, he may either plead not guilty or, refusing to plead, may ask the court to dismiss the indictment or information as insufficient in law for any one of several possible reasons shortly to be mentioned. If the court denies the request for dismissal, the defendant must plead; and if he pleads not guilty (or if, on his refusal to plead, the court, as is customary, enters a plea of not guilty on his behalf), he must stand trial. Generally speaking, no appeal from the court's refusal to dismiss the proceeding is available. The defendant, if convicted, may, however, on appeal from his conviction, urge the same legal contentions as were rejected by the trial court on his initial application to dismiss.

In the federal courts, the indigent defendant is, in a number of districts, furnished with counsel at the arraignment; in the states, generally speaking, he is not. The Supreme Court has held that where under the state procedure a crucial plea, such as that of insanity, or a crucial motion, such as one to dismiss the indictment because of the improper composition of the grand jury which returned it, can be made only at the arraignment, the state is required to furnish counsel to the indigent defendant at such arraignment;[11] but beyond this the Court has not gone.

In conjunction with the plea of not guilty, some states permit the words "by reason of insanity" or the like to be added. Whether or not thus raised

---

[10] In some states, a plea of guilty is not permitted in the case of capital charges; and in a few states the same is true in the case of offenses punishable by life imprisonment.

[11] Hamilton v. Alabama, 368 U.S. 52 (1961).

in the plea itself, the defense of insanity (a term used in this connection to cover a wide range of mental deficiency) is of course available to the defendant in the subsequent stages of the proceeding.

An alternative to the plea of guilty, found in some states and in the federal practice, is that of "nolo contendere" (refusal to contest the charge), which can be accepted only with the approval of the judge. Such a plea does not reduce in any way the liability of the defendant to punishment; but since it does not embody a confession of guilt as does the plea of guilty, it may have certain advantages to the defendant in collateral matters.[12]

6. PROCEEDINGS PRELIMINARY TO TRIAL

Between the arraignment and the trial, there is opportunity for either side, but particularly the defense, to make applications to the court either with a view to preparing for the trial, or with a view to procuring the dismissal of the charge without trial. During this period the accused may also of course change his plea to guilty, or, with permission of the court, to a plea of guilty to a lesser offense.

Dismissal of indictment

There are numerous grounds on which the defendant may contend that the indictment is fatally defective and that, hence, the prosecution must be terminated forthwith by the "dismissal" of the indictment by the court, an action which will not preclude the lodging of a subsequent valid indictment for the same offense. The grounds on which an indictment may be dismissed or ("quashed") are numerous, and some of them are too technical to mention here. The legality of the grand jury which returned the indictment may be attacked on the ground that it was not constituted according to the law, or that members of the defendant's race were systematically excluded from it. That the defendant was improperly called as a witness before it is another ground for dismissal, to which reference has already been made. The constitutionality of the statute which the indictment charges was violated may be attacked. Occasionally (but rarely) the defendant may contend that the offense named in the indictment is in substance the same as one of which he has already been convicted or acquitted, and that he is thus being subjected to "double

---

[12] Thus, in an action by a private party for damages under the federal anti-trust laws, the previous conviction of the defendant of a violation of those laws arising out of the same matters as form the basis of the civil action, may, if the conviction followed a plea of guilty, be prima facie evidence of the truth of the allegations contained in the indictment or information (cf. 15 U.S. Code, Sec. 16), while a conviction following a plea of nolo contendere may not be.

jeopardy" in violation of the constitutional prohibition.[13] In addition, it may be contended that the grand jury was guilty of prejudicial irregularity in its proceedings, or that there was no legally competent evidence before it. When a defendant presents to the court reasonable ground for believing that these latter grounds exist, but lacks adequate proof thereof, the court may in its discretion permit him to inspect the records (or "minutes" as they are often termed) of the grand jury to seek such proof. The latitude permitted in these matters, which are hardly anywhere regulated in detail by statute or rule, varies widely from one jurisdiction to another.[14]

Information furnished to accused

In the development of the English criminal law, it was not until the end of the seventeenth century that the right of the defendant to be informed, in advance of his trial, even of the nature of the accusation against him, in cases of treason and felony, was established by statute. In this country, at the time of the adoption of the Constitution this right was apparently still far from being taken for granted, as indicated by its express incluson in the list of fundamental rights of the accused (in the new federal courts) added to the Constitution in 1791. Today, not only is the accused orally informed of the contents of the information or indictment at the time of his arraignment, but it is subsequently open to his inspection, and in most jurisdictions, he must be furnished with a copy of it on request, and in almost half, apparently without request.

But in contrast to civil litigation (in which the tendency of recent years has been to encourage, if not compel, both sides to disclose in advance of the trial not merely their respective contentions but the evidence on which they rely, and to grant access by each side to evidence in the possession of the other) the field of criminal procedure is still on the whole dominated by the concept of "surprise"—the belief that the truth will more surely be disclosed at the trial if the prosecution conceals its prospective evidence from the defense, thus precluding the manufacture of rebuttal evidence.[15] This concept gives little heed to the fact that without adequate knowledge of the evidence to be presented against him an inno-

[13] In the federal courts, a defendant convicted of an offense less than that charged in the indictment or information, cannot, on his conviction being set aside on his appeal, again be tried on the original more serious charge, the conviction on the lesser charge being in effect an acquittal on the graver charge. Green v. United States, 355 U.S. 184 (1957). This has not been the prevailing view in the states in which the question has arisen.

[14] The federal Rules of Criminal Procedure permit disclosure of "matters occurring before the grand jury . . . upon a showing that grounds may exist for a motion to dismiss the indictment because of [such] matters. . . ." Rule 6 (c).

[15] The defendant, on the other hand, is not required to disclose to the prosecutor the nature of his defense. In some states, provision is, however, made for advance notice of the defendant's intention to prove an alibi.

cent defendant cannot well prepare his defense; and it is giving way, but very slowly.[16] There is characteristically, but by no means universally, provision for the disclosure by the prosecution of the names of the witnesses it intends to call, but apparently in only one jurisdiction (California) is there access as of right to the evidence given before the grand jury—a disclosure which would be regarded as self-evidently proper under the principles which govern not a few foreign systems of criminal justice.[17] In several jurisdictions, including the federal, the defendant may examine and copy (or photograph) designated documents or tangible objects obtained from the defendant or from others by seizure or process, upon a showing that the items sought may be material to the preparation of his defense.

A point often overlooked in discussion of the relative merits of the information and the indictment procedures is that the former is the more likely to be helpful to the defendant in his quest for information as to the evidence in the possession of the prosecution. If a preliminary examination must precede the filing of the information, as is so often the case, the prosecution is compelled to disclose a substantial portion of the evidence on which it intends to rely at the trial. Under the indictment procedure, by contrast, the defendant, if not arrested and given a preliminary hearing before indictment, goes to trial without having heard a single word of the testimony against him. Ordinarily, the prosecutor wishes to disclose as little of his case as possible before the trial. Therefore, he may, without arresting the prospective defendant, lay the matter before the grand jury and obtain an indictment, rather than file an information after arrest and preliminary examination. There are places where this procedure is commonplace.

Order prohibiting use of evidence by prosecution

With the development, in recent years, of new and far-reaching rules excluding evidence obtained by illegal search, or otherwise tainted with illegality or with infringement of the defendant's rights, there has been a corresponding growth in the use by defendant's counsel of a procedure formerly little favored by the courts—an application to the court in advance of the trial to forbid the use by the prosecution, at the trial, of the

[16] The question of the extent to which the defendant should be afforded further opportunity for pretrial discovery of the evidence in the possession of the prosecution is receiving increasing attention, but no marked trend toward liberalization is yet apparent, despite isolated decisions ordering the police to give the defendant access to his statements to them, and the like.

[17] Thus in Canada, reflecting the English police tradition of disclosure of evidence to the defense, the prosecution is expected to bring forward its whole case upon the preliminary hearing, and if new evidence comes to light after that hearing and prior to trail, the defendant's attorney is notified of it. Orfield, Criminal Procedure from Arrest to Appeal, 74–75 (1947).

allegedly illegal evidence (or, as the phrase is, to suppress it). The admissibility of such evidence may be of course be contested by the defendant at the trial, but its suppression in advance of the trial has obvious advantages. Latterly, because the exclusion of evidence of this character even in state proceedings has become so largely a matter of constitutional right, there has come into prominence the proceeding in a federal court to compel the suppression of evidence by the state prosecutor in a state prosecution.

Depositions

The testimony (or, as it is termed in this connection, the deposition) of a witness outside the jurisdiction, or likely to die or to be disabled from attending the trial, may be recorded in advance and read at the trial. In taking the deposition of a witness for the prosecution, however, the procedure must satisfy the constitutional requirement of confrontation. This requirement, so far as applicable to federal prosecutions, is expressed in the Constitution in these words: "In all criminal prosecutions, the accused shall enjoy the right . . . to be confronted with the witnesses against him"; and identical or similar language is found in the state constitutions. In a few states, the view is taken that all depositions for the prosecution are prohibited; the witness must confront the accused at the trial itself. In some of the remaining states, and in the federal procedure, provision is made for the taking of such depositions in the presence of the accused and his counsel with full right of cross-examination. In the absence of provision for transportation of the accused and his counsel to the scene of the examination at the expense of the prosecution—a provision found in the federal rules but not generally found in the state statutes—the right of the accused to be present, and his right to be represented by counsel, may of course be empty ones.

The procedure for depositions at the instance of the prosecution, even in the states where it exists, applies only to depositions of witnesses within the state. Hence, if one of its prospective witnesses leaves the state, whether for his own reasons or because induced to do so by the defendant, the prosecution may be seriously disadvantaged. Legislation designed to reduce this possibility—reciprocal state statutes compelling attendance of out-of-state witnesses and the federal statute punishing departure from the state to avoid giving testimony—has already been mentioned.[18]

Change of venue

Where trial is by jury, and the jury is drawn from the vicinity, a strong local prejudice against the accused obviously will make it difficult for him to secure a fair trial. Even if the trial is by the judge alone, local hostility may intimidate witnesses for the accused. Contrariwise, local feeling in-

[18] See p. 68.

tensely favorable to the accused may make a successful prosecution difficult. Hence, the provision for removing the trial to a different place—a change of venue, as the phrase is.

In state prosecutions, an application by the accused that the trial be held in a county different from that in which the crime is alleged to have been committed is a not uncommon one. The extent of the showing of local prejudice required and the procedure for passing on the proof of such prejudice vary from state to state; but the remedy exists everywhere in some form. In a few cases, the defendant has successfully appealed to the federal courts for reversal of his conviction on the ground that the refusal of change of venue by the state constituted a denial of due process of law.

State statutes also frequently permit a change of venue at the instance of the prosecutor; in some states, however, this is impossible without the consent of the accused, owing to a provision in the state constitution entitling the accused to trial in the county in which the crime was allegedly committed.

Despite the universal provision in the states for change of venue at the request of the defendant, there was until recent years, owing to the absence of any statutory regulation of federal criminal procedure, no such provision in federal prosecutions. In 1946, however, the Supreme Court, in promulgating under the authority of Congress the new uniform rules of federal criminal procedure, provided that a change of venue, even to another state, may be made because of prejudice against the defendant so great that he cannot obtain a fair trial in the district or division in which the offense was allegedly committed. Transfer to another district, even within the same state, at the request of the prosecutor is not provided for. Such transfer without the consent of the defendant is presumably prohibited by the provision of the Constitution (in the Sixth Amendment) that in federal prosecutions "the accused shall enjoy the right to a . . . trial by an impartial jury of the state and district where the crime shall have been committed, which district shall have previously been ascertained by law."

The local hostility which is frequently the ground for an application for change of venue is itself often the product of the publication before the trial of purported facts regarding the crime or the defendant. Such publication of statements made by witnesses to the police or prosecutor, or of admissions or confessions allegedly made by the defendant, may obviously prejudice prospective jurors against him, and may indeed in extreme cases make it so difficult to obtain an impartial jury in the vicinage as to make a change of venue inescapable.[19] The publication of state-

---

[19] The refusal of a court to grant a change of venue under these circumstances is a denial of due process of law. Irvin v. Dowd, 366 U.S. 717 (1961); Rideau v. Alabama, 373 U.S. 165 (1963).

ments favorable to the defendant may similarly impair the chances of a successful prosecution, though this danger is far the smaller. Despite these obstacles which pretrial publicity may thus offer to a fair trial, our legislatures and our courts (unlike the English courts) have taken no measures to curb it.[20] The press and the broadcasting media, unwilling to sacrifice the news appeal of pretrial developments in sensational cases, invoke the freedom of the press and "the right of the people to know" when any limitations are proposed. The right of the press to report the activities of the law-enforcement agencies, and the right of the public to inform itself as to those activities, are indisputable. The crucial issue, discussion of which is singularly absent from pronouncements of spokesmen for the news media on this matter, is whether it is essential, for the preservation of those rights, that information on these matters be publicly disseminated in advance of the trial. After the trial is concluded, the preparation and publication of a dispassionate inquiry into the efficiency and fairness of the pretrial activities of police and prosecutor would be a valuable public service; but it is one which, it is to be feared, the news media would regard as an unsatisfactory substitute for the day-to-day publicizing of pretrial developments, or alleged developments.

Removal of state prosecution to federal court

There are provisions of the federal statutes under which one charged with crime under a state statute may apply to the federal court, in the district in which he is charged, to remove the case for trial to that court. If the case is removed to the federal court, the judge and jury will be federal, but the prosecution will remain completely in the hands of the state. Such removals are a rarity, but they have been by no means unknown.

A defendant charged with an offense against state law may set up the claim that he performed the act charged against him as a crime in the necessary discharge of his duties as a federal officer, and seek a removal to the federal court on that ground.[21] Another possible ground of application for removal to the federal court, invoked even more rarely than that just mentioned, but likely to be invoked more frequently in the years ahead, is that the defendant "is denied or cannot enforce in the courts of such state [i.e., the state in which he is being prosecuted] a right under any law providing for the equal rights of citizens of the United States, or of all persons within the jurisdiction thereof."[22]

[20] A conviction for contempt imposed by a Maryland trial court on a broadcaster for prejudicial pretrial broadcasts was set aside by the state's high court as an undue infringement of freedom of expression. Baltimore Radio Show, Inc. v. State, 193 Md. 300; 67 A.2d 397 (1949). The Supreme Court declined to review. 338 U.S. 912 (1949).

[21] 28 U.S. Code Sec. 1442.

[22] 28 U.S. Code Sec. 1443.

Release of defendant in habeas corpus proceeding

The function of the habeas corpus proceeding in furnishing a prompt judicial remedy for illegal detention was set forth at an earlier point, in connection with police detention. The habeas corpus procedure may also be availed of, however, by one under detention by the custodial authorities, while awaiting trial, who claims that the indictment against him is fatally defective, or that the statute under which he stands charged is unconstitutional. Because other forms of application are provided for testing these contentions, and are available (as in the habeas corpus application is not) even where the defendant is not in custody (having been released on bail or on his own recognizance), the habeas corpus procedure is not favored by the courts for this purpose. If the defendant's contention is that the state statute under which he is charged is repugnant to federal law, he may also seek release from custody from the federal court, which has power to entertain a habeas corpus proceeding instituted on behalf of anyone held in custody "in violation of the Constitution or laws or treaties of the United States." Here, too, the courts are reluctant to interfere with the normal course of the state criminal proceeding, in which there is ample opportunity for the resolution of constitutional questions.[23] At this stage, a more likely intervention of the federal courts in a state proceeding by means of the habeas corpus proceeding occurs where the defendant asserts that the act with which he is charged was done in his capacity as a federal officer, or that, being a citizen and resident of a foreign state, he committed the act charged under an authority, conferred upon him by such foreign state, "the validity and effect of which depend upon the law of nations."[24]

Dismissal of prosecution at instance of prosecutor

In every jurisdiction a substantial proportion of prosecutions is terminated by dismissal at the request of the prosecutor.[25] The consent of the court must, of course, be obtained by the prosecutor; but (as in the case of a recommendation by the prosecutor that the court accept a plea of guilty to a lesser charge than that laid in the indictment or information)

[23] The statute provides that an application to the federal court by one in state custody "pursuant to a judgment" of a state court shall not be granted "unless it appears that the applicant has exhausted the remedies available in the courts of the state." (28 U.S. Code, Sec. 2254). There is no corresponding provision regarding one in custody before judgment (i.e., conviction), but the same principle is applied.

[24] 28 U.S. Code, Sec. 2241.

[25] Of the 33,110 defendants against whom indictments or informations were disposed of (by plea of guilty, trial, or dismissal before trial) in the federal courts during the year ended June 30, 1962, over 10 per cent (3,374) were discharged by dismissal of the charge. Presumably in all but a trifling proportion of cases the dismissal was at the instance of the prosecutor. 1962 Report, Administrative Office of the U.S. Courts, 234.

the court, except under unusual circumstances, is in effect compelled to accept the recommendation of the prosecutor. If the prosecutor informs the court that the evidence he has been able to obtain makes the conviction of the defendant on the offense charged, or even of any lesser offense, highly improbable, the court is virtually powerless to evaluate the truth or good faith of the statement, except perhaps by requiring the prosecutor to disclose to the court every record and exhibit in his custody, and every fact (whether recorded or not) in his possession or in that of any member of his staff. Even were such an inquiry practicable, and even were the court, as a result of such inquiry, to conclude that the evidence warranted going forward with the prosecution, the court could hardly compel the prosecutor to proceed with that degree of vigor and skill indispensable for obtaining a conviction.

The importance of this power of the prosecutor in effect to release the accused, and the possibility of its abuse by a politically motivated prosecutor, are obvious.

In this connection, it should be noted that the length of time which may elapse between the accusation and the trial is also largely in the control of the prosecutor. A prosecuting officer who has unwillingly filed an information or procured an indictment, and is not zealous to see the accused convicted, may accomplish his object by mere delay. Either by consenting to repeated adjournments or continuances requested by the defendant or by failing to move the case for trial, he may permit the trial to be delayed until public interest has died down, witnesses have become unavailable, or other difficulties of prosecution have supervened, making his subsequent request for a dismissal of the prosecution the more justifiable. It is worth considering whether a statutory requirement that the prosecutor publish periodically a list of cases awaiting trial, showing date of indictment or information and stating the reason for the failure of each case to reach trial, might not prove a useful check on such abuse of discretion by the prosecutor.

Where, however, the prisoner desires trial and the prosecutor, for reasons of his own convenience or because he has been unable to prepare a sufficietly strong case, wishes to delay the trial, the power of the court on application of the accused to compel the prompt trial of the case or the dismissal of the indictment or information is the means by which is insured the reality of the guaranty of speedy trial found in the federal Constitution and in many of the state constitutions.

In many states, the accused may apply to the court in which the case is awaiting trial for a dismissal of the indictment or information without trial on the ground that there is not sufficient evidence to justify the placing of the accused on trial.

7. TRIAL: MODE OF PROOF

Trial may be by the court alone, or by the court and a jury (commonly termed "trial by jury"). Whichever form of trial is employed, however, the central aspect of the trial—the mode of proof employed—is the same.

We speak of our courts as courts of *law*. But it would be unrealistic to regard the major function of our trial courts as the interpretation of the law and its application to the facts of the matter in hand. Their chief problem is to ascertain facts; and in a very real sense our courts (and this is equally true of our non-judicial tribunals) depend for their success on their ability to ascertain facts—in criminal cases chiefly those most elusive of facts, the facts as to past occurrences.

The adversary system

But our courts as fact-finders rest under a disability which, whatever the methods or personnel employed, seriously limits their efforts. The facts they are seeking as to past occurrences ordinarily rest largely, if not exclusively, in the recollection of witnesses. The testimony of a witness as to what he saw or heard is often at variance with what actually occurred. Quite aside from deliberate falsehood, which despite the penalties for perjury is, in a society in which the religious sanction of an oath has largely disappeared, regrettably common, the witness's observation may have been faulty; his recollection may be imperfect; he may subconsciously have a bias in favor of, or a prejudice against, one of the parties; and his ego involvement, as it has been termed, that is, his own unrecognized desire to make a good impression on the witness stand, may cause him to distort his testimony. Against all these factors making for inaccurate if not false testimony, cross-examination is a potent but by no means completely effective countercheck. Hence, much of the fact-finding of our courts is seriously defective. Equally defective is it likely to be when there are no witnesses to the events in question and they can be reconstructed if at all only from the surrounding circumstances.

In every other department of life, the search for factual information is actively conducted or directed by those who are to pass judgment on the evidence. But in our courts those charged with reaching the final conclusion as to the facts—the judge or the jurors—are almost wholly without power to direct or control the search for the necessary factual data. Their role is passive. They are, with minor exceptions, confined to such information as is placed before them by the parties contending before them. This so-called adversary system proceeds on the theory (or at any rate has been retrospectively defended on the thesis) that since each party is intent on discovering all facts favorable to its contentions, and on exposing the falsity of allegations of fact injurious to its contentions, no fact is likely to be overlooked, nor any false factual claim to prevail.

The matter is not, however, quite so simple. There is incentive indeed to discover all favorable facts, but there is also the incentive to color or even to fabricate; and the notion that such distortion or fabrication cannot withstand hostile attack is quite unrealistic. Still more, there is the incentive to suppress facts injurious to one's case. That this is no imaginary danger has been demonstrated in a regrettable number of criminal cases in which, after the conviction of the defendant, it has transpired that the public prosecutor, with resources for investigation far exceeding those of the defendant, had come upon evidence favorable to the defendant but of which the defendant had no knowledge, yet had failed to make such evidence known to the defendant or to the court. Suppression of facts by the defense is presumably much more common. To the extent therefore that the adversary system, by placing the framing of the proof in the hands of the interested parties, furnishes incentives to the coloring, the fabrication, and the suppression of evidence, it is inimical to the search for facts.

But it is easier to point out defects in the adversary system, as a system for assuring the unearthing of facts, than to suggest an acceptable alternative, at least in criminal cases. To place the sole responsibility for discovering the facts and presenting the evidence in the hands of a supposedly disinterested public agency, even one operating as an arm of the court, would leave the defendant at the mercy of the public authorities, who under pretence of conducting an imparitial investigation might be plotting his destruction. Perhaps a compromise is possible—the retention of the adversary system, checked and supplemented, however, by independent investigation by or on behalf of the court itself. In a few areas of the law, the beginning of such an approach has been made. In certain criminal proceedings, in passing on the question of the mental competency of the defendant, the court may have the assistance of court-appointed psychiatrists. A few other exceptional instances might be adduced. In the extension of this principle to non-technical matters is perhaps to be found the way to a real improvement of our tribunals as fact-finders. Certainly in the field of criminal proceedings it may be questioned whether the resources of the state for investigation of the facts, so much vaster than those of the defendant, ought to be entrusted, as they now are, solely to police and prosecuting officials who, even if quite conscientious, are likely to acquire, in the course of the proceedings, a certain subconscious desire to build up a case against the luckless suspect on whom their first suspicions happen to have fastened themselves.[26]

[26] Bertrand Russell has propsed that parallel with the law-enforcement machinery, the function of which is, as he conceives it, to prove guilt, there should be an equally

The criminal trial thus proceeds after the manner of a forensic duel, rather than that of a disinterested investigation. Essentially it is a combat between the prosecution and the defense, with the judge acting as referee to enforce the rules of the contest and the jury as umpire to announce the victor (the judge assuming this role also if there is no jury). This conception of the criminal trial as a contest has come down through the centuries from the time when prosecution for crime had not yet become a function of the community, but was merely a proceeding for redress instituted by the party wronged, or by his kin—a complexion which the criminal prosecution indeed retained in England, in many cases, till within the present century.

The judge, whether merely presiding over the jury trial, or whether himself charged with responsibility for conviction or acquittal, has however a certain measure of power to direct the investigation. He may, in some states and in the federal courts, summon a witness not called by either side; but owing to lack of funds, he may in practice be unable to call to his aid, or to that of the jury, an impartial expert witness. He may interrogate witnesses; but in a trial by jury he does so, in some states, at the peril of a rebuke or even a reversal by the appellate court, should there be an appeal. Too insistent questioning is held by some appellate courts to be inconsistent with his role, in a jury trial, of neutral referee.[27]

In the jury trial, the jurymen are not afforded all the advantages available to the judge when he alone sits as trier of the facts. The individual juryman may indeed, on being recognized for that purpose by the judge, ask a question, whether of counsel or of a witness. His position obviously precludes him, however, from exercising this privilege with anything like the freedom enjoyed by the judge; and in practice the privilege is exercised only rarely. It is perhaps one of the most curious features of our jury trial procedure, though seldom the subject of remark, that the persons charged with evaluating the testimony of the witness are thus in effect inhibited from asking him any questions. There would seem to be no difficulty in providing that, as the interrogation of each witness by the parties is completed, the jurors should be invited, before the witness leaves the stand, to put to him any question which the testimony may have raised in their minds. Such indeed is the procedure in a trial by a general court-martial (if the members of the court, so called, be regarded, as they properly may, as in effect jurymen).

The juryman may not, moreover, as may the judge, himself summon

---

powerful governmental establishment whose function would be to establish innocence. Portraits from Memory, 226 (1956).

[27] For an example, see People v. Mendes, 3 N.Y.2d. 120 (1957), reversing the conviction because the judge's questions, directed at the defendant's witnesses, tended "to indicate a communicable disbelief of their testimony."

a witness not summoned by either side; nor may the jury collectively do so.

With the calling and questioning of the witnesses thus almost completely in the hands of counsel, the full and free consultation of counsel with "his" witnesses before the trial is considered entirely proper. Its propriety is so universally accepted in the United States that its mention here at all may seem quite superfluous. It is mentioned because on the Continent (and even, to some extent, in England), there exist severe limitations on direct pretrial communication between trial counsel and witness which every member of the bar is expected to observe.

The method of proof by forensic duel in criminal trials has been termed the accusatorial method. The contrasting procedure, in which the court itself takes the lead in the questioning, relying on data furnished by the prosecution—a procedure followed in varying forms on the Continent—is termed the inquistorial.

Duty of proceeding with proof

The prosecution is required to present its proof in full before the defense is called upon to offer any proof whatever. As to certain elements of certain crimes, the uncorroborated testimony of the alleged victim, or of an accomplice, may not satisfy the requirements of the law; corroborative evidence must also be adduced. If at the close of the proof offered by the prosecution, the judge, on application of the defendant, is of opinion that the evidence offered, even if assumed to be true, does not make out the necessary elments of the crime charged, it is his duty to acquit the prisoner (or, if trial is by jury, to direct an acquittal) without requiring the defense to offer any evidence.

With respect to a limited category of criminal accusations, the duty of going forward with the proof is in effect transposed from the prosecution to the defense by the statutory creation of a legal presumption of guilt from circumstances which are consistent as well with innocence. To rebut such presumption, the defense is required to offer proof that such innocence is in fact present. Thus, one accused of fraudulently obtaining property in exchange for a check which proved uncollectible because of his lack of funds or credit at the bank, is in a number of states presumed by statute to have known the insufficiency of his funds or credit. Hence, unless he comes forward with testimony affirmatively establishing that he in good faith believed he had the necessary balance or credit, conviction must follow.[28]

[28] It is, however, unconstitutional (as a denial of due process) for a statute to create a presumption from circumstances which have no sufficiently direct connection with the fact presumed, e.g., a state statute providing that proof of insolvency of a bank creates presumption of fraud on the part of its directors, Manley v. Georgia, 279 U.S. 1 (1929), or a federal statute providing that defendant's prior conviction

Permissible types of evidence

Unless the court, under well-established rules, takes "judicial notice" of a fact, it must be proved, such proof taking the form ordinarily of oral testimony, supplemented by objects identified by the testimony (and referred to as "exhibits"). Only in exceptional cases, as already indicated, is the personal presence of the witness dispensed with and his testimony permitted to be offered in the form of a deposition; and then only on behalf of the defense, unless the prisoner was, at the time of the making of the deposition, afforded the opportunity to confront the witness. The testimony of witnesses may be supplemented, if the court deems proper, by demonstrations, experiments, charts, models, and the like, and by the judge, the defendant, counsel, and the jury, if there be one, proceeding to the scene of the events testified to, to "view" it.

Neither prosecution nor defense is free to offer every variety of evidence available. Under established rules, certain types of evidence are inadmissible; and in certain situations the testimony of a witness, though in itself admissible, must be excluded because the witness is, under some established rule, "incompetent" to give such testimony. It is the duty of the court, when the proposed introduction of any evidence by either side is objected to by the other, to exclude it if it is repugnant to the established rules; or, if it has been inadvertently introduced, to order it, on request, to be deleted from the record and eliminated from consideration. The body of "rules of evidence" thus applied exceeds in complexity and technicality those found in any other system of jurisprudence and is applied in this country with a greater degree of technicality than in England.

Historically, the development of many of our rules of evidence is closely bound up with the development of trial by jury, shortly to be discussed. The English judges of the fifteenth and sixteenth centuries were attacking a novel problem—that of obtaining reasoned decisions from a group of laymen, often illiterate, brought together only for the particular case in hand, having no organization, tradition, or experience. They early sensed the need of assisting this lay tribunal to keep clear the issue before it by thwarting attempts to introduce before it irrelevant testimony—that is, testimony as to occurrences which, while perhaps related to the subject of the action, could have no bearing on the legal rights or liabilities of the parties. Equally clear was the need of checking the invariable tendency of witnesses to relate not merely the occurrences that they themselves had seen or heard, but what someone else had told

---

of a crime of violence and his present possession of a firearm create presumption that the article was received by him in interstate commerce and subsequent to effective date of act, which makes unlawful such receipt by a person who has been convicted of a crime of violence. Tot v. U.S., 319 U.S. 463 (1943).

them about the events in question. The receipt in evidence of alleged dying declarations was also surrounded with safeguards. Rules as to the admissibility of secondary writings and records also arose. As the use of the jury and its independence and power grew, the body of restrictions on admissible testimony took shape as an extensive and increasingly technical body of doctrine. United with it was a similarly developed set of rules excluding or limiting the testimony of particular classes of persons, especially the parties, the spouses, etc.[29] It is this body of doctrine, highly elaborated by American courts during the last century, and supplemented in many states by a considerable body of statute law, that the judge must apply in determining whether the proposed testimony (as indicated by the question intended to elicit such testimony) or the proffered document or exhibit is admissible.

In theory, it is just as incumbent upon a judge sitting without a jury to exclude evidence or offers of proof which are repugnant to the rules of evidence as if a jury were present. In practice, however, there is often a disposition on the part both of counsel and the court not to insist too strictly upon the application of technical rules of evidence. As one learned in the law, the judge, it is supposed, will not, as might a jury, accord to incompetent or irrelevant evidence a weight which, in the eye of the law, it ought not to have.

Since, as we shall see, the prosecution ordinarily cannot appeal an acquittal, the judge is not too fearful of the improper admission of evidence favorable to the defendant. He is more likely to be intent on excluding evidence or witnesses against the defendant, the wrongful admission of which will be ground for a reversal of the conviction, should one ensue, by the appellate court.

Form of oral testimony

The oral testimony, which thus constitutes the chief medium of proof in a criminal case, takes the form of answers to specific questions, given by one witness at a time. The ancient English procedure of questioning two or more witnesses simultaneously has long been obsolete, and the confrontation of two conflicting witnesses, and their interrogation of each other, employed in some Continental systems, is unknown to our law. The witness is not typically permitted to tell his story in his own way; he answers questions put to him, and if, in the course of his answer to a question, he offers matter which is not strictly responsive to the question, or indulges in an expression of his opinion—the question having merely

---

[29] The rules governing incompetency of witnesses to testify, at one time of great importance, are now relatively few. Neither the accused nor his spouse was permitted to testify until the last century; and in some states the defendant's spouse may still not be compelled to testify for the prosecution.

called for a statement of what he saw, heard, or otherwise sensed—he opens himself to a possible rebuke by counsel or perhaps an admonition by the court. The method is severely logical—perhaps too logical for the man in the street. The sense of frustration and the fear of rebuke may combine to deprive his testimony of much of the content and perhaps even of the credibility which it might have in a less inhibited setting.

This much is true even when the witness is answering the questions put to him by the side which called him to the stand, and which is eager to present him as a responsible and credible witness. When he is delivered over, as he must be, to cross-examination, so called, by the other side, his case may be even worse. Effective cross-examination may often be conducted without raising the voice and with the use of questions of seemingly neutral character; but there is a temptation, which not a few attorneys find it difficult to resist, to try to break down the witness's credibility not by exposing inconsistencies or improbabilities in his testimony, but by hectoring him. At some point such cross-examination may pass permissible bounds, and call for the intervention of the court; but too often the court intervenes only long after the witness, if honestly trying to tell the truth, may well feel that he has been unjustly assailed. An observer of our system could accept this phenomenon with more equanimity were he certain that these methods are generally effective in exposing an untruthful witness. It is the melancholy fact, however, that the deliberately untruthful witness is often better equipped to maintain his poise and seeming disinterestedness under a savage cross-examination than is a truthful one.

When cross-examination is skillfully conducted, however, it may be extremely effective in unmasking false testimony; and few American students of criminal justice would be willing to see the right of cross-examination limited. No system of punitive justice can rise higher than the level set by the truthfulness of the testimony before it; and cross-examination, despite its regrettable abuses, remains one of the few instruments for intimidating and exposing intentionally false witness.

In the criminal procedure of some western European countries, cross-examination is by the court only, counsel having however the privilege of suggesting to the court questions to be put to the witness. Such a procedure, while it doubtless escapes some of the abuses of cross-examination, would encounter with us fundamental objections—the chief being that, especially when it results in hostile cross-examination of the accused or his witnesses, it tends to impair that moral position of the judge, founded on his supposedly complete impartiality, which is of the essence of the Anglo-American criminal procedure.

The solution for the dilemma posed by our cross-examination procedure is to be found only in the firmer use by our judges of their power to check abuse of the cross-examiner's privilege.

Confessions

Since, as already noted, the privilege against self-incrimination has prevented compulsory examination of the defendant before trial, the prosecution is ordinarily able to introduce evidence of pretrial admissions of the defendant only in the form of testimony by others as to the making of such admissions by him. To the extent that these are contained in a written confession alleged to have been voluntarily made by the defendant while in custody, they are of course subject to the danger of repudiation by the defendant on the claim that force or duress was used to extract the confession (or, less frequently, that the confession was obtained by promise of reward or leniency.)[30] This claim raises at once the question of whether the contents of the confession are admissible in evidence. Under the federal practice and in some of the states, the conflicting testimony as to the circumstances under which the confession was made is, even where the trial is by jury, presented only to the court. (If the court rules the contents of the confession inadmissible because coerced, the contents are not disclosed to the jury. If the court admits the contents of the confession in evidence, the defense may seek nevertheless to impugn the truth of the confession by evidence that it was coerced). In the remaining states the contents of the confession are received in evidence, and the conflicting testimony as to the circumstances under which the confession was made is presented to the jury, the court instructing the jury that if they conclude that the confession was coerced they are to disregard it—an instruction perhaps easier to give meticulously than to follow conscientiously.

As already noted, a conviction resting on a coerced confession has been held by the Supreme Court to be a denial of due process of law and thus violative of the Constitution.[31]

The absence of any provision for obtaining a prisoner's confession under such judicial safeguards as will insure its voluntary character has already been mentioned.

Defendant as witness

The defendant is not, as in England and in some Continental countries, isolated in a distinctive place in the courtroom, unable to communi-

[30] The concept of "duress" now embraces not only physical harm or threats thereof, (including threats of injury to members of the accused's family) but also undue psychological pressure. In Leyra v. Denno, 347 U.S. 556 (1954), the Supreme Court went so far as to set aside a state conviction of murder because of the reception in evidence at the trial of two apparently voluntary confessions made, in the Court's view of the record (disregarding the jury's contrary finding, implied in its verdict), under the influence of psychological pressure exerted some hours before, as a result of which the accused had made a confession which had been excluded from evidence.

[31] A conviction based on testimony as to oral admissions made by the defendant under circumstances amounting to coercion is equally a denial of due process of law. Ashcraft v. Tennessee, 327 U.S. 274 (1946).

cate with his counsel except in writing. Instead, he sits alongside his counsel at the counsel table, and may freely speak with him. If he elects to testify, he takes the witness chair like any other witness.[32]

The prosecutor is unable, by reason of the privilege against self-incrimination, to compel the defendant to testify. In the great majority of cases which reach trial in the criminal courts, the prosecutor has likewise been unable, due to the absence of any compulsory procedure therefor, to extract incriminating admissions from the defendant in advance of trial; and he has therefore obtained independent evidence of the defendant's guilt. Had he failed to do so, he would not have brought the case to trial. Consequently, the prosecutor does not at this stage ordinarily find his inability to call the defendant to the stand at the trial a serious drawback.

The effect of the statutory presumption of guilt, found in certain categories of crime, in virtually compelling the defense to go forward at the outset with affirmative proof of innocence has already been mentioned; and since such proof can generally come only from the lips of the defendant himself, the result is in effect to compel him to testify on pain of conviction.

Even where there is no such presumption, the evidence presented by the prosecution may, and quite generally is, such that for a defendant to decline to take the stand is in many cases tantamount to a confession of guilt. A guilty defendant under these circumstances might well prefer the ancient rule denying him the privilege of taking the stand; for today he has in effect only the cruel alternative of testifying, with all the risk of convicting himself on cross-examination out of his own mouth, or of remaining mute, with the risk that his mere silence in the face of the evidence against him will be accepted as proof of his guilt.

Even an innocent defendant, if he has a criminal record, may shrink from taking the stand in his own defense; for by doing so he makes possible to the prosecution an exposure of his unsavory past that is otherwise prohibited. The salutary doctrine of our law is that the prosecution, having adduced evidence that the accused actually committed the crime charged, cannot fortify its case by further evidence that the accused has a criminal record. If the accused takes the stand in his own defense, however, his credibility, like that of any other witness, may be attacked on cross-examination; and previous convictions of crime are held, whether justifiably or not, to be relevant to his credibility and hence a proper subject of questioning on such cross-examination. Manifestly, however, once admitted, the evidence of the defendant's criminal record is more than likely to influence the judge, and to an even greater extent the jury if there is one, in resolving doubts as to the defendant's guilt. There is

[32] The English practice was, however, followed until very recently in Massachusetts.

much to be said for the fairness of the English rule, which prohibits the prosecution from eliciting from the defendant, or otherwise establishing, the defendant's criminal record merely because he testifies in his own defense. Only if he, by his own testimony or by witnesses, himself places his good character in issue may his criminal record be disclosed.

That the possible cause of the accused's failure to take the stand may be the inevitable disclosure, should he do so, of his former conviction rather than of his present guilt is, however, a possibility not likely to be given much weight by the jurors, even if they are aware of it. It is, indeed, an established doctrine (except in six states)—a doctrine alleged by the courts (in what would seem to be a *non sequitur*) to follow from the privilege against compulsory self-incrimination—that the failure of the defendant to take the stand justifies no inference whatever as to his guilt. But the doctrine is so at war with everyday experience that its actual value to a defendant who fails to take the stand is negligible. As a practical matter the defendant finds it imperative to take the stand and undergo cross-examination in almost every case. In the few cases where he does not, he is almost invariably convicted. His constitutional exemption from compulsory questioning, so valuable to him while the case against him is being prepared by the police and prosecutor, is at his trial ordinarily valueless.

Failure to disclose evidence

Despite the fact that the method of proof is dominated by the adversary concept, the public prosecutor is in theory expected to subordinate his efforts to convict the accused to his obligation, as a public officer, to insure that no injustice is done. In theory, therefore, he should disclose any information in his possession which would be favorable to the accused, but of which the accused or his counsel are not aware. This would include not only information uncovered in the prosecution's investigation, but also inconsistencies between a prosecution witness's testimony at the trial and statements made by him to the authorities, or testimony given by him before the grand jury. In practice, however, this obligation of the prosecutor is doubtless more often than not disregarded; and there exists no procedure for giving any assurance that it has been honored. A requirement that the prosecutor state to the court at the close of the evidence, on his oath as an officer of the court, that he knows of nothing favorable to the accused which has not been brought forward in evidence would seem entirely reasonable.

Although there is thus no affirmative procedure for compelling disclosure by the prosecutor of information favorable to the accused, if at the trial he remains silent in the face of testimony by a prosecution witness which he knows to be false, the defendant, on learning the facts, is entitled to have his conviction set aside, as having been a denial of due process of law.[33]

No procedure has been developed to enable the defense to elicit information in the possession of the prosecution obtained in the course of its investigation; but in recent years there has been a development in the direction of facilitating the effort of the defense to establish that the testimony of a prosecution witness is inconsistent with his statements to the authorities or with his testimony before the grand jury.[34]

Expert witnesses

A witness who testifies not as a spectator or auditor of the events involved in the alleged crime but as one giving his opinion because he has special competence on some special issue—such as the sanity of the defendant at the time of the alleged commission of the offense, the cause of death, the identity of the firearm from which a particular bullet was fired—may be called by either side. Such a witness—commonly termed an expert witness—is under no compulsion to testify. He is, accordingly, almost invariably compensated for his attendance and testimony by the side which calls him. The natural result is in many cases a battle of experts, with the judge or jury understandably disposed to believe that each expert might have testified with equal positiveness for the other side had he been called by it. This unedifying aspect of criminal trials has led to provisions, in some states and in the federal courts, empowering the court to call expert witnesses (in some states, only on the issue of sanity); and in a few states the courts have exercised the power without statutory authorization. The power cannot be effectively exercised, however, unless the court is furnished with adequate funds for the compensation of the expert. Moreover, the court should not be required to assume the task of searching for an expert when the sudden need therefore arises; there should be a standing panel of experts in each of the fields commonly called upon—psychiatry, ballistics, toxicology, handwriting, etc. In a majority of the states, and indeed in the federal courts as well, hardly more than a beginning has been made in these matters.

Measure of proof

There can be no conviction unless the guilt of the defendant is established "beyond a reasonable doubt." In popular parlance, it is often said

[33] Alcorta v. Texas, 355 U.S. 28 (1958). See also People v. Savvides, 1 N.Y.2d 554 (1956).

[34] In the federal courts, by statute adopted in 1957, the court may, after a government witness has testified, order a statement or report previously made by the witness to the authorities to be delivered to the defendant, the purpose being to enable the defendant to attempt to impeach the witness's credibility should there be inconsistencies between his testimony and his pretrial statements. 18 U.S. Code, Sec. 3500.

that the defendant is assumed to be innocent until proved guilty. In strictness, there is no such presumption. The rule is simply that the defendant is not to be convicted merely because the evidence against him outweighs that in his favor; the evidence of guilt must so far outweigh the evidence of his innocence that no *reasonable* doubt of his guilt remains.

The trial setting and the witness

In every proceeding in which a witness's testimony as to past events is given, but particularly in a criminal trial, it is important that the setting of the proceeding be such as to minimize the likelihood that the witness's testimony will be unknowingly influenced by his unconscious desire to make a good impression on the audience. Experience teaches that in a quiet relaxed setting, with only those present who are directly concerned with the proceeding, a witness unaccustomed to public appearances is least likely to be influenced by this disturbing factor; and from this standpoint, it would perhaps be rational to exclude the general public from the criminal trial. The Constitution provides, however, that in a federal prosecution "the accused shall enjoy the right to a . . . public trial"; and similar provisions are found in most state constitutions and in the governing statutes in all the states.

These provisions represent, historically, the eighteenth century revolt against the abuses of criminal justice, in the service of the Crown, in the state trials of the Tudor and Stuart dynasties. They arose in a period when one tried for a felony was not entitled to be informed in advance of the accusation against him, was not entitled to have counsel, and was not permitted to testify. Under such circumstances, the opening of the court to the public, to however limited an extent, furnished some check on the excesses of judge and prosecutor in league to destroy the defendant. Under modern conditions, where the accused is represented by counsel and a stenographic record of the proceedings, available on appeal, is kept, the admission of the general public to the trial can hardly be reckoned an important protection to the accused.

The admission of the public to the trial in a small courtroom will ordinarily have little effect on the conduct of the trial. On the other hand, if the courtroom is large—and in many courtrooms a much larger portion of the space is allotted to spectators than to participants—and the trial has evoked unusual public interest, the presence of a crowded gallery may serve to heighten what might be termed the histrionic aspects of the trial. When, as is not uncommon in such circumstances, special provision is made for the accommodation of reporters (and even arrangements for the convenience of newspaper photographers have occasionally been made) this tendency is reinforced. A witness compelled to give his testimony in such a setting may well ask himself whether he has been commanded to assist in a judicial inquiry, in which the liberty or perhaps the life of a fellow citizen is at stake, or has been drafted to act in a spectacle. If in addition he is aware that his every word and every change of facial expression are being immediately communicated to untold thousands via radio and television, as has already occurred in a few of our states with the permission of the judge, it would seem that the ultimate has been reached in creating a setting in which the susceptible witness may be more concerned with how he is doing than with whether he is reproducing with exactness his recollection of what happened.

8. TRIAL BY JURY: INSTITUTIONAL ASPECTS

Trial by a jury means, ordinarily, by a jury of twelve. Smaller criminal juries are however employed in some of our states, especially in misdemeanor trials.

Origin and development trial by jury

Persistent historical researches in the nineteenth and even in the present century have failed to clear away completely the mist in which the genesis of the jury was for so long enveloped. However, there is now fairly general agreement on the chief points.

Although forms of trial resembling trial by jury in various particulars are to be found in the primitive institutions of many peoples, including the Anglo-Saxon, the institution first emerges as a definite feature of the English system of civil trial at common law in the thirteenth century. So far as its history can be traced back beyond that time, it appears to have derived not from any Anglo-Saxon institution, but from a procedure introduced by the Norman conquerors, having been carried over by them from the Continent, where it had been well developed under the Frankish kings some centuries before. This procedure, known as the inquest (in the legal Latin of the time, *inquisito* or *recognito*) consisted in the summoning by a public officer of a body of local residents to give under oath information on some local matter required by the officer for some administrative purpose—in particular for the assessment of royal taxes.

As the feudal system developed, disputes frequently arose between overlords and local lords as to their respective rights in the local lands, the services locally due the overlord, etc. Since these rights rested largely on custom, perpetuated by oral tradition rather than by writing, it became the practice, under the Franks, for the king or provincial lord to send emissaries into the several localities charged with making inquisition into these rights, and for these emissaries to summon to their aid a group of the more important freemen of the vicinage to give them information.

Transplanted to England with the Conquest (and employed on a grand scale in the compilation of Domesday Book), this procedure appears to have been extended by the sheriff, the direct representative of the king in each of the countries, from purely fiscal and administrative matters to the investigation of crimes—the forerunner of our grand jury. Thus projected into the field of law enforcement, the device of inviting the aid of a body of "freemen of the vicinage" was adopted by the royal judges, when they went on circuit, as a means of obtaining information about private disputes and even criminal charges coming before them.

It must be remembered, however, that the notion of a judgment or verdict reached only after impartial examination of all the evidence was at this time still in its infancy in England, as in Europe generally. Trial by ordeal and battle still prevailed; and heavy reliance was placed upon the supposed sanctity of oaths. Under these circumstances the function of the body of freemen of the vicinage who came to be called in by the royal judges was not merely that of giving such information as they had (or had heard, for common report was at that time regarded as proper matter for the consideration of a court), but to swear as to their opinion, based on their own knowledge or information, as to the guilt or innocence of the accused, or as to the merits of the disputes before the court.

The details of the process by which this body came, in the course of two centuries or more, to lose its functions as a body of witnesses, and to assume instead the function of judges, are still somewhat obscure; and it is clear that in criminal cases the substitution of jury trial for compurgation and trial by ordeal and battle proceeded much more slowly than did the corresponding displacement of antiquated methods of proof in civil litigation. But it is easy to surmise that, once the impaneling of the jury had become a standing feature of court procedure, occasions multiplied, with the growing complexity of medieval life, in which the jury was unable of its own knowledge or information to venture a satisfactory opinion; that witnesses from outside the vicinage might be summoned to give testimony to assist the jury; that gradually the role of the summoned witnesses became more and more important, and the judicial function of the jurors more and more predominant. By the sixteenth century, we find the doctrine well established that the jurors are to render their verdict exclusively upon the basis of the evidence.

Under the absolutism of the Tudors, the jury in criminal cases came increasingly to be seen as a protection of the subject against the oppression of the officers of the Crown. Particularly was this so because the several extraordinary tribunals created during the Tudor regime for the suppression of treason and heresy—the Court of High Commission, the Court of the Star Chamber, and the Council of the North—all operated without juries. Under the Puritan regime, the jury became established as the sole tribunal for criminal cases except for crimes on the high seas and certain other crimes connected with navigation, which were tried without jury in the admiralty courts.[35]

In the Bill of Rights, enacted in 1688 and embodied in the settlement which brought William and Mary to the throne, the right to trial by jury in criminal cases was apparently for the first time declared in statutory form, in the provision that jurors ought to be duly impaneled and returned; and thus a part of the body of basic English constitutional doctrine was formally restated.

In the struggle to establish the right to jury trial in criminal cases as a fundamental right of the Englishman, the alleged antiquity of the right was of course much stressed; and much was made of the provision in Magna Carta that "we will not set forth against him [i.e. any freeman] nor send against him unless by the lawful judgment of his peers." This provision (on whose precise interpretation scholars are still not agreed) demonstrated, it was alleged, that the English freeman was entitled to jury trial even as early as the thirteenth century. From what has been said, however, it will be apparent that at that time trial by jury as we understand it was unknown. But historical learning in this matter was still fragmentary in Tudor and Stuart times, and the mistaken belief that the phrase in Magna Carta referred to trial by jury tended to give that institution, at a time when its importance as a shield against the oppression of the Crown was being recognized, the appearance of a venerable antiquity that it did not in fact possess—so much so that by the seventeenth century it had already become customary to refer to it as an "immemorial" right.

In the eighteenth century colonies, the popular conviction that trial by jury was one of the essential liberties of the subject was intensified by the insistence of the British government that certain crimes connected with navigation were outside the province of the regular colonial criminal courts, sitting with juries, and were to be punished instead by the admiralty courts (four or five for the entire Atlantic seaboard), which were directly responsible to London and in which juries were unknown.[36]

Constitutional right to jury trial

A guarantee of the right to jury trial in criminal cases was embodied in most of the state constitutions adopted during the Revolution, and in

---

[35] Though the Puritans had abolished the Star Chamber and the High Commission, they on occasion set up special non-jury commissions of their own to try state offenses. See, for example, the trial of Liliburne, a Puritan zealot, for treason, in 1649. 4 Howell's State Trials 1292 (1816).

[36] One of the grievances recited in the Declaration of Independence is "acts of pretended legislation . . . for depriving us in many cases, of the benefits of trial by jury."

the constitutions of all the states later created. Today, such a guarantee, in one or another form, is found in the constitution of every state.

During the colonial period a fairly uniform pattern for jury trial apparently prevailed, modeled on that which obtained in England. That pattern, so far as research has up to this time disclosed it, provided for jury trial even in misdemeanors, but not in petty offenses; and this apparently was the pattern carried over into the newly independent states. In various states, in subsequent years, the right to jury trial in misdemeanors has been invaded to a greater or less extent. In no state, however, has the jury trial in felonies been abolished, being in virtually every state guaranteed by state constitutional provision.

It is solely because of such state constitutional provision that the constitutional right of jury trial obtains in our states; for it is well established that the provision in the Fourteenth Amendment prohibiting a state from depriving any person of life, liberty, or property without due process of law does not require the states to provide jury trial even in felony cases.

The right to jury trial in criminal cases in the federal courts was included in the Constitution (although the right to jury trial in civil cases was not). The form of the guarantee thus embodied in the Constitution was, however, much criticized as defective; and a more elaborate guarantee, providing that the jury should be "of the state and district wherein the crime shall have been committed, which district shall have previously been ascertained by law," was added by the amendments adopted in 1791.[37]

Present status of trial by jury

Although the right to trial by jury in a criminal case is commonly regarded as one of the chief guarantees of the individual against official oppression, it is nevertheless true that a certain proportion of defendants even in serious felony cases are tried without a jury. This comes about through the use, both in the federal courts and in more than half of the states, of the defendant's privilege of waiving a jury. In the remaining states constitutional provisions forbid such a waiver, and the defendant must be tried by a jury even though he might prefer to be tried by the judge alone. In some states and in the federal courts, the consent of the prosecution is required as well as the consent of the defendant, a rule which is difficult to justify in the light of the history of the right of trial by jury and its obvious purpose to protect the individual against a judge under the domination of the executive. In some states, capital cases are excluded from the defendant's privilege of waiving the jury.

The present tendency is toward increasing the use of the waiver of jury

[37] The constitutional provision is not applicable to the insular possessions of the United States which have not been "incorporated" into the United States. Cf. Balzac v. Porto Rico, 258 U.S. 298 (1922). In Puerto Rico, there is no jury trial for misdemeanors.

trial.[38] Students of criminal justice are inclined to believe that the extensive use of the waiver would, on the whole, greatly improve the efficiency of the trial process.

If the jury is waived, the trial is, in the federal courts and almost everywhere in the states, by a single judge. In a few places, the trial is before a bench of three judges—an arrangement found also in some places in which the jury trial of misdemeanors has been abolished. The more general substitution of such a bench for the single judge might greatly increase the frequency of jury waivers.

The motives which prompt the defendant to waive his right to a jury trial are not always easy to discover. It has been stated, however, that the defendant with a criminal record is likely to waive a jury in the belief that should that record be disclosed at the trial (as it may and doubtless will be if the defendant elects to take the stand), such disclosure is more likely to prejudice a jury than a judge, presumably schooled in confining his attention to the particular issue before the court. Again, a defendant or his counsel may feel that the judge will be less influenced than a jury by the publicity attending the case.[39] The abundance of press, and broadcast reports and commentaries which invariably precede and indeed accompany the trial of any criminal case which engages the public interest may in fact create real difficulty in procuring a jury truly open minded. But even if that is accomplished, the refusal of our legislatures and courts to take measures to control the news media in their reporting and commenting on the case as it progresses makes it extremely difficult to prevent the jurors, by any steps short of locking them up and forbidding them the use of the telephone, from being influenced by what they read and hear outside the courtroom, the admonitions of the court to the contrary notwithstanding.[40]

[38] In some of the counties of Maryland, the waiver of jury trial has become so common that trial by judge, rather than by jury, is the established routine. Comprehensive data as to the extent to which trial by jury is waived in the state courts are not available. In the federal courts, in the year ended June 30, 1962, of the 3,788 criminal trials completed, 1,090, or nearly 29 per cent, were tried without a jury. 1962 Report, Administrative Office of the U.S. Courts, 215.

[39] A commentator professing familiarity with underworld thought has offered the further explanation that the professional criminal awaiting trial has not infrequently, whether through political influence or outright bribery, obtained assurance that the judge will either acquit him or convict him only of a lesser offense; and that it is for this reason that he prefers trial by the judge alone. Cf. Maurer, The Big Con, 240 (1940). Somewhat different is the explanation offered by the experienced professional thief (Chic Conwell) whose observations were recorded by a distinguished criminologist. "It is much harder to straighten out twelve men than one. Even aside from fixing cases, the judge is better acquainted with the police and the prosecutor than the jury is and, consequently, has less confidence in their testimony and oratory." Sutherland, The Professional Thief, 134 (1937).

[40] The admonitions given by the judge to the jurors are considered by some commentators to be of trifling value. See, however, United States v. Accardo, 298 F.2d. 133 (7th Circ., 1962), in which a conviction, in a case attended by much newspaper publicity, was set aside because, among other things, the trial judge had failed to

Few would dissent from the view that the accused is entitled to trial by a jury uninfluenced by anything other than what occurs in the courtroom. It might well be contended that anything less than this is not due process of law, and that the state is thus under a constitutional duty to prevent the inundation of the court by a flood of public comment and discussion. But the highest court of one of our states has refused so to hold, declaring that an avalanche of public disclosure and comment is consistent with "the traditional concept of the American way of the conduct of a trial"; and the Supreme Court has refused, only one member dissenting, to disturb this holding.[41]

The situation now threatens to deteriorate further through the unremitting pressure of the broadcasting industries for permission to introduce microphones and television cameras into the courtroom, to enable the proceedings to be instantaneously reproduced in the homes and work places of the news-hungry public, whose chief interest, if we are to accept the assurances of the broadcasters, is to observe the administration of justice. Here, as in the case of pretrial publicity, the "freedom of the press" and "the right of the people to know" are invoked; but why the press should be free to influence the jury or why the people must enjoy the right to know what goes on in the courts at the very instant of its occurrence, when nothing whatever can be done about it by anyone but the judge and counsel, rather than after the jury has rendered its verdict, is not explained. The organized bar and the judicial conference of the federal court system have rejected such proposals decisively. The state judiciaries, while almost without exception resisting their adoption, have not taken so clear-cut and public a condemnatory position as has the federal; and in at least one state (Colorado) the highest court of the state, vested with rule-making power over the trial courts, has expressly approved the photographing, broadcasting, and telecasting of courtroom proceedings if the trial judge (who, like the judges of the high court, owes his office to popular election) approves—as he has done in several cases deemed by the media to be especially newsworthy.

Earlier, a reference was made to the undesirable effect which a large courtroom, with spectators far outnumbering the participants, may have

admonish the jurors with sufficient frequency that they were not to read newspaper accounts of the trial or listen to broadcasts relating to it.

[41] Stroble v. California, 343 U.S. 181 (1952). In a capital case, in which the trial took place, in the words of the state's high court, in the "atmosphere of a 'Roman holiday' for the news media," a change of venue was denied, the conviction and the sentence to life imprisonment were sustained by the state courts, and the Supreme Court refused to review. Sheppard v. Ohio, 352 U.S. 910 (1956). See also Irvin v. Dowd, 366 U.S. 717 (1961); Comment, The Case against Trial by Newspaper: Analysis and Proposal, 57 Northwestern U. Law Rev. 217 (1962); and Goldfarb, Public Information, Criminal Trials and the Cause Celebre, 36 N.Y. U. Law Rev. 810 (1961).

on the reliability of the testimony of certain witnesses. When there exists community hostility toward the accused, the large courtroom furnishes a setting in which such hostility can best be conveyed to the witness and the jury—not to mention the judge, who may be about to stand for re-election. It may even have an intimidating effect on counsel for the defense. A drastic reduction in the size of the courtroom, with corresponding reduction in the prominence of the public and the press, would greatly assist the fairness, not to mention the expedition and dignity, of certain types of criminal trials.

In a number of states, as already noted, the constitutional provision is so framed as to require jury trial, no waiver being permissible. Thus, in an inflamed condition of public hostility, a constitutional provision which not only guarantees the accused the right to jury trial, but goes further and compels him to be tried by a jury when he would prefer to be tried by a judge, may actually guarantee the accused not a fair trial but a lynching by jury. And in the situation, recurrent in a few of our southern states, in which community hostility to the accused is racial as well as individual, the further constitutional command, shortly to be discussed, that persons of the accused's own race be not excluded from the jury may be quite worthless; for a Negro on the jury could hardly be expected, in an explosive state of community hostility to a Negro defendant, to brave that hostility by holding out against his white fellow jurors.[42]

The procedure for change of venue, already referred to, offers some protection in this situation. It may be of little avail, however, in a time of national or regional feeling too widespread to be escaped by a mere change of locality, such as, to take an extreme example, a feeling born of war hysteria.

Nor does the federal guarantee of due process avail much here. Only if it appeared that the court and jury were in effect intimidated by a show of force by the citizenry would the Supreme Court be likely to disturb a conviction in a state court.[43]

On the whole, however, it is possible that local feeling favorable to the accused constitutes a graver weakness in trial by jury than does local hostility to him. The limited or totally absent provision in our law for change of venue at the instance of the prosecutor has already been mentioned; nor

[42] In Shepherd v. Florida, 341 U.S. 50 (1951), Justice Jackson, in a concurring opinion, said (at page 54): "Under these circumstances, for the Court to reverse these convictions upon the sole ground that the method of jury selection discriminated against the Negro race, is to stress the trivial and ignore the important. . . . this trial took place under conditions and was accompanied by events which would deny defendants a fair trial before any kind of jury. I do not see, as a practical matter, how any Negro on the jury would have dared to cause a disagreement or acquittal."

[43] Cf. Frank v. Mangum, 237 U.S. 309 (1915) and Moore v. Dempsey, 261 U.S. 86 (1923).

is it of much value, even where available, if the popular feeling involved extends over a considerable region. Under these circumstances the jury, instead of being a shield to the innocent against official oppression, becomes a refuge for the guilty.[44]

9. TRIAL BY JURY: PROCEDURAL ASPECTS

In a trial by jury, the first step is the selection of the jurors from the panel of prospective jurors (or "veniremen") who have been summoned for service. The preparation of the list of those eligible to be summoned, and the selection from that list of those actually summoned to the particular term of court (or, it may be, for the particular trial)—procedures that obviously may have a vital bearing on the character of the jurors who will ultimately be selected to try the case—will be described at a later point.[45] They take place wholly outside the control, and indeed outside the cognizance, of either the prosecutor or the defense. Nevertheless, the defense may, at the opening of the trial, object to the jury's being selected from the panel of prospective jurors thus summoned.

Challenge to the array

A ground of objection to the panel may of course be that the officers who made up the initial list, or who selected from the list those summoned to attend for jury service, failed to comply with the governing statutes. Beyond such technical objections, however, lies the possible contention that the methods employed in making up the list, or in selecting the veniremen therefrom, were such that trial by a jury drawn from the resulting panel would be unjust to the defendant—and hence a denial of due process of law. Such a contention has been successfully made, hitherto, chiefly in cases where it was alleged on behalf of the defendant, a Negro, that Negroes had been systematically excluded.[46] The contention has also been made, thus

---

[44] Those members of Congress who insisted on the inclusion in the civil rights act of 1957 of a provision for jury trial of charges of criminal contempt for violation of injunctions issued under the act (see page 166) doubtless envisaged this as the function of the jury in such cases.

[45] See pp. 403 ff.

[46] In setting aside the conviction of a Mexican on this ground, the Supreme Court declared the principle to be applicable to the systematic exclusion of any "identifiable group." Hernandez v. Texas, 347 U.S. 475 (1954). The principle is applicable also to the selection of grand jurors. If members of the defendant's race were systematically excluded from the grand jury, the indictment itself is a denial of due process, and a conviction founded on it will be reversed. Norris v. Alabama, 294 U.S. 587 (1935). Congress in 1875 made it a misdemeanor for any person charged with any duty in the selection or summoning of jurors to exclude or fail to summon any citizen "for service as grand or petit juror in any court of the United States or of any state on account of race, color or previous condition of servitude." (Act of March 1, 1875, 18 Stat. 336; 18 U.S. Code, Sec. 243.) This statute is still in effect but it apparently seldom invoked.

far unsuccessfully, that the method of making up the list of necessity produced a jury composed of persons of a higher income level than prevails in the community generally.

The challenge to the jury as not sufficiently representative of the range of economic levels in the citizenry is a recent development. The principal case in the Supreme Court arose in the state courts of New York. In that state, as in not a few others, the statutes provided for the preparation, in addition to the regular jury list, of a special list. It was alleged that, though the statute providing for the special jury lists did not indeed so provide, the administration of the statute in fact had the effect of producing a jury list predominantly, if not almost exclusively, composed of citizens of a higher economic level than those on the regular jury list, and of an economic group predisposed to be unsympathetic to the defendants in the case in question (labor union officers charged with extortion) who represented themselves to be laboring men.[47] The Supreme Court, by a sharply divided bench, affirmed the conviction;[48] but in doing so it left little doubt that had the facts disclosed as predominantly wealthy a jury as the defendants had contended, the conviction would have been reversed. It may, therefore, be regarded as accepted doctrine that in a criminal case the conviction of a defendant by a jury selected by a method which tends to produce and does produce a jury not sufficiently representative of the several economic levels of the citizenry to reflect community rather than class attitudes is, in a case where such attitudes may be regarded as having had an influence on the verdict, a denial of due process of law.

Selection of jury

The selection of the jury from among the veniremen who have been summoned is by lot.[49] If any of the twelve thus chosen is excused on examination—a procedure about to be mentioned—he is replaced by a venireman similarly chosen by lot. In the federal courts, and in a number of the states, one or two alternate jurors are chosen at the same time, to replace a juror who may during the trial become incapacitated to serve.

The prospective jurors having been thus chosen, they are questioned, either collectively or individually, or both, as to their fitness to sit in the case. This questioning is referred to as the examination of the prospective juror on his "voir dire."

Upon examination, an individual juror may either be challenged per-

---

[47] It was also contended that juries drawn from the special jury list convicted in a greater proportion of cases than did juries drawn from the general list.

[48] Fay v. New York, 332 U.S. 261 (1947).

[49] In some states the practice has been used of selecting from the panel by lot a larger number of names (e.g., 96), then permitting each side to strike from this list a certain number (e.g., 24), the jury then being chosen by lot from the remaining names. A jury so chosen is termed a struck jury.

emptorily (i.e., without cause shown) by either side, or may be excused by the court for cause at the request of either side. The number of peremptory challenges allowed each side varies from one jurisdiction to another and in some is greater in serious than in lesser crimes. Under the federal statutes, for example, the defendant is allowed twenty challenges where the offense charged is treason or a capital offense, ten in the case of other felonies, and three in the case of misdemeanors. The corresponding number allowed the prosecution is six, six, and three.

The examination of the prospective jurors in an important criminal case is sometimes extremely protracted; particularly is this true of the examination by the defendant's attorney, who may question each juror exhaustively as to his possible prejudice against the defendant, on any one of several grounds, and as to whether he has formed any opinion as to the guilt of the defendant on the basis of newspaper or other reports. The extreme latitude allowed counsel in thus questioning the juror on his *voir dire* has been much criticized, both as causing excessive delay in reaching the actual trial, and as making jury service unattractive to the citizen. In the federal courts, the examination of the prospective jurors is conducted by the judge alone (though particular inquiries may be suggested to him by counsel), with resulting expedition. It does not appear that the defendant's right to a fair trial has in any way been impaired by this procedure; and a few years ago, it was adopted in the courts of Illinois.

Opening and closing statements to the jury

The jurors are not furnished, at the opening of the trial, as might be expected, with a copy of the indictment or information on which the defendant is to be tried. They are made acquainted with its contents through the opening statement of the prosecutor, who may also, if he chooses, outline the evidence he proposes to present. The opening statement of the defense was formerly made after the prosecution had completed its presentation of the evidence, before proceeding with the presentation of the evidence for the defense; and this is still the practice in a number of states. The trend has, however, increasingly been to require the defense, if it wishes to make an opening statement, to make it immediately after the prosecution's statement. This change in the traditional sequence is intended to compel the defense to announce its version of the facts at the outset, thus depriving it of the opportunity to adapt that version to the prosecution's evidence. At the close of the evidence, the defense makes a closing statement (or "summing up"), followed by a like statement by the prosecutor. In a number of states, the closing statements actually close the trial. The jury then retires to deliberate on its verdict, the judge having given it its instructions before the closing statements. In the majority of states, however, the closing statements are followed by the judge's instructions.

During the opening and closing addresses, and indeed throughout the trial, it is the duty of the judge, either on his own initiative or on the objection of opposing counsel, to prevent any prejudicial remarks, and if any are nevertheless made, to instruct the jury to disregard them.

Directed verdict of acquittal

It has already been mentioned that the court may at the close of the prosecution's case direct a verdict of acquittal. In the federal courts and in some of the states, an acquittal may also be directed after the defendant has put in his evidence.

Instructions to the jury

If the court does not direct an acquittal, the jurymen retire to deliberate. Before they do so, they receive from the judge his instructions or "charge." In charging the jury the court always defines the elements of the crime or crimes charged against the accused in the indictment, and instructs the jurymen that they may not find him guilty on any count of the indictment unless satisfied of his guilt beyond a reasonable doubt. If not so satisfied, they must bring in a verdict of "not guilty."

Mention has already been made of the doctrine that no inference of guilt may be drawn from the failure of the defendant to take the stand in his own behalf. From this has come the rule, adhered to in some of the states, that it is the judge's duty so to instruct the jury even though not requested to do so.[50] By contrast, six states reject the doctrine itself. The court may accordingly instruct the jury that the defendant's failure to take the stand may be taken into consideration.[51]

In addition to thus instructing the jury on the law, the judge may, in the federal courts and in the courts of about a third of the states, comment on the evidence; that is to say, he may express his own views as to the truth of the matters testified to, the credibility of the witnesses, the probabilities in favor of one or another surmise permitted by the evidence on a particular matter, and the like. This power, reflecting the commanding role played by the judge in the criminal jury trial as it developed in England, characterized jury trial in all the colonies, and was at the opening of the last century still everywhere in force in this country. The tide of Jacksonian democracy brought, however, a diminution of the prerogatives of the judicial office, of which one aspect was the widespread abrogation of the

[50] The slight value, if any, of such an instruction is indicated by the fact that experienced defense lawyers sometimes expressly request the judge to refrain from giving it, for fear of underscoring the defendant's failure to take the stand. See Holtzoff, Book review, 46 Amer. Bar Assn. Jour. 539 (1960).

[51] Such an instruction is not a denial of the "due process of law" guaranteed by the Constitution. Twining v. New Jersey, 211 U.S. 78 (1908); Adamson v. California, 332 U.S. 46 (1947). In two of these states the prosecutor is also permitted to comment on the failure of the accused to take the stand.

judge's power to comment on the evidence when instructing the jury. Such power on the part of the judge to influence the views of the jury on a question of fact was felt to be in derogation of the status of the jurymen as freeborn citizens, fully as capable of judging the facts for themselves as any official whatever. In a great majority of the states, accordingly, the judges were stripped of this power. A distinct trend of informed opinion in favor of restoring it is everywhere manifest; but thus far only a few states have restored it.

In connection with the judge's charge, either side may request particular instructions. Such requests are in some jurisdictions made orally; in others, in writing. Particularly when made in writing, a request may be very lengthy and involved; yet the court on granting it will commonly read it to the jury without change. There is no need to emphasize the obvious fact that in many cases the juryman, like any layman, will have the greatest difficulty in following the precise meaning and application of an instruction given in this fashion, not to speak of his remembering it clearly when he is subsequently required to obey it in the jury room. Yet erroneous instructions (as well as erroneous refusals to give requested instructions) are necessarily, as we shall see, regarded very seriously by the appellate courts.

In nearly half the states, the judge is required, before charging the jury, to reduce his charge to writing, and then to read it to the jury. (He is usually not required, however, to deliver his manuscript to the jury for their use in the jury room.) Trial conditions ordinarily do not permit the judge to suspend the trial more than very briefly for the preparation of written instructions. The result is likely to be the perfunctory reading to the jury of well-worn generalities, supplemented by the reading of complicated instructions requested by counsel (drafted not infrequently, so far as concerns defendant's counsel, in the hope not so much of thereby improving the chances of an acquittal as of laying the foundation, on the judge's refusing the request, for reversing on appeal the anticipated conviction).

Consideration of the evidence by the jury

A striking disadvantage under which the juryman labors is that of being obliged to rely on his memory for the testimony of the witnesses— and that too in the lengthiest and most complex of cases. The jury, after it has begun its deliberations may indeed, if enough of its members so desire, notify the court, by message sent through a bailiff, of their wish to have a particular portion of the testimony read to them by the court stenographer from his notes; and the judge then returns to the bench, the jury returns to the courtroom, the stenographer locates in his notes the testimony desired, and reads it. The manifest cumbrousness of the procedure confines its use to situations where there is real disagreement among the jurors as to what was said at a particular point.

Form of verdict

Anciently it was the practice to require the jury to give its verdict in the form of answers to specific questions put by the court—a "special" verdict, a practice still occasionally followed in the civil courts, and still recognized by statute in some states as permissible for criminal cases. In practice, however, the use of the special verdict is almost, if not quite, unknown. The jury returns the verdict of guilty or not guilty (the addition of the phrase "by reason of insanity" being authorized under the law of some states).

Though the verdict of guilty connotes that the jury believes the accused's guilt to have been established beyond a reasonable doubt, the verdict of not guilty obviously does not mean that the jury believes his innocence to have been established. It may indeed have so believed, but it may equally have believed him guilty, yet have entertained a doubt. There is no regular procedure by which the jury can record its belief in the defendant's innocence, though juries have on rare occasions assumed to do so. The common reference to a defendant as having been "cleared" by the jury's verdict of not guilty is thus clearly erroneous.

Unanimity of verdict

The ancient requirement that a jury verdict may be reached only by unanimous vote, despite a strong and authoritative body of opinion in favor of its relaxation in all but capital cases, still stands virtually unimpaired in criminal trials. In some six states, however, the constitutional requirement of unanimity has been relaxed for specified cases, a verdict by five-sixths being characteristically permitted.[52]

Rather surprisingly, despite the requirement of unanimity, the jury in the great majority of cases brings in a verdict. In place of disagreement, the requirement of unanimity often results in a verdict of acquittal, or in a compromise verdict of guilty on a less serious count of the indictment or information. Should there be a disagreement, the prosecutor may bring the case on for trial anew. In the federal courts, however, and in a few states the judge may, after a disagreement, direct a verdict of acquittal.

Setting aside a verdict of guilty

Following a verdict of guilty, the defendant frequently requests the court to set aside the verdict. This power of the trial court developed at a time

[52] In Louisiana, in offenses for which the term of imprisonment may (but need not) be at hard labor, the jury numbers five and its verdict must be unanimous. Where the imprisonment must be at hard labor and in capital cases, the jury numbers twelve; but only in capital cases must its verdict be unanimous. In other cases, a vote of nine is sufficient for a verdict. La. Const., Art. 9, Sec. 19.

when there was in criminal cases no provision for appeal to a higher court. Despite the subsequent development of such a procedure the power of the trial court to set aside the verdict remained.

The established grounds on which a verdict of guilty may be set aside by the trial court are either that the verdict is contrary to law, or contrary to the weight of evidence. The verdict is declared by the court to be contrary to law if the court concludes that there exist any of the grounds on which it could have dismissed the indictment or have directed an acquittal at the close of the prosecution's case. The verdict is said to be contrary to the evidence if the prosecution has completely failed, in the opinion of the court, to establish the guilt of the defendant beyond a reasonable doubt.

In addition, the court may in most jurisdictions set aside the verdict because of errors of law committed in the course of the trial, or because of irregularities in the deliberations of the jury, or the like.[53] In the federal courts, under the rules promulgated by the Supreme Court, the trial court may set aside the verdict "if required in the interests of justice"; similarly broad provisions are found in some states.

The verdict being set aside, the court must, in most jurisdictions, order a new trial. In some states, however, and in the federal courts, is found the more rational provision empowering the judge, where the ground on which the verdict is set aside is such that a new trial would be fruitless, to enter judgment of acquittal.

10. ORDERING NEW TRIAL BECAUSE OF NEWLY DISCOVERED EVIDENCE

The convicted defendant may be granted a new trial by the trial court on establishing that since the trial new evidence has been discovered which, had it been introduced at the trial, might have caused a verdict of acquittal. The failure to discover the evidence in time for its presentation at the trial must, however, be explained to the satisfaction of the court.

On the other hand, should the prosecutor after an acquittal find new evidence of the defendant's guilt, he is powerless to bring the defendant again to trial. The provision of the Constitution, applicable to federal prosecutions, that no person shall "be subject for the same offense to be twice put in jeopardy of life or limb" is paralleled by similar provisions in nearly all state constitutions; and it has characteristically been given a very liberal construction.

---

[53] There are variations in the form and nature of the applications thus made, and in their names as well—as, motion to set aside the verdict, motion in arrest of judgment, demurrer to the evidence, and writ coram nobis. The application may also in some cases be made after sentence.

11. SENTENCE

The forms of punishment for crime fixed by our laws are, characteristically, for serious crimes imprisonment and for less serious crimes imprisonment or fine or both. In addition, the death penalty, though relatively seldom imposed, is found in the statutes of a diminishing number of states. It is found also in the federal statutes, not only for murder but also for treason, and for giving defense information to a foreign government. A variety of special penalties is also encountered.[54]

Cruel and unusual punishments are excluded from the federal laws by express constitutional prohibition; and many state constitutions also contain express prohibitions against such punishments. Whether they are also prohibited to the states by the due process clause of the Fourteenth Amendment is as yet unsettled.[55]

Criminal proceedings in the courts, be it noted, are by no means the sole form of legal proceeding by which punishment is inflicted for infraction of the law. In the courts themselves, the civil action for a monetary penalty, as a punishment for minor infractions of regulatory statutes is not infrequently used. It is to the field of administrative adjudication, however, that one must turn to find the chief instances of the infliction of severe penalties for infraction of regulatory statutes without the use of the criminal proceeding—a matter to be considered at a later point.

To a limited extent, the imposition of a fixed penalty follows automatically on convictions; the mandatory death sentence for premeditated murder found in some states is the chief illustration of this. Characteristically, however—and this is the central feature of the sentencing procedure—the sentence which may be imposed is not fixed and unalterable, but may vary within wide limits, the precise penalty being determined in the great majority of the states and in the federal courts by the judge. Even the dread choice between execution and imprisonment is by some statutes left to the judge (with the jury in most cases being permitted to make a recommendation in favor of imprisonment that is morally though not legally binding on the judge).[56] In some dozen states, however, the fixing of the

[54] Whipping is still found in one state. Forfeiture of the right to vote and to hold office are quite generally part of the punishment for a felony, as is also revocation of a license which the defendant may hold to practice law, medicine, or the like. Conviction of certain offenses involving the unlawful use of property may entail the confiscation of such property, or if it be realty, the loss of its use for a period. For the crime of "committing any act of treason against, or attempting by force to overthrow, or bearing arms against the United States," the extraordinary penalty (additional to imprisonment) of loss of citizenship—a penalty imposable even on a natural born citizen—is provided. 8 U.S. Code, Sec. 1482(a)(9).

[55] Cf. Louisiana ex rel. Francis v. Resweber, 329 U.S. 459 (1947).

[56] Under the so-called Lindbergh law, the federal statute prohibiting the interstate transportation of a kidnapped person (18 U.S. Code, Sec. 1201), the death penalty is to be imposed only if the jury so recommends—an unusual provision.

punishment is for most or all crimes entirely in the hands of the jury, and in what follows, references to the discretion vested in the judge must, as to those states, be read as referring to the jury instead.

In non-capital offenses, the choice open to the judge often ranges between a sentence of great severity and a suspension of sentence. The latter, as a practical matter, usually means a complete immunity from punishment. If, however, sentence is imposed, he may in many cases choose between imprisonment and fine; and in the term of imprisonment, or amount of fine, a large range of choice may again be open to him. Moreover, the power to compel the person awaiting sentence to comply with any one of a large variety of conditions—such as making restitution of property or joining the armed forces—on pain of receiving a more severe sentence, although not conferred by law, is also exercised as a practical matter in many cases.

The power of the judge to suspend imposition or execution of sentence for a fixed period (but not indefinitely) has been asserted by the courts of some states, even in the absence of any statutory provision, as an inherent power of the court, recognized at common law; in other states the courts have declined to assert such power. Today that question is largely academic, owing to the spread of statutes expressly conferring such power on the sentencing judge. Such statutes ordinarily provide that the judge in suspending sentence for a definite period may or must place the convicted offender on probation during such period,[57] i.e., reserve the power to terminate the suspension of sentence, if the accused is found to be misconducting himself (such misconduct not necessarily amounting to criminal activity).[58] Surveillance over the offender during such period of probation is provided for by requiring him to report regularly to the "probation officer," an officer of the court designated for that purpose. The difficult problems encountered in actually maintaining surveillance over persons on probation lie beyond the scope of this volume.

The extent of the discretion as to severity of punishment, occasionally, (though perhaps not typically), vested in the judge may be illustrated by such federal statutory penalties as imprisonment "for any term of years or for life" (second-degree murder), or "a fine of not less than $100 nor more than $5,000, or imprisonment for not more than one year, or both" (disobedience of subpoena issued by the Federal Communications Commission). In the states, the pattern is much the same; some, however, such as

[57] In a number of states, the statutes provide that habitual offenders shall not be eligible for probation. By the federal narcotics act, a person convicted of certain types of violation of the act is ineligible for probation.

[58] The power of the judge to revoke the suspension is a grave one, not being subject to any review or correction. Indeed, it has been held in a few states (though elsewhere, and in the federal courts, the contrary is provided by statute) that such suspension may be revoked without notice to the defendant and without a hearing as to whether he has broken the conditions of the suspension.

California, Indiana, and West Virginia, tend toward narrower limits than the other states generally.

In the exercise of his discretion in sentencing, the judge is ordinarily much influenced by the prosecutor. Most convictions, as already pointed out, are the result of pleas of guilty rather than of verdicts of guilty after trial—often pleas of guilty made by agreement with the prosecutor, and to a lesser charge than that laid in the indictment or information. Normally included in such agreement is a promise by the prosecutor to recommend a particular sentence to the court, a recommendation normally followed by the court. In convictions after trial, the prosecutor's views as to the severity of the sentence to be imposed similarly carry great weight with the court.

The value to a corrupt party organization of control over, or even great influence with, the prosecutor has already been emphasized in connection with the prosecutor's power to initiate or suppress prosecution. Manifestly, his value is greatly increased by his power to influence sentences. Where the judge and the prosecutor both respond to the same unsavory political machine—a condition which has not been unknown in some of our cities—individual sentences, in cases which have not engaged public interest, may be in part determined by the desire of the judge to protect himself from possible attack by imposing severe sentences on persons having no influence with the political machine, to balance the more lenient sentences meted out to those with "connections."

As a result of the wide discretion thus entrusted to the judge who happens to have presided at the trial (or, more probably, since the majority of convictions result from pleas of guilty, the judge before whom the prisoner happens to have pleaded guilty), the entire sentencing process of our courts is characterized by wide variations in length of term of imprisonment and amount of fine imposed for the same, or substantially the same, offense. Such variations stem not merely from the varying determinations of a single judge in successive cases, but also from the fact that the sentencing power is vested in so great a number of judges, with no machinery for inducing uniformity or consistency.[59]

In a great majority of the states, however, the enactment of indeterminate sentence laws has greatly reduced the control of the judge over the length of the term of imprisonment, should he impose one. These statutes typically require imprisonment for some or all offenses to be of indeterminate length, only the minimum and maximum term being fixed by the court,[60] the power to set at liberty being vested in an independent agency, usually termed the parole board. In fixing the minimum, the judge in some

[59] Those familiar with prison conditions tell us that the sense of injustice felt by prisoners who have received longer terms than their prison mates for seemingly identical offenses is a serious detriment to morale and to rehabilitation.

[60] In a few states the judge has no power to fix any minimum; it is subsequently fixed by the parole board.

states has no discretion, for the minimum is fixed by law.[61] As to the maximum term, unless it be fixed at a relatively short period the power of the judge to fix it is of little consequence, since a case in which a parole board would wish to detain the prisoner beyond the maximum term fixed by the court is so rare as to be negligible.

As to federal prisoners, the situation is substantially the same. The federal parole board, created in 1910, has power to release a prisoner on parole after he has served one-third of his term, or after serving fifteen years of a life sentence.

Despite these curtailments of the judge's power, his role in the sentencing process is still the leading one. That role was a logical one in the period when the punishment fixed for felonies was immutable and when, if discretion was permitted, it was regarded as a mere exercise of the arbitrary power of the Crown acting through a subordinate—responsive, like any non-judicial officer, to the directions of the Crown. With the development of statutory discretion in sentencing, however, and of the doctrine that all discretion must be exercised in accordance with principle, the entrusting of the sentencing power to any and every judge who may happen to preside at arraignment or at trial has been the target of a great deal of criticism —criticism all the more cogent because of the lack, except in a handful of states, of any provision for review of the judge's discretion. The obvious opportunities for political intercession for leniency of sentence furnish an additional ground for attack on the system. The proposal that the power of the judge to fix the term of imprisonment be withdrawn, and that an independent specialized agency be empowered to parole the prisoner as soon as he has served the minimum statutory term, has thus far been adopted only in California (in 1940), and by Congress with respect to youthful federal offenders.[62]

There is strong opposition, on the part not only of the judiciary itself but also of many other people, to the complete elimination from the process of the one official whose daily work in the courts may give him a different sort of insight into the mental processes of the offender from that obtained by observation within prison walls. A compromise plan which reflects this feeling, and which commands much support in qualified quarters is that embodied in the federal statue enacted in 1958. Under this statute, the power of the judge to suspend sentence (or to impose a fine rather than imprisonment where the statute permits this alternative) is

---

[61] In two states no minimum is fixed by the law.

[62] The federal act permits parole under supervision even before the minimum statutory period expires. 18 U.S. Code, Sec. 5017. The proposed transfer of sentencing discretion from the court to a specialized agency in the case of youthful offenders, proposed by the American Law Institute in a model act drafted in 1940 (Beck, 5 States, 1951), has not yet been adopted by any state.

retained. If imprisonment is imposed, however, the length of a term of imprisonment may be fixed by the judge not at the time of imposition of sentence, but after the lapse of three months, at which time he will have before him a recommendation as to length of term, prepared by a central agency functioning for all the federal courts, on the basis of an interview with the offender and of a study of all pertinent information and opinion, including his record prior to conviction, the record of the case which resulted in his conviction, and the observations made by the prison staff during his first months of imprisonment.[63]

While the judge may, and frequently does, make explanatory remarks when imposing sentence, and such remarks may be noted by the court stenographer, there is typically no provision for a formal explanatory record of the judge's reasons for the sentence he imposes—a record which would lend itself to convenient examination and which would readily disclose any gross inconsistencies in the judge's sentences and, in particular, any unduly lenient sentences or suspensions of sentence. Still less is there provision for a critical comparative review of such sentences by an impartial authority— a review which might, in addition to exposing the seemingly capricious exercise of discretion by one or another judge, bring to light inconsistencies and lack of uniformity as between sentences imposed by various judges. Our civilian courts present here a strong contrast to military justice. In the armed forces, a continuing comparative study of sentences of courts-martial is carried on, and the results are taken into consideration in the automatic review of individual sentences by the boards of review constituted by the judge advocates general.

In some dozen states, as already noted, the sentencing function has been transferred from the judge to the jury. This procedure is not likely to spread. It is obviously at odds with current doctrine, which holds that sentence should be fixed only in the light of complete information about the convicted person's history and personality; for the jury has before it only the evidence of the particular crime.

This obvious weakness of the jury as a participant in the sentencing process is especially striking in those cases in which, though the decision remains in the hands of the judge, the jury may recommend a sentence of life imprisonment instead of death, a prerogative enjoyed by the jury in capital cases even in some states in which the jury has otherwise no role in sentencing. To correct this weakness several states have in recent years by statute provided that the jury makes no recommendation at the time it announces its verdict of guilty. Instead, following that verdict, a hearing is held before judge and jury on the question of whether the jury should

[63] 18 U.S. Code, Sec. 4208. The statute permits the judge to defer final sentence for an additional three-month period.

recommend life imprisonment, evidence being admissable as to the defendant's previous criminal record, if any, together with evidence on all other matters which would be made available to a judge fixing a sentence.[64]

The appellate court has in a few states been expressly given the power to reduce a sentence which, though within the legal limits of the sentence fixed for the crime of which the defendant has been convicted, it regards as excessive; and in a few additional states, the power, while not expressly conferred, has been asserted by the appellate courts.[65] In some of the remaining states, and in the federal system,[66] no such power exists, except perhaps in extreme cases where an abuse of discretion on the part of the sentencing judge is clear.

It has been urged that a procedure for appeal from the sentence alone, with power in the appellate court either to increase or reduce the sentence, might enable it to serve as an agency to equalize sentences, and thus mitigate the wide disparity between sentences imposed by different judges for the same offense or even by the same judge at different times for the same offense. It is far from clear, however, that an appellate court is a suitable agency for correcting this weakness of our sentencing system.[67]

Viewing the sentencing process as a whole, it is not a little remarkable that our law, pervaded as it is with solicitude for the rights of the individual and with distrust of the exercise of unfettered discretion by any official, should place so vital a matter as the choice between death and imprisonment, or between fine and imprisonment, or between imprisonment and freedom on probation in the hands of a single official or, indeed, even in the hands of a plural body—the jury or parole board—with (except in a small number of states) no possibility of judicial review or correction.

12. REVIEW ON APPEAL

Nowhere in the processes of justice is there greater need than in the criminal courts for a supervisory power to check the abuses which prej-

[64] Statutes of this nature have been adopted in California (1957), Pennsylvania (1959), and New York (1963).

[65] In a few of these states, however, the appellate courts, though not assuming themselves to reduce the sentence, have asserted the power to vacate the sentence and to remand the case to the lower court for resentence.

[66] There is no statute or rule governing the federal courts in this respect. The lack of power of the federal courts of appeal to reduce a sentence (except where the sentence exceeds the statutory maximum) rests on decisions of the Supreme Court. The Court has left open, however, the question "whether a sentence may be so severe and the offence so trivial that an appellate court should set it aside. . . ." Kawakita v. United States, 343 U.S. 717 (1952).

[67] From time to time there have been statutes empowering appellate courts to increase a sentence on appeal, particularly where, in the opinion of the appellate court, the appeal was frivolous; but existing statutes of this character are exceptional and may be regarded as obsolete. Abroad, the exercise of this power by appellate courts is not unusual.

udice or even conspiracy may commit in the name of the law. Our system for appeal by the convicted defendant—so far as state convictions are concerned almost a system of dual appeal because of the powerful check of the federal judicial system on abuses in state criminal procedure—affords, to the accused able to avail himself of it, nearly as complete assurance as is perhaps practicable in any legal system against abuse of criminal process.[68] Unfortunately, it does not furnish equally complete protection against unjust conviction resulting from wilfully false testimony, mistaken identification, or convincing yet misleading circumstantial evidence, or of a community hostility fatal to a fair trial, yet too elusive to be made the basis for the reversal of a conviction by an appellate court.[69]

The criminal appeal as a matter of right is a comparatively late arrival among our legal institutions. From early times, the English practice provided for the review of a criminal judgment where there was reason to believe, on an application by the defendant, that the conviction had been contrary to law. The review would, however, be confined exclusively to matters of law appearing on the record, which did not include the evidence in the case. If on examination of the record the Court of King's Bench concluded that the conviction had been erroneous in law, the conviction was set aside and the defendant liberated, no provision existing for a new trial. Needless to say, a right of appeal so restricted was applied in but a small proportion of convictions.

The colonial practice too with respect to review of convictions appears to have been of a somewhat primitive character, appeals in many cases being allowed to the governor (or the governor and council) rather than to a court, and the reversal of conviction being accordingly regarded as the exercise of a pardoning power rather than a judicial review. It was indeed after the nineteenth century was well begun that the concept of an appeal as a matter of right in a criminal conviction became a general (though as to minor offenses not yet a universal) feature of our legal system.

[68] In addition to the appeal of the defendant from his conviction, there is found in Connecticut provision for appeal by the prosecution from the rulings of the trial court "upon all questions of law arising upon the trial of criminal cases . . . in the same manner and the same effect as if made by the accused." Under this statute, appeal was taken by the state from a conviction for second-degree murder on the ground that errors of law had been committed by the trial judge—among others, error in instructing the jury as to the difference between first- and second-degree murder. The conviction was set aside and a new trial had, at which the defendant was convicted of first-degree murder. The Supreme Court held, on appeal, that this procedure did not constitute a denial of due process of law. Palko v. Connecticut, 302 U.S. 319 (1937). Vermont has a similar statute. In some other states, and in the federal courts, the prosecution may appeal from the dismissal of the indictment or information by the court, or the setting aside of the conviction by the trial court. In a few states the prosecutor, following an acquittal, may ask the appellate court to "disapprove" a ruling on the law made by the trial court. Such a disapproval is of course without any effect on the acquitted defendant.

[69] See Borchard, Convicting the Innocent (1923); Gardner, The Court of Last Resort (1952); and Frank, Not Guilty (1957).

There is even today some opinion, though it appears to be diminishing, which regards unfavorably the criminal appeal granted as a matter of right. The execution of the sentence is in many jurisdictions deferred while the appeal is pending; and consequently, so runs the argument, the person convicted has too much incentive to prosecute an appeal merely for delay. In this view, appeal should not be permitted except on a preliminary showing that there is some merit on the appeal. Such a provision, it is urged, would insure the hearing of all meritorious appeals and would save the time now expended by appellate courts in reviewing voluminous records, hearing arguments, and reading briefs in wholly unmeritorious appeals for convictions.

Perhaps because of its dramatic possibilities, the appeal from a conviction figures prominently in the layman's picture of criminal justice; but its quantitative importance is relatively small. A majority of convictions, as already noted, result from pleas of guilty, with appeal at once excluded. Of the defendants convicted after trial, but a small fraction appeal; and in but a minority of cases, in some states a very small minority, is the conviction reversed. Thus, all but a trifling portion of the convictions, and of course all the acquittals, produced by our system of criminal justice are solely the work of the trial courts, with no participation by the appellate courts. But if the quantitative impact of the criminal appeal is small, its influence upon the daily operations of the criminal courts is omnipresent.

An appellate court reviewing a conviction may set it aside on the ground that errors of law were committed prejudicial to the defendant. Such errors of law may relate to the finding of the indictment, to the impaneling of the jury, to the admission or exclusion of evidence, to the refusal to direct an acquittal, to the instructions given by the court to the jury, to requested instructions refused, to the conduct of the jury, or to the legality of the sentence. Moreover, in all jurisdictions, the appellate court has the power to reverse a conviction where the evidence in its opinion fails to establish the elements of the crime. The reversal of a conviction by the appellate court, if based on the invalidity of the indictment or information or on the failure of the prosecution to adduce a prima facie case, means the end of the prosecution. If it is based merely on error in the conduct of the trial, however, the prosecutor may proceed with a new trial on the same indictment or information.

Once the record contains evidence which supports the conviction, the power of the appellate court further to consider the evidence is, in perhaps a majority of our jurisdictions, at an end. In the remainder it may further examine the evidence, but in some states only to determine whether, as contended by the defendant, the conviction is so contrary to the weight of the evidence as to be explainable only as the result of mistake, passion, or prejudice, in which case it may be set aside. In other states, the appellate court is empowered to go beyond this and to set the conviction aside in any case in which in its opinion justice so requires. This salutary enlargement of the power of the appellate court has made but slow progress since its introduction in the last quarter of the nineteenth century.[70]

It has been pointed out that more important perhaps than statutory or doctrinal pronouncements as to the precise limitations on the power of the appellate court to review the facts is the prevailing attitude of the judges. In jurisdictions where the older limitations still exist, the appellate court, if it desires to reverse a conviction because, on its view of the facts, justice so requires, may strain to find in the record an error of law, however minor, on which to ground a reversal.

In considering whether justice requires a reversal of the conviction, the court is almost everywhere restricted to an examination of the evidence taken at the trial. Only in a few states may it (as may the Court of Criminal Appeal in England) take additional testimony where the record before it appears to be clouded by doubt, obscurity, or omission.[71]

The position of the indigent defendant, at one time virtually barred from appeal by lack of funds (except, in certain states, in capital cases) has greatly improved in recent years. In the federal courts, a system of assigned counsel, uncompensated, has for some years been in force, though not everywhere fully effective. The states, most of which had made no provision for appellate counsel except in capital cases, were told by the Supreme Court, early in 1963, that they must, under the constitutional guarantee of due process, furnish appellate counsel to the indigent defendant in all felony cases[72]—a sweeping directive whose implementation by the states will obviously take some time. The state must also furnish the indigent defendant with copies of necessary papers.[73]

As a result, a substantial increase in the proportion of convictions appealed seems inevitable. Any attempt to reduce the number by a preliminary judicial screening of indigents' applications for counsel—a procedure often advocated—would now encounter the 1963 holding of the Supreme Court that the indigent is entitled to counsel and papers even if only for the purpose of seeking out errors which may furnish ground for appeal.[74]

[70] Thus in the celebrated Sacco-Vanzetti case the highest court of Massachusetts twice refused to overrule the action of the trial judge in refusing a new trial, on the ground that the matters in issue were within his sole discretion. Several years after the execution of the defendants, the power of the appellate court was enlarged along the lines indicated above.

[71] Perhaps the most comprehensive provision empowering an appellate court to take additional testimony is that found in the New Jersey constitution which authorizes the Supreme Court of the state to "exercise such original jurisdiction as may be necessary to the complete determination of any cause on review" (Art. 6, Sec. 5).

[72] Douglas v. California, 372 U.S. 355 (1963).

[73] Griffin v. Illinois, 351 U.S. 12 (1956). This is also done in the federal courts, though not required by statute.

[74] Draper v. Washington, 372 U.S. 487 (1963).

But though the indigent defendant has thus been placed somewhat, if not entirely, on a parity with the wealthy one, the defendant who, though far from wealthy is yet possessed of sufficient funds to bar him from public or philanthropic assistance, still confronts a formidable financial barrier, in many cases, to prosecuting an appeal. Not only the services of counsel, but the reproduction of the necessary transcripts and records—many appellate courts still insisting on printed papers despite the great improvement in cheaper and equally legible processes—may make an appeal as a practical matter hardly worth attempting. How to place the middle-class defendant on a parity with the rich and the poor is a problem to which no attention has thus far been given.

The criminal appellate process is in many places regrettably dilatory. In the larger states and in the federal system, the appeal commonly goes (except perhaps in capital cases) to an intermediate regional appellate court, whose disposition, whether for or against the defendant, may under certain limitations, of varying severity, be reviewed further by the highest court. If a substantial federal question has been raised, the affirmation of the conviction by the highest state court may in turn, as will shortly be explained, be subjected to review in the federal courts, a review process which may itself extend to half a dozen separate stages. Aggravating the delay inherent in this multiplicity of appellate proceedings is the delay imposed by the unnecesarily elaborate requirements in some jurisdictions for the reproduction of the trial record and other papers, and by the inordinately long interval, characteristic of some appellate courts, between the submission and the decision of the appeal[75]—an interval prolonged in some cases by the preparation for publication of lengthy opinions, frequently concerned with matters of fact of no juristic interest.

13. COLLATERAL ATTACK ON CONVICTION BY POSTCONVICTION PROCEEDING

Appeal in the regular course is based on errors allegedly disclosed by the record of the proceedings resulting in conviction. But the person convicted of crime, having failed to appeal, or his appeal having been unsuccessful, may launch a collateral attack, as the phrase is, on his conviction, alleging a denial of rights not reflected in the record, as, for example, that his plea of guilty was induced by the prosecutor's threats or misrepresentations as to the maximum sentence imposable on him, or that exculpatory evidence in the exclusive possession of the prosecution was suppressed or

[75] After an exhaustive review of the multiple appellate proceedings in a capital case in which an extraordinary length of time intervened between the conviction and its final affirmance, a commentator concludes that judicial indecision was the principal factor responsible for the delay. Comment: The Caryl Chessman case: A Legal Analysis, 44 Minnesota Law Rev. 941 (1960).

that he was not furnished with counsel as he should have been, or was denied a copy of the papers necessary for taking an appeal. The possibility of such collateral attack on state convictions, even if of long standing, has in recent years been greatly increased by holdings of the Supreme Court conferring on state defendants novel constitutional rights—such as the right to be furnished with appellate counsel if indigent, and the right to have excluded from evidence at the trial objects obtained by the authorities by unlawful search; and the Court has declared that the denial of such a right by a state court, even at a time when the Court itself had not yet held that the right existed, or had indeed held that it did not exist, entitles the defendant to a reversal of his conviction and to a new trial—a disposition which may well mean the end of the prosecution and the discharge of the defendant, since a new trial may be quite impracticable, owing to the death or disappearance of witnesses.

The extent to which procedures are available to reopen a conviction on such grounds varies widely. A minority of the states have virtually no such procedure. The trend is, however, for postconviction procedures to be increasingly liberalized.[76]

14. FEDERAL REVIEW OF STATE CONVICTION

If one convicted in a state court alleges a denial of a federally protected right, the case is to that extent a "case arising under this Constitution, the laws of the United States and treaties made . . . under their authority" and is to that extent within the federal judicial power. Two procedures are provided by the statutes under which the federal courts may give relief: (1) the review of the state record by the Supreme Court, and (2) a habeas corpus proceeding in the federal district court. This court may either on a review of the state record alone, or on the basis of independent proof adduced before it, or both, order the release of the prisoner (opportunity being given to the state authorities, if they so desire, to take him into custody to await retrial).[77]

[76] In some states, the habeas corpus proceeding has been held by the courts to be available for collateral attack on a conviction; in others it has been held unavailable for this purpose. Some of the courts holding the habeas corpus proceeding unavailable have held the ancient form of proceeding initiated by the writ of coram nobis to be available. Special statutory forms of proceeding are found in some states. A model postconviction procedure act proposed by the Commissioners on Uniform Laws in 1955 has been adopted by a few states. In the federal courts, the habeas corpus proceeding formerly employed for collateral attack on federal convictions has been for the most part displaced by the "motion to vacate, set aside or correct the sentence," a procedure introduced by statute in 1948 (28 U.S. Code, Sec. 2255).

[77] It will be observed that this procedure is available only to one in custody, actual or constructive. If no sentence of imprisonment was imposed following the conviction, or if such sentence, though imposed, has already been served, no application for habeas corpus will lie.

From the beginning of the federal courts and until 1916 the defendant convicted in a state court had enjoyed the right to have his conviction reviewed by the Supreme Court of the United States if he had in the state court proceedings "specially set up or claimed" any "right, privilege or exemption" under the Constitution, or under a federal statute or treaty;[78] but this right of review had been little availed of. The reason is not far to seek. The Constitution, before the enactment of the Fourteenth Amendment in 1868, gave the state criminal defendant virtually no protection; and even as late as half a century after the adoption of that amendment, the potentialities of its due process clause as a bill of rights for the state criminal defendant were only dimly appreciated by the bar, as well as by the Court itself. Hence when, in 1916, as part of a program of legislation to reduce the ever-growing docket of the Court, the right of the state criminal defendant claiming a denial of federal rights to have his claim reviewed by the Supreme Court was withdrawn, and there was substituted for it merely the right to ask the Court for such review,[79] the change drew little notice. With the vast enlargement, however, in the past half-century, of the federal rights of the state criminal defendant, the enormous significance of the change has become apparent. Today, scores of applications for review are annually made to the Court by persons convicted in the state courts, but only a handful are granted by the Court.

But as there thus developed, concurrently with an ever-growing bill of federal constitutional rights for the state defendant, an increasing inability of the Supreme Court to afford review—for the burden on the Court in other directions has also grown steadily in recent decades—there emerged from the statutes a sleeping giant, the federal habeas corpus proceeding for state prisoners. Until 1867 the federal courts had had no power to liberate one held in state custody unless he claimed to have been acting under federal authority or under the lawful authority of a foreign government; but in that year, by legislation which had its origin in concern for

---

[78] Act of Sept. 24, 1789, Sec. 25; 1 Stat. L. 85. The right to Supreme Court review was also given in any case in which "there is drawn in question [in the state court] the validity of a statute of, or an authority exercised under any State, on the ground of their being repugnant to the constitution, treaties or laws of the United States, and the decision is in favour of their validity . . ."

[79] Such a request to the Court to review the state record is known as a petition to the Supreme Court for a writ of certiorari to the state court. Such a petition sets forth briefly what the petitioner contends to be a "substantial federal question" raised in the state proceedings and decided adversely to him. The state has the opportunity of filing an answer. If as many as four of the nine justices of the Court favor granting the petition, it is granted, and the entire record is then reviewed by the Court. If in the state court the defendant successfully attacked the constitutionality of a federal statute or treaty, or unsuccessfully attacked a state enactment on the ground of its being repugnant to the Constitution or to a federal statute or treaty, he has a right to review by the Supreme Court, and need not petition for such review. The Supreme Court review is then said to be "by appeal." 28 U.S. Code, Sec. 1257.

the newly liberated Negro rather than for the state criminal defendant, the federal courts were empowered to set at liberty "any person restrained of his liberty in violation of the Constitution, laws or treaties of the United States."[80] For fifty years after its enactment, this remedy was hardly ever availed of by a state prisoner claiming a denial of federal rights in the proceedings resulting in his conviction, both because such federal rights were during that period still virtually non-existent, and because there was available an appeal to the Supreme Court as of right. Moreover, under long-established doctrines, the habeas corpus proceeding was at that time available to one imprisoned under the sentence of a court (as opposed to one imprisoned by the administrative or military officers), not to test the legality of his imprisonment, but only to attack the jurisdiction of the court imposing the sentence. Space does not permit a recounting of the successive steps by which the availability of the habeas corpus proceeding was extended by the Supreme Court, without any change having been made in the empowering statute. In brief, within the past decade it has become established as an alternative procedure for federal review of the state court record—a review made by the single judge of the federal court sitting in the district in which the prisoner is confined, with the possibility of appeal to the regional federal court of appeals, and of further review, again only by its permission, by the Supreme Court of the United States.

The review thus available in the district court may be, as in the case of review by the Supreme Court, either of the record of the proceedings resulting in the conviction, or of the record of the unsuccessful postconviction proceeding instituted by the prisoner in the state court (including in either case the record of affirmance by the state appellate court). As already noted, however, state court procedures for collateral attack on a conviction by postconviction proceedings are in some states limited or, indeed, non-existent. In such a case the prisoner, if he bases his claim of denial of federal right on matters not reflected in the record of the proceedings resulting in his conviction, may proceed directly to the federal district court, which holds a hearing and hears witnesses, including, it may be, the state prosecutor and even the state judge who presided at the arraignment or trial.

Over a thousand applications for habeas corpus are now made annually to the federal courts by state prisoners, and the number may be expected to increase. The burden placed on state law-enforcement authorities and on the federal courts by these applications, the great majority of them seemingly devoid of merit, has evoked protests from both sources. Protest has come from the state judiciaries as well, provoked in part by the impair-

[80] Act of Feb. 5, 1867, Ch. 28; 14 Stat. 385. The present provision uses the words "in custody" instead of the words "restrained of his liberty." 28 U.S. Code, Sec. 2241.

ment of the desirable finality of criminal convictions, and in part no doubt by the displeasure which some of the veteran judges of the high state courts may feel at seeing their considered judgments reversed by a single federal judge, perhaps a judicial neophyte. But more crucial than these criticisms of the procedure, however valid, is the intolerable burden it places on the state criminal defendant who has in truth been denied his federal rights by the state court—the review of his claim not by a federal court having the final word, but by a court whose determination is itself subject to review by a regional federal court of appeals, and to a further possible review by the Supreme Court. There is obvious need to make available to the state prisoner serving under an unconstitutional conviction some less protracted and less onerous procedure.

15. PARDON AND COMMUTATION OF SENTENCE

The discretion allowed the judge in tempering the punishment meted out to the convicted defendant is paralleled by the power vested in the executive branch of the government to grant either a commutation of sentence or a full pardon. The vesting of this power in the executive branch is to be explained on historical rather than rational grounds.

In the English legal system, the institution of executive clemency derived from a time when the power of the Crown was almost if not quite absolute. Transplanted to the colonies, the pardoning power was exercised by the royal governor, acting either alone or with the governor's council, as agent of the Crown to whom the royal prerogative had in this respect been delegated. As with other colonial gubernatorial powers, the pardoning power passed, in the newly independent states, to the governor.

In the creation of the new federal government, with its power to create crimes against federal law, the pardoning power was vested by the Constitution in the President (except in cases of impeachment). In the states, the vesting of the pardoning power in the governor has not, however, become universal. In a number of states the power is vested in a pardoning board, of which the governor is but one member, the remaining members being usually state officials, who sit ex officio. Even in states where the governor possesses sole power, an official advisory board may be found, and its recommendations, needless to say, are seldom disregarded.

Like the sentencing power, the pardoning power ordinarily represents the exercise of completely unfettered discretion; and the abuses and seeming capriciousness and injustice which so frequently accompany the operation of uncontrolled power have not failed to make their appearance here. Thus far, however, despite much discussion in interested quarters, there has been little progress in placing the pardoning function on a foundation of established principle, much less of binding rule.

The presidential power of pardon in federal offenses has on the whole been sparingly used. The advice of the Attorney General is invariably sought by the President; and there is no evidence of a demand for any change in the present arrangement.

From the standpoint of the wielder of political influence of a sinister nature, the pardoning authority completes the circle of opportunity for assisting the guilty to escape the vengeance of the law. Police, prosecutor, sentencing judge, parole board, governor, or pardon board—as the case comes before each of these powers in turn the mechanism of political influence may be brought to bear on an official not single in his devotion to duty. The enormous difficulties in the way of an impartial administration of our criminal justice are self-evident.

16. PAROLE

In every state, and in the federal statutes, provision is made for the conditional release of a prisoner from confinement before the expiration of the permissible term of his imprisonment, the condition being his undertaking to be law-abiding during the remainder of his term, on pain of being returned to prison. Strictly viewed, this procedure, which is known as parole, does not come within the scope of this volume, since neither the decision to release the prisoner, nor the decision to revoke his parole, is arrived at by any process of formal adjudication. Nevertheless, the parole procedure is so intimately bound up with our entire system of criminal justice that some mention of it is called for.

The several state and federal laws governing eligibility for parole exhibit numerous variations and marked differences in liberality with respcet to the time when the prisoner becomes eligible for parole.

Historically, the power to grant parole has been associated with the pardoning power and, hence, has been vested in the governor. This pattern persists in about a third of our states, the governor being usually assisted, however, by a supervisory officer or board. In a majority of the states, the power is vested in a special board, functioning for the entire state. In the remaining states, institutional boards are chiefly responsible for granting parole. Wherever the power be vested, it is a purely discretionary one, and a convict denied parole has no recourse whatever to the courts.

The methods and personnel employed in the several states, and in the federal system, to supervise parolees and to detect violations of parole—methods and personnel which vary widely in adequacy and efficiency—are matters beyond our purview.

The power to reincarcerate a parolee found to have violated his parole is usually lodged in the agency which released him on parole. In determining that a parolee has violated his parole, the agency usually (though not invariably) affords the parolee an opportunity for a hearing; but its finding that the parole has been violated is not judicially reviewable. In recent years there has, however, been observed a growing tendency for the courts to entertain applications for relief made by parolees asserting that the action of the authorities in revoking their parole was completely arbitrary.

In most jurisdictions the length of the parole period is, within limits, in the discretion of the parole authorities, who have the power to grant the parolee a final discharge from parole.

17. INDEMNITY FOR WRONGFUL CONVICTION

In Continental countries generally there has long been provision for indemnifying a person wrongfully convicted and punished, his innocence having subsequently been established; and in some countries even where he has been acquitted, but has suffered extended detention up to the time of his acquittal, he is entitled to indemnity. Despite the obvious justice of such provision for indemnifying the innocent victim of a miscarriage of justice, it is but little known in this country. Nowhere is any provision made for indemnifying a person arrested, held in custody for an extended period, and then released, even though it may be evident that he is completely innocent (as in a case of mistaken identity). As for the innocent person who actually does time in prison as the result of a wrongful conviction—and established cases of such grievous miscarriage of justice are not wanting—provision for limited indemnification is now found in the federal statutes (since 1938) and in the statutes of a small number of states, nearly all of comparatively recent enactment. It may be anticipated that similar statutes will be enacted in other states, and that the existing statutes will be liberalized. Occasionally, a special grant has been made by a state legislature to indemnify a particular person wrongly convicted.

There is no procedure for compensating a defendant merely because he has been acquitted at his trial; nor can there perhaps be without the creation of a new procedure, hitherto unknown to our law, for establishing his innocence. The verdict of acquittal, as we have seen, fails to do this, signifying in law (whatever the private belief of the jurors in the innocence of the accused), only their unanimous conclusion that the evidence does not establish his guilt beyond a reasonable doubt.

18. PROSECUTION OF PETTY OFFENSES

It has already been mentioned that the traditional pattern of English and colonial justice did not provide for jury trial for petty offenses, and that the offender is in such cases not protected by either state of federal guaranties of jury trial.

The criminal penalty for infraction of a regulatory statute may be regarded as complementary to the civil action for a penalty, provided by many statutes of this character. The more expeditious procedure available in the criminal proceeding (for the constitutional right of trial by jury oddly enough in most jurisdictions remains unimpaired in the civil proceeding), and the effectiveness of the alternative punishment of imprisonment in inducing payment of whatever fine may be imposed, have caused it to be generally preferred for dealing with such infractions.

The procedure in the punishment of petty offenses has come down to us from the practice of the justice-of-the-peace courts of England, which originated more than five hundred years ago. In the long process, begun shortly after the Conquest and still not quite complete when the thirteenth century ended, by which the English crown wrested from the local seigniorial and communal courts the power to punish offenders, an important instrumentality of the central power was the justice of the peace. A local resident, at first always an important landed proprietor, unpaid, holding his commission directly from the Crown, and responsible for the maintenance of order in his locality, he was authorized (either by himself or in concert with one or more of the other justices of the peace in the county) to try and to punish offenders against the king's peace (or, in the case of more serious offenses, to commit the suspect to prison to await the arrival of the king's traveling judges to hold the "assize" for the county). The precise extent of the powers and jurisdiction of these justices, the offenses which they could themselves try summarily as opposed to those for which they were required to impanel a jury, waxed and waned over the centuries as public order in England was disturbed or restored in the successive dynastic and other outbreaks. By the time when the growth of the English settlements on these shores brought about the gradual adoption here of the more developed legal institutions of the mother country, the power of the English justice of the peace in the punishment of offenders had been fairly well stabilized. His power of summary determination was confined to certain petty offenses specified by act of Parliament. In offenses of a criminal nature, even if not grievous, his power was limited to holding the suspect for trial by a higher court.

Transported to the colonies, where the hierarchical society in some at least of the communities gave the office at first something of its aristocratic English character, the institution of the local justice of the peace, with summary jurisdiction in petty offenses, eventually spread over the whole country. Large landed proprietors being non-existent in the frontier areas, the office tended to fall into the hands of the local storekeeper, blacksmith, or the like, or occasionally the crossroads lawyer. The pattern thus established has persisted over most of the rural areas. In the cities, the "police judge" or "police magistrate" in the course of time largely superseded the justice of the peace on the criminal side, inheriting his summary jurisdiction in petty offenses.

In the latter half of the nineteenth century, there developed, to varying degrees in the several states (and even, sometimes, in the several cities of the same state), a further growth of this summary jurisdiction. In the first place, there were embraced within it offenses connected with prostitution and soliciting, conduct which, though from ancient time regarded as morally reprehensible, had previously only rarely been specifically condemned by the law. Again, there were created new forms of infraction directed against professional criminals, pickpockets, etc., designed to discourage them from loitering in public places with wrongful intent. Finally, the summary jurisdiction was extended over infractions of the increasing number of regulatory statutes.

Whether a person charged with a petty offense is to be arrested or is merely to be given a summons, requiring him to appear before the court at a time named, is determined by local statute or ordinance. Where the charge is made by a private party, the summons is almost always employed. To an increasing extent, the officer also is required, in the case of minor traffic violations, or an infraction of building or sanitary code provisions or the like, to issue a summons instead of making an arrest. If the person summoned to appear fails to do so, an order for his arrest is issued by the court.

In theory, a police officer has no discretion as to whether or not he will take action (whether by arrest or by summons) against one who commits an offense in his presence. He must indeed pass on the question of whether an offense has been committed; but once that question is settled affirmatively in his mind (and there is of course in many cases no possible ground for doubt) he is under an absolute duty to act. In practice, in this country far more generally than abroad, police officers exercise a considerable degree of discretion in refraining from action against minor offenders.

Where the officer is authorized to arrest for a petty offense instead of issuing a summons, he may under the statutes of most states do so only if he himself witnessed the infraction. A private person witnessing the infraction is not, under the law of most states, permitted to arrest the offender (as he is, we have seen, in the case of more serious offenses). Nor may he cause an officer to make the arrest. His course is to apply to the court for a summons to be served upon the offender, or for a warrant for his arrest.

If the offender is arrested, whether under a warrant or not, he is required to be brought before the court for trial without unnecessary delay (the judicial officer presiding in the court being termed for this purpose, whatever his official judicial title, a magistrate). In our larger cities, the police are in some cases authorized by statute to admit the offender to bail overnight, or to release him on his own recognizance.

The accusation on which the defendant is tried is ordinarily a sworn complaint in writing by the officer (the oral complaint being not, however, entirely unknown in the less highly organized areas of the country). On being summoned to the bar, the prisoner is asked whether he pleads guilty or not guilty. If he pleads guilty, sentence is ordinarily imposed at once. If he pleads not guilty, the trial ordinarily proceeds at once, though adjournment may be granted.

Trial of petty offenses is in the states invariably by the magistrate alone, sitting without a jury. Congress, too, has provided for non-jury trial of petty offenses in the District of Columbia and in the territories, as well as in certain other federal territory; and such provision has been sustained by the Supreme Court.[81] The Court has declared that the constitutional guaranty of jury trial in federal prosecutions must be read in the light of the practice prevailing at the time the guaranty was framed. At that time non-jury trial of petty offenses in the states had been long established, as it had been in England for some centuries; and the framers of the constitutional guaranty cannot be held to have intended, said the Court, to do more than to assure in the federal courts the same measure of right to jury trial as was then recognized in the state courts under similar provisions of state constitutions.

The language of the opinions of the Court in the cases referred to draws no distinction, with respect to the right of jury trial for petty offenses, between offenses against statutes governing only federal territory and offenses against statutes applicable to the country at large. Nevertheless, Congress in the latter class of statutes appears not to have ventured to dispense with jury trial for any offense, however petty, except with the consent of the defendant. During the period of national prohibition (1920–1933) the unprecedented burden of criminal prosecutions, frequently minor, thrown upon the federal courts, led to repeated suggestions for the trial of minor offenses against the federal prohibition statute (popularly known as the Volstead Act) without jury; but Congress failed to act.

In the states, as already noted, the line between a petty offense, triable without jury, and a misdemeanor, triable in many states by jury, at least if demanded, is by no means uniform.

The necessity for a summary proceeding, without jury, to dispose of truly minor offenses—such as disorderly conduct, minor traffic violations, violations of sanitary ordinances, etc.—is indisputable. What is not so clear is the propriety of the extension of the summary non-jury proceeding to offenses which, at least if judged by the punishment which may be imposed, are hardly to be termed minor. In some states, the tendency thus to enlarge the criminal jurisdiction of the single magistrate appears to have gone to questionable lengths. In at least one state, the abuse by certain

[81] District of Columbia v. Clawans, 300 U.S. 617 (1937).

magistrates of the enlarged power thus vested in them has resulted in a curtailment of the summary jurisdiction formerly exercised by them.

Where the defendant is represented by counsel, the trial before the magistrate is likely to follow a formal pattern. The arresting officer or other complaining witness gives his testimony under oath and is cross-examined; he is followed by additional witnesses for the prosecution. At the close of this testimony, motion may be made for a dismissal of the charge on the ground that the testimony given does not, even if uncontradicted, establish the commission of the offense charged. If this is denied, the witnesses for the defense are next examined and cross-examined. The defendant is not required to take the stand and may not be interrogated. At the conclusion of the defendant's case witnesses may be called in rebuttal by the prosecution and in surrebuttal by the defense. The magistrate then announces his decision, which is either that of acquittal or conviction, and on conviction or thereafter imposes sentence.

Where the prisoner is not represented by counsel, the trial may follow no such formal pattern. The arresting officer (or the complainant) and the defendant are likely to be interrogated by the magistrate in a single process, the questions being directed at one or the other as the testimony develops. Although the defendant may have been and often is informed that he is not required to answer questions, questions are directed to him and he answers them. As a practical matter this can hardly be regarded as an invasion of his rights, at least where the complainant is an officer or other official, since, in these cases, if the defendant refuses to answer, the testimony of the official is almost invariably sufficient to compel a conviction.

The informal type of questioning and testimony encountered in the trial of petty offenses is regarded by some as distinctly superior, at least in these cases, to the formal question-and-answer method characteristic of judicial proceedings generally, in which, as already pointed out, the witness often feels that he has not been permitted to tell the whole story.

There has developed in some jurisdictions a procedure in traffic violations which emphasizes how far removed, despite superficial procedural resemblances, is the summary proceeding of a criminal nature from the criminal prosecution proper. In this procedure, applicable only to a limited category of traffic offenses (especially illegal parking), the person summoned has the privilege of pleading guilty by mail, at the same time remitting to the court the amount of the fine fixed for the offense (the amount being stated on the summons). Even the civil action for a penalty does not embrace this procedural convenience for the offender. We have here moved close to the long-standing procedure in effect in some Continental countries, under which the police officer is authorized, in the case of certain minor infractions, to collect the fine on the spot from the offender whom he has accosted.

The procedure for reviewing a conviction of a petty offense depends upon the nature of the record of the proceedings made before the magistrate. In our cities, the tendency is increasingly for a stenographic record to be made, in which case an appellate procedure substantially similar to that followed in criminal proceedings may be provided. It is not uncommon to designate as an appellate bench a panel of the judges of the criminal court of general jurisdiction. More common, however, because in effect unavoidable where no proper record is made of the proceedings before the magistrate, is the wasteful procedure of the trial de novo—an entirely new trial before a judge having criminal jurisdiction (sometimes, in the case of the more serious petty offenses, before a judge and jury). In part the explanation of this wasteful procedure is to be found also in the lack of professional competence of the traditional justice of the peace. As these courts are replaced by professional courts based on larger territorial units, the trial de novo may be expected to disappear.

As in the case of criminal statutes, the statutes or ordinances dealing with petty offenses frequently provide for a considerable latitude in the severity of the sentence imposed. The extent of the possible alternatives is of course less with minor infractions, where even the maximum permissible penalty is slight, than in the case of graver offenses. Nevertheless, even the magistrate exercising summary jurisdiction has a large enough measure of power in this respect to make the manner of his selection, and of his freedom from political subservience during his term, matters of prime importance.

Closely related to the summary proceeding for the punishment of minor offenses is the traditional proceeding for the prevention of a threatened breach of the peace by requiring the prospective offender to give security for his good behavior. This proceeding, of ancient lineage in England, is found in many of our states, and has, in later years, even been adopted into the federal statutes. The usual procedure requires a magistrate, before whom a complaint has been made that some person has threatened to injure the person or property of the complainant, to hold a preliminary examination of the complainant and his witnesses, and if he finds sufficient cause, to issue a warrant for the arrest of the person complained of. If, upon the subsequent hearing, the magistrate finds that there is just reason to fear the commission of the act alleged, he may require the person complained of to enter into an "undertaking," in a sum usually limited by statute to not over $1,000, with sufficient sureties, to appear at the next term of the court having jurisdiction of criminal prosecutions, and in the meantime to "keep the peace" toward the complainant. Such an undertaking may be required to be renewed for limited periods. In default of procuring the required sureties, the person complained of may be committed to prison. Although imprisonment under these circumstances is very rare, the possibility thus exists of such imprisonment without conviction of crime.

19. PROCEEDINGS AGAINST YOUTHFUL OFFENDERS

In a preceding page, mention was made of the special procedure in force for regulating the punishment for federal offenses when the offender is youthful—a procedure which has been urged, with only limited success, for general adoption by the states. The criminal prosecution itself, however, is under this plan in no wise different from that employed in the case of older persons; only at the point of sentence does the differentiation begin. We are now to consider a distinctive judicial proceeding employed in dealing with the youthful offender, a proceeding sharply differentiated from the criminal proceeding, though the offense involved be identical.

Even in the early centuries of the development of the English criminal law there appears occasionally a recognition that a youth is not to be dealt with as harshly as an adult, or near-adult; and our colonial legislation reflected this recognition quite clearly at specific points. Speaking generally, however, neither in the English law, as it existed in the seventeenth century and as it was transported to this country, nor in the law of the colonies was express recognition given to the youthful offender as a separate category. For the most part, only official and judicial mercy, exercised without any express legal warrant, stood between the youthful defendant and the extreme rigors of the criminal law. But the power of the court at common law to suspend judgment and release the defendant, his sureties guaranteeing to produce him for sentence on order of the court, was early used more frequently in the case of youthful than of adult offenders; and its use in our courts in the case of youthful offenders emerges as a regular practice early in the last century, receiving statutory recognition for the first time, apparently, in 1869.

It was not, however, till nearly the end of the century that our legislation began to give recognition to the need for separate treatment of the youthful offender, not merely as to the imposition of sentence, but as to the entire character of the proceeding against him. Today, such legislation is found in all our states, and in the federal statutes as well.

These statutes typically provide that an offender below a certain age (the age of eighteen being found in a majority of statutes, seventeen or sixteen in others) is to be proceeded against not by indictment or information but by a petition seeking an adjudication of "juvenile delinquency."[82]

[82] In some states this proceeding is to be used exclusively; in others (and in the federal procedure) the alternative use of the regular criminal proceeding is still permitted. In all the statutes, exception is made of one or more of the gravest crimes; these are still to be prosecuted by criminal proceeding only. Under the federal statute (18 U.S. Code, Secs. 5031 ff.) a juvenile is defined as one who "has not attained his eighteenth birthday." The statute also authorizes the United States attorney for the district in which a person under twenty-one has been arrested on a federal charge to forego the prosecution of such person and to surrender him to the authorities of a state (or of the District of Columbia) if it appears that he has committed

The resulting proceeding characteristically resembles an investigation into the proper disposition to be made of the offender rather than a trial of the offense—an objective greatly facilitated by the tendency of the juvenile offender to make full confession of his offense. The court, which acts without a jury[83] is permitted to adjourn the hearing at any time to "inquire into the habits, surroundings, conditions and tendencies" of the offender, to quote a typical statute; and evidence on these matters, which is of course regarded as irrelevant in the trial of a criminal charge, is freely received by the court. The exclusion of the public from the hearing room, almost invariably enforced in these proceedings, and the extensive reliance placed by the court on the advice of social workers, psychiatrists, and cognate specialists further tend to give the proceeding the character of an inquiry rather than a trial.[84]

Such is, at any rate, the situation in the distinct minority of jurisdictions where the separate juvenile court has reached full maturity. But in many places, what is styled the juvenile court is in fact merely a particular sitting of a court of general jurisdiction, or of general criminal jurisdiction. In such unspecialized juvenile courts the proceedings are likely to depart much less completely from the pattern of the ordinary criminal trial.

It is, however, in the judgment procedure that the divergence from the ordinary criminal prosecution is most striking. As has been seen, once a person convicted of crime has been sentenced to imprisonment and taken into custody by the prison authorities, he passes completely from the control of the court. His relase from prison before the expiration of the maximum term imposed by the court is in the hands of a parole board or the like, responsible to the executive, and not to the court. In the case of the juvenile offender, however, the court in many jurisdictions may, even after commitment, and on its own motion, set aside the judgment and hear the case further.

The juvenile delinquency statutes thus produce a sharp cleavage between the treatment accorded to offenders just below and those just above the statutory age; and it is not surprising that in several jurisdictions there have been efforts to provide for those just over the statutory age a

an offense or is a delinquent under the laws of that state (or the District). 18 U.S. Code, Sec. 5001.

[83] In some statutes provision is made for the impaneling of a jury (usually of six) at the request of the offender; but such provisions are rarely invoked.

[84] See the Standard Juvenile Court Act (prepared by the National Council on Crime and Delinquency), on which many of the statutes are based. Since the procedure described above is directed not toward the punishment of the juvenile offender, but toward his protection and rehabilitation, that procedure is just as appropriate to the case of a neglected or destitute child as it is to that of a delinquent one. Increasingly, the trend has been to vest in the court having jurisdiction of charges of juvenile delinquency, jurisdiction of neglected and destitute children as well. Such a court in our larger cities tends indeed to become as much a social agency as a court, a large part of the time of its staff going to cases which never come to adjudication.

procedure which while more punitive than that of the juvenile court is less severe than that of the criminal courts. In New York, where the maximum age for "juvenile" offenders is placed at sixteen, offenders over sixteen but not over nineteen are classified as "youthful"; and a special procedure is provided under which such a defendant may, instead of being convicted of the offense initially charged against him, be adjudged a "youthful offender," with appropriate amelioration and individualization of the sentence imposed. In such a proceeding there is no jury.

Provision is also found in the statutes of some states for cognate proceedings against those minors, over the age fixed for juveniles, who are charged with no specific offense, but are alleged to be addicted to intoxication, the use of drugs, or dissoluteness, the court being empowered to place the minor on probation or commit him to a reformatory institution.

In recent years there has emerged the recognition that the extreme informality of procedure which has in some jurisdictions developed in proceedings against juvenile offenders, and the exceptionally wide discretion vested in the judge in determining sentence and treatment, are not without their dangers. Question has been raised whether present procedures in all jurisdictions adequately protect the rights—indeed the constitutional rights—of the youth accused of crime. Thus in New York, by legislation enacted in 1962, the juvenile defendant may, on his request, have a member of the bar appointed as his "law guardian" (or the judge may appoint one for him without request), the statute reciting that "counsel is often indispensable to a practical realization of due process of law and may be helpful in making reasoned determinations of fact and proper orders of disposition."[85]

In view of the fact that a very considerable proportion of those arrested for larceny, burglary, and assault are brought before the juvenile courts,[86] the relatively slight attention which has been given to the procedures of those courts, as against the procedures of the criminal courts, in the latter-day emphasis on the protection of the accused, is somewhat difficult to explain. A moderate reaction from the philosophy of the past half century seems to be developing, with consequent tightening of procedures in this field.[87] This would seem to be all the more appropriate in view of the fact

[85] New York City Family Court Act, Secs. 241 ff.

[86] Of the persons arrested in 1962 for robbery in 2,188 cities having an estimated population of over 2,500 (the aggregate population of such cities being nearly 76 million), over 28 per cent were under eighteen years of age. Among those arrested for burglary (breaking and entering), larceny, and auto theft the corresponding percentages were nearly 50 per cent, over 50 per cent, and nearly 64 per cent. The percentages were computed from the figures given in Federal Bureau of Investigation, Crime Reports for the United States, 1962, 98 (1963).

[87] See National Council on Crime and Delinquency, Procedure and Evidence in the Juvenile Court (1962); Rosenheim (ed.), Justice and the Child (1962). Much emphasis is placed by some commentators on their characterization of the proceeding for adjudicating a charge of juvenile delinquency as a "civil" proceeding; since the juvenile is not charged with a "crime," so runs the argument, the safeguards pro-

that appeals from the dispositions of juvenile courts, while permissible, are in the nature of the case very rarely taken.

In the foregoing, consideration has been confined to the proceedings affecting the youthful offender who has reached what may be regarded as at least the adolescent stage, and who may indeed be approaching adulthood. But offenses are committed also by offenders too young to be regarded as entirely responsible for their acts; and their treatment by the juvenile court differs very little from that employed by the court in dealing with those children, usually also under its jurisdiction, who are not offenders at all, but are merely neglected or abandoned. While no hard and fast cleavage merely on the basis of age can be drawn between these two groups, clarity in thought on the problems of judicature involved would be enhanced by a more express recognition of the differences between them than is reflected in some of the literature of the subject.

20. IMPEACHMENT PROCEEDINGS

In the early centuries of royal government in England following the Conquest, the Great Council, or Curia Regis, exercised plenary power in judicial as well as legislative matters; and in its judicial capacity it assumed to bring before it, and to punish, high offenders against the Crown, and particularly important officers of the Crown accused of corruption or malfeasance. In due course, this judicial function of the Curia Regis passed to Parliament; and with the separation of Parliament into two chambers in the fourteenth century, the judicial function remained in the House of Lords. The function of accusation, or "impeachment," came to be vested in the House of Commons. At the time of the English settlement of America, the impeachment of high officers of the Crown (and sometimes even of private persons) was still occasionally, though infrequently, used; and the importation of the institution into the colonies followed in due course.

Although in strictness the term impeachment is confined to the accusation only (and is so used in the Constitution of the United States), it is often used loosely to include also the trial and the imposition of the penalty, which is, today, removal from office and disqualification from future office.

Impeachment was employed in the colonies only sporadically; it found place after independence in a few of the first state constitutions, being

---

vided by the law for the criminal defendant are inappropriate. A finding of juvenile delinquency may, however, like a criminal conviction of a serious nature, deprive the juvenile of his liberty for an extended period, and may inflict on him a stigma which may seriously interfere with his subsequent efforts to obtain employment, or admission to an educational institution, or even entrance to a licensed profession or occupation.

specifically limited however to the impeachment of public officers for conduct in office or relating to official acts. Incorporated also in the Constitution, impeachment has since become part of the constitution of every state but Oregon. Everywhere (except in Nebraska, whose unique unicameral legislature draws up the articles of impeachment but remits the trial to the regular courts) the upper chamber of the legislature is the trial court.

The Constitution provides that when the President is tried, the "Chief Justice of the United States" shall preside over the Senate. In at least one state, the entire membership of the highest court of the state is added to the membership of the upper chamber when it sits as a court to try an impeachment. Conviction, under the federal Constitution, requires a two-thirds vote of the senators present; and a like provision is characteristically found in the state constitutions.

In most state constitutions, the offenses for which an official may be removed by impeachment are limited to those connected with his official acts. In the remaining states, conduct prior to assuming office, or unrelated to official duties, might, presumably, also be ground for impeachment; and indeed in New York a governor has in fact been removed on impeachment for acts antedating his assumption of office.

The Constitution gives as the permissible grounds of impeachment "treason, bribery, or other high crimes and misdemeanors," language which seemingly would not preclude removal from office on impeachment for crimes wholly unrelated to the defendant's office; but in the handful of impeachment proceedings instituted by the House of Representatives, official malfeasance only has been charged.

5

Civil Proceedings: Objectives

1. OBTAINING PAYMENT OF UNSECURED DEBT. 2. OBTAINING PAYMENT OF SECURED DEBT. 3. OBTAINING MONETARY COMPENSATION FOR WRONGFUL ACT OR BREACH OF CONTRACT. 4. COMPELLING TERMINATION OF EXISTING WRONG. 5. PREVENTION OF THREATENED WRONG. 6. DECLARATION OF RIGHTS. 7. DISSOLUTION OF MARRIAGE: AWARD OF SUPPORT TO WIFE LIVING APART FROM HUSBAND. 8. OTHER SPECIAL TYPES OF REMEDY. 9. PROPOSED ADJUDICATION OF LABOR "DISPUTES." 10. CIVIL PROCEEDINGS INSTITUTED BY LAW-ENFORCEMENT OFFICERS.

We have now reviewed both criminal proceedings proper and those cognate proceedings—for the punishment of petty offenses and for dealing with youthful offenders—which are criminal in nature. All other proceedings before the courts, whether instituted by governmental authorities or by private parties, are termed civil proceedings; and to these we now turn. There will, however, be reserved for the succeeding sections of this volume discussion of those proceedings in which the court is asked either to set aside or to enforce the determination of a non-judicial tribunal, administrative, miltiary, or arbitral.

In the criminal proceeding, the judgment which the prosecution seeks in initiating the proceeding is invariable—a judgment of conviction to be followed by sentence. In the civil proceeding, on the other hand, the judgment which the party initiating the proceeding seeks may be any one of a wide variety of possible judgments—all of them, however, responding to well-defined and established categories. In the present chapter, preliminary to an examination of the procedure followed in the civil proceeding, the chief kinds of judgment which may be granted in such a proceeding are reviewed. In other words, the inquiry is: What are the possible objectives for which a civil proceeding may be instituted?

Under our system of justice a court confronted with a child and two women, each claiming to be its mother, may not, like Solomon, order the child to be divided between them. Effective as this judgment proved to be in the Biblical case, it is not one of the recognized forms of judgment sanctioned by our law; and a court may grant only recognized forms of judgment.

Diverse as may be the objectives of civil proceedings, they will be found on examination to fall chiefly into several main categories. The litigant who initiates the proceeding ordinarily asks the court either to (1) merely *declare* that he possesses certain rights, or (2) *prevent* a threatened wrong against him, or (3) *undo* a wrong already done, or (4) in lieu thereof, *award* him monetary compensation therefor. In addition, there are certain less usual types of proceeding in which the petitioner seeks special remedies not readily assimilable to the foregoing classification.

We shall examine these several categories of relief in inverse order. Logically, the function of redressing wrongs already committed might seem to follow rather than precede the functions of undoing a present wrong, of preventing a threatened wrong, and of declaring the rights of the parties. Historically, however, redress rather than prevention or mere declaration has been the earliest and the chief business of judicial institutions.

The immediate objective of a civil proceeding is to obtain the issuance by the court of a favorable judgment, decree, or order. But these documents are of value to the plaintiff only to the extent that the defendant complies with them, or may be compelled to comply with them. In connection with each type of judgment or order granted by the courts, it is necessary to consider what means are available to enforce compliance, if voluntary compliance is not forthcoming.

1. OBTAINING PAYMENT OF UNSECURED DEBT

The simplest and most usual form of judgment awarded by the courts to enforce payment of an unsecured debt is the so-called money judgment —a mere announcement of the adjudication of the sum due, and of the right of the creditor (now termed the "judgment creditor") to proceed, through the instrumentality of the officers of the court, to the collection of the amount of the judgment out of such property or income of the judgment debtor as he may be able to find.

The determination of the amount due from the debtor to the creditor (and indeed the determination of which party is the debtor and which the creditor) may, in certain situations, involve the examination not of a single transaction but of a great many, each of which results in a charge against one of the parties and a credit to the other. Typical of such a situation is that of a trust fund in which the trustee has engaged in a number of transactions over an extended period; or that of a partnership which has wound up its business, but in which the proper distribution among the partners of the partnership funds that remain is in dispute. The proceeding in which such complex accounts are to be settled by the court is termed an action or proceeding for an accounting. The resulting judgment is ordinarily a money judgment, as in the case of a single debt.

Mention has already been made, in connection with the summary proceeding to impose a fine as penalty for a petty offense, of the alternative civil proceeding for a penalty—in theory, a monetary compensation to the community for the wrong done it. This is an ancient form of proceeding, historically but no longer characteristically associated with the institution of the informer, who is entitled to a portion of the penalty collected by the proceeding—an institution not yet entirely obsolete. A judgment for a penalty, like one arising out of a debt, is enforceable only by proceedings against the property of the defendant.

The foregoing is relevant only when the proceeding is against the debtor. Where control of all the debtor's property has been taken over for distribution under the supervision of the court (as in the case of insolvency or death) the forms of proceeding and of judgment are appropriately modified.

Collection of money judgment

The money judgment, as just pointed out, is merely a declaration by the court that one of the parties is entitled to recover from the other a stated sum, and is to have the aid of the court and its officers, if he desires, in compelling the payment of that sum. This document, which remains in the court as part of the record of the case, does not, it will be observed, direct the judgment debtor to pay. A failure, even a wilful refusal, to pay the amount mentioned therein, does not, of itself, constitute a disobedience of the court.

If the judgment debtor pays the judgment voluntarily he is entitled to a formal acknowledgment of payment (commonly called a "satisfaction" or "satisfaction piece") which is, ordinarily, filed by the judgment debtor with the clerk of the court, who will thereupon note in the docket that the judgment is satisfied.

In each state there exists a system (usually, though not invariably, on a county basis) for the public recording of all instruments affecting title to real estate. A money judgment recovered in any court of the state may be made of record in any of the offices of the state where such real estate records are kept; and it thereupon becomes a lien upon any real estate in the area covered by such record office in which the judgment debtor may have (or may thereafter within a stated period of years acquire) an interest.

The judgment creditor is entitled upon the entry of a money judgment, or within a limited period thereafter, to execution of the judgment against the property of the judgment debtor, i.e., its seizure and sale by an officer of the court (most frequently the sheriff of the county). The attorney for the judgment creditor issues to the sheriff or other officer, in the name of the court (the attorney being regarded as an officer of the court for this purpose), an order known as an "execution against the property."

Although there may be nothing in the execution itself so to indicate, there are certain items of personal property which are exempt from seizure and sale under it. Such statutory exemptions vary considerably from state to state, a limited quantity of household goods and the tools of the judgment debtor's trade being almost invariably exempt.

As to real estate, there is in every state a so-called homestead exemption. In some states, the judgment debtor's dwelling is wholly exempt from sale, regardless of how valuable it may be. In a majority of the states, however, the exemption is limited by the statute to a stated amount. The varying procedures by which, under such a statute, a levy having been made on the homestead, adjustment is made of the respective rights of the judgment debtor and the judgment creditor (or purchaser at the execution sale) are beyond our present scope.

In some states, the difficulty of realizing the true value of a parcel of real estate upon a judicial auction sale thereof has resulted (in addition to the requirement that all the personal property of the judgment debtor be exhausted before his realty is proceeded against) in provisions deferring the passage of title to the realty to the purchaser at the execution sale for a specified period after the sale. If before the expiration of that period the judgment debtor tenders to the purchaser at the sale the amount, with interest, which the latter paid for the property, he is entitled to have it returned to him.

Where the property of the judgment debtor consists of money due him, the method of sale under execution is of course inappropriate. Instead, a proceeding is instituted by the judgment creditor to compel payment to himself (or to the officer of the court for his account), instead of to the judgment debtor, of the money due the latter. Such proceedings, which vary widely in detail, go under the general name of "garnishment" proceedings; and the third person who is thus compelled to pay to or for the account of his creditor's creditor, is called the garnishee.

Not only money already due may be reached in this manner, but also, in many states, money to become due as wages, salaries, income from trust funds, and the like. The statutes usually provide for garnishment of only a small portion of moneys due as wages or salaries.

However, irregular income (such as, for example, that earned by a free-lance writer or artist) cannot be reached by any type of the garnishment proceeding just discussed because it emanates from no one payor upon whom an execution may be served; and it would be impracticable and oppressive to permit the judgment creditor to submit the judgment debtor to a continuous series of examinations as to his prospective receipts. To meet this situation a special procedure has been devised and adopted in a few states. Under this procedure the court is empowered to order the debtor to pay to the judgment creditor periodically a stipulated sum, deemed by the court to be proper in relation to the income of the debtor. Failure of the debtor to obey the order is punishable by fine or imprisonment as for a contempt of court. (This procedure is to be clearly distinguished from the traditional form of decree in actions for separation or divorce in which the court awards a stipulated sum per week, month, etc., indefinitely. In the procedure here under discussion there is a lump-sum judgment.)

The method of ordering the debtor to pay a portion of his income is not satisfactory where the creditor desires to obtain the entire net income of some piece of property or business owned by the debtor. Thus, if the debtor owns a piece of real estate the rental receipts of which exceed the operating expenses of the building, the only satisfactory method for the creditor to pursue (unless he wishes to cause the building to be sold, a procedure fraught, as already seen, with expense and uncertainty of result) is to apply to the court for the appointment of someone to take possession of the premises, receive the rents, pay the operating expenses, including mortgage interest and taxes, and remit the surplus, if any, to the creditor in payment of his judgment. Again, the debtor may be operating a going business and the creditor may anticipate more effective collection of his judgment through the appropriation of the net profits of the business to its payment, than through the forced sale of the assets used in the conduct of the business, with resultant destruction of the going value of the business and the debtor's earning power. Here, too, an application to the court for the appointment of a "receiver" (as the court's appointee is called) is in order.

To enable the judgment creditor to ascertain what the assets of the debtor are, he is permitted, under procedures which vary from state to state, to institute proceedings against the judgment debtor or against persons believed to be in possession of the latter's property (or believed to be indebted to him) for the purpose of compelling a disclosure of such assets, or preventing their diversion. In its traditional form, such a proceeding is known as a judgment creditor's action. In some states, the statutes make available also a more summary type of proceeding known as a "proceeding supplementary to execution" or more briefly, "supplementary proceedings."

Obtaining enforcement of money judgment in another jurisdiction

A money judgment is regarded as creating an obligation to pay, and is thus a species of debt. Hence it may be enforced, like any other debt, anywhere.

The actual procedure in the enforcement of a state court money judgment in a state other than that in which it was obtained is simple. Assume that a money judgment has been obtained in California against a resident of New York and has not been paid. The judgment creditor now institutes in New York[1] an action "on the judgment"; that is, his complaint merely recites that he obtained judgment in California against the defendant and that the judgment has not been paid. Service of the summons and complaint must be made on the defendant in the ordinary way; or, in lieu thereof, if he has property in New York, it may, if the necessary conditions are present, be attached. If the defendant appears and defends the action, he can raise only the question of the *jurisdiction* of the California court out of which the judgment issued.[2] If he is defeated on that issue, judgment will go against him for the amount of the original judgment, with interest to date, plus the costs of the New York action. Needless to say, the judgment debtor is entitled to have any payment which he may subsequently make to the judgment creditor (and any sum which the judgment creditor may realize by sale of the debtor's property in either state) credited against both the California and New York judgments.

The courts of many countries accord reciprocal enforcement to each other as a matter of comity; and such was the situation, to a limited extent, with our own states, with respect to each other's judgments, until the adoption of the Articles of Confederation in 1791. By that instrument it was provided that each state was to give "full faith and credit" to the judicial proceedings of every other state. No provision was made, however, for enforcing this obligation. With the adoption of the Constitution, the similar clause which it contains (Article IV) was made enforceable by the provision for "the judicial power of the United States." A failure of the refusal of a state to give full faith and credit to a judgment of the courts of a sister state can be reviewed and corrected by the Supreme Court of the United States.

A money judgment obtained in a federal district court may be enforced against the property of the judgment debtor anywhere in the United States, a mere registration of the judgment being required in the district in which the property proceeded against is situated.

[1] The action may be brought either in the state courts of New York, or, if the amount of the judgment sued on, with interest, is more than $10,000 and there is diversity of citizenship (as to which see pp. 199 ff.), in a federal court in New York.

[2] As to the doctrines governing the jurisdiction of state courts, and jurisdiction by attachment, see Chapter 6.

On the Continent, it is the practice of the several countries, in most cases, to accord enforcement to each other's money judgments without the necessity of an action. The judgment creditor merely registers his judgment under a procedure provided, and execution thereunder issues automatically. Actual sale of the debtor's property does not, of course, take place immediately; and in the interim the debtor may move to cancel the registration of the judgment on the ground of lack of jurisdiction of the court which granted it. Opinions differ as to whether this more summary procedure, though apparently regarded as unobjectionable on the Continent, would under American conditions afford sufficient protection to the alleged debtor.[3] Some who favor it believe that it is within the power of Congress (in the exercise of its authority to "prescribe the manner in which [the judicial proceedings of another state] shall be proved and the effect thereof") to effect its adoption in this country by federal statute.

Whether a money judgment obtained in an American court will be enforced in a foreign country depends on the law of that country. A money judgment obtained in a foreign country may be sued on in a court here. The federal courts and the courts of a few states enforce the judgments only of those countries which enforce our judgments.

Judgment directing payment of money due

Enforcement of the money judgment is, as just shown, ordinarily restricted to action against the debtor's property or income, and not against the debtor himself. In a limited class of cases, however, the money judgment is supplemented by a form of judgment ordering the debtor to pay on pain of punishment by imprisonment until he complies. This form of judgment not merely authorizes the issuance of an order to the appropriate officer to seize and sell the debtor's property; it is in addition an order directed to the debtor himself (and in consequently described as a judgment "in personam," i.e., against the person).

The chief class of cases in which a judgment in personam will be issued to compel the payment of money due as a debt is that in which a trustee has wrongfully appropriated trust funds and has failed to make restitution, and in cognate cases of breach of trust by fiduciaries.

A state judgment in personam directing the payment of money is not enforced automatically in other states. This reluctance of the courts to enforce the sister-state judgment in personam by a similar judgment of their own may be thought to be inconsistent with the "full faith and credit" requirement of the Constitution. The seeming inconsistency, some courts have however contended, does not in fact exist. The Constitution, they

[3] See Note: Constitutionality of a Uniform Reciprocal Registration of Judgments Statute, 36 N.Y. U. Law Rev. 488 (1961).

reason, does not impose on a state any particular method of enforcing a sister-state judgment. Only recognition is commanded; the method of making such recognition effective is left to the state.

2. OBTAINING PAYMENT OF SECURED DEBT

Closely related to the ordinary proceeding for a money judgment for a debt is that in which the creditor asserts not merely his right to payment but in addition his right to have some specific piece of property sold and the proceeds applied to the payment of his claim, in defiance of the rights of other creditors of the debtor (and of the rights of the present owner of the property if the debtor no longer owns it). This right of the creditor, where it exists, is termed a lien. A simple and very widespread form of lien is the real estate mortgage lien; other common forms are the lien of the pawnbroker or other pledgee, the chattel mortgage, the lien of an artisan on the chattel entrusted to him for repair, and the lien of the warehouse or carrier on the goods stored or transported.

In certain forms of lien (e.g., the pledge), the lienor may, on default, proceed without the aid of a court to sell the property subject to the lien. In other cases, however (as, in most states, in the case of a real estate mortgage), the creditor must apply to the court to procure the sale of the property. A judgment in such a proceeding is commonly termed a judgment of foreclosure because, in addition to directing the sale of the property at auction and the payment of the plaintiff's claim out of the proceeds, it declares that, upon the sale of the property pursuant to the judgment, the interest of the owner of the property therein, and the interest of all other persons having any interest therein subordinate to the lien of the plaintiff, shall be foreclosed, i.e., extinguished.

3. OBTAINING MONETARY COMPENSATION FOR WRONGFUL ACT OR BREACH OF CONTRACT

Perhaps the most characteristic as well as the oldest of the remedies afforded by our courts is the determination that a sum of money shall be paid the injured party by the wrongdoer (using that term in its broadest sense, to include even one who has merely defaulted in the performance of a contractual obligation). The award takes the form of a money judgment identical with that granted in case of a debt, and ordinarily enforceable, as in that case, only by proceedings against the property of the judgment debtor.

In certain classes of cases (notably in the accident cases which occupy so much of the time of our civil courts) the determination of the present sum necessary to compensate the plaintiff for the bodily injury done him often requires prognostication. If a pedestrian struck by a negligently operated automobile suffers an injury which has made it impossible for him up to the time of the trial to pursue his usual occupation, the computation of his loss of earnings up to that time offers little difficulty; but the forecasting of the extent and duration of the impairment of his earning power for the future is often obviously a matter of speculation rather than of anything like certainty. Yet our law requires the judge or jury at the close of the trial to make this forecast, and translate it into dollars and cents, immediately and irrevocably. The progress of the plaintiff's condition, within a short time after the trial, may radically change his prospects, whether for better or worse; but the amount awarded him has been unalterably fixed.[4]

Much more rational is the form of award employed in a cognate type of adjudication—one entrusted, however, almost everywhere not to the courts but to special tribunals organized as part of the executive branch. In the adjudication of claims by workmen for compensation for injuries sustained in the course of employment, the injured workman receives, characteristically, not a lump sum but an award of periodical payments during the period of disability, such award being open to revision from time to time as the disability grows or lessens. Thus, in proceedings arising out of a single industrial accident, a disabled workman whose remedy falls under a workmen's compensation law will ordinarily receive an an award payable periodically during the period of disability, while an injured bystander, similarly disabled, whose sole remedy is an action for damages in the courts, will receive a lump sum.

So, too, in an action for damages for wrongful premature discharge, instituted by an employee who alleges a contract to employ him for a stated period, the determination of lump-sum damages, if made before expiration of the contract period, involves speculation;[5] while if the determination is deferred till after the expiration of that period, hardship and difficulties of proof result.

The extension of awards of periodical payments to judicial proceedings arising out of controversies of the kind instanced would seem to be highly desirable. Indeed, the elimination of the lump-sum award as compensation for prospective impairment of earning power and prospective disability generally, due to accidental injuries, would doubtless drastically

---

[4] The original determination may of course be subjected to a review on appeal; but the questions before the appellate court will refer solely to the correctness of the judgment at the time of the trial. It may not receive testimony as to subsequent developments.

[5] In Texas, apparently alone among the states, the plaintiff may recover only his damages up to the date of trial. This rule, while eliminating the element of speculation, in effect constrains the plaintiff to wait until the agreed term of employment has almost expired before bringing action, or, in the alternative, to recover less than he is entitled to.

reduce the volume of personal injury cases, arising largely out of motor-vehicle accidents, which create a difficult situation in many of our courts. It is the prospect of a large lump-sum judgment which impedes in many cases the just and prompt settlement of these cases by the parties without the aid of the courts. The failure to extend the award of periodical payments to personal injury and other suitable cases is to be attributed to inertia, rather than to any inherent impossibility, although technical difficulties, discussion of which lies beyond our present scope, doubtless exist.

In some of the states, in a very limited class of actions for damages (of which the action for damages for personal injury is the chief), the money judgment resulting may be enforced, if proceedings against the property of the debtor are ineffective, by the arrest and imprisonment of the judgment debtor for a limited period. In practice, owing to technical provisions which cannot here be set forth, the net effect of this remedy is to require the debtor to furnish bond that he will not, for the period mentioned, leave the county; and unless he does so, and the judgment creditor discovers the fact and succeeds in serving certain papers upon the bondsman before the debtor returns to the county, the creditor gains nothing. This remedy is termed an "execution against the person" and is popularly known as a "body execution."

4. COMPELLING TERMINATION OF EXISTING WRONG

Where the wrongful act or course of conduct has not yet been completed or terminated, the courts will intervene to bring it to an end (at the same time awarding monetary compensation for the wrong already done). If the wrong is caused by, or perpetuated by, the existence of a contract into which the victim was entrapped by fraud, duress, undue influence, or the like, a rescission of the transaction will be decreed.

Awarding possession of property

The simplest form of continuing wrong with which the courts deal is perhaps the wrongful possession of property, whether real property or chattel. If the person entitled to possession chooses, he may of course permit the wrongdoer too continue in possession, seeking merely a money judgment as compensation for the injury done him. If he elects he may, however, seek a judgment awarding him the possession of the property.[6]

As in the case of money awards, in most classes of cases the judgment for the plaintiff seeking possession is not directed to the defendant person-ally, but is merely an adjudication that the plaintiff is entitled to possession

[6] If the plaintiff seeks possession of real property the action is termed one in ejectment (more summary forms of action with varying names being also, however, authorized by modern statutes). If he seeks possession of a chattel, the action is termed one in replevin.

and to the aid of the officers of the court in gaining possession, by force if necessary.

Where the judgment awards the plaintiff possession of a chattel without commanding the defendant to surrender it, the possibility exists that the officer of the court, who, in execution of the judgment, attempts to take possession of the chattel in order to place it in the possession of the plaintiff, may be unable to find it. The judgment therefore usually provides that of the chattel cannot be found, the plaintiff shall have a money judgment for a sum which has been found by the court to be the value of the chattel in question. Where, however, the chattel in question is of a unique character (e.g., a painting by an old master) and, consequently, the receipt of its value in money would not enable the plaintiff to duplicate it, such a judgment is manifestly inadequate. Hence, the plaintiff may seek instead, a judgment directed to the defendant in personam commanding him to surrender possession to the plaintiff.

Awarding custody of minor

In an action for divorce or separation (shortly to be discussed) one, though not the chief, objective of the action may be a determination of the right to the custody of the minor children of the marriage.

Frequently, in the absence of any action for separation or divorce, husband and wife who are living apart have agreed, perhaps orally and quite informally, as to the custody of their minor children. Similar situations frequently result in grandparents or other relatives, by common consent, assuming responsibility for the custody of a child.

When in these circumstances disputes arise between spouses or relatives over the right to continue to have the custody of an infant, the courts will take jurisdiction of such disputes and adjudicate them. In making its determination, the court will be primarily governed, not by the agreement of the parties, but by the interests of the infant; for while the infant is initially, and in the absence of special circumstances during his entire nonage, the ward of his parents, he is also regarded by the law as the ward of the state, which may exercise its rights of guardianship, in derogation of the rights of the parents, when the interests of the child so require.

The order issued in such a case directs the person having custody of the child to surrender it to the person awarded its custody. Though the final order thus departs from the simple release order issued in habeas corpus proceedings generally,[7] the initial step is, as in those proceedings, an order for the production before the court of the child whose custody is in question; hence, this proceeding, also, has come to be termed a habeas corpus proceeding.

[7] See p. 56.

Ordering release from wrongful detention

We have already taken note of the constitutionally safeguarded right of a person illegally held in custody by the police or prosecuting authorities (or held under an allegedly illegal arrest or conviction) to apply to the courts for his release.

There are not a few situations in which custody is exercised by private persons over others. Occasionally, there are encountered cases in which persons greatly enfeebled by age or by want of full mental powers (though never adjudicated incompetent) are in effect restrained of their liberty by members of their family or by relatives. Again, there are situations in which persons have voluntarily placed themselves in the care of institutions for the mentally ill, or for alcoholic or other addicts, and allegedly find themselves beset by obstacles when seeking to leave such institutions; and so on.

The remedy in such cases is by way of an application to a court for an order directing the release of the person detained, the proceeding being known, as where the detention is by an official rather than by a private party, as a habeas corpus proceeding. Where the person whose custody is involved is of full age and *sui juris* (i.e., has not been judicially declared incompetent) such person himself is often the petitioner in the proceeding. Where the circumstances preclude his signing the petition, it may be made by some other person acting in his interest.

This proceeding may also be employed by, or on behalf of, one who has been involuntarily committed to a mental institution after due hearing, but who, it is contended, is now fully restored, to procure an adjudication of this contention.

Compelling cessation of wrongful conduct (injunction)

Passing to more complex forms of continuing wrongs, it is useful to distinguish between those situations in which the wrong consists of an affirmative course of conduct, and those in which it consists merely in failing to do what the law requires. In the former situation, a prohibitory judgment, known as an injunction, is called for. The injunction, an express prohibition addressed to the wrongdoer, is in effect a notification to him that if he continues in his wrongful course of action, or if he commits the particular wrongful acts threatened, he will, in addition to incurring liability to the injured plaintiff, bring down upon himself punishment at the hands of the court for contempt.

Illustrative of the situations in which the courts will issue an injunction is that in which a business enterprise assumes a name or a style of lettering so similar to that of an established competitor as to be calculated to confuse the buying public—a form of conduct commonly referred to as "unfair competition." The injured party in such a situation might indeed from time to time seek redress in the form of a money judgment for the damages suffered; but the near impossibility of establishing the amount of such damages, and the dubious effectiveness of that remedy, even if obtained, in bringing the wrongful conduct to an end, are obvious. In this situation, therefore, the court, in addition to awarding a money judgment for the damages already sustained, will enjoin the wrongdoer from further use of the offending name, lettering, or other device.

In addition to the types of situation in which the courts will by traditional doctrine grant injunctive relief at the instance of an aggrieved party, there are a number of special cases in which such relief is expressly provided for by statute. Notable among these are cases of patent or copyright infringement. The antitrust laws (the so-called Sherman and Clayton acts) also expressly authorize the institution of injunction proceedings both by the government and by one alleging injury as the result of a conspiracy in restraint of interstate or foreign commerce in violation of the statute.

In labor disputes, the injunction has been used to prohibit allegedly illegal strikes and boycotts, and the alleged use of violence and other unlawful means in strikes otherwise lawful; and the federal courts were for a time particularly active in this field. A determined effort by organized labor to restrict the power of the federal courts in this field resulted in the enactment by Congress, in 1914, of provisions prohibiting those courts from issuing, in connection with a labor dispute, any injunction prohibiting striking, peaceful picketing, boycotting a party to the dispute, or paying strike benefits. In 1932 these provisions were reinforced by the so-called Norris-LaGuardia Act. (Indeed, even the issuance by the federal courts of injunctions against concerted violence, if arising out of a labor dispute, was restricted by these statutes, and particularly by the latter.) However, by the Labor Management Relations Act of 1947 (the Taft-Harley law), injunctions against strikes and boycotts violative of that act are authorized (as is the injunction issued at the instance of the government to prevent a strike declared by the President to imperil the national health or safety).[8] Statutes similar to the Norris-LaGuardia Act have been enacted in about a third of the states.

Finally the injunction proceeding is used on the one hand by law-enforcement officers as a method of compelling compliance with the law, and on the other hand by private parties as a means of testing before the courts the legality of official action—matters still to be considered.

[8] All the statutes referred to are found in Title 29, U.S. Code. The 1914 statute is Sec. 52, the Norris-LaGuardia Act in Secs. 101–115, and the provisions of the Taft-Hartley Act referred to are Secs. 160(1) and 176–180. Action for an injunction against an illegal strike or boycott, as authorized by the Taft-Hartley law, may not be instituted by the employer, but only, at his instance, by the National Labor Relations Board. As to the provisions of the 1914 act and the Norris-LaGuardia Act for trial by jury of charges of contempt arising out of injunction in labor disputes, see page 167.

Compulsion

If the wrongful course of conduct is not the doing of an affirmative act, but the failure to do a required act or to pursue a required course of conduct, the problem before the courts is more difficult. There is no difficulty in framing the language of an order directing the defendant, affirmatively, to do a particular act or series of acts, or carry out a particular course of conduct, in the future; but there may be practical difficulties in enforcing it. Thus, a distributor who has agreed with a manufacturer to sell only the latter's product, and to use his best efforts to promote its sale, may readily be enjoined from selling a competitive product; and such injunction presents no difficulty of enforcement, since its violation is readily established. But the enforcement of a mandatory judgment, ordering the defendant to use his best efforts to promote the sale of the plaintiff's product would present obvious difficulties.

Directory judgments are accordingly less common than injunctions. They are, however, readily granted in a proper case. An illustration is found in the situation where one who has contracted to sell a piece of real estate wrongfully refuses to perform the contract by delivering to the buyer a deed to the property. A judgment directing the seller to deliver the deed is readily granted in such a case. The term "decree of specific performance of the contract" is usually applied to such a judgment.

It should be noted that, as a remedy for the refusal to perform an affirmative contractual obligation, the decree of specific performance of contract is highly exceptional. Ordinarily, in the view of the courts, the injury resulting from the refusal of a party to a contract to furnish merchandise, services, or the like is adequately compensated by an award of damages or possession, the conventional remedies. In the case just recited, since every piece of real estate is, at least in theory, unique, an award of damages is inadequate; the injured party will, it is true, be able to buy another piece of real estate perhaps similar to the one promised, but it will not be that one, with its unique location. Hence, the justification for the "extraordinary" remedy—the decree of specific performance.[9]

In the field of statutory enforcement, the directory judgment, like the prohibitory one, has assumed great importance. In actions instituted by the government under the antitrust laws, it has sought and obtained, in cases where monopoly and not merely wrongful practices were involved, decrees directing the defendants to dissolve corporate structures, to divest themselves of certain assets, to grant patent licenses, and the like. Clearly,

---

[9] In the jurisprudence of Continental countries, derived from Roman sources in this respect, the decree of specific performance of a contract is not regarded as an extraordinary remedy, and is thus granted rather freely in ordinary commercial cases. Such tends to be the case also in Louisiana, the civil law of which is French rather than English in origin.

in shaping decrees of this nature, the federal courts have been compelled to enter a field calling for economic wisdom as much as, if not more than, legal learning.[10] The propriety of entrusting responsibility for even the initial formulation of decrees of this nature (for they are, of course, subject to review on appeal) to any federal district judge before whom the case may have happened to come is at least open to question.

A special field for the affirmative mandate in private disputes is that of corporate affairs. Where an officer of a corporation or association refuses to perform an act which the governing statute, charter, constitution, or bylaws clearly make it his duty to do, and affords him no discretion, the courts, in the event of his refusal to act, will not hesitate to issue an order directing him to do so. The order issued by the courts in these classes of cases is termed a writ of mandamus (or mandamus order). The use of this writ in corporate disputes and the like is an outgrowth of its use in proceedings relating to the failure of a public officer to perform a mandatory duty, to be discussed at a later point.

The reluctance of our courts to issue orders directing the performance of a specific act is, interestingly, reflected in the failure of our law to develop, in cases of libel and slander, a remedy found in some Continental systems of law—a mandate to the defamer to issue a retraction in the same form as that in which the defamation was issued.

Enforcement of judgments in personam

Failure to comply with a judgment in personam subjects the disobedient party to punishment for contempt of court, such punishment being either a fine (perhaps of an amount much exceeding that usually provided by criminal statutes),[11] or imprisonment, or both, imposed through the criminal contempt proceeding described in an earlier chapter.[12] The court itself has, of course, no machinery for supervising or investigating the compliance yielded to its judgment (although a requirement for periodical re-

---

[10] In an action by the government under the antitrust laws, to enjoin the continuance of certain restrictive agreements made by an oil company with its distributors, the defendant contended that it was the government's obligation to adduce evidence warranting a firm prediction that an increase of competition would result from such discontinuance. In rejecting this contention, the Supreme Court (in an opinion by Justice Frankfurter) said that the standard of proof thus contended for was "if not virtually impossible to meet, at least most ill-suited for ascertainment by the courts," and declared that the "appraisal of economic data" that would be requisite was quite impracticable "for judges unequipped for it either by experience or by the availability of skilled assistance." Standard Oil Co. v. United States, 337 U.S. 293, 310 (1949). Justice Jackson, dissenting, said (at page 322): "I regard it as unfortunate that the Clayton Act submits such economic issues to judicial determination. . . . The judicial process is not well-adapted to exploration of such industry-wide, and even nation-wide, questions."

[11] In United States v. United Mine Workers, 330 U.S. 258 (1947), a fine of $750,000 for criminal contempt was imposed, together with a contingent fine of $2,800,000, to become payable unless the court's order was immediately complied with.

[12] See pp. 38 ff.

port of such compliance to the court may indeed be, and occasionally is, included in the judgment). It is for the party in whose favor the judgment runs to bring disobedience of the judgment to the attention of the court.

If the threat of punishment (or its actual imposition) fails to effect compliance, the court may be asked to commit the recalcitrant party to custody (ordinarily in a "civil" prison) until he does comply. The proceeding to order his commitment for this purpose is known as the civil contempt proceeding, its objective being, not as in the criminal contempt proceeding, to punish the person proceeded against for an offense against the court already committed, but to compel present compliance with the court's order.[13] In theory, the commitment, if the court's judgment continues to be defied, may continue indefinitely. While, as earlier noted, in certain types of criminal contempt proceeding the finding that the court's order has been disobeyed is made by a jury, in the civil contempt proceeding the determination that the judgment has not yet been complied with is made by the judge alone.

In aggravated cases, a punishment for criminal contempt may be imposed even after the defendant, to avoid commitment under the civil contempt finding, has complied with the judgment. Ordinarily, however, if the judgment is complied with, the offending party is regarded as having "purged" himself of the offense committed against the court by his past disobedience, and no punishment is sought or inflicted.

The federal statute, to which reference was made in an earlier chapter,[14] providing for jury trial in criminal contempt proceedings if the act prosecuted as a contempt also constitutes a criminal offense under any federal or applicable state statute, is applicable also to such a proceeding to punish the disobedience of an order or decree of a court in a civil action. However, civil actions brought by the government are excluded from this provision. This exclusion caused strong opposition in Congress to the measure, proposed in 1957, to enable the government to institute proceedings to compel the registration, by state election officials, of persons found to have been denied registration because of their race or color, in violation of the Thirteenth Amendment. To secure the passage of the measure, a compromise provision was enacted, permitting the judge to try without a jury a charge of criminal contempt for violation of a decree issued under the statute, but providing also that if he imposed a fine in excess of $300, or imprisonment for more than forty-five days, the defendant might demand a jury trial de novo.[15]

---

[13] The lack of clear demarcation, historically, of the dividing line between the civil and the criminal contempt is, however, reflected in the provision of the federal statutes that in certain classes of criminal contempt proceeding the fine imposed on the offender may be ordered by the court to be paid in whole or in part to the party injured by the act punished (18 U.S. Code, Sec. 402).

[14] See p. 40.

[15] 42 U.S. Code, Sec. 1995.

Both in the federal courts and in some of the states, one charged with criminal contempt, because of alleged violation of an injunction or restraining order issued in a case involving or growing out of a labor dispute, is entitled to a jury trial, even if the act alleged to constitute such violation is not a criminal offense.[16]

A novel aspect of the problem of enforcing the judgment in personam has been presented in connection with certain judgments of federal courts (made pursuant to the 1954 decision of the Supreme Court, declaring state school segregation laws unconstitutional), ordering state educational authorities to admit Negro students to schools theretofore, under state law, open to white students only. These judgments have in all cases been obtained in actions instituted by Negro students seeking such admission (or by their parents), for Congress has not empowered the government, despite the decade that has elapsed since the Supreme Court decision, to institute such actions. In the case of a judgment entered in such an action, in 1958, the school authorities attempted to comply with the judgment, which ordered the admission of Negro children to a certain high school, but reported to the court that compliance was being prevented by disorderly and threatening crowds congregated near the school. The court, at the request of the authorities, then issued an order forbidding certain named persons (the leaders of the hostile demonstration) and "all other persons who are acting or may act in concert with them" from hindering or obstructing the carrying out of the court's judgment. Several persons, including some not specifically named in the injunction, were subsequently found guilty of criminal contempt of court and were sentenced to imprisonment.[17] Though the entire proceeding was in form one between private parties, the Department of Justice was active in identifying those violating the injunction, and in effecting their conviction. Confusion as to the role of the executive branch of the government in the enforcement of an order entered in a proceeding nominally prosecuted by a private party, but in which the public interest is so intimately involved, was evident at the time, and again subsequently in connection with similar desegregation orders elsewhere.[18] The question is complicated by the fact that the federal statutes make it a crime to obstruct or impede "the due administration of justice" by (among

[16] 18 U.S. Code, Sec. 3692. More recently Congress, in authorizing new injunction proceedings, has provided for the right of trial by jury in criminal contempt proceedings for violation of such injunctions. 29 U.S. Code, Sec. 528 (Labor-Management Reporting and Disclosure Act, 1959) and 15 U.S. Code, Sec. 1267 (Hazardous Substances Act, 1960).

[17] The convictions were affirmed in Kasper v. Brittain, 245 F.2d 92 (6th Circ. 1957), certiorari denied 355 U.S. 834 (1957).

[18] In Arkansas the district court itself requested the Department of Justice to seek an injunction against state officers, including the governor, who were threatening to prevent compliance with the court's order to the local school authorities. On the petition of the Attorney General of the United States an injunction was accordingly issued. The contention of the state authorities that the Attorney General had no

other things) threats or force;[19] and the President not only may use federal marshals or other civilian officers to enforce the federal criminal law, but is specifically empowered by statute to use the militia or the armed forces "to suppress, in a State, any . . . domestic violence, unlawful combination, or conspiracy, if it . . . opposes or obstructs the execution of the laws of the United States or impedes the course of justice under those laws."[20] Statutory clarification would be helpful.[21]

Enforcement of injunction or mandatory judgment outside the jurisdiction

In connection with the discussion of the judgment in personam directing the payment of money, it was noted that automatic enforcement is not accorded such a judgment by the courts of other states or countries. The same is true of a judgment granting an injunction, and of a mandatory judgment.

The reasons which may cause a state court to decline to give enforcement to a sister-state judgment of this character (though giving complete recognition to the adjudication of the facts and law there made) may be various. A typical situation may be illustrated by a concrete example. If the plaintiff in an action in New Jersey has obtained a judgment enjoining the defendant from disclosing certain trade secrets obtained by him in plaintiff's employ, the New York courts, in a litigation between the same parties, if no attack is made on the *jurisdiction* of the New Jersey court, will accept as conclusive the finding of the New Jersey court that the defendant obtained the information in question while in the plaintiff's employ, that he agreed not to disclose such information, that he has actually disclosed or is about to disclose such information in breach of the agreement, etc.; but it does not follow that it will issue an injunction, as did the New Jersey court. New matters may have developed since the New Jersey decree was granted which deprive the plaintiff of his right to an injunction; the agreement in question may be regarded by the New York courts as contrary to the public policy of that state; the New York legal doctrines governing the discretion of a court in granting an injunction may be different from those of New Jersey. For these reasons, the "full faith and credit"

---

standing in the case was rejected by the courts. Faubus et al. v. United States et al., 254 F.2d 797 (8th Circ. 1958), certiorari denied 358 U.S. 829 (1958).

[19] 18 U.S. Code, Sec. 1503.

[20] 10 U.S. Code, Sec. 333. In Arkansas, and subsequently in Mississippi, federal armed forces, as well as federal marshals, were employed to prevent interference with the court's order, and to prevent hostile acts against the student plaintiff after the court's order of admission had in fact been obeyed. See Comment: Executive Powers—Use of Troops to Enforce Federal Laws, 56 Mich. Law Rev. 249 (1957).

[21] In situations arising out of school desegregation orders, the proposed legislation giving the government the right to institute actions to compel desegregation would doubtless be sufficient; but a general statute making explicit the power of the government to intervene in actions instituted by private parties, and to use government officers, civilian and military, in such cases, would seem to be desirable.

command of the Constitution is regarded as not having been disobeyed when a court undertakes re-examination of the existing situation before awarding enforcement to a judgment of this character obtained in another state.

5. PREVENTION OF THREATENED WRONG

The injunction (and to a smaller extent the mandatory decree) will be granted by the courts even in cases where the wrong against which relief is sought has not yet been committed, but is merely threatened. Needless to say a very strong showing is required before an injunction will be issued in such a case, but if the evidence is clear, the courts will act. Thus, if plans are filed for the building of a structure of a type forbidden by a covenant among the owners of the land around and including the proposed site, and preparations are under way at the site for the construction work, an injunction will issue even though no violation of the covenant has yet occurred; indeed, were the complainant owner of an adjoining parcel to wait till any substantial amount of construction had been done, his application for an injunction might be rejected because of his dilatoriness (or "laches," to use the conventional term).

6. DECLARATION OF RIGHTS

In not a few cases in which a court is asked to grant redress, or to prevent a threatened wrong, the plaintiff, and perhaps the defendant as well, is interested not primarily in the formal judgment granting redress or enjoining prospective conduct, but rather in the determination by the court of the legal rights of the contending parties. Once that determination has been made by the court adversely to the defendant, the latter, if financially responsible, will abide by it even if it is unaccompanied by any formal judgment compelling such observance. Thus, an action in form for the recovery of a month's rent under a lease may in reality be a contest over the validity of the lease, which may have many years to run. An action to enjoin the alleged infringement of a patent is ordinarily primarily a contest as to the validity of the patent.

These forms of action thus furnish a satisfactory medium for the determination of legal rights when one of the parties has acted, or is about to act, in a manner alleged by the other to be violative of his rights; but they afford no assistance to one against whom no act in violation of his supposed rights has been committed or threatened, but who would like to follow a certain course of action toward another could he be certain in advance that such action is within his legal rights and not, as that other contends, wrongful. To illustrate: A tenant under a long-term lease believes that certain acts of the landlord entitle him to notify the landlord that he elects, under the terms of the lease, to terminate the lease on a certain day specified in the notice. He notifies the landlord of such election, but the landlord, in reply, rejects the notice, alleging that the acts in question do not entitle the tenant to terminate the lease, and warning the tenant that, notwithstanding his purported notice of termination, he will be held responsible for the rent for the remainder of the agreed term of the lease. The tenant, if he vacates the premises, runs the risk that a court may uphold the landlord's contention, and hold the tenant still liable for the rent. Manifestly, the tenant can act safely only if he can procure from a court, in advance of vacating the premises, a determination that he has the right to terminate the lease.

Prior to 1921, a proceeding to obtain such a determination was not maintainable as of right, except in a few special cases. Within recent decades, however, a number of states, following the lead of New York (which in turn had but followed the model of the English statute adopted half a century before), have made the "declaratory judgment," as it is called, available in any appropriate situation. The typical statute empowers the court (usually only a court of general jurisdiction) to declare rights or other legal relations on request for such declaration, whether or not further relief is or could be claimed; and provides that such declaration shall have the force of a final judgment. In 1934 Congress enacted a similar statute applicable to the federal courts.

The action for a declaratory judgment, it is perhaps needless to emphasize, is available only where there is a genuine dispute between the parties, arising out of an existing state of fact. The courts do not permit themselves to be made the forum for litigating, under the guise of seeking an adjudication of an existing dispute, a hypothetical question as to the rights of the parties in a situation which may arise at some future time.

7. DISSOLUTION OF MARRIAGE; AWARD OF SUPPORT TO WIFE LIVING APART FROM HUSBAND

Doubtless every type of remedy available in our civil courts could, by ingenious analysis, be assimilated to one or another of the major categories of judicial relief just discussed. There are, however, a number of proceedings of so distinctive a nature that such a forced classification would be misleading rather than helpful. The number of special remedies devised by courts and legislatures to meet special types of situation tends to increase. In the remaining pages of this chapter, the objectives of some of the more common special proceedings are outlined. Among them, matrimonial actions—divorce, separation, and annulment—call for extended consideration.

Marriage and adoption represent perhaps the only cases of voluntary assumption of a legal relationship which cannot thereafter be terminated, even by common consent of both parties, without the aid of a court.

In the action for divorce, the plaintiff seeks a dissolution of the marriage bond—an adjudication which will free him or her from all further obligation to the defendant arising out of the marriage relation, and will permit him or her to remarry. The effect of such adjudication on the defendant will be to deprive him or her of all rights against the plaintiff arising out of the marriage relation; but it will not necessarily permit the defendant to remarry, the laws of the several states generally providing for a prohibition against remarriage by the defendant for a limited period or without the permission of the court. Moreover, the obligation of a defendant husband to support the divorced wife until she remarries may survive the decree of divorce.

Every action for divorce seeks primarily a judgment dissolving the marriage bond; and in many cases, particularly those in which the action is instituted by common consent, the judgment contains no additional provisions. However, where the wife is the plaintiff, the judgment (or "decree," as it is commonly termed) often also contains provision for her continued support by the defendant until she remarries. It may also award custody of the children of the marriage; and if custody is awarded to the wife, it makes provision for payment to her for their support. The order for periodical payments to the wife, or "alimony," is one directed to the husband, enforceable like other judgments in personam by commitment to jail until compliance is forthcoming. A change in the circumstances of the former husband may entitle him to have the amount of the alimony reduced; and he may apply to the court for such reduction. Should he fail to do so he is regarded as still able to pay the amount originally fixed, and may be committed for non-payment. In many cases, however, his commitment will further impair his ability to make the payments ordered. The resulting impasse, injurious equally to the wife, has resulted in some states in legislation limiting, in this situation, the period for which the delinquent may be imprisoned, thus effecting a compromise between the necessity, on the one hand, of punishing him for disobedience of the court's order and, on the other, of restoring his earning power.

As with other judgments in personam, the amount due may be sued for in the ordinary form of action for a money judgment; and this course is particularly useful where the husband is outside the jurisdiction in which the alimony judgment was made, and therefore not available for commitment for non-payment, but has property within the jurisdiction, available for levy under a judgment for arrears of alimony.

The reluctance of our state courts to grant automatic enforcement to a judgment in personam issued by the courts of a sister state has already been mentioned; and this reluctance is marked in the case of judgments for alimony.[22] The position thus taken by the courts of a number of states inflicts especial hardship on the divorced wife, who is thus remitted, in another state to which the husband may have migrated, to periodical actions for arrears only.[23] A federal statute making an alimony decree obtained in any state enforceable as such in every state (assuming that Congress has the power under the full faith and credit clause to enact such a statute) would represent a distinct improvement in the situation.

The object of the plaintiff husband in instituting an action for divorce may be solely to obtain a dissolution of the marriage, giving him freedom to remarry, without in any way impairing the defendant's wife's rights as to the custody of the children of the marriage, her rights as to the plaintiff's property which the marriage relation may give, or her right to continued support. He may obtain this objective, if the wife refuses to consent, by instituting action in another state, in which the wife does not reside, and in which he has set up a real or pretended residence, hoping that his wife will not defend the action. If she does not defend, he will obtain a divorce decree which purports to dissolve the marriage, but has no effect on any of the wife's rights above mentioned. A like course is open to the wife who wishes to divorce an unwilling husband.

This form of "divisible" divorce has come into existence only since the landmark case of Williams v. North Carolina, decided by the Supreme Court in 1942, in which, overruling previous holdings of long standing, the Court announced that a state may grant a divorce to one of its own residents even though the defendant is not a resident of the state and perhaps never set foot within its borders. The circumstances under which such a default decree against a non-resident defendant may, if attacked by the defendant, be set aside in the state which granted it, and refused recognition in other states, will be discussed in a subsequent chapter.

The action for the annulment of a marriage, though in theory the judgment is a declaration that the marriage has in a legal sense never existed, may also present problems relative to the continued support of the wife and the custody of the children. The problem of jurisdiction, as related to the obligation of a state to enforce the judgment of a sister state, is potentially almost as perplexing with respect to the judgment of annulment as in the case of the judgment of divorce; but the rarity of the annulment action has given little occasion for the examination of those problems by the courts.

[22] A special reason advanced by some courts for declining to give enforcement in personam to sister-state alimony judgments is that such a judgment is not on its face final, being always subject to revision by the court which grants it. It would, however, obviously be open to a husband, against whom the original judgment were sought to be enforced, to counter by exhibiting a revised form of the judgment.

[23] If, however, the wife has obtained a "support order" in her own state, she may be able thereby to procure a like order in the state in which her husband now lives. See p. 179.

The decree granted in an action for separation does not dissolve the marriage bond and affects only the wife's right to support. If obtained by the wife it entitles her to the continuance of such support though living apart from her husband. A decree of separation obtained by the husband relieves him from the obligation for his wife's support so long as they continue to live apart. In either case, custody of the children may be awarded.[24]

8. OTHER SPECIAL TYPES OF REMEDY

Adjudication of incompetency

It is the province of the courts to pass upon an application made to them to declare a person mentally incompetent to conduct his own affairs and to place his property and income under the management of a person appointed by the court. In some states the involuntary commitment to a hospital of a person alleged to be mentally ill also requires a court order; but in other states such commitment is possible merely by medical certificate. The problem of devising a procedure which takes account both of the necessity for prompt institutionalization of the mental patient acutely ill and of the rights of the person resisting hospitalization, of whom the psychiatrist can perhaps only say that he would be benefited by institutional care, is a difficult one, to which latterly much attention has been given.[25] In all states, the person confined in a mental institution may seek his release by habeas corpus proceedings—a remedy of limited practical value, however, unless special measures are taken to assist the patient seeking it.

Admission of will to probate

The admission of a will to probate, i.e., the adjudication that a paper offered (or, as is sometimes said, "propounded") as the last will of a deceased person was in fact executed by him, with the formalities required by the law, while possessed of testamentary capacity, and with the intention that it govern the disposition of his property, is ordinarily a

[24] In California, the courts dealing with matrimonial actions are empowered to hold a hearing for the purpose of attempting to reconcile the estranged spouses, and thereupon to "make such orders in respect to the conduct of the spouses . . . . as the court deems necessary to preserve the marriage or to implement the reconciliation of the spouses." It is also provided that "any reconciliation agreement between the parties may be reduced to writing and with the consent of the parties a court order may be made requiring the parties to comply fully therewith." For an account of the way in which this seemingly unique form of legal proceeding is conducted see Burke, An Instrument of peace: the Conciliation Court in Los Angeles, 42 Amer. Bar Assn. Jour. 621 (1956).

[25] 1952 Report, Amer. Bar. Assn., 157, 318; Lindeman and McIntyre (ed.), The Mentally Disabled and the Law (1961); Mental Illness and Due Process, Report of the special committee to study committment procedures, Association of the Bar of the City of New York (1962).

routine proceeding, requiring of the court having jurisdiction of the proceeding nothing more than surveillance to make sure that the statutory requirements as to notice, publication, etc., have ben observed. Only if objections are interposed (by those who would inherit if the deceased were held to have.left no will, or if a former purported will were instead held to be his last will) does the matter come before the court for trial.

Supervision of management of estates and of persons not sui juris

The activities of the courts in the field of private affairs thus far reviewed have concerned the adjudication of disputes. We turn now to those of their activities which might properly be called administrative, for they involve in most cases no judicial function. Indeed, their actual performance is for the most part delegated, in the daily work of the courts, to its clerical and administrative personnel, the judge himself having little or no part therein. Of these activities, the major part is concerned with the administration of fiduciary estates.

The estates of deceased persons, of incompetents, and of insolvents are administered, under our law, by persons appointed or approved by the courts and responsible to the courts for their conduct of the estate's affairs. So, too, with the estate of an infant which has come to him by inheritance, by court award, or the like.

The supervision exercised by the courts over these persons (and in addition over trustees appointed without court proceedings, as by trust instruments or by will) normally takes the form of (1) passing upon requests of the fiduciary (for so we may broadly term all the persons who hold title to property for the benefit of others) for permission to take some action with respect to the property not within his routine authority, and (2) passing upon the propriety of his past transactions. This latter function is exercised chiefly in connection with the presentation by the fiduciary of his "account" for the approval of the court. Notice of this application is given to the persons for whose benefit the fiduciary has held the property —the creditors, heirs, legatees, wards, beneficiaries, etc., as the case may be—and if any of them objects to the approval of any particular item of the account, the court passes on its propriety. Such a determination by the court may involve not merely a ruling that a particular disbursement made by the fiduciary was improper, and is not to be credited to his account, but even that a particular receipt was not as great as it would have been had the fiduciary exercised proper care and skill, and that the fiduciary is therefore to be charged with an additional sum ("surcharged" is the usual term) representing the difference between what he should have obtained and what he actually received. If, as in the case of the committee of an incompetent, he has the power to make investments, he may also be charged with losses suffered by the estate on such investments, if such losses resulted from a lack of due care and skill in making such investments, or in failing to dispose of them at the appropriate time.

A further form of supervision by the courts over fiduciaries appears in connection with an application made by a creditor or a beneficiary of the fiduciary estate for the removal of the fiduciary on the ground of misconduct.

In addition to the supervision exercised by the courts over fiduciaries, court approval is required under the laws of some of the states in particular transactions involving the property or services of infants. Under ancient doctrines prevailing everywhere in the United States, an infant may not make a binding contract; but statutes have created certain exceptions, in some cases dependent on court approval. Thus, in most states, an infant may, with court approval, sell or otherwise convey real estate which he owns. In a few, he may, with court approval, make a binding agreement to render personal services, the court, as a condition to such approval, prescribing means for safeguarding the income to be received by the infant.

Control of affairs of insolvent or embarrassed debtor

Under the federal Bankruptcy Act, a debtor may himself ask the court to adjudicate him bankrupt, to take custody of his property, to liquidate it and distribute the proceeds ratably among his creditors, and to discharge him from further liability to them.[26] Such an application is known as a "voluntary petition in bankruptcy." Contrariwise, the application for such an adjudication may originate with the creditors ("involuntary petition").

The Bankruptcy Act provides not merely for liquidation of the embarrassed debtor's property but, in the alternative, for its preservation and continued operation under the protection of the court during a limited period (all hostile proceedings being meanwhile suspended) while the debtor and his creditors may attempt a reorganization of the debtor's affairs and a readjustment of his indebtedness. Whether the debtor's situation justifies such a moratorium may be a matter of dispute between the debtor and the creditors, or between contending groups of creditors. The adjudication of such a dispute is also in the province of the court.

Under any of several provisions of the Bankruptcy Act, as already indicated, the debtor's property, instead of being liquidated, may be operated under the supervision of the court while a readjustment of the creditors' rights (in the form of a scaling down of the principal, a reduction

[26] The enactment of the Bankruptcy Act in 1898 had the effect of suspending the operation of all state insolvency statutes which were inconsistent with it. However, a state insolvency proceeding in which no discharge of the insolvent from his debts is sought is not regarded as inconsistent with the federal act; and such proceedings continue to be employed to a limited extent.

of the rate of interest, an extension of maturity dates, a release or subordination of liens, etc.) is arranged. A feature common to the several different types of provision found in the act is the necessity for the consent of a stated majority of the creditors. Where, as may be the case with an embarrassed corporation, the creditors fall into distinct classes (e.g., debenture holders, mortgage bond holders, etc.), a stated majority of each class must consent. Here, although the approval of the court is also required, such approval is likely to be more or less perfunctory where there is no serious disagreement among the creditors.

In the event of such a disagreement, however, the court may, despite the approval of the requisite majority of the creditors, disapprove a proposed plan if it seems unfair to the dissenting minority. Under the provisions governing the most important and generally the most complicated of the proceedings of this type, the proceedings for the reorganization of a financially embarrassed corporation, it is moreover provided that, if the requisite majority of the creditors, or of a particular class thereof, cannot be secured, the court may in its own discretion, impose such readjustment of the indebtedness as seems proper.

Manifestly, in exercising such discretion, a judge is required to journey much beyond the ordinary field of judicial determination, into an area in which there can be few rules, not to speak of rules of law, to guide him. It is not surprising that this power has been very sparingly exercised by the courts, the judges ordinarily presenting the interested parties, if unable to agree, with the alternative of liquidation, with attendant losses. That the function imposed on the courts in these cases is not in the traditional sense judicial is further indicated by the statutory provisions for the participation of the Interstate Commerce Commission in proceedings for the reorganization of railroad corporations and for the participation of the Securities and Exchange Commission in proceedings for the reorganization of non-railroad corporations having an indebtedness in excess of $3 million.

Partition of property held jointly; dissolution of corporations and partnerships

Where two persons own property jointly (other than as partners) neither can dispose of the property without the consent of the other; either can dispose only of his own interest in the property. The like is true where the number of co-owners exceeds two; and the right to veto a sale is enjoyed by each of the co-owners, no matter how numerous they are nor how small the interest of the dissenter.

In these situations, if real property is involved, the aid of the courts may be invoked to end the deadlock. On proper application the court will order a sale of the real property at auction, and a distribution of the proceeds among the several co-owners in proportion to their interests, account being taken of any proper disbursements made by any of the co-owners on behalf of the property. Any dispute between them on any of these matters will be incidentally adjudicated by the court. Such a proceeding is known as one for "partition."

More rarely, the court will be asked by all the co-owners of real estate physically to apportion the real estate among them in proportion to their interests, they themselves having been unable to agree either on a physical partition, or on a sale.

Analogous to the judicial sale of real property jointly held is the judicial dissolution of a corporation where opposing groups of stockholders, being equally divided in voting power, are deadlocked and unable to elect directors to carry on the enterprise. Under the corporation statutes of most states, the courts will, on application, order a liquidation of the corporation and a ratable distribution of the proceeds among the stockholders.

Similar also is the judicial dissolution of a partnership for cause, on the application of some but not all the partners, before the expiration of its agreed term.

Forfeiture of property used for illegal purposes

Reference has already been made to the use of the civil proceeding, instituted by a public officer, for law-enforcement purposes—as in the case of the civil action for a penalty. Still another type of civil proceeding in this category is the forfeiture proceeding, in which the court is asked to declare forfeited to the state property which is per se unlawful (e.g., plates used for counterfeiting currency), or which was used for illegal purposes (e.g., nets or traps set in violation of law), or possession of which was acquired without compliance with the law (e.g., smuggled merchandise). Such a proceeding is ordinarily "in rem"; i.e., the judgment sought is directed not against the owner or person in possession of the property in question (though if known he is given opportunity to contest the proposed forfeiture) but against the property itself (the "res").[27]

Control of election of officers of private associations; reinstatement of members expelled or suspended

Disputes in private associations as to the regularity of elections, eligibility of officers elected, and the like not infrequently come before the courts for adjudication. In the case of corporations, whether business corporations or corporations with philanthropic, cultural, religious, or other non-business purposes, there are generally found statutes regulating such elections to a certain extent, and conferring upon the courts express powers

---

[27] By contrast an action for a money judgment is said to be a personal one, even though the judgment itself can be enforced only in rem; for the judgment runs not against a particular piece of property but against the judgment debtor, and is enforceable against any of his property, present or future.

to intervene, upon the application of an interested party, in a disputed election, with a view to declaring invalid the results of an election found to have been irregular, and ordering a new election, perhaps under the supervision of inspectors appointed by the court. In the case of unincorporated associations, statutory provisions are usually nonexistent, and such judicial intervention as is found is based upon general rules developed by the courts over the years.

One of these rules relates to organizations in which a local unit, with its own elected officers, is nevertheless a part of a larger organization having a central board of directors and officers, with perhaps also intermediate regional boards and officers—the latter feature being not infrequently found in the larger religious bodies and labor organizations. The constitutions of these associations usually provide that appeal from the ruling of local officers or governing bodies may be taken to the national officers or governing body, appeal to the intermediate regional body being perhaps required as a prerequisite to appeal to the national body. Under these circumstances, one seeking to set aside the results of an election announced by a local body may be confronted with a delay of many months, which may even stretch out to a matter of a year or more if the final authority is declared to be, as it is in not a few religious and labor organizations, the annual, or even biennial, central convention of the organization. Notwithstanding the ineffectiveness of a procedure so dilatory, the courts have in many cases adhered to the rule that they will not intervene in the internal affairs of a private association until the person seeking the aid of the court has exhausted all the remedies open to him within the organization itself.

The adherence of the courts to this rule has undoubtedly discouraged attempts on the part of insurgent groups in officer-dominated labor union locals to upset the entrenched regime. The situation has been radically improved however (except as to that small proportion of unions whose members are employed by concerns not engaged in an industry affecting interstate or foreign commerce) by the enactment in 1959 of the federal Labor-Managment Reporting and Disclosure Act (commonly known as the Landrum-Griffin Act).[28] This act not only regulates the terms of office of union officials and the procedures for their selection, but it authorizes any member of a union who has complained of a breach of the election regulations to his union and has not obtained correction to complain, under certain limitations set forth in the act, to the Secretary of Labor, who may then bring a civil action in the federal courts to void the election.

Aside from the election of officers, the expulsion or suspension of a member or his disqualification for office doubtless furnishes the most frequent occasion for appeal to the courts for redress against the action of a private association. Here, too, the rule requiring the complainant first to

[28] 29 U.S. Code, Sec. 402

exhaust all his remedies within the organization has generally been applied by the courts.

Proceeding to compel support of dependent

The power of the courts to award alimony to the wife as an incident to the judgment in a matrimonial action has already been mentioned. In some states an independent action for support of herself and her children may be brought by a divorced wife to whom alimony was not awarded in the divorce proceedings.[29] More important numerically, however, than either of these types of judgment for support, rendered by courts of superior jurisdiction, is the support order issued by a court in summary proceedings at the instance of the wife or, in a case in which the wife or children (including adult children) are likely tot become public charges, by the welfare authorities.

Such a support order, though often issued by a court of minor jurisdiction, is enforceable, like the judgment in personam, by punishment for disobedience. Since, however, neither fine nor imprisonment of the breadwinner would be of any assistance to his needy family, punishment is rarely inflicted. Instead the delinquent is usually placed on probation for a stated period, the condition of his probation being that he shall while on probation pay periodically through the probation officials a sum, fixed by the court as reasonable, for the support of his wife or children. In the event of default in such payment, his probation may be revoked and he may be sentenced to imprisonment. The posting of security as a condition to suspension of sentence is also common. These procedures have on the whole been found quite effective.

A serious obstacle to their effectiveness, however, is the departure of the husband from the state or even from the country—an occurrence so frequent as to have necessitated the creation, some year ago, by the nation's local social agencies, of a national bureau for tracing deserting husbands. To deal with this problem the states have all in the last two decades enacted reciprocal legislation, nearly all of them adopting the Uniform Reciprocal Enforcement of Support Act drafted by the Conference of Commissioners on Uniform Laws. Under the reciprocal arrangement, the court in which the support proceeding has been filed on behalf of the wife or child enlists the cooperation of the appropriate court of the state in which the husband (or father) is found. Evidence taken in either court is made available to the other, and the court having jurisdiction of the respondent issues a support order against him if the evidence warrants. Under the support order, the defendant is normally required to pay into that court for re-

[29] In some states the courts have held that even in the absence of statutory authorization they may entertain an action by a wife solely for support, neither divorce nor separation being sought.

mittance to the wife the periodical payments ordered; if he defaults, the court, through its probation or cognate machinery, will promptly pursue him.

This ingenious cooperative arrangement, between the courts of the state in which the proceeding is initiated and the courts of the state which has jurisdiction of the defendant, has for us an interest much beyond the support proceeding. Its pattern of cooperation might well be applied to other types of situation in our legal system in which justice is hindered by the inability of the courts of the plaintiff's state to exercise jurisdiction over the desired defendant and the unsuitability of the courts of the defendant's state for the proceeding as a whole.

In the foregoing, discussion has been limited to proceedings against the husband or father only. The statutes of many of the states apply equally to the mother who fails to support her child and to the wife who, though financially able, fails under certain circumstances to support her husband. Proceedings against the mother or wife under these statutes, while authorized, are comparatively rare. In some states, provision is made for a proceeding against the delinquent mother or wife for a support order, failure of compliance with which results not in punishment, but in a civil proceeding against her property, to be brought by the authorities responsible for public charges. Similar proceedings are also found for enforcing the responsibilities for support which, in varying degree under the laws of the several states, are placed upon children, grandchildren, and grandparents.[30]

Although attention has here been given only to the process of formal adjudication, there is commonly found in the larger urban centers, where the adjudication of support proceedings has increasingly tended to be concentrated in the hands of specialized courts or court divisions, a considerable extrajudicial apparatus working in cooperation with the presiding judicial officer—social workers and psychiatrists (whether public employees or in the employ of private organizations) and in at least one city an official bureau (the head of which bears the novel title of Friend of the Court) —and having the function of attempting to rebuild the broken home which is often the occasion for support proceedings.

Closely related to the support proceeding instituted by the public authorities is the proceeding in which they seek from the court an order confiding the custody of a destitute or neglected child to an appropriate child-caring institution.

[30] In addition to the civil proceeding for a support order, the statutes of all the states provide some form of criminal proceeding as well; but the criminal proceeding, like the civil, is employed as a means of compelling future support rather than of punishing past non-support. The existence of the criminal statute makes it possible moreover to threaten with extradition the delinquent husband or father who has left the state. The Uniform Reciprocal Enforcement of Support Act (Sec. 6) provides that if the out-of-state defendant submits to the jurisdiction of the court there, and complies with its order of support, he shall be relieved of extradition on a charge of desertion or non-support in the state in which his dependents are.

9. PROPOSED ADJUDICATION OF LABOR "DISPUTES"

From time to time proposals are made that the courts be invested with power to grant a new type of remedy—the adjudication of labor disputes. Sometimes the proposal is that existing courts be invested with this power. Other proposals call for the constitution of special courts for this purpose. Whether the proposal takes the one or the other form, however, the underlying concept is the same—that we are dealing here with a species of adjudication cognate to that involved in other types of judicial proceeding.[31]

Quite obviously, however, there is no analogy between the types of dispute now adjudicated by the courts, and the type of labor "dispute" which these proposals envisage. A justiciable dispute is one in which the court, having found the facts, applies to them the appropriate rules of law which define the rights of the parties. In so far as disputes relative to their respective legal rights may arise between employers and unions, the courts (or in the field of unlawful labor practices, the special administrative tribunals which have been created by statute) already have power to adjudicate.[32] But the labor "disputes" to which the further extension of the judicial process is sought are not controversies over legal rights at all. Neither party is asserting any legal claim against the other. The dispute is a mere tug of war, resorted to because the parties cannot reach an agreement. Whether, under such circumstances, the state should step in and make their agreement for them is a political question beyond the scope of this volume. Were that question once decided in the affirmative, the question would arise whether the courts would be the appropriate state agency for thus fixing the terms of private employment. This obviously is a question so remote as hardly to justify discussion. What is essential here is to recognize that such a function would be totally foreign to the present function of the courts. They would be engaged not in adjudication but in economic legislation.

10. CIVIL PROCEEDINGS INSTITUTED BY LAW-ENFORCEMENT OFFICERS

In the foregoing account of the objectives of the civil proceeding, chief attention has been given to the use of that proceeding for adjudicating disputes—decisively its most frequent use. But one cannot overemphasize

[31] See, for example, Knox, Labor and the Law, 62 Amer. Mercury 670 (1946) and Gerhart, Labor Disputes: Their Settlement by Judicial Process, 32 Amer. Bar Assn. Jour. 752, 801 (1946).

[32] The erroneous impression frequently encountered that labor union contracts are not enforceable in the courts equally with other contracts is doubtless due to the procedural difficulties encountered in some states in bringing before the courts any unincorporated association having a large membership. See p. 232.

the importance of the civil proceeding also as an instrument of law enforcement, complementing the criminal proceeding for that purpose. The proceeding instituted by a public official for a penalty, for the forfeiture of property used for illegal purposes, for an injunction either prohibitory and mandatory, or for a declaratory judgment all play a vital role in law enforcement.

The injunction proceeding cannot be said to have yet established itself as a conventional instrument of law enforcement, even though it has obvious advantages in singling out the chronic offender and putting him, so to speak, under the surveillance of the court. Its limited use in both state and federal law enforcement is in sharp contrast to its use, in altered guise—the so-called cease and desist order—in the enforcement of those statutes in which the enforcement proceeding is initiated before an administrative rather than a judicial tribunal, a matter considered in a later chapter. Perhaps the most important instance of its use is in the enforcement of the federal antitrust laws. Those laws permit the government to prosecute violations criminally, and also to seek an injunction to prevent future violations. The far-reaching character of the decrees issued in some suits of this kind has already been mentioned.

A suit of this nature under the antitrust laws may be regarded as having for its essential purpose the conversion of the prohibitions of the statute, expressed in broad general terms, into a set of specific prohibitions and directions applicable to the particular defendant before the court. Once these specific prohibitions have been laid down, that defendant is exposed to the risk of bringing down on himself not only the civil and criminal liabilities with which the statute threatens all violators, but also the penalties for disobeying a decree of the court.

This method of enforcement has also, however, been specifically provided for in a statute in which, in contrast to the antitrust statutes, the prohibited acts are defined with complete precision by the statute itself. This is the Fair Labor Standards Act of 1938 (often referred to as the Wages and Hours Act).[33] That statute (in addition to giving the employee a right of action for double the amount of the underpayment of his wages) provides criminal penalties for its violation; but it also empowers the officer charged with its administration to seek an injunction against prospective violations; and the Supreme Court has approved the enforcement by contempt proceedings of sweeping injunctions under this provision.[34] If the statute

[33] 29 U.S. Code, Secs. 201 ff.

[34] McComb v. Jacksonville Paper Co., 336 U.S. 187 (1949). The court had required the defendant, in order to purge itself of the contempt committed by its violation of the injunction, to pay to certain employees "damages" equal to the amount of additional wages they would have been entitled to had the defendant complied with the injunction. The two dissenting justices pointed out that the injunction had not prohibited specific acts, but had merely in general terms forbidden violation of the law; consequently, the injunction, and the ensuing contempt proceedings, were in

makes a particular act criminally punishable (as the statute does in several of its provisions), and the injunction prohibits the identical act, the act apparently could be punished as a criminal contempt of court by the judge sitting without a jury, whereas the criminal prosecution provided for by the statute would entitle the offender to trial by jury.[35] The constitutional issue thus posed has not apparently come before the courts.

The use of the civil rather than the criminal proceeding for law enforcement gives to the legal officer responsible for initiating the proceedings much of the same discretionary power as the public prosecutor was found to have in the field of criminal law enforcement. A striking instance of this discretionary power is found in the field of antitrust law enforcement. It has become the accepted practice in advance of industrial mergers or major acquisitions for advice to be sought from and given by the Department of Justice as to whether the department, should the contemplated action be taken, would consider it necessary to move to undo the transaction as violative of the antitrust law.

The use of the injunction as a means of law enforcement was sanctioned by Congress, after a prolonged struggle, in the act of 1957 designed to prevent the denial of voting rights to Negroes by state election officials.[36] The Attorney General is moreover empowered by an amendment of 1960 to institute action in a federal district court to establish that there exists in a given voting registration district a pattern of denial of voting registration on racial grounds. If the court finds such pattern to exist, it may appoint a referee with power to certify, for one establishing that he has been denied registration because of his race, that the applicant is entitled to register; and the state registration official is required to honor such certificate.

There being as yet no federal statute designed to implement the 1954 decision of the Supreme Court declaring state school segregation laws unconstitutional, no federal law-enforcement agency is empowered to institute a suit for an injunction to prevent observance of such laws by state officials. The vesting of the executive with power to institute such suits would undoubtedly greatly increase their number, as they have up to this time been brought exclusively by the Negro students affected, or by their parents.

---

effect being substituted for the enforcement proceedings provided by the statute, in which the defendant would have been entitled to trial by jury.

[35] In a criminal contempt proceeding in the federal courts the defendant, even if he would be entitled to jury trial had the order which he disobeyed been issued in an action instituted by a private party, is not entitled to jury trial where the action was instituted by the government. See p. 166.

[36] 42 U.S. Code, Sec. 1971.

6

Civil Proceedings: Jurisdiction

1. CASES BROUGHT ONLY IN THE FEDERAL COURTS BECAUSE OF SUBJECT MATTER. 2. CASES BROUGHT ONLY IN THE FEDERAL COURTS BECAUSE OF THE PARTIES. 3. CASES BROUGHT IN EITHER THE STATE OR THE FEDERAL COURTS. 4. CASES BROUGHT ONLY IN THE STATE COURTS. 5. STATE IN WHICH ACTION MAY BE BROUGHT. 6. COURT IN WHICH ACTION MAY BE BROUGHT. 7. VENUE.

In the early days of some of the colonies, a single tribunal, usually the governor and his council, exercised all judicial power in the colony. Hence, the question whether the tribunal had jurisdiction in a case could hardly arise. The American lawyer of today, confronted with a multiplicity of tribunals far exceeding that found in any other country, meets jurisdictional problems at every turn. Putting to one side the question whether a particular type of relief can be given by the courts at all, he is aware that some civil proceedings must be brought only in the state courts, others only in the federal courts, and that still others may be brought in either the state or the federal courts. A proposed state court proceeding may be brought in one state but not in another. Within a given state, the proposed proceeding may be brought in one court and not in another, and in one place and not in another. An outline of the governing doctrines, necessarily condensed to the utmost, is indispensable in view of the crucial importance of the matter, one aspect of which has already been touched on in connection with the discussion, in the preceding chapter, of the enforceability of a judgment outside the jurisdiction in which it was obtained.

1. CASES BROUGHT ONLY IN THE FEDERAL COURTS BECAUSE OF SUBJECT MATTER

As already noted, the Constitution, in enumerating the classes of cases and controversies to which "the judicial power of the United States shall extend," identifies some by their subject matter and some by the character of the parties to the controversy.

Only two classes of cases are identified by their subject matter: (1) "all cases . . . arising under this constitution, the laws of the United States and treaties made . . . under their authority," and (2) "all cases of admiralty and maritime jurisdiction."[1]

Cases arising under the Constitution or under federal laws or treaties

A case "arising under" the Constitution, or under a federal law or treaty, is one in which there is necessarily involved, and must necessarily be decided to dispose of the case, a question of the construction of any provision of the Constitution or of a federal law or treaty. Such a question may be presented at the very institution of the action, by a claim asserted by the plaintiff allegedly under authority of some provision of federal law, whether in the Constitution, a statute, or a treaty. It may be presented for the first time by the answer which the defendant interposes to the plaintiff's claim; or it may arise at any subsequent point in the litigation. At however early or late a point the federal question is presented or arises, the case thereupon becomes a case "arising under" federal law, and is thus within "the judicial power of the United States"; and Congress may place it within the jurisdiction of a federal court. We are here concerned, however, only with those cases in which the question of federal law is presented at the very outset of the action, in the plaintiff's claim.

For simplicity it has been said that a case "arises" under federal law only if there is involved the construction of a federal enactment—whether the Constitution, a statute, or a treaty; and such was indeed the unquestioned understanding until 1957. In that year, however, the Supreme Court declared otherwise. Congress had in 1947 vested the federal courts with jurisdiction of suits for violation of a contract between an employer and a labor organization (in an industry affecting interstate or foreign commerce).[2] Since there was not at that time (as there still is not) any federal statute regulating such contracts, they were governed by state law. The constitutionality of the attempt to place suits for violation of such contracts within the jurisdiction of the federal courts was accordingly regarded as extremely doubtful by some commentators, and by some members of the Court as well. The Court, however, held the statute constitutional, its intent being, in the Court's view, that the federal courts shall develop a

[1] An additional class of cases is in form identified by subject matter; but it is in reality a special case of the class of "controversies between two or more states." This is the class of "controversies . . . between citizens of the same state claiming lands under grants of different states. . . ." Such a controversy is in effect a boundary dispute between the granting states, even though it takes the form of an action between private parties.

[2] 29 U.S. Code, Sec. 185.

body of federal doctrine in this field, superseding state statute or doctrine, with the consequence that a suit of this nature is one "arising under the laws of the United States."[3] This declaration that Congress may supersede state regulation in any field within the federal legislative power without enacting a federal statute, but merely by vesting the federal courts with jurisdiction of suits concerned with that field of law, and leaving the initial construction of the superseding federal law to the unguided efforts of the three hundred or so federal district judges, obviously opens vast possibilities. Fortunately, Congress has not up to this time taken further advantage of them.

Except for the class of suits just mentioned, therefore, if the plaintiff's claim is founded on federal law, it must be on some provision of Constitution, treaty, or statute—nearly always, needless to say, on a provision of statute. In enacting statutes creating federal rights of action, however, Congress has not in all cases vested jurisdiction of the action exclusively in the federal courts; in some cases it has provided that action may be brought in the state court if the plaintiff chooses. For the most part, however, where Congress has created by statute a right to sue, it has given the federal courts exclusive jurisdiction of the suit. Such is the case, for example, with the right of the owner of a copyright or a patent, granted under federal statute, to sue to enjoin the infringement thereof; or the right of one claiming to have been injured by a conspiracy in restraint of trade violative of the federal antitrust laws to sue for triple damages, or for an injunction.

As already mentioned, a statute, in addition to or instead of providing criminal penalties, may authorize the institution of a civil suit by the authorities for its enforcement. Illustrative of this is the action for an injunction to restrain activities in alleged restraint of trade in violation of the federal antitrust laws, or, to cite a newer statute, an action to restrain a secondary boycott carried on in alleged violation of the Taft-Hartley Act. An ancient form of civil action by the public authorities for the enforcement of a statute is the civil action for a penalty; and this too is found in a number of federal statutes. Actions by the government to enforce statutes are now brought exclusively in the federal courts, although actions in the state courts have in some instances been authorized by Congress, and employed.

In addition to the private rights of action expressly created by particular federal statutes, a private right of action within the federal judicial power may flow directly from the Constitution. The Constitution does not, of course, in express terms create any right of action; but the statutes confer upon the federal courts jurisdiction of any case "arising under" the Constitution (where the "matter in controversy" exceeds $10,000). With the aid of this provision the Constitution itself creates the right to bring

[3] Textile Workers Union v. Lincoln Mills, 335 U.S. 446 (1957).

action in the federal courts to enjoin the enforcement or execution of a federal statute (or treaty provision) challenged as unauthorized or prohibited by the Constitution. Such is the established doctrine of our constitutional law, now expressly recognized by statutory provisions regulating this type of action.

The assertion by the Supreme Court of its power, and inferentially that of any other court, to decline to enforce or apply a statute of Congress which it regards as unconstitutional was first made in 1803, in the case of Marbury v. Madison. The nature of that case, as well as the acquiescence of Congress and the nation in the exercise of the power thus asserted will be discussed in subsequent pages.[4] From the doctrine that the courts might refuse recognition to an unconstitutional federal statute it was but a step to the assertion that the federal courts might enjoin in advance any attempt on the part of a federal official (other than the President, who, as the head of the government, is regarded as immune from the process of the courts) to enforce the statute.[5] The power of the federal courts to issue such an injunction was long asserted without any express statutory provision therefor. In 1937, after the power had been repeatedly asserted (though in many instances the issuance of the injunction sought was refused) Congress gave statutory recognition to its exercise by the provision that an "injunction restraining the enforcement, operation or execution of any Act of Congress for repugnance to the Constitution of the United States shall not be granted by any district court or judge thereof unless the application therefor is heard and determined by a district court of three judges. . . ."[6]

The damage to the person seeking the injunction must be direct. It may well be, as he alleges, that Congress has appropriated money for a purpose not within its constitutional powers, and that a federal officer, pursuant to such unconstitutional statute, is about to disburse federal funds; yet this proposed disbursement does not threaten him with such direct damage, notwithstanding that he is a federal taxpayer, as to entitle him to maintain an action to enjoin disbursement. Such is the established federal doctrine; and since there is no other form of proceeding in which the constitution-

[4] See pp. 323 ff.

[5] A similar power exists as to injunctions to prohibit enforcement of state statutes repugnant to the Constitution or to federal statutory or treaty provisions; but as this power is also possessed by state courts, it is discussed in the section of this chapter dealing with cases which may be brought in either state or federal courts.

[6] 28 U.S. Code, Sec. 2282. Congress had, however, at an early date (1867) provided that no injunction be issued to enjoin the enforcement of a federal revenue statute. It was because of this restriction that the famous case in which the income tax law of 1892 was declared unconstitutional (Pollock v. Farmers' Loan & Trust Co., 158 U.S. 601) took the form of an action to enjoin a corporation, of which the plaintiff was a stockholder, from paying to the government, pursuant to the provisions of the income tax law, a certain portion of the dividends payable to him by the corporation.

ality of a federal appropriation act may be challenged by the citizen, the practical result is to make impossible judicial review of the constitutionality of such an act.[7]

Maritime cases

The most immediate and important effect of the Judiciary Act of 1789 upon the existing jurisdiction of the state courts was to strip from them, and to vest exclusively in the federal courts, jurisdiction over all future cases of "admiralty and maritime jurisdiction." This exclusive jurisdiction the federal courts have ever since retained.

The phrase "cases of admiralty and maritime jurisdiction" used in the Constitution indicates that what is referred to is not merely a class of cases having a distinctive subject matter but a class of cases recognized as forming a separate branch of *court jurisdiction*. The explanation is that, in the development of the English legal system, cases arising out of ocean navigation had in fact come to be adjudicated by a separate civil court known as the admiralty court, following a procedure and applying a body of legal doctrine quite distinct, and in some respects markedly different, from the procedure and doctrine of the other civil courts of England. This procedure and doctrine had been employed also by the regional admiralty courts established by the crown for the colonies; and with the disappearance of those courts on the breakdown of British authority, the state courts to which their jurisdiction passed continued to follow the same distinctive procedure and to apply the same distinctive body of doctrine.

The recognition of cases arising out of navigation and marine transportation as not merely governed by a separate body of rules of law but as constituting a separate category of jurisdiction is very ancient. To go no further back than the medieval maritime centers of the Mediterranean, we find there the development of special courts for the settlement of disputes among merchants, whether commercial or maritime in character (virtually all commerce being at that period closely bound up with navigation). In France and in the countries of the Continent bordering the North Sea and the Baltic Sea, the more marked separation of inland from ocean trade tended to bring about special courts in the seaports, concerned primarily with maritime disputes, though not wholly confined thereto; and this was the pattern followed in the ports of England as that country belatedly entered the current of international trade. On the jurisdiction of the local maritime courts which thus developed in the chief English ports, there was superimposed, in the latter half of the fifteenth century, a jurisdiction granted the admiral and the vice-admirals of the royal fleet over maritime disputes and offenses—whence the term, peculiar to Anglo-American law, of "admiralty" jurisdiction. Eventually, the

[7] Frothingham v. Mellon, 262 U.S. 447 (1923).

local maritime courts disappeared, giving way to the court of admiralty operating throughout the kingdom.

The concept of admiralty jurisdiction as distinguished from that of the other courts and as having perhaps a more direct and special interest to the sovereign—an interest very obvious in the jurisdiction of admiralty courts over prizes—was reflected in the establishment, already noted, of separate admiralty courts for the American colonies. In all other areas of colonial judicial action, the judicial system was erected within the framework of the colonial governments, each colony having its own separate set of courts; but for the adjudication of admiralty cases, courts were set up in certain of the chief seaports, having no relation to the government of the colony in which that seaport happened to be, and having jurisdiction over actions arising in a defined "district," which included several colonies.[8] The destruction of the authority of these courts by the Revolution necessitated the conferment of admiralty jurisdiction on courts in each of the thirteen states. In most of the states, following the English model, separate courts of admiralty were created, with jurisdiction distinct from that of the regular courts. So that when the framers of the Constitution referred to "cases of admiralty and maritime jurisdiction" as a branch of jurisdiction which Congress might vest in the federal courts, they were referring to a category which was in the main well defined. The precise definition of this category was, however, by no means a simple matter; and it was not till many decades had passed that such precise delimitation was accomplished by the Supreme Court.

The difficulties encountered in precisely delimiting the admiralty jurisdiction concerned, on the one hand, the kinds of cases embraced and, on the other, the physical limits to which the jurisdiction extended. The classes of cases within the jurisdiction of the English admiralty courts had been the subject of numerous changes over the centuries, some statutory, others effected by the courts alone, some excluding particular classes of controversy from that jurisdiction, others extending it to new classes of controversy. To detail these fluctuations (which corresponded roughly to the fluctuations in the balance of power between the admiralty courts on the one hand and the law courts of general jurisdiction on the other) would be little to the purpose.[9] More useful would it be, did space permit, to review the particular problems presented to the Supreme Court under this head. Suffice it to say that by the middle of the last century it had

[8] Sporadic instances of the establishment of an admiralty court by a colonial legislature did, however, occur. See 131 U.S., Appendix, xxi. An account of the British admiralty courts for the Atlantic colonies is to be found in the Introduction (by C. M. Andrews) to Towle, Records of the Vice-Admiralty Court of Rhode Island, 1716–1752 (1936). See also Ubbelohde, The Vice-Admiralty Courts and the American Revolution (1960).

[9] See Mears, The History of the Admiralty Jurisdiction, in 2 Select Essays in Anglo-American Legal History, 312 (1908).

become established by decisions of the Supreme Court that every controversy arising out of a contract relating to navigation on the high seas or on the "navigable waters of the United States" (a phrase we shall shortly discuss), or arising out of a tort occurring on those seas or waters, may be adjudicated as a case of admiralty and maritime jurisdiction.

The second problem, also long a source of controversy between the common-law courts and the admiralty courts in England, revolved about the physical boundary delimiting their respective jurisdictions. Eventually, the settled doctrine in England came to be that occurrences not only in the open sea and in the bays but even on the mouths of the rivers might be the subject of the admiralty jurisdiction, the extreme limit of that jurisdiction being reached however at the point where the river was no longer affected by the ebb and flow of the tide. Controversies arising out of river navigation above that point were subject exclusively to the law courts. The same test was accepted by the Supreme Court as late as 1848 as applicable in this country. In 1851, however, the Court repudiated this limitation, holding it inapplicable to the continental rivers of America, navigable hundreds of miles above tidewater; and it announced that controversies arising out of the navigation of any body of water forming part of a waterway or chain of waterways on which could be made a continuous voyage between two states or between the United States and a foreign country, were within the admiralty jurisdiction.[10] To such waters the term "navigable waters of the United States" was applied.

In the struggle for jurisdiction between the admiralty courts and the law courts in England, the admiralty courts never succeeded in establishing an exclusive right to adjudicate cases arising out of navigation. The law courts retained the right to adjudicate such cases should the suitor choose to apply to them instead of to the admiralty courts. This tradition of the concurrent power of the law courts was respected by Congress when it stripped the state courts of their admiralty jurisdiction and conferred such jurisdiction exclusively on the federal courts; for it added the proviso "saving to suitors in all cases the right of a common law remedy, where the common law is competent to give it." The substance of this proviso has been retained to this day. In practice, however, the suitor with a cause of action arising out of navigation on the high seas or the public waters of the United States usually brings his case in the federal court as a case of "admiralty or maritime jurisdiction." The reason is that from the standpoint of the suitor the traditional procedure in admiralty is more summary and more effective than that of the courts of law, and the sub-

---

[10] The Genesee Chief, 12 Howard 443 (1851). The Great Lakes are within the admiralty jurisdiction: The Daniel Ball, 10 Wallace 557 (1871). A canal too may be a "navigable water of the United States": Ex parte Boyer, 109 U.S. 629 (1884).

stantive rules, i.e., the doctrines by which the respective rights of the parties are determined, are in many instances more favorable to him.

In vesting in the federal courts exclusively all admiralty and maritime jurisdiction, Congress did not merely confer upon them the power to adjudicate cases arising out of navigation on the high seas or public waters of the United States, but also imposed upon them the duty to apply, in their adjudication of those cases, the historic procedures and doctrines of admiralty law, rather than the procedures and doctrines applied in other branches of their civil jurisdiction.

Even where no particular federal statute or treaty is involved in a dispute arising out of navigation, there is obviously a close relationship between navigation and water-borne commerce both interstate and foreign, which forms the subject of so much federal statute and treaty. Equally obvious is the relationship between ocean navigation and foreign relations. Finally, the extent to which aliens are likely to be parties to disputes arising out of navigation furnishes another reason for federal jurisdiction. In the words of *The Federalist* "These [maritime cases] so generally depend on the law of nations and so commonly affect the rights of foreigners, that they fall within the considerations which are relative to the public peace."[11]

It should be emphasized, however, that it would be inaccurate to say that in adjudicating cases of admiralty and maritime jurisdiction the federal courts are administering federal law. The subject matter embraced in these cases is far wider than the embraced in such statutes as Congress may have enacted. That the framers of the Constitution intended that the jurisdiction of the federal courts in this class of cases might, in the discretion of Congress, be extended to the entire range of possible maritime controversies, and not be limited to those matters which Congress might regulate in the exercise of its power "to regulate commerce among the several states and with foreign nations," seems clear from the fact that they expressly specified "all cases of admiralty and maritime jurisdiction" as within the federal judicial power, instead of merely leaving jurisdiction over such cases to be exercised under the prior language extending that power over cases arising under the laws of the United States.

No doubt many of the matters involved in the class of controversies under discussion could be regulated by Congress under its grant of power to regulate interstate and foreign commerce; but there are other matters as to which the power of Congress to regulate under that grant might well be doubted (e.g., the respective rights of two foreign vessels colliding on the high seas and thereafter making an American port). At any rate, Congress has not assumed to legislate in any but a small portion of the field of law applied in cases of admiralty and maritime jurisdiction. Over

[11] No. 80.

the remainder of the field, the federal courts apply the ancient traditional rules of admiralty and maritime law, modified as seems to them necessary to conform to modern conditions, without the aid of any legislation. Over a portion of the field indeed (e.g., contracts of employment of seamen) they occasionally apply state laws as well.

Despite the provision of the Constitution that the federal judicial power "shall extend . . . to all cases of admiralty and maritime jurisdiction," Congress might, as already indicated, had it seen fit, have withheld such jurisdiction in whole or in part from the newly created federal courts; or, in conferring such jurisdiction upon them, it might have permitted the state courts to continue to exercise jurisdiction in such cases, leaving it to the litigants in each case to elect between the state and the federal courts. Congress chose, however, to vest the *whole* of the "admiralty and maritime jurisdiction" in the federal courts and to vest it there *exclusively*. The state courts were completely ousted of the jurisdiction over these cases which they had hitherto exercised; and have never since exercised such jurisdiction.

2. CASES BROUGHT ONLY IN THE FEDERAL COURTS BECAUSE OF THE PARTIES

Those cases to which the Constitution provides "the judicial power of the United States shall extend" which are identified by the parties involved are (1) "all cases affecting ambassadors, other public ministers and consuls," (2) "controversies to which the United States shall be a party," (3) "controversies between two or more states," (4) controversies "between a state and a citizen of another state," (5) controversies "between citizens of different states," and (6) controversies "between a state, or the citizens thereof, and foreign states, citizens or subjects." Congress has conferred some jurisdiction in all these classes of cases on the federal courts, but not in all cases exclusively on them.

Classes affecting ambassadors, other public ministers, and consuls

Although, even prior to the adoption of the Articles, foreign representatives of both diplomatic and consular rank had been present in the country, the Articles made no mention of cases affecting such persons; so that such cases, if any arose, could have been adjudicated only in the state courts.

Whether the inclusion of cases "affecting ambassadors, other public ministers and consuls" in "the judicial power of the United States," and the conferring of original jurisdiction in such cases on the Supreme Court, were suggested to the draftsmen of the Constitution by any particular incident or occurrence is not clear.

The term "other public ministers" used in the Constitution has been carried over by Congress into the statute without definition; and the phrase has indeed never been authoritatively defined. In an opinion of the Supreme Court in which the point was not necessary to the decision of the case, the observation was made that the view of Congress as to the meaning of the term "public ministers" was indicated by the then existing statutory definition of the term "diplomatic officers of the United States," viz.: "ambassadors, envoys extraordinary, ministers plenipotentiary, minister, resident, commissioners, chargés d'affaires, agents and secretaries of legation and none others."[12]

Treating ambassadors and other public ministers of foreign states as a single class, Congress has provided that "all actions or proceedings against" them or "their domestics or domestic servants" which are "not inconsistent with the law of nations" shall be brought exclusively in the Supreme Court. This grant of jurisdiction is, however, nominal rather than actual since, by accepted principles of diplomatic comity, an accredited diplomatic representative of a foreign government recognized by the United States is immune from the processes of our courts, both civil and criminal. Should he commit a criminal offense, or fail to discharge a civil obligation, our government would, presumably, make representations to his government with a view to securing punishment or restitution. A like immunity extends to the personnel of his immediate household.

Actions brought by ambassadors and "other public ministers" may, under the Constitution, be brought in the Supreme Court; and by statute they may be brought also in the inferior federal courts. Moreover, since nothing in the federal statute forbids it, they may be brought also in the state courts.[13]

Cases to which the United States is a party

There have already been mentioned those cases, arising under the laws of the United States, in which the government institutes a proceeding either to compel compliance with a statute or to punish its violation. In a sense, these cases are indeed also "cases to which the United States is a party." But that phrase ordinarily connotes a quite different class of cases. The mere existence of the federal government as an organization for the transaction of governmental business gives rise to a great volume

---

[12] In re Baiz, 135 U.S. 403, 419 (1890).

[13] Actions or proceedings against consuls may by the Constitution be brought in the Supreme Court, and by statute in inferior federal courts but not in a state court. 28 U.S. Code, Sec. 1351. Consuls do not enjoy the immunity from our judicial processes accorded to diplomatic representatives and their personal entourage. Congress has not authorized a consul to bring in an inferior federal court a case not otherwise within its jurisdiction. For practical purposes, then, the consul as plaintiff is in the same position as any other plaintiff (unless indeed he should choose to invoke his constitutional privilege of suing in the Supreme Court!).

of civil cases in which the government is plaintiff in the same sense that a private person or corporation might be. As landlord, as tenant, as buyer, and as seller, the government finds it necessary, on numerous occasions, to institute civil action. The statutory provision which confers jurisdiction on the federal courts in cases in which the United States is plaintiff does not expressly provide that such jurisdiction shall be exclusive. In theory, there is no reason why a state court could not entertain such a suit should the government's attorneys see fit to institute one there; and there are occasional instances of this being done. Almost invariably, however, such actions are instituted in the federal courts.[14] Suits against the government are cognizable exclusively in the federal courts, including the Court of Claims.

Controversies between states

During the colnial period several boundary and other disputes between two or more colonies had been adjudicated by the Privy Council in London. It was not long after the destruction of the British authority that the need for a new tribunal to adjudicate disputes between states became apparent. Since a state could not be sued in its own courts without its consent, and a suit against it in another state (unless it chanced to have there some property subject to seizure) was futile, there was in effect no such tribunal.

Provision was accordingly made in the Articles of Confederation for the adjudication of "all disputes and differences now subsisting or that hereafter may arise between two or more states concerning boundary jurisdiction, or any other cause whatever" through the setting up by the United States in Congress assembled of a special tribunal for each dispute. This provision was availed of on several occasions during the life of the Articles. In the Constitution this class of cases is described simply as "controversies between two or more states."

Boundary disputes between states are of course no longer of importance, but in recent years the Supreme Court has been called upon to adjudicate several important disputes between states with respect to the use and diversion of common waters.[15]

[14] A special class of cases to which the United States is a party is that in which the government's controversy is with a state. Since this is a case in which a state is a party, the Supreme Court has, by force of the Constitution itself, original jurisdiction thereof; but Congress has not seen fit to permit such jurisdiction to be exclusive in the Supreme Court. The district courts also have jurisdiction. Where the United States is plaintiff, the jurisdiction of the federal courts is not made exclusive; hence there is nothing to prevent the United States suing a state, if the state has so consented, in the state's own courts. No case has come to notice, however, in which this has been done.

[15] A list of sixty-four cases between states in the Supreme Court up to 1946 is given in 30 Jour. Amer. Judicature Soc. 132. There have been some twenty-five cases since.

Suit by a state against a private party

Although the Constitution speaks of a controversy "between a state and the citizen of another state," language which is susceptible of the construction that the federal judicial power may be asserted, if Congress so decrees, to subject a state to a suit instituted against it in the federal courts by a citizen of another state, that construction is expressly negatived by the Eleventh Amendment to the Constitution, adopted in 1798. That amendment resulted from a decision of the Supreme Court upholding the right of a citizen of another state to sue the state of Georgia in a federal court.[16]

By the Constitution, a state may bring suit against a private party in the Supreme Court; and in several important cases in recent decades a state has brought such a suit in the Court. Congress could also, if it saw fit, confer jurisdiction of a suit by a state against the citizen of another state on the inferior federal courts; but it has not done so. On the other hand, neither has it, as it could have, withdrawn such jurisdiction from the state courts. In practice, a suit by a state against a private party outside its own courts is a rarity.

The suit by a state against a private party may be quite identical in nature with that brought by one private party against another, the cause of action arising out of the state's contractual or propietary activities. But it may also be brought by the state in its character as guardian of the welfare of its citizens. Thus, the Supreme Court has sustained the right of a state to seek from it an order prohibiting a smelter in an adjoining state from discharging noxious fumes which, passing over the border, allegedly injured crops in the plaintiff state;[17] or an order declaring the rate-making procedure of a group of railroads, whose rates, made by that procedure, were allegedly injurious to the citizens of the plaintiff state, to be a conspiracy in restraint of trade, and prohibiting the further use of that procedure.[18]

Suit against a state by a foreign state

A state may of course permit itself to be sued in its own courts by a foreign state; but if it does so the position of the foreign state is no different from that of the private citizen whom the state permits to sue it in its own courts.

[16] Chisholm v. Georgia, 2 Dall. 419 (1793).
[17] Georgia v. Tennessee Copper Co., 206 U.S. 230 (1907).
[18] Georgia v. Pennsylvania R. Co. et al., 324 U.S. 439 (1945). The interest of a state in protecting its citizens from the burden of increased federal taxation is not, however, such as to give a state standing to maintain an action to enjoin the disbursement of federal funds for an allegedly unconstitutional purpose. Massachusetts v. Mellon, 262 U.S. 447 (1923).

A suit against a state by a foreign state is in terms included in the constitutional definition of the federal judicial power, and would seem to be within the jurisdiction of the Supreme Court by force of the Constitution itself. The Court has, however, held that it is implied in the Constitution (by reason of the possibility of international complications) that a state may not be sued by a foreign state without its own consent.[19] This has apparently never been given; and Congress has seemingly not deemed it worthwhile to include such cases in its enumeration, in the current statute, of the cases in which the Supreme Court has original jurisdiction.

Suit against a foreign state

The federal judicial power extends, under the Constitution, to suits against foreign states whether by the United States, by a state, or by a citizen. The recognized doctrines of international law make suits of this kind of theoretical interest only. Congress has nevertheless conferred jurisdiction of such suits on the federal courts, when instituted by a citizen of the United States.

There remain certain cases, not yet discussed, that are within the federal judicial power. In these cases Congress has not made the jurisdiction of the federal courts exclusive of that of the state courts; and in an important class of cases indeed has not given the federal courts any jurisdiction at all. These classes of cases will now be considered.

3. CASES BROUGHT IN EITHER THE STATE OR THE FEDERAL COURTS

As may be seen from the review just made, the cases within the federal judicial power, jurisdiction of which Congress has not vested exclusively in the federal courts, are of two main categories—cases arising under federal law (using that term as before to embrace the Constitution and federal statutes and treaties) and controversies between citizens of different states. These two classes of cases may in some instances be brought in either the federal or the state court at the option of the plaintiff; in others, they may be brought only in the state courts.

Cases arising under federal law: claim based on federal law

Where the plaintiff's claimed right to sue is expressly given by federal statute, Congress has, already stated, usually vested jurisdiction of the suit exclusively in the federal courts; but there are important classes of cases in which it has not done so, and the suit may consequently be brought in the state courts as well, if the plaintiff so elects. Thus Congress, in

[19] Monaco v. Mississippi, 292 U.S. 313 (1934), in which suit was brought on the defaulted bonds of Mississippi, issued in 1833!

creating a new right of action in favor of private parties, has sometimes provided that action thereunder may be brought "in any court of competent jurisdiction." The words "any court" are intended to include state courts as well as federal, and have been so construed. If a state court possesses, for example, jurisdiction of actions for damages generally, it is, if the federal statute so provides, a court of "competent jurisdiction" to take cognizance of an action for damages recoverable under the federal statute. So, too, if the federal statute creating the right of action is, as has occasionally happened, completely silent as to the court in which suit to enforce that right is to be brought, suit may be brought in either the federal court or in any state court of competent jurisdiction.[20]

That Congress, in creating a new right of action, may require a state to enforce such federal right of action through its existing courts of competent jurisdiction, is now well settled.[21] The enforcement of the federal cause of action is a function of "the judicial power of the United States." That power is by the Constitution vested (aside from the Supreme Court) "in such inferior tribunals as Congress shall . . . ordain and establish." To the extent that Congress may require existing state courts of competent jurisdiction to enforce a right of action created by Congress, it has "ordained" such state courts as tribunals vested to that extent with "the judicial power of the United States."

Whether Congress could assume to impose upon any state court a compulsory jurisdiction which it does not possess under state law is a quite different question—one which up to the present has been academic and which, in view of the enormous practical difficulties that any such attempt would involve, is likely to remain so.

Perhaps the most important instance of a private right of action created by federal statute, which may by the terms of the statute be enforced "in any court of competent jurisdiction" is that found in the Fair Labor Standards Act of 1938 (often colloquially referred to as the Wages and Hours Act). By the provisions of this act, an employer is required to pay an employee within the coverage of the act a minimum hourly wage and, for any hours worked in excess of a weekly maximum fixed by statute, wages at the rate of one and one-half times the basic rate. An employee paid lass than the minimum wage, or paid for such overtime at a lower rate than the statute requires may bring action against the employer "in any court of competent jurisdiction" for double the amount of the underpayment.[22] In practice, the greater part of such suits have been brought in minor state courts.

Similarly, the Securities Act of 1933 (which requires, in connection

[20] Claflin v. Houseman, 93 U.S. 130 (1876).
[21] Mondou v. N.Y.N.H. & H.R.R.Co. 223 U.S. 1 (1912); Testa v. Katt, 330 U.S. 386 (1947).
[22] 29 U.S. Code, Sec. 216(b).

with certain public offerings of securities, the filing of a so-called registration statement and, under certain circumstances, additional documents) imposes upon any person knowingly making or causing to be made a false or misleading statement in any such filed document a liability for damages to any person who relied on such statement in purchasing the security concerned (a provision subjecting to possible liability a wide group of persons whose liability to the purchaser was under ordinary rules of law doubtful or clearly nonexistent); and the statute then provides that "a person seeking to enforce such liability may sue . . . in any court of competent jurisdiction."[23]

Where an action under these statutes, which could have been instituted in the federal courts,[24] is brought in a state court, the defendant has the right to have the case at once transferred (or as the statutory phrase is, "removed") to the federal district court of the district in which the state court is situated.[25] The action then proceeds as if it had been instituted in the federal court.

Just as the Constitution is itself the source of the right to bring action to enjoin the enforcement of a federal statute repugnant to the Constitution, it equally creates the right to enjoin the enforcement of a state statute (or state constitutional provision) repugnant to the Constitution, or to a federal statute or treaty—all declared by the Constitution to be "the supreme law of the land." The inferior federal courts may entertain an action for such an injuction by reason of their statutory jurisdiction of cases arising under the Constitution; while the state courts also entertain such actions even without express statutory authorization, being expressly bound by the Constitution (Article VI) to honor "the supreme law of the land . . . any thing in the constitution or laws of any state to the contrary notwithstanding."

In connection with an application to a federal court for an injunction against the enforcement of a state statute, Congress (as in the parallel proceeding, already referred to, to enjoin the enforcement of an allegedly unconstitutional *federal* enactment) has made provision for a three-judge court. Congress has also provided, because of past abuses in this field, that, "where a plain speedy and efficient remedy may be had in the courts of the state," a federal court shall not, because of alleged repugnance to the federal Constitution, enjoin or restrain "the assessment, levy or

[23] 15 U.S. Code, Sec. 77(k).

[24] Even though the plaintiff's cause of action arises under the Constitution or the laws or treaties of the United States, the suit may not, except when otherwise specifically provided by statute, be brought in the federal courts if the amount involved does not exceed $10,000 (28 U.S. Code, Sec. 1331). The statutory exceptions are, however, so comprehensive that this limitation is of little importance. Both the cases mentioned doubtless fall under the statutory exception of case arising under statutes affecting interstate or foreign commerce (28 U.S. Code, Sec. 1337).

[25] 28 U.S. Code, Sec. 1441(b).

collection of any tax under state law"[26] or "the operation of, or compliance with, any order affecting rates chargeable by a public utility and made by a state administrative agency or a rate-making body of a state political subdivision."[27] Moreover, even in cases not falling within these statutes, the Supreme Court has laid down the rule that a federal court should refrain from exercising its statutory power to enjoin state officers where the state courts are capable of giving relief.[28]

As a result of these limitations, it is in most cases no longer possible to obtain an injunction against a state body in the federal courts. Instead, the plaintiff must first exhaust remedies in the state courts, and after the matter has been passed upon by the highest state court available, seek review by the Supreme Court of the United States of the federal question involved.

Controversies between citizens of different states

The inclusion in the Constitution of "controversies between citizens of different states[29] "in the classes of cases to which "the judicial power of the United States shall extend" represents a striking exception to the general statement that all the categories of federal jurisdiction have a manifestly close relationship to the national interest and are associated, either by subject matter or by the nature of the parties, with matters entrusted to the care of the national government. In this category, neither the subject matter nor the parties have any direct relation to national interests. The sole ground of federal jurisdiction is merely that the plaintiff is not a citizen of the same state as the defendant.

In view of the exceptional character of this category of federal jurisdiction, it is indeed remarkable that the contemporary records throw so little light upon the reason for its inclusion. Only one of the three original plans for a constitution submitted to the Convention—Randolph's —contains any suggestion of such a jurisdiction, and none of the several sets of notes of the proceedings of the Convention which have survived makes reference to any discussion upon it. In the *Federalist*, Hamilton designedly evades any specific discussion of the necessity for such jurisdiction, assimilating it, in a general plea for the necessity of impartial tri-

[26] 28 U.S. Code, Sec. 1341.

[27] 28 U.S. Code, Sec. 1342. The provision is restricted to cases in which the state rate order does not interfere with interstate commerce, has been made after reasonable notice and hearing, and can be corrected by a plain, speedy, and efficient remedy in the courts of the state.

[28] Alabama Public Service Commission v. Southern Railway Co., 341 U.S. 341 (1951).

[29] Though the Constitution here and elsewhere refers to a citizen of a state, it nowhere defines what constitutes state citizenship. By the Fourteenth Amendment, however, adopted in 1868, citizens of the United States are also "citizens of the State wherein they reside." For the use of the term "domiciled" instead of the word "reside," see note 44 below.

bunals unaffected by local prejudice, to the quite different category of controversies between a state and citizens of another state;[30] and that the necessity for this jurisdiction was seriously questioned by contemporary opinion is evident from the proceedings of the ratifying conventions in the several states.[31]

With the provision for federal jurisdiction in diversity of citizenship cases thus incorporated without limitation in the Constitution, Congress, if it considered that to insure against local prejudice the reservation of some federal control of controversies between citizens of different states was necessary, might nevertheless have provided merely for an *appellate* review of such cases by the federal courts, where the non-resident losing party set up a claim of such local prejudice. On the other hand, Congress might, in conferring *original* jurisdiction on the federal courts, have divested the state courts completely of that jurisdiction.[32] It chose a middle course, conferring original jurisdiction on the federal courts *concurrently* with the state courts. The parties were permitted, if neither one preferred to have the case litigated in the federal court, to proceed in the state courts as before; the plaintiff being permitted to sue in either state or federal court, and the defendant, if sued in the state court in a state of which he was not a citizen, being permitted to have the case forthwith removed to the federal court.

Moreover, Congress, in conferring on the federal courts concurrent jurisdiction in diversity cases limited it, in 1789, to cases involving more than $500—a figure which has since been successively increased to $2,000, $3,000, and $10,000.

The pattern of diversity of citizenship jurisdiction thus laid down by Congress in the original Judiciary Act has remained substantially unchanged.[33] In 1844 occurred, however, a further development which has

[30] Federalist, Number 80: "in order to insure the inviolable maintenance of that equality of privileges and immunities to which the citizens of the Union will be entitled, the national judiciary ought to preside in all cases in which one State or its citizens are opposed to another State or its citizens."

[31] In the amendments proposed to the Constitution by the ratifying conventions of Virginia and North Carolina, this branch of federal judicial power was proposed to be eliminated—a proposal not made with respect to any of the other categories of federal jurisdiction; while in the proposals of the ratifying convention of Massachusetts the jurisdiction, while retained, was proposed to be limited to cases involving $1,500 or more, and in those of the New Hampshire convention it was proposed to be limited to appellate jurisdiction in cases involving $3,000 or more.

[32] Since Congress has never attempted to divest the state courts of all jurisdiction in diversity cases, its power to do so has never been expressly passed upon by the Supreme Court. The Court has, however, expressly stated that Congress may vest exclusively in the federal courts jurisdiction of *any* class of cases declared by the Constitution to be within the judicial power of the United States. See The Moses Taylor, 4 Wallace 411, 429 (1867) and Chicago R. Co. v. Whitton, 13 Wallace 270, 288 (1871).

[33] The present provisions are found in 28 U.S. Code, Secs. 1332 and 1441. After the Civil War the right of removal was given even in cases in which less than the

had the highest significance for our legal system. This was the ruling by the Supreme Court of the United States that within the meaning of the word "citizen" as it occurs in the phraseology of the Constitution defining "the judicial power of the United States" (but not as it occurs anywhere else in the Constitution) a corporation is to be treated as if it were a "citizen" of the state in which it is incorporated.[34] This extraordinary extension of the federal jurisdiction to a vast category of cases manifestly not within the intension of the farmers of the Constitution or the draftsmen of the original Judiciary Act, could, of course, readily have been set at naught by Congress through a mere amendment of the relevant provision of the statute, expressly limiting the term "citizen," as used in that provision, to natural persons. Congress, however, acquiesced in the decision, and the federal jurisdiction of actions by or against corporations solely on the basis of diversity of "citizenship" continues to this day, constituting a substantial element in the business of the federal courts.

It will be observed that the diversity jurisdiction has no necessary reference whatever to any federal right or statute, extending to ordinary commercial and tort litigation. It is under this jurisdiction that there chiefly took place, prior to the enactment of the Norris-LaGuardia Act in 1932, the activity of the federal courts in the issuance of injunctions in labor disputes, the jurisdiction of federal courts being invoked because the plaintiff employer was a citizen of a state other than the state of residence of the employees or union officials sought to be enjoined. In not a few of the injunction cases, the plaintiff employer was a corporation doing business chiefly in the state of residence of the employees or labor union officials enjoined, but incorporated under the laws of some other state, e.g., Delaware or New Jersey.

The federal courts were, for some years before and after the turn of the century, regarded by some, and not wholly without justification, as citadels of corporate privilege. There consequently developed in some quarters a strong opposition to their exercise of jurisdiction in cases in which a

---

minimum statutory amount was involved, if the defendant could show to the satisfaction of the federal court that by reason of local prejudice he could not expect justice in the state court; this provision, seldom used, was repealed in 1948. By statute enacted in 1949 it was provided that for the purpose of federal jurisdiction in diversity cases the word "states" includes the District of Columbia. The Supreme Court held this extension of the federal jurisdiction constitutional in Nat. Mut. Ins. Co. v. Tidewater Transfer Co., 337 U.S. 582 (1949). In 1956, a similar provision was enacted with respect to Puerto Rico.

[34] Louisville, Cincinnati and Charleston R. Co. v. Letson, 2 Howard 497 (1844). A serious limitation which Congress has from the beginning placed upon the diversity-of-citizenship jurisdiction of the federal courts is the prohibition against collusive assignments for the purpose of invoking such jurisdiction. (See 28 U.S. Code, Sec. 1359.) This provision makes fruitless the assignment by a claimant of a claim subsisting against a citizen of the same state, to a citizen of another state, solely for the purpose of invoking the jurisdiction of the federal courts.

corporation had invoked that jurisdiction solely on the ground of diversity of "citizenship." With the liberalization of the federal bench in recent decades, this opposition has declined.[35]

The hostility to the federal courts also found expression in certain states in laws assuming to inflict penalties upon a foreign corporation doing business within the state which resorted to a federal court in a controversy with a citizen of the state (either in bringing action in such court, or by removing to such court an action against it brought in a state court), such penalty being either a monetary one or the revocation of the corporation's license to do business in the state. These attempts by states to hamper resort to the federal courts have, however, been set at naught by the Supreme Court as an unconstitutional state interference with the federal judicial power.[36]

In practice, the preference of a party for the federal court springs perhaps less frequently (even in the case of a non-resident party) from the fear of prejudice or local influence than from the belief that the procedure of the federal court, or the identity of its judges, the caliber of its jury, or the state of its trial calendar promises some advantage; and for converse reasons the other party is likely to prefer the state court.[37]

On the whole, it is to be doubted whether the retention of the diversity-of-citizenship jurisdiction in its present extensive form is defensible.[38] It is worth considering whether original jurisdiction in diversity cases should not be restricted (1) to cases in which it appears, on the showing of either plaintiff or defendant, that a fair trial in the state courts is unlikely, and (2) to those special classes of cases, shortly to be discussed, in which a federal court may accomplish results not open to state courts. As a further safeguard, there could perhaps be reserved to the federal appellate courts a power to review the judgments of state courts in diversity cases upon a clear showing by the non-resident appellant of prejudice or local influence.

The special cases in which the federal diversity jurisdiction should be preserved and even extended are those in which, the necessary parties de-

[35] By statute of 1958 a corporation is, for purposes of diversity jurisdiction, a citizen also of the state in which it has its principal place of business. This legislation was prompted by a desire to reduce the caseload of the federal courts, rather than by opposition to the corporation diversity jurisdiction as such.

[36] Insurance Co. v. Morse, 20 Wallace 445 (1875) is first of a series of such decisions.

[37] As to the divergence, until 1938, between state and federal courts, of rules of law applied in certain cases, and consequent "forum shopping" see p. 357.

[38] See concurring opinions of Justice Frankfurter in Sutton v. Lieb, 342 U.S. 402, 413 (1952) and in Lumbermen's Casualty Co. v. Elbert, 348 U.S. 48, 53 (1954); American Law Institute, Study of the Division of Jurisdiction between State and Federal Courts (1936); Doub, Time for Re-evaluation: Shall We Curtail Diversity Jurisdiction?, 44 Amer. Bar Assn. Jour. 243 (1958).

fendant being scattered over two or more states, no state court is capable of bringing them all before it and thus determining the entire controversy and the rights of all the parties in a single proceeding. This a federal court, if properly empowered by Congress to bring before it all necessary parties wherever they may be in the United States, may readily do. A striking example of the superiority of the federal court in a case of this kind is furnished by a situation quite common in the field of life insurance —the simultaneous presentation to the insurance company of claims to the same insurance proceeds by two or more claimants (each usually claiming to be the next of kin of the deceased insured or beneficiary). In general, where a debtor is confronted with demands for payment from two or more persons, each claiming to be the sole creditor, he may institute a proceeding (known as an "interpleader" proceeding) against all the claimants jointly, pay the amount of his debt into court, and leave the rival claimants to fight it out among themselves. Unfortunately, this is possible only where all the contending claimants are within the jurisdiction of the same court, which thus has coercive power to bring them all before it. In the case of the insurance claims in question it frequently happened that the contending claimants resided in different states, and it was thus impossible to bring them before a state court in any one state. Each might sue the insurance company in his own state; and each might there recover judgment. To remedy this situation, Congress, in 1926, provided that the insurance company might institute proceedings in the federal court in the district in which any one of the claimants resided, depositing in the court the fund in dispute and requesting the court to bring before it the adverse claimants wherever in the United States they might be. In addition, that court was authorized to enjoin any of the claimants from instituting (or from further prosecuting if already instituted) any other suit on account of the fund in controversy in any other court, state or federal. More recently this interpleader jurisdiction of the federal courts has been extended to cover also cases in which a party other than an insurance company holds a fund to which there are adverse claimants in different states.[39]

It will be noted that since the controversy here is in reality between the several contending claimants, and the petitioner is only nominally a party to the controversy, the statute confers jurisdiction on the federal court whenever the several claimants are citizens of different states, even though

[39] 28 U.S. Code, Sec. 1335. The federal interpleader jurisdiction could usefully be extended to an action by an executor or administrator against the tax officials of two or more states which claim to have been the domicile of the deceased, to determine which was the domicile. Unfortunately, however, this would be under prevailing doctrine an action by a private party against a state and, hence, not within the federal judicial power. See p. 195.

the petitioner and one of the claimants may be citizens of the same state. A different question would be presented were Congress to attempt to give federal courts jurisdiction of a class of cases in which such jurisdiction would seem to be highly desirable—civil cases in which there are two or more defendants allegedly jointly liable, but resident in different states. An illustrative case would be one in which action is brought on behalf of a corporation against the directors of the corporation to obtain restitution for the alleged waste or improper diversion of corporate funds. If the directors, as frequently happens, reside in different states, it is now in effect impossible to join them as defendants in a single action in either a state or a federal court. They cannot be sued in the same state court, because, as we shall see, a state cannot in such a case confer on its courts jurisdiction over non-residents who choose to remain outside its boundaries; nor in any one federal court, because Congress has not seen fit, in diversity-of-citizenship cases generally, to give to a federal district court jurisdiction over any non-resident of the district who chooses to remain outside its boundaries. A change in the statute to permit the plaintiff in a diversity action to bring before a single federal court all the defendants jointly liable would confront the difficulty that in many cases one or more of the defendants are of the same state citizenship as the plaintiff, and hence, as between the plaintiff and such defendant or defendants, there is no controversy "between citizens of different states." Could Congress nevertheless constitutionally give the federal court jurisdiction over such defendants as being "necessary and proper" for effectuating the federal jurisdiction over "controversies between citizens of different states"? No certain answer to this question is to be found in the rulings of the Supreme Court on related questions.

There is, moreover, a class of "controversies between citizens of different states" to which Congress has never extended the jurisdiction of the federal courts, but which the federal courts might well adjudicate to greater advantage than do the state courts, in whose hands exclusively it now rests. This is the class of divorce actions in which the plaintiff, suing in a state court, and claiming to be a resident of the state, alleges that the defendant is a resident of another state. Where, as in the great majority of such cases, the action has been brought in accordance with an agreement in advance between the spouses, there is perhaps no strong case for withdrawing jurisdiction from the state courts. Where, however, the defendant has not consented to the action, this unilateral termination of the defendant's marriage by a court in another state may do grave injustice to the defendant and create troublesome uncertainties regarding the status and rights of both plaintiff and defendant. The nature of these uncertainties will be considered in the next chapter.[40]

[40] See pp. 247 ff.

4. CASES BROUGHT ONLY IN THE STATE COURTS

Any case not falling within the federal judicial power must of course be brought, if at all, in the state courts. The qualification "if at all" is necessary because certain actions which may be brought in some states may not be brought in others. A familiar example is the action for damages for breach of promise of marriage, an action at one time open to the female plaintiff in every state, but which has been abolished in some of the states.

Of the cases falling within the federal judicial power which may be brought only in the state courts, the only important class is that of controversies between citizens of different states in which either no money is involved (as in the action for divorce) or the amount in controversy does not exceed $10,000.

It has been noted that both in suits on claims based on federal law and in diversity-of-citizenship cases in which federal and state courts have concurrent jurisdiction, Congress has provided that if the plaintiff elects to institute his action in the state court, the defendant may in certain cases remove it to the federal court. Congress has also provided for removal by the defendant to the federal court in certain classes of cases in which the federal court does not have concurrent jurisdiction, and which could not consequently have been instituted in the federal court. The principal class of cases thus removable is that of actions commenced in a state court against federal officers for acts done in alleged performance of their duties.[41]

Since, as already seen, a case which can be brought only in the state courts may, at any stage of the proceeding, become a case "arising under" federal law, though the emergence of a decisive federal question, Congress could, in theory, have provided that the case should thereupon be removed to the federal court. Congress has not done so. Instead, the case continues in its course through the state courts, including the appellate courts; and if at that stage the federal question is still decisive (as it may no longer be, the case having been decided purely on state law grounds against the party claiming rights under the federal law), review of the state courts' disposition of the federal question may be had, either as of right or by permission, from the Supreme Court.

5. STATE IN WHICH ACTION MAY BE BROUGHT

A sovereign state (e.g., France) may assume to regulate by legislation any persons or property within its borders, to adjudicate through its courts any controversies it may see fit, and to execute, within its own boundaries, any resultant judgments or decrees issuing from these courts.

[41] 28 U.S. Code, Sec. 1442; and 50 U.S. Code, Sec. 738.

Its sovereign powers under these heads are controlled only by its treaties with foreign countries.

In our own country, although each state is in theory sovereign within its own borders when dealing with matters not withdrawn from state control by the Constitution,[42] the attempt by a state to assume like powers is seriously limited by the Constitution. A state may have invested its courts with jurisdiction over a controversy, and with power to execute the resultant judgment or decree; but the party aggrieved by such assumption of jurisdiction may nevertheless challenge it on the ground that the state is, under established doctrines of jurisprudence, wholly without jurisdiction, and that a judgment against him rendered in the controversy in question would deprive him of life, liberty, or property "without due process of the law" in violation of the Constitution.

This possibility exists even where the attempt to enforce the judgment is confined to the territory of the state from whose courts it issued. Should the attempt be made to secure its enforcement or its recognition in another state, and should the courts of that state, despite the constitutional requirement that such judgment be given "full faith and credit" by every state, refuse it enforcement or recognition, the question of its validity is again a federal question, the ultimate determination of which rests with the Supreme Court of the United States.

By reason, therefore, of the "due process" clause and of the "full faith and credit" clause, it has thus fallen to the Supreme Court, as ultimate arbiter, to develop, as it has in a series of decision extending over nearly a century, the permissible limits of the power of a state to confer jurisdiction upon its courts; and the resultant doctrines will now be briefly summarized.

As already indicated, the limitation under which each state rests in its assumption of jurisdiction of a controversy is found in no express language of the Constitution but is implied in the provision, added in 1868, that "no state shall . . . deprive any person of life, liberty, or property, without due process of law." The Supreme Court has laid down the principle that by this provision there has been written into the Constitution, as limitations

---

[42] It is not uncommon to speak of the state, in the American frame of government, as a "sovereign" state which has yielded a portion of its sovereignty to the federal government. Though this is a convenient form of words, it does not correspond with the historical facts. The repudiation of the British authority by the several colonies may indeed be regarded as having converted each of them into a sovereign state; but they were already linked, however loosely, in a confederation under the name of the United States, conducting war and diplomatic relations under a central authority. By the adoption of the Articles of Confederation each state further limited its own powers, including, as we have seen, its judicial powers; so that the original thirteen states entered the regime of the Constitution already shorn of some of their sovereign powers. Of the remaining thirty-seven states, only one, Texas, entered the union as a formerly sovereign state. Almost all of the remaining states were created by Congress from territory theretofore under the exclusive control of Congress; instead of their conferring on the national government part of the sovereign power they had formerly possessed, the national government conferred on them part of the sovereign power it had formerly possessed.

upon the states, those time-honored principles of jurisprudence regarding jurisdiction which had theretofore been accepted, in greater or lesser degree, not as limitations imposed from without but merely as self-denying ordinances, by the courts of all Western nations. In a succession of cases precise delimitation of this doctrine has been made by the Supreme Court, so that it is now possible to mark with some assurance the limitations which surround each state in assuming to give its courts jurisdiction over controversies otherwise clearly within the field of state judicial power.[43]

As will appear, the power of the state to authorize the adjudication of a controversy by its courts ordinarily depends either upon the presence in the state of the property that is the subject of the controversy; or upon the physical presence of the defendant, if a natural person, within the state; or upon his residence in the state, notwithstanding temporary physical absence therefrom. (In the case of a corporate defendant, there are of necessity, since a corporation, as distinguished from its property or its agents, has no physical being, special doctrines, equating its activities to physical presence or residence, which will be examined in due course.)

The concept of residence in a state (or "domicile," as the courts have now come to call it)[44] is a fundamental one in this context. A person who maintains no home in any state, and spends no greater length of time in any one state than in another, or who even has for many years spent no time in any state, having been abroad, is nevertheless regarded for this purpose as a resident of a particular state if he regards that state as his home and has the intention of ultimately returning there. A person who maintains two or more homes, each in a different state, is a resident only of that state which he regards as his home, and to which he intends to return—this regardless of the fact that he may spend less time there than in the other state or states. Finally, most elusive of all, a person who leaves his home state with no intention of returning to it, and proceeds to another state with the intention of settling there, becomes a resident of the latter state at the moment of his arrival there.[45] Should he subsequently change his mind and go elsewhere, he has nevertheless been, no matter how short his sojourn in

---

[43] The first such case was Pennoyer v. Neff, 95 U.S. 714 (1878).

[44] Although the Constitution (Fourteenth Amendment, Section 1) declares that citizens of the United States are citizens of the state wherein they "reside," and a similar usage is found in many statutes, the courts have favored the use of "domicile" rather than "residence" to identify the place which a person (regardless of where he may at one time or another be sojourning, even for extended periods) regards as his permanent home, and to which, if absent, he intends to return. Hence, one may be spoken of as a "domiciliary" of a particular state or country, rather than as a "resident."

[45] A minimum period of residence in the state may nevertheless be required, after such acquistion of residence, as a prerequisite to the enjoyment of certain privileges incident to such residence (e.g., the right to vote); and all the "quickie divorce" states have such a requirement as a prerequisite to instituting action for divorce in their courts. The period is in these states apparently a compromise between the desire to detain the newly acquired "resident" as long as possible in the interest of the state's tourist industry, and the fear that competitor states may offer a shorter period.

the state to which he first migrated, for that period a resident of that state. The difficulty, in some cases, of reaching a firm conclusion as to the residence of a person (particularly if the determination must be made after his death) is obvious.

In addition to the cases in which, on the grounds just enumerated, jurisdiction may be exercised by a state notwithstanding that the defendant resists such exercise of jurisdiction, there are as we shall see certain classes of cases in which jurisdiction may be exercised though none of these grounds exists, on the ground that the defendant has expressly or impliedly consented to the jurisdiction of the state.

Exclusive jurisdiction of subject matter

By well-settled doctrine where a controversy concerns the title to or possession of real estate, jurisdiction over the subject matter of the controversy rests exclusively with the state in which the real estate is situated. Such being the case, that state may adjudicate the claims of all persons whatsoever as to the title to such real estate, or as to the right to its possession, regardless of where such persons may reside or be.

Where the controversy concerns the title to or possession of tangible personal property (i.e., movable property) the subject matter, not being permanently situated in any one state, is not exclusively within the jurisdiction of any one state. In practice, however, the result is often otherwise. In many classes of action affecting the title to such property, the practice is to obtain, simultaneously with the institution of the action, an order impounding the property in the hands of an officer of the court pending the final disposition of the action. Where this has been done, the property is, for the purpose of the action, just as completely immobilized as is real estate, and whatever the theoretical right of the defendant to seek an adjudication in another state, in practice the state whose courts hold the property exercises exclusive jurisdiction.

Certain classes of intangible property may be treated in much the same way. Thus, if the ownership of a debt is the subject of controversy, the courts of the state where the debtor is may, by enjoining him from paying the debt pending adjudication, in effect immobilize it in that state; the possibility existing, however, that the debtor may leave the state, rendering enforcement of the injunction impossible.

It is also established doctrine that the state in which a person has his residence at the time of his death has exclusive jurisdiction of all controversies relative to his will (if any), or relative to the distribution of his estate, whether under the will or in intestacy (i.e., death without leaving a will). If, however, the deceased left real estate situated in some state (or country) other than that of which he died a resident, the courts of that state (or country) have exclusive jurisdiction over any controversy relative to the passage of title to such real estate, whether under a will or in intestacy.

General jurisdiction of defendant

Where a controversy does not concern the title to property, but merely the right of one party to obtain a money judgment against another (as in an action on a debt or for damages for breach of a contract or for damages for a tortious injury) or to enjoin another from committing an alleged wrong, or other analogous remedies, the subject matter is regarded as having no particular situs; and hence any state may in general assume jurisdiction over the subject matter if it has jurisdiction of the defendant. In controversies affecting such subject matter, the right of a state to invest its courts with jurisdiction over the controversy therefore depends solely upon whether that state has jurisdiction of the person of the defendant.

A person resident in a particular state is subject to the jurisdiction of its courts; and he cannot evade that jurisdiction either by secreting himself within the state so as to avoid personal service of process if such is required by the statutes of the state, or by remaining outside the state with like intent. If a court is satisfied that he is doing either, it may order its process served upon him by some other method, the precise method being a matter of detailed statutory regulation. Such service, being a substitute for the personal service otherwise required, is in many jurisdictions termed "substituted" service.

Even though a person may be a resident of another state, or of a foreign country, the moment he crosses the borders of a state he subjects himself, as to controversies of the kind under discussion, to the jurisdiction of that state, and makes himself amenable to the process of its courts; and if such process is duly served upon him while in the state, he is brought within the jurisdiction of the court out of which the process has issued and is bound by any judgment or decree resulting from the action or proceeding thus instituted.[46]

Just as a state at all times possesses jurisdiction over its residents, a *domestic* corporation (i.e., one incorporated under the laws of the state) is at all times within the jurisdiction of the courts of the state, and can be subjected to the jurisdiction of a particular court by the service of process issuing from that court upon a proper agent of the corporation, or, in most states, upon a designated state official, who, in turn, forwards the process by mail to the office of the corporation.

Upon what grounds can an analogous jurisdiction be asserted over a *foreign* corporation (i.e., a corporation incorporated under the laws of another state, or of a foreign country)?[47] Having no physical existence, the

[46] The statutes, however, generally exempt from the jurisdiction of the courts of the state a person who has voluntarily entered the state to respond to the process of a court, either as a witness, or to plead to a criminal charge or the like, such exemption remaining in force, if he promptly leaves the state, until he has left.

[47] Corporations incorporated under the laws of a given state are termed in that state "domestic corporations." All other corporations (whether incorporated in

corporation cannot be "physically present" in the state. The courts have answered that the analogy to physical presence is, in the case of a foreign corporation, the *doing of business* within the state. The mere physical presence of one or more of its agents within the state is not sufficient; the agents must be "doing business" in the state on behalf of the corporation. By so "doing business," and as long as it continues so to "do business" the corporation subjects itself to the jurisdiction of the state and to the process of its courts as fully as if it were a domestic corporation or as if it were a natural person physically present in the state.

A mere isolated transaction within a state by the agents of the corporation does not subject the corporation generally to the jurisdiction of the state (although it may, as we shall see, subject it to jurisdiction in an action arising out of that transaction); a regular course of business is required for this purpose. Needless to say, borderline cases arise in which, despite voluminous litigation, there is great difficulty in determining whether the activities of the corporation's agents within the state are sufficiently regular to constitute the "doing of business."[48] The current tendency is distinctly in the direction of resolving all doubts against the foreign corporation.

For the purpose of giving the courts of the state general jurisdiction of the foreign corporation, it is immaterial that the regular activities carried on by its agents in the state may be concerned solely with interstate business (such as the making of contracts for goods to be shipped into the state).[49] If the foreign corporation's business in the state is, however, in whole or in part intrastate in character (such as the rendering of professional services wholly within the state), the state, in addition to possessing general jurisdiction of the corporation, may (and every state does) require the corporation to obtain from the state (in the form of a document frequently termed a "certificate of authority") permission to do such intrastate business within the state. In making application for such permission, the foreign corporation is required by the governing statute to acknowledge its submission to the general jurisdiction of the courts of the state

another state or territory or in the District of Columbia or in a foreign country) are termed "foreign corporations" and receive identical treatment. A corporation incorporated by Congress (e.g., Union Pacific Railroad Company) may be treated by state statutes and courts as either a domestic or a foreign corporation, in some states being treated as domestic for some purposes and as foreign for others.

[48] See "What Constitutes Doing Business," a digest of decisions on this point published annually by the Corporation Trust Company, New York.

[49] However, in the case of actions against foreign railroad corporations and other foreign carrier corporations, where the sole activity of the corporation's agents in the state is that of solicitation of business, the Supreme Court has laid down the doctrine that if the cause of action does not arise in the state and the plaintiff is not a resident of the state, the assumption, by the courts of the state, of jurisdiction over the carrier may constitute an unreasonable burden upon interstate commerce. For discussion of the principles involved, see International Milling Co. v. Columbia Transportation Co., 292 U.S. 511 (1934).

until such time as the corporation surrenders its right to do intrastate business in the state and revokes its submission to the state's general jurisdiction. Where such a submission is in force, it becomes immaterial whether the corporation is in fact "doing business" within the state. If in seeking to effect service of process on an agent of the corporation, no agent can be found, service may, under the statutes in question, be made on a designated official of the state (ordinarily the secretary of state), the foreign corporation having, in its application for permission to do intrastate business within the state, consented that service might be made in this manner.

Special jurisdiction of non-resident or of foreign corporation in action arising out of activity within the state

Although a state has no general jurisdiction of a non-resident not physically present in the state, or over a foreign corporation not "doing business" in the state (and not bound by a general submission to the jurisdiction of the state), it may yet so far have jurisdiction of such absent non-resident or such foreign corporation as to require them to answer in actions arising out of their activities in the state. Several distinct varieties of this category of jurisdiction are to be noticed.[50]

One of them, applicable only to foreign corporations, arises out of the grant by a state to a foreign corporation of permission to do intrastate business within its borders. We have already seen that in applying for such permission, the corporation must submit itself to the general jurisdiction of the courts of the state. When it ceases to do intrastate business within the state, it may apply for a revocation of the permission granted it, and for a like revocation of its submission to the jurisdiction of the state's courts. Under the statutes of most if not all of the states, however, it must simultaneously consent to remain nevertheless subject to the jurisdiction of the courts of the state with respect to any action which may be instituted in those courts by a resident of the state (or a corporation incorporated in that state) to enforce a claim arising out of the activities of the corporation during the period when it was doing business in the state.

A second and very important form of special jurisdiction over a non-resident, or over a foreign corporation, exists in connection with actions arising out of the alleged negligent operation of motor vehicles on the public highways of a state. Under statutes in force in every state, a non-resident driving a motor vehicle on the public highways of the state thereby submits himself to the jurisdiction of the courts of the state with

[50] An additional type of jurisdiction, somewhat analogous to the types here treated, is discussed at page 552. This is the jurisdiction exercised by the courts of a state, in an action against a non-resident, for the conversion into a judgment of the court of an award made by arbitrators, the defendant having consented, in the arbitration agreement, that the courts of the state in question should have that jurisdiction.

respect to any action instituted against him in those courts, arising out of any accident in which it is claimed such non-resident was involved while so driving; his submission being implemented by his impled consent, imputed to him by the statute, that service of summons in such an action may be made on him by delivery of the summons to an official of the state (usually the secretary of state) who is charged with mailing it to the non-resident. Under the statutes of some states, if the operator of the vehicle is an employee of (and operating the vehicle on behalf of) a non-resident or foreign corporation, the employer is likewise deemed to have submitted to the jurisdiction of the state. A similar submission is made, under the statutes, by the non-resident of foreign corporation owner of a motor vehicle who permits such motor vehicle to be driven by another on the highways of the state.

A third category of special jurisdiction arises under statutes permitting suit against persons doing business through agents to be instituted by service of process on the agent instead of the principal. Such statutes, to be found in a number of states, typically provide that a person having an agency for the transaction of business in a county in which he does not reside may be sued in that county in all actions growing out of or connected with the business of that agency, service of process being made on the agent. Such a statute, so far as it applies to residents of the state, or to non-residents physically present in the state, is not relevant to the present discussion. Once the attempt is made to apply it, however, to a non-resident without the state, the constitutional question of the power of the state obviously arises. The Supreme Court has decided the question in favor of the power of the state.[51] It is to be noted that the statutes in question do not assume to authorize the exercise of general jurisdiction over the absent non-resident, but jurisdiction only in actions growing out of or connected with the business conducted by the non-resident. This is to be contrasted with the general jurisdiction asserted by the states, and approved by the Supreme Court, over a foreign corporation doing business within the state. It is more than doubtful whether a like assertion of general jurisdiction over a non-resident would be sustained by the Court.

Within recent years there has emerged, with increasing importance, a new category of statutory jurisdiction of suits by state residents against non-residents or foreign corporations. In these cases, there being in the plaintiff's state no agent of the defendant, nor any state official whose appointment for the purpose as agent of the defendant has been either expressly or constructively assented to, service of process may under the statute be made on the defendant in the defendant's home state. The basis of the jurisdiction thus asserted by the state in which the suit is brought is that the claim sued on arises out of a transaction entered into, or an oc-

[51] R. L. Doherty & Co. v. Goodman, 294 U.S. 623 (1935).

currence within, or a liability incurred, in that state. Thus, to take an extreme instance, in at least one state a statute (whose constitutionality has not yet been passed on by the Supreme Court) authorizes suit in the state on a claim arising out of injuries caused to a resident by allegedly defective merchandise shipped to him from another state; and the Supreme Court has approved a state statute asserting jurisdiction of an out-of-state insurance company in a suit by a resident on an insurance policy negotiated entirely by mail.[52]

Submission of defendant to jurisdiction of court in a particular proceeding: "appearance"

In all systems of civil procedure, provision is made whereby a person named as defendant in an action may notify the plaintiff or the court that he acknowledges the jurisdiction of the court over him and is prepared to defend the action. By such a notice (termed an "appearance") the defendant subjects himself to the jurisdiction of the court for the purposes of that action, and it becomes immaterial to inquire whether he was physically within the jurisdiction of the state (or in the case of a corporation, whether it is domestic or foreign, and if the latter, whether it was doing business within the state) and if so, whether process was properly served, if indeed it was served at all.

Correspondingly, a non-resident or a foreign corporation not subject to the jurisdiction of the state courts may, by entering those courts as a plaintiff, thereby confer jurisdiction on the court in which the action is instituted to entertain a claim asserted against the plaintiff by way of counterclaim in such action. The rules which prescribe the kinds of counterclaims which may be asserted in a particular kind of action vary from state to state and are in any case beyond our scope. Cases are not unknown however in which a foreign corporation (or non-resident) has been as it were provoked into bringing an action in a state, only to find itself (or himself) unwittingly subjected to the jurisdiction of the court with respect to a counterclaim greatly exceeding in magnitude the claim sued on.

Jurisdiction of matrimonial actions

The foregoing discussion has failed to take account of an important class of controversies, namely, actions for separation, annulment, and divorce (collectively termed matrimonial actions).[53] The doctrines which

---

[52] McGee v. International Life Insurance Co., 355 U.S. 220 (1957). These statutes are an outgrowth of the doctrine, first enunciated in International Shoe Co. v. Washington, 326 U.S. 310 (1945), that the state has jurisdiction of the defendant in the particular suit if the defendant had "sufficient contacts or ties with the state . . . to make it reasonable and just . . ."

[53] The nature of these actions is explained at page 171.

have developed regarding the extent of the jurisdiction of the state in this field have been developed almost wholly in connection with the action for divorce. Questions did not present themselves to any significant degree till the turn of the century. Since that time a succession of decisions has built up a body of doctrine which it is quite impossible to restate accurately in the space here available. The general outlines may, however, be indicated.

In perhaps the great majority of divorce proceedings, both parties are residents of the state in which the proceeding is instituted and the defendant is personally served with process in the state, so that no doubt as to the jurisdiction of the state can arise. The question arises in those cases in which the defendant is not alleged to be a resident of the state or to have been served with process in the state. May a state entertain jurisdiction of an action for divorce against such a defendant?

The answer is that it may, if the plaintiff is a resident of the state.[54] Such is the law as it was laid down by the Supreme Court in 1942, in the historic case of Williams v. North Carolina.[55] The state of which the plaintiff is a resident may, under this holding, grant the plaintiff a divorce against a defendant who is not and never has been a resident in that state, and has indeed never been physically within the state.

The rationale of this holding is that since the state has an interest in the marital status of its residents, it may deal with the marital status of one of its residents through its courts, even though the other party to the marriage is not otherwise subject to the jurisdiction of the state. For some decades prior to the announcement of this holding by the Court it had been understood, in consequence of earlier decisions of the Court, that in the absence of personal jurisdiction of the defendant the only state which could assert the power to dissolve the marriage without the defendant's consent was the state of so-called marital domicile, i.e., the state in which both the parties had last resided. Under this doctrine the marriage relation was analogized to tangible property located in a state, over which the courts of that state may exercise jurisdiction, regardless of the where-

[54] In a few states are found statutes purporting to confer jurisdiction on the courts of the state of actions for divorce in which the plaintiff has been in the state for a minimum period, no claim of his being resident or domiciled there being required. (Some of these statutes are intended for, and may be availed of, only by a serviceman stationed in the state.) The constitutionality of such statutes has never been passed upon by the Supreme Court. The Arkansas statute has been held constitutional by the highest court of that state. Wheat v. Wheat, 318 S.W.2d 793 (1958). A decree obtained under such a statute on default of the out-of-state defendant in defending the action would, if challenged by the defendant, undoubtedly be held void by the Supreme Court, the state being wholly without any claim of jurisdiction over either the defendant's or the plaintiff's marital status.

[55] 317 U.S. 287 (1942). Previous to this case the Court had held that the plaintiff's state had no jurisdiction of the non-resident defendant unless the parties had last lived there as husband and wife. Haddock v. Haddock, 201 U.S. 562 (1906).

abouts of anyone who may have a claim on the property, in an action in rem. Under the present doctrine it is not the marriage relation between the two parties, but merely the marital status of the resident plaintiff, that apparently may be regarded as the res.

Correspondingly, the jurisdiction of the state is *limited* to the issue of marital status. Only if the defendant submits to the jurisdiction of the court by acknowledging its jurisdiction (by "appearing" in the action, as the phrase is) may the court go beyond the mere dissolution of the marriage bond and adjudicate the rights of the spouses in relation to property, support, and custody of children. Otherwise the "ex parte"[56] divorce is, as already noted, "divisible," the marriage no longer existing but the defendant's rights created by the marriage remaining unimpaired. The practical consequences—and practical difficulties—that flow from this anomalous form of divorce arise, of course, chiefly in proceedings in other states than that in which the divorce was decreed—most frequently in the state in which the parties both formerly resided and in which the divorced defendant still resides. Discussion of those consequences will therefore be deferred to the next chapter, in which is considered the general question of the obligation of a court to accord recognition to the judgments of courts in other jurisdictions.

As just indicated, the non-resident defendant may appear in the action and seek its dismissal,[57] one of the possible grounds for such dismissal being that the plaintiff is not a bona fide resident of the state, but has merely set up a pretended residence there for the purpose of instituting the divorce action. However, in the typical situation in which the husband, unable to procure his wife's consent to a divorce, sets up residence in a distant state and there institutes action, it is often beyond the wife's means to contest the action there. More important, if she does so, thereby submitting to the plenary jurisdiction of the court, she runs the risk of an adverse decree, not only dissolving the marriage but perhaps stripping her of

[56] An "ex parte" proceeding is strictly one in which the party instituting the proceeding is the only party, the order sought from the court if granted having no adverse effect on the rights of any other person. An application to a court for an order changing one's name is thus an "ex parte" proceeding. A divorce decree granted on the failure of the defendant to answer after being served with process is thus a "default" decree rather than an ex parte decree. The latter term has, however, come into use for divorces of the type under discussion because of the flimsiness of the jurisdiction of the state granting the decree.

[57] In most states, a defendant wishing to challenge the jurisdiction of the court need not, by appearing for that purpose, thereby subject himself generally to such jurisdiction. He may appear "specially," and if the court sustains its own jurisdiction, he may then permit judgment to be taken against him by default, with the intention of again challenging the jurisdiction of the court, and hence the validity of the judgment, when the attempt is made to enforce the judgment, or to secure its recognition in another jurisdiction. In some states, however, the statutes do not authorize such "special" appearance.

rights of support, property rights, and even, it may be, of rights to the custody of the children of the marriage. Consequently, in this situation the wife is commonly advised to permit judgment to be taken against her by default.

Jurisdiction by attachment

Finally, attention must be given to the exercise by a state of jurisdiction over a controversy in which it does not enjoy exclusive jurisdiction over the subject matter and in which the person of the defendant is not subject to the jurisdiction of the courts of the state. This special exercise of jurisdiction by a state is possible where property of the defendant, even though wholly unconnected with the controversy in suit, is within the state. Any person owning property, real or personal (including intangible property such as monetary claims), situated in a given state consents that such property may be subjected to the process of the courts of that state. Hence, if an action is sought to be instituted against the owner of such property in the courts of that state, even if the controversy in nowise concerns the property in question, the plaintiff may procure a seizure and impounding of the property by an officer of the court (commonly called an "attachment"). Notice of such seizure (and of the action) having been duly given to the defendant, whether within or without the state, the resultant judgment will be binding on the property so seized, though not on any other property of the defendant, whether within or without the state. In most states, the property of a resident may not be thus attached except under special circumstances but the property of a non-resident may be attached in every case; and for the purpose of this remedy, a foreign corporation is treated precisely like a non-resident natural person, even though it may, in fact, have its principal or even its sole place of business in the state in which the attachment is had.

If the defendant fails to defend the action and judgment goes against him by default, the plaintiff may cause the property which has been attached to be levied upon and sold, and may satisfy his judgment only out of the proceeds of such sale. If the defendant desires to prevent this result he must "appear" in the action and defend. Once he does this, however, he has, as already seen, subjected himself completely to the jurisdiction of the court; and any money judgment thereafter resulting is enforceable against him by the seizure and sale not only of the property attached, but of any other property owned by him (even, as we shall see, property owned by him in another state or in a foreign country). The choice thus presented to a non-resident defendant where a limited amount of his property has been attached—the choice between permitting judgment to go against him by default, thus forfeiting the limited value of the property attached, and defending the action, thus risking an adverse judgment for a larger amount—is often a hard one.

6. COURT IN WHICH ACTION MAY BE BROUGHT

If an action is to be brought in the federal courts, the problem of the appropriate court in which to bring it does not (except as to the appropriate geographical division) ordinarily arise. A single type of court, the district court, has, with minor exceptions,[58] jurisdiction of every variety of federal civil case.

In the states, by contrast, a multiplicity of types of civil courts is everywhere found—in a few states, a bewildering multiplicity—each with its own specially defined jurisdiction, there being differences not only with respect to the type of remedy which they may grant, but, even among those which may grant only the money judgment and cognate simple remedies, as to the maximum amount of the judgment they may grant.

With respect to the type of remedy available in them, the chief cleavage is between those courts which may grant only the money judgment and the like, and those which may grant injunctions, mandatory decrees, and other more sweeping remedies, or, to use the conventional terminology, between those which may grant only "legal" remedies and those which may grant "equitable" ones.

Courts of law and courts of equity

The English system of civil justice, as it existed at the time of the British colonization of these shores, exhibited on the one hand an extreme centralization of its civil courts in London, and on the other hand, an extreme fragmentation of jurisdiction among those courts. If we take 1650 as a convenient point at which to examine this structure, and if we confine ourselves only to the leading civil courts, we find side by side in London (in addition to the Admiralty Court, and to the ecclesiastical courts, having jurisdiction over decedent's estates) the Court of King's Bench and the Court of Common Pleas (both known as "courts of law") and the Court of Chancery (known as the "court of equity").[59]

The two courts of law already had behind them, by the middle of the seventeenth century, some four centuries of development, whereas the Court of Chancery was but two centuries old. It had originated in the

[58] Certain classes of claims against the government can be sued on only in the Court of Claims. 28 U.S. Code, Secs. 1346, 1491 ff. In the District of Columbia, actions involving less than $10,000 must in certain cases be brought in the Court of General Sessions of the district.

[59] For a full account of the English courts at this time (as set forth by Coke in his Fourth Institute) see Pound, Organization of Courts, 4 ff. (1940).

practice of referring to the king's chancellor such petitions as were from time to time submitted to the king, praying for his aid in securing justice for the petitioner. Despite the growth of the royal courts during the preceding century, and the continued extension of their jurisdiction, petitions to the king for relief in particular cases, based on the unwillingness or inability of the royal courts to give redress, were in the fourteenth century increasingly numerous. These petitions came to be quite commonly referred to the chancellor, a high officer of the king, invariably a churchman, who also served as a sort of secretary to the king's council. In about the middle of the fourteenth century, by royal decree, the chancellor and the keeper of the privy seal were designated as the sole officials to whom such petitions ("petitions of grace") should be referred. The next century witnessed the concentration of this duty in the chancellor, and the emergence of the Court of Chancery as a formal court rather than a mere informal agency of the king's council, and by 1474 we have a recorded case in which the chancellor makes a decree by his own sole authority.

The usual plea in these petitions was that the royal judges had refused to grant relief to the petitioner because the existing rules of law made no provision for such relief and the judges professed themselves powerless to change the rules. Sometimes however, the plea was that the petitioner, seeking redress against some powerful person, had in effect been barred from the local sittings of the royal courts by force or threat of force, or that the judges or officers of the court had been overawed by like means— a complaint especially common during the dynastic disorders of the fifteenth century.

The rigidity that had come to characterize the courts of law arose from the fact that as royal courts they had from the first proceeded only when set in motion by a royal writ. Such writs, though issued in the name of the king, had of course come to be issued as a matter of routine by his officers (the chancellor and his clerks being in fact the officers primarily charged with this duty), and had in the course of decades assumed a standardized form. By reason of conflicts of jurisdiction between the several royal courts, and perhaps also in certain cases between the secular and ecclesiastical courts; by reason also perhaps of the jealousy of the king's council of too great an extension of the power of the royal courts; and, no doubt of equal importance with any of these factors, the universal tendency of institutions to become petrified—for all these reasons, and perhaps others which have escaped the researches of historical scholars— the types of redress dispensed by the royal courts had come to be confined exclusively to those available under the several traditional types of writs. An extremely static, inflexible, and extraordinarily technical system of justice had developed in the royal courts; and a legal profession had rapidly grown up, a large part of whose skill was expended in ingenious efforts at demonstrating to the judges that a particular situation could, or could not, be redressed by a particular standard form of action, predicated on a particular writ, and within the rigid rules of decision determined by precedent. It was this system that caused the increasing volume of "petitions of grace" to the king, resulting, as we have seen, in the development of the Court of Chancery.

A simple case will illustrate the function of the Court of Chancery in shaping new remedies. A contract has been made for the sale of land; but on the day fixed by the contract for the delivery of the deed to the buyer, the seller refuses to deliver it, announcing that he has changed his mind. He is willing to pay a certain sum in damages to the buyer; but the buyer refuses, having had special reasons (such as contiguity to another piece of land he has concurrently contracted to buy) for desiring that particular piece of land. Under such circumstances, however, a court of law, with its limited sheaf of remedies, could offer the buyer only a judgment for damages, which he did not want. Petitions to the Court of Chancery, in such cases, however, resulted in the creation of a new form of remedy— an order directing the seller, on pain of imprisonment for disobedience, to deliver a deed to the buyer.

Here it is essential only to note the coexistence in England at the time in question of a dual civil court structure. As distinguished from the admiralty and ecclesiastical courts, each of which had exclusive jurisdiction of a special class of matters, both these parts of the main court system had a general jurisdiction over civil matters, but differed in the form of remedy they could afford, and thus in the type of proceeding they could entertain.

In course of time the procedures and doctrines which the Court of Chancery applied came to be known as "equitable," in contradistinction to the great body of rules applied by the ordinary courts, which were termed "legal." The same distinction, in another form, developed in the terms "equity" and "law." The Chancery Court, and subsequently any court in this country exercising similar powers, became known as a "court of equity," while the ordinary civil courts were termed courts of "law." In English, and subsequently in American, legal nomenclature the term "law" continues to be used in the narrow technical sense just indicated, while retaining also its original non-technical meaning, in which it embraces not only the legal doctrines and procedure of equity as well as of law courts, but also those of the courts of admiralty and of the ecclesiastical courts and their modern successors.

In the development of the legal systems of the colonies during the eighteenth century (for during the seventeenth century their legal institutions were for the most part rudimentary), the governor and designated members of his council were in several states constituted a separate court of chancery. In the remaining colonies the distinction between legal and equitable remedies was, however, by no means ignored. The "extraordinary" remedies available in the Court of Chancery (for so they had come to be termed) were not committed to the minor courts but were reserved to the superior courts. Consequently, the former could grant only legal remedies, while the latter could grant both legal and equitable remedies. After the Revolution, separate chancery courts were created in several of the states; and even some of the states later admitted created separate courts of chancery. In the second half of the nineteenth century, however, separate courts of chancery were largely abandoned, and their powers vested in the superior courts of law. Today only Arkansas, Delaware, Mississippi, and Tennessee still maintain separate chancery courts. Hence, generally speaking, all civil courts may entertain an action for damages, resulting in a money judgment—a legal remedy—while, for example, an action to compel the performance of a contract, resulting in a decree directing the defendant to perform on pain of punishment—an equitable remedy —can be maintained only in such of the higher civil trial courts as have been vested with equitable jurisdiction.

Other important traditional remedies available only in a court clothed with equity powers are the injunction, an order forbidding the defendant to do a particular act, and the judgment ordering a trustee or other fiduciary to surrender funds or property adjudicated to have been wrongfully taken or suffered to be lost, or the equivalent thereof. Moreover, as additional special forms of remedy have been introduced into our law, their administration has in some states been entrusted only to courts enjoying equitable powers; so that though they were in fact unknown to the Court of Chancery these newer remedies have come in those states to be assimilated to the purely historic category of equitable remedies. Illustrations are the decree of divorce (a remedy unknown to the Court of Chancery) and the declaratory judgment, a declaration of the legal rights of the parties to a dispute (a remedy dispensed by the Court of Chancery only in a very limited class of cases).

Inferior and superior courts of law

The money judgment, already mentioned as a typical "legal" remedy, is by no means the only one. Closely associated with it (though quantitatively far less important) is the judgment awarding the plaintiff the right to possession of property in the possession of the defendant (the action for such a judgment being termed, if the property is realty, an action in ejectment, and if it is personalty, an action in replevin). Both these judgments, be it noted, take the form not of an order to the offending party to pay the money or to surrender possession of the property; they merely adjudicate that the money should be paid or the property surrendered, and make available to the victor the aid of the officers of the court (sheriff, marshal, constable, bailiff, or the like) in obtaining payment by levy on the property or income of the judgment debtor, or in obtaining possession of the specific property, if it can be found, by physical seizure. In contradistinction, the judgment of a court of equity is directed, characteristically, to the defendant himself, and non-compliance with the judgment will subject him to fine or imprisonment. It is for this reason that it is often said that a court of equity acts "in personam," i.e., against the person, while a court of law merely acts "in rem," i.e., against the thing (the property) of the litigant.

In addition to the proceedings resulting in the two common types of judgment at law just referred to, there are a number of special proceedings cognizable in the courts of law, in each of which a specialized remedy is appropriate. Among such proceedings may be mentioned proceedings for the release of a person from private custody or from the custody of officers of the law (the so-called habeas corpus proceeding), a determination of the right of contending parents or relatives to the custody of an infant, determination of the value of property condemned, the appraisal of the shares owned by a dissenting stockholder in certain corporate proceedings, and the dissolution of corporations.

Some of these proceedings, and their corresponding remedies, are part of the ancient tradition of the courts of law; others have been the product of later legislation, which has specifically extended the jurisdiction of the courts of law to embrace them.

The law courts of the lowest stratum—the rural justice courts and their urban counterparts—have not been invested with jurisdiction over the entire range of proceedings and remedies at law. On the contrary, their power is ordinarily limited to the award of a money judgment (not exceeding a stated amount) and the award of possession of property. Even within this limited area, there are ordinarily further limitations. Actions for money judgments, even if the sum demanded is within the modest monetary limits of the court's jurisdiction, are ordinarily withdrawn from these courts if the claim arises out of anything other than a contract or an injury to person or property; for example, actions for damages for defamation or for wrongful arrest or imprisonment are ordinarily not cognizable by these courts.

Where there exists an intermediate level of civil courts, the courts on that level are generally invested with jurisdiction over nearly the whole range of proceedings and remedies at law. There are a few such proceedings and remedies, however, sometimes termed "extraordinary," which are commonly reserved for the trial courts at the highest level. Among these are a proceeding to compel a public officer to perform an act required by law (mandamus proceeding) or a proceeding to procure the release of a person unlawfully held in custody (habeas corpus proceeding). Indeed, in a few states, even the highest trial court is not entrusted with the power to entertain mandamus proceedings against public officers, that power being reserved for the highest court of the state, whose functions are in all other types of proceeding purely appellate.

Probate courts

There is one type of special proceeding which is in some states entrusted to a special court, namely, a proceeding for the admission of a will to probate; and the supervision of the management and distribution of the estate of a deceased person by the executors of his will (or the administrators appointed by the court) is also commonly entrusted to this court. Quite frequently proceedings regarding the adoption of children, and in some states cases regarding the administration of the estates of incompetent persons, are also cognizable only by this special court. Its basic jurisdiction relates, however, to the estates of deceased persons.

The reason for thus erecting separate courts for the disposition of this particular type of proceeding is historical only, since there is nothing in the nature of the proceeding which calls for such separate jurisdictional organization. In the development of the English legal system, the estates of deceased persons occupied a special place. It was not until the sixteenth century that wills of real estate were given recognition in the English law; previous to that time the descent of real property was regulated by the law. Earlier, however, there had developed the doctrine that personal property[60] could be bequeathed by will provided that a stipulated portion was left to the church. There resulted a system of administration of the personal estates of decedents by the ecclesiastical authorities; and in the course of time there developed in these ecclesiastical tribunals a considerable body of law regulating the distribution of the personal property of decedents who died intestate and the probate and execution of wills of personal property. Such was still the situation at the time of the English settlement of America; and thus we find in some of the colonies, as for example, in New York, the arrangements for the jurisdictional control of decedents' estates being withheld entirely from the regular courts and assumed by the governor, in his character as deputy of the Crown and in that capacity the representative of the king as the head of the Church of England. Had there developed in this country a single established church for all the colonies under the dominion of the Church of England, such an institution might have taken over the jurisdiction of decedents' estates. Instead, the separate probate jurisdiction thus initiated survived in the form of the separate probate courts already mentioned. Such separate

[60] In Anglo-American legal nomenclature all property (intangible as well as tangible) which is not realty is termed personal property.

courts are still found in many of our states. In not a few areas, however, the separate existence of the court dealing with decedents' estates is more formal than real, the separate court which apparently exists, commonly termed a probate court, being in fact merely a registry of papers and proceedings affecting decedents' estates, and any questions calling for judicial determination arising in connection with such estates being handled by the regular civil courts of superior jurisdiction.

7. VENUE

In the organization of any system of civil courts for an extensive area, the question of the territorial jurisdiction within which the process of each court shall be effective is a difficult one. Constitutionally, a state may, of course, vest a court in any part of the state with power to bring before it a defendant from any other part of the state no matter how distant; and in certain types of proceeding there is sound reason why this should be done. On the other hand, to permit a litigant in any part of the state to institute a proceeding at the point most convenient to him and require his adversary to respond there, no matter from what part of the state, would, except perhaps in our few small states, be manifestly unjust. To arrive at a proper compromise between these two considerations is not easy. In most states at the present time in the ordinary civil proceeding the defendant, if a natural person, can be summoned to answer only in the county in which he resides. Where the defendant is a corporation, it may be required to answer, in some of the states, not merely in the county or counties in which it has its establishments, but even in the most distant counties.

In the much vaster area of the federal court system, the problem is still more difficult. The solution arrived at by Congress is in most classes of cases to subject the individual to suit only in the federal court district in which he resides.[61] In diversity cases he may also be sued in the district in which the plaintiff resides, if he is there served with process (where he could, of course, be sued also in the state courts at the plaintiff's election). If the defendant is a corporation, it may be sued in the federal courts in the district in which it is incorporated, or in which it is licensed to do business, or is doing business.[62]

[61] If there are two or more defendants, and they reside in different districts of the same state, the action may be brought in any of such districts. If, however, they reside in different states they may not be sued in any one state. The resulting impossibility of procuring an adjudication in a single proceeding against defendants jointly liable but residing in different states—a defect of our system which Congress could cure—has already been commented on (pp. 202 ff.).

[62] However, Congress in 1948 authorized a district court "for the convenience of parties and witnesses, in the interest of justice," to transfer any civil action to any other district where it might have been brought. 28 U.S. Code, Sec. 1404(a). This

In actions under the federal antitrust laws (jurisdiction of which, as already noted, is vested exclusively in the federal courts), Congress has authorized the bringing of suits, both by the government and by private parties, in districts in which the defendant in not amenable to suit in other classes of actions.[63] Proposals have for some time been advanced in Congress to permit suits in all cases to be brought in the district in which the transaction or occurrence on which the suit is founded took place—proposals reflecting no doubt the belief that the increased speed of travel minimizes the inconvenience to the defendant of responding in a distant court.

---

provision has, as intended, largely, abated the practice of bringing nuisance actions against corporations (railroads particularly) in a federal district court remote from the scene of the occurrences or transactions involved.

[63] An action by a private party for damages under the antitrust laws may be brought in any district in which the defendant is "found," or has an agent. 15 U.S. Code, Sec. 10. In an action for an injunction under the antitrust laws, if it appears to the judge before whom the action is pending "that the ends of justice require that other parties should be brought before the court, the court may cause them to be summoned" regardless of where located. 15 U.S. Code, Sec. 25.

7

Civil Proceedings: Procedure

1. DEVELOPMENT OF CIVIL PROCEDURE. 2. THE RIGHT TO SUE. 3. ACQUISITION OF JURISDICTION. 4. STAGE OF PROCEEDING. 5. PROVISIONAL REMEDIES. 6. DEFINING THE ISSUES OF LAW AND OF FACT. 7. THE LAW APPLICABLE TO THE ISSUES OF LAW. 8. READJUDICATION OF MATTERS ALREADY ADJUDICATED. 9. JUDGMENT IN ABSENCE OF ISSUE OF FACT: SUMMARY JUDGMENT. 10. TRIAL OF ISSUE OF FACT: PREPARATORY STEPS. 11. TRIAL OF ISSUE OF FACT: MODE OF PROOF. 12. TRIAL OF ISSUE OF FACT BY JURY: INSTITUTIONAL ASPECTS. 13. TRIAL OF ISSUE OF FACT BY JURY: PROCEDURAL ASPECTS. 14. JUDGMENT BY DEFAULT: CONSENT JUDGMENTS. 15. APPLICATION FOR NEW TRIAL ON GROUND OF NEWLY DISCOVERED EVIDENCE. 16. APPELLATE REVIEW: THE RIGHT TO A REVIEW. 17. APPELLATE REVIEW: JUDGMENT ENTERED ON VERDICT OF JURY. 18. APPELLATE REVIEW: OTHER JUDGMENTS. 19. APPELLATE REVIEW: PROCEDURE. 20. DELAY. 21. COSTLINESS.

Perhaps more markedly than is the case with criminal procedure, the procedure in the more diversified field of civil proceedings displays numerous variations in detail as we move from state to state. But the civil procedures of all the states (except Louisiana) and of the federal courts have a common ancestry; and to a very considerable extent nineteenth century—and even twentieth century—reforms in the states have been widely made on the basis of fairly uniform statutes. Our civil procedure thus displays a marked uniformity of basic patterns, and frequently of detail as well.

These basic patterns themselves are the product not of a logical design but rather of a process of growth some centuries old; hence, before entering on their examination, it will be of value to take some account of the historical factors.

1. DEVELOPMENT OF CIVIL PROCEDURE

In the multiplex civil court system of seventeenth century England, each of the separate sets of courts—the courts of law, the court of chancery, the ecclesiastical courts, and the admiralty courts—had its characteristic procedure, developed by it independently of the others. Present-day civil procedures represent an imperfect and as yet incomplete fusion of these diverse systems. Despite a process of unification and homogenization which has been at work for more than a century and which has been notably accelerated in recent years, our civil procedures still reflect the diverse origins from which they stem.

The procedure of the law courts in civil cases developed, like those courts themselves, more or less as an indigenous product of English soil, or rather in its early stages, of the Norman judges operating on English soil. With the development of the jury in the courts of law (a development which, as we have seen, required several centuries for its completion) the civil trial procedure of those courts was, like the criminal trial procedure, in very considerable degree shaped by the fact of the participation of the jury. The admiralty, ecclesiastical, and equity courts, however, developing independently of the law courts, proceeded wholly without juries; and their procedures, though differing one from another, all have in common the fact that their trial procedure was a non-jury procedure, and that their procedures were not developed indigenously but derived from the Roman procedure.

Each of these four systems of procedure has contributed in greater or less degree to the procedures in force today. Thus, although no ecclesiastical courts as such were transplanted to this continent, the courts which inherited the ancient jurisdiction of the ecclesiastical courts in the administration of decedents' estates still show traces of the traditional procedure in their exercise of that jurisdiction. The procedure employed in an admiralty proceeding today retains to a marked degree features peculiar to the separate admiralty courts of English and colonial days.

The process of conforming the two most important of these four systems of procedure—law and equity—as far as possible to a single pattern received its first important impetus in the adoption by the legislature of New York in 1848 of a code of simplified civil procedure designed to supersede the complex and multiplex procedures which had developed through the centuries, and in particular to free our procedure from historical deposits laid down under conditions peculiar to the development of the several English courts and to their competition for jurisdiction, and serving no purpose in a rational system of procedure. This code (often known as the Field Code after its chief proponent and draftsman, David Dudley Field) was widely copied in other states and is regarded as one of the major events in the history of American procedural reform. Today, in not less than half of the states, the civil procedure is in greater or less degree derived from this code; and the process of rationalization and simplification of civil procedure continues unremittingly, if slowly.

In the federal courts, while the procedure in admiralty cases still retains much of its distinctive traditional character, the procedure in other civil cases is a model of latter-day simplification. A distinctive federal procedure in equity existed almost from the beginning (the Supreme Court having been authorized at the very outset to promulgate rules for the procedure in all federal courts in actions in equity); but the procedure in actions at law varied from state to state, Congress having from the first provided that in such actions the federal court should conform "to the practice pleadings and forms and modes of proceeding existing at the time in like causes in courts of record of the state" within which the federal court might be sitting. In 1938, however, the Supreme Court, acting under authority given it by Congress in 1934, promulgated the Rules of Civil Procedure for the District Courts of the United States which not only provided for the first time a single procedure for all federal courts in civil actions at law, but conformed the procedure at law and in equity as nearly as practicable to a single pattern. These rules, like the New York Code of nearly a century before, have served as a model for procedural reform in an increasing number of states.

The codes of procedure adopted in the last century in the various states represented an immense advance toward simplicity and efficiency. It must not be thought, however, that the technicalities and idle forms characteristic of the ancient system have given way to a regime of complete simplicity and directness. The code system has developed technicalities and refinements of its own; and though these do not have the scholastic and artificial flavor of their ancient predecessors, they have been widely criticized as tending to delay and obstruct the administration of civil justice.

The responsibility for this condition has been very generally laid by critics at the door of the legislatures. The code of procedure enacted by the legislature should, in this view, comprise a few basic procedures only, outlined in general terms, the detail to be supplied by the higher courts of the state, and even as framed by those courts, to allow a large measure of discretion to the judge in a particular case. In many code states, however, the legislature has elaborated the code to a high degree, with the result that needed changes come slowly, and the ability of the courts to deal expeditiously with procedural problems is greatly impaired.

A definite movement for a return to the higher courts of the states of the "rule-making power" anciently exercised by the English courts, and even by our own early courts, is now under way. As already stated, the

Supreme Court of the United States has been vested by Congress with the power to make procedural rules for all cases in the federal courts. The example thus set by Congress is finding increasing favor in the states.[1] It must be admitted, however, that in some states in which the highest court has long enjoyed rule-making power, there has been little disposition on the part of the court to make a vigorous use of the power for the improvement of procedure.

To the extent that the inertia of the legislature in matters of procedural reform has been due to lack of current expert guidance, the creation, in a number of the states, of a standing advisory board, usually designated as the judicial council of the state, to study procedure and recommend reforms, has effected a substantial improvement.

The need for procedural improvement in the civil courts is a subject of much current interest and effort on the part of the organized American bar, as well as of judicial and other official agencies. It is fair to state that a steady progress in the improvement in civil procedure is being made. It is doubtful, however, whether any efforts at reform, no matter how sincere or how long continued, can reduce our civil procedure to that degree of simplicity which the layman is likely to think it ought to have. The situations which rules of procedure are designed to meet are in many cases rather complicated; and the framing of "simple" rules to control complicated situations too often results not in simplicity, but rather in uncertainty and ambiguity, the resolution of which in turn entails the exercise of uncontrolled, and in procedural matters virtually unreviewable, discretion by the judge.

The layman's conviction that procedural elaboration is unnecessary stems often from a somewhat naive feeling that both parties to a litigation are really seeking the same thing and that judicial red tape merely gets in their way. The fact is, of course, that virtually every procedural device was born of the necessity of checking some attempted abuse of the process of the court by one or another party. When both parties are in fact sincerely desirous of a quick adjudication on the merits, procedural requirements create little difficulty or delay.

Partly as the result of their historical origins and partly because of their special setting, certain types of civil proceeding are characterized by variations in procedure, and even more often in nomenclature, peculiar to themselves. Nevertheless, despite such variations, it is possible to identify in all civil proceedings certain features common to all, and it is to these basic features that we shall direct our attention, giving primary

[1] In New Jersey, the state constitution confers the rule-making power on the state supreme court "subject to law." That court has held that this phrase does not empower the legislature to override by statute the rules laid down by the court—that the words "subject to law" mean merely subject to the substantive law. Winberry v. Salisbury, 5 N.J. 240, 74A.2d 406 (1950).

emphasis throughout, however, to that proceeding which is quantitatively at least far the most important—the ordinary form of action at law.

In our account of procedure in criminal cases, we took note of the overriding importance of the requirement of the Constitution, applicable both to federal and state proceedings, of "due process of law." This requirement is, needless to say, applicable equally to civil proceedings. In that field, however, there is manifestly less occasion for the application of the due process concept. Indeed, its chief significance is in the principle that all procedural forms must be so designed as to give the party proceeded against reasonable notice of the several steps and issues in the proceeding and reasonable opportunity to protect his interests therein.

The several stages of a civil proceeding under which we shall consider civil procedure are (1) the acquisition of jurisdiction, (2) provisional or conservatory steps, (3) the framing of the issues, (4) proceedings preparatory to trial, (5) trial, and (6) proceedings subsequent to trial. In a proceeding in which there is no dispute as to any issue of fact, the necessity for a trial and for some of the preliminary steps in connection therewith of course disappears.

2. THE RIGHT TO SUE

Basically, our courts, state and federal, are open to all persons of full age. The right of natural persons to have access to the courts is indeed doubtless a constitutional one, protected as to both federal and state courts by the due process clauses of the Constitution. The right of a citizen of one state to have access to the courts of any other state equally with the citizens of that state is moreover specifically protected by the "privileges and immunities" clause of the Constitution (Article IV, Section 2).[2] Finally, any attempted interference by a state with the right of access to the federal courts is unconstitutional; and presumably, though the case has never arisen, an attempted interference by Congress with the right of access to state courts for redress wholly within the sphere of state judicial power would be equally unconstitutional.[3]

The privileges and immunities clause of the Constitution, just referred to, provides that "the citizens of each state shall be entitled to all privileges and immunities of citizens in the several states." Inasmuch as a corporation is not a citizen, however, this provision affords no protection against the refusal of a state to permit a corporation incorporated in another state to sue in its courts; and not uncommonly, state statutes im-

[2] This provision does not, however, disable a state from requiring that a nonresident citizen, suing in its courts, shall post bond to insure payment to the defendant of any costs that may be awarded him. As to costs, see below, pp. 285 ff.

[3] In time of war enemy aliens may be (as indeed to a limited extent they have been in both world wars) prohibited by Congress from suing in our courts.

pose as a penalty upon such a corporation, which has assumed to do intrastate business in the state without having obtained authority to do so pursuant to statute, the denial of the right of suit in the state courts.

Notwithstanding the failure of the constitutional provision quoted to afford protection to a foreign corporation against exclusion from the courts of a state, an exclusion too drastic or arbitrary might well encounter the condemnation of the courts as a denial of "due process of law" or of "equal protection of the laws," forbidden by the Constitution.

Still another limitation upon the power of the state to regulate access to its courts is to be found in treaties of commerce and amity between the United States and foreign countries. A typical provision of such a treaty reads: "The citizens or subjects of each of the High Contracting Parties shall have free access to the courts of justice of the other in pursuit and defense of their rights: they shall be at liberty, equally with the native citizens or subjects of the most favored nation, to choose and employ lawyers, advocates, and representatives to prosecute and defend their rights before such courts."

Even though a given controversy falls within the constitutionally permissible area of state judicial power, the state may decline to vest its courts with jurisdiction thereof, or it may vest its courts with power to decline jurisdiction thereof. In the exercise of this latter power, state courts generally refuse to accept jurisdiction of actions between non-residents arising out of torts allegedly committed outside the state, of actions between non-residents relative to the internal affairs of foreign corporations, and of other types of action in which neither the parties nor the subject matter have any connection with the state. Under doctrines enunciated by the Supreme Court, however, as will shortly be pointed out, a state, by reason of its constitutional obligation to give "full faith and credit to the public acts" of another state, may be compelled against its will to permit its courts to take jurisdiction of such a matter where the right of action is created by the statute of another state.

In various types of proceeding, the person instituting the action alleges not a wrong suffered by him individually, but rather one done to a class in which he is included, or to a community of which he is a member (hence the term "class action"). Thus a stockholder may allege injury done by the directors or officers of the corporation to the stockholders generally; a local taxpayer may under certain statutes allege injury to the public treasury to which he is a contributor. The right thus to institute a proceeding in a representative capacity ("standing" to sue, as the phrase is) is subject to diverse restrictions, variously applied in the several states and in the federal courts.[4]

[4] As to standing of federal taxpayer to sue, see pp. 188, 293, and 314.

3. ACQUISITION OF JURISDICTION

We have already considered in previous chapters the permissible and actual scope of both federal and state judicial power, and have noted the concentration of federal jurisdiction in a single type of court of original jurisdiction, and the typical distribution of jurisdicton of the several classes of cases within the state judicial power among the courts of the state.

Given a certain class of cases within the jurisdiction of a given court, we are now concerned with the procedure by which that court acquires jurisdiction of a particular case within that class. If the judgment sought is to run against the defendant, so that all his or its property (or even his person) is to be bound by it, the court must acquire jurisdiction of the defendant; if the judgment sought is to bind only some particular item of property, the court need acquire jurisdiction only of that property.

Jurisdiction of defendant: service of process

The first step in the institution of a proceeding in which jurisdiction of the defendant is desired is the giving of written notice to the defendant of the institution of the action, such notice usually, though not necesarily, embodying a statement of the plaintiff's claim, and a demand on the defendant that he answer the plaintiff's statement.

With respect to a defendant resident in the state, the traditional method of service of the initial process, if the defendant is in the state and does not evade such personal service, is delivery of the process to him in person, the delivery, under some procedures, being preceded by a reading of the process to him. In many states, however, and in federal proceedings, the delivery of a copy of the process at the defendant's abode is deemed adequate; and service of process by mail is permitted in an increasing number of states. In the case of a non-resident defendant, service within the state is ordinarily necessary. Exceptions are found, however, in cases covered by the motor-vehicle or other cognate statutes, under which the state assumes jurisdiction of an action against a non-resident by reason of the activities carried on in the state by the non-resident in connection with the subject matter of the action, and in divorce actions instituted by residents against non-resident.

In those states in which personal service of the process on the defendant is still requisite, the statutes commonly provide that if a resident of the state absents himself from the state for an extended period, without designating an agent upon whom personal service may be made in his absence, it is ordinarily possible, under the governing statutes, to effect service by delivering the process to his residence or place of business, or by serving him personally outside the state.

In connection with these varied methods of giving notice to the defendant of the institution of the action, as well as in connection with the forms of notice employed in other situations about to be mentioned, the alleged inadequacy of the form of notice provided may be attacked as constituting a denial of due process of law; and in some cases judgments by default have been set aside on this ground. The question is one ultimately for decision by the Supreme Court; but relatively few cases raising the question have come before that tribunal.

Service of process on a corporation may involve technical questions not merely of the state's jurisdiction of the corporation, referred to in the previous chapter, but of the proper selection of the particular officer or agent of the corporation on whom service may be made. Where the defendant is an unincorporated association with a great many members, such as a labor union, service of process must under traditional doctrines be made on all the members of the association. In a number of states, by statute, service may however be made on the officers of such an association (some of the statutes specifically mentioning labor unions), and the resulting judgment will bind the property of the association, though not the individual property of the members. In states where such statutes have not been enacted, and where the traditional rule still obtains, large associations are for practical purposes immune from suit. From this has arisen the wholly unfounded notion that a labor union is immune to suit. The practical difficulty, however, in the states still following the traditional rule, of holding a labor union financially responsible for breach of contract (as where a strike is called in violation of the no-strike pledge in an agreement with an employer) caused Congress to insert in the Labor-Management Relations Act of 1947 (popularly called the Taft-Hartley Law) a provision making a labor organization representing employees in an industry affecting interstate or foreign commerce suable in the federal courts for violation of its contract with an employer (or with another labor organization), and providing that the service of the process of the federal court upon "an officer or agent of a labor organization, in his capacity as such, shall constitute service upon the labor organization."[5]

Jurisdiction of property proceeded against

Where the judgment sought in a proceeding would not bind the defendant's person, or his property generally, but only his rights in some property within the exclusive jurisdiction of the court, jurisdiction of the defendant is unnecessary. All that is required is that he be given timely notice of the proceedings by direct communication or, if that be impracticable, by publication. A particular piece of property is within the exclusive jurisdiction of the court either because as real estate it is perma-

[5] 29 U.S. Code, Sec. 185(d).

nently situated there, or because it has been seized under order of the court, such seizure constituting indeed in the proceedings under discussion the step by which the court acquires jurisdiction. The property thus seized may be the property which is the subject of the dispute to be adjudicated (as where the plaintiff, alleging that possession of an item of property is wrongfully withheld by the defendant, institutes an action for its repossession by procuring the seizure of the property); or it may be property on which the plaintiff claims a lien arising out of the claim in dispute (as when a seaman suing for wages in admiralty institutes the suit by causing the vessel on which he served to be "arrested");[6] or it may be property which has no relation to the dispute (as when the plaintiff seeking a money judgment against a non-resident institutes his action by attaching some property of the defendant within the jurisdiction of the court). In all these cases, the jurisdiction thus acquired by the court is a jurisdiction in rem only; but as already pointed out, if the defendant appears in the action, the jurisdiction of the court is enlarged and becomes a jurisdiction of the defendant, so as to enable the court to enter judgment where appropriate against him also, and not merely against the property initially proceeded against.

Exclusive jurisdiction of subject matter

Where a particular subject matter, though intangible, is exclusively within the jurisdiction of a single court, the methods of giving notice to the parties in interest are of the same character as employed in proceedings in rem. In bankruptcy proceedings and under many state laws in proceedings affecting probate and decedents' estates, notice by ordinary mail is all that is required.

Jurisdiction of non-resident defendant in divorce action

As pointed out in the preceding chapter,[7] the doctrine which permits a divorce action to be instituted in a state in which the defendant does not reside and is not present, the sole ground of jurisdiction being the plaintiff's residence in the state, may be regarded, though not expressly so stated by the Supreme Court, as an action in rem, the plaintiff's marital status being the res. It is presumably on the basis of such a concept, though nowhere so expressed, that the Court has given its approval to the employment in such cases of service by publication—i.e., the publication of a copy of the

---

[6] Such an "arrest" has the effect of impressing the special rights of the claimant (when, as, and if established) upon the vessel, and of immobilizing the vessel until the claim is disposed of or until suitable bond is furnished. The judgment for the libelant (as the plaintiff in an admiralty suit is called) confirms the libelant's lien on the vessel, but does not further bind the owners of the vessel unless the court has by service of process on them, or by their appearance, acquired personal jurisdiction of them.

[7] See p. 214.

summons in a newspaper published in the place where the court sits—as meeting the constitutional requirement of "due process"; and despite the obvious precariousness, in this situation, of this method of bringing home to the defendant notice of the institution of the action, it is sanctioned by the statutes and court practice of many of the states.

4. STAGES OF PROCEEDING

In the history of any type of civil proceeding, several distinct stages may be noted; and a recognition of those stages, sometimes so distinct from one another that each stage may indeed be regarded as a separate proceeding, is helpful. However, no uniform listing of such stages is practicable. The course of the proceeding is determined by its objective, and the variety of possible objectives outlined in the preceding chapter may call for corresponding variations in the procedural design.

A basic line of cleavage may, however, be drawn between those proceedings in which a single determination is sought, and those in which a series of successive determinations is called for. Typical of the first category is the action for a money judgment, a proceeding numerically more important than all other types of civil proceeding combined. Such an action exhibits, potentially, three stages, in the first of which the judgment sought is either granted or denied. If appeal is taken, a second stage ensues. If the judgment is granted (and affirmed on appeal if any), a further stage may ensue, that concerned with the collection of the judgment.

In the category of proceedings in which a succession of determinations may be required, the bankruptcy proceeding furnishes a ready illustration. The first stage is concerned with adjudicating the debtor bankrupt—a stage which may be essentially perfunctory or may entail a bitter litigation. The adjudication of bankruptcy having been made, there may ensue a succession of stages, often spaced over considerable periods of time—the election by the creditors (and appointment by the court) of a trustee of the bankrupt's assets, the recovery by the trustee of hidden assets and preferential payments, the determination of the validity and accuracy of claims of creditors, the determination of priorities, if any, of particular creditors, the reduction of the assets to cash, the distribution of the proceeds among the creditors, and finally, the determination of the right of the bankrupt to a discharge from his debts, or from some of them. At each of these stages, the court (in the person of the referee in bankruptcy, by whom these matters are initially decided) may be called upon to adjudicate what is in effect a subsidiary litigation; and the judgment is thus not a single determination but the aggregate of a series of determinations.

In what follows, emphasis is on the typical procedure in an action in which a single determination is sought. It would not be profitable to trace in this volume the modifications which this procedure may undergo in the multiple-stage type of proceeding, matters of interest only to those professionally concerned.

Moreover, the procedure outlined is that followed in a court of general jurisdiction. In courts of limited jurisdiction, where the subject matter is of small value, a more informal procedure is permitted and the more elaborate procedures here outlined, even if available under the governing statutes, are seldom employed. In the small claims courts constituted in cities, and in the rural justice's courts in many states, a further simplification is found, a simplification extending indeed not merely to procedure, but even to rules of evidence.[8]

To the layman, a civil litigation is, essentially, a trial. In point of fact, however, many litigated controversies never heach the stage of trial, being disposed of on questions of law. Moreover, the shape and importance of the trial itself depend on matters which occur in advance of the trial. An understanding of these matters is as essential as a familiarity with the techniques of the actual trial—perhaps more essential.

5. PROVISIONAL REMEDIES

Provisional remedies (also known as "conservatory remedies") are, as their name implies, procedures available to the plaintiff while the proceeding is pending, designed to make more secure and certain the remedy which will be granted him should he prevail in the proceeding. Their purpose is to minimize the possibility of an empty victory—a judgment which cannot effectively be enforced because the defendant, or his property, or the subject matter of the action has, pending its determination, escaped the control of the court.

Since this process obviously involves an invasion of the rights of the defendant before it has been determined that the plaintiff's cause is just, the law requires the plaintiff who seeks such provisional relief to give security (usually in the form of a bond) for the payment of the damages which will have unwarrantably been inflicted on the defendant should he prevail in the action.

The objective of the procedure may be either to immobilize the defendant's person, so to speak, or to immobilize his property, or to immobilize the status of the subject matter of the proceeding.

The various procedures for the seizure of property[9] which have been

[8] Thus for example, in proof of the value of work done for the claimant (for which he seeks reimbursement from the defendant), a bill rendered to claimant may be admitted in evidence in a small claims court. Under the accepted rules of evidence, proof would have to be made by the oral testimony of a person experienced in the type of work in question.

[9] If the property is realty, no seizure is necessary, the mere filing of a notice in the public office where real estate records are kept being sufficient.

described as methods of instituting a proceeding and thereby giving the court jurisdiction in rem—replevin, arrest of a vessel in admiralty, seizure of property for foreclosure of a lien thereon, and attachment—are also to be regarded as provisional remedies. They may be resorted to by the plaintiff—and often are—even though it is quite practicable for him to make service on the defendant, or he has indeed already made it.

A provisional remedy much less frequently employed is the arrest of the defendant, and his release on bond. Originally employed in all actions for debt, it is now permitted, characteristically, only in actions for fraud, or for personal injuries. Its technical aspects are beyond our province.[10]

Temporary injunction

In many situations the plaintiff, simultaneously with the institution of the action, applies to the court for an order restraining the defendant from doing certain acts until the action shall have been determined. A simple situation in which such an application would be appropriate is presented where the plaintiff seeks the restoration of property sold by him, alleging that he was induced to part with it by fraud. In such a situation there is danger that the rights of the plaintiff (assuming his allegations are eventually found to be true) may be defeated by the sale of the property, while the action is pending, to an innocent third person; for in that case, as between the plaintiff and the innocent purchaser, the law would leave the property with the latter. To forestall this possibility, the plaintiff will, therefore, simultaneously with the institution of the action, apply to the court for an order restraining the defendant from disposing of the property pending the determination of the action. Such an order is termed a temporary (or preliminary) injunction (in contradistinction to an injunction embodied in the final judgment entered at the conclusion of an action, which is often termed a permanent injunction).

In the illustration just given, the remedy sought in the action itself is not a permanent injunction, being indeed a remedy at law. A temporary injunction is, however, perhaps more frequently sought in actions where the primary, if not sole, purpose of the action is to obtain a permanent injunction of the same tenor. Thus, a plaintiff who alleges that the defendant is guilty of unfair competition (i.e., of acts designed to mislead the public into believing that the establishment or wares of the defendant are those

[10] The bond which the defendant must furnish, insures, contrary to what might be expected, not that the defendant will pay any judgment that may be obtained against him (though such is indeed its provision in a limited class of cases) but rather that he will obey any mandate which the court may subsequently issue to him. Since, as already seen, the ordinary money judgment does not constitute a mandate directed to the judgment debtor directing him to pay, the bond in question obviously does not insure such payment. The procedure for arrest has a close relation to the remedy of body execution which has already been discussed. It is not favored by the courts, and is but rarely used.

of the plaintiff) and asks that the defendant, after trial of the action, be permanently enjoined therefrom is likely also to make application, simultaneously with the institution of the action, for a temporary injunction, alleging that he will suffer irreparable injury during the pendency of the action unless the defendant is forthwith restrained.

An application for a temporary injunction is typically determined by the judge, to whom it is made without hearing the testimony of witnesses. Instead, he has before him affidavits submitted by both sides. These affidavits are, like affidavits in legal proceedings generally, usually prepared by the attorney for the party in whose behalf they are submitted rather than by the persons who sign and swear to them, and are unchecked by cross-examination, that potent device for curbing and exposing falsehood. The unreliability of affidavits as a means of discovering where the truth lies in hotly controverted issues of fact is generally recognized. Temporary injunctions should accordingly be granted on affidavits only in the clearest cases. If the merits of the application are not quite clear, and if no grave emergency exists, the proper course is for the judge, if he is convinced that the situation calls for prompt disposition, instead of granting a temporary injunction, to set the case down for early or immediate trial. If immediate action on the application for temporary injunction seems called for, a hearing, rather than a reading of affidavits, is the proper way to resolve disputed facts.

A field in which this rule was, however, formerly too frequently disregarded is that of labor disputes. The typical action arising out of a labor dispute was one wherein the employer brought action to obtain a permanent injunction to restrain the officers and members of the labor union, engaged in conducting a strike against the employer's establishment, from allegedly unlawful intimidation of those working for, or seeking to obtain work from, the plaintiff, such unlawful intimidation usually being alleged to consist in violence, or threats of violence, made by pickets or emissaries of the union, allegedly on so large a scale as to be beyond the control of the police authorities. While the purpose of the action was thus ostensibly to obtain a permanent injunction, quite generally the real object of the plaintiff was to obtain a temporary injunction. If the temporary injunction were obtained, the situation had ordinarily so changed by the time the action came on for trial that the plaintiff was then probably indifferent to the permanent injunction, which was the ostensible objective of the action. The real conflict thus centered about the granting of the temporary injunction; and thus the controversy was in effect finally adjudicated on affidavits rather than on the testimony of witnesses. In the Norris-LaGuardia Act of 1932, already referred to as having severely limited the power of the federal courts to grant injunctions in labor disputes, this affidavit procedure was abolished. The act provides that no temporary injunction may be issued in a labor dispute by a federal court "except after hearing the testimony of witnesses in open court (with opportunity for cross-examination) in support of the allegations of a complaint made under oath, and testimony in opposition thereto, if offered."[11] Substantially similar provisions have since been enacted by the legislatures of about a third of the states.

Ex parte restraining order

A special procedural question of considerable importance in connection with temporary injunctions concerns the issue of the so-called ex parte restraining order—i.e., a restraining order issued without previous notice to the person restrained that any application for such an order is being made. This question has received especial attention in the field of labor injunctions.

At first sight it may seem curious that a restraining order should under any circumstances be issued without an opportunity having been given to the party restrained to protest or to controvert the allegations made. Nevertheless, there are instances in which such a procedure is not only justifiable but indeed indispensable. Reverting to the illustration already given, of an application made simultaneously with the commencement of the action, to enjoin the defendant from disposing of property alleged to have been fraudulently obtained, it is clear that the entire purpose of the application might be defeated if the defendant were to utilize the interval between the service on him of notice of the application and the time at which the court hearing on the application is to be held for the very purpose of disposing of the property, thereby coverting not merely the application itself but the entire action into an idle ceremony—a very real possibility even if the interval is one of only a few days, as it ordinarily is. Under these circumstances, it has long been the practice of our equity courts upon a proper showing to grant ex parte a temporary restraining order to be in force for a few days only, until the party restrained shall have had an opportunity to appear before the court and show cause why the restraint should not be continued in the form of a temporary injunction pending determination of the action.

Though the ex parte restraining order thus has its legitimate place in a system of civil procedure, it is a remedy rather susceptible to abuse in the hands of a prejudiced judge; and there can be little doubt that in labor disputes such orders were in some cases issued with little or no justification. As a result of the demand of labor organizations that the powers of the courts in granting ex parte orders be limited, the Norris-LaGuardia Act expressly provides that in the federal courts an ex parte restraining order may be issued in a labor dispute only upon testimony under oath (instead

[11] 29 U.S. Code, Sec. 107.

of, as formerly, upon affidavit) and shall be effective for not more than five days. The legislatures of several states have adopted cognate provisions.

Receivership

Reference has already been made to a method sometimes employed for the purpose of enforcing collection of a money judgment—the assumption by the court of control over income-producing property of the judgment debtor, such control being exercised by the court through an officer appointed ad hoc and known as a receiver. The same procedure may be employed at the very outset of an action for the purpose of maintaining the status quo pending the determination of the action, where an injunction alone is not appropriate to the purpose. Illustrative of such a situation is that which arises when two partners fall out, each accusing the other of misconduct, perhaps amounting to actual conversion of partnership funds, and each announcing his complete loss of confidence in the other. One of them, perhaps by common consent, institutes action against the other, demanding a dissolution of the partnership, a winding up of its affairs, and an accounting; the other counterclaims in like vein. The determination of the action may not be had for weeks, perhaps months. Neither is willing, in the meantime, to have the other manage the business, and they cannot, in the present state of their relations, manage it jointly. Application is therefore made to the court for the assumption of control of the business by the court during the pendency of the action through the appointment of a receiver.

Bankruptcy proceedings furnish another illustration, the court appointing a receiver to take possession and exercise control of the bankrupt's property until the selection by the creditors of a "trustee," whose function it is to liquidate the estate and make a pro rata distribution to creditors.[12]

6. DEFINING THE ISSUES OF LAW AND OF FACT

In the adjudication of a civil controversy, a possible method is for the tribunal to proceed at once, without any preliminary statement from the parties, to hear their testimony and arguments, and, as the hearing proceeds, to identify the points at issue between them, both as to the facts out of which their controversy arises, and as to their rights to redress or relief. Such is the method of primitive tribunals. As a system of adjudication takes on a more developed form, however, there invariably emerges a

[12] In a proceeding (under the Bankruptcy Act) for the reorganization of the indebtedness of a corporation, which may extend over several years, control of the corporation's property is in the hands of the court. The court exercises its control through an appointee who is in effect a receiver, but is termed by the statute a "trustee."

preliminary procedure for ascertaining, on the basis of formal statements of the transaction, occurrence, or situation out of which the controversy arises, the points at which the factual allegations of the contending parties are at variance; or for ascertaining their conflicting contentions as to the legal consequences thereof; or both.[13] In our system, such preliminary statements of the parties are, except in petty courts, embodied in formal writings, which are collectively termed the pleadings.

Pleading procedure

The plaintiff's initial pleading (commonly called the complaint or petition) contains not only a statement of the facts on which he relies,[14] but also a demand for the judgment to which he conceives himself entitled.

It is possible to suppose a system for the adjudication of controversies between private parties in which a person who conceives himself injured by the conduct of another comes before the court and merely states the facts, leaving to the court the question of the redress to be afforded him, after the manner of the suppliant of tradition who throws himself at the feet of the sovereign and cries, "Justice!"; and there is much to be said in favor of such a system. This, however, is not the practice in our system. It is for the petitioner to state to the court at the outset the precise form of redress which he seeks. Thus, the question posed in the litigation is not what the abstract rights of the parties are, but whether the plaintiff is entitled to the particular form of redress he seeks. Traditionally, the plaintiff was held with great strictness to his initial demand for relief. Recent decades have witnessed, however, a very general relaxation of requirements in this respect, with amendment of the pleadings to enable a revision of the demand for relief permitted rather freely.

The varieties of forms of redress which have been developed in our law, and the limitations which surround the grant of particular types of redress by the court, have already been noted; and we have also seen that

[13] If there is no disagreement between the parties as to the facts, but only as to the law, and they desire to cooperate in procuring a determination of their legal rights, they may under the procedures of many jurisdictions collaborate in preparing a joint pleading, setting forth the facts and requesting an adjudication of their rights.

[14] Traditionally, the statement of facts was required to be sufficiently detailed to show that, if the allegations made were established, the plaintiff would be entitled to the relief sought. Thus, in the codes of procedure in force in a majority of the states, the plaintiff was required to set forth in his complaint "the material facts" on which he relied. In recent years, the tendency has been toward a relaxation of requirements in this respect. Thus the rules of civil procedure for the federal district courts, promulgated by the Supreme Court in 1938, merely call for a "statement of the claim showing that the pleader is entitled to relief." Those who argue for greater latitude in the complaint and other pleadings contend that it is sufficient for the adverse party to be put on notice as to the general character of the claim asserted against him (whence the term "notice pleading").

even when the particular type or measure of redress sought is appropriate and permissible, the particular court in which the action has been instituted may not have power to grant that redress.

Manifestly, if the plaintiff seeks a form of redress to which, under established doctrines, even if all the factual allegations of his complaint be assumed to be true, he is not entitled (at any rate from that court), there would be no point in the court's proceeding further with the case, unless the plaintiff is willing to amend his complaint so that it asks for a different, and permissible, form of redress. Again, as often happens, even if the factual allegations of the complaint are assumed to be true, the court may hold that the plaintiff is nevertheless not entitled to any form of relief (as, for example, where he alleges a contract, and the breach thereof, but it appears on the face of the complaint that the contract was an unlawful one). A defendant confronted with a complaint thus defective may ask the court to dismiss the case without proceeding further. (The court before making such dismissal final will ordinarily permit the plaintiff to amend the complaint if it appears that the legal objections thereto can be overcome by such amendment). Through such an application to the court, the chief questions of law arising out of the controversy —whether the events that are alleged to have occurred entitle the aggrieved party to judicial redress and if so of what nature—are thus often decided at the very outset.

If the complaint is not thus attacked, or resists attack, the defendant, unless he is willing to have judgment go against him by default, responds with a statement (commonly called an "answer") giving his version of the facts and asking for a dismissal of the action with costs. If he relies merely upon a denial of the plaintiff's version, an "issue of fact" is now presented which must be "tried." He may, however, instead of or in addition to his denials, interpose an "affirmative defense," i.e., he may add allegations of further matters which, he contends, would in any event defeat the plaintiff's right to redress. To illustrate: A defendant sued for damages allegedly sustained by the plaintiff by reason of default by the defendant in the performance of his obligations under a contract with the plaintiff, may in his answer deny that he was guilty of a default; and he may further allege, as an affirmative defense, that even if the court should find that he did default, he would yet be free of liability, in that the orginal contract was an unlawful one which the courts will not enforce.

It is now open to the plaintiff to attack the legal sufficiency of such "affirmative defense," and if the defendant's answer relies solely on such defense, admitting the plaintiff's version so far as stated by the plaintiff, the court may, on finding such alleged defense legally insufficient, even if true, "strike out the answer" and award judgment for the plaintiff. (If the affirmative defense in the answer is not stricken out, the plaintiff responds to the new allegations in the answer, his response being usually termed a "reply.")

If the case is not thus disposed of (by dismissal or by judgment for the plaintiff) "on the pleadings," the pleadings now furnish the basis for identifying the "issues of fact" to be resolved by the trial. Since every allegation in the complaint should, under the governing practice, be specifically admitted or denied in the answer, and every new allegation in the answer be likewise admitted or denied in the reply, it should be possible, and ordinarily is, by a comparison of these documents, to identify what allegations are at issue between the parties. It is to the questions of fact thus put in issue, and only those, that the subsequent "trial of the issues of fact" is to be confined. Such is the rationale of our system of pleading.

It is readily apparent that a procedure of this kind runs the risk of being turned into a paper war, in which the resolution of the controversy on its merits is delayed and obscured by the syllogistic clamor of the contenders; and such was notoriously the case with the almost incredibly artificial system of special pleading, so called, developed in England, which flourished during the eighteenth century and even in some of our jurisdictions well into the nineteenth. There are some who regard even the more rational system of pleading of today as unduly artificial and as calculated to hinder rather than advance the prompt and orderly disposition of the controversy. These critics point to the forms of pleading in use in Continental courts as evidence of the practicability of their proposals. Whatever view one may take of the matter—and it is one appropriate for detailed consideration only by those acquainted with it at first hand—it would be erroneous to suppose that characteristically our system of pleading is a source of difficulty or delay. In the ordinary action it functions smoothly enough. Its abuses, such as they are, are the exception.

Counterclaim

For the sake of simplicity it has been assumed in the foregoing that the defendant, in answering the complaint, seeks merely to defeat the claim made against him by the plaintiff. The defendant may, in addition, take advantage of the occasion to set forth a claim which he has against the plaintiff and which, should he establish it, will entitle him to reduce the amount to which plaintiff may be entitled and possibly to offset it completely (and conceivably will even entitle him to an affirmative judgment in his favor).

Where the counterclaim thus interposed by the defendant arises out of the same transaction or occurrence as is the foundation of the plaintiff's claim, the trial of the action differs little, if at all, from what it would be were there no counterclaim present. Thus, if the plaintiff sues for the balance of the purchase price promised by the defendant, and the defendant counterclaims for damages sustained by him through the allegedly fraudulent representations made to him by the plaintiff in inducing him to make the purchase, the trial will involve in the main no different an inquiry into the transaction than had the defendant not interposed his counterclaim, but had merely resisted payment of the plaintiff's claim.

Should the counterclaim, however, arise out of a totally different transaction or occurrence, an examination into its merits upon the trial in effect requires the court to try a second case simultaneously with the first. To permit this to be done without any restriction would, of course, be impracticable; for a counterclaim in equity would thus be tried simultaneously with an action at law, and vice versa. Moreover, actions on contract would be tried simultaneously with claims arising out of wholly disconnected torts. To prevent these results, statutes and traditional doctrines often impose limitations upon the counterclaims which may be interposed by the defendant.

7. THE LAW APPLICABLE TO THE ISSUES OF LAW

In identifying and passing upon the issues of law raised by the pleadings, as just outlined, and indeed at various later stages of the proceeding as well, a state court may be called upon to apply, instead of the law of the state under whose authority it sits (conventionally termed "the law of the forum"), the law of some other state or of some foreign country; for though the occurrences involved in the dispute may have all taken place within the state, it may be that the status or capacity of one or another party depends upon occurrences, unconnected with the present dispute, which took place elsewhere, and must be examined in the light of the law of the jurisdiction in which they took place. Thus, it may be necessary to determine the marital status of one of the parties involved; and that determination of necessity requires the application of the law of the place in which the alleged marriage took place. Again, it may be necessary to determine whether a corporation, whose acts form part of the facts of the dispute, possessed the legal capacity to perform the acts in question; and if the corporation was created under and derived its powers from the laws of some other state or country, examination and application of those laws are of course necessary.

Still more is such an examination called for when the transactions or occurrences involved in the dispute took place in some other state or country. Assume a written contract executed in France between two American citizens, residents of New York and Massachusetts, respectively, whereby one, a musical artist, engages to appear under the management of the other in concerts and recitals in the principal cities of the United

States; assume further that in the course of the tour made pursuant to such contract, a dispute arises between the artist and the manager as to their respective rights and duties; that the manager cancels all future dates and announces that he regards the contract as terminated; and that one of the parties brings action against the other for damages in the state of the defendant's residence, in which none of the alleged breaches occurred. Obviously, the court in that state will have before it the possibility of applying, as one or another of the questions of law is presented to it in the course of the litigation, either the doctrines in force in that state or those in force in the country where the contract was made, or those in force in the several states where the several alleged breaches of contract occurred, assuming there to be divergencies in such doctrine.

The necessity of a choice as between the law of two different jurisdictions, neither of them necessarily the jurisdiction in which the case is being adjudicated, may also arise in tort cases (as between the law of the state where the wrongful act was committed and that of the possibly different state in which the consequences took place); in cases of inheritance (as between the law of the state in which the personal property of the deceased was situated at the time of his death and the law of the state of which he was a resident); in cases involving domestic relations (as between the law of the state where the spouses resided and that of the state where an antenuptial or separation agreement was entered into), etc.

Out of the number of cases in which a choice of this character has become necessary, there has been developed a body of rules or doctrines (upon which also, unfortunately, there exist considerable divergencies of opinion) which guide the courts in choosing which of the possible alternative doctrines should be applied to the case in hand. The branch of legal learning which deals with these canons of choice is called "conflict of laws." The term is unfortunate, since it suggests that two conflicting legal rules are applicable to a single situation, whereas in truth only one of the two is properly applicable, the problem being to determine which is the more appropriate.

It will be recalled that the Constitution requires each state to give "full faith and credit" not merely to the "judicial proceedings" of every other state, but also to its "public acts," which include its statutes. Thus, while the application of the law of a foreign country is a matter wholly within a state court's discretion, the application by it of the statutes of another state may well be a mandatory obligation imposed by the Constitution; and the Supreme Court has indeed, though thus far only in a very limited class of cases, on the basis of the full faith and credit clause, required the state courts to apply the statutes of other states. A notable line of such cases is that of suits on fraternal society insurance policies, in which, because of delay in bringing the action, the suit is outlawed by the statutes of the state in which the fraternal order is incorporated but is not yet outlawed by the statutes of the state in which the action is brought. In these cases, the Supreme Court has laid down the rule that the statutes of the state of incorporation are controlling and must be accorded "full faith and credit" by every other state.[15]

Federal law in state courts

In the foregoing discussion, for simplicity, no account was taken of the fact, never to be lost sight of, that the law in force in each state is not merely the state law, but the federal law as well, and that the state court must continually apply it. Thus, in cases in the state courts arising out of contract, the question is frequently presented whether the contract was for a purpose, or founded on a consideration, illegal under federal law, as is also the question whether federal tax requirements necessary to give the transaction validity (e.g., the revenue stamp on a real estate deed) were complied with. In tort cases, too, federal statutes may require application. Thus, in an action against a railroad in a state court by a passenger injured in an accident through the alleged negligence of the railroad, the question may arise whether the railroad complied with all the federal statutes designed to promote safety on railroads (such as those requiring the installation and maintenance of certain safety appliances or limiting the number of hours of labor of locomotive engineers, etc.), a failure so to comply constituting presumptively negligent operation. In a variety of actions, the defense may be interposed that the claim in suit has already been discharged in bankruptcy by a federal bankruptcy court. The disposition of this defense requires the construction and application by the state court of the federal bankruptcy act, and of the proceedings had thereunder. Further examples could readily be multiplied.

State and foreign law in federal courts

In a great part of the cases coming before the federal courts in the exercise of their original jurisdiction, no question of state or foreign law is involved. In cases of one class, however, it is not uncommon to find questions of state (or foreign) law exclusively involved. These are the cases of diversity of citizenship.[16] In these cases (and in other cases in-

---

[15] Order of Travelers v. Wolfe, 331 U.S. 586 (1947). The Constitution, in addition to imposing the obligation of "full faith and credit" on the states, expressly authorizes Congress to prescribe "by general laws . . . the effect thereof." It has been suggested that this language gives Congress power (thus far never exercised) to enact a uniform body of rules as to which of the statutes of two or more states possibly applicable a state court shall apply.

[16] Diversity cases constitute, however, by no means the only class of federal cases in which state law must be applied. Thus in bankruptcy proceedings, which are conducted exclusively in the federal courts, claims of creditors must be adjudicated chiefly under state law, and the rights and priorities of lienors must be determined

volving state law) the federal courts have from the beginning applied state statutes where applicable and have also, since 1938, followed state decisional law.[17] This does not mean, of course, that a federal court must apply the law of the state in which the federal court happens to sit. Like the courts of that state, the federal court may apply the law of some other state (or of a foreign country where applicable).

8. READJUDICATION OF MATTERS ALREADY ADJUDICATED

Even though a state has, within the doctrines already discussed, jurisdiction over a particular controversy, a limitation may exist upon its right to adjudicate an issue involved in that controversy—perhaps the sole issue involved in such controversy; for such issue may already have been adjudicated in another country or in another state.

It is a settled doctrine of jurisprudence that, an issue having once been fully tried between two parties and adjudicated by a court having jurisdiction, another court will not, even though possessed of power to do so, again try the issue. Instead, it will accept the determination theretofore made by the other court. This doctrine is commonly termed the doctrine of *res adjudicata* (or *res judicata*). It is applied by the courts not only in cases in which the issue has been previously adjudicated in the courts of the same jurisdiction as that in which it is now being raised anew, but also where it has been adjudicated in another jurisdiction. Thus, a federal court will not readjudicate an issue already adjudicated by a state court in a controversy between the same parties, and vice versa; a state will not readjudicate an issue adjudicated in another state; and as a matter of comity neither state nor federal courts will ordinarily adjudicate an issue already adjudicated in the courts of another country.

The duty of the court to recognize an adjudication made by a court in another jurisdiction is, however, limited, as in the case of the duty to enforce the judgment of such other court, to adjudications made by a court having *jurisdiction*. It is thus the privilege of every state court when called upon to give recognition to a matter already adjudicated in a court in another jurisdiction to determine, if the jurisdiction of the court which made such adjudication is questioned by the party against whom such ad-

---

by state law. Cases affecting consuls must also be determined ordinarily exclusively by state law; and even cases in which the United States is a party may, where the government is involved in a purely proprietory capacity, also be determinable by state law. Finally, even in deciding cases of admiralty and maritime jurisdiction, the federal courts in many instances have given effect to substantive rights created by state statutes, as for example the right of the next of kin to sue for wrongful death, a right unknown to the traditional law of admiralty.

[17] See p. 357.

judication is offered, whether such court possessed jurisdiction. If the adjudication was made by a court of a sister state, the question is, under the full faith and credit clause of the Constitution, ultimately one for the Supreme Court of the United States.

Recognition of divorce decrees

The recognition of a divorce decree granted in another jurisdiction is governed by the same general principles as are applied in the case of other judgments, the recognition of decrees granted abroad being governed by principles of comity, and the recognition by a state of a decree granted in another state by the constitutional obligation to give it full faith and credit. Only in the case of a divorce decree granted by a state against a non-resident defendant who was not served with process within the state and who did not appear in the action are special problems present.

The jurisdiction of the state[18] in such a case depends, as already seen, on the residence of the plaintiff in the state at the time of the institution of the action. If extra-state recognition of the decree is opposed on the ground that the plaintiff was not in fact a bona fide resident of the state at that time, there is involved an inquiry into the facts and into the good faith of the plaintiff in setting up his seeming residence there. If the court of the sister state resolves the question in favor of the jurisdiction of the granting state, it must accord recognition to the decree, but only, as previously noted, to the extent that it must treat the marriage as dissolved; it need give the decree no effect in a determination of the rights of the defendant spouse to support, property, or custody of children.

In practice, however, the mere recognition of the decree as having dissolved the marriage may effectively deprive a wife thus divorced of the right to support. In a majority of the states, an action for support may be brought only by a wife, not an ex-wife. The only way in which a wife thus divorced ex parte may seek to obtain support is to contend that she is still a wife—that her husband's alleged establishment of residence in the state which granted the decree was a pretense and a fraud on the court, that the state was consequently without power to empower its courts to entertain the action, and that the decree is consequently a nullity. Such a contention may be very difficult to establish even if well founded; and it is in many cases without foundation. The remedy is to be found in the enactment by the states of statutes giving the divorced wife, if divorced ex parte, the right to bring action for support. Thus far, although it is

[18] In the great majority of "migratory" divorces the defendant does appear, the action having been instituted by concert of the parties. The resulting judgment is entitled to full faith and credit in every state; the court of another state may not inquire whether the plaintiff was in fact a resident of the granting state. Coe v. Coe, 334 U.S. 378 (1948).

now more than twenty years since the Supreme Court declared an ex parte state divorce decree entitled to recognition, only a small number of legislatures have taken action.

Under certain circumstances the contention that the ex parte decree is not entitled to recognition is first advanced after the death of the spouse who obtained the divorce. In these circumstances, the difficulty of reaching a firm conclusion as to the good faith of the deceased in establishing residence in the state which granted the divorce is compounded by the doctrine, already mentioned, that residence in the state to which one has migrated does not depend on the length of time during which one remained there, but on the intention one had in going there.

The attack on the validity of the ex parte divorce decree after the death of the spouse who obtained the decree may arise under varying circumstances. If that spouse remarried and dies "intestate" (i.e., leaving no will), controversy may arise between the children of the first and those of the second marriage as to the right of the latter to share in the deceased's estate. The children of the first marriage may assert that they alone are entitled to share, the children of the second marriage being, they contend, illegitimate; the first marriage of the deceased, they declare, was never dissolved, the purported divorce decree being, for reasons already mentioned, a nullity. Again, if the second spouse and the deceased lived in a state where there is in force a system of "community property," under which each spouse has certain rights in the property acquired by the other during the marriage, the rights of the second spouse in such property may be similarly attacked.

Even, however, if the ex parte divorce decree is of unquestioned validity, its "divisible" character gives rise to various legal questions. One such is presented by the situation in which the wife, before the husband obtained the decree of divorce, and at a time when both parties resided in the same state and the courts of that state thus had unimpeachable jurisdiction, had herself obtained from those courts a decree of separation awarding her alimony. If she seeks to compel payment of arrears of such alimony accruing after the divorce decree, may her former husband defeat such attempt by demanding that the state in which she institutes such proceeding give "full faith and credit" to the ex parte divorce decree and regard the alimony decree as automatically voided? The Supreme Court has answered that he may not, at least if the proceeding for arrears has been instituted by the wife in the state which granted the original alimony order; and, on principle the same result would seem to be called for if she proceeds in some other state—even, indeed, in the state in which the divorce was granted. Still not entirely certain is the right of the spouse divorced ex parte to share in the estate of the plaintiff spouse on the latter's death. Doubtless, much litigation of such matters as these still lies ahead.

As has already been suggested, it would seem that the manifold complexities and injustices created by the ex parte divisible divorce could be eliminated by a federal statute limiting the jurisdiction of the state courts in divorce actions between citizens of different states to cases in which the the defendant, served outside the state, voluntarily appears in the action, and conferring jurisdiction on the federal courts in all other actions for divorce between citizens of different states. The practical result of such a statute would be to leave in the state courts jurisdiction in all divorce actions between citizens allegedly of different states where the defendant is cooperating with the plaintiff, but shift to the federal courts all cases in which the defendant does not cooperate.

In this class of cases, where so much confusion and injustice result from present state court jurisdiction, the federal courts writing on a clean sheet could develop rules as to the applicable state law, and as to the place of trial, which would cure much of the present evil.[19]

There is danger, however, of overrating the importance of this aspect of our law of divorce in relation to the total subject. While no statistics are available, it is a matter of common knowledge that the overwhelming majority of divorce decrees are obtained in states in which both parties reside and have resided, so that no question of jurisdiction arises. Moreover, it is also unquestionable that even in the case of migratory divorces, the great majority may be characterized as divorces by consent in the sense that the action is instituted by the plaintiff (almost invariably the wife) with the consent, if not with the assistance, of the defendant, and the defendant, though under no obligation to do so, accordingly appears in the action, with resultant virtually total validity of the ensuring divorce.[20]

[19] See Mayers, Ex Parte Divorce: A Proposed Federal Remedy, 54 Col. Law Rev. 54 (1954). There appears to be no constitutional obstacle to the investment of the federal courts with such jurisdiction. The complete absence of federal court jurisdiction in divorce actions between citizens of different states results not from any constitutional exclusion, but from the fact, already noted, that the statute defining the jurisdiction of the federal courts in diversity cases has from the beginning limited it to cases in which the matter in controversy exceeds a certain sum of money. In an action for divorce, the matter in controversy cannot be measured in terms of an amount of money; it is whether the plaintiff is entitled to have the marriage dissolved. Where the wife is plaintiff, the judgment may award her ailmony; but alimony is not *the* matter in controversy.

[20] The reason couples desiring a divorce resort to the courts of Nevada, Florida, and other "quickie divorce" states is often not chiefly that the grounds of divorce in their home state are too exacting (all the states except New York permit divorce on the ground of desertion, and perhaps a score permit it without proof of desertion where the parties have lived apart for a certain period), but that under the laws of the "quickie" state the decree when granted becomes effective immediately, without a waiting period being required, as in the home state, before the expiration of which the parties may not remarry (and a contemplated marriage forthwith is of course in many cases the immediate occasion for the institution of the divorce action).

It is thus only in the numerically small (but nevertheless highly important) class of unilateral migratory divorces that problems chiefly arise.

9. JUDGMENT IN ABSENCE OF ISSUE OF FACT: SUMMARY JUDGMENT

As already noted, if it appears from the pleadings that there is no necessity for a trial of any issue of fact (either because they raise no issues of fact or because the only issues of fact raised are legally irrelevant) judgment may be rendered forthwith. But what if the pleadings on their face raise merely an ostensible or pretended issue of fact, which in truth does not exist?

Where a measurable interval elapses between the exchange of pleadings between the parties and the hearing of the testimony by the court, a defendant who has in fact no meritorious defense to the claim asserted against him is under the temptation nevertheless to interpose a perfunctory defense, thereby postponing the day of reckoning until the trial comes on. Particularly will he be likely to do so in those cases where he is engaged in attempting to put his property beyond the reach of the plaintiff. Various methods have been employed to combat this abuse by the defendant of his right of defense. Of these the chief is the procedure known as "summary judgment." Developed in Great Britain shortly after the middle of the last century, this procedure was not adopted in this country until well into this century. It has rapidly gained acceptance, however, and where it is already in effect the tendency is to extend its application. In 1938, it was extended to the federal courts in comprehensive form.

In essence, the summary judgment procedure is designed to "smoke out" a defendant whose answer to the complaint, while on its face raising an issue of fact and therefore entitling him to have such issue duly tried by the court, is in fact a mere sham. This is accomplished by requiring him on the application of the plaintiff to submit to the court, supplementing his formal answer, a detailed affidavit setting forth in full his version of the facts, and answering with particularity the allegations made by the plaintiff in the affidavit which he submitted when asking for summary judgment. If, upon reading these affidavits, the judge is satisfied that the defendant, notwithstanding the technical sufficiency of his answer, has in fact no defense, he may strike out the answer and grant summary judgment for the plaintiff.

This drastic remedy, which denies to the defendant the right to the presentation of his proof by witnesses and to the production of the plaintiff's witnesses for cross-examination, has in different degree in different jurisdictions been applied to the several kinds of action. It is especially favored in actions on negotiable instruments and on other obligations.

Though thus developed originally to prevent delay in obtaining judgment on a meritorious claim, the summary judgment procedure has subsequently been extended in some few jurisdictions to serve an entirely different purpose—to enable a defendant to rid himself promptly and without the necessity of trial of a wholly unmeritorious claim.

Despite the current tendency towards its extension, the summary judgment procedure remains of course an exceptional one. In the typical case, the issue having been defined by the pleadings, judgment can be had only after trial.

It is to be noted that in the summary judgment procedure the judgment is rendered without the intervention of a jury, despite the fact that the action is usually one at law, in which, as we shall shortly see, jury trial is everywhere constitutionally guaranteed. The summary judgment procedure, it is everywhere accepted, is nevertheless entirely constitutional; for the function of the jury is to pass on controverted issues of fact. The granting of summary judgment upon affidavits is a determination by the court that there is in truth no real issue of fact to be passed upon—that the issue of fact seemingly raised by the pleading attacked is in reality a mere pretense.

It is indicative of the extent to which the procedure in admirality cases tends to cling to its special traditions that the summary judgment procedure, adopted for all other classes of cases in the federal courts in 1938, was not extended to admiralty cases until more than twenty years later—this despite the fact that the rules of procedure in admiralty cases are, like the rules of procedure in other cases in the federal courts, promulgated by the Supreme Court.

The summary judgment procedure may be employed also to give partial judgment without trial, judgment as to the remaining items at issue being deferred to await the outcome of the trial.

10. TRIAL OF ISSUE OF FACT: PREPARATORY STEPS

If on the pleadings or as a result of the various applications already referred to, which may be made to the court on the basis of pleadings, it appears that a trial of one or more issues of fact is called for, that trial may be and often is the next step in the proceeding. A party may, however, wish to employ one or another of several available preparatory procedures. Of these the most important is the procedure for "discovery and inspection."

Discovery and inspection

The compulsory disclosure in advance of trial by one of the parties to the other, or perhaps by each party to the other, of certain of the testimony and records to be offered upon trial, is a phase of our civil procedure which, while long familiar in equity and admiralty proceedings, is of comparatively recent development in its application to actions at law. The federal rules of civil procedure, adopted in 1938, made a complete departure from the tradition of marked illiberality which had previously characterized the federal procedure in this respect, and provided for the utmost freedom of examination by both parties of each other, of prospective witnesses, and of records. The extent to which such disclosure may be compelled in the state courts varies greatly from state to state. In the procedure of those states which, while recognizing the right to compel disclosure before trial, have tended to keep it within strict bounds, only the testimony of the adverse party may be compelled; and even that must be confined within certain definite limits. The examination must characteristically be confined to matters which are "material and necessary" to the party seeking the examination. There is, however, a distinct tendency toward relaxation of these doctrines, both in the direction of enlarging the scope of the inquiry open to the plaintiff, and of extending the right of examination to the defendant. In these states a witness not a party to the action may also be examined where circumstances exist which make it unlikely that he will be available as a witness at the trial. In the absence of such circumstances, however, a mere witness may not be examined before trial.

In strong contrast to the practice of these jurisdictions is that of the federal courts, initiated by the rules adopted by the Supreme Court in 1938 already referred to. By those rules "the testimony of any person whether a party or not may be taken at the instance of any party by deposition for the purpose of discovery or for use as evidence in the action or for both purposes . . . the deponent may be examined regarding any matter, not privileged, which is relevant to the subject matter involved in the pending party or to the claim or defense of any other party. . . ." The court may, however, on application limit or terminate the examination if it appears that it is being conducted "in bad faith or in such manner as unreasonably to annoy, embarrass or oppress" the deponent or party, or is being used to compel the disclosure of trade secrets or other matter the secrecy of which the law protects.

In a clear majority of the states the practice in this matter is now quite liberal, though not necessarily characterized by the extreme liberality of the federal practice; and in those states, as in the states adhering more closely to traditional restrictions, the debate on liberalization continues. The opinion of the bar is still divided. Proponents of liberalization urge its merits in bringing into the open, before trial, all the contentions of either side, thereby making the trial itself a full and fair inquiry instead of a series of tactical maneuvers; while opponents see in it a powerful weapon added to the armory of the unscrupulous litigant, who will be enabled thereby to harass his innocent adversary, pry into his affairs, and, though lacking any meritorious claim, yet club him into an undeserved settlement. They see in it, too, an encouragement to the manufacture of evidence in order to meet, at the trial, evidence the existence of which was unknown to the examining party prior to the examination, and which, but for it, would have taken him by surprise at the trial, with devastating effect. The divergent views found in this field will illustrate the difficulty, found throughout the field of judicial procedure, of devising a remedy for the honest litigant which will not be susceptible of abuse by the unscrupulous; but the prospect is definitely for the spread of liberalization.

For simplicity, discussion has been confined to oral examination before trial. Almost equally important is the right to examine the books and records of an adverse party in order to elicit information allegedly necessary for the proof of the matters on which the party seeking the examination has the duty of going forward and the burden of proof. This privilege is susceptible of greater abuse than is the privilege of oral examination before trial, and is accordingly more zealously safeguarded.

Where the plaintiff's rights of examination and inspection before trial are skillfully and thoroughly exercised, he is not infrequently able, upon the trial, to prove his entire prima facie case without calling any witnesses of his own, merely by adducing the admissions made by the defendant on his examination before trial and the transcripts made before trial of the defendant's own records.

Obtaining testimony of witnesses outside jurisdiction

A state may not compel the presence at a civil trial of a witness who is outside the state; and even within a state, a court frequently has no power, under the governing statutes, to compel the presence at the trial of a witness who though within the state is beyond the territorial limits of the court's jurisdiction—such limits being, in the typical case, the county in which the court sits, or even, in the case of a special city court, the city limits. In the federal courts, the power of the district court in a civil case to compel the attendance of a witness at the trial is limited by the provision that the subpoena—i.e., the process requiring the attendance of a witness at a hearing or trial—may not be served at any place outside the district that is more than 100 miles from the place of the hearing or trial.

To meet this difficulty, which is not peculiar to our own legal system, courts have adopted the device of cooperating with one another, the court within whose jurisdiction the witness is found lending its aid, if necessary, to procure from him a deposition to be used upon the trial in the distant jurisdiction.[21] The actual procedure is for a party who seeks the testimony of a witness who is beyond the jurisdiction of the court in which the trial

[21] As to criminal cases, see p. 94.

is to be had to make an application to that court for the issuance by it of a commission directed to some official or attorney in the jurisdiction where the witness is, empowering him to take the deposition of the witness and forward it to the court. The deposition may take the form either of answers to written questions and cross-questions prepared by the attorneys for the parties, or of oral examination and cross-examination—obviously a more costly procedure.

If the witness named in the commission refuses to attend before the person named therein, that person is, of course, himself powerless to compel such attendance; but application may be made to the courts of that jurisdiction to compel such attendance, assuming that those courts recognize the authority of the commission. The courts of some foreign countries, unlike those of our states, do not do so; and in such cases the American court is asked to issue, instead of a commission, a request to a court in the foreign country to cause the witness to be examined ("letters rogatory"). Where letters rogatory are issued by a federal court, and the witness, being a citizen or resident of the United States, fails to appear before the foreign court, the federal court may issue a subpoena to him to appear in this country, before the federal court itself, and may punish him for contempt if he fails to appear.[22] So long as he remains out of the country, such punishment is, of course, limited to a fine, enforceable by the seizure of any property he may have in the United States.

Severance of issues for trial

It not infrequently happens that, among the several issues of fact raised by the pleadings, there is one such that a decision thereon may make it unnecessary to pass upon any of the remaining issues. For example, let us suppose that the defendant, in addition to contesting the various allegations made by the plaintiff designed to charge him with liability, has further alleged that, even assuming the truth of the plaintiff's allegations, they are immaterial since subsequent to the time of the alleged events, the plaintiff duly released the defendant from any liability he may have had; to which the plaintiff has replied that although he admittedly executed and delivered to the defendant a paper purporting to release the latter, such paper was procured from him by the defendant by fraud and deceit and with the corrupt connivance of the plaintiff's own attorney. Manifestly, if the issue of the validity of the release is decided favorably to the defendant, the controversy is at an end.

Accordingly, provision is found in some modern procedural codes, for a severance of the issue of release, or cognate dispositive issues, from the remaining issues of fact in the case for separate prior trial.

But it is not merely in the minority of cases in which the defendant

[22] 28 U.S. Code, Secs. 1783–1784.

thus interposes some special affirmative defense, having no relation to the transaction in chief out of which the action arises, that disposition of one issue may dispose of the entire case. In even the most common types of action—the action for damages for negligent injury to person or property (of which motor-vehicle accidents furnish the chief source) and the action for damages for breach of contract—the issues ordinarily are twofold: first, whether the defendant is liable at all; and second, if the defendant *is* liable, the extent of the injuries suffered by the plaintiff or his property and the amount of money required to compensate him. Only if the first question is decided against the defendant does the second question arise at all. On purely logical grounds, one would suppose that the trial would thus be conducted in two stages—the second being of course dispensed with should the outcome of the first stage so permit.

In actions in equity, the two-stage trial is commonplace. The ordinary patent infringement action in our federal courts, a modern variant of the action in equity, will serve as an illustration. Here the plaintiff, the owner of the patent, ordinarily asks first that the defendant, who is alleged to have infringed the patent, be enjoined from continuing such infringement, and secondly that he be required to make an accounting and reimbursement of the profits alleged to have been made by him through the alleged infringement. When the case comes on for trial the evidence will be limited to the issue of whether there has been an infringement of the plaintiff's patent. If the court finds that there has been no infringement of the plaintiff's patent (or that the plaintiff's patent is invalid), the case is, of course, terminated at this point. If, on the other hand, the court finds that there has been an infringement, it will issue an injunction and in addition order an accounting to be had. This means there will in effect be a further trial, quite separate and distinct from the one just concluded (and usually held before a referee or special master rather than before the judge himself), such trial being exclusively on the question of the amount of damages to be awarded the plaintiff. A similar procedure prevails in admiralty cases.

In actions at law, on the other hand, the two-stage trial was, despite occasional statutory encouragement, almost unknown until recent years. Even today, despite scattered experience which seems to indicate its applicability to the personal injury litigation which occupies much of the time and personnel of our trial courts, its use is exceptional. Its failure to come into use more rapidly appears to be closely bound up with the development of trial by jury in actions at law, a matter shortly to be considered, and the difficulty, particularly in the presence of constitutional guarantees of jury trial, of departing from the established pattern of such trial. This factor has doubtless been largely responsible for the failure of severance of issues for trial, and in particular the severance of the issue of liability from the issue of damages, to gain acceptance in actions at law even where the parties have waived a jury and the trial is by the court alone.[23]

Preliminary examination of issues by court

In the traditional procedure, if neither party has sought to have his adversary's pleading stricken out or dismissed as insufficient in law, the court is not apprised of the issues presented by the pleadings until the very opening of the trial—indeed, in a jury case, until after the jury has been impaneled. A modern development, however, has been the preliminary examination of the issues by the court or by a special officer of the court, in the presence of the opposing attorneys, to reduce the area of contention.

Experience demonstrates that at such a preliminary, and somewhat informal, canvass of the issues, without any adjudication thereof being imminent, the opposing attorneys are more likely to make reciprocal concessions of fact and to consent to procedures for facilitating the development of necessary evidence, particularly documentary evidence, than were the effort made in the contentious atmosphere of the trial. This preliminary procedure (commonly referred to as "pretrial procedure") has long been employed with excellent result in the higher English courts. It has in recent years made marked progress in this country. Its effectiveness is greatly increased by insistence upon the advance disclosure of proposed proof in much greater detail than is required in the conventional initial pleadings.[24]

11. TRIAL OF ISSUES OF FACT: MODE OF PROOF

The methods of proof employed in civil trials do not differ essentially from those of the criminal trial, already described.[25] Certain features of

[23] See Mayers, Severance for Trial of Liability from Damage, 86 U. of Pa. Law Rev. 389 (1938); Miner, Court Congestion: A New Approach, 45 Amer. Bar Assn. Jour. 1265 (1959). For the view that severance is unsuited to jury trials in personal injury cases see Weinstein, Routine Bifurcation of Jury Negligence Trial, 14 Vand. Law Rev. 831 (1961).

[24] The pretrial procedure in addition affords an opportunity for the parties to negotiate a settlement with the assistance, or at any rate the encouragement, of the judge. Since settlement, rather than judgment, is the real objective of the plaintiff, and the wish also of the defendant, in many of the actions instituted in our courts, the procedure of the courts should be aimed at encouraging settlement and expediting it. On the other hand, there is an understandable reluctance on the part of many judges to go very far in this direction. It diminishes the stature of the courts and of the judiciary, it is felt, to convert the court into a market place for haggling as to the amount or terms of a settlement. The dilemma has not yet been resolved. There is respectable opinion in favor of recognizing settlement more frankly as one of the functions of the machinery of civil justice, and of placing the settlement process in the hands of officials supervised by, if not part of, the courts.

[25] Not much over a century ago there still survived in England, in certain controversies respecting relationship to a decedent, a method of proof radically different from that to which we are accustomed. The tribunal did not in the first instance receive proof offered by the parties; on the contrary, an agent of the tribunal sought

the presentation of proof in the civil proceeding, however, warrant mention.

Sequence of proof

The presentation of proof in a civil proceeding is, under our system (in contrast to that typically employed in Continental systems) a single continuous process, no adjournment ordinarily being permitted to enable a party to collect additional evidence to counter the evidence produced by the other side.[26]

The trial may require the determination of several quite distinct issues of fact (the "severance" of an issue for separate trial being, as already indicated, very exceptional). In such a situation the proof is not taken, as might be supposed, issue by issue. On the contrary, one side (ordinarily the plaintiff) presents the proof on all the issues on which it has the "duty of going forward" (a matter shortly to be explained); the other side then presents its proof in rebuttal on all those issues, as well as its proof in chief on all the issues on which it has the duty of going forward. Thus, instead of all the evidence on both sides relevant to a given issue (e.g., the manner in which an accident occurred) being heard in sequence, there is interposed, between the plaintiff's evidence on that issue and the defendant's evidence on the same issue, the plaintiff's evidence on entirely different issues (e.g., the nature of the injury done to plaintiff's property or to his person and the proper monetary compensation therefor). This sequence is virtually never departed from in jury trials, and only very rarely in trials by the court.

Familiar as this sequence is, it has little other than tradition to recommend it. Not only would a better scrutiny of the evidence result from a trial of the case issue by issue; but where a single issue, if decided adversely to the plaintiff, would put an end to the entire case, the case could be dismissed at the end of the plaintiff's evidence on that issue, if he had failed to establish it even prima facie. Under present procedure, such a dismissal of the plaintiff's case can be made only after he has put in all his evidence on all the issues; for since he is not required to announce the completion of his evidence on the single dispositive issue, it is only when all his evidence is in that it can be assumed that all his evidence on that issue is in.

---

out proof, traveling to wherever a witness or evidence seemed likely to be found, interrogating witnesses in private, the witness being sworn not to disclose his testimony.

[26] Such adjournments, it is thought, tend to encourage the manufacture of evidence. On the other hand, denial of an adjournment may prevent the party seeking it from obtaining incontestable documentary proof that the evidence offered by the other side is false. Where a party "pleads surprise" (that is, represents to the court that the evidence introduced by the other side could not reasonably have been anticipated), the court may in its discretion grant an adjournment.

Duty of going forward; burden of proof

The duty of going forward with the proof on a given issue (sometimes termed "the burden of evidence") is ordinarily, but not invariably, on the party on whom rests the "burden of proof" on that issue—that is to say, the party on whom rests the obligation to establish his allegation on that issue by a preponderance of the credible evidence. The party who initiates the proceeding has the burden of proof on the issues raised by the allegations of his pleading. As already noted, however, the defendant, in his answering pleading, may have interposed a so-called affirmative defense, not merely denying his adversary's allegations but alleging new matters, such as fraud. On that issue, he and not his adversary has the burden of proof. In certain situations, however, the party having the burden of proof on an issue enjoys a presumption of law in favor of the allegation made by him; and until that presumption has been rebutted by proof offered by his adversary, he is under no duty to go forward with the proof of his allegation.

Expert testimony and advice

In connection with the criminal trial, there was pointed out the absence of any provision for furnishing the trier of the facts, whether judge or jury, with the advice of experts not in the employ of either side. A like situation exists in the civil proceeding. However, with respect to many types of issue of fact in the civil proceeding, it would be far more troublesome, assuming it were desirable, for the court to obtain impartial expert testimony than is the case with respect to the relatively few types of issue on which expert opinion is commonly required in the criminal trial. An outstanding exception, however, is the issue of the nature and extent of personal injuries. This issue is regularly the subject of a battle of partisan experts in the negligence cases which occupy much of the time of our civil courts. Here a system of impartial experts at the service of the court is at long last making its appearance.[27]

It is perhaps not commonly appreciated how considerable a proportion of the time of our civil trial courts is occupied by the presentation of evidence as to the nature, extent, and probable future effects of personal injuries. This kind of evidence bulks large not only in actions for damages for accidental injuries (of which a heavy proportion arise out of motor-vehicle accidents), but also in actions against physicians and surgeons for damages for injuries allegedly caused by professional imcompetence or neglect ("malpractice" actions). The latter, while much less numerous than accidental injury actions, have in recent years grown rapidly.

The adversary system of proof was developed in an age when the factual issues before the courts were chiefly as to what had occurred in the past.

[27] See Symposium on Impartial Medical Testimony, Tenn. Law Quart. 357 (1961).

How explain the retention of this system, unchanged, for the resolution by laymen, whether judges or jurors, of difficult questions of medical diagnosis and procedures and of problems of medical prognosis the evaluation of which must in many cases even at best be highly speculative? It can be explained only by the inertia of our judicial institutions, especially when there is at hand the convenient excuse that change is really beyond the realm of the practical because of constitutional guarantees of the right of trial by jury.

Closely associated with the persistence of this indefensible method of resolving abstruse medical issues is the traditional lump-sum award already mentioned, which compels a prognostication covering the entire remainder of the expected life of the injured person (even though he be a small child), instead of a periodical re-evaluation of his condition.

In cases presenting technical issues other than medical, the need for public provision of expert advice to the court is not so urgent. Nevertheless, there is a useful place for such provision, not necessarily taking the form of expert testimony, however. In the English admiralty courts, an expert adviser on maritime practices (usually an experienced naval officer) sits on the bench with the judge;[28] and in some Continental countries, the judge may seek expert advice in any field. Another method, more consistent with our traditional procedures, which could well be employed, would be the appointment of experts as referees to take testimony and report to the court on particular technical issues—a method of course much more readily applied to non-jury than to jury trials.[29]

Witness's refusal to give incriminating answer

It has already been pointed out in connection with criminal proceedings that the constitutional privilege against self-incrimination extends to every variety of testimony given under compulsion and, hence, to testimony in civil proceedings. As a result, it not infrequently occurs in the trial of a civil case (and, perhaps equally important, in an examination before trial in such a case) that answers to vital questions are unobtainable. It might be thought that, on the refusal of a witness to answer a question, a justifiable surmise as to what the truthful answer would be is just as serviceable as the answer itself. In many of the practical affairs of life this reasoning doubtless governs. But under our system of proof surmise cannot take the place of evidence. If the desired answer is refused, the link is missing, and unless it is otherwise supplied, the chain of evidence cannot be forged. Only if the witness is a party to the action (and in a civil trial a party may be called to the stand by his adversary) do the courts permit an unfavorable

[28] In our own admiralty courts, it has long been the practice for the judge to call upon experienced masters of vessels for expert opinion.

[29] See p. 264.

inference to be drawn from the refusal to answer; and some courts decline to permit it even in this situation.[30]

Decision

At the conclusion of a trial by the court, if the case is in equity, the traditional practice is for the judge to reduce his holdings to a formal writing, commonly termed a decision, which sets forth the specific facts found and the specific legal conclusions drawn from those facts, including the precise nature of the relief to which the successful party is entitled (the two corresponding parts of the decision being known respectively as "findings of fact" and "conclusions of law)." Upon this decision, the judgment of the court is entered.

Where the case is one in which the parties though entitled to trial by jury have waived it, the practice with respect to the judge's decision varies. In some jurisdictions, he is required to make a formal decision as in an equity case; in others, he may merely give his decision in terms similar to those of the general verdict of a jury, shortly to be described.

References

A court trying a case without a jury sometimes, instead of itself trying the issues of fact, refers them, or some of them, to a person not holding judicial office for trial by him. Such a person is called in some states a referee, in others (and in the federal courts) a "special master" (or in admiralty cases a "commissioner"). Other terms are also found in some states. In some states, provision is made for the appointment of former members of the judiciary as "official referees" on a salary; but everywhere private citizens, almost invariably lawyers, are also called upon by the courts to act as referees, their compensation being chargeable ordinarily to the unsuccessful party in the litigation.[31] The referee may be empowered to give judgment just as would the court; or he may be merely empowered to make recommendation to the court.

---

[30] In some states, however, the court may direct the witness to answer, at the same time informing him that he will receive immunity from subsequent prosecution with respect to the matter as to which he testifies. Statutes permitting this are obviously susceptible of abuse, enabling a person subject to criminal prosecution to obtain immunity by procuring himself to be subpoenaed to testify in a civil proceeding (a proceeding which he may have even designedly procured to be instituted). For a discussion of this problem in New York, see New York State Law Revision Commission Report for 1942, 367. Curative legislation followed this report.

[31] Referees are also appointed to take testimony and report in connection with preliminary examinations and with applications connected with the form of the judgment to be entered. The Federal Trade Commission Act provides that in any suit in equity brought by the government under the antitrust acts, the court may, if it concludes that the complainant is entitled to relief, refer the suit to the commission "as a master in chancery, to ascertain and report an appropriate form of decree therein." 15 U.S. Code, Sec. 47.

12. TRIAL OF ISSUE OF FACT BY JURY: INSTITUTIONAL ASPECTS

The trial of the issues of fact in a civil proceeding may be either by the court (almost invariably by a single judge) alone, or by a jury with the judge presiding. In equity, admiralty, and bankruptcy proceedings the trial is in most cases by the court alone; in actions at law, though the right to trial by jury is almost everywhere a constitutional one, the right is waived in a considerable percentage of cases. It has been asserted that the jury is no longer, as it once unquestionably was, employed in the majority of civil trials.[32] Nevertheless, it is undoubtedly still employed to a greater degree than is the case perhaps in any other country whose legal institutions are of English origin. In countries whose legal traditions are Roman rather than English, the civil jury is virtually unknown.

The factors which determine the presence or absence of the jury in a civil trial are quite different from those applicable in a criminal proceeding, and call for more extended consideration.

Right to jury trial

We have already noted the existence in England, at the time of its colonization of America, of a structure of multiple civil courts—courts of law, of equity, of admiralty, and of probate. Of these, only the courts of law employed a jury; and basically today, despite the more or less complete merger of those separate courts in this country, the distinction between actions at law, on the one hand, and proceedings in equity, admiralty, and probate, on the other, still chiefly controls in determining the right to jury trial in a civil proceeding.

In the federal courts the right to jury trial in civil cases rests in the first instance on the constitutional provision (found not in the Constitution as originally adopted but in the Seventh Amendment) that "in suits at common law, where the value in controversy shall exceed twenty dollars, the right of trial by jury shall be preserved. . . ."[33] There is thus no constitutional right to jury trial in the federal courts in suits in equity or admiralty, nor in the wholly statutory proceedings in bankruptcy. Congress has, however, in a limited number of cases provided for jury trial as a matter of right even where no constitutional right thereto exists.

[32] No country-wide data are available. In the federal courts, of the 6,260 civil trials completed in the year ended June 30, 1962, only 2,925, or less than 47 per cent, were jury trials. 1962 Report of Administrative Office of U.S. Courts, 215.

[33] In Puerto Rico there is no jury trial in civil cases. See p. 114, note 37. In Pennsylvania, despite the state constitutional guarantee of jury trial in such actions, an action in which the amount claimed is less than $1,000 may by court rule be ordered to be tried first by an arbitrator appointed by the court. A party dissatisfied with the arbitrator's award has, however, the right to demand a trial de novo by a jury, provided he first pays the arbitrator's compensation. See Zal, Philadelphia's Municipal Court Eliminates Backlogs, 47 Amer. Bar Assn. Jour. 1101 (1961).

As in criminal trials, the Constitution confers no right whatever to jury trial in civil cases in the state courts. There is some diversity in the provisions of state constitutions guaranteeing the right to trial by jury in civil actions; but typically the guarantee extends to all actions at law.[34] In two states there is no constitutional guarantee of jury trial in civil cases; but the pattern of civil jury trial in those states seems substantially the same as in states where the right is constitutionally protected.

In a number of states are found statutes, varying widely from state to state, creating new types of proceeding and extending to them the right to jury trial. On the other hand, in most states the institution of a system of workmen's compensation has been accompanied by the replacement of jury trial, theretofore enjoyed as a matter of right in an action by an injured workman against his employer, by trial before an administrative tribunal (in practice, ordinarily, before a single hearing officer).

In the ordinary action at law, as well as in other cases in which the statute so provides, the right to trial ordinarily extends to all the issues of fact in the entire action. All the issues of fact are tried before the judge and jury; the judge then instructs the jury upon the law, and the jury, in theory at least applying that law to the facts, brings in a verdict disposing of the entire case.

Jury trial in discretion of court

In addition to cases in which jury trial is a matter of right, there are cases in which, under the diverse procedures of the several American jurisdictions, jury trial, either of the case as a whole, or of a particular issue thereof, may be ordered in the discretion of the judge. Under the federal rules, even in cases where the parties have no right to jury trial (as in the ordinary action in equity) the court, with the consent of both parties, may order a trial by jury.

Where a jury trial is thus ordered by the court in a case where a jury is not a matter of right, the verdict or finding of the jury is in some procedures merely advisory or, as it has been phrased, "for the information of the conscience of the court" while in others it is conclusive. Thus in the federal procedure just referred to, the verdict of the jury is given "the same effect as if trial by the jury had been a matter of right." Even where the verdict is purely advisory, however, it is seldom rejected by the court in any but the most exceptional cases.

Jury trial of particular issues only

In certain classes of cases, moreover, in which jury trial is not constitutionally guaranteed, the statute confers the right to trial by jury, limited,

---

[34] It has become routine in certain places to insert in leases and other standard forms of contract provisions waiving the right to jury trial in actions arising under the contract.

however, to a particular issue of fact only. In this procedure, the adjudication of the case as a whole is the responsibility of the judge; but a particular issue of fact is referred to a jury, and upon receipt of the jury's findings on that issue of fact, the judge proceeds to the disposition of the case, which may require him to try additional issues of fact. Thus, in a bankruptcy proceeding instituted by creditors, the alleged bankrupt may demand a jury trial of the issues of whether he is insolvent or has committed an act of bankruptcy; but all other issues of fact which may arise in the proceeding (and they are frequently numerous) are decided by the judge or by the referee acting under his supervision.

The future of the civil jury

It will be apparent from the foregoing that in civil cases the extension or withdrawal of the right to jury trial, and the presence or absence of the jury, correspond to no rational principle but represent, rather, the result of historical accident. In some states, the history of civil jury trial has been (except for the workmen's compensation system) that of a more or less irregular and sporadic extension beyond the limits originally assigned to it in England. The civil jury, however, may now be regarded as having entered a period of decline—a decline presaged by its abandonment, almost to the point of extinction, in England itself. There is an increasing tendency in the industrial states to dispense with the jury trial even in actions at law (particularly in actions on contract) through provisions designed to make jury trial more expensive to the litigant than trial without jury, and provisions requiring him to demand trial by jury and pay the jury fee very promptly at an early stage of the litigation, failing which he is deemed to have waived his right to such trial.

The growing movement to permit jury verdicts in civil cases by less than unanimous verdicts—a matter shortly to be discussed—may also be regarded as tending, when combined with the other procedures mentioned, in the direction of eliminating the jury.[35] A litigant who sees in the requirement of unanimity ground for hoping that he will escape judgment, and who therefore demands jury trial, may be less likely to insist upon a jury trial where unanimity is not required.

As already indicated, the chief invasion of the field of jury trial, though not commonly so recognized, has been the institution of specialized administrative tribunals outside the regular judicial structure, for the trial of claims for workmen's compensation. Actions by employees for injuries sustained in the course of their employment formerly constituted a very important class of litigation; and indeed such actions by railroad employees

[35] A cognate development is the use of juries of less than twelve (six being a usual number). Where, however, the right to jury trial is constitutional, and no mention is made in the constitutional provision of juries of smaller size, a party may insist on a jury of twelve.

(such employees not being embraced as yet in any system for workmen's compensation) still represent a substantial field of litigation. Such actions were and are almost invariably tried before juries, the plaintiff employee generally believing, and no doubt with reason, that a jury is more likely to render a substantial verdict than is a judge.[36]

Indeed, it has been said, though with doubtful foundation, that it was the costly verdicts returned by juries that aligned enlightened industrialists in favor of the movement for workmen's compensation laws; for those laws, though benefiting the employee by eliminating the necessity for proof of negligence on the part of the employer, represent a marked diminution of the employee's rights in serious cases, in that they embody a schedule of maximum awards for the several classes of injuries and for death distinctly lower than the verdicts sometimes recovered in actions at law, in which no fixed maxima exist (the verdict of the jury being, however, subject to reduction by the court as excessive).

The current proposals for a system of compensation for injury or death sustained in automobile accidents, similar to the workmen's compensation system, would of course if adopted constitute a further very substantial invasion of the province of the jury. Similarly, commercial arbitration, to the extent that it develops, displaces chiefly actions at law and, hence, jury trial.

The increasing frequency of litigations presenting intricate questions of finance and of technology difficult for the layman to comprehend has confronted our trial judges with a grave problem, now under careful study. The problem is obviously aggravated when the facts are tried not by a judge but by a random group of citizens. The suggestion of jury panels of experts in particular fields, sometimes heard, fails to take account of formidable constitutional, and in many jurisdictions practical, difficulties. The proposal that the testimony dealing with such technical problems be heard not by the jury but by an expert referee, who would then testify as a witness before the jury, endeavoring to "explain the unexplainable" in terms understandable to laymen, is ingenious, and, assuming constitutional obstacles overcome, doubtless represents an improvement over the present situation; but it is at best an unsatisfactory makeshift. It is occasionally employed in the federal courts and in some of the states.[37] Despite its cumbersomeness, it has its uses, and it is not clear why it is not more widely used.

[36] For the same reason, doubtless, in many personal injury actions arising out of shipping, the plaintiff, instead of suing in admiralty, sues at law, the statute (known as the Jones Act) having extended to such jury trial actions the doctrines of the Employers Liability Act (see p. 493, note 6).

[37] It issued sparingly, and chiefly in cases in which complex financial accounts are involved. The report of the "auditor" or "master" is presented to the jury as evidence, to be evaluated by it like other evidence. The federal rule of civil procedure permitting its use is Rule 53(b).

Undoubtedly, the present drift is strongly away from jury trial in civil cases; but constitutional provisions and the strong hold which the institution undoubtedly has on the popular mind (which does not readily differentiate between the role of the jury in civil and in criminal cases) make it unlikely that it will soon disappear.[38] The readiness of the electorate to acquiesce in the partial or complete elimination of the civil jury depends largely on the degree of public confidence which the judiciary enjoy. This in turn varies from place to place and from court to court, a primary factor being, needless to say, the extent to which the selection and retention of judges is controlled by political considerations. It is doubtless true, however, that the man in the street would be less likely to regard the civil jury as an indispensable agency of justice were he more fully aware of the extent to which already, and indeed for centuries past, in equity, admiralty, and probate cases, judges have acceptably administered justice.

No doubt, too, the prevalence of the single judge, rather than a bench of judges, as the alternative to the jury, is a factor of importance in the popular view of this question. The bench of judges is today encountered only at isolated points in our system. This is the more remarkable in view of the wide use of the multijudge court in Continental (though not in English) practice, and its fairly frequent use in our own earlier tribunals. In the federal system, the single-judge system prevails throughout the district courts except for one feature: the constitution of a special three-judge bench to hear applications to enjoin a state or federal officer. In the state systems, too, the bench of judges sitting as a court of first instance in civil cases is a distinct rarity. Undoubtedly, radical proposals for the reduction of the use of the jury in civil cases would more readily secure adoption did they also contemplate the replacement of the single-judge court by a bench of judges.

13. TRIAL OF ISSUES OF FACT BY JURY: PROCEDURAL ASPECTS

The function of the judge in the civil jury trial is essentially the same as in the criminal trial. He rules on the admissibility of evidence and on the competency of witnesses, passes on motions made at the close of the defendant's case for a dismissal of the action for failure to establish a cause of action, passes on motions for a directed verdict at the close of the evidence, and instructs the jury before they retire to arrive at their

[38] The concept that the jury reflects the sense of the community more accurately than does the judge is put forward by Justice Brennan, in his dissenting opinion in Kingsley Books v. Brown, 354 U.S. 436, 447 (1957), as warranting the voiding, as a denial of due process, of a state statute authorizing the issuance of an injunction against the distribution of an obscene publication where the issue of obscenity was passed upon by the judge, and not, as Justice Brennan would have it, by a jury. In this view, jury trial is an indispensable safeguard in civil actions bearing on freedom of expression.

verdict. The other procedural features which in a civil case accompany trial by jury do not differ in most respects from those already encountered in connection with the criminal jury trial. Several distinctive aspects of the civil jury procedure should however be noted.

Form of verdict

At the conclusion of the evidence request may be made by either side that the jury be directed to answer certain specific questions of fact put to it by the court—to render, as the phrase is, a "special" verdict. Since this procedure is, in an action at law, quite exceptional, its consideration is deferred to a later page, and attention here confined to the so-called general verdict, in which the jury merely finds for the plaintiff or for the defendant and, if the action is for a money judgment and the verdict is in favor of the party seeking such judgment, states the amount to be awarded.

Judge's instructions to the jury

As in a criminal case, the jury is given no instructions by the judge as to the applicable law until all the evidence is in. The legal issues in a civil case are, however, likely to be more numerous and complex than in a criminal case; and hence despite the explanations of the legal aspects with which the attorneys for the parties may interlard their opening statements to the jury, the jurymen not infrequently listen to the evidence without any clear understanding of the relevancy of certain matters.

In framing his charge, the judge must determine which are the issues of fact to be determined by the jury, and which are questions of law to be determined by the judge himself. Thus, for example, if the action is one to recover damages for personal injuries sustained by the plaintiff in an accident allegedly caused by the negligence of the defendant, the question whether the defendant was negligent (as also the correlative question whether the plaintiff was free from contributory negligence) while usually a question of fact may in a given case be in whole or in part a question of law. Thus if one of the elements of negligence alleged is the failure of the party allegedly negligent to observe some law or legal regulation such as a traffic regulation (the facts as to what the party actually did being undisputed) the question whether such action did or did not constitute a violation of the law is a question of law for the judge. So, too, in a case arising out of an alleged breach of a written contract, if the contract is ambiguous and the parties differ as to the meaning of the writing, the determination of what the parties are to be held to have meant by the writing is ordinarily a question of law for the judge.

Having defined the issues of fact, the judge proceeds to the applicable rules of law. He must instruct the jury as to which side has the burden of proof on each issue of fact, and as to the necessary elements of the plaintiff's case (or defendant's defense or counterclaim, if any). He must also in an action for damages instruct them as to the "measure of damages"— i.e., the elements which the law permits to be taken into consideration in fixing damages.

Vote required for verdict

At common law, a civil verdict could be reached by the jury as in a criminal case only by unanimous vote. In recent years, several states have dispensed with the necessity for unanimity in civil cases, invariably requiring however more than a mere majority for a verdict (some requiring in a jury of twelve, the concurrence of ten jurors, others of nine, and one only of eight). In the federal courts, in actions at law where the amount in controversy is $20 or more, the requirement of unanimity is implicit in the constitutional provision that "the right of trial by jury"— i.e., trial by jury as known at the time of the adoption of the provision in question—"shall be preserved"; and Congress, in extending the right of trial by jury to cases other than suits at common law, has, by failing to make any different provision, preserved the requirement of unanimity in those cases also. The federal Rules of Civil Procedure provide, however, that in all cases of jury trial, the parties may stipulate "that a verdict or a finding of a stated majority of the jurors shall be taken as the verdict or finding of the jury." A similar provision is found in some of the states.

Direction or setting aside of verdict

The seemingly plenary power of the civil jury is qualified by the power of the court to direct its verdict (a direction which is forthwith recorded by the clerk as having been complied with) or to set aside the verdict it has rendered. This power of the court is to be exercised, in theory, only in a case in which in the court's view the evidence is completely (or so nearly completely) on one side that there is in truth no real issue of fact for the jury to pass upon,[39] or in which it appears from the evidence that the party seeking judgment has, in law, no right thereto.[40]

It may be thought that if the judge takes the view that there is no foundation in the evidence or in the law for a verdict for the plaintiff, for example, it is his duty not to let the case go to the jury at all, i.e., that it is fruitless for him to permit the case to go to the jury and then, should

[39] Where the court sets the verdict aside on this ground it is conventionally said that the verdict is "against the evidence" or "contrary to the weight of the evidence," and the rationale is said to be that the verdict was so completely at variance with the evidence that the jury must have been prejudiced or corrupt or must have misunderstood the court's instructions on the law. A cognate ground on which a verdict may be set aside is that of inconsistency between its several parts—a situation encountered ordinarily only when there are two or more defendants.

[40] The court may also dismiss the case on this ground at the close of the plaintiff's case.

the jury nevertheless bring in a verdict for the plaintiff, to set such verdict aside. On closer examination however, this turns out not to be the case. The judge may indeed believe that there is no question for the jury. Should he however, acting upon his view, direct a verdict for the defendant and should an appellate court subsequently decide that he was in error in his view, a new trial will be necessary. If, instead, he submits the question to the jury, and, if, on its finding, contrary to his anticipations, for the plaintiff, he sets the verdict aside, an appellate court, if it regards his view as erroneous, need not order a new trial, but can merely reinstate the jury's verdict. Moreover, if the jury, as anticipated, finds for the defendant, the desired result is achieved without raising the possibly troublesome legal questions which a direction of the verdict might have created. The result now rests, not on a perhaps debatable ruling by the judge that there was as a matter of law no question of fact for the jury, but on the finding the jury itself on whatever tenuous issue of fact may have been present.

Particularly if the judge is empowered not only to set the verdict aside, but to substitute for it the verdict which he would have directed had he not permitted the case to go to the jury, there is little reason for his exercising his power to direct a verdict, with its attendant risks. In the federal courts, and in an increasing number of states, he now enjoys this power of substitution.

Provision is also made in the practice of many jurisdictions for the setting aside of a verdict on the ground that it is inadequate or excessive. The setting aside of a verdict on the ground of inadequacy is comparatively rare; but the setting aside of verdicts deemed excessive is, particularly in action for damages for personal injuries, by no means infrequent. Usually, the court stipulates that unless the successful party consents to a reduction of the verdict to a figure specified by the court, the verdict is to be set aside and a new trial ordered. The court may not itself reduce (or increase) the verdict.[41]

Improvement of jury trial by use of special verdict

In the ordinary action at law, the principal area of civil trial by jury, the submission to the jury of the case as a whole, and the rendition by it of a general verdict, as just described, are now the standard, indeed almost

[41] It might be supposed that if the prevailing party refuses to consent to the reduction demanded by the court, the new trial ordered by the court will ordinarily concern itself with the issue of damages only. However, the traditional aversion to the severance of issues in the trial by jury of actions at law has in some jurisdictions prevented the severance of issues even in so obvious a situation as this. Instead, the new trial, ordered merely because the jury went astray in fixing the amount of damages, must also repeat, before a new jury, all the evidence bearing on the issue of whether the defendant is legally liable for the damage—an issue which the court has already determined was properly decided by the first jury.

the invariable, procedure. Yet the general verdict is a comparatively late development in the history of jury trial. In its genesis, as already seen, the jury was a device for procuring answers to particular questions, and as it gradually changed from a group of witnesses to a panel of judges of the facts, its verdict continued in many cases to have the form of responses to particular questions of fact, the judge then rendering judgment by applying the law to the facts found by the jury. For a long period there appears to have been no fixed rule, at least in civil cases, as to whether the verdict of the jury should take this form, or should be a "general" verdict, making no finding on the facts, but merely awarding, or refusing to award, redress to the plaintiff.

The development, in the seventeenth and eighteenth centuries, in both England and America, of the feeling that the power of the jury, as an institution reflecting the popular will in opposition to the bureaucratic power of the judiciary, should be enlarged, led to the establishment of the general verdict as the virtually exclusive form of jury pronouncement. This development received further reinforcement, even up to the middle of the last century, in the pioneer communities of this country, where the supremacy of the jury accorded well with the prevailing feeling that common sense and fairness rather than legalism should govern the settlement of disputes, and that, one man being as good as another, the jury were as competent as the judge to make a just disposition of the case. After a brief interlude in which it was in some places the rule that the jury was the judge of the law as well as the facts, the principle was virtually everywhere recognized that the jury was to accept from the judge instruction as to the law, and was to apply the law, as laid down by him, to the facts as it found them; and this continues to be the theoretical basis of trial by jury today.[42] Nevertheless, it is obvious that under the general verdict procedure it is impossible in many cases to ascertain what facts the jury found (if indeed it took the trouble to find any), and consequently whether or not it correctly applied the law to the facts. In many cases, consequently, whatever the theory of the matter, the jury is at liberty in effect to rewrite the law to suit itself—a phenomenon which one jurist has dubbed "juries-prudence."[43]

For some years past legal scholars have urged a return to the original form of jury verdict, in which the jury merely gave responses to questions of fact—the "special" verdict as it is now called; and statutes permitting

---

[42] In Louisiana, the civil jury was engrafted upon an alien system of procedure. The curious result has ensued that the jury is there the judge of the law as well as of the facts. On appeal, however, the appellate court is free to re-evaluate the evidence and revise the jury's verdict in any way it sees fit. The result has been that the civil jury is little used. Montgomery, Practice of Law in Louisiana, 3 Harv. Law School Bulletin, No. 5, p. 10 (1952).

[43] Frank, J. in Skidmore v. B. & O. R. Co. 167 F.2d 54, 59 (1948).

such verdicts instead of general verdicts are now found in a number of states and in the federal rules. However, only in Texas does the statute require the judge to call for a special verdict on demand of one of the parties. Elsewhere, the matter is within the discretion of the judge; and since the formulation of the questions to be asked the jury is sometimes a difficult process, fraught with possibilities of reversible error, it is not surprising to learn that the special verdict is ordered relatively infrequently. It seems likely that its use will increase, even under the present unsatisfactory statutes. Statutory provision making it mandatory is, however, greatly needed. Were it to supersede the general verdict and become the characteristic procedure, much though by no means all of the current dissatisfaction with jury trial in civil cases would doubtless be allayed.

14. JUDGMENT BY DEFAULT: CONSENT JUDGMENTS

It has been assumed, in the foregoing, that the defendant has answered the complaint and has thereafter gone to trial on the issues thus joined. In not a few cases, however, the defendant fails to answer the complaint ("defaults in answering," as the phrase is), and not infrequently, after having answered, he fails to appear at the trial. In either situation, judgment may be granted against him by default.

If the complaint demands judgment for a sum of money fixed by agreement between the parties, a default judgment for that sum may be entered by the court without a hearing. If, however, the complaint demands a sum of money as damages, the amount of the damages to which the plaintiff is entitled can be fixed only by the court, and a hearing is ordinarily required; and so too with other special forms of judgment.

Even where the framing of the judgment requires no hearing, public policy may require it, in order that the court may be satisfied that the plaintiff is entitled to a judgment and that the failure of the defendant to defend does not stem from a collusive agreement with the plaintiff. This principle finds its chief application in connection with undefended actions for divorce. It can hardly be said, however, that the insistence on a hearing is in fact very effective in preventing collusive divorces. Apparently, the effect is frequently rather to cause the plaintiff, who has already committed perjury in swearing to the complaint, to aggravate the offense by false testimony, or by procuring the false testimony of others, at the hearing. To check this abuse, the statutes of some states require the public prosecutor (or, in a few states, a specially appointed officer) to investigate the facts and participate in the trial of uncontested divorce cases; but in some, perhaps in most, of these states such participation is quite perfunctory.

To be grouped with the judgment by default is the judgment entered with the consent of the party against whom the judgment runs. This type of judgment has been extensively used in injunction actions brought by the government under the antitrust laws, the consent decree (the term "decree" being traditionally used for a judgment in an equity action) setting forth with particularity the specific practices which the defendant agrees to discontinue, or the specific divestments of property or control it agrees to effect. Actions brought by stockholders in behalf of corporations, seeking restitution from officers or directors for losses suffered by the corporation through their neglect or misfeasance, have also frequently been compromised, after trial in whole or in part, by consent judgments. In entering such judgments, an interesting procedure has been employed by some courts—the notification to all stockholders of the intended judgment, with opportunity to voice objections before final entry.

15. APPLICATION FOR NEW TRIAL ON GROUND OF NEWLY DISCOVERED EVIDENCE

As in a criminal case, an application may be made at any time after a trial for a new trial on the ground of newly discovered evidence. The questions before the court on such an application are first, whether there exists evidence of a substantial nature which was not introduced upon the first trial; second, whether such evidence, had it been so introduced, might have changed the result; third, whether the failure of the losing party to discover such evidence in time for its presentation upon the first trial is excusable. Where all these questions are answered in the affirmative, it is the duty of the court to grant a new trial.

16. APPELLATE REVIEW: THE RIGHT TO A REVIEW

We have seen that in criminal proceedings the right of the convicted defendant to a review of the proceedings by an appellate court is in effect a nineteenth century development. The right of the losing party in a civil proceeding to procure a review by a higher court developed much earlier; and today, despite limitations in come jurisdictions on appeals from judgments of the lower courts, it is correct to say that the right to a review of the judgment in a civil proceeding is a pervasive feature of our procedure.

Indeed, in some jurisdictions, the right to a review embraces not only judgments, but also many types of intermediate orders made in the course of the proceeding—such as the order to the plaintiff to furnish further particulars of the allegations made in his complaint (a "bill of particulars," as the phrase is), or an order to the defendant to permit an inspection of his records. In other jurisdictions, and in the federal courts, the right to appeal from intermediate orders is very much more restricted.

As a substitute for the appellate review of the record of the lower court, there is found, in most states, with respect to the proceedings before justices of the peace and cognate inferior courts, as in proceedings to punish minor offenses, provision for a retrial of the case—"trial de novo" —in a higher trial court.

Upon a trial de novo, the court of course has the same freedom of action as if the trial in the petty court had never taken place. Upon an appeal, however, the appellate court functions under sharp restrictions as to the extent of the matters it may review and of the action which it may take. These limitations differ according to the character of the proceedings in the trial court.

In a number of state court systems there are found, in addition to the highest court of the state, intermediate appellate courts; and in some of the larger cities there are special appellate benches for appeals from the special city courts. There is wide variation in detail in the provisions governing the right to further review, by the higher appellate court, of the determination made by the lower appellate court. Seldom is such further review a matter of right in all cases. Illustrative is a provision in one state giving such right of further review where the lower appellate court has reversed the judgment of the trial court, or where the affirmance of the judgment has been by a divided court; in all other cases review may be had only by permission, granted either by the lower or the higher appellate court.

In the federal court system, appeals in a few cases go directly to the final appellate court, the Supreme Court. In all other cases, they go to one of the intermediate regional appellate courts, known as courts of appeals. From a court of appeals, there is no right of appeal to the Supreme Court except where a party has relied on a state statute and the court of appeals has held such statute invalid as repugnant to the Constitution or to a federal statute or treaty. In all other cases, the Supreme Court may grant review (by "writ of certiorari") on application (or "petition") being made, showing why the case deserves this exceptional further review.[44]

A similar situation exists with respect to further review by the supreme Court of the decision of a state court (such review being in any case available only after the party seeking it has exhausted all possible appellate review in the state courts). The right to such Supreme Court review (confined in all cases to the questions of *federal* law, whether arising under the Constitution or under a federal statute or treaty, raised in the state court) is given only where the state court has declared a federal statute or treaty unconstitutional (a rare case indeed), or has upheld a state

[44] 28 U.S. Code, Sec. 1254.

statute attacked as unconstitutional because repugnant to the Constitution or to a federal statute or treaty. In all other cases, Supreme Court review is available only by permission of the Court.[45]

Some have criticized the Supreme Court for exercising so extensively its discretionary power to deny further review in cases decided by the federal courts of appeals and, to a more limited extent, in cases decided by the state courts. The motive for such denial, these critics assert, has by no means always been merely the desire to keep the court's docket clear of inconsequential issues. Some of the denials, it is said, are to be explained rather by an uwillingness of the court to confront difficult issues, and to make unpopular or even politically undesirable decisions.[46] Appraisal of this criticism within the space here available would be impracticable.

In many of states, and in the federal system, review, even where not available to the parties, may be sought by the lower appellate court itself, a step resorted to, needless to say, only where there is a close, or perhaps even an equal, division of opinion. Such a request by the lower court in most jurisdiction takes the form, not of a general request that the case be reviewed by the higher court, but of a "certification" to the higher court of the legal questions involved, the case remaining with the lower appellate court for disposition in accordance with the answers given by the higher court to the certified questions.

17. APPELLATE REVIEW: JUDGMENT ENTERED ON VERDICT OF JURY

In the development of English legal procedures, provision for the review of civil jury verdicts makes its appearance very early. But the jury at this period is still a body of witnesses rather than of judges. Accordingly, the appeal from the jurors' findings takes the form of an attack not on the correctness of their appraisal of the evidence, but rather on their good faith and honesty. Thus there developed the procedure known as "attaint of judgment," an accusation of misfeasance brought against the jury. Though in form an accusation, it was in fact a retrial of the original issues by a new jury, larger, and perhaps more consequential in its membership, than the first jury. Its verdict could not only supersede the first verdict, but also subject the members of the first jury to punishment.

The notion that a finding of fact by a jury could not be set aside by the judges, but only by another jury—a notion logical enough during the period when the jury was still deciding issues of fact on the basis of its

[45] 28 U.S. Code, Sec. 1257.

[46] See, for example, annual critiques on this point by Harper and others in 1950–1954 in U. of Pa. Law Rev., vol. 99, p. 293; vol. 100, p. 354; vol. 101, p. 438; and vol. 102, p. 427. And see, for a contrary view, Bickel, Foreword, Supreme Court, 1960 Term, 75 Harv. Law Rev. 46 (1961).

own knowledge as much as if not more than on the basis of the evidence adduced before it—persisted even after the jurymen had become simply weighers of the evidence. It was reinforced by the feeling that the jury, at least in prosecutions or proceedings instituted by the officers of the Crown, was a shield against oppression, the juror being presumably less susceptible to improper pressure from the royal officers than was the judge. Thus from the fusion of ideas drawn from these two diverse and essentially irrelevant sources there emerged the doctrine that the finding of a civil jury on a question of fact, in a trial in which the judge had committed no error of law, was final and could not be reviewed on appeal. It is this doctrine which is, so far as our federal courts are concerned, elevated to the dignity of a constitutional principle by the provision in the Constitution that "no fact tried by a jury [in a action at law] shall be otherwise reexamined in any court of the United States, than according to the rules of common law"; and which in our state courts, even where not expressly enunciated in the state constitution or even in statute, still commands general obedience by the judiciary as part of the essential fabric of our traditional law.

It has been seen, however, that the trial judge is under a duty, when there is no real issue of fact for the jury, to direct a verdict; and if he permits the case to go to the jury and the jury returns a verdict which is so completely contrary to the weight of the evidence that it is explainable only on the ground that the jury did not understand the judge's instructions or was motivated by prejudice or corruption, he is under a duty to set it aside. Correspondingly, if in the trial the judge erred in failing to direct a verdict, and to set aside the verdict rendered as against the weight of the evidence, the appellate court may correct the trial judge's error of law by itself setting aside the judgment entered on the verdict.

Thus in theory the appellate court, like the trial court, leaves undisturbed the jury's supremacy in the field of questions of fact, intervening only when there is in truth no question of fact. In practice, however, as reflection will readily show, there can be no clear-cut line between the case in which the evidence is so overwhelmingly one-sided that no question of fact really exists and that in which it is preponderantly on one side, but not so preponderantly that no question of fact exists. In the actual business of the appellate courts, therefore, one encounters a proportion of cases in which the judgment entered on the verdict runs too strongly counter to the view of the evidence which the appellate judges themselves take for them to permit it to stand.

The appellate court has of course the same power to reverse the judgment as had the trial court to set the verdict aside, on the ground of excessiveness, inadequacy, or inconsistency of the verdict, and the same lack of power to correct the verdict or the judgment entered thereon. In those jurisdictions in which the trial judge has the power, on setting aside the verdict of the jury, to enter judgment contrary to the verdict, the appellate court possesses the like power.

From the foregoing it will be apparent that, as a corrective to erroneous findings by a jury on issues of fact, the field of usefulness of our appellate courts is distinctly limited. In the exercise of the other branch of their function—that of correcting errors of law made by the judge in the conduct of the trial—no such limitations exist.

Errors of law may be of either of two kinds. The first relates to alleged errors made by the judge in the conduct of the trial—errors in *procedure*. The second relates to the alleged errors made by him in applying the proper legal rules to the facts of the case—errors in *substantive* law.

Errors in procedure

Possible errors in procedure cover a wide range, extending in some cases even to the stages of the proceeding before the trial. In the conduct of the trial itself the possibilities of procedural errors are more numerous in the case of a trial by jury than in a trial without a jury; for in the jury trial there are the numerous possibilities for error in the process of summoning and impaneling the jury already referred to in connection with criminal trials. In civil cases however, these matters are relatively rarely made the ground of complaint on appeal. More frequent is the contention that the trial court committed prejudicial error in admitting improper testimony, or excluding proper testimony.[47]

Errors in substantive law

In a jury trial, occasions for the judge to pass on the substantive law of the case may occur at several stages of the trial: (1) At its opening, an application may be made to him by the defendant to dismiss the case on the ground that the allegations of the complaint, even if proved, would not entitle the plaintiff to the relief he seeks (or a similar application by the plaintiff for the dismissal of a counterclaim interposed by the defendant). (2) At the close of the plaintiff's case, an application may be made by

[47] In passing upon the allegedly erroneous exclusion of oral testimony—i.e., the refusal of the court, upon objection made, to permit a witness to answer a question put him—the appellate court does not know whether the answer to the question, had it been permitted, would have been helpful to the appellant. Hence, although perhaps in fact it would have been of no assistance whatever to his case and would even have been harmful, the court is obliged to assume that it *would* have been helpful. There is in most states no procedure by which the court may ascertain what answer would have been made to the questions propounded, had the witness been permitted to answer. With respect, however, to writings offered as evidence, but rejected by the court, the appellate court is usually in a position to pass on whether the wrongful exclusion of such writings was damaging; for the writings, if "marked for identification" are part of the record before the court.

the defendant to dismiss the case on the ground that the evidence adduced by the plaintiff, even if believed, does not establish the allegations of the complaint. (3) At the close of the evidence, an application may be made by either side in a jury case for a directed verdict. (4) After denial of such a motion, the court must instruct the jury as to the law to be applied to each of the several possible views which they may take of the facts. (5) After the rendition of the verdict in a jury case, an application may be made to set aside the verdict as against the evidence. (Under headings 3 and 5, it will be observed, the question before the judge is not in reality one of law but one of fact—the question whether there is in truth any question of fact for the jury. This question is, however, conventionally treated as if it were really a question of law.)

Of the several occasions thus presented for the application of rules of law, the most important, and from the standpoint of the judge frequently the most difficult, is that of giving instructions to the jury, and the reviewing function of the appellate courts is correspondingly important at this point. Attention has already been called, however, to the frequently unrealistic character of that review, based as it must be on the assumption that the jury understood, remembered, and faithfully applied the instructions of the court, an assumption which reaches sheer absurdity when the instructions have taken the form of a perfunctory reading of lengthy and complicated statements of law framed by counsel.

Allegedly improper conduct of judge

Occasionally, but infrequently, the appellate court is asked to vacate or modify the judgment of the lower court entered on the verdict of a jury not because of alleged errors made by the presiding judge, but because of his allegedly improper conduct at the trial. The refusal to permit an attorney to conduct in the usual maner the examination of the witnesses called by him, the court itself taking the witness out of the hands of the attorney, the refusal similarly to give an attorney adequate opportunity to cross-examine witnesses produced by his adversary, the making of uncalled-for comments, particularly of a hostile character, upon the witnesses, or upon the attorney—these are some of the types of misconduct which have particularly moved appellate courts to order new trials, where the conduct of the judge has been such as materially to impair the proper and adequate presentation of the case, and adversely to influence the jury. As already indicated, however, it is proper for the judge, at a jury trial, to question a witness.

Relation of general verdict to appellate review

Throughout the process of appellate review of a judgment entered on a general verdict, the appellate court is often confronted with a frustrating obstacle; it has no way of knowing how the jury viewed each of the several issues of fact before it and, hence, no way of knowing whether the erorrs of law made in the admission or exclusion of testimony had any influence on the jury's verdict. It may well be that, even had the improperly admitted evidence not been given at all the jurymen would have been fully convinced of the contention to the proof of which the improperly admitted evidence was directed, so that the evidence, although improper, in no way prejudiced the losing party. It may well be that the answer to the improperly excluded question, had it been admitted, and had it been fully as favorable as anticipated by the questioner, would have been of no benefit to the losing party, since the jury was in any event satisfied of that party's contention on the point in issue, the adverse verdict having been due to their view on a different issue.

So too in connection with erroneous instructions to the jury. Not knowing the view of the jury on any of the several issues of fact, the appellate court, when it concludes that a substantial error has been made, is often compelled to assume, without any foundation therefor, that the erroneous instruction in question influenced the jurors in reaching their verdict or that an instruction erroneously refused, if given, would have done so. Since such an assumption may be safely assumed to be false in a fair proportion of cases, it follows that numberless verdicts of juries have been set aside by appellate courts for errors in the trial which in no wise influenced the verdict. This enormous defect of our system of civil jury trial can be cured only by substituting the special verdict for the general verdict.

Ordering retrial of particular issues

When a judgment entered on a general verdict is reversed and a new trial ordered, such retrial is almost invariably a retrial of all the issues. This may be unavoidable since, as already seen, it is often impossible to ascertain, from a general verdict, what the jury's findings were on any particular issue; hence, all issues must be retried. Such, however, is the inertia generated in our appellate courts by the limitations surrounding them when reviewing a judgment entered on a general verdict, that they decline, in a number of jurisdictions, to order the retrial of particular issues only, even in a class of cases in which the error of the jury is manifestly confined to a single issue only—the amount of damages. This phenomenon can be explained only by the hold still possessed by the concept of the jury verdict as an almost mystic pronouncement, to be superseded, if at all, only by another jury verdict.[48]

---

[48] A retrial of all the issues is, however, called for where the amount of damages awarded by the jury clearly represents a compromise between opposing views of liability.

18. APPELLATE REVIEW: OTHER JUDGMENTS

In reviewing an equity judgment the appellate court does not labor under the restrictions present in the review of a judgment entered after jury trial in an action at law. It is at liberty to reverse the judgment because it takes a different view of the facts than did the trial judge. It is perfectly true that the findings of the trial judge, based, if there was oral testimony, partly on his personal observation of the demeanor of the witnesses, are entitled to great respect at the hands of the appellate courts, which has before it only a transcript of the testimony. Nevertheless, if, after making due allowance for this factor, the appellate judges feel that the findings of fact made by the trial judge are clearly erroneous, they may disregard his findings, and substitute findings of their own. If additional evidence was in their opinion required, they could, in English and early American practice, order the taking, or themselves take, such additional testimony, and upon the basis thereof make the appropriate findings of fact. This power to take additional evidence in equity appeals is still found in a few of our states, but for the most part the power of our appellate courts in this respect has been curtailed. Consequently, as in appeals from judgments entered on jury verdicts, they are powerless to take new evidence.

The appellate court may in most jurisdictions itself modify the erroneous judgment or decree made by the trial court. If it chooses, however, it may and often does remand the case to the lower court with directions to take appropriate action.

Appellate review in admiralty and probate cases, like that in equity cases, had in England, and also in our colonial period, a development quite distinct from that of appellate review in cases at law. In general, the development resembled that of equity appeals; and what has just been said of appellate review in equity, as distinguished from that at law, is true, in the main, also of admiralty and probate appeals. In admiralty appeals, the power of the appellate court to take additional evidence remains in full vigor.

Falling into no traditional pattern, with respect to the scope of appellate review, is the review of the judgment rendered by a judge in an action at law in which a jury has been waived by the parties. In perhaps a quarter of the states, the appeal is in theory still treated as if the judgment had been entered on the verdict of a jury; if no error of law is found, the judgment is not to be disturbed unless completely unwarranted by the evidence. In the remaining states and in the federal courts the judgment is treated like an equity judgment, reviewable on the facts as well as the law. However even in those states in which in theory the judgment is as sacrosanct as one entered on a jury verdict, it is in practice, at least in some of these states, less so.

19. APPELLATE REVIEW: PROCEDURE

In the development of English judicature, appellate review was at first obtainable by what was in effect a separate proceeding—an application to a higher court to order the trial court to transmit its record of the case to the higher court for examination as to alleged errors of law committed by the trial court—a "writ of error" as the phrase was. This cumbersome procedure has given way in all but a few jurisdictions to a procedure in which the defeated party merely serves notice on the successful party of his intention to appeal, and files a like notice in the court. If an appellate court has already passed on the case, and review is now sought from a higher appellate court, permission must, as already noted, in many cases be obtained from the higher court before appeal may be taken.

Stay of enforcement of judgment pending appeal

The filing of a notice of appeal from the judgment does not of itself suspend the enforcement of the judgment. If the judgment has awarded a sum of money to the plaintiff, the mere fact that the defendant files notice of appeal does not relieve him from the necessity of paying the judgment, or from the risk of having his property seized and sold to satisfy such judgment if he does not pay. To prevent this result he must give security (usually in the form of a bond furnished by a surety company) for the payment of the judgment, should it be affirmed on appeal. The alternative course would be to pay the judgment and, should the judgment subsequently be reversed on appeal, to seek restitution from the respondent, that is to say, the party against whom the appeal was taken. Such a course is, needless to say, followed only where the respondent is of unquestioned financial responsibility.

Where the judgment appealed from provides for something other than the payment of money, a stay of the enforcement of the judgment pending appeal is not thus automatically obtainable on filing bond but must be granted by the court. Such a stay will nearly always be granted; but again if there is any danger that the respondent may be injured thereby, the granting of the stay will be made conditional on the appellant's furnishing appropriate security for the satisfaction of or compliance with the judgment if affirmed, and for the payment of any damages which the respondent may suffer by reason of the delay in such satisfaction or compliance.

Record on appeal: briefs and oral argument

The appeal procedure having been thus initiated, it is now for the appellant to procure preparation and submission to the appellate court and to the respondent of a record of the case—that is to say, a transcript of the pleadings, the judgment, or order, etc., and the testimony and documentary evidence.

In many cases the questions which the appellant intends to raise upon the appeal can be properly answered from an examination of a limited part only of the record. Provisions exist in most jurisdictions, whereby portions of the record not material to the appeal may be eliminated; but, for a variety of reasons, these provisions are not always fully made use of. That the needless fullness of appeal records is no new evil in legal procedure may be inferred from a reference by a fifteenth century French writer to a record on appeal in a contemporary case "which is contained in six huge volumes and several writings, of which three-quarters does not count for anything, either pro or contra."

The court also has before it statements of the contentions advanced by the respective parties. Such statements, known as "briefs," sometimes run to a hundred pages or more. Nevertheless, it is the practice of appellate courts to hear the attorneys for the parties orally; and some of them insist on such oral argument.

20. DELAY

The law's delay, included by Hamlet in his short list as one of life's chief public ills, is to some extent unavoidable. A certain deliberation of tempo must characterize all judicial proceedings if the parties are to have a full and fair opportunity to present their case. But indubitably our civil litigation moves in many cases at much too slow a pace.

Delay in civil litigation may be caused by an inadequate number of judges, or by the lack of industry or competence on the part of a seemingly adequate bench, or both. With these causes of delay we have at this point no concern. Assuming courts adequately and competently manned, the speed with which a case runs its course toward final disposition will depend partly on the procedural rules applicable and partly on the extent to which the parties, and particularly the plaintiff, are desirous of having it disposed of.

On the whole, it cannot be said that our civil procedure produces avoidable delay. Unquestionably, it affords opportunities for a party seeking delay to abuse certain of the procedures provided; but the procedures themselves are for the most part indispensable. The cure for their abuse would seem to lie in the imposition of more severe monetary penalties (in the form of "costs," a term shortly to be explained) where completely unmeritorious applications are made to the court, obviously only for purposes of delay.

One respect in which our procedural rules tend to defer the conclusion of an action unnecessarily is in the inordinate time now allowed for the taking of particular procedural steps. The time scale applied in this respect in many courts is an ancient one, coming down from the days of the quill pen and the stage coach. A drastic reduction could be effected on the time allowed for many of the routine steps in the ordinary litigation.

Excessive allowances of time are particularly common in our appellate procedures. But the most important factor in delaying the final disposition of a case on appeal is, where it exists, the double appeal. The necessity for the intermediate appellate tribunal, with resultant possibility of double appeal, is examined at a subsequent point.

There is another aspect of the problem of delay which might also be termed procedural, though the cause lies in the absence of a rule, rather than in its presence. This is the failure of the court to act with reasonable promptness in announcing its decision. This phenomenon, often the result not of indolence or procrastination, but of indecision, is encountered in trial courts in the decision of non-jury cases, and perhaps even more markedly in the appellate courts, where the delay in the announcement of the court's decision stands in such marked contrast to the practice of the high appellate courts of England, which customarily announce their disposition of the appeal promptly after the conclusion of the argument, even without leaving the bench. In some states are found statutory provisions designed to compel prompt disposition by judges,[49] and these have a certain effectiveness. In most states, however, and in the federal courts, the matter rests wholly in the pleasure of the judges themselves.

When one speaks of delay attributable to the parties themselves, rather than to the procedure, one must distinguish clearly between delay caused by one side in despite of the other, and delay, so to speak, by common consent.

Where, despite the ample time allowed by the governing procedure, one of the parties seeks further delay, the extent to which delay is permitted depends greatly on the presiding judge. It is at this point that some form of supervision of the individual judge is again of great importance. The lenient or indolent judge who too readily grants requests for adjournment or extensions of time is, under even the simplest system of supervision, readily identified; and if there be a strong hand at the helm his weakness in this respect is not difficult to correct.

It is, however, delay by common consent, rather than delay by one side in despite of the other, that is chiefly responsible for the leisureliness with which many litigations pursue their way to a conclusion. Unwillingness of either party to bring the matter to a decision accounts for delay

[49] In some states there is a statutory requirement that each judge file, as a prerequisite to his receiving payment of his salary, an affidavit that he has disposed of all matters that have been before him more than a certain length of time, as, for example, three months.

to an extent hardly appreciated by the layman. It is not uncommon, even in courts in which the calendar is most congested, that when a case is eventually reached for trial neither side is ready to proceed.

The extent to which actions are instituted with no intention to press them to final disposition, with the intention indeed in some cases to resist any attempt on the part of the defendant thus to press them, is perhaps not commonly appreciated by those who have no first-hand contact with these matters. This phenomenon is particularly marked in the field of personal injury claims (of which motor-vehicle-accident claims form so large a part), which occupy much of the time of our courts (including, chiefly by reason of their diversity jurisdiction, the federal courts). The great majority of such claims are settled by the responsible insurers without action having been instituted by the plaintiff. Of the remainder, the great majority are settled after action has begun, but before, sometimes just before, trial. Action was begun, in most of these cases, in the hope and expectation of settling, rather than of trying, them.

The institution of the action gives each side facilities for exploring the strengths and weaknesses of the other's position, and makes it easier for the defendant's counsel, in some cases, to procure his client's agreement to a settlement than it would be in the absence of a pending action. Much the same is true of many classes of commercial claims.[50]

In the case of personal injury actions moreover, a special factor enters —the uncertain extent of the plaintiff's injuries and of the permanent damage done to his earning capacity. The lack of any procedure, in our courts of law, for making periodically reviewable partial awards instead of a single lump-sum award has already been pointed out. In consequence, in many cases, the plaintiff in such a situation does not desire a speedy disposition of his claim; he wishes to delay the final disposition until matters have become better clarified. From this standpoint it might even be said that our procedure, far from delaying the disposition of a case, compels a speedier disposition than is desirable if justice is to be done.

21. COSTLINESS

The cost of legal procedure to the litigant is twofold; on the one hand, necessary disbursements for court fees and witness fees; on the other, the

---

[50] Not infrequently, this failure of a litigation to progress toward a conclusion reflects the convenience of the attorneys, rather than the interests of the parties. Continuances and extensions of time, reciprocally granted, are the device by which attorneys smooth out the highly irregular curve which their caseload would otherwise present. Within limits, this is not to be condemned; but there is needed a stricter supervision by the court than is commonly exercised in such matters to insure that the interest of the client is not being sacrificed to that of the attorney. There is much interest at present in the problem of disciplining attorneys who unduly delay a proceeding. The power of the court to punish the attorney for contempt is doubtful; and no other power of punishment has in general been provided by statute.

expense of retaining counsel (and possibly also accountants, investigators, expert witnesses, and the like). Expenditures of the first category do not ordinarily bulk very large, in relation at least to the matter in controversy. It is expenditures of the second category which make litigation costly. A prime objective should therefore be a simplification of the procedures in small claims cases (and a more active role for the judge) to eliminate as far as practicable the need for attorneys, whose fees, however modest in relation to time consumed, are disproportionate to the amounts involved.[51] Much has been done in this field, but not nearly enough.

When one passes to litigations of more consequence, the problem of reducing the cost to the litigant of the professional services mentioned becomes much more difficult. Indeed it is difficult to see how that cost to the litigant can be much reduced, short of its assumption by the community.[52]

Laymen who have had little to do with litigation are apt to entertain the notion that the law is unnecessarily complex and that if it were simplified the litigant might be able more frequently to conduct his case without the aid of counsel. This notion is unfounded in both its branches. It would not be practicable to simplify the law over most of its area, its complication being in the main the necessary result of the complexity of the subject matter with which it deals, rather than of ineptitude on the part of legislators or courts (though indeed of ineptitude there is no lack); and even where the legal issues in a litigation may be relatively simple, it is common experience that the layman quite frequently lacks the time and capacity to organize the factual materials, whether in the form of documents or of oral testimony to be elicited from witnesses, for satisfactory presentation to the court. If the trial is by jury, the procedures involved in selecting the jury, and other technical steps which the presence of the jury necessitates, make it especially difficult for the layman to dispense with counsel.

Granting the services of an attorney to be necessary in a litigation, such services could of course be furnished by the state, either by way of a salaried staff, or by payment out of the public funds of the fee of the

---

[51] There is room in this country for an institution found in some Continental countries—the legal clerk. This craftsman, who makes his headquarters in the vicinity of the minor civil courts, is not authorized to give legal advice; his function is to prepare for litigants unrepresented by counsel such simple writings as the court may require.

[52] A proposal to make legal services generally, including counsel in civil litigation, more readily available to persons of moderate means contemplates the establishment by the local bar association, in its own headquarters, of a legal service office for handling matters which do not call for the higher order of legal ability. See Smith, Legal Service Offices for Persons of Moderate Means (1947), a report to the Survey of the Legal Profession conducted by the Amer. Bar Assn. See also Cheatham, A Lawyer When Needed: Legal Services for the Middle Classes, 63 Col. Law Rev. 973 (1963).

attorney retained by the litigant.[53] The objections to the former alternative, from the standpoint alike of the lawyer and the client (who would necessarily forego much if not all of what freedom in the choice of his counsel he now enjoys) are fairly obvious. The second alternative, wholly without precedent in this country, has been adopted on a limited basis in Great Britain, so far as concerns the plaintiff of small means who has an apparently meritorious claim.

With respect to the plaintiff, there is available, in certain types of action, the possibility of retaining an attorney on a contingent basis—an arrangement under which the plaintiff agrees to advance or be liable for all necessary disbursements in the litigation, and the attorney agrees to serve without any liability on the part of the plaintiff for payment of a fee, the attorney to share, however, to an agreed extent (normally from 33⅓ to 50 per cent) in the plaintiff's net proceeds, if any, by way of recovery or settlement. This type of arrangement is obviously subject to abuse at the hands of unscrupulous attorneys, and in some foreign countries it is prohibited by law or by the courts. In this country, its use has in certain jurisdictions been regulated by the courts with a view to preventing the expolitation of ignorant or immature clients;[54] but in principle it is generally defended as enabling a person without adequate means nevertheless to retain competent counsel to prosecute a meritorious claim. It may be regarded as a crude form of insurance, under which the unremunerated services of counsel in the cases in which he obtains little or nothing for his client (and hence for himself) are paid for by the more fortunate client, who parts with a larger share of his proceeds than the services rendered him in that particular case might by themselves warrant.

The contingent fee is in fact, as is well known, employed to

[53] The activities of philanthropic legal aid societies in the civil courts have largely been confined to a few types of cases such as are characteristic of the low-income clientele which these societies service—cases involving rent of living quarters, unpaid wages, security deposits withheld, installment sales, personal loans, and the like. Once this level is left behind, no provision whether public or philanthropic exists for easing the cost burden on the litigant. In New Jersey, the state bar has undertaken a program for establishing under local bar association auspices a legal aid society in each county for civil business. Such a program might ultimately cover all forms of legal services on the civil side which cannot sustain the cost burden of the ordinary client-lawyer relationship. See Bell, Legal Aid in New Jersey; The Answer to a Socialized Legal Profession, 36 Amer. Bar Assn. Jour 355 (1950).

[54] Thus, in New York, one of the four regional appellate courts having supervisory powers over the bar has required that all retainer agreements for a contingent fee be filed in court upon being entered into, and that the fee agreed upon shall not exceed 50 percent of the first $1,000 of the judgment, 40 percent of the next $2,000. 35 percent of the next $22,000, 20 percent of the next $25,000 and 15 percent of any amount over $50,000. The rule applies only to actions for personal injury or death. There have been proposals that contingent fees be made unlawful; but proposals for a workable substitute in personal injury and death actions brought by persons of small means have not been forthcoming.

provide for the cost of attorney's services to plaintiff's in a large class of litigations—indeed the largest class, numerically, to be found in our state courts. This is the class of cases arising out of the alleged negligence of the defendant or his employees, of which again cases arising out of automobile accidents form the larger part.

In actions for separation, divorce, and annulment there is found a special provision for insuring legal service to the wife—an order of the court issued on a proper showing at or shortly after the institution of the action, requiring the husband to pay to the wife's attorney a counsel fee fixed by the court.

That attorney's fees in the typical commercial litigation (which furnishes the chief source of business of the civil courts other than actions for negligence) are not excessive would seem to be indicated by the zealous efforts so often exerted by the attorneys in such litigation to settle matters out of court—efforts motivated by the desire of the attorneys to escape the time-consuming and to them little profitable labor of paper work, preparation for trial, and trial itself.

All in all, having in mind the high cost under which the attorney himself operates, there seems little possibility of reducing the cost of his services in the typical civil litigation.[55]

The expense of expert witnesses, however, is one item of cost that might well be reduced by a reorganization of the methods employed, along the lines suggested at an earlier page.[56]

Costs recoverable by prevailing party

Closely connected with the problem of financing the cost of the lawyer's services and other expenses of litigation is that of the reimbursement to be made by the losing party in a litigation to the successful party for his necessary disbursements.

These disbursements include the cost of serving process on the adverse party, the cost of serving subpoenas on witnesses, fees and travel allowances paid to witnesses when subpoenaed, as required by law, filing fees paid to the clerk of the court on filing certain papers, jury fees, fees paid to the sheriff, marshal, or other like officer on delivery to him of an execu-

---

[55] A field of litigation in which the cost of litigation has been criticized as being almost prohibitive is that of actons against labor unions by members claiming to have been wrongfully expelled. The Landrum-Griffin Act of 1960 empowered the Secretary of Labor to institute action on behalf of a complaining member in cases of allegedly improper elections, but did not extend this form of aid to cases of expulsion. Under the National Labor Relations Act, an employee can enlist the aid of the National Labor Relations Board when complaining of an unfair labor practice by an employer; but the act does not cover wrongful action of a labor organization against a member. The jurisdiction of the Board could readily be expanded by statute to cover such "unfair labor practices" also.

[56] See pp. 258-259.

tion, expense of advertising in cases where such is required, cost of making a search of title to property in certain cases where such search is a necessary preliminary to the action, etc. These disbursements the prevailing party is entitled to include in the judgment in full.

The other disbursements often necessary to the successful prosecution of an action are not, however, taken cognizance of by our courts in an ordinary litigation. These include counsel fees and fees to accountants, investigators, and expert witnesses, as well as expense incurred by these persons, or by the party himself, in preparing for trial. By way of an offset to these expenses, a certain sum is allowed to the prevailing party according to a schedule fixed by law, the amount usually depending chiefly on the number of terms of court at which the case appeared on the calendar, and on the number of days occupied by the trial.

These allowances are termed "costs." In equity cases the allowance even of costs to the prevailing party is within the discretion of the court.

In the case of "difficult and extraordinary" actions, the court may in some states make an additional allowance for costs, but this is rarely done. In some states, statutory provision for allowance of a reasonable attorney's fee is specifically made in certain classes of actions, such as actions against insurance companies brought to recover losses claimed to be payable under policies of insurance, and actions against railroads for causing fire. Moreover, it is not uncommon for certain routine contracts —in particular, promissory notes and drafts—to contain a provision consenting that in the event of non-payment, the person liable thereon shall pay in addition to the amount of the instrument the costs of collection, including a reasonable attorney's fees. Such stipulations are enforced by the courts.[57]

Generally speaking the scale of costs in the American courts is quite low. Hence, even though the prevailing party scores a complete victory, and even though it may appear that the institution or the defense of the action by the losing party was wholly without justification, the prevailing party may fail to recover nearly enough by way of costs to compensate him for his necessary or unavoidable expenses. The injustice of this situation has caused many to urge that our scale of costs be increased, or that at any rate there be instituted a system of punitive costs to be awarded against the unsuccessful party where it appears that there was

[57] Analogous to the allowance of costs proper is the allowance to the plaintiff, provided for in the statutes of some states, for an additional sum as the "damages" resulting from his having been compelled to sue. Such provisions are chiefly found in insurance statutes, with reference to suits by the insured or the beneficiary or a policy of insurance against an insurance company, to recover a claimed loss under a policy. The amount of the "damages" thus awarded to the plaintiff is generally fixed by the statute at a percentage of the amount in suit, 10 to 15 per cent being perhaps the typical percentage, though in certain instances it runs as high as 25 per cent.

no real justification for his instituting or defending the action, as the case may be.

Proponents of reform usually point to England as furnishing an example worthy of imitation. In its courts a much more severe scheme of costs exists. A severe scale of costs, so goes the argument, tends on the one hand to discourage the institution of unjust suits and on the other to discourage the defense of suits by defendants who have no substantial ground of defense. The difficulty with this view in the minds of many students of the subject is that it makes the litigation of even a bona fide dispute too costly a risk to be undertaken by any but a person of ample means, and thus in effect constitutes a denial of justice to persons of limited means. The best opinion seems to be that the American system of costs should be made somewhat more severe with a view to an approximation to real reimbursement to the prevailing party particularly where the losing party is thought to have instituted or defended the action without sufficient cause; but that it should avoid going as far as the English system.

Were one able to feel certain that the successful party is in all cases the one who ought to have succeeded, and that the defeated party has no claim on the leniency of the court, it would be easy to accept the proposal for a very stringent scale of costs. Experience teaches, however, that not infrequently the unsuccessful party is the one who has had justice and law on his side, having failed of success rather for lack of available proof than for want of merit in his case.

A proposal that has recently received increasing attention is that, in certain types of action at least, there should be a procedure for the filing with the court of a formal offer of settlement by either party. If the offer is not accepted, and the outcome at the subsequent trial of the action is not more favorable than the offer, the party who refused the offer should be saddled with the costs of the action subsequent to the time of the offer. It is quite possible that in this direction is to be found a satisfactory compromise between the conflicting considerations above reviewed.

Quite distinct from the question of the proper amount of the costs to be awarded to the prevailing party is the question of their collectability. The situation is not infrequently encountered in which a party wholly without financial responsibility institutes litigation against a responsible party, without much prospect of success (whether from want of justice in his claim, or from lack of the evidence necessary to substantiate it, or both). The defendant under these circumstances has no alternative but to prepare his defense, often at great expense, though he well knows that even if he succeeeds in having the suit dismissed at the trial he will probably be unable to collect from the plaintiff any part of even the inadequate costs that may be allowed. The unfairness of this result has led to the suggestion that in every action the plaintiff should be required to furnish security (as in the form of a bond or guarantee executed by a person of accepted responsibility or by a surety company), for the payment of any bill of costs which may be found against him. This suggestion, however, has not as yet received adoption in any American jurisdiction. In many jurisdictions there is found, however, a provision which requires a plaintiff to furnish a bond for costs if he is a non-resident of the state, or, if the court has jurisdiction over only a particular part of the state, a non-resident of that part.

For simplicity, discussion of the cost of litigation has been confined to proceedings in courts of original jurisdiction. But appellate proceedings also entail a heavy burden of cost, not only for counsel fees but often quite as much or more for furnishing the judges of the appellate court with the record of the proceedings in the lower court and the briefs of counsel, a cost which is, as noted in connection with criminal appeals, susceptible of great reduction where the appellate courts are willing.

Despite the continued increase in certain special types of action, such as personal injury actions, medical malpractice actions, and triple damage suits under the antitrust laws, civil litigation as a whole appears to be declining in volume relative to the growth of the population and business of the country. The explanations are various. Important among them is the tendency toward vertical integration in business, with its attendant conversion into intercompany or interdepartmental routines of what would formerly have been a negotiated transaction between parties dealing at arm's length; and the related tendency for business transactions increasingly to become transactions with "other people's money," so that emotions are less keenly aroused and settlement without resort to litigation made more likely. Doubtless, too, the costliness and delay of litigation, though perhaps no greater than formerly, are favoring the growth of commercial arbitration.

8

The Courts as a Check
on Executive Action

1. JUDICIAL REVIEW OF VALIDITY OF ADMINISTRATIVE REGULATIONS.
2. JUDICIAL REDRESS FOR DENIAL OF RIGHTS GIVEN BY LAW. 3. JUDI-
CIAL PROCEEDING TO COMPEL PERFORMANCE OF DUTY OWED TO PUBLIC.
4. JUDICIAL CHECK ON DISCRETIONARY AWARD OF BENEFITS. 5. JU-
DICIAL REDRESS AGAINST PUBLIC OFFICERS FOR INJURIES TO PERSON. 6.
JUDICIAL REDRESS FOR INJURIES TO PROPERTY BY PUBLIC OFFICERS: SEI-
ZURE OR DESTRUCTION. 7. JUDICIAL CHECK ON EMPLOYMENT OF
TROOPS IN DOMESTIC DISORDER. 8. JUDICIAL CHECK ON THE EXECUTIVE
IN TIME OF WAR.

The role of the courts in checking unlawful action of the executive
—using that term to embrace all officers of the executive branch—appears
in two settings. In the one there is before the court a proceeding, civil or
criminal; and the legality of some official action, bearing on the subject
matter of the proceeding, is questioned as an incident to the determination
of the central issue.[1] In the other, the proceeding before the court is one
instituted against the public official, by the private party alleging himself
injured, or threatened with injury, by the unlawful action or inaction of the
official.

One aspect of this matter is however reserved for subsequent chapters.
In so far as administrative agencies engage in formal adjudication, they
are themselves tribunals rather than administrators, and the function of
the courts in relation to them is appellate rather than original. Hence, the
extent to which the courts act as a check in this field is examined in connection with the account of administrative tribunals, at a later point.
Similarly, the extent to which the courts exercise a check on the proceedings

---

[1] The rules to which reference has been made in earlier chapters, prohibiting the
reception in criminal trials of evidence illegally obtained by law-enforcement officers,
may be regarded as a form of judicial check, though perhaps one of dubious effectiveness, on executive action.

of military tribunals is examined in subsequent chapters in connection with an account of such proceedings.

It is one of the distinctive, perhaps unique, characteristics of Anglo-American law that the validity or legality of acts of public officers may be questioned in any proceeding whatever in which the question of such validity or legality becomes relevant, and that the ordinary forms of civil proceeding, in the ordinary courts, are in general available equally against public officers as against private parties—the action for an injunction or for a declaratory judgment, the action to recover possession of property, the action for damages (as for a wrongful arrest), the action for debt (as for the recovery of a tax wrongfully collected), and so on.[2]

But to institute and prosecute a judicial proceeding of this character the aggrieved citizen requires the assistance of able counsel. In connection with the prosecution of criminal offenses, the obligation of the state to furnish counsel to the indigent accused was recounted. There is an analogous need in the field of the administrative action. The individual who is the victim of abuse of official authority, and who would seek judicial redress is deterred by the expense of retaining counsel; and even the individual who is not without means may shrink from the expense of a judicial proceeding where the injury done him, however serious a departure from the rule of law, is not financially serious to him. The suggestion has accordingly been made for the creation of an independent officer having the special function of entertaining and investigating complaints of administrative illegality, and of instituting executive or judicial proceedings for their correction.[3] Whether or not the specific suggestion be regarded as meritorious, it indubitably emphasizes a real weakness in the practical application of our vaunted doctrine of the supremacy of law. There are signs that recognition of this weakness is growing; so curative measures may not be far off.

1. JUDICIAL REVIEW OF VALIDITY OF ADMINISTRATIVE REGULATIONS

It is perhaps true that, of the total body of legal prescriptions to which the citizen must give heed at his peril, the greater portion is to be found

[2] A self-denying ordinance has in the past limited the extent of the control of the courts in this field—the doctrine that the chief executive, whether of the state or the nation, is not subject to the process of the courts and, hence, may not be personally enjoined, directed, or held liable. In recent years, however, the federal courts have in several cases enjoined the governor of a state (e.g., the cases cited at p. 299, note 18); and the action of a federal court in enjoining a federal official who was acting as the personal agent of the President, and not in the exercise of any power conferred on him or on the President by statute, was upheld by the Supreme Court. Youngstown Steel Co. v. Sawyer, 343 U.S. 579 (1952).

[3] Davis, Ombudsman in America, 109 U. of Pa. Law Rev. 1057 (1961). The ombudsman is an official found in the Scandanavian countries, with extensive powers to redress abuses of authority by administrative officers.

not in statutes or ordinances enacted by legislative bodies, but in regulations promulgated by agencies of the executive branch, acting under the purported authority of legislative enactments. Manifestly it is of prime importance, in a government by law, that some procedure exist for determination by a disinterested tribunal, if challenge is made, whether the regulations so promulgated fall within the authority thus conferred on the agency. In our system, this power is vested in the courts, to be exercised, if at the instance of the party alleging himself aggrieved, through the conventional forms of civil proceeding—ordinarily by an action for an injunction to restrain the enforcement of the regulation, or an action for a declaratory judgment, declaring the regulations invalid.

For the most part, however, the courts exercise their supervisory powers over the executive arm in this area not through proceedings instituted by the aggrieved party, but rather through proceedings instituted by the agency concerned. Inasmuch as statutes often provide penalties for violation of administrative regulations, to be imposed through either civil or criminal proceedings before the courts, such proceedings furnish a ready opportunity for review by the courts of the validity of such regulations. Moreover, as will be seen in subsequent pages, administrative agencies are in some instances empowered by statute themselves to impose penalties for violation of their own regulations, or to issue prohibitory or mandatory orders designed to compel compliance with such regulations. In proceedings before the courts to review the propriety of penalties thus imposed or orders thus made, the validity of the regulations themselves may likewise be questioned.

In the Emergency Price Control Act of 1942 there was employed a novel device—the concentration in a single court of power to set aside administrative regulations issued under the act. By that act, a special bench of federal judges (known as the Emergency Court of Appeals) was created with exclusive jurisdiction to enjoin the enforcement of a regulation issued under the act; and if in a civil or criminal proceeding in any court arising out of an alleged violation of such a regulation the defendant pleaded the invalidity of the regulation, the proceeding was to be stayed pending the determination of the question of the validity of the regulation by that special bench. Though this procedure is unexceptionably logical in design, it has been criticized as imposing upon the defendant an unjust burden—that of in effect instituting a separate proceeding before a distant tribunal (for the special court sat only in Washington).[4] The device was nevertheless retained in the statutes until 1960.

---

[4] The device was attacked as unconstitutional in depriving one prosecuted criminally for violation of a regulation of the opportunity to contest the validity of the regulation before the trial court; but the Supreme Court upheld it. Yakus v. United States, 321 U.S. 414 (1944). See Fraenkel, Can the Administrative Process Evade the Sixth Amendment? 1 Syracuse Law Rev. 173 (1949).

2. JUDICIAL REDRESS FOR DENIAL OF RIGHTS GIVEN BY LAW

Where an official omits or refuses to do something which the law clearly requires him to do, the courts, on application of a party adversely affected by such inaction, will direct him to do so (the conventional proceeding for this purpose being known as a mandamus proceeding). If, however, the governing statute does not unequivocally require the official to act in the given circumstances, but confers on him a measure of discretion as to whether or not he shall act, the courts will not interfere by substituting their own discretion for his. They will interfere only if his refusal to act is so arbitrary, so devoid of any proper basis in fact or in law, as to constitute not an exercise of discretion, but an abuse of discretion.

An action for a declaratory judgment, declaring that the plaintiff is entitled to the action sought, is sometimes also an appropriate form of proceeding in this situation.

A federal statute, enacted nearly a century ago, imposes both civil and criminal liabilities upon any one who "under color of any law, statute, ordinance, regulation or custom willfully subjects" another "to the deprivation of any rights, privileges or immunities secured or protected by the Constitution or law of the United States."[5] The ambiguities of this statute have, however, greatly limited its effectiveness—ambiguities which Congress, despite a succession of cases in the Supreme Court revealing irreconcilable differences of construction among its members,[6] has failed to clarify.[7]

It has been suggested that school authorities in districts in which racially segregated schools are still maintained, under state laws clearly unconstitutional under the Supreme Court desegregation decision of 1954, are under an inescapable duty to desegregate such schools without waiting, as so many of them have been, for judicial compulsion; and that school authorities failing to take such action consequently open themselves to liability, civil and criminal, under the statute just cited. This view is based on the holdings in several cases involving violence against persons in custody, in which the officers who had them in charge were held liable under the statute for failure to protect them. The analogy is, however, open to serious question.

A novel form of federal statute granting judicial redress for denial by

[5] 18 U.S. Code, Sec. 242. A parallel statute provides for civil redress. 42 U.S. Code, Sec. 1983.

[6] See, particularly, U.S. v. Williams, 341 U.S. 58 (1951) and Williams v. U.S., 341 U.S. 97 (1951).

[7] The history of the enforcement of this statute is traced in Carr, Federal Protection of Civil Rights: Quest for a Sword (1947). See also Putzel, Federal Civil Rights Enforcement, 99 U. of Pa. Law Rev. 439 (1951); and 347 U.S. 153–154.

state officers of rights under state law is found in a provision added in 1960[8] to the civil rights act of 1957. It is designed to curb state election officials found to have followed a pattern or practice of racial discrimination in their administration of state laws prescribing qualifications for voting (a type of discrimination that has been especially common in the administration of literacy requirements). The statute provides that if, in an action instituted by the Attorney General in the federal court, the court finds that there has existed in the voting registration district concerned a pattern or practice of refusing registration to qualified citizens because of their race or color, it may appoint a referee to whom any citizen denied registration may apply for a certificate of qualification as a voter, and upon presentation of such certificate to the state registration officers his registration is mandatory. The statute permits the federal court thus to supersede the recalcitrant state official only after a preliminary finding of disregard of federal rights in a suit brought by the Attorney General; but presumably Congress could equally provide for such supersession merely at the instance of the aggrieved citizen himself.

The right of Congress to enact this legislation rests upon the power specifically given it in the Fifteenth Amendment to enforce the provisions of that amendment "by appropriate legislation." An identical power is conferred upon it with respect to the Fourteenth Amendment, which places incomparably more far-reaching limitations on the states than does the Fifteenth.

3. JUDICIAL PROCEEDING TO COMPEL PERFORMANCE OF DUTY OWED TO PUBLIC

It is not only where a right enjoyed by an individual is denied that judicial intervention may be sought. In many cases, even if the duty which the official neglects to perform is one owed only to the public as a whole, the courts will, at the instance of a citizen, order its performance. The question in such cases is whether the particular plaintiff has, under the governing doctrines and statutes, "standing" to sue. In many jurisdictions (including the federal) neither a member of the public nor a taxpayer, merely as such, is regarded as being adversely affected by official inaction to a sufficient extent to give him standing to invoke the interference of the court. In other jurisdictions, however, any taxpayer may ask the courts, by a proper proceeding, to compel official action of a mandatory character. Under the statutes of some states the "taxpayer's action," as the phrase is, is available only against municipal and other local officials, but not against state officials—a somewhat irrational differentiation.

[8] 42 U.S. Code, Sec. 1971(c).

4. JUDICIAL CHECK ON DISCRETIONARY AWARD OF BENEFITS

A field of administrative action in which the courts are able to exercise only a slight check is that of the discretionary distribution of benefits.

There are certain types of benefit (as, for example, unemployment insurance benefits) to which the beneficiary, if he satisfies the statutory requirements, is entitled as a matter of right; and as to these, the courts will come to the aid of one claiming to be denied his rights, either by the type of proceeding already discussed, or, where there exists a process of formal administrative adjudication of the claim, by the proceedings discussed in a subsequent chapter. Where, however, the benefit is of such a type that no would-be beneficiary can be said to have a right to it, since it is not available to every person who satisfies the stated requirements, a large measure of discretion must be accorded to the agency empowered to select the fortunate beneficiaries. The allocation of housing accommodations in a public housing project is perhaps the clearest example of such a benefit. The very valuable privilege of obtaining one's housing for less than its economic rent can be extended to only a part of the people seeking it; and it has seemed to be, and doubtless is, impracticable to select the successful applicants by any system of competitive scoring attended with complete publicity of the data. The necessary result is to invest administrative officials with a type of discretion which in the nature of the case cannot be reviewed by the courts. Aside from the inherent difficulty of a judicial review of so clearly discretionary an administrative act, there is lacking a suitable plaintiff for such a proceeding; for the unsuccessful applicant cannot well demonstrate that he individually is adversely affected by the alleged abuse of discretion. In an extreme case, a taxpayer's action is conceivable in this situation; but none has come to attention.

Cognate forms of discretionary government benefits are found in the field of government loans (such as those made by the Small Business Administration), the award of government contracts without competitive bidding (a form of discretionary benefit—though benefit to the contractor admittedly is not the purpose in awarding a contract—of immense importance), and the award of government employment.

5. JUDICIAL REDRESS AGAINST PUBLIC OFFICERS FOR INJURIES TO PERSON

Although not commonly so thought of, an arrest on a criminal charge constitutes an administrative action against a private party without his having had an opportunity to contest it. Hence the restrictions on the power of the peace officer to make an arrest without a warrant, and the requirement that the officer promptly bring a person arrested before a magistrate —matters discussed in a preceding chapter.

Further protecting the individual against wrongful arrest and detention generally is the fact that the courts are open for an immediate inquiry into the legality of any detention by public officers, and are armed with the power to order the immediate release of a person found by them to be illegally detained. In some jurisdictions this proceeding—termed, as we have already noted, the habeas corpus proceeding—is further strengthened by provisions penalizing the judge who fails, on proper application made to him, promptly to issue the necessary order (or "writ") to the person detaining in custody the person by whom or on whose behalf the proceeding is instituted.[9]

As has already been pointed out, however, the circumstances of illegal detention by the police are sometimes such that the person detained is unable either himself to petition a court for his release or to communicate with anyone who might institute the proceeding on his behalf. In such a situation, existence of the right to a writ of habeas corpus if of course useless to the person detained. His remedy is only for subsequent redress.

Such redress takes the form of an action for damages against the officer who committed the illegal arrest. In theory, the liability of the peace officer for damages to the person illegally arrested or detained by him should be a powerful deterrent to illegal arrests and detention; in practice its deterrent force, though by no means negligible, is relatively weak. The action for damages is one at law, and the parties are entitled to jury trial. Juries are traditionally reluctant to return substantial verdicts against peace officers in these cases, unless there were aggravating circumstances. In the larger cities, the members of the police forces are commonly banded together in organizations to promote their common interests; and these organizations not infrequently undertake the defense of members sued for alleged illegal arrest.

Where the governing statutes permit, an action for false arrest will lie not only against the arresting officer, but against the municipality or other governmental unit employing him.

Not only a wrongful arrest or confinement, but excessive force used in making an arrest, or force used to extort a confession, renders the participating officers liable in damages to the person aggrieved. Here, however,

[9] It is a circumstance seldom commented on that although the Constitution forbids the withdrawal of the privilege of resorting to the federal courts for a writ of habeas corpus, it nowhere actually confers that privilege; and indeed, though the federal courts are in fact empowered to issue the writ, their power in every case (except perhaps in a case originating in the Supreme Court under its constitutional original jurisdiction) derives from statute and not from the Constitution. It did not in fact exist, with respect to persons in *state* custody in violation of federal right (except in a few special cases), until less than a century ago.

the difficulties of proof frequently make the remedy theoretical rather than actual.

On the whole, the resort to the courts must be rated as relatively ineffective in checking abuse of power by peace officers. It should be supplemented by better provision for administrative investigation and punishment by an agency standing outside the line of authority over the peace officers involved. The subjection of the wholly autonomous police establishments of cities and towns to some form of state supervision—a development already urged on other grounds—would be a powerful deterrent to the abuse by local officers of their powers of arrest and detention.

In the search for a more effective check on police abuses, some commentators have advanced the somewhat farfetched contention that such abuses as coercion to obtain confessions, delay in bringing the arrested suspect before the magistrate, and searches without warrant constitute a contempt of court, and may be punished as such.[10] Far more within the realm of practicality would seem to be a statute giving to appropriate courts jurisdiction of proceedings to discipline police officers for unlawful behavior. Such proceedings would be instituted by the court itself on a sworn complaint being laid before it, showing probable cause, or on there coming to the court's attention, in a case before it, evidence of apparently unlawful action. So far as known, no such statute now exists in any jurisdiction.

Despite their ambiguities, the federal statutes condemning the denial of constitutional rights "under color of any law," referred to in a preceding page, have been successfully invoked in some cases against police and other law-enforcement officers guilty of brutal treatment of prisoners in their custody, and in some cases of illegal treatment of persons not in custody.[11]

6. JUDICIAL REDRESS FOR INJURIES TO PROPERTY BY PUBLIC OFFICERS: SEIZURE OR DESTRUCTION

When property allegedly repugnant to the law is seized by an officer acting not under judicial mandate but in the exercise of his own discretion, such seizure is usually merely for the purpose of impounding the property pending a determination, whether by a judicial or an administrative tribunal, as to its forfeiture; and procedures may be available to the owner of the property for invoking judicial determination summarily, without waiting for the outcome of the proceeding instituted by the authorities.

[10] Cf. Blumrosen, Contempt of Court and Unlawful Police Action, 11 Rutgers Law Rev. 526 (1957).

[11] In Monroe v. Pape, 365 U.S. 167 (1961) the Supreme Court, reversing the lower federal courts, held that a person alleging maltreatment by police officers had the right to sue for damages under the federal statute even though the police had not taken him into custody.

There is a limited class of cases, however, in which the officials charged with responsibility for public health and safety must be vested with wide discretion to deal with urgent situations; and here authority is vested in such officials not merely to impound property but to destroy it summarily, without awaiting a determination by judicial or administrative process. Thus, health authorities are commonly vested with power to seize and destroy food found unfit for consumption, and fire-fighting authorities are vested with authority to demolish structures when necessary to check a conflagration. The Secretary of the Army is authorized to remove obstructions to navigation; and appropriate authorities of cities are likewise frequently empowered to remove encumbrances from public highways. In the nature of the case, injunction proceedings to halt the destruction of property in these situations are often impracticable. The law affords redress for an unlawful or unwarranted destruction by way of suit either against the officers responsible, where their action was grossly negligent or malicious, or against the governmental entity under those authority they assumed to act. Where the destruction is warranted, the extent to which the owner of the propery destroyed may be entitled to compensation depends upon a variety of factors beyond our province.[12]

7. JUDICIAL CHECK ON EMPLOYMENT OF TROOPS IN DOMESTIC DISORDER

The employment of troops (in almost all cases, state militia, though the employment of federal troops has also occurred) for the restoration of public order in times of natural catastrophe, violence arising out of labor disputes, or the like, raises no legal questions if the troops are merely placed at the disposal of the authorities regularly responsible for preserving order. Under such circumstances the civil authorities exercise their established statutory powers (which may include the making of appropriate regulations to prevent the congregation of people on highways and public places), and the military merely patrol the area, arrest offenders under the same limitations as govern civilian peace officers, and promptly deliver persons arrested to the civil authorities, to be dealt with according to established law and procedure.

Use of state militia

On not a few occasions, however—chiefly during the decades immediately preceding and following the turn of the century, a period of widespread industrial strife—the state militia has been called out by the

---

[12] Instances in which property is seized not for destruction but for other treatment are also found. Thus, the appropriate federal or state authorities may take possession of a bank believed unsafe and liquidate it. In time of war the President has been empowered to seize and sell the property of enemy aliens.

governor not to assist the local authorities, but to supersede them, the militia commander acting as the immediate deputy of the governor. The legal basis asserted for such assumption of authority by the governor has been a provision in the state constitution or statutes empowering the governor to call out the militia to suppress insurrection.[13] The term "insurrection" often implies not merely a defiance of the authorities responsible for public order, but an attempt to overthrow and supersede the existing government. Needless to say, in none of the industrial disorders in question was there any such attempt made or contemplated. Nevertheless, the language in question was invoked, and with it, in some cases, there was asserted the power, drawn from the analogy of a state of war, to supplement or even supersede the established law by "martial law," a phrase which, in its origin, means the will of a military commander exercising complete dominion over a zone of combat. Assuming thus to promulgate new regulations and not merely to enforce existing law, the governor, or the military commander as his deputy, has on occasion issued prohibitory orders to the population, forbidding the carrying of arms, the use of the public streets after certain hours, the use of the public highways by particular classes of vehicles, and the like.[14] In addition, orders have been issued to the troops to arrest not only persons violating these prohibitory orders, but also persons believed to be likely to violate them—a form of "preventive arrest" wholly repugnant to our criminal law (though sometimes resorted to, as already suggested, by police officers in disregard of the law); even orders to shoot persons refusing to halt on command, a power not vested in peace officers, have been issued. On at least two occasions, moreover, "martial law" has been construed by the military commander, with the approval of the governor, as authorizing him to constitute summary military tribunals for the trial of persons violating his prohibitory orders, and the sentencing of persons convicted by such tribunals to terms of imprisonment —matters to be considered at a later page.[15]

On the powers thus assumed by the state executive (for there is no instance in which a military commander has assumed such powers without the full support and approval of the executive), powers manifestly capable of gross abuse, the courts have on the whole declined to exert any effective check, declaring the existence of the "insurrection" to be a question to be determined solely by the executive. On a few of the occasions

[13] In perhaps the first such incident in our history, however (the so-called Dorr Rebellion in Rhode Island in 1842), the legislature had expressly declared the existence of a state of martial law. A diversity-of-citizenship case, in which damages were sought for injuries inflicted by the military, reached the Supreme Court of the United States. Luther v. Borden, 7 Howard 1 (1848).

[14] In addition to issuing regulations, military commanders have seized property and closed industrial plants. In one case, however, the closing of a plant was carried out, on orders of the governor, by the state police, not by the military.

[15] See p. 536.

in question, the governor, though not expressly authorized to do so by statute, has assumed to suspend the issuance by the state courts in the "insurrectionary" area of the writ of habeas corpus; and the courts have aquiesced in such suspension.[16] Even where there has been no purported suspension of the writ, however, the courts have in general refused to order the release of persons arrested by the military (and indeed in one case the release of persons sentenced to terms of imprisonment by the military tribunals); and they have been equally reluctant, with one or two notable exceptions, to enjoin the military, or to grant redress subsequently in the form of damages for wrongful arrest or imprisonment, or to sustain criminal prosecution of members of the military who have injured or killed civilians, or of the officers under whose orders they acted.[17]

It must be remembered that the cases enunciating the doctrines just reviewed, so anomalous in a system of government by law, have been few in number, and the handiwork chiefly of only a few state courts, and these, for the most part, not of states to which the courts of the country look for leadership; to which it must be added, however, that the federal courts, including the Supreme Court, in the few cases in which their interposition has been invoked, have done little to moderate these extreme pronouncements.[18] Moreover, the extreme doctrine of executive prerogative accepted by these courts—a doctrine which destroys any possibility of judicial protection against or redress for even the most flagrant abuse of power by the executive—was enunciated by them for the most part in the early years of the present century, in cases in which the issues arose out of the use of the militia in labor conflicts, chiefly in mining areas. In the industrial climate of today such violent episodes are hardly likely to recur. Nevertheless, there is clear need for a re-examination of the whole problem of the power of the state executive, or of the military commander acting as the deputy of the executive, to enact emergency regulations in

[16] Even though the privilege of the state writ of habeas corpus stands suspended, with or without proper authority, and the state courts honor such suspension, the federal courts are open for an application by the person arrested for his release, through habeas corpus proceedings, on the ground that his confinement constitutes a deprivation of his liberty without due process of law.

[17] The cases are reviewed in Rankin, When Civil Law Fails (1939) and in Fairman, the Law of Martial Rule (2d ed. 1942).

[18] At one point only has the Supreme Court interposed a check. While apparently subscribing to the doctrine enunciated by a few of the state courts, that the question whether an "insurrection" exists is one solely for the governor and that his determination is not subject to review by the courts, the Court has said that where, in the absence of any alleged disorder, the executive calls out the militia to seize private property as a means of compelling compliance with a regulatory statute by the owners of the property more speedily than might be the case were the ordinary processes of law enforcement resorted to, such seizure constitutes deprivation of property without due process of law, contrary to the Constitution, and will be enjoined by the courts. Sterling v. Constantin, 287 U.S. 378 (1932). See also Powers Mercantile Co. v. Olson, 7 F. Supp. 865 (1934).

time of public disorder and to restrict the liberty of the individual in ways not countenanced by our law under ordinary conditions. What is wanted is a precise legislative enactment, sharply defining the limits of the extraordinary powers to be invoked, the conditions under which they are to be invoked, and the extent of judicial control to be permitted and of subsequent judicial redress to be granted.

Use of federal troops

The Constitution expressly authorizes the use of federal troops to assist the state authorities in suppressing domestic disorder involving resistance to state authority; for it provides that "the United States shall protect" every state "on the application of the legislature, or of the executive (when the legislature cannot be convened) against domestic violence." The occasions on which this provision has been invoked by a state have been few, and have given rise to no judicial intervention.

The provision is sometimes read to mean that the federal government is powerless to use troops within a state to combat "domestic violence" unless the state requests their presence. But what if the domestic violence is directed also, or even solely, against the execution of the federal laws, or the enforcement of the orders of federal courts, and the state authorities fail to control it (or even condone it, as has recently occurred)? The propriety, in this situation, of the use of federal troops (the term being used to include state militia units called into the federal service) is self-evident; and the existing statutory authority for their use for these purposes has already been mentioned.

There is another situation in which the statutes authorize the use of federal troops without the request and indeed over the protest of the state authorities. This is the situation in which domestic violence within a state "so hinders the execution of the laws of that State, and of the United States within the State, that any part or class of its people is deprived of a right, privilege, immunity or protection named in the Constitution and secured by law, and the constituted authorities of that State are unable, fail, or refuse to protect that right, privilege, or immunity, or to give that protection."[19] Despite the reference to the laws of the United States, the provision could obviously be invoked even though only the execution of state laws were hindered.

Although the warrant, both constitutional and statutory, for the use of federal troops in these cases without the request of the state is clear, the extent of the power of the President, when troops have been sent into a state under these statutes, to prescribe regulations and otherwise to supersede the civil authorities by military authority is no clearer than it is in the case of the use of state militia by the governor; and statutory clarifica-

[19] 10 U.S. Code, Sec. 333; and see pp. 167-168.

tion would be equally welcome.[20] Thus far, in the few instances in which federal troops have been employed under these statutes, no action seeking judicial intervention against arrests or other action of the troops has apparently been brought, or if brought has apparently failed to reach the appellate courts.

8. JUDICIAL CHECK ON THE EXECUTIVE IN TIME OF WAR

By the Constitution, Congress is given power to declare war and to provide armed forces, and to make all laws necessary and proper in connection therewith. Hence, though the President is, by the Constitution, the commander in chief of the armed forces thus provided by Congress, it might be assumed that his powers as commander are only such as Congress has defined by law. This is indeed the accepted rule with respect to many matters affecting the armed forces, in war as well as peace. Nevertheless, during wartime it has been assumed by the President on several occasions, with subsequent acquiescence by the Supreme Court, that as commander in chief he possesses certain powers not expressly conferred upon him by statute. The precise extent of the constitutional, as opposed to the statutory, power thus possessed by the President in wartime in his character as commander never having been authoritatively defined, it will be of value to review briefly the chief occasions in which it has been asserted, either by the President himself or by a military commander with the President's approval, as the basis for action against individuals.[21]

The crucial importance in this field of the power of the courts, through habeas corpus proceedings, to liberate persons arrested by executive order has already been seen. In the federal field, the power to suspend the privilege of the writ of habeas corpus "when in cases of rebellion or invasion the public safety may require it" is expressly recognized by the Constitution; but the language employed does not specify who is empowered to suspend the privilege in those cases, leaving it at least arguable that the President enjoys this power.

[20] The statute cited in the preceding note empowers the President to use not only the armed forces but also "any other means," and to "take such measures as he considers necessary," an authorization which would seem to include the power to issue regulations and to provide for punishing their breach, and even to provide for preventive arrest and detention. The attempted exercise of such power would, however, doubtless invite litigation.

[21] A historic clash between the military and the judiciary on domestic territory took place shortly after the battle of New Orleans which General Jackson refused to honor a writ of habeas corpus issued on behalf of an editor whom he had caused to be arrested for an editorial denouncing the continuance of martial law in the city. Inasmuch, however, as Jackson had not yet received official notice of the conclusion of peace, and there was theoretically still a possibility that the British attack on the city might be renewed, the episode is technically one involving the exercise of military power in a zone of combat.

Shortly after taking office, Congress not being in session, Lincoln authorized the commanding general of the army, at any point where he encountered resistance in the mobilization or movement of troops, to suspend the privilege of the writ of habeas corpus or (as Lincoln himself put it) "in other words, to arrest and detain without resort to the ordinary processes and forms of law such individuals as he might deem dangerous to the public safety." A small number of arrests were made by the military under this authorization; and attempts by some of those arrested to procure release by resort to the federal courts proved unavailing, the writ being either refused by the court or, if issued, defied by the military.[22]

When Congress convened in special session shortly after these events (on July 4, 1861), Lincoln laid the situation before it, saying: "Whether there shall be any legislation upon the subject, and, if any, what, is submitted entirely to the better judgment of Congress." Congress took no action, however, either at that session or in the regular session in the first months of 1862. In September 1862, Congress again being in recess, Lincoln went much further. He authorized the military not only to arrest and detain, but to try and punish, persons interfering with the draft or discouraging volunteer enlistment (acts not condemned by statute); and he declared the writ of habeas corpus suspended as to all persons so taken into custody by the military.[23] When Congress reconvened in regular session (December 1862) it expressly conferred upon the President the power to suspend the writ of habeas corpus; but (a point often overlooked) it at the same time provided, as to persons held by the military, another form of proceeding under which a person arrested by the military (while denied the right to a preliminary examination, and to release on bail if held to answer) was entitled to be ordered discharged by the federal courts if not promptly indicted by a grand jury.[24] Although this provision, for reasons not clear, seems not to have been widely invoked,[25] it greatly reduced the importance of Lincoln's suspension of the privilege of the writ of habeas corpus; and, perhaps on this account, no case involving the suspension ever reached the Supreme Court.

During World War I there was no suspension of the writ of habeas

[22] The principal instance of such defiance was that in which the judge issuing the writ was indeed the Chief Justice (Taney) sitting as a circuit judge (a duty then regularly discharged by members of the Supreme Court). He placed on record a formal protest asserting that the suspension of the writ by the President was unauthorized by the Constitution, Congress alone having, in his view, the power to suspend the writ. Ex parte Merryman, 17 Fed. Cases No. 9,487 (1861). See also In re McDonald, 16 Fed. Cases No. 8,751 (1861).

[23] Proclamation of Sept. 24, 1862, 13 Stat. 730.

[24] Act of Mar. 3, 1863, 12 Stat. 755.

[25] Thus it was not apparently invoked in the case of Vallandingham (see page 534, note 1) which arose shortly after the enactment of the statute. It was, however, invoked by Milligan, who was discharged from military imprisonment pursuant to the statute (page 534, note 3).

corpus; nor was there during World War II, in the continental United States. In the territory of Hawaii, however, the writ was suspended directly after the attack on Pearl Harbor, as part of the assumption of complete governmental power by the general commanding the territory, with the assent of the civil governor of the territory, whose complete surrender of power to the military was made under the purported authority of the organic act of the territory. The later court proceedings attacking the action of the military will be discussed in a subsequent chapter, in connection with an account of the military tribunals set up by them.[26]

On February 19, 1942 a little over two months after the outbreak of the war with Japan, President Roosevelt, acting without any express statutory authority, empowered the Secretary of War, and any military commanders the Secretary might designate, to restrict the right of any person to enter, remain in, or leave any military area, so called, which the Secretary or military commander might define.[27] A month later, at the request of the Secretary of War, Congress by statute declared it a misdemeanor, punishable by fine or imprisonment, or both, for any person knowingly, in violation of the restrictions so promulgated, to enter, remain in, leave, or commit any prohibited act in a military area so defined.[28]

In requesting the enactment of this statute, the executive in effect rejected the alternative, which was no doubt urged by some, of setting up military commissions to try offenses against regulations promulgated by the military. The President thus opened the door to the possibility of the assumption by the federal courts, in proceedings before them for the prosecution of such offenses, of the power to review the judgment of the military as to the military necessity for the regulations breached.

By this enactment, Congress in effect delegated to the President and to such subordinates, civilian as well as military, as the President might designate, the power to declare any part of the United States a "military area" and to regulate the movements of all persons in such area. Both before and after this enactment, various military commanders, and in particular the commander of the Western Defense Command, consisting of the Pacific coast states and adjacent areas, established extensive military areas. In some of these areas curfew regulations, applicable to all enemy aliens and, also, to all persons of Japanese ancestry, were promulgated. By subsequent orders of the commander of the Western Defense Command all persons of Japanese ancestry were in effect compelled, on pain of violating prohibitions issued by the commanding general, to give themselves up to the custody of the military, by whom they were in turn delivered over to an agency—the War Relocation Authority—nominally

---

[26] See p. 536.
[27] Executive Order No. 9006, 7 Fed. Reg. 1407.
[28] Act of Mar. 21, 1942, 56 Stat. 173, 18 U.S. Code, Sec. 1383.

civilian, but in fact functioning in close concert with the military, which supervised their further confinement. Release from such confinement was obtainable on an individual basis by such of the American citizens confined as were found, by administrative investigation, to be of unquestioned loyalty. Such release was afforded, however, only if the loyal citizen agreed to certain conditions as to his or her future movements.

The question of the validity of these relocation proceedings did not reach the Supreme Court until 1944. It then sustained, by a divided court, the conviction of an American citizen of Japanese parentage who had failed to leave a military area as required by regulation, remaining instead in his long-established home.[29] In substance, the majority of the Court expressed its willingness to acquiesce, virtually without reservation, in the judgment of the executive, acting under Congressional authorization, as to military necessity. The minority, on the other hand, pointing out that other concurrent regulations made it impossible for the defendant to obey the exclusion regulation except by surrendering himself for imprisonment in a relocation center, declared that such mass imprisonment of citizens, particularly on the basis of race, was forbidden by the Constitution (the particular provision violated not being identified, however), and that though a civilian court, when it could discern no reasonable relation between the danger apprehended and the measures taken by the military to meet it, might hesitate to interfere, it was under no obligation to enforce the orders of the military by means of a criminal proceeding.[30] Even the minority justices, however, were apparently in agreement with the majority as to the lack of potential effectiveness of the courts in checking the military if the latter really took the bit in their teeth—a view expressed by Justice Jackson (of the minority), thus: "I would not lead people to rely on this Court for a review that seems to me wholly delusive. The military reasonableness of these orders can only be determined by military superiors. If the people ever let command of the war power fall into irresponsible and unscrupulous hands, the courts wield no power equal to its restraint. The chief restraint upon those who command the physical forces of the country, in the future as in the past, must be their responsibility

[29] Korematsu v. U.S., 323 U.S. 214 (1944).

[30] On the same day, however, the Court unanimously ordered the release of an American citizen of Japanese ancestry who had been declared loyal and therefore eligible for release, but who had refused to assent to the conditions sought to be attached to such release. The action of the Court was based on the proposition that the further detention of admittedly loyal citizens had not been in fact authorized by the President, or within the contemplation of Congress when it gave penal sanction to the orders of the President and the military commanders. The justices who had dissented in the first case reiterated their view that neither Congress nor the President could constitutionally authorize the indefinite detention, on the plea of military necessity, of a body of citizens against whom individually no evidence whatever of disloyalty existed. Ex parte Endo, 323 U.S. 283 (1944).

to the political judgments of their contemporaries and the moral judgments of history."[31]

Should war again come, the executive will be armed with a statutory power which it did not possess in previous wars. By act of 1950,[32] Congress authorized the President to proclaim an "internal security emergency" in the event of war, invasion, or insurrection in aid of a foreign enemy. During the emergency thus proclaimed, the President, acting through the Attorney General, is authorized to apprehend and detain any person "as to whom there is reasonable ground to believe that such person will probably engage in, or probably conspire with others to engage in, acts of espionage or sabotage." A person apprehended is to be given a prompt hearing before a hearing officer, and if ordered detained, may appeal to a detention review board to be established by the President. This board not only may vacate the detention order, but it may order the payment of indemnity to any person found to have been wrongfully detained. The orders of the board are reviewable by the United States Court of Appeals for the circuit where the petitioner resides or is detained, and upon such review the usual finality is to be accorded (as in other administrative proceedings) to findings of fact supported by substantial evidence. It is expressly provided that nothing in the act is to be construed to authorize the suspension of the privilege of the writ of habeas corpus.

[31] Korematsu v. United States, 323 U.S. 214, 248 (1944). See also Rostow, The Japanese American Cases: A Disaster, 54 Yale Law Jour. 498 (1945) and ten Broeck, Barnhart, and Matson, Prejudice, War and the Constitution (1954).
[32] Title III of Act of Sept. 23, 1950, 64 Stat. 987; 50 U.S. Code, Secs. 811 ff.

9

The Courts as a Check on Investigation

1. GROUNDS FOR CHALLENGING DEMAND OF INVESTIGATIVE AGENCY.   2.
REFUSAL OF COURT TO ASSIST INVESTIGATIVE AGENCY.   3. REFUSAL OF
COURT TO PUNISH WITNESS.

The function of the courts as a check on the investigatory activities of police and prosecutor have been considered in earlier chapters.[1]
In the present chapter will be examined the manner in which the courts
act as a check on those investigative agencies, executive and legislative,
described in an earlier chapter, which are authorized to summon witnesses
and to interrogate them under oath.

An investigating agency, though empowered to subpoena witnesses, to
put the witness on oath and to question him, does not itself ordinarily
enjoy the power to punish a failure to appear in response to its subpoena,
or the refusal of a witness to answer a question.[2] It is compelled to resort
to the courts, to seek the court's aid either in compelling the witness's
compliance or his punishment for his disobedience or recalcitrance.[3] Since

[1] Chapter 3, Secs. 3 and 4. Mention is also made in that chapter of the occasional
investment of a judicial officer with power to conduct an investigation into unlawful
acts. In addition, a judicial tribunal sometimes authorizes an investigation into the
conduct of attorneys, or other matters affecting the conduct of judicial proceedings,
which may involve no infractions of law; and the investigator (usually a judicial
officer) may be empowered by the court to subpoena witnesses and records. Such
an investigation is ordinarily ordered by a court only if statutory warrant for such
order exists.

[2] In Brimson v. Interstate Commerce Commission, 154 U.S. 447 (1894) the
Supreme Court declared, though such declaration was not necessary to its disposition
of the case, that Congress could not constitutionally vest an administrative agency
with the power to punish disobedience of its orders (including a subpoena), but that
recourse must be had to the courts. In the states, however, there is occasionally
found an administrative officer with such power. See In re Groban, 352 U.S. 330
(1957).

[3] Congress, however, possesses the power to punish disobedience of its subpoenas,
or refusal to answer its questions, without the aid of the courts: it may direct its own
officers to arrest the recalcitrant, to bring him before the bar of the House, and

306

in any of these types of proceeding the person subpoenaed or questioned may challenge the demand of the investigating agency as unwarranted, the courts may exercise a potent check on the abuse of the power of investigation.

1. GROUNDS FOR CHALLENGING DEMAND OF INVESTIGATIVE AGENCY

A challenge to the validity of a subpoena issued by an investigating agency may correspondingly be made in either of two settings: in a civil proceeding brought by the agency to compel compliance (or one brought by the person subpoenaed to quash—or "vacate"—the subpoena), or in a criminal proceeding (either a criminal contempt proceeding or a criminal prosecution) to punish disobedience of the subpoena. A challenge to the right of the agency to require an answer to a particular question, or to require the production of a particular paper or object, may be made in similar manner. The availability of one or another proceeding to challenge the subpoena or the question depends in every case on the governing statutory provisions.

A subpoena can be challenged, of course, on the ground that the agency issuing it has not been vested with the subpoena power—obviously, a ground seldom available—or that the subject matter of the investigation in connection with which the subpoena is issued is not within the scope of the agency's authority. A subpoena calling for the production of books and papers, or of physical objects (a subpoena "duces tecum") may moreover be challenged on the ground that the papers or objects called for have on the face of the matter no relevance to the subject of the investigation—a challenge manifestly not available as to the questions which may be asked the subpoenaed witness until he has appeared in obedience to the subpoena and a question has been put to him.[4]

In addition to challenging a question asked of him on the ground just

---

to confine him. This power, asserted on the basis of power of this nature long exercised by the houses of Parliament, has been exercised by both houses of Congress, the latest occasion having apparently been that of the attachment by the Senate, in 1927, of one refusing to appear before one of its committees. See McGrain v. Daugherty, 273 U.S. 135 (1927). As the result of a holding, however, made by the Supreme Court in 1821, that the confinement of a person committed for contempt by one of the houses of Congress could not extend beyond the adjournment of that house (Anderson v. Dunn, 6 Wheaton 204), Congress in 1857 made contempt of Congress a criminal offense. Punishment by Congress itself is now virtually obsolete.

[4] In 1958 an attempt was made to withdraw from the federal courts, in a criminal prosecution for refusal to answer a question put by a congressional committee, the power to pass upon whether the question was pertinent to the subject under investigation. 85th Cong., S. 2646, and proposed amendments. The constitutionality of such an enactment is very doubtful.

stated, the witness may refuse to answer a question on the ground that his answer, were he to give it, might tend to incriminate him. The demand that the witness produce a particular paper or object may be challenged on the like ground.

If the challenge goes to the agency's authority to investigate the subject in connection with which it seeks testimony or physical evidence, the challenge may be based, if the agency is an administrative one, on the claimed unconstitutionality of the statute authorizing the agency so to investigate. More commonly, however, the contention will be that the statute itself fails to give the agency the authority claimed by it[5] In connection with legislative investigations, a quite different kind of question presents itself. The authority of a legislature to investigate is seldom expressly set forth in any constitutional provision and, hence, must be derived from a power expressly conferred upon it. Express powers of the legislature, or of one of its chambers, that clearly imply a power to investigate and, hence, to compel testimony necessary to such investigation are the power of each chamber to "judge of the elections, returns and qualifications of its own members" (to use the language of the Constitution), and the power to impeach and to try impeachments. Equally clear is the power of the legislature, or a chamber thereof, to investigate the manner in which the public business has been or is being transacted—an area of investigation obviously essential to the framing of legislation regulating that business. When, however, one leaves these matters and considers legislative investigations ostensibly ordered for the purpose of collecting information to aid in the framing of legislation in some general area, the power of the legislature to compel the testimony of witnesses not in the public service is by no means so clear, and was indeed, until a century ago, a subject of dispute in Congress. Today, however, the existence of the power seems to be everywhere accepted as self-evident.

Since the power of a legislative committee or agency to interrogate private parties regarding matters not connected with public business can be justified only if the information sought has a legislative purpose, there is no power where there is no ostensible purpose to legislate.[6] Even where the investigation has been authorized for a proper legislative purpose, if the information sought to be elicited by a question is clearly of no value for legislative purposes, the question being obviously asked only for the

[5] In a few cases arising out of legislative investigations the challenge to the subpoena or to the question has been on the ground that compulsory disclosure would be an invasion of the right of privacy as to one's political beliefs, or the right of free association for political purposes, both these rights being claimed as constitutional rights implicit in the First Amendment protection of freedom of speech and press, and of the right to assemble and petition for redress of grievances. See Redlich, Rights of Witnesses before Congressional Committees: Effect of Recent Supreme Court Decisions, 36 N. Y. U. Law Rev. 1126, 1151 (1961).

[6] Kilbourn v. Thompson, 103 U.S. 168 (1881).

purpose of exposing the witness to obloquy, a refusal to answer will be upheld by the federal courts at least.[7]

The doctrine that the witness has the right to refuse to answer a question on the ground of possible self-incrimination, as developed by the English and subsequently by our own courts, had no application to legislative investigations; hence, to the extent that such a right is possessed by the legislative witness it must rest on statutory or constitutional provisions. State constitutional provisions protecting against self-incrimination are, as was noted in an earlier chapter, in many cases so phrased as seemingly to apply only to the accused in a criminal proceeding; but they have in a number of states been construed as applying also to the witness, not only in all judicial proceedings, but in all administrative proceedings as well. Whether a state constitutional provision of this kind protects also a witness before a legislative committee is a question that has thus far been raised in only a few states, and the answer there has been in the affirmative.

The self-incrimination clause in the Constitution (in the Fifth Amendment), applicable only to federal matters, protects one against being compelled to be a witness against himself "in any criminal case"; but as already noted the quoted words have in effect been deleted by the Supreme Court, and it has long been settled that the witness in any federal administrative investigation enjoys the constitutional privilege. Whether it is equally enjoyed by the witness in an investigation held under the authority of Congress, or of one of its chambers, was not passed upon by the Supreme Court utnil 1955. In a case which came before it in that year the Court assumed, without discussion, that the congressional committee witness is protected by the constitutional privilege.[8]

Immunity statutes, protecting the witness in an administrative investigation against prosecution for any offense connected with the matter as to which he testifies, are common;[9] indeed, the power of the federal administrative agencies to compel incriminatory testimony by virtue of such statutes is much more extensive than that of the federal courts. Similar statutes applicable to legislative investigations are also found in some states; but there is no such general statute applicable to congressional investigations.[10]

[7] See Redlich, note 5 above, at p. 1147.

[8] Quinn v. United States, 349 U.S. 155 (1955).

[9] The danger that an administrative agency may improvidently confer immunity upon a witness has resulted in an enactment in New York requiring an agency to give notice to the attorney general of the state and to the local district attorney before proceeding with the examination of a witness who claims the privilege against self-incrimination. Penal Law Sec. 2247.

[10] In congressional investigation in matters involving the national security, treason, sabotage, etc., the congressional committee may, by a two-thirds vote of all its members, and with the concurrence of a federal district court, notice having first been given to the Attorney General, confer immunity on a witness who pleads fear of self-incrimination. This provision was enacted in 1954. 18 U.S. Code, Sec. 3486.

2. REFUSAL OF COURT TO ASSIST INVESTIGATIVE AGENCY

A number of statutes, particularly those governing the federal revenue and regulatory agencies, authorize the agency, on the failure of the person subpoenaed to appear (or on his failure, if he appears, to bring with him the books or objects whose production is called for by the subpoena duces tecum served on him), to apply to the courts for an order directed to the person so disobeying, commanding him to comply with the agency's subpoena on pain of being in contempt of court. In many cases such applications are made ex parte, and are granted as a matter of routine by the courts without any real scrutiny of the dishonored subpoena to determine whether it complies with the statute governing the agency. Only if the court's order is in turn ignored, and the agency then asks the court to enforce the subpoena by committing the recalcitrant until he complies, will the court have before it a contest as to the validity of the subpoena. In such a case the court may refuse to enforce the subpoena if it finds that the reasons advanced for resisting it are well taken. The court may also in such case suitably modify the demands of the agency and order commitment of the witness unless he complies with the subpoena as modified.

In some cases the attack on the validity of the subpoena occurs before the court issues its initial order, the witness taking the initiative and applying to the court to void (or "vacate") the subpoena. This procedure is invoked chiefly in connection with subpoenas duces tecum.

The procedure described has thus far seldom been authorized with respect to legislative inquiries; and there is no provision for its invocation in connection with congressional investigations.

Where, instead of challenging the validity of the subpoena itself, the person subpoenaed appears as a witness but challenges the right of the agency to demand an answer to a particular question put to him, the agency, if authorized by statute, may similarly request a court to compel the witness to answer the question, on pain of commitment. This procedure is not available in congressional investigations nor, apparently, in state legislative investigations, except in a few states.[11] Obviously, so cumbersome a procedure will be resorted to by the agency only if it deems the anticipated answer sufficiently important. Ordinarily, the danger in which the witness stands that the courts, in a subsequent proceeding to punish him for his refusal to answer, may hold his refusal to have been unwarranted, is sufficiently effective for the agency's purposes.

The question of the right of the legislative committee to require the answers to questions, needless to say, has more frequently been raised in congressional investigations than in those conducted by state legislative committees. The plenary rights of the congressional witness to refuse an

[11] As, for example, New Hampshire. See Sweezy v. Wyman, 354 U.S. 234 (1957).

answer on the ground of fear of self-incrimination are now well established. His cognate rights under the First Amendment are as yet by no means so clear. Neither is it clear how far the Supreme Court is prepared to go in permitting the courts to pass on the relevancy of the question asked to the particular subject under investigation, as stated by the committee to the witness, or to pass on the relevancy of that stated subject to the scope of the committee's authority to investigate. The congressional witness who, on his own view of the law, takes it upon himself to refuse to answer a question thus runs grave risk that, if he is subsequently prosecuted, his view will be rejected by the courts. There has, consequently, been substantial support for the proposal, embodied in bills that have several times been before Congress, that, on a witness's refusal to answer, the propriety of the question be tested at once by an application to a federal court to commit the witness unless he answers. Congress has, however, failed to display any interest in this proposal.

3. REFUSAL OF COURT TO PUNISH WITNESS

The statutory provisions empowering the courts to entertain proceedings for the punishment of a witness for failure to obey the subpoena of an investigative agency, or to answer its questions, vary widely. In the federal statutes, provisions for the summary punishment of the disobedient witness before an administrative investigative agency, as if the offender were guilty of disobedience of an order of the court, are found in the case of some agencies; and provisions for criminal prosecution, in the case of some others. In the case of witnesses before Congress or before congressional committees, criminal prosecution only is provided for, the offense charged being known as contempt of Congress.

Although, in the criminal prosecution, the right of trial by jury is of course present in the federal courts, there is seldom in these cases any question of fact for a jury, since the witness's disobedience is a matter of record. The sole defense open to him is thus the contention that as a matter of law the subpoena was invalid, or that the question asked, or the demand for production of papers, was improper; so that in either form of punitive proceeding, it is the judge who decides.

In several cases involving refusal to answer questions put by a congressional committee, the disposition of the case has taken the form of a dismissal of the indictment before trial on the motion of the defendant, the court accepting his contention that the recital of the committee's authorization in the indictment discloses that the question asked was not within the scope of that authorization. The Supreme Court has moreover held that the witness is entitled to be informed, before being interrogated, of the subject matter under investigation, in order that he may be in a position to judge both whether the stated subject matter is within the committee's province and whether the questions asked him are relevant to that subject matter.[12] These holdings have caused prosecution of the recalcitrant congressional committee witness to be requested by Congress, and to be undertaken by the Department of Justice, with more circumspection than was formerly the case.

In several prosecutions of congressional committee witnesses for refusal to answer a question, the witness having given as the ground for his refusal his fear of self-incrimination, the courts, in sustaining the refusal, have given the witness's privilege against self-incrimination a latitude as great as they have given it in judicial proceedings—indeed, perhaps even a greater latitude.[13]

[12] Watkins v. United States, 354 U.S. 178 (1957).

[13] See, for example, Simpson v. United States, 355 U.S. 7 (1957), reversing the conviction of a congressional committee witness for refusing, on the ground of possible self-incrimination, to disclose his former residence or his age.

10

The Courts as a Check on Legislation

1. VOIDING OF STATE ENACTMENT AS REPUGNANT TO STATE CONSTITU-
TION: "STATE" JUDICIAL REVIEW.   2. VOIDING OF STATE ENACTMENT AS
REPUGNANT TO FEDERAL LAW: "FEDERAL" JUDICIAL REVIEW.   3. VOID-
ING OF FEDERAL ENACTMENT AS REPUGNANT TO FEDERAL CONSTITU-
TION: "NATIONAL" JUDICIAL REVIEW.   4. THE HISTORIC ROLE OF THE
SUPREME COURT.

At various points in the preceding pages reference has been made
to the action of the courts in declaring void statutes deemed by them repugnant to constitutional provisions. In this chapter will be briefly outlined the genesis and development of this distinctively though not uniquely
American function of the courts.[1]

Although, for brevity, this power of the courts is commonly referred
to (as it was a few lines back) as that of declaring statutes repugnant to
constitutional provisions, it embraces also the power to declare state constitutional provisions void because repugnant to federal law, as contained
either in the Constitution or in federal statutes or treaties. Since such constitutional provisions in virtually all the states require approval of the
electorate, and since in some states even statutes may be enacted by
popular vote without the intervention of the legislature, it is apparent that

---

[1] The power of courts to invalidate legislation has existed in limited form in some
other countries for some time, and has also been introduced in some of the newer
nations. However, statements sometimes encountered, that the American system is
being imitated elsewhere, commonly ignore the crucial difference between the power
of our Supreme Court and that of the courts of any other country, arising from (1)
the far greater difficulty, indeed in some respects the near impossibility, of amending
our Constitution, the result being that the Court's holdings can be changed only by
itself; and (2) the vagueness of the provisions of our Constitution, permitting a freedom in interpretation not found elsewhere. See Haines, Some Phases of the Theory
and Practice of Judicial Review of Legislation in Foreign Countries, 24 Am. Pol.
Sci. Rev. 583 (1930) and McWhinney, Judicial Review in the English-speaking World
(2nd ed. 1960).

with respect to state enactments the courts thus exercise a check not only on the legislature, but on the electorate itself.

Again, although it is customary to speak of the power of "the courts" to declare enactments unconstitutional, only the highest courts of the states and the Supreme Court of the United States have that power in any real sense. A decision on a constitutional question by any but the highest court is merely an exploratory or preparatory process, designed to clear the way for the highest court.[2] Indeed, in some systems having intermediate appellate courts, provision exists for expediting the determination of constitutional questions by bypassing, in cases involving such questions, the intermediate appellate court, the appeal going from the court of first instance direct to the highest court.

There is no special procedure for invoking the power of a court to declare an enactment void because of unconstitutionality. The contention that the enactment should be disregarded by the court because repugnant to the governing constitutional provision is raised by one of the parties in a civil litigation, or by the prosecution or defense (ordinarily the defense) in a criminal proceeding, precisely like any other relevant contention of law, to be passed upon by the court in precisely the same way. Only if there is before it an actual, not a moot case, between parties having a genuine special interest in the outcome, and a decision on the alleged repugnance of the statute to the constitutional provision is essential to the disposition of the case, will the court consider the issue of constitutionality.[3]

From this it results that a statute may be in theory unconstitutional, but in practice immune from judicial action because there is no one in a position to institute a litigation to challenge its constitutionality. Thus, in the federal sphere, the Supreme Court has, as already noted, held that a federal taxpayer has no standing to institute an action to enjoin the disbursement, under statutory direction, of federal funds for a purpose which the taxpayer asserts is beyond the constitutional sphere of action of the federal government. Some of the state courts have taken a more lenient view of the right of a citizen, not peculiarly aggrieved but coming forward merely as the self-appointed spokesman of the body of the citizenry, to challenge the constitutionality of state legislation; but on the whole this doctrine that the constitutionality of an enactment can be attacked only by one having proper standing as a litigant has, at least as respects the question of the constitutionality of an expenditure of public funds, thus far

---

[2] The losing party in a case in which the trial court has declared an enactment unconstitutional may of course decide not to appeal. As a practical matter, however, this possibility may be ignored.

[3] In five states however (chiefly in New England), by constitutional provision, either house of the legislature may ask the opinion of the state's highest court as to the constitutionality of proposed legislation.

constituted an important limitation of the power of the courts to void legislation—a limitation self-imposed, it should be noted.

Another self-imposed limitation repeatedly affirmed by the courts, but repeatedly disregarded by them—sometimes indeed in the very act of affirming it—is the doctrine that an enactment should not be declared void unless its repugnance to the constitutional command is indisputably clear. It is a matter of common knowledge, however, that in cases of the first importance, the Supreme Court has declared a statute void by a majority of one, the majority judges blandly asserting its indisputable and self-evident repugnance to the Constitution, despite the insistence of their dissenting brethren that such repugnance was at least very questionable if not indeed non-existent; and some high state court majorities have exhibited an equal nonchalance. For practical purposes therefore the self-denying ordinance in question may be regarded as having merely ritual significance.

All this is doubtless well understood by even the moderately sophisticated layman. What is perhaps not equally well understood is that with respect to some of the most important federal constitutional limitations affecting both state and federal enactments (and the same is true less importantly of some of the limitations imposed by state constitutions), a clear and indisputable repugnance to the constitutional command is inherently impossible, since the words in which constitutional command is couched are of the vaguest, and what is omitted and implied is of equal importance with what is expressed. Doubtless the most important phrase in the Constitution, from the standpoint of judicial review of legislation, has in our time been and continues to be "due process of law." When isolated from their historical context—an isolation the Supreme Court did not attempt until a century after the phrase was first employed in the Constitution (in the Fifth Amendment)—the words are doubtless vague. It is this vagueness which has enabled the Court to erect, on so precarious a verbal foundation, a vast and versatile conceptual engine, capable of demolishing the most diverse legislation.

The power of the courts in this field must thus be conceived of as exercised on two quite separate planes. On one plane stand those constitutional provisions which are precise and unequivocal, such as that no state shall impose duties of tonnage; on the other loom such vague commands of "due process" and "equal protection of the laws," and such inferential doctrines (nowhere expressed in the Constitution) as that no state shall "burden" interstate commerce.

The courts, be it noted, have moreover the power to translate a provision from the lower to the higher plane. Thus, as has been seen, the specific provision in the Constitution that no person "shall be compelled in any criminal case to be a witness against himself" has been converted by the Supreme Court (and identically specific provisions in state constitutions have similarly been converted by state courts) into an omnipresent concept of exemption from compulsion to give self-incriminatory testimony in any type of proceeding or investigation whatever.

As already indicated, the ostensible purpose of a proceeding is hardly ever to declare an enactment void; its ostensible purpose is to vindicate some alleged right of one of the parties to the litigation. The unconstitutionality of the statute is "declared" only in that it is assigned as the reason for the court's grant, or refusal, of particular relief to a particular party. But since the reason given is equally applicable to all other cases, the world is on notice that enforcement of the enactment in question must henceforth be denied by the courts—at least unless and until the high court reverses itself, as the Supreme Court has indeed occasionally done.

In a case before either a state or a federal court, the court may be asked to invalidate a state enactment as being repugnant either to the state constitution ("state" judicial review) or to the Constitution or a federal statute or treaty ("federal" judicial review). Similarly, in a case before a state or federal court, the court may be asked to invalidate a federal enactment as repugnant to the Constitution ("national" judicial review).

1. VOIDING OF STATE ENACTMENT AS REPUGNANT TO STATE CONSTITUTION: "STATE" JUDICIAL REVIEW

The constitutions framed by eleven of the thirteen revolting colonies during the early years of the Revolution represented a complete novelty in the history of their governmental institutions—a charter emanating not from a ruler but from the sovereign people themselves (or, more accurately, from the limited electorate of the period) through representatives; and in these unprecedented instruments were included limitations on the power of the legislature—restrictions, not as in colonial times emanating from the Crown and enforced by it, but emanating from the sovereign people[4] and to be enforced—how?

In most of the newborn states during the process of formulation of the new constitution not much thought or public discussion apparently was given to this question of how these new limitations on the legislatures were now to be implemented—specifically, whether they were mere exhortations to the legislature or whether they were legal commands, to be enforced by the courts. This is not perhaps too surprising if one remembers that these constitutions were in most cases not framed as state constitutions are today, by a convention specially elected for the purpose, its handiwork subject to approval by the electorate. Instead, they were promulgated by the

---

[4] The English Bill of Rights, by contrast, was in effect a set of limitations on the Crown, exacted from the Crown by the legislature.

revolutionary legislatures themselves. That their provisions were regarded to some extent as counsels of legislative self-restraint rather than as judicially enforceable restrictions on the legislature would seem to be indicated by the inclusion, in the "declaration of rights" attached to some of them, of injunctions which, in the words of Hamilton, "would sound much better in a treatise on ethics than in a constitution of government."[5]

In two states—Pennsylvania and Vermont—provision was made in the constitution for a special representative body outside the legislature which, while not empowered to declare laws unconstitutional, had the duty of bringing their repugnance to the state constitution to the attention of the legislature

The adoption of these expedients—in both cases rather short-lived[6]— indicated that while the existence of the problem of assuring the adherence of the legislature to constitutional commands was appreciated by the public men of the day, the notion that the courts in their disposition of ordinary cases could assume to declare laws unconstitutional was as yet unfamiliar. When, during the early years of independence, the possession of such a power was suggested, even if not expressly asserted, as it was by the courts in several states, there was in every case violent criticism, and in some cases threats of removal of the judges—threats by no means empty, since in a number of states the judges held office for relatively short terms, and appointment, if not by the legislature, required legislative approval. The supremacy of the legislature—an echo of the struggle of Parliament for control not only of the ministers of the crown, but of the royal judges as well—was the accepted dogma of the period; and indeed inasmuch as the participation of the electorate in the process of state constitutional amendment was still in its infancy, the clear-cut supremacy of constitution over statute, today axiomatic, was by no means so obvious. Under these circumstances, the doctrine that state judges had power to void state laws made little progress in the eighteenth century and even in the first quarter of the nineteenth. When asserted, it tended to be confined to cases in which the judiciary were defending their own functions from legislative or executive encroachment.

The legislative excesses of the second quarter of the nineteenth century appear to have created a climate more favorable to the state judiciaries, and their assertion and exercise of the power to void legislation increased in frequency. It was not, however, till after the Civil War that the power came to be exercised as a matter of course. It reached its peak during the decade preceding and following the turn of the century—a period of new

[5] Federalist, No. 84.

[6] In New York, until 1849, the highest court of the state was the Court of Errors, consisting of thirty-six members, of whom only four were judges. The remainder were the members of the upper house of the legislature. Needless to say, they did not declare any laws unconstitutional!

departures in social legislation, not a few of which were voided by the high state courts as repugnant to the state constitution. The result was an outcry against the whole institution of judicial review, with proposals, at both state and national levels, to curb the courts. This movement bore fruit in the adoption in Ohio, in 1912, of a constitutional provision, still in force, providing that no law should be held unconstitutional without the concurrence of all but one of the judges. Provisions of similar import were subsequently adopted in North Dakota (1918) and in Nebraska (1920).[7] The period was marked also by the enactment, in the form of constitutional provisions, of legislation which in statute form had been held unconstitutional, or seemed likely to be so held.

With the twenties, the revolt against state judicial review appears to have subsided. The relaxation of the constitutional amending process, even in the states in which old obstacles to amendment had long survived, doubtless contributed to this result. Where amendment of the constitution is relatively easy, the state courts may briefly delay, but cannot permanently prevent, legislation for which there is a general demand. Moreover, in the current climate of opinion, the voiding of social legislation by state courts on the ground of its alleged repugnance to laissez-faire concepts supposedly embodied in state constitutions is relatively rare. There are thus few occasions for the exercise by the high state courts of their power to declare legislation invalid under the state constitution; and the ground for such action is more likely to be an inconsistency between the statute and some detailed provision of the state constitution than the repugnance of the statute to fundamental principles expressed in the constitution.

2. VOIDING OF STATE ENACTMENT AS REPUGNANT TO FEDERAL LAW: "FEDERAL" JUDICIAL REVIEW

The original Constitution contains several express limitations on the power of the states; and the Thirteenth, Fourteenth, Fifteenth, and Nineteenth amendments have added further restrictions. Equally important are the restrictions implicit in the provisions conferring particular powers on the federal government—powers whose exercise is more or less clearly inconsistent with the exercise of concurrent power in the states. In small part, these limitations on state power are enforced, and the exercise of state power in fields committed to the federal government is regulated, by Con-

---

[7] See Cushman, Constitutional Decisions by a Bare Majority of the Court, 19 Mich. Law Rev. 771 (1921). In Ohio, however, if the act has already been declared unconstitutional by a regional appellate court of the state, affirmance by the highest court of the state requires only the customary majority. For a full account see Aumann, The Course of Judicial Review in the State of Ohio, 25 Am. Pol. Sci. Rev. 367 (1931).

gress, whether through federal legislation or through assent to interstate compacts. In chief, however, it is regulated without congressional intervention, through the power of the courts, state as well as federal—but ultimately through the power of the Supreme Court—to declare unconstitutional state enactments repugnant to the Constitution or to federal statutes or treaties.

The power, and indeed the duty, of the state courts in this field is expressly declared by the Constitution itself, in the provision that the Constitution itself and the federal laws and treaties shall be "the supreme law of the land, and the judges in every state shall be bound thereby anything in the constitution or laws of any state to the contrary notwithstanding" —a provision reinforced by the one requiring all state judicial officers to "be bound by oath or affirmation, to support this Constitution." But manifestly, reliance on the state courts alone would be futile. Some suprastate authority must be provided.

In the Convention, the proposal was made that Congress have the power to veto state laws "contravening, in the opinion of the national legislature, the articles of union, or any treaties subsisting under the authority of the union"; but the Convention rejected the plan.[8] It substituted no other specific plan, however. The Constitution thus contains no express provision for federal control of repugnant state legislation.

Little attention appears to have been given to the subject while the ratification of the Constitution by the states was in progress, but it quickly came to the fore in the first Congress, in the framing of the Judiciary Act of 1789. The draftsmen of that basic act (who had in part been members of the Convention) unequivocally adopted the view that the task of compelling the observance by the state judiciaries of their duty to nullify "anything in the constitution or laws of any state to the contrary" of "the supreme law of the land" was for the Supreme Court. Relying on the provision of the Constitution which places within the federal judicial power "all cases in law and equity, arising under this Constitution," the act empowered the Supreme Court to re-examine and reverse a judgment or decree of a state court upholding (after all available state appeal) "the validity of a statute or authority exercised under a state" which had been "drawn in question" in the case "on the ground of their being repugnant to the Constitution, laws or treaties of the United States."[9]

The attack in the state courts on the validity of state statutes as repugnant to federal law was apparently not long in developing. No data are readily available as to the cases in the state courts during this early period in which state statutes were nullified on this ground. Such cases, under the

[8] Documents Illustrative of the Formation of the Union, 234 (1927).
[9] Sec. 25. 1 Stat. 85.

provision of the Judiciary Act just quoted (a provision which remained in the statutes until 1914), could not be appealed to the Supreme Court. The first case in which the state court refused to nullify a state statute asserted by a party to be repugnant to federal law reached the Supreme Court in 1812,[10] and was followed by a considerable number of others in the first half of the century.

In 1816 a litigant challenged the power of Congress to invest the Court with power to reverse a state court judgment upholding a state statute;[11] and seven years later a state itself renewed the challenge.[12] The Court, however, in sweeping terms affirmed the power of Congress to vest the Supreme Court with final power of decision of constitutionality of state statutes in all cases "arising under the Constitution"; and the power has never since been seriously questioned. However, numerous proposals to limit or abolish the court's power to review state court judgments were from time to time introduced in Congress prior to the Civil War.[13]

But it was not only through the Supreme Court that federal judicial review of state statutes was exercised. Although neither the Constitution nor the Judiciary Act made any express mention of the matter, the federal courts from an early date assumed, and the Supreme Court concurred, that in diversity and admiralty cases and in cases based on federal statutes, they too were commanded by the Constitution to disregard state enactments repugnant to federal law.[14] Nor did the Eleventh Amendment, adopted in 1795, denying to the federal courts jurisdiction of suits against states by private parties, long prevent those courts from entertaining suits against state officers alleged to be acting, or to have acted, under an unconstitutional state enactment. The Supreme Court in 1824 announced the principle that such a suit is a suit against the officer in his individual capacity and not as a representative of the state (this despite the fact that at the time the suit is instituted it has not yet been determined that the enactment is in fact unconstitutional) and hence is not withdrawn from the jurisdiction of the federal courts.[15] Despite latter-day limitations imposed by Congress,[16] the federal courts remain an important forum for initial proceedings to test the validity of state enactments attacked as repugnant to federal law.

But whether the initial proceeding be in a state or a federal court, it

[10] New Jersey v. Wilson, 7 Cranch 164, (1812).

[11] Martin v. Hunter, 1 Wheaton 304.

[12] Cohens v. Virginia, 6 Wheaton 264 (1821).

[13] See Culp, A Survey of the Proposals to Limit or Deny the Power of Judicial Review of the Supreme Court of the United States, 4 Indiana Law Jour. 386, 474, (1920).

[14] The first such case was Fletcher v. Peck, 6 Cranch 87 (1810), in which, in a diversity case, the lower federal court had held unconstitutional a state statute as "impairing the obligation of contract."

[15] Osborn v. Bank of U.S., 9 Wheaton 738 (1824).

[16] See pp. 186 ff.

is, as already set forth, only the decision of the Supreme Court which really governs.

During the first century of its existence the Supreme Court declared void some 175 state statutes[17]—over 100 of them in the two decades following the Civil War.[18] The number declared void in the years since 1889 may be estimated at over 500.[19] The increase during this period is to be explained largely by the enactment, in 1868, of the sweeping limitations—for so they proved to be—on the power of the states erected by the "due process of law" and "equal protection of the laws" clauses contained in the Fourteenth Amendment, and by the enlargement, in 1876, of the jurisdiction of the federal courts to permit suit to be instituted in them solely on the ground that a federal question affecting a state enactment was involved.[20]

However, the high state courts, too, for a century and a quarter after the adoption of the Constitution, played a role in this field. The Judiciary Act of 1789, as has been seen, permitted appeal from the state courts to the Supreme Court, when state action was attacked as void on federal grounds, only if the state court upheld the validity of state action. If the state court declared the state action invalid, no appeal to the Supreme Court was possible. In this state of the law, a state court sometimes invalidated, on federal grounds, a state statute which, had the question been permitted to come to the Supreme Court, would doubtless have been upheld. This anomalous state of affairs did not, however, evoke much criticism until the opening decade of the present century. During that decade several state courts declared invalid, under the Fourteenth Amendment, as a deprivation of property or of liberty (i.e., freedom of contract), state statutes in the field of economic regulation which, had they come before the Supreme Court, would almost certainly have been upheld. The resultant protest was effective in causing Congress, in 1914, to enlarge the appellate jurisdiction of the Supreme Court to enable it to review a state court decision on the validity of state action attacked on federal grounds even when the decision was against such validity.[21] Since this enactment, the function of the state courts in this field is preparatory only; the last word, on all questions of the compatibility of state action with federal law, rests with the Supreme Court.

[17] The count is based on the list of state statutes declared unconstitutional in 131 U.S. (Appendix ccxxxvii.)

[18] Of this latter number, however, no less than 16 were Louisiana statutes constituting a single group.

[19] The estimate is based chiefly on figures given in Bullitt, The Supreme Court and Unconstitutional Legislation, 10 Amer. Bar Assn. Jour. 417 (1924); and Wright, Growth of American Constitutional Law, 108 (1942).

[20] Previously, such suits could be brought only in the state court; and if the alleged repugnancy of the state statute to federal law was involved, and the state court held the state law unconstitutional on this ground, there was no appeal to the Supreme Court.

[21] The present statute is 28 U.S. Code, Sec. 1257 (3).

3. VOIDING OF FEDERAL ENACTMENT AS REPUGNANT TO FEDERAL CONSTITUTION: "NATIONAL" JUDICIAL REVIEW

The Constitution, as we have seen, expressly proclaims the supremacy of federal over state law. There is no corresponding declaration of the supremacy of the Constitution itself over federal enactments. Similarly, though the Constitution expressly empowers the state judiciary, and inferentially the federal judiciary, to disregard state enactments repugnant to federal law, it is completely silent with respect to the power of the judiciary to disregard federal enactments.[22] The power, now and for a century and a half past, asserted by the courts—or more realistically by the Supreme Court—to declare unconstitutional a federal statute deemed repugnant to the Constitution rests wholly on the ratiocination of the Supreme Court itself.

There is disagreement as to the extent to which the fifty-five members of the Constitutional Convention of 1787,[23] or the twenty-five or so members who were chiefly responsible for its work, foresaw the problem of possible unconstitutional legislation by Congress, or expected that the power to nullify such legislation would be assumed by the courts.[24] Perhaps the more important question is the state of public opinion generally on these matters in the widespread debate which filled the period of nearly a year between the promulgation of the Constitution by the convention and its ratification by the requisite number of states. On the one hand, it cannot be said that there was no discussion of the issue (which, as we have seen, had indeed, as to the cognate power of state judges to declare state enactments void as repugnant to state constitutions, already been the subject of acriminous discussion in several states). But the issue had not been a prominent one, and such discussion as there was did not always distinguish clearly between the possible exercise of "federal" and of "national" judicial review by the federal courts. It is safe to say that when Congress opened its session in April 1789, not a few among its members were quite unaware of the possibility that the Supreme Court, yet to be created, would assert and acquire the power to set their acts at naught.

The Judiciary Act, enacted in September, was as lacking in express provision on this point as had been the Constitution. However, it contained

[22] The oft-quoted words of Gouverneur Morris (generally credited with a major role in the authorship of the final draft of the Constitution), written thirty years after the event, are perhaps relevant: "On that subject [the judiciary] conflicting opinions had been maintained with so much professional astuteness, that it became necessary to select phrases which, expressing my own notions, would not alarm others nor shock their self-love. . . ." 1 Elliot, Debates in the Several State Conventions, etc., 507 (2nd ed. 1836).

[23] Of the fifty-five who at one time or another attended, however, only thirty-nine signed the proposed constitution.

[24] The diverse conclusions which have been reached on this question are reviewed at length in Haines, American Doctrine of Judicial Supremacy, 126 ff. (2nd ed. 1932).

a provision certainly susceptible of the construction that it recognized both the power of the state courts to declare an act of Congress unconstitutional, and of the Supreme Court, on appeal, to affirm the decision of the state court; and such has been the general, but not the unanimous, view of the provision.[25] Presumably, the federal courts, with the Supreme Court at their head, were to have a power at least equal to that of the state courts. It would thus seem that the framers of the Judiciary Act envisaged, fairly clearly, the position of the Supreme Court as ultimate arbiter of the constitutionality of acts of Congress.

In the first decade of the new federal court system (1790–1800) only a single case was decided by the Supreme Court in which was involved the power of the court to refuse enforcement to an act of Congress found to be repugnant to the Constitution. Though the Court enforced the act, it was apparently assumed, both by the parties (of whom one was the federal government) and by the majority of the Court that the Court possessed the power to refuse enforcement.[26]

The first case in which the Court unequivocally asserted its power to refuse enforcement to an act of Congress arose in 1803; and it will be of value to review this case somewhat fully, particularly since it presents other features relevant to an understanding of the American legal system.

The case in question, Marbury v. Madison,[27] involved an application to the Supreme Court as a court of original jurisdiction. The original jurisdiction of the Supreme Court as specified in the Constitution is limited to (1) cases involving ambassadors, other public ministers, and consuls, and (2) cases in which a state is a party; and Congress, in the Judiciary Act of 1789, did not, in defining the original jurisdiction of Court, specifically include in that definition any classes of cases other than the two classes

[25] The Act (Sec. 25) provided that a state court judgment (after appeal through the state courts) in a suit "where is drawn in question the validity of a treaty or statute of or an authority exercised under the United States, and the decision is against their validity . . . may be reexamined and reversed or *affirmed* in the Supreme Court of the United States upon a writ of error" (italics supplied). For the contention that the word "affirmed" was, however, not intended to apply to the quoted portion of the section, but only to other portions, see 2 Crosskey, Politics and the Constitution, 1029–1035 (1953).

[26] Hylton v. United States, 3 Dallas 171 (1796). This was an appeal in an action brought by the government in an inferior federal court to recover a statutory penalty from the defendant by reason of his failure to pay a tax (on carriages) imposed by Congress. His defense was that the tax law was unconstitutional, because it enacted a direct tax not apportioned among the several states in proportion to their population, as required by the Constitution. Only four of the six justices apparently took part; all agreed that the tax was not a direct tax. In addition to this case there was a refusal of one circuit court to enforce an act of Congress providing that applications for invalid soldier's pensions should be made to the federal circuit courts, and that the determination of those courts should be subject to review by the Secretary of War and by Congress. Hayburn's Case, 2 Dallas 409 (1792). A like opinion was expressed in two other circuits.

[27] 1 Cranch 137 (1803).

enumerated in the Constitution. It did, however, empower the Court to issue, among other types of process, writs of mandamus to persons holding office under the authority of the United States.

In the case in question, the petitioner who instituted the proceeding sought from the Court a writ of mandamus to compel the Secretary of State to deliver to him a commission naming him to a certain office. This commission had been signed by outgoing President Adams and thereafter transmitted to the State Department for delivery to the petitioner, but had not been delivered to him; and Secretary of State Madison, appointed by Jefferson, the new President, now refused to deliver it. Manifestly, this application to the Supreme Court did not fall within either of the two classes of original jurisdiction defined by the Constitution; and the petitioner thus in effect contended that Congress had, by the provision empowering the court to issue writs of mandamus, enlarged the original jurisdiction of the Supreme Court beyond these two specified classes. If this was the intention of Congress, the question was presented whether such enlargement of the original jurisdiction of the Court was consistent with the constitutional definition of that jurisdiction. The Court could, of course, and according to accepted doctrines should, have ruled that such was not the intent of Congress; that the provision of the Judiciary Act in question was merely procedural in character, intended to aid the Court in any case properly within its jurisdiction in which it might become necessary to issue a writ of mandamus to a federal officer.[28] Instead of doing this, however, the Court accepted the petitioner's contention that the intent of Congress in enacting the provision was to enlarge the original jurisdiction of the Court as defined in the Constitution and, having accepted that unnecessary premise, declared that such enlargement was beyond the power of Congress.[29] Accordingly, the provision of the act of Congress allegedly extending the original jurisdiction of the Court to cases not included in the definition of that jurisdiction contained in the Constitution was held unconstitutional and void; and the case was dismissed for lack of jurisdic-

[28] The provision authorizing the Court to issue writs of mandamus is in fact part of the same sentence in which it is authorized to issue the writ of prohibition to inferior courts—a writ which in its nature could not enlarge the original jurisdiction of the Court, but could aid it in protecting its existing jurisdiction.

[29] This construction of the constitutional provision, however unnecessary to the disposition of the case, is the accepted one. It is reasoned that the original jurisdiction of the Court is limited to these two classes of cases by necessary implication from the immediately following provision that "in all other cases it shall have appellate jurisdiction." That provision is, however, qualified by the words "with such exceptions as Congress shall make." The accepted view is that this merely permits Congress to withdraw some or all of these "all other cases" from the Court's appellate jurisdiction; but the contention has in recent years been put forward that it also empowers Congress to place a case so withdrawn from the Court's appellate jurisdiction within its original jurisdiction. See 2 Crosskey, Politics and the Constitution, 1041 ff. (1953).

tion.[30] In thus disposing of the case the Court made it the occasion for a fundamental pronouncement from the pen of Chief Justice Marshall, asserting the power of the courts (and thus in effect of the Supreme Court, since the final word would lie with it) to refuse enforcement to acts of Congress which they deemed unconstitutional.

During the succeeding half century, the Court heard argument and passed upon the validity of several acts of Congress; but it sustained all of them, not pronouncing another such act invalid till the Dred Scott case in 1857.[31] In the following decade, it pronounced but two more acts void.[32]

Despite its sparing exercise, the power of the Court did not escape attack during this long period. The mild political furor created by the decision in Marbury v. Madison quickly subsided; but as the increasing use of the Court's veto on state legislation provoked, as already noted, numerous proposals for a limitation on its power in that direction, its power to invalidate acts of Congress was also embraced in some of these proposals. But no serious threat to its power materialized; and indeed in 1868 a striking evidence was given that even the powerful Reconstruction Congress, then riding roughshod over the executive, was unwilling to engage in a contest with the Court on this issue. While the Court had under consideration an appeal, already argued, in a habeas corpus proceeding in which was questioned the constitutionality of one of the reconstruction acts (creating military government in the formerly seceded states), Congress, fearful that the Court might declare the act unconstitutional, but unwilling to challenge the Court's power, resorted to the device of withdrawing from the Court's appellate jurisdiction appeals in certain classes of habeas corpus proceedings, including the pending proceeding.[33]

The remaining decades of the last century witnessed the voiding of a score of additional congressional enactments. In at least two of these—the civil rights cases in 1883 and the income tax cases in 1895—fundamental limitations on congressional power were announced; but in neither case, though proposals for reform were again agitated, was there any

[30] It is an obvious rule of judicature that where the jurisdiction of a court is challenged, that question is to be disposed of before any other question is considered; for should it be determined that the court is indeed without jurisdiction there is no longer any question before it. In this case, however, the Court, composed of Federalists, could not resist the opportunity covertly to rebuke the Jefferson administration for its refusal to deliver to a Federalist appointee a commission issued to him by the outgoing Federalist President; and in disregard of the rule of procedure referred to, first considered the propriety of the conduct of the respondent (Madison) and declared it unlawful.

[31] Dred Scott v. Sandford, 19 Howard 393 (1857).

[32] Gordon v. U.S. 2 Wallace 561 (1865) and Ex parte Garland, 4 Wallace 333 (1867).

[33] 15 Stat. 44. This act was acquiesced in by the Court and the appeal dismissed for want of jurisdiction in Ex parte McCardle, 7 Wallace 506 (1869).

serious disposition in responsible quarters to undermine the power of the Court. In the first third of the present century, during which the Court voided nearly forty federal statutes, a number of them dealing with minor provisions of the revenue acts, there was much public discussion of the propriety of the Court's power, and some proposals for reform attracted much attention; but the issue never became a major one.[34]

With the advent of the Roosevelt administration in 1933, however, there came a marked change. In a series of some ten or eleven decisions, during 1935 and 1936, the Court invalidated, in most cases by a divided court, major portions of the New Deal program, including the National Industrial Recovery Act (its oil-regulation provisions included), the Railroad Retirement Act, the Bituminous Coal Conservation Act, and portions of the Agricultural Adjustment Act and of the acts regulating the bankruptcy of municipalities and of farmers. The grounds advanced by the court for its action were various—the lack of power in Congress to deal with the subject matter, the undue delegation by Congress to the President of the legislative power which it did possess, or the repugnance of the legislation to the prohibitions of the Constitution.

Early in 1937 President Roosevelt recommended to Congress the enlargement of the membership of the Court from nine (the number fixed in 1868) to fifteen. The ostensible reason for the proposal was that the nine-man Court was overburdened; the actual objective was freely conceded to be a change in the ideological complexion of the Court by the addition of six Roosevelt appointees. The ignominious rejection of the proposal by a Congress otherwise readily responsive to the Roosevelt leadership demonstrated clearly the position the Court holds in the political creed of the American people. Aware that its individual members may have a definite political background, the citizen nevertheless regards the Court as collectively above the battle; and even those citizens who appreciate that its function is in large measure not judicial but legislative, and therefore political, are unwilling that it should be made an instrument of the designedly political branches of the government.

The attempt to "pack" the Court—for so Roosevelt's plan was freely characterized—led to the proposal that the size of the Court's membership should be fixed by the Constitution itself, instead of by statute. Despite influential support in legal quarters, this proposal has made little progress, presumably because another court-packing attempt in the foreseeable future seems quite improbable.[35]

[34] The so-called LaFollette Amendment, proposed by Senator LaFollette, presidential candidate of the Progressive party in 1924, was incorporated in the platform of that party in the campaign of that year. It proposed that Congress, by re-enacting a law which the Court had declared unconstitutional, could nullify the action of the Court.

[35] However, Joint Resolution 44 of the Eighty-third Congress, known as the Butler amendment, passed the Senate, but failed to reach the floor of the House. In the

There is open to Congress another possible method of limiting the Court's power to declare acts of Congress unconstitutional—the method actually employed, as already noted, during the Reconstruction period. Congress may deprive the Court of its appellate jurisdiction in any particular class of cases—as, for example, all cases arising under a particular statute. In 1957, proposals to withdraw from the Court appellate jurisdiction in certain cases gained substantial support in Congress,[36] but no legislation resulted, and the proposals have not been revived. On the other hand proposals continue to be made from time to time to withdraw from Congress the power to diminish the appellate jurisdiction of the Court by fixing that jurisdiction in the Constitution itself.[37] These proposals likewise have failed to enlist any widespread popular support.

The brief period between the court-packing episode and the outbreak of the war witnessed a shifting of the Court's majority in such a way as to save the National Labor Relations Act, one of the most controversial of the administration's measures, from invalidation; and the Fair Labor Standards Act, representing perhaps the furthest Congress has yet gone in regulating manufacturing (and even merchandising) within the states, was similarly upheld. The relation of this shift to the court-packing attempt has been the subject of interesting speculation.

In recent years the Court has not, except in its holdings on courtmartial jurisdiction, significantly exercised its power to void federal statutes.[38]

4. THE HISTORIC ROLE OF THE SUPREME COURT

As we have seen, despite the common reference to the power of "the courts" to nullify legislation, the power to nullify acts of Congress and the power to nullify state enactments on federal grounds are in effect exercised only by the Supreme Court. That court consequently has played and

---

Eighty-fourth Congress, Joint Resolution 45, of similar import, failed to pass either house. These resolutions would have fixed the membership of the Court in the Constitution itself at nine, the present number.

[36] In the Eighty-fifth Congress, Senate bill 2646, known as the Jenner bill, proposed to withdraw from the Supreme Court appellate jurisdiction in certain cases arising under statutes or executive regulations dealing with subversion, cases arising out of congressional committee action, and cases relating to the admission of persons to the bar of a state. Apparently the appellate power of the several courts of appeals in these classes of cases was to be left undisturbed.

[37] Some proposals contemplated that the Supreme Court should be given plenary appellate jurisdiction in all cases within the judicial power of the United States, the Court having power to make exceptions. The Butler amendment (see note 35) proposed that the Court's jurisdiction in constitutional questions only be made constitutional.

[38] For a list of federal statutes declared unconstitutional see Corwin (ed.), The Constitution of the United States, Analysis and Interpretation, 1241 (1953). A singular omission from this list is the limited immunity statute of 1868, declared unconstitutional in 1892. See note 40.

continues to play the major role in shaping our constitutional structure. A glance, necessarily cursory, at the results of its work in this role will assist in understanding its present position.

The pronouncements of the Court have shaped our constitutional system at almost every point. But in chief the Court's role has been twofold. On the one hand, it has served as arbiter between the federal power and the states, tracing in detail that difficult boundary between central and local power, of which the Constitution provides merely the chief landmarks. On the other hand, it has served as the umpire between the citizen alleging governmental invasion of his constitutionally protected rights of person or property, and the governmental power, whether state or federal, threatening such invasion.

The Court as arbiter between state and national power in economic life

During the decade and a half which preceded the initiation of the new national government, the states had exercised plenary power over economic affairs—not merely over their internal economic affairs but also over their commerce with each other and with foreign countries. This plenary power of the states was subjected by the Constitution to but few express prohibitions. As respects their interstate and foreign commerce, they were merely forbidden to levy duties on imports or exports or duties of tonnage, to make war, or to enter into compacts with one another without the consent of Congress. On the other hand, the new national government was vested with power to coin money, to levy import duties and internal taxes, and to "regulate" interstate and foreign commerce.[39] Clearly these brief constitutional phrases provided but meager tools for drawing, in necessarily intricate and detailed design, the line which would have to be drawn, in the years to come, between permissible state and national exertions of the power of economic regulation. The task of tracing that line fell to the Supreme Court.

In this task, the central question was for a century or more the extent to which state statutes might go in "regulating" interstate or foreign commerce. That a state statute must yield to any federal statute on the subject was axiomatic. But Congress, in the first century of national life, passed but few statutes regulating interstate commerce. Hence, it was not congressional action that chiefly guided the Court. Instead it was the doctrine, early announced by the Court itself, that the states were prohibited, not indeed by any express provision of the Constitution, but by its implied intention, from "burdening" interstate commerce. It is under this gloss upon the Constitution that the Court has invalidated perhaps a greater

[39] The words "interstate commerce," now so familiar, do not appear in the Constitution. The phrase used is "commerce among the several states." For the novel contention that these words were intended to embrace all domestic commerce, intrastate as well as interstate, see 1 Crosskey, Politics and the Constitution, 50–83 (1953).

number of state statutes than it has under any of the express prohibitions of the Constitution.

With the second century of national life, Congress entered upon a more positive regulation of the national economy, relying chiefly on its power to regulate interstate and foreign commerce. But in a series of decisions at the turn of the century the Court made clear that the mining, manufacture, or agriculture production of goods destined for shipment in interstate or foreign commerce was not itself "commerce" within the meaning of the Constitution, and thus was not itself directly subject to federal regulation.

Proceeding piecemeal with the work of negation, the Court did not clearly perceive (nor did the country at large) that it was creating an area of economic life exempt from governmental control—exempt from state control because state regulation would constitute a burden on interstate commerce; exempt from national control because national regulation would be a regulation not of interstate commerce alone but of intrastate industry as well. Eventually, in the late 1930s, following a few earlier tentatives, the Court in a series of decisions in effect discarded the doctrines it had constructed a few decades before. It now announced in effect that Congress possessed the power to regulate any phase of ecomonic life that could be said to be even remotely related to interstate commerce—as indeed almost every phase can; so that today, and presumably for the indefinite future, the role of the Court in this field is that of a check on the states alone.

Reviewing the historic role of the Court in this field, one is likely to be brought to the conclusion that, however indefensible may be thought to be the investment of a judicial tribunal with the function of constructing, case by case, the constitutional boundaries within which the several components of a federal system must operate, the Court, except for the period already referred to, has accomplished an extraordinarily difficult task in a statesmanlike manner. Indeed, one must confess, perhaps with chagrin, that it has accomplished the task more satisfactorily than it probably would have been accomplished by a more logical organ. A constitutional amendment, or successive amendments, substituting for the vague and brief phraseology of the Constitution a precise delimitation of the respective spheres of state and national power (or investing Congress with power to make such delimitation) would, of course, have greatly reduced the necessity for the function of the Court. However, the enormous difficulties which would have attended the framing of constitutional amendments, and their acceptance by Congress and the states, are only too obvious.

The Court as arbiter between the legislature and the individual

The Constitution contains a number of provisions designed to safeguard the individual against abuse of power on the part of the federal government. For the most part, however, they relate to the rights of the accused in a criminal proceeding; and it is accurate to say that outside the field of criminal prosecution the Supreme Court, in the century following its first announcement of its power to declare federal enactments void, did not invalidate a single act of Congress as a prohibited invasion of the rights of the individual. Even in the field of criminal procedure, it had only one important ocasion to pronounce an act void—an act purporting to compel self-incriminating answers from witnesses in federal proceedings by the grant of a limited immunity only.[40]

During the present century also, the Court has on but few occasions vetoed a congressional act as an invasion of individual rights. In the early decades, in two cases long since overruled, it did so in the name of freedom of contract;[41] and in at least one of the cases invalidating New Deal legislation, invasion of property rights was the ground assigned.[42] Today neither ground retains much potency in the field of economic regulation. In the field of federal criminal prosecution Congress has delegated to the Court itself chief responsibility for regulating procedure. The decisions of the past decade which voided the statutory provisions conferring on courts-martial jurisdiction of certain civilians in peacetime[43] were of major importance; but further invalidation of statutory provisions governing military justice is unlikely. In the field of freedom of expression and of religion, federal legislation is likely to have little impact. Nor is the court likely to be confronted with the question of the constitutionality of federal aid to church-related schools as long as present doctrines denying to the federal taxpayer the right to challenge federal expenditures are adhered to. All in all, then, the protection of individual rights against Congress has been, and continues to be, among the less significant aspects of the Court's function.[44]

Quite otherwise is it where state legislation is concerned. As the Constitution stood at the time of its adoption, and as it remained for four score years thereafter (for none of the first twelve amendments made any change in this respect), it contained few prohibitions designed to protect the indi-

[40] Counselman v. Hitchcock, 142 U.S. 547 (1892).

[41] Adair v. United States, 208 U.S. 161 (1908) and Adkins v. Children's Hospital, 261 U.S. 525 (1923).

[42] Louisville Land Bank v. Radford, 295 U.S. 555 (1935).

[43] See p. 511.

[44] An exception should be noted with respect to the Court's role in checking Congress in its investigative, as opposed to its legislative, function. See Chapter 9. Moreover, though the Court has not invalidated the Smith Act of 1940, it has, since its initial decision in 1951 sustaining the constitutionality of that act (Dennis v. United States, 341 U.S. 494), construed it so narrowly as to render it largely ineffectual. More recently it has followed the same pattern of extreme narrowness in interpretation, rather than outright invalidation, in dealing with the other chief attempt by Congress to legislate against the Communist party and its affiliates, the Internal Security Act of 1950.

vidual against state action. The states were forbidden to pass any bills of attainder or ex post facto law or any law impairing the obligation of contracts; and each state was required to extend to the citizens of other states the "privileges and immunities" enjoyed within its borders by its own citizens. Save for these few limitations, the individual enjoyed no federal protection against state legislation when dealing with a subject wholly within the area to state power—such as criminal prosecution, the control of the press and of education, or the regulation of local business.

During the first half-century under the Constitution, the "contracts" clause was on a number of occasions invoked against state legislation to protect vested property rights; and the holding of the Court in 1834—in the Dartmouth College case[45]—that a corporate charter was a contract between the state and the corporation, the obligation of which the state was consequently powerless to impair, promised for a time to shackle the states in their legislation affecting the growing corporate segment of economic life. But the decision proved of less consequence than anticipated, as the states in rapid succession wrote into their statutes and constitutions a reservation of power to alter or repeal all corporate charters thereafter granted. The Court, moreover, in subsequent decisions, somewhat limited its earlier liberal construction of the contracts clause. Well before the end of the last century, that clause had ceased to have major importance. Nor did the Court lay down any other important limitation on state action against the individual on the basis of any of the few other provisions of the Constitution, restrictive of state power.

But for the Civil War, perhaps, the situation would have remained unchanged. It was one of the changes in the Constitution resulting from that struggle, embodied in a single sentence of the Fourteenth Amendment, that furnished the Court with the constitutional text out of which it forged its latter-day restrictions on state action. Some there are who insist that even had there been no Fourteenth Amendment, the Court would have found a way to protect private property against confiscatory or even unduly oppressive state legislation; and there can be found indeed, here and there in opinions written by its members shortly before the Civil War, expressions hinting at such a possibility. But it is difficult to see how these views could have been given effect had there been no language in the Constitution to support them. Indeed, even after the adoption of the Fourteenth Amendment in 1868, nearly two decades were to elapse before the Court, using that text as its justification, extended the shield of federal protection to property rights invaded by the states.

The Fourteenth Amendment introduced into the Constitution three clauses protective of the right of the individual against state action. No state is to "abridge the privileges or immunities of citizens of the United

[45] Dartmouth College v. Woodward, 4 Wheaton 518 (1819).

States; nor shall any state deprive any person of life, or property, without due process of law; nor deny to any person within its jurisdiction the equal protection of the laws."

Of these three clauses the first has proved of relatively little consequence, owing to decisions of the Court reducing to relative unimportance the "privileges and immunities of citizens of the United States" which are thus placed under federal protection against the states. It is the "due process" and "equal protection" clauses—above all the "due process" clause—that have furnished the textual groundwork for a constitutional revolution of the first magnitude.

It has already been seen how in the field of state criminal procedure the Court has taken the conventional phrase "due process of law," which, as a restriction in the Constitution on the federal government, had slumbered almost unnoticed, as it were, for a century and more, and has expanded it to become synonymous with fundamental fairness. Here the effect of the numerous reversals of state criminal convictions which the Court has made has been (aside from the correction of what it deemed to be abuses of power by state law-enforcement authorities) chiefly not to invalidate existing state statutes but to impose on the states new requirements—such as those calling for the furnishing of counsel to indigent defendants—for which existing state statutes made no provision.

In the field of state economic regulation the Court has, by a textual gloss perhaps even more fragile, extended a cognate federal supervision. Under its hand "due process of law" and "equal protection of the laws" became, once it had been announced by the Court in 1886 that a corporation was a "person" within the meaning of the amendment,[46] within the space of two decades or more, a prohibition of confiscatory regulation of public utility rates and of any unreasonable invasion of the freedom of private contract, or of the use of private property, the Court being the arbiter of reasonableness. The restrictive effect of these doctrines on state economic regulation, at one time regarded as a major issue in our political life, proved in the event short-lived. Under a barrage of criticism leveled at some of its decisions, (especially those, however, in which the regulatory statutes held void were federal rather than state enactments) the changing membership of the Court, while stoutly maintaining the correctness of the basic doctrines, applied them so charily that by the end of the 1930s the states had in effect almost regained a free hand. Only the requirement that utilities be not deprived of a fair return on their property survived as a permanent restriction on state power.

Meanwhile, however, the Court had begun, in the 1920s, the expansion of its supervision of state legislation, again under the authority of the due process clause, into an entirely new conceptual area—an area even less

[46] Santa Clara County v. Southern Pac. R. Co., 118 U.S. 394 (1886).

present, it may be hazarded, to the minds of the generation which added the Fourteenth Amendment to the Constitution than was the field of state economic regulation. Freedom of expression and of religion, the Court announced, are also protected against state invasion by the due process clause; and not long after, the principle of separation of church and state was added to the list.[47]

With a greater measure of textual support, the Court has undertaken a task of supervision of state legislation in quite another field—that of state legislation requiring racial segregation in the use of transportation facilities, public educational institutions, and the like—legislation found, needless to say, almost exclusively in the southern states, and applying to the segregation of the white and Negro races. The Constitution contains no express restriction on state action in this field, and the clause of the Fourteenth Amendment protecting the "privileges and immunities of citizens of the United States" against abridgement by the states, which might be thought to apply, was early held by the Court to be inapplicable. The clause prohibiting a state from denying to any person "the equal protection of the laws" was then invoked. It would have been entirely defensible for the Court to have taken the position that these words, in their context, had reference only to laws intended to afford *protection* to the individual, and not to laws regulating the use of public facilities, and thus to have entirely excluded from the sphere of federal supervision the whole problem of state segregation laws, leaving the evil to be attacked from other directions.

The court, however, did not hold the clause inapplicable. But neither did it hold that the clause forbade racial segregation laws. Instead, it enunciated the doctrine, but dubiously grounded either textually or historically, that the intent of the clause was that the segregated Negro population of the southern states was constitutionally entitled to receive public accommodations and facilities equal to those furnished the white population. It would unduly extend this discussion to trace the way in which this doctrine, first announced in 1896 with respect to transportation, was declared thirty years later to apply also to public education; how during the next two decades it was, in the field of public higher education, given verbal endorsement but was in specific cases declared inapplicable because the facilities offered the Negro student were not in fact equal to those available to the white student; how, in 1954, in perhaps the most far-reaching decision ever rendered by it, the Court declared the segregated

[47] The basis for thus incorporating the principle of separation of church and state into the Fourteenth Amendment is found by the Court in the First Amendment, a prohibition against Congress. The language of that provision forbids only a "law respecting an establishment of religion," but the Court has declared that it was intended to build "a wall of separation" between church and state. Leading cases are McCollum v. Board of Education, 333 U.S. 203 (1948); Zorach v. Clauson, 343 U.S. 306 (1952); and Engel v. Vitale, 370 U.S. 421 (1962).

Negro school, however equal in other respects, to be inherently unequal from the standpoint of its psychic impact on the Negro pupil;[48] and how, shortly thereafter, discarding completely all consideration of equality of facilities, it declared segregated public facilities, whether parks, libraries, or any other, to be unconstitutional, thus announcing the final destruction, after sixty years, of its own unhappy creation, the doctrine of "separate but equal."

In less than a decade, the Court announced a doctrine only less far-reaching than its repudiation of the "separate but equal" doctrine. The inequality of representation in the state legislatures, as between urban and rural areas, difficult if not impossible to correct through the state legislative organs themselves, had on several occasions been attacked in the courts as repugnant to the "equal protection of the laws" provision of the Fourteenth Amendment; but the Supreme Court had declared the problem to be a political one, beyond judicial cognizance. In 1962, however, by a divided court, it held that the courts had power to order the removal of at least gross inequalities in representation.[49] The suits which followed, in both state and federal courts, raised, as had been expected, a host of problems, both substantive and procedural, the outworking of which will doubtless occupy some years to come.

The Court as a political organ

Even when the Court was not yet half a century old, the acute observer could perceive that "although its constitution is essentially judicial, its prerogatives are almost entirely political";[50] and succeeding decades made this increasingly clear. However, in the past century the Court's constitutional decisions had in almost every case a textual foundation so clearly related to the constitutional issue as to give its pronouncements, however political in essence, somewhat of the color of a judicial determination. But the developments of the present century have made it clear to even the less sophisticated that, though functioning as a judicial tribunal in its routine labors, the Court, when imposing new fundamental restrictions on the states, and commanding them to adopt new procedures in criminal justice, purportedly in obedience to the mandate of the Constitution embodied in such vague phrases as "due process of law" and "equal protection of the laws," is making political decisions of the first importance.

Surely few phenomena in political history are more striking than this. A great nation, historically and in the present era the protagonist before the world of responsible representative government, yet acquiesces in the exercise of virtually uncontrollable political power—a power acquired,

[48] Brown v. Board of Education, 347 U.S. 483 (1954).
[49] Baker v. Carr, 369 U.S. 186 (1962).
[50] 1 de Tocqueville, Democracy in America, 151 (1831; Bradley ed. 1945).

moreover, chiefly by a remorseless process of self-aggrandizement—by a small irremovable chamber, its lifetime members responsible only to their own consciences.

In his first inaugural address Lincoln protested that "if the policy of the government upon vital questions . . . is to be irrevocably fixed by decisions of the Supreme Court . . . , the people will have ceased to be their own rulers, having to that extent practically resigned their government into the hands of that eminent tribunal." Never has the truth of his words been more strikingly demonstrated than in the 1954 desegregation mandate. The segregated school system of the South, developed initially on a pattern already familiar in the North (surviving even in such states as New York and New Jersey for two decades after the adoption of the Fourteenth Amendment), had been given implicit approval by the Court in 1896 (when it cited the segregated school as a justification for upholding the constitutionality of segregation in public transportation), and had been given express unanimous approval thirty years later,[51] so long as it conformed to the requirement of "separate but equal." The abolition of this hateful system, inevitable in the long run, presented to the nation a political problem so thorny that its resolution by our representative organs, even in the national capital, had not even begun to be attempted.[52] Overnight, the Court cut the Gordian knot.

The assertion by the Court of its power (and of the power of the state and lower federal courts under its supervision) to correct inequalities in state legislative apportionment was likewise a political decision, without any but the most fragile textual foundation. The imposition on the states, in rapid succession, of new mandates and prohibitions in law enforcement

[51] In the opinion of the Court in the school segregation case (note 48 above), the 1927 case in question (Gong Lum v. Rice, 275 U.S. 78) is said not to have involved the issue of the constitutionality of school segregation because "the plaintiff, a child of Chinese descent, contended only that the state has misapplied the doctrine by classifying him with Negro children and requiring him to attend a Negro school" (p. 491). The Court could indeed have disposed of the case on the narrow ground urged by the plaintiff, at the same time making clear that it did not pass on the constitutionality of school segregation itself. Instead, the opinion of the Court is a lengthy dissertation on the obvious constitutionality of segregated schools, citing as authority high state court opinions in Massachusetts and New York, among other states, and characterizing the case decided thirty years earlier, upholding segregation in public transportation (Plessy v. Ferguson, 163 U.S. 537 [1896]) as having presented a more difficult question.

[52] It is generally assumed that Congress was powerless to act, except to initiate a constitutional amendment. However, under the power expressly conferred on it by the Fourteenth Amendment, to "enforce, by appropriate legislation, the provisions" of that amendment, Congress could have enacted legislation for the desegregation of the schools. The previous holdings of the Court, sustaining segregation in certain cases in the absence of federal legislation on the subject, would not have required it, even in strict theory, to hold that federal legislation could not override state legislation in this field. At any rate, Congress possessed unquestioned power to repeal its own statute requiring segregation in the public schools of the District of Columbia.

and in criminal prosecutions, has similarly been political, not juristic, action.

These vast exertions of political power on the part of the Court have given rise to an unprecedented outpouring of commentary and criticism. Two years after the school segregation decision, 101 senators and representatives from the southern states joined in a declaration condemning the justices of the Court for having "substituted their personal, political, and social ideas for the established law of the land." In 1958 the state chief justices, in conference assembled, by a large majority, urged the Court to recognize and give effect to "the difference between that which, on the one hand, the Constitution may prescribe and permit and that which, on the other, a majority of the Supreme Court, as from time to time constituted, may deem desirable or undesirable." The Council of State Governments, in 1962, proposed constitutional amendments overruling the Court's decision on state legislative apportionment, and superseding the Court, in questions of national versus state power, by a court composed of the state chief justices. Even highly respected jurists, above any suspicion of state parochialism, have voiced grave doubts.[53] But academic commentators have been almost unanimously favorable.[54] Indeed, their writings have in some instances revealed a degree of reliance on the Court as the guardian of the national interest unequaled even by those defenders of nineteenth century laissez-faire capitalism who extolled the Court as a bulwark against socialism.

But how reconcile this anomalous institution with a polity otherwise dominated by the concept of the responsibility of political power to the electorate? How reconcile one's faith in the democratic process—a faith professed by all these commentators—with the exercise of vast political power by a small irremovable council in office for life? The Court, these commentators insist, is nevertheless a democratic organ, which, in a manner not elucidated, ascertains and then gives effect to a national consensus (or, as some would have it, the promptings of the national conscience) unable to find expression through our representative institutions. Others, emphasizing the "ambiguities" of the Constitution—ambiguities largely created by the Court itself—find in it the indispensable organ for reconciling the

[53] See especially Hand, The Bill of Rights, 38 ff. (1958). Even one of the present members of the Court, Justice Harlan, appears to have some doubts. See 48 Amer. Bar Assn. Jour. 324 (1963).

[54] Almost all the works by academic authors listed in this connection at page 565 are highly favorable. Space does not permit citation. One troubled legal scholar asks how the Court, in making essentially political determinations, can function as a court of law, rather than as a naked power organ; how its holdings "can be asserted to have any legal quality." His answer is that they have this quality if they are "entirely principled." Wechsler, Toward Neutral Principles of Constitutional Law, 73 Harv. Law Rev. 1 (1959). Surprisingly, one of the few academic dissenters, and perhaps the only one who calls for a curtailment of the Court's power to veto legislation, confines his attack to its power over federal laws, now of minor importance. Hook, The Paradoxes of Freedom, 102 ff. (1962).

"conflicting ideals" reflected in those ambiguities, a task beyond the capacity of the organs responsible to the electorate.

The debate continues. But, conceivably, its chief significance is that of a commentary on the historical role of the Court, rather than of a controversy as to whether its future role should be curtailed. As already noted, the great issues of national power were settled several decades ago, and the major issues of constitutional restrictions on the states have now been resolved in their fundamentals. No new issue of comparable magnitude is on the horizon. Quite possibly, the political importance of the Court is now at its zenith, and moves toward its decline.

11

The Courts as Molders of the Law

1. COLONIAL FOUNDATIONS OF AMERICAN LAW. 2. THE HISTORIC ROLE OF COURT AND LEGISLATURE. 3. THE ROLE OF PRECEDENT. 4. LIMITATIONS ON THE POWER OF THE COURTS TO IMPROVE THE LAW. 5. ROLE OF THE COURTS IN MOLDING CRIMINAL PROCEDURE AND IN REGULATING LAW-ENFORCEMENT METHODS.

In that period of American political thought in which it was deemed essential to construct sharp and clear-cut lines of demarcation between the respective functions of the three departments of government, it was customary to announce that the legislature made the law, while the courts merely applied it. In the theoretical elaborations of this thesis, the existing body of doctrine was conceived as containing within itself the rule applicable to any possible state of facts. The facts being established, the court had only to find the applicable rule. The task was one not of creation, but of research and syllogism.

It needs but slight acquaintance with our legal institutions to appreciate how completely fallacious is such a concept of the work of the courts. Despite the formidable bulk of the body of existing legal rules, whether expressed in statute or in received doctrine, cases daily arise for which no applicable rule can be found; and rapidly as new rules may be formulated, the ever-changing fabric of business practice and of technology continually creates the need for new rules. In large part the need is of course met by legislation; but rare indeed is the statute or the regulation drafted with such minuteness of detail, and with such clairvoyance, as to anticipate every situation which may arise under it. Under statutes, no less than in those areas of the law in which the entire body of rules is traditional, the elaboration of new rules is an inescapable concomitant of the judicial process.

However, to speak of the courts generally as agencies for the development and creation of the rules of law is to overlook the wide divergence between the trial courts and the appellate courts in this respect. It is the

338

essential function of the trial courts to dispose of particular controversies; only to a very limited extent, and only tentatively, do their judges develop or create new law. The appellate courts, on the other hand, are largely concerned with the development of the law and the creation of new law. True, a court, unlike the legislature, can exercise this function only as opportunity offers through the presentation to it of a particular case. Moreover, the frequency with which such opportunity offers depends also on the extent to which the legislature has left questions open, failing to make statutory provision in advance for their ready determination. But everywhere the area still open to the appellate courts further to develop the law, or to make new law, is extensive.

The role of our courts in developing legal doctrine, and the relation of the courts to the legislature in this field, represent, as do so many other aspects of our legal system, the outworking of a historical process going back in England nearly a millennium; and a brief review of the American phase of that process is therefore called for.

1. COLONIAL FOUNDATIONS OF AMERICAN LAW

Our law is of English descent. The English settlers carried with them to these shores, in however truncated a form, the law of the mother country; and it was on the foundation of the meager elements of English law which they had first found it necessary to incorporate in their institutions, and of legal doctrines subsequently imported from England and here elaborated, that the independent structure of American law was reared. The body of doctrine—it can hardly be called a system—thus transplanted to the Atlantic shores by the English colonists steadily extended its sway westward and southward.

This was true not only of the areas in which the original settlers carried the English law with them; it was true also, though perhaps less completely, in those areas in which the English law had to displace the French, Spanish, or Mexican law already established there—in the settlements north of the Ohio, which came under British dominion in 1763, in the settlements already existing at the mouth of the Mississippi and at its junction with the Missouri when the Louisiana Territory was acquired in 1803, in Florida (acquired in 1819), in Texas (which, when it joined the United States in 1845, had but recently been part of Mexico), and in the territory acquired from Mexico in 1848. Only in New Orleans did the English law fail to displace the law already well established there at the time of its acquisition. That law persisted and spread to the remainder of the area which later became the state of Louisiana; and even the century and a half that has since elapsed has not sufficed, at least on the civil side, to do much more than overlay that law with an Anglo-American veneer. In the region which subsequently became the states of Washington, Oregon, and Idaho, Anglo-American legal institutions of a rudimentary character had from the first been planted by the British and Americans who had settled there while its sovereignty was still in dispute between Great Britain and the United States. Thus, despite their multiplicity and diversity, all the systems of state law (except that of Louisiana) and within its narrower limits the federal law as well bear the unmistakable imprint of their common English parentage. Because of that parentage, we may appropriately begin with the English law as it existed during the period of English colonization of North America.

Since the first permanent English settlements on this continent occurred in the early years of the seventeenth century, it might seem logical to infer that the colonists brought with them the English law as it stood at that time. In fact, however, it was not an early seventeenth century body of doctrine which the English colonists transported to these shores; rather was it the law of the closing years of that century, or of the early years of the eighteenth century. The primitive English settlements which developed in the first half of the seventeenth century at Jamestown (settled 1607), at Plymouth (1620), at Boston (1630), in Rhode Island (1636–1639), on the Connecticut and at New Haven (1636–1638), in Maine (1635–1640), and on the Chesapeake (1634) had in their early years little need for refined legal doctrine; and in some of these colonies indeed the theocratic principles which animated the settlers precluded a reproduction of English models. Comparatively simple codes of law were in not a few cases adopted by their legislatures or governors which sufficed for some decades. It was only gradually, with the development in the colonies of extensive commerce with the mother country, with one another, and with the West Indies, that the need for elaborated legal doctrines manifested itself; and the need, as it grew, was supplied by the adoption and assimilation, with modifications, of the contemporary English rules. The later settlements in New Jersey (1660–1670), the Carolinas (c. 1660–1680), and Pennsylvania (c. 1680) were still primitive when the eighteenth century opened. New York, though one of the earliest settlements, did not pass under English rule, and hence did not receive English institutions, till 1664.[1] Hence the developing law of the colonies was modeled chiefly on the English law as it existed at the end of the seventeenth century.

The fact that the essential reception of English law took place at the end, rather than at the beginning, of the seventeenth century had important consequences for colonial, and hence for American, law. At the

[1] In the capitulation of New Amsterdam it was stipulated according to a judicial author that "the Dutch should remain in the enjoyment of their own customs regarding their inheritances, and that all differences of contracts and bargains made before the 27th of August, 1664, should be determined according to the manner of the Dutch." 37 N.Y. 253 (1867).

opening of the century, Elizabeth was still on the throne and the legal system was still encumbered with many survivals, both institutional and doctrinal, that had accumulated in the five and a half centuries since the Conquest. By the end of the century, much of this had been swept away. Aside from the inevitable changes which a developing commercial economy necessarily brought about in a system whose bases were feudal, that century saw the reforming zeal of the Puritans, the changes which accompanied the Stuart restoration, the abdication of the last of the Stuarts, and the adoption of the Bill of Rights. The English law as it stood at the end of the century had begun to take on a semblance of modernity. Much of the detail of its earlier history had ceased to be of interest to any but the antiquarian.

That law had behind it five centuries of development. It was not until about the beginning of the thirteenth century, after the power of the Norman conquerors, built for a century and a half, had firmly extended itself into all the ramifications of English economic and social life, that there began definitely to emerge in England a national system of justice to supplement and ultimately to supplant the system of communal and seignorial courts which prevailed at the time of the Conquest. By means of itinerant royal judges who periodically examined into the proceedings of the local courts and also held court themselves in the several counties, and by means of central courts in London exercising power over the whole kingdom, the local courts were welded into a national system, and the seignorial courts were gradually displaced. By the middle of the fourteenth century, England had a substantially uniform system for the administration of justice and a body of rules of law nationwide in their application—a "common" law as opposed to the diverse local rules or customs which had formerly been applied by the communal and feudal courts and which continued to be applied by them until their eventual disappearance. It was on account of its national applicability that the system of legal doctrine and procedure thus established and developed, through the succeeding centuries, came to be known as the "common law." By the end of the seventeenth century, this had come to be a highly elaborated body of doctrine, mainly in the fields of real property law, of the law of torts, and of criminal law. In other branches of the law, particularly in the fields which now go by the name of contract and quasi contract, there had been little development; and to the fields of commercial law—the law of mercantile transactions, of negotiable instruments, of insurance, and the like—the common law was still largely a stranger.

The somewhat one-sided body of doctrine which had thus come to be known as the common law, and which governed the adjudications of the courts of law, had no close kinship with the systems of legal doctrine prevailing on the continent of Europe. It was largely an indigenous English product, developed by English judges who, at least in the centuries immediately following the Conquest, in not a few cases were unacquainted with the rich legal heritage of Rome, and in some cases were determined to have none of it. This is not to say that ideas of Roman origin did not find their way into the structure built by the architects of the common law; but they formed no part of the foundation. In those branches of English law which were thus developed by the courts of law, a distinctive terminology and a distinctive group of concepts continue to set the law of England, and of all countries, including our own, which inherited their law from England, apart from that of Scotland and of the Continent, and of those non-European countries which have inherited or appropriated their law from Continental sources. On the civil side—and the discussion is relevant only to the civil side of the law, for on the criminal side the law of the several Continental states can hardly be said to have a common character—there have thus come to be in the Western world, and in the countries beyond which have borrowed their law from it, two great bodies of doctrine, the one of English, the other of Roman, origin: the "common" law and the "civil" law.[2]

But, as noted at previous points, the courts of law shared the field of civil proceedings with other courts. The courts of law, the Court of Chancery, the Court of Admiralty, and the ecclesiastical courts each participated independently in the development of different branches of legal doctrine, with no workable machinery for coordinating and reconciling their efforts.[3]

The extraordinary sequence of events through which the Court of Chancery had come into existence and established itself as the most powerful of the civil courts and as the creator of new branches of legal doctrine has already been reviewed. In addition to special bodies of doctrine affecting such matters as guardianship and trusteeship, it developed pervasive equitable doctrines, so called, applicable to many of the fields of doctrine built up by the law courts. Dominated in its formative period by churchmen, its procedure and not a little of its doctrine

---

[2] The somewhat confusing use of the term "the civil law" (the expounders and practitioners of which are thus frequently referred to as "the civilians") to designate the civil law of Roman ancestry as opposed to the civil law of English ancestry, is to be traced to the title of the historic compilation of the Roman civil law, made under Justinian and his successors, termed the "Corpus Juris Civilis."

[3] The House of Lords did indeed enjoy appellate power over all the courts of England; but it did not sit as a court with sufficient frequency or regularity to mold the law with a firm hand. (The development by which there was in time to be constituted, under the name of the House of Lords, a supreme court of the kingdom composed of the most distinguished judges of the land, was still more than a century off.) On the criminal side, however, the Court of King's Bench exercised almost exclusive power to formulate doctrine and procedure.

derived from the canonical law, itself developed on Roman foundations.

The doctrines applied by the admiralty court, while not specifically Roman in origin, were yet derived chiefly from Mediterranean sources, and were thus alien to the common law. Since the admiralty law has been subjected to relatively little statutory change, divergencies between the doctrines of the common law and those of admiralty law, applicable to substantially parallel situations on land and water, respectively, persist— divergencies the more striking when, as in our federal courts, both sets of doctrine may be applied in the same day by the same judge, with divergent results.

A fourth body of doctrine, and this too of Roman rather than of English origin, was applied by the ecclesiastical courts. These courts, a part of the hierarchical organization of the Church of England, enjoyed, at the period of which we speak, only a remnant of the extensive jurisdiction, criminal as well as civil, which their predecessors, the ecclesiastical courts of the Roman Catholic church, had possessed in the period following the Conquest. During the Middle Ages, the ecclesiastical courts had been progressively shorn of jurisdiction, and the jurisdiction of the courts of law correspondingly extended; and the Reformation left them only jurisdiction over matrimonial actions (i. e., support, separation, and annulment, judicial divorce being still in the future) and over the probate of wills of personal property and the administration of decedents' estates. Thus, while the Court of Chancery was developing the law governing one class of fiduciaries—trustees—the ecclesiastical courts were developing their own parallel doctrines regarding the duties and liabilities of another type of fiduciary—the executor or administrator of the estate of a decedent.

Although, as has been seen, the diffuse and complex judicial structure of England was nowhere transplanted in the colonies, all the four bodies of doctrine just mentioned were inevitably drawn upon as the needs of the developing society of the colonies demanded. But (except for the field of admiralty law, in which the Crown retained direct control of adjudication[4]) the English rules were by no means taken over unaltered. Aside from the few statutes which Parliament expressly made applicable to all the colonies, the law of the several colonies was shaped in large measure by the statutes passed by their own legislatures. But despite the divergencies in law from colony to colony, its substructure remained that of the contemporary English law.

The maintenance of a common legal base in all the colonies was not entirely due to their community of English origin and English tradition.

---

[4] The British admiralty court exercised also, in the period under discussion, a limited criminal jurisdiction which, however, was never fully instituted in the colonial admiralty courts and disappeared after the Revolution.

So far as concerned colonial statutory law, the Crown, acting through the Privy Council, exercised, though sparingly, the power of veto to enforce the provision, found in each of the colonial charters, that the laws enacted by the colonial legislature should be consistent with the law of England. Nor were the colonial courts entirely free to depart from English doctrine at their pleasure. Appeal lay from the highest court in each colony to the Privy Council, where the claim was that the colonial court had failed to conform to fundamental principles of English law, or to applicable British statutes.[5] In addition, certain acts of Parliament regulating particular matters of judicial procedure in the colonies helped to give them, to a limited extent, a common procedural base. Moreover, uniformity in statutory law was aided by the temptation to copy an existing statute rather than confront the labor of creating another and perhaps better one—a factor responsible, indeed, for a considerable portion of what uniformity is to be found today in American statutory law.[6]

Indubitably, without this development under English dominion of a firm common base for the jurisprudence of the colonies—a body of doctrine that might justifiably be called American law—the subsequent history of our law, under a regime in which the states have been subject in this field to virtually no central control whatever, would have been one of far greater diversity than has actually been the case.

2. THE HISTORIC ROLE OF COURT AND LEGISLATURE

To an extraordinary extent English law as it stood at the beginning of the eighteenth century was judge-made law. Although royal edicts and acts of Parliament had made their contribution, it had been constructed chiefly by the judges over the centuries, not by any process of deliberate enactment, but piecemeal, case by case, until in one area after another there emerged something resembling a rational set of principles. Needless to say, under this procedure principles developed in one field of the law were not always consistent with those developed in another; and if a general characterization of the body of English doctrine as it stood at the opening of the eighteenth century were attempted, it would be fair to say that it consisted of a number of separate bodies of doctrine each applicable to a particular field. The work of the colonial legislatures did little to integrate these somewhat disjointed bodies of doctrine into a system; nor

[5] For an account of the appellate jurisdiction over the American colonies see Hazeltine, Appeals to the Lords of Trade from Colonial Courts, 1894 Report of the Amer. Hist. Assn, 299; Schlesinger, Colonial Appeals to the Privy Council, 28 Pol. Sci. Quart. 270, 433 (1913). Appellate review of the judgments of the courts of the British colonies is still exercised by the Judicial Committee of the Privy Council.

[6] That this process of borrowing is not a recent invention is suggested by the provision of the Northwest Ordinance of 1787 (Sec. 5) directing the governor and judges to "adopt and publish . . . such laws of the original States, criminal and civil, as may be necessary."

did the colonial judges, dependent on the royal governors, leave any noticeable impression on our law.

In the formation of the new state governments that ensued upon the breakdown of the royal authority, the establishment of the judiciary as a separate branch of government was a notable feature. Only to a limited degree were the judicial powers of the governor and his council, or of the legislature, so characteristic a feature of the colonial governments, retained.[7] By the opening of the new century there existed in most of the states a strong court of last resort. Thus was provided the agency for the development of an independent American law, no longer a subsidiary but a rival of the English law in the world of the common law.

But in the early decades of the Republic it was by no means everywhere that men were willing to entrust to the judiciary the shaping of the law of the new nation. The rising spirit of equalitarianism was intolerant of lawyers as a special order, and of the judiciary as leagued with it. The notion that the law was not properly the possession of a monopolistic profession, but was equally understandable by any man of intelligence, was so congenial to the spirit of the times that in several states men wholly without legal training were elevated to high judicial office. The common sense of the legislature was looked to as adequate to the formulation of a new code of law to supplant the judge-made English law of the colonies, now, like everything English, condemned as unfit for a free nation.[8] The people, through their elected representatives, and on the basis of common sense instead of precedents largely developed in a semifeudal society, would provide a new code of laws congenial to republican institutions.

During the early decades of the century, much was done to repeal colonial statutes deemed archaic, and to discard by statute rules of law no longer suitable to the growing commercial society of the new century; the ancient land law was cleared of many feudal survivals; not a few new legal inventions were effected by statute. A beginning, and in some states more than a beginning, was made toward the reform of the antiquated criminal justice of the colonial era. But the comprehensive legislative reconstruction envisaged by early enthusiasts did not materialize.

The failure of the legislative process to fulfill the expectations of its

[7] In New York, however, the upper house of the legislature, numbering thirty-four, together with the highest judges of the state, numbering four, constituted the court of last resort (the Court of Errors) till 1849. In Connecticut we read that in 1814 a defendant convicted of a capital crime "applied to the General Assembly for a pardon, or for other relief; alleging some informalities in the proceedings of the court preparatory to his trial" and that "the General Assembly thought fit to order a new trial." Lung's Case, 1 Conn. 428 (1815).

[8] Hostility to things English reached such a point in the post-Revolution decades that in several states the citation of English decisions made after the Declaration of Independence was forbidden. See Aumann, The Changing American Legal System, 78 ff. (1940).

early panegyrists is to be explained chiefly by the inherent difficulty of envisaging in advance the legal needs of a developing society; in large part however it was due to the absence, in our legislative framework, of that element of permanent professional personnel which was responsible for the ambitious legislative projects of Napoleonic France and of other Continental countries. Thus to the courts fell the task of remolding the law to the needs of the new time.

Particularly in the field of commercial law, in which the English courts had, up to the time of the separation, made little more than a beginning, did the courts of the first half, and particularly of the second quarter, of the last century play a creative role. Drawing heavily on the writings of the Continental jurists in this field, they created a firm base on which has been reared, partly by legislation and partly by further judicial elaboration, the unprecedentedly complex structure of the commercial law of our day.

No small part of the materials out of which the courts reared this structure was supplied to them by a constellation of American legal commentators, some of them judges, but most of them practitioners, and hardly any of them of that type of purely academic legal scholar which has played so large a role in the development of the law of the Continent, and is today increasingly important with us also. Chief among the commentators perhaps, were Joseph Story, long on the Supreme Court of the United States, and James Kent, long Chancellor of New York; their labors were encyclopedic. In a number of special fields, other writers made important contributions. It is indeed to these commentaries, on which the judges of all the states drew as from a common source, that is due much of the basic uniformity of American law.

By the middle of the century the foundations of American law had been firmly laid, and a substantial superstructure erected. The century that has since passed has been one of incessant elaboration, both by the courts and by the legislatures. New fields of law have been opened up, and here the structure has for the most part been built by the legislature, the work of the courts being merely that of elaboration. In the older areas of the law, however, the legislature has for the most part been content to leave substantially untouched the legal edifices built by the courts over the years. To an extent that astonishes the Continental observer, these branches of our law still repose not in statute but in a tradition that has come down to us through the years, in some instances through the centuries, in the opinions written by the courts in particular cases and in the books written by the commentators.[9] Nor does there seem much like-

---

[9] It will be apparent that the term "unwritten" sometimes applied to these doctrines is inapt (the more so since the written records of the development of English and American legal doctrines extend unbroken over a longer period, and are char-

lihood that these areas of the law—the law of contracts, of torts, of agency, of trusts, of real estate in large part (the list is merely partial)— will in the near future be removed from the category of the traditional, and reframed in the form of statute.

The term traditional as applied to these areas of our legal doctrine is here used merely to emphasize their non-legislative character. It is not intended to convey the impression that such legal doctrine is necessarily ancient. Much of it has indeed come down, with only minor alterations, over a period of some centuries. On the other hand, much of it is of recent and some of it even of contemporary origin. Despite the unremitting invasion by legislation of areas formerly entirely traditional, and despite the incessant labor of the courts in settling questions hitherto undecided, the necessity for further developing legal doctrine continues, even in such well-traveled fields of our traditional law as the law of contracts, of torts, and of agency.

3. THE ROLE OF PRECEDENT

A conventional American law library, such as is found in law schools or in the larger bar associations, contains complete sets of the reports of the opinions handed down by the highest courts of each of the states, and by the Supreme Court of the United States (with additional sets, perhaps, of the reports of subordinate appellate courts, state and federal). These volumes, aggregating thousands, contain in turn hundreds of thousands of cases.

To the layman, each of these cases is likely to be pictured as a "precedent" controlling the court in its disposition of a case presenting similar facts. Only a small—indeed a minute—portion of these cases (many of which in any event deal with statutes, doctrines, or subject matters long since obsolete) could, however, answer this description. Relatively seldom does a case present facts so nearly identical with those of some reported case that the previous holding can be used automatically, so to speak, to decide the instant case. It is not as a storehouse of "precedents" in this

---

acterized by a greater fullness and abundance, than is the case with any other modern legal system). What is intended to be conveyed by the term "unwritten" is that none of the doctrines forming this body of law has been authoritatively formulated in a single statement. Our non-statutory law is also often referred to as "case law." This term fails to reflect the important place accorded, as a source of our traditional law, to the writings of commentators. The term "case law" is by no means properly applicable exclusively to the doctrines enunciated by the courts in the fields in which the law rests only on a traditional base. In those fields in which statutory enactment forms the base of the law (eg., the field of workman's compensation) there is also a vast body of "case law"—the sum of the doctrine and distinctions which the courts and administrative tribunals have developed in applying the statutory provisions to particular cases.

sense, but as a source of reasoned doctrine, that the reports of previous cases are chiefly important. In stating in its "opinion" its view as to what legal doctrine is applicable to the case before it, and how that doctrine should be applied to facts of that case, the court—and it is chiefly the appellate courts that write such opinions—is in effect presenting a commentary or gloss on some traditional doctrine, or on some statutory provision, amplifying it, refining it, distinguishing it from some related rule. Thus our legal rules, both traditional and statutory, are subjected to a ceaseless process of re-evaluation and minor modification, sometimes of erosion, sometimes of accretion. The name by which a rule is known may remain unchanged for decades, but meanwhile its content may, by almost imperceptible steps, have been materially changed.

Thus, the courts are continually but slowly making and remaking the law by degrees. Abrupt changes can come ordinarily only by legislative action. There are, however, some rules of law which cannot be modified by degrees—a choice must be made in favor of one or another of two possible rules, and the choice once made may not be undone by the courts except by a complete reversal, unequivocally announced. Such a reversal, though within the power of the courts—or at least of the highest court in each jurisdiction—is, however, seldom made. The courts guide themselves by the accepted doctrine of "stare decisis." This doctrine originally appears to have meant no more than that the court, having decided in a given way a case presenting a given state of facts, should "stand" on its decision when subsequently confronted with a case presenting substantially similar facts. In time however the doctrine has passed on from the limited sphere of the *decision,* i.e., the actual disposition of the case, to the *opinion,* i.e., the reasons announced for making such disposition, or in short, the rule or doctrine then announced. Having announced its adherence to a given rule or doctrine, the court is under an obligation to adhere thereto. Drastic reversal is improper. Peripheral modifications and qualifications, distinctions, refinements may be resorted to, to ameliorate the rigor of the rule, as originally announced; but repudiation is permissible only in exceptional cases.[10] Such at least is the received doctrine, to which obeisance continues to be made by bench and bar alike. In recent decades, however, there has become manifest a marked tendency on the part of some of our high courts to ignore settled rules in hard cases without announcing an outright repudiation, asserting instead, sometimes with dubious justification, that the problem before them is different from those presented to their predecessors who framed the rule. Professional literature recurrently carries complaints

[10] The Supreme Court of Georgia, which has seven judges, makes it a rule not to overrule previous decisions unless at least five of the judges concur. See Wheatley v. State, 114 Ga. 175 (1901).

that the resulting lack of certainty in the law makes it impossible for the lawyer to advise his client with any confidence.[11]

The lawmaking function of the courts is thus twofold. On the one hand, they interpret and thereby elaborate—sometimes they indeed in effect nullify—the statutory enactments (including many state constitutional provisions essentially statutory in character) from which so much of our present-day law takes its starting point. On the other hand, they develop, modify, and occasionally radically change the law which rests not on statutory enactments but on traditional doctrines, much of it, as we have seen, going back to English doctrines of pre-Revolutionary vintage.

It would be impracticable to attempt any quantitative statement designed to indicate the extent to which the law under which we live is traditional rather than statutory. In some areas—particularly in the field of regulatory statutes and in newer fields of private redress, such as workmen's compensation—the statutory element obviously bulks far larger than it does in such ancient fields as the law of partnership or of real property. But in virtually all fields, there is an interpenetration of the statutory and the traditional, making a quantitative generalization impossible. Suffice it to say that a considerable part of the work of the courts, doubtless much the greater part, deals not with matters of traditional legal doctrine, but with the construction and application of enactments—constitutions and statutes, both federal and state, treaties with foreign countries, interstate compacts, municipal and other local ordinances, and with the great mass of regulations issued by administrative agencies, federal and local, to which has been delegated, under the statutes or ordinances authorizing their creation, the power to promulgate such regulations supplementary to the statutes or ordinances.

The study of a legal problem, therefore, varies sharply accordingly as the matter is or is not governed by an enactment—whether constitution, statutes, treaty, ordinance, or regulation. If it is, the analysis begins with a study of the enacted provision, and of the decisions and opinions of the courts in cases involving that provision, traditional doctrines of law being resorted to only where these fail to resolve the problem. If, on the other hand, no enacted provision is involved, the examination may range over any part of the body of traditional doctrine in which the searcher thinks light may be found.

Even where a matter is controlled by statutory provision, however, it

---

[11] The Supreme Court of the United States has displayed greater willingness to overrule previous holdings than have the high courts of many of the states. As long ago as 1944, Justice Roberts of that Court declared that the tendency to disregard precedent "has become so strong of late as, in my view, to shake confidence in the consistency of decisions, and leave the courts below in an uncharted sea of doubt and difficulty . . ." Mahnich v. Southern S. S. Co., 321 U.S. 96, 113.

by no means follows that the body of traditional doctrine antedating the statute is irrelevant to the problem. Not a few statutes, particularly in the field of commercial law, are in large part attempts to codify, in systematic form, rules of law which existed as traditional doctrine for many decades, in some cases for centuries, prior to the enactment of the statute; and in difficult problems arising under such codified provisions resort to the antecedent doctrine is often extremely helpful. Moreover, even in statutes which attempt to break new ground, traditional phrases or expressions are employed, having a wealth of meaning developed in connection with long-standing doctrines; and in using them, the legislature has in effect imported into the new statute as much of the traditional meaning of the established phrases as is pertinent to the new statutory rule.

The extent to which a statutory enactment will call for judicial construction depends in part on how clearly it is drafted, but in perhaps equal or greater part on how detailed are its provisions. If the draftsman of a statute successfully attempts to anticipate as exhaustively as possible the various categories of concrete fact likely to arise under it, and provides specifically for each situation, little is left for the courts. If, on the other hand, the statute is couched in general terms, expressing merely what might be termed its theory or rationale, the burden of amplification laid upon the courts is enormous. The Sherman Antitrust Act of 1890 furnishes a striking illustration. It denounced merely "every contract, combination . . . or conspiracy in restraint of interstate and foreign trade or commerce" and "every person who shall monopolize or attempt to monopolize . . . any part of such trade or commerce. . . ." Later amendments have specifically condemned a few enumerated practices (such as certain interlocking directorates); but in the main, the determination of what is and what is not condemned by the statute has been made, ex post facto, by the Supreme Court. After nearly seventy-five years it is still often impossible to know, with respect to particular forms of business activity or association, whether or not they are condemned by the statute; the best one can do is to prognosticate the probable view of the Supreme Court should the question finally reach that tribunal.[12]

[12] A new area of the law, in which not even the slightest guidance is provided by the statute, was placed in the hands of the federal courts, and thus ultimately of the Supreme Court, by the provision of the Labor-Management Relations Act of 1947 (the Taft-Hartley law) giving the federal courts jurisdiction of "suits for violation of contracts between an employer and a labor organization representing employees in an industry affecting [interstate or foreign] commerce." 29 U.S. Code, Sec. 185. As construed by the Supreme Court this grant of jurisdiction of a class of cases formerly cognizable by the federal courts only if diversity of citizenship and a requisite monetary issue were present, the federal court in such a case being obligated to apply state law, was "transmuted into a mandate to the federal courts to fashion a whole body of substantive federal law appropriate for the complicated and touchy problems raised by collective bargaining." Frankfurter, J., dissenting in

In the absence of a controlling precedent in its own state, a court is free to follow the views of a court elsewhere (the courts of England, Canada, or any other common-law jurisdiction being regarded as proper sources of light, equally with those of this country) or to formulate its own view without reference to authority. Traditionally, the courts of the older states, or those in which there has been a great deal of litigation with consequent resolution of many problems, have been the path-breakers, and have been followed by the courts of the newer and less populous states. At one period in our legal history, the highest courts of New York and Massachusetts had each its following, so to speak, among the courts of the less populous states; and in the characteristic divergence of opinion by those two courts on a number of legal doctrines lies the explanation for the lack of uniformity in those doctrines today.

4. LIMITATIONS ON THE POWER OF THE COURTS TO IMPROVE THE LAW

Although the courts have been permitted, through failure of the legis-latures to act, to make the law over considerable areas of legal doctrine (and, in the fields declared by the courts to be governed by the constitu-tional requirement of due process of law, they have made law which it is beyond the power of the legislatures to change), the power of the courts to effect, even within those areas, any substantial improvement of the law has been and continues to be very limited. Unawareness of the governing limitations is responsible for much of the criticism occasionally directed at the courts for their supposed failure in this field.

The overriding limitation on the power of the courts to improve the law is that they have no power of initiative—they must wait for a case to be presented to them. Since, in effect, judicial lawmaking is practicable only for the appellate courts, and an appeal can be taken only at the instance and at the financial risk of the losing party in the court of first instance, the pervasive character of this limitation is painfully obvious.

But even within the framework of the cases presented to them, the power of the courts to improve the law is severely limited. Specifically (to enumer-ate the three chief areas of law improvement) our courts have but limited power to correct erroneous doctrines, they have virtually no power to make the law more uniform among the several states, and they have no power to codify the law.

Textile Workers Union v. Lincoln Mills, 353 U.S. 448, 461 (1957). Congress could of course create a federal law in this field by statute, but it has not attempted to do so. See Bickel and Wellington, Legislative Purpose and the Judicial Process: The Lincoln Mills Case, 71 Harv. Law Rev. 1 (1957).

Correction of erroneous doctrine

It has already been pointed out that the outright repudiation by the courts of a doctrine previously announced by them is regarded as unwarranted except in extreme cases. Two considerations readily suggest themselves in support of this conservative use of power by the courts. The first is, in theory, unanswerable: If the rule adopted by the court has been left undisturbed by the legislature, which at all times has plenary power to abrogate it and substitute another rule by statute, the legislature must be assumed to have determined that the rule is satisfactory and calls for no correction. The element of unreality present in this reasoning will be apparent to anyone familiar with the legislative process. We shall shortly return to this matter.

The second consideration is, however, in its application at least to many legal doctrines, firmly planted in reality. When the highest court of the state announces a doctrine, the legal profession, and all those whose affairs are affected by such an announcement, govern their future transactions and decisions accordingly; a subsequent refusal of the court to apply that doctrine, on the ground that it seems, on reconsideration, a mistaken one, would work serious injury on those who had acted in reliance upon it. Let us assume that the court has clearly announced the doctrine that one who is reasonably careful in selecting an independent contractor to perform a given piece of work is not liable for injuries negligently inflicted by such contractor on another in the course of such performance. Relying on the doctrine thus announced, one who has carefully selected a contractor refrains from insuring himself against possible claims against him arising out of the contractor's negligence. He is nevertheless sued by a person injured by the negligence of the contractor. Should the court, now concluding that the doctrine formerly announced was unsound to begin with, or has become obsolete through the change of conditions under which work of the kind in question is today performed, refuse to abide by its former pronouncement, the uninsured defendant is burdened with a liability he readily could and would have insured against, but for his reliance on the only existing authoritative definition of his liability.

Guided by these considerations, the highest court of the United Kingdom, the House of Lords, has steadfastly refused to repudiate, or even seriously to modify, a rule of law, or a statutory construction, once deliberately announced. It regards such a change as exclusively a legislative function. Our own courts have not, on the whole, taken so consistently logical a position. Outright repudiations of announced rules have been few, but they have from time to time been made. The favored doctrine controlling the courts in this matter is that they will not disturb a settled rule where property rights have been established in reliance on it. Where property rights are not involved, they will do so with reluctance.

The Supreme Court of the United States has contributed some of the most complete and far-reaching repudiations of established doctrine known to our legal history. In 1938, in the case of Erie Railroad v. Tompkins, as will shortly be noted, it repudiated a construction of the federal rules-of-decision act which had remained unquestioned for nearly a century—unquestioned not only as the correct construction of that act, but unquestioned also in the sense that little, if any, attempt had ever been made in Congress to procure an amendment of the act itself. In 1943, in the case of Williams v. North Carolina, it expressly repudiated the doctrine announced almost forty years previously (in Haddock v. Haddock) as to the lack of jurisdiction in a divorce action of the plaintiff's state of residence if that state was not also the state of matrimonial domicile—a doctrine in reliance on which, doubtless many a deserted wife had, on advice of counsel, ignored divorce proceedings instituted against her in another state by her fugitive husband.

In sum, if a high court overturns an established rule, it may work injustice to interests created in reliance on the rule; if it clings to an unjust role it often lays the foundation for further injustices. To solve the dilemma the suggestion has been put forward that the court might, in a given case, uphold the established rule but announce that as to all transactions entered into or occurrences taking place after the date of its decision, it would follow a different rule, which it would simultaneously formulate and announce; and a few state courts of last resort have in fact employed this device in special classes of cases.[13] The difficulty with this suggestion is that a new rule of private law should, ordinarily, take effect not immediately upon its announcement but at a later date, announced in advance; the interval being necessary to enable those concerned to learn of the new rule and to prepare to act in accordance therewith. Moreover, a high court, pressed by its judicial business, is hardly a suitable agency for the enactment of new legislation. Finally, an announcement by the court of its future intentions would not be binding upon its membership, even if still composed of the same individuals, at a later date. The remedy is thus to be sought from the legislative rather than from the judicial branch; unless the judges of the high court were indeed vested within prescribed areas with express legislative power.

It has been pointed out that it is unrealistic to infer, from the failure of the legislature to change a doctrine or a statutory construction promulgated by the courts, that the legislature approves of it. Such an inference is no doubt permissible where, as frequently happens, a determined effort has been made in the legislature to change the judicial doctrine, and has failed. Where no such effort has been made, however, the only inference to be drawn from legislative inaction is that the judicial doctrine, even if un-

[13] The Supreme Court has held that such a procedure by a state court raises no federal question. Great Northern Ry. v. Sunburst Oil Co., 287 U.S. 358, 366 (1932).

satisfactory, has evoked no such active opposition as to generate a successful drive for reform.

Where a rule judicially announced creates unsettlement and inconvenience in an important section of the business community or of organized labor, or runs counter to the views or convictions of important religious or racial groups, or to the practices or administrative policies of important government officials, or otherwise evokes concerted criticism or opposition, attempts at legislative correction usually follow promptly. Where, on the other hand, the rule, though patently obsolete or unwise, trenches on no important group interest but only on the interest of scattered individuals, and evokes condemnation only from the academic critic, the individual legislator is unlikely to bestir himself even to introduce corrective legislation, much less to press its enactment upon the party leaders in charge of the legislative program; while the latter are far too occupied in trying to placate and reconcile the contending special interests, industrial, trade union, agricultural, philanthropic, educational, religious, ideological, and racial—all intent on their particular legislative projects or hostilities—to take the initiative or even to give much aid to law reform proposals that have nothing to recommend them except that they are in the general interest.[14]

Two illustrations from the legislative history of New York will perhaps illustrate the point. In 1925 the highest court of that state decided that the innocent purchaser of a stolen "bearer interim certificate"—a paper issued by an underwriting house to a subscriber to a bond issue, acknowledging payment and undertaking to deliver the bonds subscribed for when received from the issuing borrower—had no rights therein as against the person from whom it was stolen. This decision, based on a technically correct construction of the Negotiable Instruments Law, ran counter to the understanding and the established practice of the New York financial community with respect to a large class of securities, of which the particular security in question, the "interim certificate," was merely one type. Accordingly, these interests promptly procured the passage of legislation in effect changing the rule. On the other hand, that same court had in 1895 declared that if a debtor in good faith pays the creditor's customary agent, unaware that the creditor has died, and without ready means of ascertaining that fact, and if the agent fails to remit the money paid him to his deceased principal's executor or administrator, the latter may exact a second payment from the debtor. The injustice, under modern conditions, of this ancient rule was recognized by the court, which declared however that a change could be made only by the legislature. The rule has been repeatedly criticized since, but thus far has not been changed. Debtors are not an organized group.

[14] See Note: Congressional Reversal of Supreme Court Decisions 1945–1957, 71 Harv. Law Rev. 1324 (1958).

The inertia in matters of law reform thus characteristic of our legislatures has led to the view that there should be established in every state and in the national government a permanent and influential governmental agency for law reform, adequately staffed to explore the need for change in existing rules, whether traditional or statutory, to draft proposals for revision, and to press for their enactment.[15] In several states, such an agency already exists, and substantial improvements in the law of those states has resulted. Limitations of staff, and, perhaps still more importantly, an inherent limit on the amount of corrective legislation which the legislative machinery can tolerate in a given legislative session, have made impossible the enactment of more than a portion of the proposals advanced by these agencies; and doubtless many more could profitably have been advanced. It becomes increasingly clear that basic improvement in this field can be expected only from a reform of the whole system of legislation, so as to relieve the legislature from the almost impossible task of enacting all the laws which need enacting.

It is beyond the province of this volume to explore this question. This much may, however, be pointed out. Delegation by the legislature of power to amplify legislation has hitherto been confined to those fields of law that require administration by public officials, such administrative officers being then also vested with power to promulgate regulations supplementary to statute. In those fields in which there is no occasion for administration but only for adjudication by the courts—the whole field of private law—there has been no delegation of legislative power. There has indeed been what might be called a delegation by default: the courts, in the absence of statute, have made the law over wide areas. But they have made it only incidentally, in deciding established cases; they have not expressly promulgated it as law. The question presents itself whether there is not room in this field, as in the field of regulatory legislation, for a delegation of legislative power to some agency better qualified for the task than is the legislature; and that agency might well be one in whose determinations the courts participated to an important extent.

This discussion of the limitations on the power of the courts to correct erroneous doctrine would be incomplete did one not, in concluding, take note of a factor prone to inhibit the exercise of that power by the courts even where its exercise is not open to the difficulties above reviewed. Judges of courts of last resort are characteristically of ripe years. Their minds were formed in the professional climate of a previous generation. They have been educated in a profession whose habits of thought and indeed whose function is conservatory. Although many of them retain great flexibility of mind, and are quite accessible to ideas of change, as a group they are not the kind of people who supply the motive power by which new advances are made.

[15] See Friendly, The Gap in Law-making, 63 Col. Law Rev. 787 (1963).

Promotion of uniformity of law among the states

With the destruction of the British authority in America disappeared those legal institutions which alone had imposed some degree of uniformity upon the jurisprudence of the several colonies—the statutes enacted by Parliament, and the veto power and appellate jurisdiction of the Privy Council. Thenceforth, each state was free to develop as it chose its own body of doctrine. Nor did the coming of the Constitution change the situation. That instrument provided no means for reconciling the divergencies in legal doctrine which had even then begun to develop among the several states, and which have continued to develop. Only to the limited extent to which the Constitution made possible the transfer from the field of state legislation to that of federal legislation the rules governing particular subjects, did the Constitution hold out any prospect of substituting nationwide law for the discordant law of the several states.[16]

American law, it has consequently been said, is merely a "geographical expression"—a picturesque way of emphasizing that there is in the United States (if we exclude the limited field of federal statutory law and the traditional admiralty law administered exclusively by the federal courts) no body of law having authority over the whole country, but rather fifty separate bodies of law, each autonomous within its own state[17] (not to mention the additional bodies of local law, each distinctive, found in the District of Columbia, Puerto Rico, the Canal Zone, and the Virgin Islands).

Yes, despite its seeming fragmentation, the law of this country, however great may be the divergencies at particular points, exhibits a basic uniformity. The key to this community of legal pattern is to be found chiefly in two factors—on the one hand, the common ancestry of nearly all the half-hundred separate bodies of doctrine, giving them a large measure of family resemblance, and on the other, the extent to which they have borrowed one another's garments. Not only have the judges in each state, when confronted with a doctrinal problem, sought guidance from the solutions reached by their judicial brethren in other states; the legislatures have also borrowed freely from one another, a successful statute in one state often being copied widely in others. Moreover, in some fields, as we shall see, the states have consciously cooperated to bring about uniformity in law. Thus it results that while it is never safe to assume without investigation that a particular rule of law, or a particular statutory provision,

[16] For the unorthodox view that it was in fact the intention of the framers of the Constitution that the national government should have power, through the federal courts as well as through Congress, to create in most fields a national law to supersede state law, see 1 Crosskey, Politics and the Constitution, 509 ff. (1953).

[17] Mention has already been made, however, of the duty imposed by the Constitution upon each state to give "full faith and credit" to the "public acts" of each state, and its consequent obligation, in certain cases, to enforce the law of other states rather than its own.

is in force in any given state, it is nevertheless true that doubtless the very great majority of legal rules are found in substantially uniform effect in most of the states, and that a substantial similarity of content, even if not of language, is to be found over most of the states on a large number of subjects regulated by statute. In this sense, therefore, there is a common core, and more than a core, of doctrine and statute, the country over; and it is in this sense that one may use the term "American law."

In one connection, indeed, the system created by the Constitution resulted, for almost a century of our history, in creating even further divergencies in our law. As has already been noted, a diversity of citizenship case, if the amount involved reaches the minimum provided by the federal statute, may be adjudicated in either a state or a federal court. Congress in the original Judiciary Act provided that "the laws of the several states except where the constitution, treaties or statutes of the United States shall otherwise require or provide shall be regarded as rules of decision in trials at common law in the courts of the United States in cases where they apply." So far as concerns state statutes and the construction given to such statutes by the state courts, the mandate of this provision (often termed the "rules-of-decision act") has been followed from the first; and in many cases, the decisional law of the states was similarly followed by the federal courts. Beginning with 1842, however, following the decision of the Supreme Court of the United States in the historic case of Swift v. Tyson,[18] the federal courts no longer regarded themselves obligated, in diversity cases, to conform to a holding of the appropriate state court on a question of "general law" and particularly on one of "general commercial law." Hence, in a given diversity case which turned upon such a question, the victory might go to the plaintiff if the action were adjudicated in the state court, but to the defendant if it were adjudicated in a federal court, or vice versa; and whether it was adjudicated in one or the other might in turn depend on the amount involved and on the skill of maneuver of the contending parties. Alongside of the discordant rules developed by the state courts, there thus emerged on a number of questions the "federal rule," which was often in accord with the minority rather than the majority of the state courts, and which indeed, in not a few instances, differed somewhat from both. This extraordinary situation came to an abrupt end in 1938 when the Supreme Court decided, in the landmark case of Erie Railroad v. Tompkins,[19] that the phrase "laws of the several states" in the rules-of-decision act includes, and under the Constitution must include, all the decisional law of the states as fully as their statute law. Except possibly as to questions on which no state decision exists, the "federal rule" in diversity cases is a thing of the past.

[18] 16 Peters 1 (1842).
[19] 304 U.S. 64 (1938).

The divergencies among the states extend into all fields of the law and are found both in the decisional and the statutory law. Over a large part of the field these divergencies cause perhaps no major inconvenience. In the important field of real estate law, whatever the divergencies, the rule governing rights in any particular piece of real estate can never be the subject of doubt; those rights are exclusively governed by the laws of the state in which the real estate is situated, and it matters not, except to lawyers and others from outside the state who may have occasion to deal with its real estate law, how divergent the rule of that state may be from the rule of other states. Other fields could be instanced in which the lack of uniformity in the legal rules of the several states causes no more than minor inconvenience to a limited class of persons. When we enter the field of commercial transactions, however, the situation is quite otherwise. Business operations, of course, disregard state lines, and every departure from uniformity in the laws of the states creates the likelihood that the law by which the rights of the parties may ultimately be decided will fail to correspond with what was in their minds at the time they entered into the transaction. Hence, for many decades there has been agitated the matter of seeking uniformity in the commercial law of the country. It has been said that the United States is the only country in the world which has no national commercial law.

Manifestly, the courts can do little if anything to cure this situation. In so far as it is the result of divergent court decisions in the several states, rather than of divergent statutes, it is difficult to see how it could have been avoided, once the courts of each state court became wholly autonomous. It is hardly to be wondered at that the highest court of a state, confronted with the responsibility of laying down for the first time the authoritative rule on a difficult question, should have declined to adopt a rule of which its judgment disapproved, merely because that rule had been enunciated in another state, in which the question had earlier happened to present itself for decision. Divergence of opinion on numerous points was bound to arise; and further divergencies may be expected in the future.

Dissatisfaction with divergencies in the law, particularly in the field of commercial transactions, led some eighty years ago to the proposal that the several states should each enact identical statutes, particularly in the field of commercial law, drafts of such statutes to be prepared by some central body cooperatively created. This proposal resulted in the creation, in 1890, of a Conference of Commissioners on Uniform Laws, members of which, several from each state, are appointed by the governor of the state pursuant to state statutory authority. These commissioners, a wholly extraconstitutional body, entirely without legal power, have prepared a number of proposed statutes affecting matters as to which they believe there should be uniformity, many of them outside the field of commercial law. Their success in procuring the enactment of these drafts by the legislatures of the several states has been varied. The Negotiable Instruments Act proposed by them in 1897 was enacted in every state and territory. The Sales Act, the Warehouse Receipts Act, and the Bills of Lading Act have also enjoyed widespread adoption. Some other proposals developed by them have met with indifferent success.

In collaboration with the American Law Institute, a non-official body shortly to be mentioned, the Commissioners on Uniform Law in 1952 submitted to the states a proposed Uniform Commercial Code, designed to supplant the statutes just mentioned and to provide new statutory law over a considerable portion of the field of commercial law. This code differs markedly from the uniform commercial laws hitherto proposed by the commissioners in that, while the former laws were in effect a restatement in systematic statutory form of doctrines which had been developed by the courts, the code embodies a number of radical proposals for change, none of which have hitherto been developed by the courts or by any legislature. The acceptance of the code by the state legislatures was at first very slow, but more recently has grown markedly. By 1963, twenty-eight states had adopted it. Until all do, the law on some commercial subjects will be less uniform than it was before the code was proposed.

Among the uniform laws enacted by the various states is one which has been also enacted by Congress, the Uniform Bills of Lading Act. Congress has made this statute applicable to all interstate railroad shipments. An attempt has been made to procure the enactment by Congress of the Uniform Sales Act but thus far without success. For a time the resistance to federal enactment of the Uniform Sales Act was no doubt attributable in part to the doubts entertained by many as to the constitutionality of such a federal enactment. Under early decisions of the Supreme Court, it was open to question whether, merely because a sale of goods contemplated an interstate shipment of the goods, the reciprocal rights and liabilities of buyer and seller thereby became a proper subject of federal regulation. The tendency of the Supreme Court in recent years to approve, as a proper exercise of the power to regulate interstate and foreign commerce, legislation regulating labor relations and working conditions in industries whose product enters interstate commerce, suggests that a federal sales act would today find no difficulty in resisting an attack upon its constitutionality. Indeed, it is difficult to believe that any portion of the Uniform Commercial Code, were it enacted by Congress to be applicable to all interstate and foreign transactions, would encounter constitutional obstacles. There appears to be no disposition on the part of the sponsors of the code, however, to seek federal enactment at this time.

It should be noted that the enactment of uniform statutes does not assure uniform law. It is virtually impossible to draft a statute in fields like those covered by the uniform laws with such elaboration and detail as to preclude the possibility of the necessity for a judicial construction of the statute in determining its application to particular cases. There can be no assurance that the courts of all the states before which such a provision may come for construction will construe it identically.[20] In connection with the Negotiable Instruments Law divergencies of construction on certain points caused the Commissioners on Uniform Law to propose clarifying amendments. But the difficulty of procuring enactment of such amendments by all the legislatures which enacted the original statute is obvious.

Codification

American law differs markedly from that of the Continent and indeed latterly even from that of England, in the extent to which its doctrines in basic areas still remain without authoritative form, to be collected, as already indicated, only by bringing together a plurality of opinions of judges and dicta of commentators. The proposal of the Commissioners of Uniform Laws in a particular field often represents—quite apart from the possibility of making the law more uniform—an attempt to codify a branch of the law which has hitherto reposed almost exclusively in the scattered opinions of the judges; to express in systematic, precise, comprehensive, and uniformly authoritative form a body of doctrine formerly unsystematic, sometimes uncertain, often incomplete, and nearly always compounded of contributions from courts and commentators of varying degrees of authoritativeness.

The foregoing, it should be noted, has reference only to substantive legal doctrine. On the procedural side, as we have already seen, our law is on the whole well codified, though exception must be made as to a few states.

The same master hand that drafted the New York procedural codes in the middle years of the last century, and thereby laid the foundation for modern American procedural law, attempted also a codification of substantive doctrines in the principal areas of the traditional law. But here he met failure in his own state, and in the country generally. Only California, and subsequently a few of the mountain states, adopted the Field code of substantive law. Even in the states which adopted it, its broad statements of principle were found, in practice, of little more help to the courts than the equally broad generalizations already to be found in legal handbooks. A code which would adequately cover these fields would call

[20] There would seem to be a place for a body, necessarily extraconstitutional, as is the Conference of Commissioners on Uniform State Laws itself, whose function would be to recommend the construction to be given to particular provisions of the uniform laws, especially the Uniform Commercial Code, as soon as question arose. The Conference of State Chief Justices could well assume responsibility for such a development.

for far more than the labor of a single individual—even one as capable as was Field. No significant attempt at such a code has been made since his time.

At the present time, although codification has its advocates, particularly in academic quarters, it may accurately be said that there exists no appreciable movement for comprehensive codification in either professional, judicial, or legislative circles. Imperfect and seemingly unscientific as the present system is, it is not apparently found so unworkable or time consuming, or so productive of uncertainty, as some of its critics contend.

Without attempting here to debate the relative gains and losses to be anticipated from a codification of one or another branch of our traditional legal doctrine, it may be pointed out that, with respect to certainty, it can hardly be said with accuracy that the essential doctrinal principles in these fields are at all uncertain, or would be renedered more certain by such express formulation as codification involves—such express formulation indeed running the risk that the diverse meanings or shades of meaning which ingenious minds may seek to give the particular words or phrases used my produce uncertainty where none existed before. Greater certainty is a desideratum not with respect to essential principles but rather with respect to the application of those principles to rather complicated states of fact; and a codification in any of these fields, so voluminous as to embrace specific rules readily applicable to the inexhaustible variety of fact situations presented to the courts, has never been drafted, nor is it likely to be: the practical difficulties are well-nigh insurmountable.

The writings of proponents of codification sometimes give the impression that a thoroughgoing codification of the basic doctrines of our law would eliminate the major part of the tremendous volume of decisional law to which the lawyer is now compelled to resort. The accuracy of this impression is open to question. As already indicated, a vast amount, quite possibly much the greater part, of the outpouring of opinions by courts and administrative tribunals, bears on questions arising not in the uncodified branches of the law, but rather under statutes. Not only would these not be eliminated by codification of our traditional law, but experience with such codifications as we have had, such as the Negotiable Instruments Law, now over half a century old, makes clear that codification itself does not put an end to, or perhaps even seriously check, the flood of decisional law.

In discussion of codification, attention is often drawn to the contrast between the relatively uncodified state of our own doctrinal law and the highly codified doctrinal law of Continental and other countries. The fact is sometimes lost sight of that foreign codes characteristically were brought into being not, as would be the case with us, merely to reduce existing law to more ordered form, but to replace existing law with new law, or to create law in fields where none existed. The Continental codes typically represented the creation of a national body of law to displace the numerous varied and confusing local bodies of law then in force. The adoption of codes, usually appropriated in bulk, by the nations of the East which arrived late on the commercial stage set by the Western countries, represented the filling of a vacuum. Even the adoption of the Field codes by California and by some of our mountain states is to be explained largely by the need to replace quickly the Spanish-Mexican legal rules which had previously prevailed there. Since under our system there is no way, short of constitutional amendment, of replacing the diverse law of the several states, on subjects exclusively within state cognizance, with a single law, the device of uniform state laws, already noted, has been resorted to; and it is in this effort to displace diverse local law with uniform law that, as on the Continent, our chief progress in codification has been made.

In the foregoing, attention has been confined to the field of traditional law. Codification has, however, an important role also in the domain of statutory law. The history of almost every body of statutory law exhibits, in its initial period, a succession of uncoordinated statutory provisions, enacted at different times, bearing on the same or related subjects, and amended from time to time in particular provisions, without comprehensive consideration of the effect of such amendments on related provisions. Eventually, the inconsistencies, perhaps conflicts, of the several provisions, together with the purely practical difficulty of physically assembling for examination all relevant statutory provisions bearing on a particular matter, compel a systematic codification. Such a codification, if competently made, and if thereafter used by the legislature as the starting point for all further statutory change, represents an immense improvement both in convenience and clarity.

In our federal statutory law, a codification was first attempted in 1874, under the name of the Revised Statutes of the United States. Congress, however, failed to conform the legislation of succeeding years to the pattern laid down by this codification; so there speedily accumulated a new body of statutory law, outside the Revised Statutes, unrelated to it, and eventually of equal if not greater size. In 1926, a new codification was adopted, under the name of the United States Code; and this code is now annually revised.

Restatement of the law

In some of the chief branches of the law in which legal doctrine still rests on a traditional rather than a statutory base, there have been developed, within recent decades, authoritative but non-statutory formulations known as "restatements." Such restatements exist in the branches of legal doctrine known as contracts, agency, torts, trust, property, restitution, and conflict of laws. These restatements have been issued by a group of some three hundred distinguished lawyers, judges, and law teachers organized since 1923 under the name of the American Law Institute. The work of restating the law of a given subject was entrusted to a "reporter" assisted by a committee of advisers, whose work was in turn reviewed by the governing body of the Institute, and by its membership. The resulting restatement thus represents in each case a far more authoritative formulation of existing doctrine (or, where existing doctrine is in doubt or confusion, a more authoritative formulation of preferred doctrine) than has previously been available. Moreover, whereas previous attempts to state the law had confined themselves almost wholly to questions on which adjudicated cases were available, the restatements have not hesitated to propose solutions of problems which, though perhaps never presented in reported cases, may nevertheless have arisen in non-litigated connections or may even have been litigated on more than one occasion before a trial court, the adjudications of which do not ordinarily enjoy publication.

The restatements, some of which have in recent years undergone revision, have been widely cited by the courts. In many of the cases in which a particular principle enunciated in a restatement has been cited by a court, that principle was already well established, in the body of law governing that court, by authoritative decided cases. Consequently, its presence in the restatement could hardly be regarded as having influenced the court in its decision. In not a few cases, however, particularly in states having but a meager body of decisional law, and in which the profession is consequently compelled to look chiefly to the decisions in other jurisdictions for guidance, the courts have adopted a statement of principle in the restatement as sufficiently authoritative to warrant its adoption without such exhaustive scrutiny and weighing of precedents from other jurisdictions as might formerly have been thought necessary.[21] No case has come to notice in which any court has abandoned a rule well settled by authoritative decisions in its own state in favor of a contrary rule chosen by the restatement.

5. ROLE OF THE COURTS IN MOLDING CRIMINAL PROCEDURE AND IN REGULATING LAW-ENFORCEMENT METHODS

In the preceding pages emphasis was placed on the limitations under which courts labor in reforming the law. An important qualification must be noted, however, with respect to procedural law, particularly where it touches upon constitutional rights, as it so often does in criminal proceedings. As is apparent from our discussion of those proceedings in earlier chapters, the courts, and more particularly the Supreme Court, have in

[21] The code of laws enacted by the legislature of the Virgin Islands in 1957 provides (Sec. 4) that the principles of the common law, as expressed in the Restatements, shall govern the courts in the absence of local laws to the contrary.

recent decades, and especially in the past decade, been engaged in remolding the law in that area to an unprecedented extent. Their function has been not so much to change existing rules of law as to promulgate new rules where none existed before.

Perhaps the most striking example of the lawmaking role of the courts in this field is that furnished by the history of the rule, now in force everywhere, that evidence obtained by the authorities through unlawful search of the defendant's person or premises is inadmissible at his trial.

This rule obviously has no relation to the fairness of the trial; the materiality or significance of the evidence is totally unaffected by the fact that the search which revealed it was made without the authority of a warrant rather than, as the court now rules it should have been, under such authority.[22] Consequently, courts in England and in this country, and of the countries of the common law generally, have customarily admitted physical objects in evidence, despite the possible irregularity of the search in which they were obtained. A quarter-century ago, however, the Supreme Court announced that in federal proceedings evidence obtained by unlawful search would be inadmissible.[23] It did so, it declared, not because the introduction of the evidence against the defendant deprived him of his life or liberty without due process of law and was therefore unconstitutional, but because it was improper for a federal court to permit itself to be used as an instrument for furthering the illegal process set in motion by the law-enforcement authorities when they made the unlawful search. It seemed quite apparent, however, that the real, as opposed to the good, reason for the Court's action, which was to have such far-reaching effects on our criminal justice, was its expectation that the new rule would tend to make federal officers more careful to observe the law; and in due course the Court indeed announced, in applying the rule in another case, that it acted in the exercise of its "supervisory powers over federal law enforcement agencies,"[24] powers nowhere conferred upon the Court by statute or by the rules which it has itself promulgated with congressional approval.[25]

---

[22] Some cases have even gone to the extreme of suppressing evidence obtained by a seemingly lawful search under authority of a warrant issued by a judicial officer empowered to issue such warrant, on the ground that the papers submitted by the law-enforcement authorities in support of their application for a warrant were defective, and the warrant itself therefore inoperative. See Rea v. United States, 350 U.S. 214 (1955).

[23] Weeks v. United States, 232 U.S. 383 (1914).

[24] Rea v. United States, 350 U.S. 214, 216 (1956). See Note: The Supervisory Power of the Federal Courts, 76 Harv. Law Rev. 1656 (1963).

[25] The activities of law-enforcement officers, when not acting under a warrant of arrest, or a search warrant, are not part of any judical proceeding, and thus not subject to regulation by the courts. Nevertheless, the Supreme Court in 1946, in promulgating, pursuant to the authority conferred upon it by statute, the rules of procedure for the federal courts in criminal proceedings, included a provision that a person arrested (an arrest without a warrant being specifically included) should

A few high state courts had already promulgated a like doctrine; and in succeeeding decades an increasing number of state courts adopted it, assuming the same power to supervise state law-enforcement authorities as had the Supreme Court with respect to the federal. That Court refused, however, to extend the rule to the states generally, emphasizing that no denial of due process was involved.[26] In a majority of the states the courts, refusing to assume supervision of the law-enforcement authorities, declined to adopt the rule. In some of those states, repeated attempts to procure the enactment of the rule by legislation met with failure. Those who opposed the rule held that ways of curbing unlawful searches should be employed which would not result in the escape of persons guilty of crime, and which would not open the door, as the rule unquestionably does, to protracted pretrial attacks on the admissibility of evidence in the possession of the authorities, as well as to time-consuming interruptions of the prosecution's presentation of the evidence at the trial itself. In 1961, however, as already stated,[27] the Supreme Court announced that the due process requirement did after all compel the exclusion of evidence seized without benefit of warrant, (and also, presumably, as in the federal courts, of evidence seized in full compliance with a warrant subsequently held to have been issued on insufficient papers), and that the federal rule would now be binding on all the states as well.

This episode has been treated at some length because it illustrates so clearly how the Supreme Court, and those high state courts that have followed its example, after taking upon themselves the responsibility for promulgating new rules governing the conduct of criminal proceedings in the courts, have gone on to impose new rules intended to regulate the conduct of the law-enforcement authorities. The objective of the courts in thus assuming to legislate in the field law-enforcement administration is of course in the highest degree a laudable one; but authoritative commentators have nevertheless deplored the assumption of these responsibilities by the high courts, contending that they, the Supreme Court included, lack the opportunity and the facilities for that thorough exploration of the vexing practical considerations that should be taken into account in promulgating rules in this field[28]—opportunities and facilities which a legislative committee,

---

be taken "without unnecessary delay" before the committing magistrate, a provision obviously not governing "the procedure in the courts of the United States and before United States commissioners" (Rule 1). Congress, however, did not exercise its power to veto this provision when the rules were laid before it.

[26] Wolf v. Colorado, 338 U.S. 25 (1949).

[27] See p. 60.

[28] See, for example, Barrett, Book review, 23 U. of Chi. Law Rev. 730, 735 (1957); and Waite, Judges and the Crime Burden, 54 Mich. Law Rev. 169 (1955). In his dissenting opinion in Upshaw v. United States, 335 U.S. 410 (1948), a holding which reaffirmed the rule first announced in McNabb v. U.S. (see p. 51), Justice Reed of the Supreme Court said: "Such condemnation of even the restricted McNabb

or an advisory commission acting under legislative authority, would have in ample measure.

When the courts promulgate new rules favorable to the criminal defendant, without holding that the new rule is required by constitutional provision, no question of retroactivity arises, any more than it would were a statute to confer new rights on the criminal defendant. In those cases in which the new protection is declared to be one required by a long standing constitutional provision, however, there is presented at once the question of the rights of those who were convicted before the announcement of the new rule. The question was first presented to the Supreme Court in acute form in connection with its holding in 1956 that one convicted of crime in a state court may not be denied an appeal, open to all defendants, merely because of his inability to afford the cost of a transcript or other record required to be filed by an appellant[29]; and the Court answered that one convicted previous—even many years previous—to that holding was nevertheless entitled, on a proper showing, to a belated appeal, with the necessary papers furnished free of cost by the state.[30] More recently it has, without express pronouncement, seemingly declared retroactive also its 1963 holding that trial counsel must be furnished on request to every criminal defendant who is unable to retain counsel.[31] The retroactive application of this and cognate holdings, it is said by an apparently dubious member of the Court, "may well require the reopening of cases long since finally adjudicated in accordance with the then applicable decisions of this Court."[32]

---

rule by those immediately responsible for the enactment and administration of our criminal law should make this Court, so far removed from the actualities of crime prevention, hesitate long before pushing farther by judicial legislation its concepts of the proprieties in criminal investigation" (p. 435). The condemnation referred to was that elicited by the inclusion of the rule of the McNabb case in a provision of the preliminary draft of the rules of criminal procedure for the federal courts. In the rules as finally promulgated this provision did not (and still does not) appear.

[29] See p. 133.

[30] Eskridge v. Washington State Board, 357 U.S. 214 (1958).

[31] Pickelsimer v. Wainwright, 375 U.S. 2 (1963), remanding a group of ten cases to the Supreme Court of Florida "for further consideration in light of Gideon v. Wainwright, 372 U.S. 335."

[32] Id., p. 3. The quotation is from the opinion of Justice Harlan, who dissented from the Court's "summary disposition" of the ten cases involved, urging that one or more of them should have been set for argument; because the question presented "is deserving of full-dress consideration." He expressly disclaimed any intimation as to how the question should be decided.

12

Court Organization and the Administration of Justice

1. CONSTITUTIONAL VS. STATUTORY ORGANIZATION. 2. TRIAL COURTS.
3. APPELLATE COURT STRUCTURES.

A defective court structure may have untoward effects in either or both of two quite different directions: it may be excessively costly to the public treasury; and it may impair the quality of the justice dispensed by the courts. Movements for court reorganization characteristically have as their objective both the improvement of justice and the elimination of wasteful expenditure. With the latter of these goals, the present volume is not concerned, except to the extent that an image of the courts as wasteful affects the attitude of the public toward judges and the administrative of justice.

But whether the emphasis be on the reduction of costs or on the improvement of judicature, it is essential in an era of incessant change that the court structure be correspondingly susceptible to change. To the extent that its form is embedded in constitutional provisions, rather than in statute, change is likely to be more difficult.

1. CONSTITUTIONAL VS. STATUTORY COURT ORGANIZATION

Except for the constitutional provision for the limited original jurisdiction of the Supreme Court, a provision of little practical importance, the federal court system is wholly statutory. The number of justices of the Supreme Court, their salary, and their appellate jurisdiction are left entirely to Congress. As to the remaining federal courts, the Constitution does not even command their creation by Congress, and their very existence is wholly statutory, from which it follows that their organization and jurisdiction are likewise entirely within legislative control.[1]

[1] The Constitution provides (in the Sixth Amendment) that "in all criminal prosecutions the accused shall enjoy the right to a trial by an impartial jury of the

By contrast, state constitutions characteristically create the highest court of the state, prescribing its jurisdiction, the number of its judges, their mode of selection, and their salaries; and in a number of states the constitution also goes into like detail with respect to the courts of general original jurisdiction, sometimes with additional detail regarding boundaries of districts and the like. Even considerable prescription with respect to inferior courts of first instance is found in some constitutions.

There is general agreement that although in some states detailed constitutional prescriptions of court organization may have curbed a tendency to legislative tinkering for political reasons, such detailed prescription is unwise because of the ensuing difficulty of making needed changes even, in the case of some states, in such petty tribunals as the justice-of-the-peace courts. The better plan is to provide in the constitution only the general framework of the state court structure.

In several states, the provisions of the constitution concerning the courts have undergone extensive amendment in recent years. In these revisions, the tendency has been to give the legislature a freer hand than formerly. In none of them, however, has the legislature been vested with the virtually plenary power given to Congress over the federal court system.[2]

The task of improving the court structure, a task always in progress somewhere,[3] in some places on a comprehensive scale, is in fact two distinct tasks, one dealing with the trial courts, the other with the appellate.[4] "Trial court" is here used, as is common, as a convenient designation for a court of original jurisdiction, despite the fact that, as already seen, in a considerable proportion of the proceedings instituted in such a court there is no trial.

2. TRIAL COURTS

At first blush it might seem that the over-all design of the trial court structure, whether state or federal, has little relation to the quality of the justice dispensed by any particular trial court in any particular case; but

state and district wherein the crime shall have been committed." This provision does not, however, require the creation of a court for each state, but only the impaneling of the jury (and presumably the holding of the trial) in the state where the crime was committed.

[2] The Model Judicial Article for state constitutions proposed by the Section of Judicial Administration of the American Bar Association in 1962 vests in the state's highest court virtually complete control over the organization of the other courts of the state for which the article makes provision—intermediate appellate courts and two levels of trial court, one of general and the other of limited jurisdiction.

[3] The progress of court reorganization in the several states since 1942 can readily be traced in the volumes of the Annual Survey of American Law, in the articles on judicial administration.

[4] A detailed up-to-date account of the courts of each state is to be found in the Martindale-Hubbell Law Directory, published annually.

the fact is far otherwise. The quality of those who seek judicial office, and of those who attain it, is likely to be affected by the design of the court structure. An ill-designed court structure may inflict on litigants and law-enforcement authorities wasteful controversies over jurisdiction and venue. A wastefully organized structure creates vested interests, both of judges, subordinate court personnel, and, it may be, lawyers and others connected with particular courts, which impede the reorganization of the structure to cope with increasing business. If, instead of reorganization, it is proposed, as it often is, to increase the number of judges, the already excessive cost is an obstacle to such increase; and it is not made. In all these ways, and others to be noted, a defective design of the trial court structure impedes the due administration of justice.

Courts of general and of limited jurisdiction

In the federal court structure, there is only a single type of trial court, the district court, established in each of the eighty-eight districts (at least one in each state), into which the country is divided.

In no state, however, is there an equally simple trial court structure. In every state there is found at least a lower and a higher level. The lower level is in many states still occupied, at least in the rural areas, by the local justice-of-the-peace court; in the remaining states, as already noted, this has been replaced by an integrated district court system, manned by full-time judges. The upper level is occupied by the court of general jurisdiction, in most states known as the superior or circuit court. The separate structure of courts of minor jurisdiction, their civil jurisdiction restricted to actions at law and to claims of limited amount, and their criminal jurisdiction extending only to petty offenses or minor misdemeanors, is everywhere accepted as necessary. The possibility of integrating these minor civil and criminal cases into the operations of the courts of general jurisdiction, perhaps by the use of commissioners or masters attached to those courts and supervised by their judges, seems to have been given little consideration.

In only a few states does this simple two-tier structure exist. In all the others, there is found a trial court of intermediate jurisdiction. Established in most cases on a county basis, such a court has a civil jurisdiction larger than that of the courts at the lower level, but still limited as to the amount of money judgment it may render and the remedies it may give; on the criminal side, it has in some states plenary jurisdiction. It is difficult to perceive the necessity for this intermediate level of courts as found in some states. Like the justice-of-the-peace courts, they seem to have been the product of an age when travel was difficult and the visit of a judge of a court of general jurisdiction to the county seat was an undertaking justified only by cases of great consequence. Even in some of the well-populated areas, the business emanating from a single county is insufficient to occupy a full-time judge, and the county judge practices law as well. Like other local courts, however, the county court is prized by the local party organization, and hence shows great powers of survival.[5]

In some states, these by no means always the most populous, even three tiers of trial courts have not seemed sufficient to the legislature. A fourth set of courts with overlapping jurisdiction is intruded even in the rural areas; and in some cities, one finds special courts, often again with some overlapping jurisdiction, perhaps displacing within the city, in part or in whole, the state-wide pattern of courts of limited jurisdiction.

State versus local courts

The relation of court structure to the administration of justice is perhaps most strikingly illustrated in the rural areas, in the contrast between a state in which the autonomous village court still prevails, and one in which it has been replaced by a state-wide court of limited jurisdiction, holding sittings at larger places. The one entails, of necessity, a part-time judge, often a layman, often compensated only by fees, and often holding court in a makeshift courtroom. The other permits a full-time professional judge, with adequate supporting personnel, presiding in a dignified setting.

But it is not only in the rural areas that local autonomy of the courts of limited jurisdiction tends to produce inferior justice. In the cities, the more closely such a court is associated, in the governmental structure, with the local government, the more likely it is that partisan influence in the selection of its judges will be strong. The more completely the trial judge is removed from local selection, the more likely is it that the better qualified aspirant will achieve judicial office. Almost everywhere, however, even in states in which the courts of general jurisdiction constitute a unified and integrated state-wide structure, covering the cities as well as the less densely populated areas, the courts of inferior jurisdiction are strictly local, with perhaps complete local autonomy and with the power of appointment of judges vested in the mayor, or, if the post of judge is elective, with the designation of party candidates by the local party machine. This type of arrangement doubtless accounts in part for the needless multiplication of special city courts so often encountered. This multiplicity is difficult to explain except by the need of the local party organizations, in a bygone day, for additional court posts, both judicial and subordinate, with which to reward the party faithful. In the truly large city, which plays a dominant role in the state in which it is located, such local selection is doubtless inescapable and indeed justified. But in the remaining cities, there is no

---

[5] With respect to its subordinate personnel—clerks, bailiffs, etc.—the county court, like the special city court, is in many places the last stronghold of the spoils system.

reason why justice should not be administered in the city, as well as outside it, by judges attached to an integrated court system and detached as much as possible from local selection. The administration of justice is not a local or municipal function.

In the courts of general jurisdiction as well, even though their structure be an integrated state-wide one, local selection of judges is virtually universal. In ideal theory, a state trial judge should be elected or appointed not to a court in a particular place in the state, or to a particular county or group of counties, but simply to the court of the state; and his selection should correspondingly be on a state-wide instead of on a local basis. But this ideal is nowhere even approached in any of our states. Whether selection be by appointment or election, and if by election, whether by partisan or nonpartisan procedures, it is local; and the judge appointed or selected is a local man.

Aside from the likelihood of better-qualified candidates being selected on a state-wide than on a local basis, if the judge is the judge not of the court in a particular place, but merely of the court of the state, he is more readily available for service in any part of the state. Arrangements for the assignment of the judge of a court in a particular place to a court elsewhere which is in need of additional judges are of course in wide use; but the assignment of a judge to a court other than that to which he was elected or appointed is regarded as exceptional. This is not to suggest that trial judges should be perpetual itinerants. A middle course is possible. But the desirability of freeing the trial judge not only from local political contacts, but from too constant contacts with the same coterie of local lawyers (and the converse desirability of requiring the favored local lawyer to appear more often before a strange judge) will be self-evident to those with first-hand acquaintance with these matters.

Though not commonly thought of in this connection, even our federal judiciary would be the better were its members each appointed to a national corps, instead of to a particular one of the country's eighty-eight districts. The unlikelihood of this coming to pass is, however, self-evident.

Finally, it is the tradition of local autonomy that is chiefly responsible for the almost complete lack of supervision under which most of our state judges still function—a lack of supervision without parallel in any other area of government. The conversion of the autonomous local court, whether of minor or of general jurisdiction, into a unit of a state-wide integrated structure makes possible the designation of an administrator—usually the chief judge of the court—empowered to keep close watch on the progress of judicial business in each locality in which the court sits, to transfer judges for temporary service where needed, and to make inquiries and if necessary administer rebuke when a particular judge seems to be dilatory or indolent (or perhaps merely incompetent). If, in turn, the several state-wide court systems are placed under the supervision of the chief justice of the state, as has been done for example in New Jersey, a fully integrated state court structure at length emerges. The creation of a judicial council or conference, usually composed of judges at various levels, but in some instances having lawyers also among its members, further aids integration. Developments of this nature are steadily making progress, though at an uneven pace from state to state and in the federal structure.

In addition to its tendency to improve the quality and the performance of its judges, the integration of a court system works powerfully for procedural improvement. It permits the ready mobilization of judicial manpower for the study of procedural problems, and facilitates the exchange of experience and the dissemination throughout the state system of improvements achieved by the more alert and inventive members of the court.

Specialized courts

Not withstanding the desirability of keeping the court structure simple, of resisting the multiplication of courts and fragmentation of jurisdiction which has, regrettably, characterized many of our court structures in the past, there are certain classes of cases calling for specialized skill; and if the volume of such cases is sufficient, the creation of a special court unit for them is justified.

In the federal trial court structure, a field in which many have thought that a specialized court is called for is that of patent infringement cases. In the practice of the law, patent law is an entirely separate specialty. The members of the bar who have not specialized in that field are ordinarily almost wholly unacquainted with the law involved (and indeed with the knowledge of chemistry or engineering requisite for a proper application of the law in particular cases). Mere membership in the bar is indeed insufficient to entitle one to prosecute an application for patent before the United States Patent Office, which requires of those appearing before it proof of special competence in the field of patents. Nevertheless, actions to enjoin infringement of a patent, which in their nature require the application of both patent law principles and technical knowledge on a level higher than that involved in the application for a patent, are heard exclusively in the district courts of the United States, many a judge of which is, on assuming office, totally ignorant of and wholly without previous experience in this field and deficient in basic scientific education.

A compromise between the present system of unspecialized diffused tribunals in this highly specialized field, and a complete centralization of jurisdiction in a specialized tribunal would be the retention of jurisdiction in the United States district courts, with provision for the possibility of removal of the case to a more specialized tribunal upon the application of either party, on a showing that the case involved complicated technical questions.[6]

In the state trial courts, specialized local courts are practicable only where the volume of cases in the special category is large. A state-wide or regional specialized court means that the case must either be tried at a distant point or await the visit of the specialized court. There are few classes of cases which warrant these disadvantages. In the larger cities, however, there may be sufficient business to warrant specialization. A usual division is that between civil and criminal cases. It is questionable whether this has any advantage over a unified city court, with certain parts designated for civil and other parts for criminal cases. This not only has the advantage of flexibility, permitting the assignment of judges where needed (a result usually much more difficult to achieve with separate courts, though by no means impossible), but more important, it helps to combat the deplorable tendency of the lower criminal courts in the city to become exclusively the province of those who have no contact with civil justice. Moreover, the post of judge in courts having both civil and criminal jurisdiction will ordinarily be more attractive to the qualified judicial aspirant than will the post of criminal court judge.

A specialized court found in all the larger and even some of the smaller cities is the juvenile court, with its special staff of probation officers and social workers and a judge owing his selection primarily to his known interest in and competence for the problems of youth rather than for his juristic distinction. In some cities, the juvenile court is part of a larger specialized court which deals with cases of non-support, filiation, and the like. Some have proposed that actions for divorce and separation, everywhere cognizable only in the courts of general jurisdiction, be also placed within the jurisdiction of this specialized "family" court, and that even cases of disorderly conduct and the like, cognizable in the courts of minor criminal jurisdiction, be transferred to it where it appears that the episode involved arose out of a marital quarrel. These proposals reflect the point of view that all family difficulties should be resolved if possible by conciliation and

[6] It is notable that Canada, though without a generalized system of federal courts (matters of Dominion law being adjudicated in the first instance in the courts of the several provinces) has nevertheless found it expedient to vest patent jurisdiction in a single Dominion-wide court of first instance, which sits at various places in the Dominion. It has also been suggested by a distinguished federal district judge that special courts for personal injury cases be set up within the federal court structure (such cases falling within the federal jurisdiction chiefly on the ground of diversity of citizenship, but also when arising out of injuries to seamen, longshoremen, and railroad workers in the course of their employment). Wyzanski, Address, Proceedings of the Attorney General's Conference on Court Congestion, 1958. The reason advanced for the proposal is not, however, that the trial of such cases calls for special qualifications on the part of the judge, but that, on the contrary, it calls for so little that a federal district judge should not be wasted on it.

by the help of social workers, marriage counselors, and perhaps psychiatrists, before either spouse is permitted to insist on an adjudication of his or her legal rights. In general, this point of view has yet to win acceptance from the legislative organs of the states.

The problem of extending specialized services, not to speak of the services of specialized judges, to the considerable number of juvenile cases which arise in the rural areas and in the smaller towns has thus far received only incidental attention.

3. APPELLATE COURT STRUCTURES

In the organization of appellate courts, two distinct objectives are present, the demands of which are not easy to reconcile. It should be possible to subject the determination reached in a court of original jurisdiction to speedy and inexpensive review—a desideratum which calls for appellate courts at convenient places and in number sufficient promptly and finally to dispose of appeals presented to them. On the other hand, since it is only in appellate proceedings that the rules of law are authoritatively laid down and statutes authoritatively construed, it is desirable that there be only a single appellate court in each legal system, whether federal or state, to make such authoritative pronouncements. Our appellate structures reflect the difficulty that has been experienced, in the federal court system, and in the larger states, in satisfying these two opposing requirements.

In the federal court structure, the solution adopted has been the obvious one of establishing intermediate regional appellate courts, to which go virtually all appeals from the district courts. Appeals in a few special classes of cases (the chief being that of injunctions granted by three-judge district courts) go instead to the Supreme Court. There are eleven regional courts of appeals. They dispose annually of some three thousand appeals from the district courts and from the various federal administrative tribunals whose orders are, as will be set forth in a subsequent chapter, reviewable by them. As already noted in connection with both criminal and civil appeals, in only a small proportion of these is further appeal to the Supreme Court a matter of right; and of the requests made to that court (by petition for writ of certiorari) to review decisions not reviewable as of right, only a small proportion are granted. The total number of court-of-appeals holdings annually reviewed by the Supreme Court typically does not thus exceed perhaps 5 per cent of those holdings. In the overwhelming proportion of federal proceedings in which appeal is taken to a court of appeals, the disposition made by that court is final.

The appellate organization found in the majority of the states is of the simplest—a single appellate court for the entire state. In the remaining states, however (not all of them, contrary to what might be expected, in the front rank as respects population or presumably volume of litigation), we find subordinate appellate courts of diverse kinds.

In five states, there is a subordinate appellate court whose decision is final in particular classes of cases, unless the higher appellate court sees fit, on application, to remove the case to its own docket, or to review the determination of the subordinate appellate court when made. In eight other states there is a structure of regional appellate courts (the number of such regional courts ranging from as few as two to as many as eleven) to which most appeals go in the first instance, with a limited right of further appeal to the supreme appellate court of the state. In Oklahoma and Texas, there are two coordinate appellate courts of last resort—one for civil and one for criminal cases. In a few of the states having metropolitan areas, there are, supplementing the state-wide system of appellate courts, special appellate benches to hear appeals from the special inferior courts sitting in the metropolitan area.

In some of the states having regional appellate courts, those courts are held by judges especially elected or appointed to them. In other states, the judges sitting in the regional appellate courts are designated for such service (usually by the governor) from among the judges of the superior court of general jurisdiction.

The limitations found, in the several states having subordinate or regional appellate courts, on the right to a further review by the highest court are too varied and technical to admit of discussion here. In general their effect is to make the subordinate or regional court of appeal the court of last resort in the great majority of the cases brought before it.

In addition to reviewing determinations already made by the subordinate or regional appellate benches, the highest appellate courts in all these states entertain appeals directly from the trial courts in particular classes of cases. Thus, capital cases and cases involving constitutional issues characteristically go directly to the highest court.

Review by panel

In some of the more populous states having only a single appellate court, the ability of that single appellate court to handle all the appellate business of the state is to be explained by the fact that, as to all but a small fraction of the cases coming before it, the court is not in fact a single court but rather two or even three separate courts. This is accomplished by the organization of the court into what are in effect three-judge committees (commonly called "divisions"), to whom is entrusted the final disposition of all but a small portion of the appeals taken, consideration by the full bench being reserved for cases of exceptional importance or those which, on petition for rehearing after the decision by a division, are judged worthy of further review by the full bench. It will be observed that there is no essential difference between this arrangement and that of regional or subordinate courts, since in either arrangement the final disposition is made in most cases by a tribunal other than the highest court. Under the divisional system, the circumstance that the members of that tribunal are also members of the highest court may serve to mask this fact; and perhaps the circumstance that announcement of the decision of that tribunal is made in the name of the highest court produces a greater feeling of satisfaction with the finality of the decision. Reflection makes it clear, however, that the determination made by three judges of a bench of seven or nine, for example, is not much more likely to represent the views of a majority of that bench than would a determination made by an entirely different tribunal of three. Whether, on a rehearing by the full court, the presence on the bench of the members responsible for the initial determination tends to impair the chances of reversal is a question to which a reliable answer is difficult.

Whether the regional, subordinate, or divisional system of intermediate appellate review is to be preferred has been the subject of sharp difference of professional opinion. The proponents of the divisional system claim for it a greater economy and simplicity than is provided by the other systems. In the largest states, however, the number of regional appellate courts is so large that were it replaced by an equal number of divisions of the highest court, and were each division to consist of the usual three judges, the aggregate number of judges of the highest court, all of whom would presumably be expected to participate in the consideration of cases requiring further review, would be quite excessive as judged by prevailing practice, which is to have five or seven.

The Supreme Court of the United States does not employ the divisional system, even petitions for certiorari being passed on by every member of the Court. However in the federal courts of appeals, though the judges of the court may number as many as nine, cases are heard and disposed of by a panel of three, with the possibility of their disposition being reviewed, in exceptional cases, by the court sitting "en banc," i.e., with all its members participating. A panel to sit for a particular period is ordinarily determined well in advance;[7] but there has occasionally been complaint that a panel has been made up to hear a particular case, or group of cases, the members being chosen because of their known views.[8]

---

[7] The chief judge (the senior of the judges not yet seventy years old) usually makes up the panels; but the practice is not uniform.

[8] On July 30, 1963, one of the judges of the Court of Appeals of the Fifth Circuit filed in the court a protest against the course pursued by the chief judge of the court in designating panels to hear school segregation cases. Armstrong v. Board of Education, 323 F.2d 333, 358 (1963). An experienced practitioner declares that "the panel problem . . . turns the court of appeals review into a lottery in so many circuits." Wiener, Federal Regional Courts: A Solution for the Certiorari Dilemma, 49 Amer. Bar Assn. Jour. 1169, 1170 (1963).

Specialization of appellate courts

An alternative to the creation of regional, subordinate, or divisional appellate benches is the establishment of specialized appellate courts. If appeals could be classified by subject matter in such fashion that a single court could dispose of all appeals in a particular category, the obvious expense and delay entailed by double appeals would be obviated. The possibilities of such a reorganization of our larger appellate court structures do not appear to have been explored, at least in any authoritative way. In actual practice, only the obvious separation of criminal from civil appeals (as is done in England) appears to have been undertaken, and this only in Oklahoma and Texas. A similar separation in the federal system would be entirely practicable; it is quite possible that a single court would be able to dispose of federal criminal appeals for the entire country, making further appeal to the Supreme Court, to the extent permitted at all, very rare.

The economy of time and expense which a system of single appeals might effect has been mentioned; but this is perhaps less important than the greater consistency and uniformity of decision that result when all cases are disposed of by a single appellate tribunal rather than by a number. Despite the possibility, necessarily limited, of a further appeal from an intermediate appellate court to the final appellate court in the system, most appeals are necessarily decided by the intermediate courts; and their views of questions of law may not be uniform. It is indeed the fact that the decision of certain federal cases may depend on the particular part of the country in which they arise. In the rules which the Supreme Court has promulgated, indicating the considerations which will influence (but not control) it in consenting to review further a decision of one of the regional courts of appeals, one of the enumerated considerations is indeed an inconsistency in the treatment of the same question of law by different courts of appeals. But by no means every such inconsistency is resolved promptly, or perhaps at all, by further review by the Supreme Court.

In the federal field, perhaps even more markedly than in the states, specialization of appellate courts would have the additional advantage of providing judges who were as familiar with the intricacies of the legal problems presented as are the specialized counsel who argue appeals before them—a condition impossible of realization under the present structures. Finally, the creation of a specialized court of appeals of sufficient stature would make it possible to give the decisions of that court finality, precluding further review by the Supreme Court (which is quite unequipped to adjudicate certain of these classes of cases—e.g., patents),[9] except in the rare case where an issue of constitutionality might arise.

[9] As to the desirability, in patent cases, of specialization even in the court of first instance, see note 6, above.

The introduction of specialized appellate courts into the federal appellate court structure, for the disposition of appeals from the district courts, is thus well deserving of consideration. Much more obvious, however, is the need for the creation of a specialized appellate court (or courts) to relieve the courts of appeals from the responsibility for reviewing the orders of the highly specialized federal administrative agencies, a matter to be considered at a later point, in connection with administrative adjudication.

That ours is a country of great distances is no real obstacle to the replacement of the existing regional appellate courts in part at least by nationwide specialized appellate courts. Only a portion of the cases which would come before such specialized appellate courts really call for oral argument; and for those that do, it would seem entirely practicable for the court, or a panel of its members, to travel about for the purpose (peripatetic state high courts have long existed in some of the states). Indeed, perhaps our appellate courts when desiring oral argument may in time adopt the arrangements long familiar in the business world, whereby meetings of committees whose members are widely separated are held by telephone, to which closed circuit television will no doubt in due course be added, if it has not already been. By such means, the necessity for a peripatetic court may in large measure be obviated.

In state appellate structures too, in which double appeals are now found, there is room for the replacement of those structures, in whole or in part, by specialized appellate courts to which alone appeal could be taken, and whose disposition would be final. Mention has already been made of the possible creation of a specialized court for criminal appeals—a field in which the elimination of double appeals, and the speedy final determination of the defendant's fate, are especially to be sought. It is worth considering whether, in a state where the volume of such appeals would warrant it, civil appeals might not in turn be divided between two or even three courts, each with sole and final appellate jurisdiction in the classes of cases entrusted to it. Among the special categories of civil appeals to which recognition could readily be given in such an allocation of appeals between two or more civil appellate courts are those relating to trusts and decedents' estates, real property, divorce and separation, torts, and public administration. The design of such a novel appellate system would no doubt present problems, but hardly intractable ones; and their solution would fully repay the effort.

13

The Personnel of the Courts:
Judges, Jurors, and Lawyers

1. CAREER JUDICIARY VS. JUDICIARY DRAWN FROM THE BAR.   2. STATE
JUDGES: COURTS OF GENERAL JURISDICTION.   3. STATE JUDGES: LOCAL
COURTS.   4. STATE JUDGES: APPELLATE COURTS.   5. FEDERAL JUDICI-
ARY: DISTRICT COURT JUDGES.   6. FEDERAL JUDICIARY: APPEALS COURT
JUDGES.   7. FEDERAL JUDICIARY: JUSTICES OF THE SUPREME COURT.
8. JURORS.   9. LAWYERS.   10. PROSECUTORS.

No legal system, no matter how logical its design or how elegant its
procedure, can rise higher than the personnel who administer it. In the civil
courts the personnel are threefold—judges, jurors, and lawyers. Moreover,
in the field of criminal justice we must add a fourth category—the prosecutor.

1. CAREER JUDICIARY VS. JUDICIARY DRAWN FROM THE BAR

Of all the factors which determine the complexion of a judiciary, perhaps the most significant is this: Is entrance to judicial office possible
only at the lowest rank, all the higher ranks being filled by promotion from
the lower? Or is it drawn in all ranks, characteristically, from the mature
members of the bar? The career judiciary, as is well known, characterizes
the Continental countries;[1] in the English-speaking countries, including our
own, it may be said to be non-existent. Characteristically, judges in the
middle and higher ranks are drawn from the more experienced members
of the bar. Moreover, the passage of a judge from a lower to a higher court,
though by no means unusual, cannot be said to be the rule; there is neither
firm tradition nor system to facilitate it.

---

[1] In some Continental countries, the aspirant for a judicial career must enter
the judicial bureaucracy immediately upon his graduation from law school. In
others, he may enter it only after a minimum period of practice; but in either case
he enters it only at the lowest level.

The introduction of a career judiciary has seldom been advocated here, even by the academic critics of the American judiciary. One reason has doubtless been that such a system is practicable only where the administration of justice is centrally controlled over a large territory, making it possible for the judicial novice to be assigned first to a tribunal of petty jurisdiction, and then promoted to courts of increasing importance. This condition has not existed in our federal court system because it has no courts of petty jurisdiction; while in our states, the complete autonomy of the local lower courts and their manning by local residents, have precluded any possibility of the career system. With the growing integration of our state court systems, the feasibility of something like a career judiciary in the states begins to emerge. However, the American tradition of local selection of the judiciary presents an obvious obstacle to the introduction of such a system, except possibly in the judicial apparatus of a few of the larger metropolitan areas. A like obstacle is the tradition of the independence of the judge, his freedom from control by any higher authority—even judicial authority.

Such difficulties aside, the institution of a separate judicial order raises more fundamental questions. A bureaucratic service—for a career judicial service, with its indispensable machinery for assignment and promotion, must unavoidably take on the character of a bureaucracy—exercising such vital power over the fate of the citizen as does the judiciary, is repugnant to American traditions; and while it must be admitted that the American people have accepted with perhaps unexpected submissiveness the erection of essentially bureaucratic systems of administrative adjudication in the national government, the jurisdiction involved has been a narrow one, affecting only particular groups. An extension of this type of judicial organization to the everyday business of the courts would evoke widespread resistance.

Nor are there wanting those who oppose, on other counts, at least the filling of the higher trial court benches by promotion. The experienced practitioner, elevated to an important bench, so runs the argument, brings to his judicial work a firsthand knowledge of life and of men that the career judge, insulated at an early age, can seldom have. Moreover, the career judge, until he reaches such an age and position that the desire for promotion is no longer a major motive, is dependent for his professional future wholly upon the approval of his superiors (even if they be judicial superiors, and not, as in the Continental countries, bureaucratic superiors in the ministry of justice). He is thus in reality less independent, it is urged, than is the judge who has come from the bar and can return to it if need be, who does not, characteristically, expect or hope for higher judicial office, and who can discharge his duties without fear of reprisal or hope of reward.[2] That the American trial judge in many instances does not corre-

---

[2] For an illuminating discussion of the effect of the career system on the personality of the judge see von Mehren, The Civil Law System, 843 (1957).

spond to this description as closely as he should does not impair the force of the argument.

Since the members of the judiciary are recruited from the members of the bar, the discussion might logically begin with an inquiry into our methods of legal education, our standards of admission to the bar, and the like; but space forbids.

Aside from the quality of the bar itself, obviously a prime factor in the quality of the judges drawn from it, the problem of recruiting a capable judiciary presents two distinct phases—attracting qualified aspirants, and rejecting unqualified ones. The governing factors of compensation, tenure, prescribed qualifications, and method of selection may best be considered separately for state and for federal judges.

2. STATE JUDGES: COURTS OF GENERAL JURISDICTION

The state judiciaries fall into three fairly distinct groups. Justices of the peace, police magistrates, and judges of other minor courts comprising one group; the judges of trial courts of general jurisdiction, another; and the judges of appellate benches, a third. It will be convenient to discuss first the judges of the trial courts of general jurisdiction.

Qualifications

The governing statutes or constitutional provisions quite generally fail to prescribe any special qualifications for the office of judge. Indeed, even the requirement that the judge be a member of the bar is often absent; but whether prescribed or not, membership in the bar is of course almost invariable.[3] What is not equally universal, however, is extended experience in legal affairs, and more particularly, in the type of legal affairs which the particular judicial office calls for. It is probably fair to say that were a set of job qualifications prepared by competent hands for the post of judge in each of our courts (of the same type as are prepared by the personnel departments of large business organizations, or by civil service commissions for the public services), by no means a negligible percentage of those currently appointed or elected to the run of judicial offices would but dubiously answer the specifications. Indeed, the absence of a more precise definition of those qualifications, against which the attainments of a pro-

[3] Laymen are still occasionally found sitting even in county courts, where questions of considerable technicality may arise. Cf. Craig v. Harney, 331 U.S. 367 (1947). In New Jersey until 1947, when its archaic judicial structure was by constitutional amendment replaced by its present advanced judicial design, six lay judges sat with the Chancellor and the nine members of the Supreme Court to form the highest court of the State. The presence of these lay members is traced to the fact that in the colonial period the governor and his council constituted the court of last resort of the colony.

posed appointee or nominee to judicial office might be checked, creates a real difficulty for bar associations, the press, and other public-minded critics when challenging a proposed appointment or nomination. Though seldom found as an item in a program of judicial reform, statutory prescription of minimum qualifications for the judicial office would do much to eliminate unqualified aspirants.

Compensation

Compensation is not perhaps a primary factor determining the quality of a judiciary, unless its scale is so low as actually to debar a substantial proportion of the qualified bar from the possibility of accepting judicial office. Such a scale actually exists, however, in not a few of our states at the present time, largely because of the retention of nineteenth century statutory salaries in the face of living costs that have tripled. Although the situation in this respect is improving, much more radical improvement is needed if the run of judicial offices in these states is not to be partitioned solely between the incompetent and the wealthy members of the bar.[4]

It hardly needs arguing that nowhere in the field of public service is a pinchpenny policy more fallacious than in judicial compensation. Aside from the fact that an inadequate salary constitutes a standing temptation to partiality or worse on the part of a judge lacking in complete integrity, there are few offices in which the difference between a more competent and a less competent incumbent is reflected more strikingly in the speed and economy with which the public business is dispatched. In terms of the time of litigants, witnesses, and lawyers, and of the services of clerks, attendants, stenographers, and other courthouse personnel, the more competent trial judge is actually worth several times the less competent one. In the appellate courts, the monetary aspect is less striking, but the results for the legal system generally are more so.

Concurrently with the tendency to increase inadequate state judicial salaries has gone the development of retirement and disability pensions for judges; but here too much remains to be done.

Quite generally, constitutional provisions protect the state judge against reduction of his salary while in office. Whatever may have been the importance of such provisions in an earlier day, their significance today is purely symbolic. Quite aside from constitutional provision, public opinion would hardly tolerate such a reduction by the legislature.

Tenure

Lack of life tenure is not in the case of judicial office so serious a factor in reducing the number of aspirants as it is in many other types of public

---

[4] See Skoler and Janewicz, A Survey of Judicial Salaries in the United States and Canada, 45 Jour. Amer. Judicature Soc. 233 (1962).

office. At the bar, the added prestige enjoyed by a former judge is such that many a lawyer would unhesitatingly abandon an established practice for even a short career on the bench, counting on readily re-establishing himself at the bar when his term was over. Only occasionally does the judicial aspirant fall into this category, however; typically he looks forward to a long judicial career. Where the term of office is short he must resign himself to having his judicial duties recurrently punctuated by the uncertainties and the political activities incident to the impending expiration of a term of office, and the quest for reappointment or re-election. Under this necessity, needless to say, a judge of weak moral fiber will in each case before him tend to have in mind the possible influence of his conduct in or disposition of such case on his chances of renomination or re-election. Perhaps no single reform would do more to improve the caliber of the judicial aspirant in some of our states than the radical lengthening of the brief terms of judicial office which their laws now prescribe.

The actual length of term of judges of courts of general jurisdiction ranges from only two years in Vermont to life in Rhode Island and Massachusetts.[5] The fact that extremes are thus found in adjacent states suggests the difficulty of any regional generalizations.

Between these two extremes, terms of 4, 5, 6, 7, 8, 10, 12, 14, and 15 years are to be found. The characteristic terms are, however, 4 and 6 years, the 4-year term being found in no less than 18 states for some or all of the judges of courts of general jurisdiction, and the term of 6 years in no less than 16. In New Jersey is found the unique but sensible provision, applicable to Superior Court judges, that their initial term is 7 years, but on reappointment the term is for life.

The vice of a short term of judicial office may be mitigated by the existence of a strong tradition that a sitting judge if competent is to be retained in office. Such a tradition exists, in varying degrees of strength, in a number of jurisdictions. It is more readily established where judgeships are filled by appointment rather than by popular election.

Selection

The judges of our state courts of general jurisdiction are either appointed by the governor (subject to confirmation by one or both houses of the legislature, or by the council), or are elected by the legislature, or are popularly elected.[6]

Appointment by the governor, the predominant method till the middle of the last century, is now found in only eleven states, five of them in New

[5] In New Hampshire the term is to age seventy.
[6] The statements in this chapter as to the methods of selection of judges are (except as to the new constitutional provisions in Iowa and Nebraska) based on The Book of the States, 1962–1963, page 124.

England.[7] The process of shifting from the appointive to the elective method in the older states, and of adopting the elective method in the newer states, was essentially complete well before the turn of the century. Since that time there has developed a movement for a return to the appointive method. Both Alaska and Hawaii adopted this method on becoming states; and Iowa and Nebraska have since adopted it.

Election by the legislature is found in only four states.

The remaining thirty-five states employ popular election—a method of judicial selection unknown outside of the United States.[8] Here we find several distinct patterns. In eighteen of these states the names of the judicial candidates appear together with those of party candidates for non-judicial office, under a party listing, at the regular election. In four additional states, though on the ballot the candidates are listed without party designation, they are nevertheless party candidates, having been named at party primary elections. There thus remain twelve states in which not only the ballot at the election, but the process of nomination as well is wholly free from party designation of candidates.[9]

Even where popular election prevails, initial selection to the bench is to a considerable extent made by the governor, in the exercise of his power to fill vacancies occurring through death, resignation, retirement, or removal. The percentage of elected judges who for one or another of these reasons fail to complete their term of office varies considerably from state to state, being dependent on the length of term and on the tradition of re-election. In states where the term is long, and judges are ordinarily re-elected without opposition, death, disability, or the compulsory retirement age is likely to overtake a judge before his term has expired. The judge appointed to replace him will ordinarily receive the party nomination—sometimes a bipartisan nomination—at the ensuing election. In a group of six states in which by tradition the governor's interim appointee is usually elected without opposition for a full term, more than half the judicial offices, it has been computed, are thus filled.[10]

The primary effect of the varied methods of selection just described

---

[7] In Alaska, Iowa, and Nebraska the governor's appointee, to continue in office, must be confirmed by the electorate at an ensuring general election; in Maryland he must run as a party nominee at an ensuing election in opposition to the nominees, if any, of other parties.

[8] In California, superior court judges are elected; but any county may substitute appointment by the governor, subject to veto by a board consisting of the chief justice, the presiding justice of the regional appellate court, and the attorney general. No county has yet so acted.

[9] In nine of these states, a place on the ballot is secured through a nonpartisan primary election (designed to limit the number of contestants in the election) and in three states, by a mere petition of candidacy, without primary election. In four of these states, the nonpartisan character of the judicial election is further emphasized by its not being held at the same time as the general election.

[10] Vanderbilt, Minimum Standards of Judicial Administration, 8 (1949).

is to eliminate from consideration for the great majority of the judicial posts in question all members of the bar who have not been active in the party organization, Appointment by the governor is ordinarily confined to members of the governor's party and, in most cases, represents not the free choice of the governor but rather the choice of those powerful in the party organization, of whom the governor is ordinarily one. A truly non-political appointment by a governor, that is to say, the appointment of a lawyer who has taken no part in the active work of the political organization, is a rarity. Election by the legislature of course takes place ordinarily against a similar background of party control. Where judicial candidates are voted on party tickets (as they are in twenty-one states), only party members with a history of party activity can hope to secure nomination—and this is almost as true in the eighteen states in which the party nominees are chosen at a party primary election, as in the three in which they are chosen by a party nominating convention. In the four states in which the party primary is combined with the nonpartisan election ballot, the same is true.

That the exclusion from these judicial posts of all lawyers without political support deprives the bench of access to a vast source of capable judicial material is obvious. Such exclusion is nevertheless defended on principle by some, the contention being that lawyers who have not so far interested themselves in public affairs as to be active in a political party have thereby evidenced a lack of that concern for the public welfare which the judge should have.[11] The argument overlooks the fact that interest in public affairs may express itself equally by activity in nonpartisan organizations. Moreover, the lawyer active in one of the minority parties, whose disinterested zeal for the public good is self-evident from his association with a party whose present function is chiefly educational, is debarred as effectively as one totally inactive. Finally, the proposition that the lawyer who is active in one of the major parties is presumptively motivated by concern for the public welfare can be accepted only in a Pickwickian sense.

The exclusion of the non-political lawyer from the bench does not perhaps of itself seriously impair the quality of the judiciary. Among those active in politics is ordinarily to be found a more than sufficient number of lawyers well qualified for judicial office. Unfortunately, however, it is by no means the best qualified among them who is most likely to be chosen by those who control the party machinery. Rather may the choice (especially in metropolitan areas where the contenders for the nomination are often quite unknown to the general public and little known even to the bar) be determined by the devious machinations of intraparty cliques; and

[11] See for example Peck, The Bar, Politics, and Judicial Selection, 24 N.Y. State Bar Bull. 32 (1952).

in a few metropolitan centers rumors persist that generous but secret contributions to the party treasury, with attendant opportunities for malversation by those in control, have played a major part in the choice.

Even where the history of his designation is entirely honorable, the judge who owes his appointment or nomination to the favor of particular groups or individuals within the party enters upon his office under a load of political debt; and however high-minded he may be, he will find it almost impossible to resist completely the importunities of his creditors for payment through judicial favors—sometimes slight, sometimes not so slight. Moreover (life tenure of judicial office being almost unknown in our states), unless there has been established, as there has been in many places, a firm tradition that a capable sitting judge is to be reappointed or renominated on the expiration of his term, regardless of which party is then in power, the judge can practice complete independence of those in power in the party only at the risk of failing of reappointment or renomination when his term expires.

The judicial favors which can be dispensed by a judge seeking to repay political debts (or to build up a political credit balance against the day when reappointment or renomination becomes necessary) are varied. In a civil case he can favor a party or attorney with political connections (or able to procure political intercession) either in minor procedural matters, incidental to the substantive controversy, or more rarely, in the final substantive determination itself, any inclination to the latter being, however, in matters of consequence, much inhibited by the possibility of reversal on appeal. It is noteworthy that the judge who pretends to no great legal learning is nevertheless (indeed perhaps all the more) sensitive to reversal of his determinations on appeal. Whatever his pre-judicial practice and circle, his elevation to the judiciary tends to reorient his life within a new framework, in which a record free of reversals, or of an excessive number of reversals, takes on an importance which to the bystander seems much exaggerated. The freedom of appeal characteristic of our system undoubtedly is a very useful check on gross favoritism in civil determinations.

In the field of criminal proceedings, it is the prosecutor rather than the judge, as we have seen, whose favor is chiefly important to the suspect or to the defendant under charges. (Favor to the complainant is, in the whole, a minor factor in criminal proceedings.) In dropping a prosecution already begun, however, or in accepting a plea of guilty to a lesser offense than that charged, the prosecutor requires the consent of the judge; and here political pressure on the judge may be valuable. To the extent to which he supervises the grand jury in its investigation of a particular crime or situation, the judge also has an opportunity to extend political favor. It is, however, in the sentencing procedure that the power of the judge to confer political favors is most important; and here too the resistance to pressure from the politically important is most difficult.

Judicial discretion may moreover be politically motivated in an area quite removed from the merits of a particular controversy or prosecution—the area of judicial patronage. This is found in the lower courts chiefly in the selection by the judges of such auxiliary personnel as secretaries, clerks, bailiffs, and the like (although increasingly, especially in the cities, these posts are filled by merit system procedures, and in some places, whatever the selection procedure, by officials other than the judges). When we reach the higher trial courts, judicial patronage embraces an entirely new group—referees, guardians of infants or incompetents, receivers, and the like. The political organization abounds in lawyers seeking these often lucrative appointments. Moreover, if a political personage, not himself a lawyer, is able to procure the designation to a profitable refereeship, receivership, or guardianship of a particular lawyer, he is in a position to arrange in advance with the designee sponsored by him for a share of the proceeds—or perhaps in some cases the better term would be spoils. For there can be no doubt that the scale of the compensation awarded by the courts to persons appointed to the posts in question is ofttimes very generous—far greater indeed in certain cases than would be tolerated were the payment coming out of the public purse instead of the pockets of the litigants.

The power enjoyed by the judges of the superior trial courts in the appointment of these officers of the court, combined with the readiness with which political plums may thus be distributed without any perceptible injury to the public—for these appointees though frankly political may nevertheless be entirely competent—is indubitably one of the chief reasons for the intense interest displayed by the political organizations in the selection of the judges in question, and for their hostility to reforms looking to non-political selection. One might suppose accordingly that in a program for a non-political judiciary the elimination of judicial patronage, by the institution of something in the nature of a merit system in the appointment of referees, guardians, receivers, and the like, would find an important place—as would also perhaps a plan for standardizing, and in the process reducing, the allowances made to these officials. But these matters are largely ignored in the movement for non-political selection of judges.

That movement, which has for decades had the virtually unanimous support of the organized bar and of lay civic organizations, has for its premise that the function of the judge is a non-political one, that his function is to apply the law, not to make it. Even as to the judges of the higher appellate courts this premise has considerable validity, since to the extent that they do make the law, the areas within which they make it are almost wholly technical, so technical that the questions presented can only in a scholastic sense be termed political. So far as the trial judge is concerned, the premise that his function is non-political is believed to be amply supported by a realistic appraisal of his work, as reflected in earlier chapters. Surprisingly, however, this premise has in recent years been challenged by some political scientists, who, recognizing no distinction between appellate and trial courts, affirm their conviction that "the judicial function" is "necessarily political" and that consequently "the policies of the people" can be assured of execution only by partisan selection. Obviously, the phrase "the judicial function" has no correspondence with any reality unless the particular type of court in which "the judicial function" is exercised is identified. In considering, therefore, whether the machinery for the selection of a judge of a court of general jurisdiction should be partisan or non-political, it is not "the judicial function" but the function of the judge of such a court that should be examined. The political scientist, in forming his picture of that function, would presumably wish to rely, not on generalizations uttered with the higher appellate courts chiefly in mind, but on an intensive survey of the activities of the typical judge in this category. Such a survey does not appear to be available, at any rate in published form; but to one with firsthand acquaintance with these courts the picture is sufficiently familiar. As the judge presiding at jury trials in the staple negligence or commercial actions which occupy so great a proportion of the time of our trial courts, his role—chiefly that of ruling on objections to offers of evidence and giving routine instructions to the jury at the close of the evidence—is important chiefly in giving dignity and authority to the proceedings; and the same is true of criminal jury trials. When he tries a case without a jury, the issue before him is more likely to be one of fact than one of law; if legal issues are involved, they are in most cases technical and narrow ones. If novel or important issues of law are present, his determination of them is more than likely to be merely preliminary; the appellate court will have the last word. In passing upon interlocutory motions, he deals almost exclusively with narrow procedural issues. The large measure of discretion, unlikely to be subjected to appellate review, which he enjoys in these matters, in the acceptance of pleas of guilty to reduced charges and in fixing sentences, has already been mentioned. How he exercises this discretion will be determined, his mentality and personality aside, by the degree to which he is honorable and independent. The process will be in no sense political (unless indeed he has partisan obligations and commitments, in which case his dispositions will be political in the sense in which that word is used by the club-house politician).

Seemingly responsible for the notion that the trial judge's function is political is the misconception, derived largely from a few engaging discourses that had much vogue in the thirties, that our rules of law are merely a verbal mask, behind which the judge makes the law anew in each case as he pleases. Whatever validity this view may have when applied to the higher state courts, and particularly to the Supreme Court when dealing with constitutional issues, it is, as applied to the judge of a court of first instance, a gross distortion of the reality. It is true only in the sense that a judge who very much wants to reach a given result can sometimes, but by no means always, find something in the books which he can, if he is sufficiently devoid of intellectual and moral honesty, distort to give seeming support to that result. It is to be remembered, however, that in the great majority of cases that come before him he has typically no desire to reach one result rather than another; and of course one way to insure that this shall be so to as great an extent as possible is to have him mount the bench free of those ties and obligations to the party chiefs which partisan selection almost invariably entails.

Of course, if the judge of a court of general jurisdiction is really discharging a political function, if partisan selection is necessary to insure that he will carry out "the policies of the people," logic would demand that he run for re-election at short intervals; and, a fortiori, the highest appellate judges at still shorter intervals![12]

In the attempt to eliminate, or at any rate reduce, the role of the party organization in judicial selection, various expedients have been adopted: nomination by petition instead of by the party machinery; the removal of party designations from the ballot, both in primary and in general elections; the abandonment of popular election in favor of appointment by the governor; and the initial preparation by a special nonpartisan nominating board of a small list of eligibles from which the governor must choose his appointee.

Nonpartisan election procedures offer the voter a more clear-cut opportunity than do partisan elections for exercising deliberate choice among the several judicial candidates; and the choice is in many cases

[12] The argument for partisan selection of judges here discussed is found (together with the quoted phrases) in Wormuth and Rich, Politics, The Bar, and the Selection of Judges, 3 Utah Law Rev. 459 (1953). One would not be justified in supposing that a single article reflects a view common among political scientists; but in a voluminous collection of readings intended for college political science courses, compiled by two distinguished political scientists (Murphy and Pritchett, Courts, Judges and Politics, 1962) this article is the only discussion of the problem of selecting state court judges deemed worthy of inclusion. A succession of texts issued in recent years, intended for college use, dealing with what is commonly styled "the judicial process," displays a like tendency to treat all courts, from the lowliest trial court to the highest appellate court, as engaged essentially in the same "process" and, hence, made in the same image, that image being derived, astonishingly, in large part from a court utterly unique not only in this country, but in the great globe itself—the United States Supreme Court.

doubtless other than it would be had the same candidates been presented under party designations. The greater willingness of the voter to make a choice can be turned to advantage however, only by something comparatively rare under the regime of partisan elections—a vigorous judicial election campaign, distasteful to the type of lawyer best suited for judicial office, and financially burdensome. Nor is there any reason for believing that even a studious voter, after such a campaign, is really qualified, unless the difference between the contending candidates is striking, to make an intelligent choice. Nor is the nonpartisan primary election without its weaknesses. Despite the nonpartisan character of the formal machinery in these states, there is nothing to prevent partisan activity in the solicitation of signatures to designating petitions, with the result that among the candidates filing petitions for a place on the primary ballot certain ones may be well known to the electorate as the candidates of a particular party. Again, whatever be the method employed for securing nomination to elective judicial office, such nomination, like nomination to non-judicial office, can be obtained only through organization, with concomitant expenditure of energy and funds. If it is not obtained through the regular political organizations, it can be obtained only through an organization created by the candidate himself, or by his associates. In neither case does the successful candidate mount the bench without a sense of obligation to the organization responsible for his nomination.

Moreover, since anyone who can procure the requisite number of signatures to a petition may enter the primary, a sitting judge may find himself confronted, in a nonpartisan primary, with a contest which would not have occurred under a party primary system. Some have accordingly contended that whatever its merits with respect to contests between candidates not holding judicial office, the nonpartisan primary tends to force the sitting judge whose term is expiring into far greater political activity than does the party primary or party convention method.

Those who urge that popular election be replaced by gubernatorial appointment recognize that such appointments are ordinarily no less politically motivated than are nominations by party leaders; but they urge that the necessity under which the governor rests, of accepting personal responsibility for the selection made, tends to compel the application of a higher standard of fitness than is deemed needful by the more or less conspiratorial participants in the party cabals. Where the governor is a man of character and independence, this is doubtless true. Where he is not, his selection can in no event be worse than that of the party leaders, for it will in fact be dictated by them. As opposed to the system of partisan nomination and election, therefore, the system of appointment, at least for judicial posts in metropolitan areas, as to which no intelligent choice or even critical evaluation by the electorate is to be hoped for, seems clearly preferable.[13]

A more radical position is taken by those who, premising that the judge's function is wholly non-political, seek to eliminate politics entirely in his selection. They advocate, not a career judiciary on the Continental model, but the selection of judges from a small list of eligibles prepared by a non-political nominating board. This is the essence of the plan. Given such a list of eligibles, the actual selection could be made by any method, including popular election; the method actually proposed is, naturally enough, appointment by the governor. This is the plan in force in Alaska, Iowa and Nebraska, and in some counties of Missouri.[14]

The heart of such a plan is, manifestly, the method of selection of the purportedly non-political nominating board. In Alaska, there is a single selection board for the entire state, consisting of the chief justice of the state (as chairman), three lawyers appointed by the organized bar of the state, and three laymen nominated by the governor and confirmed by the legislature. In the other states, district selection boards of cognate composition are constituted.[15] In some boards, staggered terms are provided as an additional safeguard against political party control. The designation of the nominating board by the organized bar of the state was the chief feature of a proposal defeated—doubtless largely because of this feature—by the voters of New Mexico in 1953. The composition of the Alaskan selection board would seem open to little criticism.

The nominating board plan has been urged by the American Bar Association since 1937, but only for states not having an appointive judiciary. Presumably the failure to recommend its application also to states having an appointive judiciary reflects tactical considerations rather than any supposed difference in principle. As thus applied to states having popular election, the association's plan provides for appointment by the governor from the list prepared by the nominating board. It further provides, however, that the electorate shall be given the power to disapprove the appointment of the judge selected by the governor: at the election following the first year of the appointee in office, the question of whether

[13] In a state where judges are appointed, if a single party retains the governorship over a long period, the judiciary tends to become largely of that party. But a party dominant in the state is likely to be the minority party in certain parts of the state; hence, where popular election of judges on a district basis prevails, the state judiciary as a whole is more likely to be bipartisan in complexion.

[14] In Iowa and Nebraska the constitutional amendments creating the nominating board procedure for judicial selection were ratified by the electorate in 1962 and went into effect at once.

[15] The composition of the nominating boards is, except in Iowa, substantially the same as in Alaska. In Iowa there is no provision for division of the board between legal and lay members.

he shall be continued in office is submitted to the voters. A like question is put to the voters at the expiration of each incumbent's term. Popular election is thus in effect replaced by the power of popular recall at stated intervals. This is the plan in effect in the states mentioned.

Removal

It is doubtless true that by and large an unfit judge finds it easier to retain his office than does any other incompetent official, holding an office of comparable importance and required, as is the judge, to perform his duties in person rather than through deputies. The reason is twofold; on the one hand the judge is subject, characteristically, to no supervision; on the other, his removal is likely to be a cumbersome and difficult process.

The tradition of the judge's freedom from supervision gives way only slowly, for it has deep historical roots. Its development is closely associated with the pattern of decentralization which long characterized virtually all our judicial structures, and as noted in the preceding chapter, has only in recent years begun to alter. In the colonies, the royal authority had favored the centralization of the judiciary, still closely associated with the governor of the colony, in the seaboard centers. The decades following independence, marked as they were by rapid settlement of the western country, brought an increased demand for the erection of new local courts of superior juris-diction. The contact between the judges of the remoter local courts thus set up and the judges of the existing courts in the larger centers was, as was perhaps natural under the conditions of travel and communication of the times, for the most part quite tenuous. Each court was in organization a legal principality in itself. Thus was developed that pattern of extreme decentralization of judicial power, and of power over the administration of the judicial machinery, which in so many states (and in the federal system as well) characterizes our court organization to this day, and which pre-sents so marked a contrast to the judicial organization of the Continental countries and of Great Britain.

The lack of supervision under which the judge of a court of general jurisdiction typically functions is notorious. He is by law free from personal financial liability for losses resulting from his incompetence or neglect in the discharge of his duties. Even in urban areas in which he is a member of a multimembered court, headed by a chief justice, he is usually free from any effective supervision by his colleagues or by his chief, the latter's administrative functions being ordinarily confined to the making of assign-ments and the supervision of the court's auxiliary personnel. No one has the duty of appraising the judge's efficiency or industry, much less his judicial demeanor, his impartiality, his knowledge of the law, and his ability to apply it correctly to a case before him. Even in those few states in which an efficient control over the assignment of judges, coupled with effective records of the disposition of the cases before them, has for the first time assured the industry of the judges, no effective check on the quality of their work exists. This is not to suggest that the development of such a check is easy; on the contrary, it presents grave difficulties.[16]

Under these circumstances, only in the case of a notoriously incompetent or corrupt judge is the demand for his removal likely to arise. At this point, the short term, condemned on all other grounds, may prove of value; the expiration of the unfit judge's term may accomplish—especially in the rural areas where the party organization cannot count as it can in the large cities on the ignorance and apathy of the voters—what under a longer tenure can be effected only by removal proceedings.

Since judicial independence must be preserved at all costs, removal procedures in this field are necessarily surrounded with heavy safeguards. In all but one state, impeachment—removal by the upper branch of the legislature on charges brought by the lower—is available where specific charges of misconduct (usually defined as constituting treason, felony, or other high crime or misdemeanor) is made. Though in over one-third of the states no other method of removal for misconduct is available, state judicial impeachments have been so rare as to be virtually non-existent. Almost equally rare, though less cumbersome, and available even in the absence of specific charges of misconduct, is the use of the method of removal on joint legislative resolution, found in about a quarter of the states sometimes with the requirement of a two-thirds or three-fourths majority. In some six states, the highest court of the state has power to remove the judges of the trial courts, including the courts of general jurisdiction—again a power rarely exercised. In New York, a special tribunal of higher court judges may be convened by the chief judge of the state—an innovation still too recent to permit an appraisal of its effectiveness.

Rare and exceptional as must be the removal of a judge of a court of general jurisdiction, it would doubtless occur more frequently were there available some agency directly charged with responsibility for investigation, on its own motion, whenever grounds for suspicion of unfitness or corruption are alleged to exist. In 1961, such an agency was established in California. A standing commission, composed of judges, lawyers, and laymen, is empowered to receive and investigate complaints against judges, to cause evidence to be taken, and to recommend to the state high court that it

[16] Though in several states the higher courts have been given power to remove judges of lower courts for misconduct, nowhere does a higher court appear to have been vested with responsibility for appraising the efficiency or industry of lower court judges. The New Jersey plan of state-wide power of assignment of judges by the Chief Justice, coupled with a power to require reports of progress on unfinished cases, appears to be the nearest approach to such a system.

either remove or recommend the voluntary retirement of a judge found unfit.[17]

The organized bar has thus far created no standing machinery, as it well could, for the same purpose. A procedure for systematic and continuing appraisal of each sitting judge by the organized bar would in many cases bring about the resignation of an unfit judge, or at any rate his decision not to seek renomination or reappointment, making removal proceedings unnecessary.

3. STATE JUDGES: LOCAL COURTS

In the special local courts found in our larger cities, and in many smaller ones, the quality of the judges, as might perhaps be expected, tends to be lower than that of the judges of the courts of general jurisdiction. This is not merely because their salary scale is usually lower; it is chiefly because their selection is even more completely political and their contact with the local political machine closer. For reasons already indicated, a local political machine of the baser sort has a special interest in close association with the judges who sit in the preliminary examination of persons arrested on criminal charges.

It is hardly doubtful that in many places a substantial elevation of the caliber of the judges sitting in the local courts would be effected did they, instead of being selected locally (whether by appointment or election), constitute part of a state-wide corps, sitting in a particular locality only by assignment. The possibilities of such a substitution of a state corps for local judges, though already realized in several states in connection with the rural justices of the peace, have received, apparently, little attention in discussions of the quality of the judiciary in city courts.

To the general characterization of the city judiciaries above made, important exceptions must be noted. In the larger metropolitan centers, the special local courts, particularly if integrated into a single court with central administrative control, as in Chicago, Detroit, and New York, may have an importance and a stature much exceeding that of the courts of general jurisdiction in a rural area; and the judges are of corresponding quality.

Outside the larger cities, the quality of the minor judiciary exhibits wide variations. In some of the small towns and villages, the part-time judge may be a good lawyer and a man of respectable stature. In the rural areas, being chiefly occupied with some other calling, he is very unlikely to have much legal knowledge, though in some states programs for giving

[17] Frankel, Removal of Judges: California Tackles an Old Problem, 49 Amer. Bar Assn. Jour. 166 (1963). In some other states intermediate appellate courts may remove petty judges. In eight states are found provisions for "recall" of judges by popular vote—a method virtually never used.

legal instruction to the rural justices of the peace has effected a substantial improvement in this respect. He is in many, perhaps most, places politically active. His partiality in traffic cases and perhaps others, in some places due to his sharing in the fines collected, has already been mentioned.[18] In general, he is not likely to be of impressive stature.[19] Where the part-time rural justice has been replaced by a corps of full-time judges, with legal training, it has proved quite practicable, despite the minor character of the jurisdiction exercised, to recruit sufficiently able men for the post of judge.

4. STATE JUDGES: APPELLATE COURTS

In general, the method of selection of appellate judges is the same as for the courts of original jurisdiction. In three states, however, where trial judges are elected, appellate judges are appointed by the governor. In California, one of these states, appointments are subject to veto by a commission on qualifications. Intermediate appellate benches are in some states filled not by initial election or appointment to the appellate court, but by designation from among the judges of the courts of general jurisdiction, such designation being in most states made by the governor.

In no state is there a requirement that one appointed or elected to any appellate court shall have had prior judicial experience; and in point of fact many appellate judges have had none prior to mounting the appellate bench. Many others have had such experience; but no numerical data are available. In some states are found provisions designed to insure that the court of last resort shall be bipartisan in membership; and in several states where no such provision exists, tradition favors the maintenance of a bipartisan balance in the court.

The compensation of appellate judges, needless to say, is somewhat larger than that of trial judges, but in not a few states is still woefully inadequate. Term of office also tends to be slightly longer—in a number of states one or two years longer.

On the whole, the evils of the partisan participation in the selection of judges, regarded as so serious in the case of trial judges, are much less so in the case of appellate judges. The pressure on an appellate judge for political favors is much less severe than on a trial judge, both because he has few if any favors to dispense, and because he is only one of a bench. Moreover, there is an aura of power, dignity, and remoteness around most appellate courts that tends to insulate a member of the court from political influences, even though his political activities may have persisted up to the day of his selection for office.

[18] See Lee, Emergence and Evolution of Constitutional Right to a Fair Trial before a Justice of the Peace, 20 Fed. Bar Assn. Jour. 111 (1960).

[19] See Sunderland, Study of Justices of the Peace and other Minor Courts (1948).

Except for removal by a higher court, the provisions for removal of appellate judges are in general similar to those existing for trial judges.

5. FEDERAL JUDICIARY: DISTRICT COURT JUDGES

The federal district court judges represent the most clear-cut example of a judiciary drawn from the bar. To their courts, as we have seen, come a greater variety of matters than come to any state court, and ordinarily they are matters of some importance, often of great importance. Yet federal district judges are rarely drawn from the state judiciary (the only judiciary from which they could be drawn, since there are no inferior federal trial courts); almost invariably they are drawn from the bar (including in that term lawyers in government service).

The compensation of the federal district judge, and the provision for retirement, while much improved in recent years, are still on a level which debars some able men from seeking the office. On the other hand, the constitutional life tenure (or more accurately, tenure "during good behavior")[20] offsets in a measure the inadequacy of the compensation.

Selection

District court judges are, by statute (not by the Constitution), appointed by the President with the approval of the Senate. By long-standing tradition, senatorial courtesy—i.e., the traditional, though not perhaps invariable, refusal of the Senate to confirm an appointment to a local office if the senator from the state, being of the same party as the President, objects—governs here as with administrative presidential appointments. Hence, the senators from the state in which the vacancy exists, if of the same party as the President, ordinarily initiate the suggestion for the name sent by the President to the Senate; while if the senators from the state in which the vacancy exists are not of the President's party, the name will ordinarily be suggested by those in power in the President's party in that state. Needless to say, even where the senator suggests the name to the President, that name ordinarily represents the selection of the party rather than the senator's personal selection. In recent years, the Attorney General has apparently also taken the initiative in suggesting names to the President on occasion; and on still rarer occasions a name put forward by bar associations has been favorably acted on. On the whole, however,

---

[20] Congress may, however, abolish the court in which the judge holds office, so that his office ceases to exist. It may also, apparently, abolish the office even without disturbing the court. This is no longer a practical possibility; but it was actually done in 1801, when the Jeffersonian party, on gaining control of Congress, abolished a number of judgeships created by the Federalists in the previous year. The judges holding these judgeships lost their offices and had no recourse.

it is still the party organization which makes the initial designation. Occasionally, such a designation, after investigation made for the President (usually by the Department of Justice) and sometimes after adverse comment by the local press or bar associations, is withdrawn; but the substitute designation will again ordinarily be made by the party organization.

Under these circumstances, the quality of the federal district judges varies considerably from one area to another, according as the quality of the political organization in the area is higher or lower. The post is so attractive, from the fact of its life tenure[21] and the importance of the matters which come before the court that, despite the inadequacy of the compensation, some extremely able men have been attracted to it. On the other hand, the remoteness of the appointing machinery and of the court itself from the community as a whole has made possible some extremely weak appointments.

There is one small group of federal judges whose appointment has been somewhat less influenced by politics. This is the group of judges in the federal courts of the District of Columbia. Since senatorial courtesy does not operate in these appointments, and the political organizations of the voteless district are nominal, the President has a comparatively free hand in making these appointments; and they have in recent years been used on several occasions to reward faithful service of career men in the legal departments of the government—to such an extent indeed as to evoke the criticism that this bench, by reason of the allegedly bureaucratic background of its members, is biased in favor of the official viewpoint in the numerous controversies regarding administrative action which because

[21] Congress, in establishing certain courts, has failed to provide life tenure for the judges. Such a court is, for example, the United States District Court for Puerto Rico, the judges of which hold office for eight years. The power of Congress to create such courts derives not from Article III of the Constitution, which requires that the judges of the inferior courts authorized by it shall hold office during good behavior, but from its power (Art. I, Sec. 8) to make all laws necessary and proper for carrying out any of the powers vested in the federal government. American Insur. Co. v. Canter, 1 Pet. 511 (1828). Courts created under Article III are known as "constitutional" courts; those created under Article I, as "legislative" courts. Although the judicial power of the United States, vested by Article III in the constitutional courts, "extends" to "all cases" arising under the Constitution or federal statutes or treaties, Congress has vested legislative courts with jurisdiction of some of the classes of cases in this category. The seemingly irreconcilable repugnance of such jurisdiction to the Constitution (as well as the characterization by Congress of certain courts— e.g., the Customs Court—as courts "established under Article III of the Constitution" despite the fact that the matters entrusted to them are but dubiously "cases" arising under federal law) has been the subject of several Supreme Court opinions, themselves not by any means easy to reconcile. The latest of these opinions, rendered in Glidden Co. v. Zdanok, 370 U.S. 530 (1962), appears to represent an attempt by the Court to dispose definitively of all objections to existing legislation in this field. In the opinion of some, however, the attempt was unsuccessful. See Amer, The Legislative Court Problem: A Proposed Solution, 38 N.Y. U. Law Rev. 302 (1963).

of the location of the court in Washington come before it.[22] Whatever the validity of this criticism, the bench in question represents the nearest approach in the federal system, or indeed in the entire American legal picture, to a career-man judiciary, though not a career judiciary.

The senatorial power of veto of a nomination to the office of district judge is rarely employed.[23] However, the practice of public hearings on such nominations, by the Senate committee to which the nomination is referred—a practice instituted as recently as 1929—has doubtless caused a more careful scrutiny of candidates by the executive in advance of their nomination. Such hearings invite attacks on the candidate, often unfounded, both by those inspired by personal motives and by those averse to his supposed political philosophy. The propriety of examining the political philosophy of a nominee for district judge has been defended on the ground that he is in part a political functionary with legislative power—this because of the power of the courts to declare laws void as unconstitutional, and their power to make law in the interpretation of novel statutes setting up new forms of governmental control.[24] The supposed power of a district judge to declare a law unconstitutional is, as we have seen, merely a shadow without substance. His power to make law is likewise severely limited by the power of the appellate courts promptly to unmake the law he has made. In any event, the attempt to insure at the time of his appointment, in a judge who holds office during good behavior, the possession during his entire term of the "correct" political philosophy is manifestly condemned to failure.

The constitutional amendment which in 1913 transferred the selection of United States senators from the hands of the state legislatures to those of the electorate represented merely the final stage of a reform which had been long in progress, for by means of pre-election senatorial pledges the members of the state legislatures had long, in a number of states, been committed in advance to the designation as senator of a person popularly selected. Nevertheless, it was still true at the beginning of the century that senators were in many states selected without much reference to the electorate; and it was equally true that they tended to reflect, to a much greater degree than is true today, the views of the banking and industrialist classes. This was naturally reflected in their choice of persons to be

[22] The growth, even outside the District of Columbia, in the number of federal judges whose chief if not sole legal experience has been in the Department of Justice, has also evoked protest. See 1952 Annual Report Amer. Bar Assn. 212–213.

[23] There is no constitutional requirement that federal judges (save members of the Supreme Court) be appointed by the President with the advice of the Senate. Like other federal officers, they could, did the statute so provide, be appointed by the President alone, a head of department (e.g., the Attorney General), or the courts of law.

[24] Cole, The Role of the Senate in the Confirmation of Judicial Nominations, 28 Am. Pol. Sci. Rev. 875, 892 (1934).

suggested to the President for federal judgeships; and during the early years of the century the federal courts were generally regarded as citadels of conservatism, if not of reaction. The issuance by some federal judges of sweeping injunctions in labor disputes was a factor of importance in creating this public attitude. Within the past few decades, however, the membership of the federal bench has been almost completely changed; and the new appointees have as a whole reflected a more varied background, and a less intimate past connection with corporate and banking interests, than had formerly been the case. The weakness of the federal bench lies rather in the indifferent quality of those of its members who owe their appointments to the inferior sort of party organizations.

Because of the remoteness of the appointing power, the advice of a local non-political selection board would seem to be more clearly needed in federal than in state judicial selection.[25] The patronage interests of the senators in these district judgeships are, however, so deeply rooted that the selection board plan cannot now, or perhaps for some years to come, be regarded as a practical issue. In the meantime, vigorous counter pressure by bar associations seems to be the only force available for combating the political pressure for mediocre or even unfit appointees. The actual extent of the participation of the bar in the selection process varies greatly from district to district.

Since the President almost invariably bestows his nominations to the federal district bench on lawyers of his own party, the district courts tend to reflect, if either political party has long retained the presidency, the political complexion of that party. Thus, when the twenty-year period of possession of the presidency by the Democratic party ended in 1953, the federal district judges who had been drawn from that party were heavily in the majority. During the succeeding eight years of a Republican presidency, the balance was restored. The advent of a Democratic president in 1961 was marked by an unprecedented enlargement of the number of district court judgeships,[26] virtually all of which were filled by the appointment of Democrats, thus again creating a heavy Democratic majority. This condition has been lamented by some, the contention being put forward that appointments should be so balanced that the district bench would be

[25] In 1958 the House of Delegates of the American Bar Association recommended to the President the establishment of an independent commission as an agency of the President, to originate suggestions for nominations to the federal bench "of persons deemed highly qualified," and called on the members of the Senate to restrict themselves "in a spirit of unselfish public service" to merely passing on the nominations submitted. 1958 Report Amer. Bar Assn. 183. The matter has not been further pressed by the association.

[26] The need for the creation of additional judgeships had been urgent for some years past, but the Democratic majority in Congress, holding fast to the traditional concept of federal district judge nominations as party perquisites, refused to provide judgeships until they were certain the judgeships would not be filled by a Republican President.

"bipartisan," by which it is apparently meant that there should not at any time be a heavy majority of district judges coming from one party. The rationale of this criticism is somewhat elusive, since the judges do not in any case carry out party policies.[27] It is perfectly true that were federal judges selected solely on the basis of merit, their party affiliations, if any, would probably be divided fairly evenly between the two parties; but such a method of selection would be not bipartisan but nonpartisan—a method which some of the critics of the present outcome would perhaps be the last to favor.[28]

At an earlier page it was suggested that a more effective use of the judicial manpower of the federal district courts would be possible were each judge merely appointed to a nationwide federal judicial corps, instead of to a particular district. Such an organization of the district courts would also make it much easier to attain a nonpartisan method of selection of these judges. The suggestion is, however, too far removed from present-day realities to warrant more than mere mention.

Removal

Federal judges, by constitutional provision, hold office "during good behavior." Like all federal officers, they are removable on impeachment for "treason, bribery or other high crimes and misdemeanors"; Congress has provided no other method for their removal. The impeachment process has been resorted to on perhaps half a dozen occasions, removal generally following. There have been not a few cases, however, in which notoriously unfit federal district judges have continued in office because of the cumbrousness of the impeachment process. Proposals have accordingly been made that a supplementary removal procedure be instituted, removal by a bench of appellate federal judges being strongly urged by some students of the subject. To date, however, neither Congress nor the bar has shown any appreciable interest in this desirable change.

A perplexing problem is presented by the judge whose faculties have become impaired—a circumstance to be expected in a corps having life tenure—but who, unaware of his own unfitness, continues on the bench. The problem is not insoluble, but no attempt to set up a procedure for

---

[27] In appointments to the district courts in the southern states since 1960, the restriction of appointments to Democrats, committed by party connections to the doctrine of racial segregation, has, however, been clearly reflected in the reluctance of some of the judges appointed to implement wholeheartedly the 1954 Supreme Court decision requiring school authorities to desegregate their schools "with all deliberate speed." See Lewis, Federal Judges in South Scored, New York Times, July 19, 1963, p. 8.

[28] The discussion has reference solely to courts of original jurisdiction. In high appellate courts, particularly in the states, a bipartisan complexion is highly desirable because of matters of election law and other matters of party interest which come before them for final adjudication.

dealing with it appears to have been made. Less difficult is the case of the judge who is unable to discharge his duties because of physical ailments long continued and seeming incurable. Whether it constitutes "good behavior" for such a judge to insist on retaining his office, instead of retiring under the generous provision now available to him, may well be questioned.

6. FEDERAL JUDICIARY: APPEALS COURT JUDGES

A large number of the judges of the eleven federal courts of appeals served their judicial apprenticeships as federal district judges. In recent years, however, the practice of filling these judgeships from the district bench has tended to decline. The appointment of an outstanding lawyer or legal scholar to one of these courts, while not intrinsically objectionable, should be exceptional if the morale of the district bench is to be preserved, and if the appeals bench as a whole is to have, in the cases which it reviews, that realistic appreciation of what has gone on in the trial court that comes best from experience as a trial judge.

With respect to the other matters discussed in connection with district judges, the judges of the courts of appeals present no important differences.[29]

7. FEDERAL JUDICIARY: JUSTICES OF THE SUPREME COURT

In the case of the justices of the Supreme Court, appointment by the President with the consent of the Senate is prescribed by the Constitution, not by statute. The tradition has from the first been against the promotion to the Supreme Court of judges of the lower federal courts. The creation, in 1893, of the system of intermediate appellate courts might have been expected to modify this tradition but it did not.

Without doubt, some of the ablest jurists of the past generation were to be found on the federal appellate benches; their outstanding qualities were recognized by the virtually unanimous opinion of the bar and of academic legal scholars. But in appointments to the Supreme Court they were repeatedly passed over in favor of appointees of mediocre quality and without previous experience on an appellate—or indeed on any—tribunal. Of the present members of the Court, only three had previously served on appellate courts, and their service had in each case been brief.

All this is not to suggest that appointment to the Court should be

[29] The large role commonly understood to be played by the Attorney General in the promotion of district court judges to the courts of appeals has been criticized on the ground that district judges hopeful of such promotion are likely to lean to the side of the government in the cases, numerous in the district courts everywhere and numerically very important in some, brought before them by the Department of Justice.

confined to jurists with experience on appellate benches. Some of the
ablest members of the Court in this century were without any judicial
experience (as were also most of the less distinguished). The prime
requisite is that the appointee, if his presence on the Court is to contribute
to that confidence in the Court's essentially political decisions that is so
desirable, shall at the time of his appointment already have demonstrated
to the country his high stature as a legal thinker and statesman. Service
on a high state court, or on the federal intermediate appellate bench, gives
an exceptional opportunity for doing this; and there are few other equal
opportunities for doing it.[30]

Throughout our history, the choice of justices of the Supreme Court
has been the resultant of diverse forces—partisan, geographical, personal,
and ideological. The vast political power exercised by the Court sets it
apart from all other courts in the land, and makes it impossible that juristic
ability should be the sole consideration in selecting its members. Nevertheless, one reviewing the history of appointments to the Court in recent
decades cannot but feel that it would have been possible to give due
weight to the political role of the Court and yet have found a greater
measure of juristic ability than has characterized the Court as a whole.
Without assuming to appraise the stature of the present membership of
the Court, it is accurate to say that hardly any of its incumbents enjoyed
any special juristic reputation at the time of his appointment.[31]

In the history of the Court only one of its members has been im-
peached—Samuel Chase. The violent Federalist partisanship exhibited

[30] Moreover, an appellate judge has in most cases seen service as a trial judge.
In view of the function which the Court has assumed of supervising the nation's
law-enforcement officers, state as well as federal, through the promulgation of new,
exclusionary rules of evidence in criminal trials, it would be helpful, in view of the
Court's complete lack of contact with law-enforcement problems, and its lack of
expert advice, for a greater proportion of its members to have had even that peripheral contact with these matters that a trial judge encounters.

[31] An aspect of the nomination of Supreme Court justices that has more recently
drawn attention is that of the recess appointment of a justice, followed by his nomination, when Congress reconvenes, for appointment "during good behavior." The
conflict between a recess appointment and the obvious intent of the Constitution, that
a federal judge shall, by virtue of his assured tenure, be wholly independent of the
executive and of Congress (and indeed of public opinion) in his adjudications, has
caused some to urge that the constitutional provision for recess appointments was not
intended to apply to the judiciary, or at any rate should not be applied to them.
With respect to Supreme Court appointments, the undesirability of recess appointments is of course much more marked than with respect to the inferior federal
courts. Such appointments have, however, increased in frequency in recent years, and
the number of cases heard and decided by the Court while recess appointees sat on
it has increased even more markedly. In 1960 the Senate adopted a resolution "expressing the sense of the Senate that recess appointments to the Supreme Court of
the United States should not be made except under unusual circumstances." 86th
Cong., S. Res. 334. See Note: Recess Appointments to the Supreme Court—Constitutional but Unwise?, 10 Stan. Law Rev. 124 (1957).

by him when sitting as a trial judge (as Supreme Court justices then did) brought about his impeachment in 1803 by the House; but the Senate refused to remove him.

The provision, now in effect for some years, whereby a member of the Court may retire on full salary, has reduced, though it has not eliminated, the danger that a justice will remain on the bench after his powers have begun to fail, a danger that several times in the Court's history has been very real.

8. JURORS

Though the improvement of the quality of the judge is a perennial theme in the literature of legal reform, the improvement of the quality of the juror is given relatively little attention. Yet it must be apparent, from the account given in earlier pages of the role of the jury in our courts, that the intelligence and probity of the juror are of vital consequence.

No improvement in methods of jury selection will produce a jury really competent to pass upon some of the more complicated and technical issues of fact which some present-day civil litigations present. However, a vast improvement of the quality of the juror can unquestionably be effected in many jurisdictions by unremitting efforts to improve the selection procedure.

In such efforts, it is important to have clearly in mind that the need is for jurors of intelligence, probity, and understanding; that that need can be met only by a process of fairly strict elimination not only of those lacking in native intelligence but also of those lacking in that type of intelligence which comes from a reasonable amount of education, whether acquired by schooling or by self-instruction. This criterion encounters, however, the opposition of those to whom the jury is not primarily an agency of justice, but rather a safeguard of democratic institutions. Though it is not considered to be repugnant to the nature of a democratic society to insist that its public officials generally should be of a high order of intelligence, jurors, who are after all discharging a public office of the gravest importance, are in this view in a special category.

The origin of the jury, as we have seen, was not even remotely related to any notion of democracy. As the English jury was gradually transformed from a panel of persons speaking of their own knowledge into a bench of triers of the fact, it became a jury of freeholders, and in the towns, a jury of householders and merchants. In our colonial period, the property qualification was universal for jurors, as it was for voters. The notion that a jury should be representative of all economic levels, now in effect accepted as a constitutional requirement, would have been quite strange to the draftsmen of our first constitutions. Yet so far has this concept of the jury as a democratic device taken hold, that to some a jury confined to the more intelligent, even if representative of all economic levels, is obnoxious as undemocratic.[32] If such be the premise from which the attempt to improve the quality of the juror must proceed, the limit of improvement will soon be reached.

The juror who sits in the jury box has arrived there as the result of three successive steps. The last of these steps—the selection of a jury from the larger panel of veniremen who are in attendance at the court awaiting service—has already been described; it is a process of weeding out, by challenges, from a group which has been selected by lot from among those summoned to the court for jury duty, those unsatisfactory to either side, and replacing them with others, also drawn by lot. While this process may occasionally eliminate a juror deficient in elementary qualifications—such as adequate knowledge of the language—it cannot materially improve the quality of the jury.

Neither can the preceding one of the three steps improve the quality of the jury. This is the selection of veniremen from the basic list of those subject to jury duty. Typically, this selection is also by lot.[33]

It is the first step in the process—the preparation of the list from which veniremen are to be selected by lot—to which efforts at improvement must be directed. This list obviously fixes the level above which the quality of the jurymen ultimately selected for service cannot rise. To insure that that list shall include a due proportion of the more intelligent members of the community, the starting point should be a complete list of all, or virtually

---

[32] "The vice lies in the very concept of 'blue ribbon' panels—the systematic exclusion of all but the 'best' or most learned or intelligent of the general jurors. Such panels are completely at war with the democratic theory of our jury system, a theory formulated out of the experience of generations." Justice Murphy, dissenting, in Moore v. New York, 333 U.S. 565, 569 (1948). This was a criminal case, but the language of Justice Murphy's opinion in this case and in Fay v. New York (see p. 119) is not limited to criminal juries. It is interesting to note that Justice Murphy, and perhaps some of those who joined him in his dissents in these two cases, while aware that the Constitution does not require trial by jury in the states, hold that once it is employed it must be "democratic." Thus, the concept of a "fair" trial, created by the Court, is transformed into a "democratic" trial. See Foley, Class Discrimination in Selection of Jurors, 5 Cath. U. Law Rev. 157 (1955).

[33] Where, however, the choice is left to officials, there is ordinarily no authority and no machinery for making the selection on the basis of the comparative qualifications of the persons on the list. Indeed, discretion entrusted to officials at this stage has often had the contrary result: the development of a class of "professional" jurors—individuals who are summoned for jury service with such frequency, and who are so willing if not eager to serve, that their presence on the jury selected to try a particular case, or to sit on all cases tried within a given month or other like period of jury service, can often safely be predicted. The opportunities for and temptations to the corruption of prospective jurors offered by such a system have resulted, in a number of instances, in jury scandals. The selection of veniremen from the jury list by lot is a minimal requirement for a proper jury system.

all, the eligible citizenry. Such a list is unfortunately hardly anywhere in existence, in default whereof, the list of registered voters may be used. The selection from this list of such number of names as experience indicates will be required over a given period may then be made a purely mechanical process, as by selecting every twentieth, thirtieth, or fortieth name. In this way, the possibility that the list will contain an undue proportion of members of one or another race, religion, or economic class or that it will be weighted in favor of any particular political group, is obviated.

The next requisite is the removal from this list of unfit or exempt persons. This it has been found can effectively be done only by summoning each person on the list to appear before a properly qualified official. The result is a list on which every name is that of a person qualified to serve—a list which can be used with a minimum of delay by the trial court.

In contrast to the method described, the jury list is still made up in most jurisdictions, and in the federal courts,[34] by a process which combines the initial listing and a preliminary screening in a single operation, subject to the unregulated discretion on the part of the officials in charge (in most states, the county commissioners or supervisors; in the larger centers, special jury officials; in the federal courts, the clerk assisted by a "jury commissioner" appointed by the judge). The officials make up the list by selection, random or deliberate, from assessment rolls or other available lists, from names suggested to them or solicited by them, and by adding names of persons personally known to them. Under such a procedure, the quality of the list depends largely on the conscientiousness of the official; and it is likely to omit an appreciable number of persons thoroughly qualified for jury service.[35] On the other hand, it facilitates the efforts of the "professional juror" type to get on the list. Such a list is, moreover, likely to contain some persons who are unfit or exempt; consequently, a further screening of the list after the veniremen have been summoned for service is essential. This not only places a needless burden on the court, but insures that the screening will not be thoroughly done.

Reform of the jury list procedure along the lines suggested has made progress in some of the larger cities; but the small size of the entire operation in the smaller cities and in the rural counties works against that greater formalization and impersonality of procedure which is so essential. What appears to be needed is not merely a state-wide statute (for in not a few states the matter is still left largely to the counties, sometimes under special statutes for particular counties) but a state-wide administrative

[34] See the exhaustive report on the jury system in the federal courts made by the Committee on the Operation of the Jury System to the Judicial Conference of the United States, 26 F.R.D. 409 (1961).

[35] It is at this point that the exclusion of Negroes from jury service, found in some states, is commonly effected.

agency either to supervise the operations by the county officials or itself to take over those activities. Undoubtedly, a career official, responsible perhaps to the state high court, traveling from county to county to take charge of or to supervise the preparation of jury lists, would in many counties produce an improved list.

An obstacle to jury improvement is the exemption from jury duty of large classes of persons who would make excellent jurors. Exemptions differ widely from jurisdiction to juridiction—lawyers, physicians, dentists, pharmacists, teachers, and clergymen being almost everywhere exempt. In a number of states, printers, railroad employees, telegraph and telephone workers, journalists, government officials, firemen, policemen, etc., are also among the exempt classes. Some of these exemptions are of questionable validity. In others, a qualified rather than a total exemption would be sufficient. Moreover, the holding of a proportion of jury trials in the later hours of the day would doubtless make possible the service of many now exempt.

Any plan indeed which would place the juror's service on a part-time rather than a full-time basis would greatly improve the average quality of the jury panel by reducing the urge to escape jury duty now so prevalent. In the cities certainly it would be entirely practicable for many a juror of the most desirable type to serve half a day in the courts and still be able to make a substantial amount of progress in his own affairs in the remaining hours of the day. Indeed, it may be questioned whether the entire time schedule of the urban courts in their trial sittings is not out of step with the conditions of modern life—whether a sitting beginning at a much later hour than does the business day, and ending correspondingly later, would not better meet the convenience not merely of the juror but of all concerned.

Still another factor responsible for the desire to escape duty is the utter inadequacy of the compensation paid. The disparity between the typical juror's daily fee and the amount which a day is worth in wages or in earning capacity is notorious; and it has been steadily increasing. The burden is not perhaps intolerable if the juror is to serve but a few days. In many jurisdictions, however, he serves at least a fortnight; and if he happens to be selected in a lengthy case he may have to serve for many weeks. As a result, service in lengthy cases is especially avoided or evaded by those who might be best qualified to try them.

The matter of increased compensation for jurors, and of extra compensation for jurors in lengthy cases, is one that urgently needs attention.[36]

[36] Much of what is said here as to the trial juror is equally applicable to the grand juror. In the selection of the grand jury another factor is specially to be guarded against—the "packing" of the jury to secure a panel favorable or hostile to the public officials of the county, or its former officials, with a view to a politically motivated investigation, or suppression of investigation, of official conduct.

9. LAWYERS

Under our adversary system of judicature, the attorney is in most types of judicial proceeding as indispensable as is the judge or the juror.

Even under those Continental criminal procedures in which the court takes the lead in the questioning of witnesses, the attorneys, both for prosecution and defense, have an active role in the trial; and the preparation of the case is of course chiefly in their hands. The practicability of a judicature functioning without advocates continues to be an interesting subject of speculation; and such systems have indeed proved their practicability in a setting of great simplicity of social organization. For the present purpose, however, the need for, and the indefinite continuance of, the institution of advocacy in all but the simpler types of judicial proceeding may be assumed.[37]

In theory the attorney is an officer of the court, intent, like the judge, on eliciting the truth.[38] But an advocate inevitably becomes a partisan. Moreover, unlike the judge, he has a personal interest in the outcome of the case. Even if his fee in the particular case has already been fixed regardless of the outcome—a practice which is supposed to make the English barrister disinterested—victory, in addition to being more satisfying than defeat, is more helpful in procuring further retainers.

How to reconcile the personal interest of the advocate in victory, with his ostensible character as a servant of justice, is a perennial dilemma of judicature. In a considerable proportion of cases the dilemma has been resolved for at least the advocate on one side (and curiously enough, sometimes for the advocates on either side) by the conviction that the truth is completely with his side. In the remainder, however, the advocate is either aware that there is much truth on both sides, or that there is little or none on his side.

The form of oath of admission to the bar administered in some states obligates the lawyer not to counsel or maintain any suit or proceeding which appears to him to be unjust, nor any defense except such as he honestly believes to be debatable under the law of the land. The ideal thus set forth is adhered to with substantial completeness by a large percentage of the bar; to expect universal observance of so high a standard

[37] See, generally, Assn. of Amer. Law Schools (ed.), Select Readings on the Legal Profession (1962).

[38] See Cohen v. Hurley, 366 U.S. 117 (1961), in which the Supreme Court refused to set aside, as a denial of due process of law, the disbarment of a lawyer by the New York courts by reason of his refusal, because of danger of self-incrimination, to answer a question regarding his professional conduct. The question was put to him in the course of an inquiry ordered by the court into unprofessional conduct prevalent in connection with "ambulance chasing." While the lawyer enjoyed the (state) constitutional right to refuse to answer, such refusal disqualified him from continuing to be "an officer of the court."

would be utopian. In criminal cases, its observance would in effect require the lawyer to refuse to represent a client who had admitted his guilt, but who wished to plead not guilty and to stand trial; it would at any rate bar the lawyer from offering evidence which would tend to raise doubt as to his client's guilt. That such is not the code of the lawyer whose chief practice is in the criminal courts of the larger cities goes without saying.

To the generous imagination of many a youth dreaming of a legal career, such a lawyer wears an aura of chivalry. He is a knight-errant coming to the aid of the innocent victim of deceptive circumstantial evidence, of malevolent enemies, or even of official miscreants. No doubt every urban criminal lawyer from time to time finds occasion for the exercise of his talents in defense of such unfortunates; but realistically, the staple of his clientele is the professional lawbreaker, and his daily work consists less in dramatic courtroom appearances than in negotiations with the prosecutor on the terms on which the latter will accept a plea of guilty to a lesser offense and will recommend leniency to the court. If his clientele includes the racketeer, his ostensibly professional labors may include intimate collaboration in the necessary arrangements with corrupt police and prosecuting authorities.

The bar is often reproved for not cleaning its house of these enemies of society, garbed in the colors of an honorable profession. But the critics have seldom put forward a practical program of action. Proof of unlawful conduct on the part of such a practitioner is ordinarily impossible to obtain. His known offense is his continued representation of the underworld, which raises a presumption that his character and methods are unworthy of a member of the bar; but to found a disbarment proceeding on this ground alone is obviously difficult.[39]

A lawyer of this type shows no hesitancy in protesting to the court, the jury, and the prosecutor the innocence of a client whom he knows to be guilty beyond question. But what of the lawyer of character? If he knows a client to be guilty, may he properly enter a plea of not guilty on his behalf, and at the trial introduce evidence, truthful so far as it goes perhaps, but intended to sow doubt in the minds of the jurymen; may he cross-examine prosecution witnesses whom he knows to be truthful with the object of causing the jurymen to suspect them of untruth; and may he then in his summing up strive to reinforce these doubts? There are without question many lawyers of character who would answer all these questions in the affirmative; but it is difficult to adduce any defense for such

---

[39] The most effective cure is to make his services unattractive to his clientele. It should not be difficult for a prosecutor, and indeed the court, to give the inhabitant of the underworld to understand that the retainer of a lawyer of this category injures his defense.

conduct on the part of one who is in theory at least an officer of the court. The organized profession has taken no position on this question. In a formulation of proper standards of professional ethics adopted by the American Bar Association in 1908, and in this respect still unchanged, the position is taken that "it is the right of the lawyer to undertake the defense of persons accused of crime, regardless of his personal opinion of the guilt of the accused; otherwise innocent persons, victims only of suspicious circumstances, might be denied proper defense." It is obvious that all this relates only to the situation in which the client has protested his innocence to the attorney; it has no relevance to the situation in which he has confessed his guilt. As to that the statement is silent.

Certainly, even if it be thought proper for the advocate to carry on a defense of the character described, he should go no further. Clearly improper is it for him falsely to represent to the jury that he is personally convinced of his guilty client's innocence. The Canons of Professional Ethics adopted by the American Bar Association declare that "it is improper for a lawyer to assert in argument his personal belief in his client's innocence or in the justice of his cause."

A quite different question with respect to the lawyer's obligation is that presented when he is asked to undertake the representation of one, particularly a defendant in a criminal case, to whom, or to whose cause, the community is hostile, so that, associating the lawyer with his client, it will be so unfriendly to the lawyer as to threaten his future professional success in that community. The question has been presented acutely in connection with the defense of those accused of subversion or spying, and, in the southern states, those charged with participating in demonstrations, picketing, sit-ins or the like, in connection with campaigns for desegregation of facilities. Because of allegations, apparently well-founded, that such defendants have in some cases experienced extreme difficulty in obtaining representation, it has been urged that the principle should be recognized in this country, as it is said to be in England, that a lawyer asked to undertake the defense of a person charged with crime may not refuse.[40]

The tradition of unbridled advocacy which prevailed in an earlier day (and with it the histrionics which often characterized the summing up to the jury) is on the decline. Its complete disappearance, which is much to be desired, depends chiefly on the judiciary. A firm judge can quickly convey to the attorneys before him that any show of emotion or personal interest and any resort to irrelevancy are out of order. When thus restrained,

[40] See Rostow, A Lawyer and His Client, 48 Amer. Bar Assn. Jour. 25, 146 (1962); Report on Professional Responsibility by the Joint Conference on Professional Responsibility established by the American Bar Association and the Association of American Law Schools, 44 Amer. Bar Assn. Jour. 1159, 1216 (1958).

advocacy has its legitimate place in most forms of judicial proceeding.[41]

But every useful institution is open to abuse; and few are as liable to it as is the institution of advocacy. A major factor making for its abuse is the overcrowding of the bar; for the lawyer, like other professional men, is ordinarily less likely to play an ignoble part when his professional position is secure. Since public opinion would reject, and rightly so, any attempt to limity arbitrarily the number of new entrants to the calling, the remedy for overcrowding, if remedy there can be, is to be sought rather in severe standards of entrance. This is not to be confused with merely increasing the number of years of college study prerequisite to entering law school; such requirements set up a test of endurance rather than ability, since virtually anyone devoting the necessary time can meet them. What is wanted is a complete revision of the tests given for admission to the bar, to test thoroughly the ability to do the tasks that the lawyer is called upon to do, rather than as now, the ability to reproduce the legal doctrines set forth in the books. Such a test, it is believed, would substantially reduce the rate of new entrants to the profession. It would be idle to hope, however, that it will reduce it to a point where the number of those holding license to practice wil be equal only to the real need for legal service. The surplus lawyer will continue, as now, after a shorter or longer attempt to continue at the bar, to turn to other pursuits.

Despite its English ancestry, the American bar completely failed to develop the separate class of specialists in advocacy, found in the higher English courts. From the first, the American lawyer almost everywhere combined advocacy with the other, quantitatively far more important, activities of a lawyer's work—the negotiation of business affairs, the drawing of documents, counsel on business and family problems having a legal aspect, supervision of trusts, settlement of controversies, preparation of litigation, and in more recent times, representation before administrative agencies.

The absence of a recognized class of advocates, corresponding to the English barrister, has been deplored by some. The inexpert conduct of court-

---

[41] Much of the time of the civil courts, however, is consumed and, correspondingly, much of civil advocacy is devoted to a class of cases in which the equipment of the lawyer is largely superfluous. This is the class of so-called negligence suits—i.e., actions brought to recover damages for injuries sustained in accidents. Such actions, largely arising out of automobile accidents, today constitute a principal part of civil litigation, federal as well as state. The placing of compensation for injury, in all the usual forms of accident which constitute a universal hazard of modern life, on the same legal principles as now govern in industrial accidents to workmen (a reform which does not necessarily involve the transfer of responsibility for adjudication from the courts to administrative tribunals) would greatly reduce the need for lawyers in this field, with resultant saving to the public and enhanced prestige to the profession. In the field of petty civil litigation, too, the lawyer's education, his methods of work, and the expense which they necessarily entail are increasingly out of proportion to the need. In a number of cities, in the small claims courts, lawyers are unknown; and in this field the number of people who are capable of presenting the facts without the aid of counsel tends to increase.

room proceedings by lawyers who enter the courtroom only occasionally, so runs the argument, tends to clog the work of the courts. Undoubtedly, inexperience of counsel not frequently exhibits itself in American courtrooms. To remedy this, however, it is hardly necessary to confine courtroom representation to a separate order of lawyers—a method which, as the English experience proves, adds substantially to the cost of litigation and is in any event practicable, in the trial courts, only in those of major jurisdiction and in a closely settled area, where much litigation is concentrated in a relatively small number of centers. It would be sufficient if law school graduates were better grounded in courtroom procedure, and the legal novice, thus equipped, were required to gain adequate experience in the lower courts before being permitted, as he is today, sometimes to waste the time of the higher trial courts while learning the rudiments of trial work.

10. PROSECUTORS

In earlier pages, the well-nigh dominant position occupied by the public prosecutor in the administration of criminal justice has been emphasized: his power to determine that a prosecution shall or shall not be instituted, his power to procure dismissal by the court of a prosecution already instituted, or to procure the acceptance by the court of a plea of guilty to a lesser offense than charged, and his power to influence the severity or leniency of the sentence to be imposed. As an able student of the prosecutor's role has well said: "Nowhere is it more apparent that our government is a government of men, not of laws. Nowhere do the very human elements of dishonesty, ambition, greed, lust for power, laxness or bigotry have more room for development. Also, there is no office where an able and honest public servant can be more effective."

All this, however, as already indicated, is much more unequivocally true of the state prosecutor than it is of the federal prosecutor; and it is to the character of the state prosecutor therefore that chief attention should be given.[42]

Characteristically, the public prosecutor in the states is, as already noted, an elected local official, either responsible to no one, or responsible to the governor or attorney general in practice only for aggravated nonfeasance or misfeasance. He runs for office, ordinarily, on a party ticket. His term is nowhere longer than eight years; two years is the term in a number of states. In many of the country's rural counties, the limited demands of the office (even when it carries with it, as it frequently does, responsibility for the civil legal business of the county as well) and the

[42] In some of the larger cities, much or all of the responsibility for prosecuting charges of violation of municipal ordinances and the like falls on the city attorney rather than the county prosecutor. Prosecutions of this kind are in most cases, as already noted, criminal in form only.

correspondingly low compensation make it essentially a part-time office, the incumbent continuing his private practice. At the other extreme, in a county embracing a large city the office may be a most exacting one, entailing the direction of a large number of subordinates, rather than the personal conduct of an investigation or a prosecution.

However it may be assessed on theoretical grounds, the system characteristically produces, in the average rural county, a moderately satisfactory type of prosecutor. There is, in such a county, ordinarily no underworld to interest itself in control of, or even influence in, the party organizations of the county; the county funds are not large, and their raising is too directly a concern of the residents of the county for peculation to remain unprosecuted. Ordinarily crime too is a matter of direct interest to the citizenry, and lack of vigor in its prosecution is promptly resented. A prosecutor in such a county is thus under direct pressure from the electorate to be alert and active, and is under no strong temptation ordinarily to suppress prosecution. The office thus appeals to the young lawyer, particularly if he has ambitions for public life, as an opportunity to establish himself in the eyes of the local community as a man of character and ability.

But there are also major weaknesses in the institution as it is found in the rural counties. Typically the county prosecutor on assuming office is wanting in extended experience in criminal prosecution—perhaps, indeed, is wholly without such experience. He seldom remains in office long enough to acquire it. Instead, he leaves for more lucrative office, or to devote his entire time to his growing private practice. If, as is usually the case, he has political aspirations, he can further them only by procuring well-publicized convictions: a decision not to prosecute, based on honest doubts of the guilt of the suspect, however laudable as a victory of conscience, will gain him few votes when next he runs for office.

These weaknesses can be overcome only by basing the prosecutor's office, in the rural areas, on a larger territorial unit than the county—as is indeed done in a few states. With a unit large enough to warrant a full-time prosecutor and an assistant, something more nearly approaching a career office is possible, even if popular election is retained; and with a larger constituency, the prosecutor's interest in procuring a conviction at all costs in a well publicized local case would be reduced.

In the cities (or more accurately, in the counties in which the cities are situated) the prosecutor's office is sought by lawyers of longer experience, and typically by lawyers who have had long connection with one of the dominant party organizations. Occasionally, a citizens' reform crusade will succeed in electing a lawyer who has had no political activity; but typically the urban prosecutor has come up through the party organization, often having served in a subordinate post in the prosecutor's office, a post also obtained through party influence. He is thus not likely to be of the independent mind and character that are so much to be desired in a public prosecutor. Though he be in no sense corrupt, the energy he puts forth in investigating suspected violations of the law, the decision whether to prosecute, and the rigor of prosecution are all likely to be influenced by his ties to the party organization and through that organization to the elements that have influence within it—including, it may be, gambling, vice, and racketeering elements.

In the colonial period, and for some decades thereafter, the prosecutor's office was in fact an appointive one, appointment being in some cases by the governor, in others by the judges; and the method survives in five of the original states, appointment being by the governor in four of them and by the judges in Connecticut. As with judicial office, however, appointment almost everywhere gave way to popular election in the democratic upsurge of the early decades of the nineteenth century; and it became the universal pattern in the newer states.

A return to the method of selecting the public prosecutor by appointment, rather than by election, at least in the counties comprising the larger cities, would produce a type of prosecutor less completely dependent on the local machine, and one less susceptible to sinister influences. Such a change would, however, sacrifice the advantage possessed by local election of giving opportunity for the occasional citizens' crusade for the election of a non-political prosecutor—the opportunity for which poses an ever-present threat to the political machines. Moreover, to deprive the city electorate of the choice of the local prosecutor, while permitting the rural electorate to retain that choice would obviously be difficult. To deprive the electorate generally of a privilege which on the whole has been exercised satisfactorily would be even more difficult. The substitution of appointment for election is in the case of the prosecutor therefore hardly a practical question. The situation illustrates in striking fashion the empire of habitual patterns of thought in the shaping of public institutions; for in those few states in which the office of prosecutor has continued since colonial times to be an appointive one, a change to the elective system would doubtless likewise now meet strong popular opposition.

Two measures which would tend to discourage the nomination by party organizations of inferior characters may, however, be mentioned. First, selection of most of the legal and investigating personnel of the prosecutor's office should be on a merit basis, with permanency of tenure. Even in jurisdictions in which the merit system is well established and pervasive, the prosecutor's office is almost invariably exempt from its requirements; and there seems litle disposition to question this exemption. The unexpressed feeling appears to be that since the responsibility for results is the prosecutor's, he should have a free hand in the selection of his assistants. This assumes, which is of course not the case, that the party organization to which he owes his own nomination permits him a free hand. Moreover, his appointees, dependent on him for their continuance in office, are in no position to exercise independence; and it is precisely their indepedence, as a check on his own lack of independence, resulting from his political selection, that is wanted. A permanent, experienced, non-political staff, secure from party reprisal, would make it extremely embarrassing, even though not impossible, for a prosecutor to yield unduly to the demands of the party or its affiliated interests.

A second measure, which would tend to make the prosecutor's office in the larger centers less attractive to the time-serving political type of lawyer would be the provision, now found only in those states in which public officers generally are subject to "recall," for the removal of an incumbent prosecutor by popular vote, in a special election initiated by petition. Whatever view may be taken of the soundness of this procedure with respect to public office generally, it has a special appropriateness to the office of prosecutor. All the other elected officers of government are in some sense under the supervision of the prosecutor—at least in the sense that he may draw the possible illegality of their conduct, on the criminal side, into question and under investigation; and the criminal side, in this connection, covers a much wider area than is involved in criminality involving moral turpitude, there being in every state statutes imposing criminal penalties on acts of official misconduct which may not involve moral turpitude. The prosecutor, on the other hand (except in the relatively few states in which the statutes may place some measure of supervision or control in the hands of the governor or of the attorney general of the state) is immune from this supervision. It is consequently especially appropriate that he be subjected, more directly than the other officers of government, to the possibility of removal by the electorate.

If with these measures there were coupled the enlargement of the power of the governor or the attorney general to intervene in local prosecution, and to supersede or remove the local prosecutor in extreme cases, the inefficient, the insincere, and the corrupt local prosecutor would tend to become much rarer.

The federal prosecutor is ordinarily, like the county prosecutor, a political lawyer, owing his appointment to the sponsorship of the local political organization. However, the Attorney General of the United States, without whose recommendation the President (in whose hands rests the formal power of appointment) never acts, serves as a potential and often actual powerful countercheck on the local political organization. When the Attorney General is an able one (and the power and prestige of the office attract able men to it) the local political powers are unable to procure the appointment of an unsuitable candidate; and occasionally they may be completely deprived of the initiative. The very remoteness of the Attorney

General's position indeed makes his a more valuable check on the local political organization than that of the state attorney general in the states where county prosecutors are appointed.

The appointment of the subordinates of the federal prosecutor is also in large measure influenced by politics, neither the merit system nor any statutory security of tenure being in force for these posts. To an increasing extent, however, traditions of merit recruitment and of tenure appear to be developing in this field. As with the situation in the larger county prosecutor's offices, the placing of these offices on a completely non-political career basis is greatly to be desired.

The Canons of Professional Ethics promulgated by the American Bar Association declare that "the primary duty of a lawyer engaged in public prosecution is not to convict but to see that justice is done. The suppression of facts or the secreting of witnesses capable of establishing the innocence of the accused is highly reprehensible." There is an almost total absence of machinery, and even of statutory provisions, which might help in making of these principles more than a pious wish. In one respect, however, machinery is available. The judge presiding at a criminal trial possesses ample power to check a prosecutor whose tactics in the courtroom reflect a determination to secure a conviction at all costs. Too frequently, however, the judge considers that he is doing his full duty if he depends on counsel for the defense to protest the prosecutor's tactics.

PART II ADMINISTRATIVE TRIBUNALS AND THEIR SUPERVISION BY THE COURTS

In the preceding part of this volume, attention was given to the role of the courts in checking the unlawful exercise of power by administrative officials, and in compelling action by them when they unlawfully refuse to act. There were excluded from consideration, however, those forms of administrative action which take the shape of formal adjudication—in which the administrative agency, in other words, acts as a tribunal discharging judicial functions, making adjudications indeed in many cases indistinguishable in purpose from types of adjudication carried on in the courts. It is to this vast field of adjudication by administrative tribunals that we now turn.

That the function discharged by the administrative tribunal is essentially judicial in nature tends to be obscured by the circumstance that such a tribunal is not termed a "court." In the popular mind, the judicial function and the judiciary are indissolubly linked; and even some commentators have not been entirely free from the empire of this concept. There have resulted various suggested differences in function between an administrative tribunal and a court, which on scrutiny appear to have little substance.

At the outset, it is necessary to free oneself from the notion, so common a result of the oversimplification almost invariably propounded by the writers of elemenatry texts on civics, that there is a sharp line of demarcation between the functions of the executive and of the judicial branches, with judicial power committed exclusively to the judiciary, that is, to the judges of the regularly constituted courts. We need not perhaps go so far as did the distinguished scholar who declared that there are but two functions of government—the legislative and the administrative: all functionaries, including the judiciary, however dissimilar otherwise, being engaged in the application to particular cases of the general rules laid down by the legislature.[1] But it is clear that when one attempts to trace with precision along its entire extent the line separating the administrative from the judicial function, real difficulties appear. The point will be abundantly illustrated in what follows. Here it is sufficient to refer only to familiar instances —such as the adjudication by the Patent Office of priority of invention as between the contending applicants for patent on the same improvement, or the infliction by numerous administrative agencies of such severe punishment for alleged violation of law as is involved in the revocation of a license without which the culprit cannot continue in business. Such familiar instances sufficiently indicate at this point how important is the role played by so-called administrative agencies in the adjudication of private controversies and in the punishment of law violators, functions ordinarily thought of as judicial.

Nor is there much value in the term "quasi-judicial," not infrequently applied to administrative tribunals.[2] When engaged in the process of formal adjudication, the "administrative" tribunal is discharging a function fully as judicial as is that of a court engaged in a similar process of formal adjudication; and there is no more reason, from the standpoint of function, for the use of the qualifying term "quasi" in one case, than in the other. Our administrative tribunals have not been vested, as have our courts, with the power to punish disobedience of their mandates by committing the offender for contempt; they must invoke the aid of the courts for this purpose. But this circumstance can hardly be regarded as rendering the adjudicatory function of the administrative tribunal any the less judicial. Again, the determination of an administrative tribunal is never final. It is in every case subject to review in greater or less measure; and the function of final review is in every case entrusted to a court, not to an administrative tribunal. In this respect, however, the administrative tribunal does not differ from the judicial tribunal of first instance. Except in those rare cases in which the Supreme Court of the United States or the highest court of a state sits as a court of original jurisdiction, there is hardly any case in which the initial determination of a controversy by a judicial tribunal is final; it is almost always subject to review by another judicial tribunal.

A further distinction sometimes suggested is that the judicial tribunal is concerned solely with adjudication, while the administrative tribunal, so called, is in reality an administrative agency, having administrative functions of which its adjudicatory functions are merely part. This, even if true, would not alter the judicial nature of the adjudicatory function involved; and it is in fact not true with respect to those administrative tribunals

---

[1] Goodnow, Politics and Administration, Ch. 1 (1900).

[2] Cf. the oft-quoted phrase of Justice Holmes (speaking of the powers of the Interstate Commerce Commission): "legislative, judicial and executive acts, only softened by a quasi." Springer v. Philippine Islands, 277 U.S. 189, 210 (1928).

which, from the standpoint of number of adjudications made and number of individual litigants affected, perhaps overshadow all other administrative tribunals combined—the tribunals responsible for the adjudication of claims of injured workmen arising under workmen's compensation laws, state and federal. Indeed it is not significantly true even of some administrative tribunals before which enforcement proceedings are heard.

Neither is there much substance in the distinction sometimes suggested, that while courts adjudicate disputes, administrative tribunals enforce statutes. If an administrative tribunal is, as in the case of the National Labor Relations Board, engaged solely in adjudicating disputes, it can hardly be said, merely because the disputed claim under adjudication is bottomed on a statute, that the tribunal is "enforcing" the statute; in that sense the courts also are heavily engaged in "enforcing" statutes. In point of fact, instances may be found in which the private dispute administratively adjudicated concerns no statutory right whatever; thus the Secretary of Agriculture is empowered to adjudicate claims asserted by shippers of produce against commission merchants arising out of alleged fraudulent practices—claims not founded on any statute and from time immemorial cognizable by the courts of law. Nor is the specialization ordinarily found in the administrative tribunal inherently less appropriate to the judicial tribunal, as is demonstrated, for example, by the specialized probate courts of not a few of the states.

Quite clearly, then, whatever the differences in concomitant functions, or in incidental power, the administrative agency when acting as a tribunal[3] —when engaged, that is, in formal adjudication—discharges a function indistinguishable from that of a court of first instance. The administrative tribunal is termed "administrative" not because its function is any less judicial than is the function of the judicial tribunal, not because it may be charged with administrative as well as judicial functions, but simply because it is structurally not part of the independently organized judicial branches of our national and state governments, but is structurally part of the administrative branch.

Discussion of the problems of administrative adjudication has tended to give relatively little attention to the great number of state agencies which engage in adjudication, and to concentrate on federal activities; and within the federal field, again, there has been a marked tendency to take little or no notice of the highly important and variegated adjudicatory activities carried on by departmental tribunals—as in the Departments of State,

---

[3] Sometimes, the administrative tribunal is so wholly remote from the operations of the administrative agency under which it functions that it may properly be said to be merely located in that agency rather than to be part of it. Such, for example, is the case with the tribunal which, in the name of the Postmaster General, issues orders barring the receipt of mail by persons adjudged to be using the mails to defraud. The official who constitutes this tribunal has no connection whatever with postal management.

Treasury, Justice, Agriculture, and Health, Education and Welfare—and to consider chiefly if not solely the independent agencies. Here, again, the distinction between the adjudicatory and the non-adjudicatory functions of the independent agencies is frequently ignored, both being comprehended in a single discussion, with resultant confusion.

A distinct further contribution to the confusion is made by the practice of characterizing the independent agencies as a whole as "regulatory" agencies. The Interstate Commerce Commission, the Federal Power Commission, the Federal Communications Commission, and the like, are truly regulatory agencies. Their chief, even if not their sole, function, is in each case to formulate detailed policies, under the governing statute, for the regulation of a particular industry or industries. They promulgate regulations, and in the case of the two first named, fix rates and classifications. They have thus no resemblance to the Federal Trade Commission, for example, in its functions in connection with the unfair methods of competition condemned by its governing statue; for that commission has no power to promulgate regulations defining what are such unfair methods of competition. It does not in this connection regulate any particular industry, but merely institutes and adjudicates proceedings against anyone in any industry whom it has reason to believe to be employing unfair methods of competition, just as the Department of Justice institutes, and the courts try, proceedings against any one in any industry who is believed to be party to a combination in restraint of trade. Neither, to take another example, is the National Labor Relations Board, doubtless one of the more important of the federal administrative agencies, in any sense a regulatory agency. Not only does it have no power to issue regulations; it does not even have the power to institute proceedings before itself, but must, like a court, merely deal with the complaints registered with it by private parties. Some regulatory agencies are indeed entrusted with adjudicatory functions, which are, however, quite peripheral to their primary function of regulation and could perhaps be just as well entrusted to another agency or to the courts —as, for example, the adjudication by the Interstate Commerce Commission, in a so-called reparation preoceeding, of the claim of a shipper against a carrier for refund of allegedly excessive freight charges. Other regulatory agencies have adjudicatory functions more closely related to, but still quite distinct from, their regulatory function. Since our concern is solely with adjudication, it is only to the limited extent that they engage in adjudication that the "regulatory agencies" come within our purview.[4]

Perhaps equally inimical to clear thinking in this field is the invocation

[4] Hence no reference is made in this discussion to the well-known Landis report of 1960 (Senate Committee on Judiciary, Subcommittee on Administrative Practice, Report on Regulatory Agencies to the President-elect, 82nd Cong., 2nd Sess.) or to the earlier Hector memorandum (Problems of the CAB and the Independent Regulatory Comissions, 69 Yale Law Jour. 931 [1960]), both of which dealt with the regulatory rather than the adjudicatory functions of the federal agencies.

on all occasions of the comprehensive phrase "the administrative process" —a phrase frequently so employed as to convey that there is involved a certain element of mystique. The "administrative process" is defined by one of the most authoritative commentators in this field as "the complex of methods by which agencies carry out their tasks of adjudication, rule-making and related functions."[5] The use of the word "complex" suggests, as does the term "process," that there is some inherent integration between the task of adjudication carried on by an administrative agency and the "related functions" which it discharges. On scrutiny, however, it is difficult to discover such integration. In truth, in those administrative agencies which in addition to their adjudicatory function also discharge other functions, whether rule-making, prosecuting, or rate-fixing, the totality of the agency's activities appears to be an aggregate rather than a complex, and the term "the administrative process," as applied to such an aggregate, to be correspondingly devoid of content.

Few areas of our legal system have in recent years been the subject of as much discussion as has the area of administrative adjudication. Much of the extensive literature of the subject, academic as well as polemical, suffers, however, from too great a generality—a failure sufficiently to appreciate that the problems of administrative adjudication present themselves with wide variations of importance and content as we pass from one type of administrative adjudication to another. It is believed that a just appraisal of the place of administrative justice in our legal system can be gained only by recognizing clearly the several distinct types of proceeding which are administratively adjudicated, and considering separately the problems encountered in each such type of proceeding.

Broadly speaking, these proceedings fall into three main classes. In the first, government is proceeding against the individual; in the second, the individual is seeking from government some permit, benefit, or dispensation; in the third, government is neither prosecutor nor benefactor, but merely umpire, the contest being, as in an ordinary civil judicial proceeding, between private parties.

In the first of these classes—proceedings by government against the individual—we encounter a type of proceeding clearly distinguishable from all other in this category. This is the proceeding before an administrative tribunal to compel compliance with the law or to punish non-compliance —a proceeding essentially similar to one instituted by an administrative officer or agency before a judicial tribunal with a like purpose, with the crucial difference, however, that here the prosecuting agency and the tribunal are one. It is this type of proceeding which has in recent decades occasioned much, though by no means all, of the discussion of administrative adjudication; and it is to this type of proceeding, which may be termed an enforcement proceeding, that attention may well first be given.

[5] 1 Davis, Administrative Law Treatise, 2 (1958).

14

Enforcement Proceedings

1. DEVELOPMENT OF THE ADMINISTRATIVE ENFORCEMENT PROCEEDING.
2. CONSTITUTIONALITY OF ADMINISTRATIVE ADJUDICATION IN ENFORCE-
MENT PROCEEDINGS. 3. ORGANIZATION. 4. DECISION NOT TO PRO-
CEED. 5. CONDUCT OF PROCEEDING. 6. DECISION. 7. ENFORCEMENT
OF ORDER. 8. JUDICIAL REVIEW OF ORDER: AVAILABILITY. 9. JUDI-
CIAL REVIEW OF ORDER: SCOPE OF REVIEW. 10. JUDICIAL REVIEW OF
ORDER: MECHANISM OF REVIEW. 11. THE NEED FOR THE ADMINISTRA-
TIVE ENFORCEMENT PROCEEDING. 12. UNION OF PROSECUTING AND
ADJUDICATING FUNCTIONS. 13. UNION OF ADJUDICATORY FUNCTION
WITH THAT OF LEGISLATION.

In our system the traditional method by which law-enforcement
officers may seek to enforce upon the individual compliance with the law
has been the judicial proceeding—the civil proceeding to compel compliance and the criminal proceeding (or the civil penalty proceeding), to
punish non-compliance. In many of the newer fields of law enforcement,
however, initial resort to the judicial enforcement proceeding is virtually
unknown. Instead, a variegated array of administrative tribunals issues
directory and prohibitory orders, forbids the carrying on of business or the
operation of establishments, imposes monetary penalties, denies the use of
public facilities, withdraws eligibility for public benefits, and even con-
demns the alien resident to expulsion from the country. Our legal history
shows few developments of equal importance with this, so largely the
work of the present century.

1. DEVELOPMENT OF THE ADMINISTRATIVE ENFORCEMENT PRO-
CEEDING

To the statement that the judicial rather than the administrative
tribunal has been the traditional forum for law-enforcement proceedings,
there has from early time been an outstanding exception: in the field of

422

licensed occupations or establishments, the revocation of a license for failure to comply with the statute governing the licensed occupation or establishment has traditionally (though not invariably) been entrusted to administrative officers rather than to judicial tribunals—ordinarily to the same officers as were empowered to issue the license now to be revoked.[1]

We are so accustomed to this exception to our traditional scheme of law enforcement that unless our attention is directed to it, we are not likely to regard it as an exception at all; we regard it as natural and logical that the agency which isues a license should have the power to revoke it. But slight reflection makes clear that the two determinations are widely different in character. The issuance of a license is in many fields a routine matter, involving a determination merely that the prospective licensee possesses the prescribed qualifications. The revocation of a license for improper conduct or for failure to observe the conditions of the license may call for the sifting of conflicting testimony, the weighing of evidence, and the application of the law to complex facts.

With the increasing extension of the license requirement to fields formerly unlicensed, this type of administrative adjudication in law enforcement has grown apace; and over large areas of business and professional life administrative tribunals hold very nearly the power of economic life or death. The magnitude of the monetary loss which may thus be inflicted by administrative action in a case, of which there have been instances, in which a revocation or suspension of license has destroyed the going value of a large business, exceeds that of the fines or civil penalties generally imposable by the courts.

When proposals to extend the licensing process to new fields are under consideration—and such proposals are ever current—attention is usually concentrated on the licensing procedure and its apparent benefits; there is a tendency to overlook the concomitant investment of the administrative agency with the sometimes drastic power of revocation of the license it grants.

Federal administrative enforcement proceedings

Congress early exercised the licensing power in the field of navigation, licensing vessels, masters, crew, and pilots, and providing for the administrative revocation of licenses for cause. This long remained virtually the sole field for the use of the federal licensing power as a means of regulation (the various license taxes imposed solely as a means of revenue being irrelevant in this connection). In the early decades of this century, however, legislation requiring the licensing of various classes of persons engaged in the marketing and processing of agricultural products and livestock

---

[1] It was formerly, however, quite usual to vest in the courts the power to revoke the licenses of liquor establishments violating the law.

marked a notable extension of the federal licensing authority. Somewhat later, the advent of radio transmission and air transportation have brought with them a vast extension of the federal licensing power, and correspondingly, of the proceeding for revocation of license as an important administrative proceeding. The latest important extension of federal licensing has been in the field of securities marketing.

Aside from the revocation of marine licenses, the field of customs administration furnishes perhaps the earliest illustration of federal administrative enforcement powers. By the tariff act of 1842 the customs authorities were authorized, if they concluded that an importer had intentionally undervalued his merchandise, to impose a penalty amounting to 20 per cent of the duty payable; and parallel provisions have been contained in all subsequent tariff acts.

The postal service was the next federal administrative agency to be vested with independent enforcement powers. The antilottery legislation which marked the period following the Civil War not only made lottery matter unmailable, but, by act or 1872 empowered the Postmaster General to refuse all delivery of mail to any person whom he found "upon evidence satisfactory to him" to be using the mails to conduct a lottery. An administrative official was thus empowered to inflict upon the individual, without judicial proceedings, a penalty far more severe than would be the imposition of a fine of considerable amount. This power persists, having been extended to apply as well to persons using the mails to defraud, or to sell obscene matter.

The immigration act of 1903 introduced into our law a further extension of the administrative enforcement proceeding—its use for the imposition of a fine. That act made it the duty of those transporting immigrants to this country by sea to refuse passage to an immigrant afflicted with any of several diseases enumerated by the statute; and should the physician of the immigration service who examined the immigrants on their arrival in this country find an immigrant afflicted with one of those diseases, and should he further be of opinion that the diseased condition could have been detected at the time of embarkation, the immigration authorities were empowered to impose on the operators of the vessel a fine of $100 for each such case, and the vessel was to be detained till the fine was paid.

It was by that act also that the most drastic administrative enforcement proceeding known to our law—the alien deportation proceeding, or to term it more accurately, the banishment proceeding[2]—was effec-

---

[2] The term "deportation" is also applied to the physical act of placing an alien on a vessel, aircraft, or railroad train bound for a foreign country. As so used it is equally applicable to an alien who has never been in the country but has been barred on arrival. The term is, moveover, inapt as applied to a resident alien who, on being ordered to leave the country, does so. The term "expulsion proceeding" has been suggested as a substitute for "deportation proceeding"; however, the latter term is now statutory.

tively instituted. The deportation proceeding had first made its appearance in 1882 in the Chinese exclusion legislation; but those laws had provided for a judicial, not an administrative, proceeding.[3] Provision for administrative deportation had first been made in 1888, in the statutes prohibiting the immigration of contract labor, but had been employed to only a trifling extent. A very limited authority to deport aliens likely to become a public charge had been conferred on the immigration authorities in 1891; but no power was given to arrest the alien. By the act of 1903 (since reinforced and extended by later legislation) that power was conferred; so that today, as to all classes of deportable aliens, an administrative agency is empowered to arrest the alleged alien resident in this country and then determine that he shall be expelled from it on the ground either of his unlawful entry or of his subsequent criminality or indigence—an "alleged" alien, because even the issue of whether he is in fact an alien may be determined in the administrative proceeding.

At about the same time the administrative enforcement proceeding was extended to a new field—that of railroad regulation. By act of 1906, the Interstate Commerce Commission, which had been created as an investigative, prosecuting, and rate-making agency some twenty years earlier, was given the power to issue orders directing compliance with the Interstate Commerce Act—orders whose disobedience was punishable by penalty.[4] This act may be said to mark the beginning in the federal field of the institution which has since come to bulk so large in the field of governmental regulation of business—the issuance of a mandate by an administrative tribunal, either prohibitory or directory, disobedience of which is punishable through judicial proceedings.

The development of the federal administrative enforcement proceeding as thus far traced was confined to fields in which the government was already engaged in administration—shipping, customs, postal service, immigration, railroads; and the administrative enforcement proceeding in lieu of the judicial was resorted to by Congress as an extension (though not necessarily a logical one) of the existing powers and duties of administrative officers. The next step was the extension of the administrative enforcement proceeding by Congress to fields in which there was no existing administrative function, the administrative agency being brought into existence primarily to sit as a tribunal in enforcement proceedings. This

---

[3] The constitutionality of even the judicial proceeding prescribed by these laws, as applied to Chinese who had entered the United States lawfully but who had subsequently failed to obtain a certificate as required by the act, was attacked, but was upheld by a divided court in Fong Yue Ting v. United States, 149 U.S. 698 (1893).

[4] Under the Act of 1887 disobedience of the so-called orders of the commission carried no penalty; and on its application to the courts for aid in enforcement, its findings were merely prima facie evidence of the facts found by it.

step was taken in the Federal Trade Commission Act of 1914, creating a commission with large investigatory powers (including extensive sub-poena powers) and empowering it, after due hearing accorded, to order any person or concern found by it to be using any unfair method of competition in interstate or foreign commerce to cease and desist from using such method.[5] By a companion act (the Clayton Act), certain particular methods of unfair competition tending to monopoly were enumerated, but, more important for the present purpose, power to issue orders prohibiting the use of such methods was conferred not merely on the newly created trade commission, and on the Interstate Commerce Commission where common carriers were the respondents, but on the recently created Federal Reserve Board.[6]

In recent years the creation with each new piece of regulatory legislation of a new administrative tribunal to enforce it (or, as notably in the case of the Department of Agriculture, the authorization of administrative enforcement proceedings before some existing agency) in lieu of leaving its enforcement proceedings to the courts, may almost be said to have become a pattern. Thus, to enumerate only the major examples of this practice, the Warehouse Act of 1916, the Packers and Stockyards Act of 1921, and the Commodity Exchanges Act of 1922, imposing upon the affected activities a wide variety of novel statutory prohibitions, entrusted the issuance of prohibitory orders and the punitive revocation of licenses to the Secretary of Agriculture. The Securities Act of 1933 empowered the newly created Securities Commission (now the Securities and Exchange Commission) in effect to enjoin the sale of a security, the registration statement relating to which the commission deemed incomplete or misleading. The National Labor Relations Act of 1935 (the Wagner Act), setting up wholly new restrictions upon the labor practices of employers, created the National Labor Relations Board to adjudicate complaints of violation and issue appropriate enforcement orders. The power to issue orders prohibiting unfair competitive practices, already enjoyed by the Federal Trade Commission, the Interstate Commerce Commission, and the Federal Reserve Board in their respective fields, was conferred also upon the Federal Communications Commission, the Federal Power Commission, and the Civil Aeronautics Board. The postwar Defense Production Act, while providing for enforcement of its price stabilization provisions by conventional judicial penalty and injunction proceedings, also empowered the President to prescribe that a payment made to settle a liability arising from violation of the act should be disregarded in determining gain for tax purposes; and the persistence of the pattern is evidenced by the creation by Congress in 1950 of a Subversive Activities Control Board, in which it

[5] Act of Sept. 26, 1914, 15 U.S. Code, Sec. 41 ff.
[6] Act of Oct. 15, 1914; 15 U.S. Code, Sec. 21.

vested the power to condemn an organization, on the application of the Attorney General, as being a Communist-action or a Communist-front organization, with resultant drastic consequences to the organization and its members, and the authorization by Congress of the creation in time of war emergency of a Detention Review Board, to order the continued detention or release of persons suspected of intending sabotage or espionage.

State administrative enforcement proceedings

The extension of the administrative rather than the judicial enforcement proceedings to new fields of regulation which has thus characterized the federal government has been paralleled, but much less markedly, in the states. In part this has been due to the less rapid expansion of state regulatory legislation, in part to the more express emphasis in state constitutions upon the separation of powers, tending to inhibit the vesting of judicial functions in administrative agencies. In the field of licensing of occupations, establishments, and businesses, however, the states have been even more active than the national government; and the administrative proceeding for revocation of license looms large as a weapon of state law enforcement. In the cities, and in many cases in the counties as well, are also found numerous licensing agencies vested with the power to suspend or revoke the licenses they grant. The judicial licensing of liquor-selling establishments, with its attendant judicial proceeding for revocation of license, once not uncommon, has given way completely to administrative licensing, with its almost invariable concomitant, administrative revocation.

A field of licensing in which suspension and revocation proceedings have assumed major importance is that of motor-vehicle operators' licenses. In at least one of the larger states, the volume of such proceedings is such as to require a staff of traveling hearing examiners.

Since a particular form of state or local licensing is ordinarily of interest only to those immediately affected, relatively few are conscious of the ubiquitousness and magnitude of the total licensing and license-revoking machinery, or of its proportionate importance in our system of adjudication.[7]

Diversification of administrative enforcement orders

The suspension or revocation of license was for many decades virtually the sole form, and it continues to be one of the chief forms, of enforcement decree imposed by administrative process—a decree of drastic character in that it requires no judicial aid for its enforcement. The order suspending or revoking a license may in fact inflict a monetary loss far

[7] See Chapter 3, "The Right to Make a Living," in Gellhorn, Individual Freedom and Governmental Restraints (1956).

exceeding the amount of any conventional monetary penalty or fine; yet, characteristically, an agency empowered to suspend or revoke a license lacks the power to impose any monetary penalty whatever. Where the licensee is found to have committed a relatively minor offense, even a brief suspension of the license may be too severe a penalty, and there will be reluctance to impose it. Hence, it has been urged that licensing authorities vested with the power of suspension or revocation ought also to have the alternative power to impose monetary penalties.[8]

There has indeed been an apparent reluctance to vest administrative tribunals with the power to impose direct monetary penalties. In a few fields, however, as in the field of customs and of regulation of vessels bringing immigrants into the country, the power has been given.

The prohibitory (or "cease and desist") order—the equivalent of the injunction in a judicial enforcement proceeding—introduced in the second decade of this century has become one of the chief forms of enforcement order; and express authority was given for a directory order—the analogue of the mandatory injunction—by the National Labor Relations Act of 1935. That act indeed authorized the tribunal created by it to require a person found by it to have engaged in an unfair labor practice "to take such action . . . as will effectuate the policies of this Act."[9]

A development of recent years is the infliction, by administrative tribunals, of the penalty of ineligibility for governmental benefits otherwise available. Thus, in the typical state unemployment insurance statute, provisions are found withdrawing eligibility for benefits under the law, for limited periods, from persons who have made false statements or otherwise wrongfully obtained prior benefits, such ineligibility being adjudicated by the unemployment insurance authorities. By the federal act of 1936 (the so-called Walsh-Healy Act) which regulates wages and working conditions in industrial plants producing goods under government contract, the Secretary of Labor is empowered, on finding that a contractor has failed to comply with the provisions of the act, to declare the contractor ineligible to receive any further government contract for a period of three years—a penalty which, in a period when certain materials are available only to government contractors, might well mean that the contractor would have to go out of business. In connection with the licensing of exports of strategic materials, another development of recent years, the licensing

[8] See, for example, Benjamin, Administrative Adjudication in New York, 266 (1942).

[9] Still another aspect of the directory power of the National Labor Relations Board deserves mention. The board, where it finds that an employee has been discharged for reasons condemned by the act, is expressly empowered to order his reinstatement. This is in sharp contrast to the lack of power of the courts, under existing doctrines, in suits against the employer arising out of his allegedly unjustified discharge of the employee prior to the expiration of the agreed term of employment, to order reinstatement.

authority (the Department of Commerce) has been authorized by the President, acting under statutory authority,[10] in the case of an exporter adjudged guilty by that agency of having made false representations in his application for a license already issued as to the ultimate destination of goods exported, to place on him a "blacklist" for a stated period, rendering him unable to procure any export license during that period.[11]

A form of administrative penalty occasionally found is that denying to a wrongdoer the use of public facilities. In 1950 a novel type of administrative penalty made its appearance. The Defense Production Act, as already noted, provided that a payment administratively determined to have been made to settle a liability under the price stabilization regulations might if so decreed by the President be disregarded in determining tax liability, the administrative finding being thus potentially equivalent to an enormous fine—a potentiality in fact realized in several cases.

2. CONSTITUTIONALITY OF ADMINISTRATIVE ADJUDICATION IN ENFORCEMENT PROCEEDINGS

Despite the acceptance of the broad doctrine of separation of powers as one of the cornerstones of our constitutional structure, there is nothing in the Constitution which expressly precludes the exercise of judicial functions by federal administrative agencies. It nowhere lays down the command that judicial functions shall be exercised only by the courts for whose creation it provides. Whatever may be the limitations which the judicial article of the Constitution (Article III) may place upon the power of Congress to vest in other courts than those provided for in that article the classes of cases and controversies enumerated in that article,[12] there is nothing in the Constitution which precludes the investment of other tribunals—whether denominated courts, commissions, or boards, and whether comprising a plural membership or a single official—with power to adjudicate in statutory proceedings which do not constitute such "cases" or "controversies."

[10] 50 U.S. Code, Sec. 2023(a).

[11] By the Act of 1872, already noted, the Postmaster General is empowered to refuse mail delivery to a person found by him to be using the mails to conduct a lottery (and, by later provisions, also to a person found by him to be using the mails for a fraudulent enterprise or to sell obscene matter). The immigration act of 1903 gave to the Secretary of the Treasury the power to deny the privilege of landing alien immigrant passengers at United States ports to any transportation company which has persistently violated the statutory provisions prohibiting the solicitation of immigration by such a company. A limited form of "blacklist" is that provided for by the Wool Labeling Act, under which the Federal Trade Commission is empowered to prohibit one whom it has found to have violated the act from importing any wool product except upon the filing of a bond in a sum double the value of the import plus duty, conditioned upon compliance with the act. 15 U.S. Code, Sec. 68 f.

[12] See p. 397, note 21.

The question of the power of Congress to invest administrative officials with power to impose penalties was raised as early as 1853, in connection with the provision of the tariff law of 1842, already referred to, authorizing the imposition by the customs authorities of penalties for under-valuation and was answered affirmatively by the Supreme Court.[13] It was not raised again until half a century later, when the statute authorizing the administrative imposition of a penalty on a vessel negligently bringing diseased aliens to this country was challenged, unsuccessfully, before the court.[14] The National Labor Relations Act, enacted in 1933, empowered the board created by it to order the reinstatement, with back pay, of an employee dismissed in violation of the prohibitions contained in the act. This provision, so far as it authorized the imposition on the employer of a monetary liability, was attacked as violative of the constitutional right of jury trial in "suits at common law" in federal tribunals, but the Supreme Court rejected this contention; the proceeding created by the statute, it held, did not fall within the constitutional guarantee.[15]

In the light of the decisive holdings in these and related cases, that the exclusive constitutional investment of the courts with jurisdiction over the classes of cases and controversies mentioned in the Constitution does not preclude Congress from entrusting to administrative officers the adjudication of a subject matter which might also be the subject of a "case" or "controversy," there has been little disposition to question the constitutionality of subsequent federal statues authorizing administrative enforcement proceedings.

State constitutions present numerous variations in the provisions whereby they parcel out the power of the state to the governor, the legislature, and the constitutional courts; and in some of them is found an express statement of the doctrine of separation of powers—such statement being in many cases limited, however, to the agencies created by the constitution itself. Without attempting any review of the applicable state constitutional provisions, it may be said that in general, while there are some states in which the courts have tended to apply these constitutional limitations with a degree of strictness, there is no state in which those provisions have been found by its courts to preclude a considerable exercise of judicial functions by administrative agencies.

3. ORGANIZATION

The administrative agency before which an enforcement proceeding is brought is in only a minority of cases organized merely as a tribunal,

[13] Bartlett v. Kane, 16 Howard 263 (1853).
[14] Oceanic Steam Nav. Co. v. Stranahan 214 U.S. 320 (1909).
[15] National Labor Relations Board v. Jones & Laughlin Steel Corp., 301 U.S. 1, 48 (1937).

unconnected with any function other than that of adjudication. Instead, the tribunal is characteristically part of an administrative agency responsible for investigating non-compliance with the statute, and for instituting the resulting proceeding (as well as, in many cases, for promulgating regulations, fixing rates, granting permits and dispensations, etc.). The head of the agency (usually a board rather than a single individual) is thus on the one hand the chief of the various divisions of the agency discharging these functions,[16] and on the other hand the chief of its adjudicatory activities, both as supervisor of the subordinate adjudicatory personnel, and as itself the tribunal with final power of decision.

As an organization for adjudication, the adjudicatory division of the administrative agency usually presents a sharp contrast to the typical judicial organization. Most marked is its restriction to cases arising under a single statute or group of statutes, as opposed to the variety of cases usually cognizable by even the more specialized types of court. But even if the comparison be made with a class of courts engaged in adjudicating only cases arising under a particular statute—as, for example, the probate courts of a state which has a more or less complete structure of separate specialized courts for this purpose—the difference is apparent. Each of the separate courts exercising probate jurisdiction in the state is autonomous, and its decision is final unless modified on review by an appellate court. In the administrative field, by contrast, there is typically but a single tribunal for the entire state, or, in the field of federal administration, for the entire country. In lieu of local courts, we find local hearings, conducted ordinarily by itinerant hearing officers dispatched for the purpose from the tribunal's headquarters, whose initial decision or recommendation goes to the head of the agency for approval.

In a few administrative enforcement tribunals, we find a total absence of provision for local hearings. The tribunal sits only in the capital and anyone wishing to contest before it the proceedings instituted against him must appear there. In the federal field, where the failure to provide for local hearings is of course more likely to be burdensome on the respondent than in state proceedings, the fraud order proceeding before the Post Office Department furnishes a striking illustration of this practice.

In the organization of an agency charged with adjudication, there is seldom at first any sharp cleavage, in the subordinate ranks, between investigating, prosecuting, and adjudicatory functions. The same individuals are assigned from time to time, as the demands on the agency may dictate, to investigate a complaint, to prepare a case for prosecution, to preside at a hearing and make recommendation for decision, or to review a recommendation already made. Indeed, the one individual may even be

[16] In some agencies headed by a board, the chairman of the board, rather than the board collectively, is responsible for prosecution and investigation.

called on to investigate and subsequently to adjudicate the same complaint. This confusion of functions was one of the chief points in the decade-long barrage of criticism of federal administrative adjudication in legal quarters —criticism to which the enactment of the Administrative Procedure Act of 1946 was chiefly due. By that act[17] each adjudicating agency (with important exceptions) is required to have a separate category of employee— termed by the act an "examiner"—to preside at the taking of evidence and to make an initial or recommended decision on the basis thereof. Such employees are to "perform no duties inconsistent with their duties and responsibilities as examiners," and are not to "consult any person or party on any fact in issue unless upon notice and opportunity for all parties to participate"; nor are they to be "responsible to or subject to the supervision or direction of any officer, employee, or agent engaged in the performance of investigative or prosecuting functions. . . ."[18] The rationale of these provisions is discussed, and their effectiveness evaluated, at a subsequent point in this chapter.

4. DECISION NOT TO PROCEED

Statutes providing for enforcement by administrative proceeding frequently make that proceeding, to be instituted only by the administrative agency itself, the sole remedy under the statute. Under such a statute, should the agency conclude, on the basis of its own investigation, that there is not sufficient evidence to warrant its instituting a proceeding against the individual suspected of offending against the statute, it closes the matter; and its decision not to proceed, reached without any hearing, is final.

The fact just stated is on the face of it so self-evident that the reader may well ask himself why it is stated at all. It is stated because it is not always appreciated that in thus closing a matter without a hearing, on the basis of its own views of the evidence or the law, the agency, in exonerating the party under investigation, may be cutting off the rights of another private party—the person who considers himself aggrieved by the conduct of the person investigated and who perhaps drew the attention of the agency to the matter in the first instance.

When the public prosecutor, after investigating a complaint of unlawful conduct, decides not to institute a prosecution, his action usually puts an end to the possibility of a criminal proceeding—a result quite

---

[17] 5 U.S. Code, Secs. 1001–1011.

[18] Morever "No officers, employee, or agent engaged in the performance of investigative or prosecuting functions for any agency in any case shall, in that or a factually related case, participate or advise in the decision or recommended decision. . . ."

analogous to that effected by the administrative agency in the situation just described.[19] But the refusal of the public prosecutor to prosecute never deprives the complainant of his right to institute a civil proceeding on his own account. (Indeed, in the case of minor offenses, he has the right to institute a summary criminal proceeding also, without being required to obtain the permission of the prosecutor.)

In contrast to this, if the proceeding by and before the administrative agency is the only form of proceeding authorized by the governing statute (as is the case, for example, with the unfair-methods-of-competition provisions of the Federal Trade Commission Act) and that agency refuses to proceed, the matter is at an end. There is no form of redress to which the complainant can resort without the collaboration of the agency. A court, on a claim that the refusal of the agency to proceed was arbitrary, capricious, discriminatory, or corrupt, might perhaps order the agency to proceed—a dubious remedy. No case has come to my attention in which such judicial relief has been granted.[20]

5. CONDUCT OF PROCEEDING

Even were there a total absence of statutory provision, there exists, as we have seen, a traditional body of practice which would give to the procedure of our judicial tribunals a substantial uniformity. The procedure of administrative tribunals has no corresponding body of tradition. Nor has the lack of a traditional body of procedural practices been made good by any detailed statutory code of procedure. Characteristically, statutory regulation of the procedure in administrative proceedings is sketchy.

The earliest federal statutes authorizing administrative enforcement proceedings in the customs, postal, and immigration fields contained no procedural provisions whatever. The act of 1887 creating the Interstate Commerce Commission provided that its proceedings should "conduce to the ends of justice." Subsequent statutes affecting this and other administrative agencies went somewhat further than this pious injunction. It was not till 1946, however, that Congress attempted any comprehensive regulation. The Administrative Procedure Act of that year lays down, albeit in quite general terms, requirements (applicable to all agencies not excepted by statute) as to notice, pleading, the right to be heard and to be represented by counsel, subpoenas, evidence, record, and statement of

---

[19] However, where the grand jury sits regularly, the complainant may bring his complaint directly to the attention of that body.

[20] A policy adopted by the National Labor Relations Board of refusing to entertain any complaint falling in a particular class was, however, held to be beyond the statutory power of the board. The policy involved was the refusal to consider complaints against labor organizations made by the employees of such organizations. Office Employes Internat. Union v. Nat. Labor Rel. Bd., 353 U.S. 313 (1957).

grounds of decision.[21] The possible further codification of the procedure of the federal agencies, as well as its improvement, has been the subject of several official studies, and of legislative proposals, during the past decade.

In the states, the development has been similar. However, it has not yet resulted, in a majority of the states, in a general statute regulating administrative proceedings. At least twelve states now have statutes,[22] based in whole or in part on the Model State Administrative Procedure Act proposed by the uniform law commissioners in 1946 and revised by them in 1961.[23] The movement for procedural improvement in administrative adjudication in the states is making progress, but hardly at a gratifying rate.

Pleadings

There is in the special statutes governing federal administrative enforcement proceedings characteristically no detailed prescription as to the contents of the initial notice to the respondent of the institution of the proceedings—commonly termed the complaint. The Attorney General's Committee reported in 1941 that "agencies not infrequently set out their allegations in general terms, perhaps in statutory terms, thus failing fully to apprise the respondents and to permit them adequately to prepare their defenses."[24] The Administrative Procedure Act of 1946 now requires that the notice shall set forth "the legal authority and jurisdiction under which the hearing is to be held" and "the matters of fact and law asserted"—provisions which hardly seem calculated to insure an improvement in the situation described by the Attorney General's Committee. In particular, the notice should clearly inform the respondent what action against him is contemplated by the agency should it sustain the complaint.

The situation among state administrative agencies apparently gives equally little certainty that the notice will give the respondent adequate information.[25]

In a judicial proceeding, the initial pleading has a further function. Should the party against whom it is directed deem the allegations made, even were they admitted to be true, to be insufficient in law, he may forthwith invoke the decision of the court on the question of such legal sufficiency. In short, legal sufficiency of the allegations may be determined at the outset by an independent tribunal. In an administrative enforce-

---

[21] The act itself contains several saving clauses; and in addition, several special exceptions to its requirements have subsequently been enacted.

[22] See especially the very comprehensive California act (Govt. Code, Secs. 11370–11445, and 11500–11528).

[23] 9C Uniform Laws Annotated.

[24] Report of Attorney General's Committee, 63 (1942).

[25] Cf. Benjamin, Administrative Adjudication in the State of New York, 30–34, 77–83 (1942).

ment proceeding, however, the agency itself has prepared the complaint, and the chance of procuring from the hearing examiner at the outset of the proceeding a dismissal of the complaint for legal insufficiency is remote. Nor can a refusal so to dismiss be brought for review to a judicial tribunal; judicial review, as will shortly appear, is limited to final orders. The proceeding must go forward to its conclusion; only then may the legal sufficiency of the administrative agency's theory of the proceeding be judically passed upon.

The answer of a respondent to a complaint in an administrative enforcement proceeding is ordinarily a mere denial, serving no purpose other than to inform the agency that its proposed order against the respondent is to be contested.

Compulsory attendance of witnesses and production of papers

Statutory provisions governing the powers of administrative tribunals to compel the appearance of witnesses and the production of papers vary in detail, but they all follow the pattern already described in connection with investigatory agencies, all of them requiring the aid of the courts to compel obedience or to punish disobedience.

Right to counsel

The right to be represented by counsel (or indeed by a qualified representative not a member of the bar) is universally recognized in administrative enforcement proceedings. The right of an indigent respondent to be furnished with counsel at public expense is, however, nowhere recognized. In many types of administrative enforcement proceeding, needless to say, the latter problem does not present itself. There are some such proceedings, however, in which it may present itself in acute fashion. The proceeding against an alien to deport him from the country is the most obvious of such cases. In connection with the current efforts to insure adequate provision of counsel for indigent defendants in federal criminal proceedings, attention might well be given to providing counsel also for the friendless and penniless alien threatened with deportation by the immigration authorities. Particularly is such provision called for in view of the fact that in the deportation hearing the official holding the hearing is not required, as in the case of enforcement proceedings generally, to sit in a purely judicial capacity, the evidence being presented to him; instead he is denominated by the statute a "special inquiry officer," who shall "present and receive evidence, interrogate, examine and cross examine. . . ."[26]

[26] 8 U.S. Code, Sec. 1252(b). Moreover, the closed character of the hearing, as contrasted with the public trial required in criminal proceedings, makes the need for counsel especially acute.

Oral presentation of evidence; cross-examination

In judicial enforcement proceedings, whether civil or criminal, the party proceeded against is, as has been seen, invariably afforded an opportunity for cross-examination of the witnesses produced on behalf of the government and for oral presentation of his own evidence. Such opportunity is characteristically afforded also in administrative enforcement proceedings. In federal enforcement proceedings it is now (since the adoption of the Administrative Procedure Act of 1946) the law that "every party shall have the right to present his case or defense by oral or documentary evidence . . . and to conduct such cross-examination as may be required for a true and full disclosure of the facts." The state administrative procedure codes characteristically contain similar provisions.

For the effective presentation of his case the respondent may require the testimony of witnesses who will not testify voluntarily. The Administrative Procedure Act requires federal administrative tribunals to issue subpoenas "to any party upon request and . . . upon a statement or showing of general relevance and reasonable scope of the evidence sought." In state proceedings a similar rule generally governs. The procedure for taking depositions is still, however, in a rudimentary state for some federal as well as state agencies.

Evidence

In connection with judicial proceedings, mention was made of the body of exclusionary rules of evidence which form a characteristic element of Anglo-American law. It was pointed out that these rules were originally developed in connection with trial by jury, with a view to keeping from an inexperienced, often only moderately literate, body of laymen any evidence (aside from the credibility of the witness) requiring qualitative evaluation; and that these rules were in due course extended even to non-jury proceedings. It was stated, however, that in non-jury judicial proceedings the tendency is to apply these rules with less meticulousness than in the case of jury trials. In administrative enforcement proceedings this tendency may be carried to the extent of disregarding the exclusionary rules altogether;[27] and in not a few statutes the administrative tribunal is expressly relieved of the necessity for observing these rules. The Administrative Procedure Act provides that "any oral or documentary evidence may be received."

But though the administrative tribunal may not be bound by the exclusionary rules applicable to judicial proceedings, it does not follow that the evidence admitted before the administrative tribunal, which would be

---

[27] By contrast, exclusionary rules intended to prevent disclosure of confidential communications, as those between husband and wife, or by patient or client, are enforced just as strictly in administrative as in judicial proceedings.

excluded by judicial tribunal, is of equal value with that which is acceptable in judicial proceedings. Hearsay testimony—that is, testimony offered to establish that something occurred, given however not by a person who himself observed the occurrence, but by one who was told about it by the actual observer—even if received by the administrative tribunal is obviously not of the same value as the testimony of the actual observer, subject to cross-examination, which would in like circumstances be insisted upon by the judicial tribunal; and indeed, an enforcement order based solely on hearsay evidence has been condemned as a denial of due process of law.[28] So, too, with certain types of secondary records which the courts view with such distrust as to exclude them. Hence, in reviewing the findings of administrative tribunals—and the nature of that review will shortly be considered—the courts search the record of the evidence which was before the administrative tribunal to make sure that, when there is put to one side all the evidence which would have been excluded had the proceeding been before a judicial tribunal, there still remains what has been called a "residuum of legal evidence" to sustain the findings. There must be in the record some evidence of a kind that would have been regarded in a judicial proceeding as having probative value; and the federal Administrative Procedure Act provides that "no sanction shall be imposed or . . . order be issued except upon consideration of the whole record or such portions thereof as may be cited by any party and as supported by and in accordance with the reliable, probative, and substantial evidence."

Official notice

Mention should be made of still another aspect in which the record of the evidence before an administrative tribunal may differ from that before a judicial tribunal. The latter may, as already noted, accept a certain thing as true without proof—or as the phrase is, "take judicial notice" of its truth. The precise limits of permissible judicial notice are of course difficult of definition; but in general, the court may not take judicial notice of anything not a matter of common knowledge. On the other hand, administrative tribunals sometimes make clear in their decisions that they have taken into account information obtained by the members of the tribunal in their capacity of administrators—a capacity in which they have made independent investigations for the purpose of determining policy (to be expressed either in regulations formulated by them, or in advice on policy given by them to the legislature or the executive). The information thus considered by them when sitting as a tribunal is not information regarding the particular party whose case is before them; it is information regarding the general framework of data—usually data relating to a particular type of industry or of industrial practice—in which the regulatory legislation they are enforcing operates. There is, of

[28] Cf. Bridges v. Wixon, 326 U.S. 135 (1945).

course, no reason why such data should not be considered by the administrative tribunal; the vice of the procedure appears when the data in question are not presented in the course of the hearing, making it impossible for the party being proceeded against to know what they are and thus possibly to offer evidence to show that they are inaccurate or incomplete.

6. DECISION

The procedure followed in promulgating the decision in an administrative enforcement proceeding varies according as the tribunal has itself presided at the reception of evidence, or has delegated that task to a hearing officer. In the former case, no further procedural steps ordinarily intervene between the hearing and the announcement of the decision. This is the procedure found in many state proceedings for the revocation of an occupational license, where it is quite usual to find the full licensing board sitting in revocation proceedings.

In most of the federal enforcement agencies, however, and in many of the larger state agencies, as already noted, a hearing officer presides at the reception of evidence as the deputy of the tribunal vested with the power of decision. Here the practice is for the hearing officer either initially to make the decision, which becomes the final decision unless modified by the tribunal, or to make a recommended decision which can become final only by affirmative action of the tribunal.

The Administrative Procedure Act provides that the former of these methods is to be employed unless the tribunal orders otherwise, either by general rule or in specific cases. To an increasing extent, the agencies affected have by general rule elected the latter procedure.

Whichever procedure is employed, it is important that prompt access to the initial or recommended decision be given the respondent and that he be afforded an opportunity, before it becomes final, to state and argue the objections he may have to it. In most of the federal agencies, it is now required by the Administrative Procedure Act that the respondent shall be afforded an opportunity to submit to the head of the agency exceptions to an initial or recommended decision, and his own proposed findings and conclusions.[29] Such a procedure is by no means universal in state enforcement proceedings; and it has been objected to as unnecessarily elaborate and time-consuming in certain cases.[30]

The procedure for formulating the final decision just described is in many cases in effect equivalent to an appeal. In some cases, the govern-

[29] The provision is not applicable where the governing statute does not require the agency to afford a hearing.

[30] Benjamin, Administrative Adjudication in the State of New York, 229 (1942). In a case decided before the Administrative Procedure Act, the Supreme Court held, however, that the failure to afford the respondent an opportunity to examine and

ing administrative regulations provide a formal appeal procedure, within the agency;[31] and some statutes also make such provision.

The statutes creating administrative enforcement tribunals in most cases authorize them to issue specific types of order—one or the other of the types of order referred to in a preceding page. By the Administrative Procedure Act, however, it is provided that each agency "is authorized in its sound discretion, with like effect as in the case of other orders, to issue a declaratory order to terminate a controversy or remove uncertainty." Similar provision is found in some of the state administrative procedure codes; and even in the absence of statute, the use of the declaratory order by administrative tribunals is increasing, though slowly.

7. ENFORCEMENT OF ORDER

The orders issued in administrative enforcement proceedings are in some cases self-executing: upon the entry of the order no further action by the agency is required, except perhaps suitable directions to its own personnel, or notice to other agencies which will honor its orders. Thus an order revoking a license requires no further action; an order of the Postmaster General denying postal delivery to a person adjudged by him to be using the mails to defraud requires merely the dispatch of a copy of the order to the post office at which the respondent's mail is delivered.

In the deportation proceeding, an administrative proceeding indeed without parallel in other respects as well, the administrative agency which adjudicates the case has, as part of its own personnel, officers empowered to arrest the alleged alien, to detain him, and to place him physically over the border or on board a foreign-bound craft.

In perhaps the majority of enforcement proceedings, however, the order issued is prohibitory or directory in character, addressed to the respondent himself. If not complied with, it can be enforced only by punishing the recalcitrant. But not only has the administrative tribunal empowered to issue such orders ordinarily not been furnished by the legislature, as have all courts above the pettiest, with officers subject to its order, empowered to seize the offender or his property to enforce compliance; typically it has not even been vested with power to adjudicate that its order has not been complied with. It must complain to a court

---

object to the initial decision made by a subordinate was a "vital defect" in the proceeding, requiring the resultant order to be set aside. Morgan v. U.S., 304 U.S. 1, 22 (1938).

[31] Thus, in alien deportation cases, the report of the local immigration inspector recommending expulsion is reviewed by the Commissioner of Immigration. If he decides in favor of expulsion, his determination is further reviewed by a board of three (the Board of Immigration Appeals), which has been created, without statutory requirement therefor, by the Attorney General. In certain cases the determination of the board may be further reviewed by the Attorney General. 8 Code Fed. Reg. Ch. 1, Part 6 (1958).

that such is the case, request the court so to find, and invoke the aid of the court in compelling compliance or punishing non-compliance.

It would be difficult to find a more striking illustration of the persistence of customary habits of thought in the design of novel institutions. An administrative tribunal may be empowered to adjudge that the respondent has violated the law and to revoke his license, inflicting immediate and it may be extended damage to the respondent. But for an administrative tribunal to adjudge that the respondent has failed to comply with its own order is apparently to exercise a power too like that of a court to have gained the approval of the legislature.

The agency, in asking a court to adjudicate that its order has not been complied with, and to assist it in effecting compliance, may request the court to issue its own order enjoining the non-complier from further disregarding the agency order on pain of punishment for contempt. Should the court's mandate in turn be disregarded, the agency seeks from the court the punishment of the non-complier as for a contempt of court. The punishment sought is ordinarily that of a monetary penalty. As we have seen, however, imprisonment as a penalty for contempt of court is by no means unknown even in civil proceedings; and it has occasionally though rarely been sought and obtained by an administrative tribunal intent on vindicating the authority of its prohibitory orders.

It may be that the governing statute does not empower the agency itself to institute a judicial proceeding for a mandatory order. In such a situation the agency must enlist the cooperation of the government's legal department—a condition encountered in state and local governments, as well as in the federal government.[32]

Where the governing statutes so provides, the agency may, instead of seeking a court order implementing its own order, or in addition thereto, seek to have a monetary penalty imposed upon the recalcitrant. Both the Interstate Commerce Act and the Federal Trade Commission Act provide for such penalties.

On the whole, it must be said that the machinery that has thus typically been developed for enforcing compliance with prohibitory or directory orders of administrative enforcement agencies—a compound of administrative and judicial elements—is a cumbersome one. However, it works more satisfactorily than might be anticipated.

8. JUDICIAL REVIEW OF ORDER: AVAILABILITY

It has been seen that in some types of administrative enforcement proceeding, the order issued is self-enforcing, that in others the administrative

---

[32] The legal department will ordinarily not press the case before the courts if it believes the agency has failed to comply with the applicable laws or has overlooked essential facts.

agency possesses its own enforcement machinery, and in still others, the agency must secure judicial aid to compel compliance.

Orders requiring judicial aid for enforcement

In the last category of cases, in the judicial proceeding instituted by the agency to compel compliance (whether it be one for an injunction or mandatory order, or a proceeding to impose a penalty for non-compliance) the person proceeded against may attack the legal validity of the order he has allegedly disobeyed. No statute, state or federal, has come to notice in which a court, in a proceeding before it to compel compliance or punish non-compliance with an administrative enforcement order made by an administrative tribunal, is commanded to proceed to judgment automatically, on a showing of non-compliance, without affording the alleged recalcitrant an opportunity to challenge the validity of the order. There has consequently apparently been no occasion for the Supreme Court to pass directly on the question whether such an attempted denial of the right to challenge the validity of the administrative enforcement order would be a denial of due process of law. In some of the opinions of the court bearing on collateral questions, however, there is to be found language suggesting that it would be.[33]

Congress and the state legislatures have in general refrained from making it a crime to fail to obey an administrative enforcement order, though such statutes are seemingly constitutional. Congress has, however, made it a felony for an alien against whom a deportation order is outstanding, and who is awaiting deportation, to "willfully fail or refuse to depart from the United States" within the period allowed by statute or to "willfully fail or refuse to make timely application in good faith for travel or other documents necessary to his departure," or to "willfully fail or refuse to present himself for deportation."[34]

Self-executing orders

In cases in which the order of the administrative tribunal is self-executing or is executed by the administrative agency without judicial aid, the governing statute may itself provide that the person against whom the order is directed may apply to the court for a review of the legality thereof, and for a stay pending such review.

In some of the states, a general statute authorizes such proceedings; and in the federal field the Administrative Procedure Act authorizes judicial review in cases where no special statutory provision has been made.

[33] In Colting v. Kansas City Stock Yards, 183 U.S. 79, 102 (1901), it was suggested but not decided, in the case of a state administrative order, that the imposition of a severe penalty for non-compliance, before opportunity for judicially testing the validity of the order has been afforded, may amount to a denial of this opportunity and may, therefore, be a denial of due process. See also Wadley So. Ry Co. v. Georgia, 235 U.S. 651 (1915).

[34] 8 U.S. Code, Sec. 1252(e).

Even in the absence of express statutory provision, however, whether general or special, the courts have everywhere asserted their power, under traditional doctrines, to give relief against an invalid order in enforcement proceedings. Whether the courts could constitutionally be precluded by express statute from undertaking such review of an enforcement order is perhaps an unsettled question. Such a statute is occasionally encountered;[35] but no case involving the constitutionality of such an attempted denial of judicial review appears to have come before the courts. It has been seen that the courts have upheld, as not wanting in due process, statutes empowering administrative officials, in urgent situations where the public welfare so demands, to proceed directly against persons and property without affording those proceeded against any opportunity for hearing. Once, however, the statute, by affording an opportunity to be heard by the administrative tribunal before the issuance of the order, recognizes that there is no emergency requiring immediate action, there would be presumably be no reason why a further opportunity to contest the legality of the enforcement order before a judicial tribunal could not also be afforded without injury to the public welfare. A statute expressly denying such opportunity, one would therefore be justified in supposing, should be held wanting in due process;[36] but it is by no means certain that, should the question arise, the Supreme Court would so hold with respect to either federal or state enforcement proceedings.[37]

Doctrines restrictive of judicial review

The availability of judicial review of an administrative enforcement order is limited by several doctrines, in the nature of self-denying ordi-

[35] Cf. Va. Laws of 1934, Ch. 94, Sect. 25. (1950 Va. Code 4–37 d): "The action of the [Alcohol Beverage Control] Board in suspending or revoking any license pursuant to the provisions of this section shall not be subject to review by any court nor shall any mandamus or injunction lie in any such case."

[36] The classic statement of Justice Brandeis, in St. Joseph Stock Yards Co. v. U.S., 298 U.S. 38, 72–77 (1936), is often cited in this connection: "The inexorable safeguard which the due process clause assures is . . . that there will be opportunity for a court to determine whether the applicable rules of law . . . are observed. . . . There must be the opportunity of presenting in an appropriate proceeding at some time to some court every question of law raised. . . ." An authoritative commentator declares, however, that "this rule has not received in its application the same clean-cut adherence from the courts which would correspond to its statement by Mr. Justice Brandeis." Dickinson, The Judicial Review Provisions of the Federal Administrative Procedure Act, in Warren (ed.), The Federal Administrative Procedure Act and the Administrative Agencies, 582 (1947). In Barsky v. Board of Regents, 346 U.S. 442 (1954), a case arising out of the suspension of a professional license by a state administrative agency, Justice Frankfurter, in his dissenting opinion, declared that "there is nothing in the United States Constitution which requires a State to provide for judicial review of the action of such agencies" (p. 470). He further declared, however, that arbitrary action by such an agency is a denial of due process of law— in effect, a declaration that federal judicial relief is available in every such case. In the case in question, the state law provided a limited judicial review.

[37] It should be noted that judicial review of a self-executing order may be pre-

nances, developed by the courts, which result in their refusing to undertake a review of the order although not expressly forbidden by statute to do so. Perhaps chief among these is the doctrine that if the procedure of the administrative agency provides for review of an order within the agency itself, the courts will not intervene at the instance of the respondent unless and until he has exhausted the possibility of obtaining relief within the agency itself. The rationale of this rule (commonly referred to as the rule of exhaustion of administrative remedies) is obvious. It has been criticized, however, and indeed rejected by some state courts as productive of useless delay and injustice in those cases in which the only question to be reviewed is one of law. Still more open to criticism is the extreme application of the doctrine, particularly by the federal courts, to cases in which the procedure of the agency provides no stay of the order pending its further review by the agency, the respondent being thus compelled to comply with an order which may subsequently be set aside as unlawful or unwarranted, without any provision for redress for the injury meanwhile done him.

Allied to this doctrine of exhaustion of administrative remedies is the principle observed in most jurisdictions that only the final order in an enforcement proceeding will ordinarily be reviewed. The Administrative Procedure Act, while not expressly forbidding review of preliminary, procedural, or intermediate rulings or orders, does so by implication, since its express grant of the right of review (where not otherwise given by statute) refers only to final action.

Costliness of judicial review

There is still another factor restrictive of judicial review of the administrative enforcement proceeding to which reference is seldom made—its costliness. The chief item of expense involved in challenging the order of an administrative tribunal is the cost of the services of counsel; the cost of preparing for the court, where needed, a transcript of the record of the proceeding before the administrative tribunal—a cost sometimes not a little increased by the vaunted liberality of that tribunal in receiving evidence of dubious probative value—may also be substantial.[38]

In earlier pages was mentioned the proposal that in proper cases the

---

cluded, even in the absence of a statute expressly precluding it, if there is no court which has jurisdiction of the proceedings necessary for bringing the order to the court for review. Where the legislature has complete control of the jurisdiction of the courts (as Congress has of the jurisdiction of the federal courts) it may thus preclude judicial review in such fashion as to make the question of the constitutionality of such preclusion an extremely difficult one to raise.

[38] In the case of some but not all of the federal administrative tribunals, the statute provides that upon the filing in court of a petition that the order of the tribunal be set aside or modified, the tribunal itself shall file in the court a complete transcript of the proceedings before it. Cf. 15 U.S. Code, Sec. 45(b); 29 id., Sec. 210(a). In state proceedings, such provisions are very exceptional.

public treasury bear the burden of securing judicial redress for illegal action by administrative officers, and for the defense of indigent persons proceeded against before administrative enforcement tribunals. It may be questioned whether there is not some place for this principle even in the field of judicial review of the administrative enforcement proceeding—a proceeding which may result in the revocation of a license, or in other penalty, having catastrophic results for a person of small means.

9. JUDICIAL REVIEW OF ORDER: SCOPE OF REVIEW

As in the review by an appellate court of the judgment of a trial court, so in the review by a court of the order of an administrative tribunal in an enforcement proceeding: the power to review determinations of law is plenary, but as to findings of fact the review may be severely limited.

Review of questions of law

The most sweeping ground of attack, purely legal in character, on the order of the administrative enforcement tribunal is that the statute under which it acts is unconsitutional. If the issue of constitutionality is not present, the most fundamental legal objection is that the agency had under the governing statute or regulation no jurisdiction of the person or subject matter involved in the proceeding. Jurisdiction conceded, the claim may be that the order issued is of a character not authorized by the statute. Another ground of attack may be that the procedure followed by the administrative tribunal deviated so widely from that commanded by the statute as to vitiate the entire proceeding—a ground successfully invoked against federal agencies in several cases arising subsequent to the enactment of the federal Administrative Procedure Act in 1946.

To the statement that the review of questions of law is, as in the review of judicial proceedings, plenary, one reservation may be noted. In certain of its decisions the content of which it is not practicable to discuss here, the Supreme Court has expressed a reluctance to review the determination of a legal question of a technical nature made by an administrative tribunal having special competence in the particular statutory field in which the question arises.[39] While especially relevant to tax questions, this doctrine has occasionally been invoked by the courts also in reviewing enforcement orders.

In the case of the orders of a few agencies, still another element, neither of law nor of fact, may come under review—the nature of the

[39] The doctrine was first enunciated in Dobson v. Commissioner, 320 U.S. 489 (1943), in which the Court said (at p. 502): "In deciding law questions courts may properly attach weight to the decision of points of law by an administrative body having special competence to deal with the subject-matter."

order issued. This element is presented perhaps most clearly in the case of the National Labor Relations Board, which is empowered, on finding that unfair labor practices have been engaged in, to order such action as it deems calculated to "effectuate the policies" of the act. The determination of the board that a particular form of order will further the policies of the act is not of course wholly beyond judicial control. An order having no clear relation to the purposes of the act may be annulled by the courts as not within the lawful power of the board. But once it is conceded that the order has indeed a relevancy to the purpose of the act, the courts are reluctant to disturb it because of the seeming harshness of the order. Similar views have been taken by state courts under state statutes granting similarly broad powers to administrative enforcement tribunals. This is in contrast to the control exercised by an appellate court over the shape of the decree issued by the trial court in an equity case; there the appellate court feels free to modify such a decree in its own discretion.

Review of findings of fact

The earlier federal enforcement statutes—the statutes authorizing revocation of licenses, imposition of penalties on importers, denial of postal service, etc.—made no mention of the possibility of judicial review, and hence were silent as to whether the findings of fact made by the administrative officers vested with adjudicatory power were to be conclusive. In the Interstate Commerce Act, under which, after 1906, a carrier failing to comply with an order of the Interstate Commerce Commission could be proceeded against in the courts for a penalty, it was merely provided that the finding of the commission as to the facts should be prima facie evidence thereof. By the Federal Trade Commission Act of 1914, however, there was introduced the principle that the findings of the administrative tribunal "as to the facts, if supported by evidence, shall be conclusive." This principle, expressed in varying language, is found in not a few later federal statutes providing for administrative enforcement proceedings, and in a great number of cognate state statutes. Today, the principal governing federal statute is the administrative Procedure Act of 1946, which commands that the evidence on which the administrative tribunal acts shall be "reliable, probative and substantial" and requires the courts, on reviewing the order of the tribunal, to "review the whole record or such portions thereof as may be cited by any party," to take "due account" of "the rule of prejudicial error" in the erroneous exclusion or admission of proof, and to set aside the order of the administrative tribunal if "unsupported by substantial evidence." The emphasis of the statute on the necessity for a review of "the whole record" has checked the alarming tendency which had developed in the federal courts, with the seeming blessing of the Supreme Court, to sustain administrative finding of facts whenever it was possible to discover anywhere in the record evidence which, taken in isolation, would support the finding. In the states, some statutes lay down a rule similar to that enunciated by the federal act; where the statute does not do so, judicial gloss has generally accomplished the same result even in the face of statutory commands that administrative findings of fact be treated as conclusive.

Precisely how far the courts should go in thus according greater weight to the findings of fact of an administrative tribunal than to those of a judge, or even a multijudge bench, sitting in an equity case has been expressed in diverse ways. The position which has now been arrived at by the Supreme Court, and which has received the general but not universal assent of the state courts, may be stated thus. It is not sufficient merely to search the record for some possibly isolated element of proof which lends support to the findings; the whole record must be considered, and the question whether the supporting proof relied on is in truth of a substantial character must be answered in the light of the whole record.

This is not to say, however, that the court may examine the whole record to determine where the preponderance of the evidence lies, and set aside the order on the ground that it is against the weight of the evidence; on the contrary if the administrative tribunal makes findings of fact supported by substantial evidence, yet contrary to the weight of the evidence, such findings must receive affirmance, even if reluctant affirmance, by the court.[40]

As has just been indicated, it is by no means in all administrative enforcement proceedings that the governing statute discloses an intention to give finality to the findings of fact made by the administrative tribunal. In many cases, the statute is silent as to the effect to be given to such findings. In the early days of administrative enforcement, the courts could presumably have taken the position that where the statute is thus silent, or where it makes no provision for judicial review, the court may properly review the entire record to determine for itself where the preponderance of proof lies, and set aside an administrative finding contrary thereto; and in some early cases this was in fact done. For some decades past, however, the courts have uniformly declined to do so, and have of their own motion governed their review of facts, where no statute controls, by substantially the same principles as in the cases governed by statute.

In the opinions of the courts in which this doctrine of deference to

---

[40] The point was illustrated in unusual fashion when the U. S. Court of Appeals for the Sixth Circuit upheld the findings of a jury awarding damages to an employer against a union for acts constituting a secondary boycott declared unlawful by the Taft-Hartley law, after having upheld shortly before a contrary finding of fact by the National Labor Relations Board in a companion case, in which that tribunal had found that the acts complained of had not been committed by the defendant union. Recognizing the inconsistency of its affirmance of both findings, the Court explained that each was supported by substantial evidence. United Brick and Clay Workers v. Deena Artware, Inc., 198 F.2d 637 (1952).

findings of fact made by administrative agencies has been developed, reference has frequently been made to the special competence of the administrative agency to find the facts, owing to its expertness in the field and the technical character of the subject matter. Whatever the accuracy of this characterization in the particular cases where it has been made, the fact is that the courts have shown an equal willingness to give substantial finality to findings of fact by administrative agencies in fields where no technical knowledge is required and no expertness is called for. The proceeding for the deportation of an alien resident, already mentioned as one of the gravest of administrative enforcement proceedings, obviously is of this non-technical character. So also is the proceeding to deny postal service to one engaged in a fraudulent enterprise. Other varieties of administrative enforcement proceeding, particularly proceedings for suspension or revocation of many types of occupational license, could readily be cited, in which the issues of fact involved ordinarily call for little or no expert competence.

At one stage in the development of the doctrine of the finality of administrative findings of fact in enforcement proceedings, the Supreme Court sought to place in a separate category those issues of fact which raised question as to whether the administrative tribunal had jurisdiction, and to enlarge the power of the courts to make independent evaluation of the facts involved in such issues. The attempt was, however, eventually abandoned as impracticable; and today in the federal courts and in some state courts as well the findings of the administrative tribunal on "jurisdictional" facts are accorded the same degree of finality as are other findings. There still remains, however, an unsettled area in which the finding of facts involves a constitutional right of the person proceeded against.

In the review of an order of the Attorney General for the deportation of an alleged alien, the courts, on an application for the review of the order, make independent determination of the question of fact, if one exists, as to whether the petitioner is in fact an alien; and there are expressions in some opinions of the Supreme Court indicating that, because the right of the petitioner, if he is indeed a citizen, is a constitutional one, such an independent determination of the facts by the courts (as contrasted with merely inquiring whether the finding of the Attorney General is supported by substantial evidence) is a constitutional imperative.[41] Congress has not, however, in the case of deportation orders, as it has in the case of some other orders of administrative tribunals already mentioned, expressly limited judicial review to the inquiry whether the questioned order is supported by substantial evidence; so that it cannot be confidently stated, though such seems to be the case, that the findings of fact of an administrative tribunal may not by statute be given finality, so as to preclude an independent determination of an issue of fact by the

[41] Ng Fung Ho v. White, 259 U.S. 276 (1922).

reviewing court, where the party seeking such review presents to the court grounds for questioning whether he may not have been deprived of a constitutional right by the allegedly erroneous finding. This is a question of importance in connection with several other types of administrative adjudication, shortly to be discussed.

As has been noted, only a small fraction of the enforcement orders issued by administrative tribunals are brought to the courts for review, and of these only a minority are set aside. Indubitably, the virtual finality accorded to the findings of fact made by the administrative tribunal is a principal factor in discouraging appeals to the courts, and in defeating such appeals when made. In this connection there have frequently been quoted the words attributed to Chief Justice Hughes: "An unscrupulous administrator might be tempted to say 'let me find the facts for the people of my country and I care little who lays down the general principles.' "

Thus increasingly, as the legal questions arising under the regulatory statute governing a given agency tend to become clarified, the findings of fact made by the agency tend to become the sole determinant of the action taken by it. Correspondingly, the importance of judicial review of such action decreases, and the agency tends increasingly to become autonomous in the field of regulation entrusted to it. The history of several of the federal regulatory agencies illustrates this tendency.

From the foregoing, it might be assumed that the courts, in reviewing the orders of enforcement tribunals, always draw a clear distinction between questions of law and questions of fact, and then apply the appropriate limitation. They do indeed generally do so where the distinction is obvious; in less clear-cut cases there is a disposition, in recent years, to ignore the distinction and describe the function of the court as being to inquire whether the administrative determination under review has a "rational basis."

10. JUDICIAL REVIEW OF ORDER: MECHANISM OF REVIEW

As already noted, the form of proceeding for the judicial review of an administrative enforcement order is in many cases provided by the statute itself. Where it is not so provided, the person proceeded against may resort to traditional forms of proceedings. Of these, the most familiar in federal practice is the injunction proceeding, in which an order will be issued to restrain action threatened against the property of the petitioner by an administrative agency, where, allegedly, irreparable injury will be caused thereby. In state procedure, the certiorari proceeding, in which in contrast to the injunction proceeding the court has before it only the record made before the administrative tribunal, is more generally employed. Where a license has been suspended or revoked, a proceeding for an order directing its restoration (termed either a mandamus proceeding or a proceeding for a mandatory injunction) is appropriate. In the sole administrative enforcement proceeding in which arrest is authorized—the alien deportation proceeding—the statute declares the administrative determination to be final; and the habeas corpus proceeding, instituted only after arrest, long afforded the only possibility of judicial intervention. In 1955, however, the Supreme Court ruled that one threatened with arrest for deportation might bring an action for a declaratory judgment—an action in which the court is free to make an original determination of the facts, instead of inquiring merely whether the administrative determination already made is supported by substantial evidence.[42]

Where resort to the courts is authorized by no statute, the courts merely asserting their power of review under traditional doctrines, jurisdiction in review proceedings is exercised by all the courts of general jurisdiction; and where resort to the courts is provided for under a general statute, it is not perhaps surprising to find the jurisdiction of those courts confirmed. Where, however, a statute governing particular enforcement proceedings limits the function of judicial review of such proceedings to particular courts it would be reasonable to expect that a single court would be designated for the review of the determinations of a given agency. Such has indeed been the scheme adopted in a few cases; in general, however, such statutes fail to concentrate such proceedings in a single court. Conspicuously is this the case in the review of federal enforcement proceedings.

In the Interstate Commerce Act of 1887 Congress designated the federal circuit courts, one or more of which then sat in each state, as the forum to which the Interstate Commerce Commission might resort for enforcement of its orders. Dissatisfaction with this diffuse arrangement led to the creation, in 1910, of a Commerce Court, to have exclusive jurisdiction of the review of such enforcement proceedings. Unfortunately, this court, composed of five federal judges designated by the President to sit upon it for stated terms, endured only till 1913, when for reasons hardly related to the merits of the plan it was abolished. Jurisdiction of proceedings to enforce the commission's orders was then returned to the federal district courts (the circuit courts having in the meantime been abolished). In the Federal Trade Commission Act adopted in the next year, however, Congress created a new pattern of judicial enforcement of administrative orders which it has since followed in a succession of statutes creating administrative agencies. Proceedings to procure enforcement of orders of the Trade Commission were to be brought, not as in the case of the Commerce Commission in the district courts, but in the court of appeals "within any circuit where the method of competition in question was

[42] Shaughnessy v. Pedreiro, 348 U.S. 48 (1955).

used or where any such person, partnership or corporation resides or carries on business." Cognate provisions now govern the judicial review of the proceedings of a number of other agencies having enforcement powers.[43]

The scheme of initial judicial review of federal enforcement orders by the district courts, or by the regional courts of appeals, thus applied where the agency seeks enforcement of its order, is also applied by the governing statutes to cases where the respondent takes the initiative in attacking the order. Where the agency order is self-executing (as in the case of deportation orders, or of fraud orders issued by the Post Office Department) Congress has made no specific provision for judicial review, and the person proceeded against must consequently resort to the district court, with its attendant possibility of appeal to the courts of appeals.

The federal system of review of enforcement orders has been characterized as an "inverted pyramid" of judicature. It is indeed extraordinary that, in this field, the accepted design of appellate systems is reversed, and instead of the determinations of a plurality of inferior tribunals being channeled into a smaller number of appellate tribunals, or a single one, the stream of decision issuing from a single tribunal is distributed among eleven courts of appeals (or, if the district court has jurisdiction, among several score district courts) to be reunited on rare occasions (for only occasionally is leave for such appeal granted) in a final review by the Supreme Court.

The irrationality of the design is heightened by the fact that the administrative agency whose decisions are thus scattered for review to the four winds is in many instances itself an appellate tribunal passing on decisions made by its hearing officers. Perhaps the extreme is found in the system prevailing in the review of deportation orders. Here the initial decision of the Commissioner of Immigration (based on the report of a hearing officer) has been reviewed by a three-man Board of Immigration Appeals, and again, frequently, by the Attorney General or one of his chief assistants; but the judicial review of the order begins in the federal district court, with probable further review by the regional court of appeals and final review, perhaps, by the Supreme Court. Contrasted with such a procedure, entailing five separate review proceedings, the double appeal so often criticized in the field of ordinary civil or criminal proceedings seems relatively expeditious.

But it is not merely expedition that suffers under the present system. In some fields of federal administrative enforcement the factual material and the detailed regulations which must be mastered by the reviewing

[43] These include the Secretary of Agriculture, the National Labor Relations Board, the Federal Power Commission, the Federal Communications Commission, the Civil Aeronautics Board, the Federal Reserve Board, the Securities and Exchange Commission, and the Subversive Activities Control Board.

court before it can intelligently consider the questions presented in the particular proceeding before it are formidable. Yet every judge of a court of appeals (or it may be every district judge) must be prepared to master this material on short notice.

From time to time proposals have been advanced for a single federal court, to have sole jurisdiction of all judicial proceedings for the review of federal administrative proceedings. Such a court, with a large membership, sitting ordinarily in specialized divisions but convening its full membership for the consideration of important issues, would give to the process of judicial review greater expertness, expedition, and finality. In deference to the feeling that the Supreme Court should have the last word on all questions—a feeling which despite its irrationality cannot well be ignored by Congress—that court could continue as at present, on petition, to review such cases as it deemed important.

Such a plan, whatever its details, would represent a decisive improvement in design. It encounters, however, one formidable, though often unstated, obstacle. The present arrangement, irrational though it is, or perhaps it would be more accurate to say because of its very irrationality, insures the injection of what might be called the lay point of view. The administrative tribunals, it is felt, have a narrow if not a prejudiced approach because of their specialization; the review of their determinations by an unspecialized court or, rather, congeries of courts, furnishes a salutary check on this parochial tendency. A specialized court, it is said, would run the same danger of narrowness of perspective as does the administrative tribunal itself.

One may concede a certain degree of validity to this view without accepting the conclusion that the present irrational system should continue. Were the judges of the court of administrative appeals to be designated from among the federal judiciary, perhaps by the Supreme Court, to sit on the court for limited staggered terms, and were there to be a certain amount of rotation during such term of service from one to another of the specialized divisions of the court, any tendency on the part of the judges to become administrative-minded, so to speak, would be held to a minimum.

A like irrationality of design characterizes the machinery for judicial review of administrative proceedings in some of the states, particularly in those having intermediate courts of appeal. On the whole, however, since administrative enforcement proceedings, other than revocation of licenses, have been less resorted to in the states than in the federal government, the need for improvement cannot there be regarded as equally pressing.

Where the order of a state administrative enforcement tribunal is challenged on the ground that it or the statute under which it issues is violative of federal law—i.e., of the Constitution or of a federal statute, regulation, or treaty—it may be directly attacked in the federal courts, as by a proceeding to enjoin its enforcement, without first attempting such challenge in the state courts. The limitations which the Supreme Court has however placed on access to the federal courts in such cases have already been mentioned.[44]

11. THE NEED FOR THE ADMINISTRATIVE ENFORCEMENT PROCEEDING

As one reviews the striking development of administrative in place of judicial enforcement of regulatory statutes, so largely the work of recent decades, and asks whether this radical departure from traditional patterns was necessary, and whether it has realized the expectations of its designers, it speedily becomes apparent that though generalizations are the rule in the literature of the subject—contributed alike by the champions and the denigrators of administrative justice—no easy generalization is in fact possible. At an earlier page it was pointed out that understanding of the problem of administrative justice is not furthered by confounding in a single discussion proceedings quite diverse, such as those directed to enforcement of regulatory statutes, the assessment of taxes, the grant of benefits and privileges, and the adjudication of private disputes. Similarly, even within the field of the enforcement proceeding itself, it will shortly be apparent that only confusion can result from assimilating in a single statement the diverse types of agency engaged in adjudicating such proceedings, and the diverse types of statute to be applied.

Since the Federal Trade Commission was the first federal agency created to exercise solely the function of administrative adjudication, it might be supposed that an examination of the contemporary documentation would reveal a systematic exposition of the reasons for this departure from traditional methods of law enforcement. But nothing of the sort is to be found. Both the presidential message which proposed the creation of the commission, and the congressional committee reports which recommended the passage of the act creating it, are barren of anything but the vaguest phrases. In the first scholarly study of the commission's work, made after it had been operating for about a decade, the author, after a thorough search of all contemporary material, was unable to explain the reasons for the commission's creation as a tribunal outside the judicial structure, or for its investment with the function of initiating proceedings under the act, in place of the traditional method of imposing that duty upon the Department of Justice.[45]

The reasons commonly advanced for the use of the administrative

[44] See p. 198.
[45] Henderson, The Federal Trade Commission, 16–24, 328–329 (1924).

rather than the judicial tribunal are (1) more expert application of the statute and (2) greater expedition. To what extent are these advantages realized in the administrative enforcement proceeding?

Need for expert application of the statute

In the discussion of administrative enforcement tribunals, one frequently encounters the thesis that the administrative rather than the judicial enforcement proceeding is needed because the statute to be enforced is, unlike those enforced by judicial proceedings, expressed in general terms and thus unsuitable for judicial enforcement, requiring instead the expert touch. Even the Attorney General's distinguished committee endorsed this generalization, which finds only qualified support in the texts of the relevant statutes. The statutes entrusted to administrative adjudication, said the committee in 1941 "necessarily describe in general terms, and with emphasis upon tendency or effect, those practices which are forbidden. It . . . must be left to the administrative agencies to apply these prohibitions to a great variety of conduct."[46] Yet the lottery and fraud order statutes, and the immigration statutes, the two early examples of drastic administrative enforcement, are framed in terms of complete definiteness, and the subject matter is one calling for no expertness whatever. In the field of license revocation, the instances are many in which the statute whose violation is ground for suspension or revocation of license is expressed in the ordinary phrases which are the daily business of the criminal and indeed the civil courts.

Even where the statute which the administrative tribunal is required to apply contains language of greater generality, the language is no broader than that of some statutes whose enforcement is left to the courts. The phrase "unfair methods of competition" employed in the Federal Trade Commission Act doubtless lacks the venerable age, and accompanying body of judicial interpretation, enjoyed by the phrase "combination in restraint of trade" contained in the antitrust laws and left to the sole

[46] Report of the Attorney General's Committee on Administrative Procedure, 59 (1941). It may be questioned, moreover, whether in some cases, instead of the administrative tribunal being needed because the statute is necessarily vague, the statute has not been left needlessly vague with the dubious purpose of giving the administrative tribunal a freer hand in developing its meaning—the unstated premise being that the tribunal to be appointed would be "sympathetic" to the objectives of the act. That case-by-case development of the content of a regulatory statute, particularly by a "sympathetic" expounder, breeds uncertainty among those regulated, and may inflict actual hardship on those legal guinea pigs who happen to be the parties to a case in which new content is added to the statute, is obvious. However, even the qualified independence of an administrative tribunal empowered to interpret a statute is a source of regret to the true believers in executive government, because the "development of administrative adjudication on a large scale has caused a substantial dissipation of the President's ability to supervise the execution of public policy"! Emmerich, Essays on Federal Reorganization, 36 (1950).

ADMINISTRATIVE TRIBUNALS

interpretation of the judiciary; but it is to be doubted whether, in the context of modern business practices and of the actual trust and monopoly cases with which the courts have had to deal under those laws, ancient learning is of much assistance.

Assuming, however, the existence of a statute describing "in general terms, and with emphasis upon tendency or effect, those practices which are forbidden," the question remains whether an "administrative agency" is able "to apply these prohibitions to a great variety of conduct" more expertly than is a court. The answer to this question clearly varies with the extent to which the agency is also charged with regulatory and administrative functions with respect to the subject matter involved. At one extreme is such an agency as the Civil Aeronautics Board (more useful as a simple example than is the Interstate Commerce Commission, which covers several diverse industries instead of a single one). The regulatory powers exercised by Aeronautics Board over air transport embrace all the varieties of governmental function: it legislates (prescribing safety standards, regulating liability for baggage, rate practices, etc.); it administers (granting franchises for air routes, issuing licenses to pilots, etc.); it investigates, it prosecutes, and it adjudicates (issuing cease and desist orders against unfair and monopolistic practices). At the other extreme is found such an agency as the National Labor Relations Board, which has only the function of adjudication.[47] Clearly, such an "administrative" tribunal as the latter has inherently no greater potential for expertness than would a judicial tribunal similarly charged only with adjudicating enforcement proceedings under a single statute.

Between these two extremes lie perhaps the great majority of administrative enforcement tribunals, which do indeed have functions other than adjudication but which do not, contrary to the impression often encountered, have any such regulatory or administrative functions with respect to the subject matter of their adjudications as to give them any expertness. One source of the prevalent confusion is that not a few adjudicatory agencies do have an administrative function but only with respect to the *penalty* inflicted by their adjudication.

A clear illustration is to be found in the power of adjudication exercised by the Postmaster General in proceedings to deny mail delivery to a person engaged in a lottery or fraudulent enterprise. That official has no more power to regulate lottery or fraudulent enterprises, or any enterprises likely to become or suspected of becoming such, than has the federal

[47] By the Labor-Management Relations Act of 1947 (the Taft-Hartley law) complete responsibility for prosecution was vested in an official termed the General Counsel of the Board—a total misnomer, since he is appointed by the President and is completely independent of the board, which has no authority over him. To remove misconceptions on the part of the public on this point, the office of general counsel should be completely separated from the board and given an appropriate independent name. Were that done, the purely judicial character of the board's work would more clearly emerge.

prosecutor who institutes criminal proceedings against persons conducting such enterprises through the mails, or than has the judge or jury who try a person thus proceeded against. The fact that the Post Office Department happens to be responsible for the postal service is wholly irrelevant. Its *postal* functions give it no special knowledge of fraudulent schemes.

A review of the federal agencies before which enforcement proceedings are tried will disclose that not a few of them—including the agency charged with the most drastic proceeding of all, the deportation proceeding—are in the same position as is the Postmaster General with respect to the fraud order proceeding. In the states, too, it will be found that many of the agencies empowered to revoke licenses are in the same situation: they have no power of regulation or administration of the conduct for which the license may be revoked.[48]

A further source of confusion is found in the fact that administrative enforcement tribunals are usually responsible for the investigation and prosecution of the cases that come before them, and may thus give the superficial but false impression of having regulatory and administrative powers over the subject matter they adjudicate. The position of the Federal Trade Commission in the enforcement of the statute prohibiting "unfair methods of competition" is illustrative. The commission investigates complaints made to it or initiates investigation on its own account; it initiates a proceeding against the person thought to be engaged in unfair practices, prosecutes, and adjudicates. Beyond this it may do nothing to regulate methods of competition; it has no power to promulgate regulations defining fair or unfair methods of competition, or to license or otherwise authorize the use of any particular method. It is prosecutor and judge—nothing more.[49]

In sum, it is believed that a review of the statutes entrusted to administrative rather than judicial enforcement will disclose only a minority, perhaps a small minority, which call for any more specialized knowledge than do the run of statutes enforced through the courts; and that an examination of the functions of administrative agencies entrusted with adjudication in enforcement proceedings discloses many that have no such functions of regulation or administration of the subject matter they regulate as would give them specialized knowledge were it required.

If one confines attention to the relatively small area of enforcement proceedings in which the text of the regulatory statute, and the complexity

[48] The administrative proceeding to suspend or revoke the license of a motor-vehicle operator is numerically very important among state administrative enforcement proceedings; but the motor-vehicle licensing agency, characteristically vested with the power of suspension or revocation, ordinarily has no power whatever to regulate the manner of operation of motor vehicles.

[49] The commission does have large powers of investigation in this field and the power to require periodical reports from corporations engaged in interstate or foreign commerce. It also has power to issue regulations under some of the special acts it enforces.

of the subject regulated, do indeed call for expertness, the question remains whether that expertness can be possessed only by those who are simultaneously engaged in regulation and administration of the subject matter. So far as concerns the subordinate adjudicating personnel, it is now conceded on all hands that they should *not* engage in regulatory or administrative activities. The head of the agency, in any case, ordinarily depends on subordinates for expert advice.[50] If specialized knowledge is required, may it not then equally be found in a tribunal entirely divorced from regulation and administration, its members selected from those experienced in the field, their own knowledge fortified by the tribunal's own expert research staff and expert corps of referees? Such a tribunal, needless to say, could readily be organized as part of the judicial establishment rather than of the administrative branch, should that be desired.

It should be emphasized that the foregoing discussion has reference solely to enforcement proceedings. When one comes to other forms of governmental proceeding against the individual (such as tax assessment or collection) or with proceedings in which the individual is himself seeking some grant or benefit at the hands of public authority—proceedings shortly to be discussed—the considerations just reviewed must be reappraised and may indeed be found quite inapplicable.

Expedition

If, in choosing between the judicial and the administrative enforcement proceeding, one rather than the other is to be preferred on grounds of fundamental principle, the secondary factor of expedition can hardly be permitted to affect the choice. Whichever proceeding is chosen on principle, expedition should be sought in its conduct. Yet expedition is sometimes discussed as if it were of the essence.

Implicit in some of this discussion is the notion that the judicial, as opposed to the administrative, proceeding is inherently incapable of expedition. The rules of pleading and of evidence applicable to the judicial proceedings (usually cited as responsible for its supposed dilatoriness) are assumed to be unalterable. In point of fact, as noted in earlier pages, the rigor of these rules is greatly relaxed in certain types of judicial proceeding; and did the legislature, in conferring upon the courts jurisdiction

[50] The provisions of the Administrative Procedure Act, prohibiting the personnel connected with the prosecution of a case to participate in its adjudication (see p. 418) may indeed deprive even an administrative tribunal of needed expert advice in arriving at its decision and framing its order. A chairman of the Federal Trade Commission, where such a situation appears to have developed, suggested that it be remedied "by attaching economic advisers directly to the Commission, and possibly to the hearing examiners, to perform economic functions in the same manner as the General Counsel performs legal functions." Howrey, The Federal Trade Commission: A Revaluation of its Responsibilities, 40 Amer. Bar Assn. Jour. 113, 115 (1954).

in a particular type of enforcement proceeding now administratively adjudicated, wish to free the court from procedural rules to the same extent it has the administrative tribunal, no constitutional objection could in most cases be offered.

But the notion that the freedom of the administrative tribunal from procedural restrictions does in fact automatically insure expedition is itself unfounded. A congressional study of the Federal Trade Commission's adjudicatory activities, made in 1951, commented on its "laborious and protracted processes of administrative adjudication" and stated that "a person making a typical complaint to the Commission should not, on the basis of its past record, expect to secure relief for several years. Major cases have occasionally required a decade."[51] It should come as no surprise to one familiar with the multiple causes of delay in judicial proceedings, in no wise related to rules of procedure or of evidence, that similar conditions should develop in administrative justice.

Nor does the liberty to disregard the exclusionary rules of evidence considered controlling in judicial proceedings (and to depart also from the interrogatory pattern followed in those proceedings) automatically ensure that the administrative tribunal conducting the hearing will at once come to grips with the essential issues before it, and expeditiously elicit the necessary facts. Just as a capable judge, operating within the judicial rules, can compel the proceeding before him to move expeditiously, so an administrative hearing officer of indifferent interest or ability may, despite the greater freedom he enjoys, permit the proceeding before him to bog down needlessly. Thus an authoritative official survey of federal agencies made in 1949 reported that "the hearings by some of the commissions have been sharply criticized as unduly lengthy and drawn-out. The record tends to be loaded with repetitive and cumulative evidence; with long statements of counsel and witnesses which are primarily argumentative; and useless cross-examination."[52] Despite repeated ventilation of the problem, both by official bodies and by the bar, the situation appears to have improved but little.

From the foregoing, it is apparent that the current tendency to entrust the enforcement of new regulatory statutes to administrative rather than judicial agencies calls for reappraisal; and that even in the case of such long-established administrative enforcement proceedings as the license revocation proceeding (federal, state, and local), the fraud order proceeding, the deportation proceeding, the unfair labor relations practice

[51] Antitrust Law Enforcement by the Federal Trade Commission, H. Rept. 3236, 81st Cong., 2nd Sess., 21 (1951).

[52] U.S. Commission on Organization of the Executive Branch, Report, Appendix N, 55 (1949). It is significant that the Conference on Administrative Procedure created by the President in 1953 has devoted much attention to the problem of reducing the voluminousness of records of hearings.

proceeding, and not a few others, there is wanted a fundamental reexamination of the need for tribunals standing outside the independently organized judicial branch, to which the vast majority of enforcement proceedings is still entrusted.

12. UNION OF PROSECUTING AND ADJUDICATING FUNCTIONS

It remains to consider one other usual aspect of the administrative enforcement proceeding (absent from most other types of administrative adjudication) that has been the target of incessant criticism, which still continues. This is the union in a single hand of the power of the prosecutor and of the judge—a concentration of power of course totally at variance with the traditional scheme of judicial enforcement in which the judge and the prosecutor are completely independent of each other, and of any common superior.[53]

However much the union of responsibility for both prosecution and adjudication in a single agency may offend against the traditional concept that no man should be judge in his own cause, it does not, as has been seen, in the view of the courts violate the constitutional principle of separation of powers. That principle relates to the legislative, executive, and judicial departments as the primary divisions of a government. Within each of those departments, a certain admixture of the functions primarily vested in the other departments is unavoidable.

Moreover, it is necessary to recognize that, technicality aside, the combination of prosecuting and perhaps judicial functions in a subordinate agency of government, itself wholly the creature of the legislature and subject to control by the courts, is something quite different from the union of these powers in a single sovereign organ of government. The theory of checks and balances, which is at bottom the basis for the doctrine of separation of powers, seeks to make despotism impossible by entrusting to no one sovereign organ of government the whole of the governmental power. A subordinate administrative agency is, however, hardly capable of playing the role of despot. When a Lord Chief Justice of England characterized the development of administrative agencies in Great Britain as "the new despotism," he was referring to the agencies of a sovereign government in the organization of which the theory of checks and balances, as of separation of powers between the executive and the legislative, finds virtually no recognition.

This having been said, the fact remains that this concentration of functions impairs public confidence in the impartiality of the administrative tribunal, and may impair the impartiality of the tribunal itself. Even if he is able to rise above the urge for victory, the administrative

[53] This subject is exhaustively treated in 2 Davis, Administrative Law Treatise, 171–249 (1958).

prosecutor who is also the judge may be animated (to use the words of a distinguished British official investigating committee) by that "bias from strong and sincere convictions as to public policy" which "may operate as a more serious disqualification than pecuniary interest." It is not surprising, therefore, that demands for the complete separation of adjudication from prosecution have been recurrent.

As early as 1931 the National Commission on Law Observance and Enforcement had recommended complete separation in the only area of administrative enforcement which it had investigated—the alien deportation proceeding.[54] In 1937 the distinguished Committee on Administrative Management appointed by President Roosevelt recommended completely separate prosecuting and adjudicating agencies throughout.[55] The equally distinguished Attorney General's Committee on Administrative Procedure, which reported in 1941, divided on the question. Opposing the proposal, the majority declared:

Of prime importance is the danger of friction and of a break-down of responsibility as between the two complementary agencies. This is a danger to private interests no less than to public ones. To create a special body whose single function is to prosecute will almost inevitably increase litigation and with it harassment to respondents. At present the added responsibility of deciding exercises a restraining influence which limits the activities of the agency as a whole. . . . The situation is likely to be different where the function of prosecuting is separated out. First, a body devoted solely to prosecuting often is intent upon "making a record." It has no responsibility for deciding and its express job is simply to prosecute as often and successfully as possible. Second, it must guess what the deciding branch will think. It can explore the periphery; it can try everything; and meanwhile the individual citizen must spend time and money before seome curb can be exercised by the deciding branch. And, it should be noted, a separation of functions would seriously militate against what this Committee has already noted as being, numerically and otherwise, the lifeblood of the administrative process—negotiations and informal settlements. Clearly, amicable disposition of cases is far less likely where negotiations are with officials devoted solely to prosecution and where the prosecuting officials cannot turn to the deciding branch to discover the law and the applicable policies.[56]

Three members of the committee, however, disagreed with these views. They commented:

It is said, in the Committee report, that there would be a division of responsibility for policy if one agency could settle cases by consent but only a separate agency could decide disputed cases, yet this is what the Department of Justice and the courts do in the judicial system as we know it and it is what takes place in the administration of the tax, customs, and criminal law. It is said that sepa-

[54] Report, Part V, 8, 178.
[55] Report, 41–42. The President in transmitting this report to Congress praised it highly and expressed no dissent.
[56] Report, 58–59.

ration would mean hindrance of "amicable disposition of cases" and a "breakdown of responsibility." But this has not been true of the Department of Justice, which must go to the courts with contested cases, nor of the Bureau of Internal Revenue, which must go to the Board of Tax Appeals with contested tax matters. . . .[57]

In the intervening years, much has been written on the issue, and several proposals have been advanced for transferring to judicial tribunals the functions now vested in the major federal administrative tribunals (the proposals usually calling for a specialized court or courts);[58] but little has been added to the views expressed in these two excerpts. Without attempting any definitive choice between the opposing points of view which they put forward, the opinion may be ventured that, on the one hand, the reasons advanced by the majority of the Attorney General's Committee (which embraced all forms of administrative adjudication) have in fact no application to numerous types of administrative enforcement proceedings; and that, on the other hand, if the validity of the reasoning be accepted, it would equally call for the removal of the traditional cleavage between prosecution and adjudication which characterizes the enforcement of those innumerable regulatory statutes in which the judicial enforcement proceeding is still relied on.[59]

The action of Congress in commanding the separation, in the subordinate ranks of the agency, of the prosecuting from the adjudicating personnel, recounted at an earlier page, may be regarded as a concession, even if not a very rationally conceived one, to the principle of separation. But it is separation at the subordinate level only. The head of the agency, whether a single individual or a board, is in most cases responsible not only for adjudication but also for vigorous prosecution, and for the successful over-all enforcement of the statute involved. In numerous situations,

[57] Ibid., 206–207.

[58] In 1955, the distinguished Task Force on Legal Services and Procedure, created by the second Hoover Commission (the Commission on the Organization of the Executive Branch of the Government) reported in favor of transferring the adjudicatory functions of the federal administrative agencies to regular or specialized courts as a matter of policy, there being some differences of opinion among its members as to the immediate practicability of certain particular transfers (Task Force Report, 249–250). The commission, confining itself to more generalized recommendations, endorsed the position of the Task Force, declaring that "where the proceeding before the agency is strictly judicial in nature, and the remedy afforded by the agency is one characteristically granted by the courts, there can be no effective protection or private rights unless there is a complete separation of prosecuting functions from the functions of decision." Legal Services and Procedure, 84–85.

[59] A comment by a qualified French observer is of interest: "[American] administrative commissions endowed with judicial powers . . . constitute a regrettable confusion of powers, the more surprising since American public law has always been attached to the doctrine of the separation of powers. . . . Although situations of this sort are not unknown in French law, it has never carried so far the confusion of the functions of decision, prosecution, and judgment in the same agency." Auby, Book review, 2 Amer. Jour. Comparative Law 573 (1953).

the decision to prosecute has been made in the first instance by the head of the agency (perhaps, as in some Federal Trade Commission proceedings, by the full commission after thorough examination). The proceeding is then referred to the hearing examiner who, though a subordinate, is expected to pass on the merits of the complaint with the same complete impartiality as if it had been laid before him by someone unconnected with the agency. Recognizing the unreality of looking for judicial impartiality in this setting, Congress has sought to protect the independence of the subordinate hearing examiner by novel devices. Though he remains an employee of the agency, appointed "subject to the civil service and other laws," he is, in contrast to federal employees generally, who are removable by the department head, removable "only for good cause established and determined by the Civil Service Commission, after opportunity for hearing and upon the record thereof." The compensation of examiners too is to be "prescribed by the Commission independently of agency recommendations or ratings."[60]

Moreover, Congress has attempted to regulate the procedure for assigning cases to examiners, so as to prevent the head of the agency, presumably, from assigning a case to an examiner believed to possess views on the issues involved more or less in accord with those of the agency head. To this end the Administrative Procedure Act provides that cases shall be assigned to examiners in rotation; and it entrusts to the Civil Service Commission the promulgation of regulations for carrying this mandate into effect. The regulations adopted by that body have been attacked as negating the purpose of the act in this respect, but the Supreme Court has upheld them.[61]

Even had this elaborate structure of dubious devices to protect hearing officers from their enforced association with fellow employees engaged in prosecution and from improper pressures from the agency head become completely effective, as clearly it has not,[62] one might still wonder why Congress did not adopt the simpler and more effective plan (recommended by at least one member of the distinguished Attorney General's committee which reported in 1941) of constituting hearing officers not merely a separate category within each agency, but as themselves a separate corps, not part of any agency. The position of the hearing officer in relation to the agency would thus be not that of a subordinate employee of the agency, but rather that of a member of an independent corps, for the time being

[60] 5 U.S. Code, Sec. 1010.

[61] Ramspeck v. Federal Trial Examiners Conference, 345 U.S. 128 (1953).

[62] Though doubtless improved since it was termed a "paper system" by an authoritative commentator in 1953 (Schwartz, A Decade of Administrative Law, 1942–1951, 51 Mich. Law Rev. 775, 793), it was still found wanting by the Task Force on Legal Services and Procedure of the second Hoover Commission in 1955, and subsequently by a special committee of the American Bar Association.

attached to the agency. The first loyalty of the adjudicator would thus be not to the agency to which he is attached, albeit fairly permanently, but to the adjudicatory corps of which he is a member, and of which the dominating interest is judicial impartiality and efficiency, rather than the furtherance of the special objectives of one or another of the administrative agencies to which its members are attached.[63] The experience of California with such a corps, created in 1945, to serve primarily those agencies which cannot themselves provide a full-time hearing officer divorced from investigation and prosecution, has demonstrated its value.

The organization and control of such a corps would present novel problems, but by no means difficult ones. As has been seen, the Administrative Procedure Act has given the Civil Service Commission a measure of responsibility for the examiners as a corps by vesting in it control over their compensation and a veto on their dismissal (as well as the selection of examiners for loan by one agency to another to relieve a temporary shortage). That commission is, however, ill-adapted to exercise control of such a separate corps of hearing officers as is here suggested. Much more appropriate perhaps would be a judicial tribunal.[64]

The attention which has been given to the status of the hearing officer should not be permitted to obscure the fact that, however the independence and dignity of that officer's position be safeguarded, his power is only that of initial decision or recommendation, and that the ultimate power of decision is in the head of the agency, the very officer or officers whose judicial impartiality is, as the elaborate precautions against the use of improper influence demonstrate, by hypothesis suspect.[65]

In the field of state administrative adjudication, likewise, the separation of prosecuting from adjudicating agencies is little known. In California, the creation of an independent corps of hearing officers, to preside at

[63] A bill which would make the hearing examiners a separate corps., but would nevertheless assign each examiner virtually permanently to a particular agency—a feature which would seem to negative the very purpose of establishing a separate corps—was proposed in 1957 by the American Bar Association (S. 932, 85th Cong.,). It failed to gain any significant measure of congressional support.

[64] So far as federal hearing examiners are concerned, their appointment by a judicial tribunal would encounter no constitutional obstacle, the Constitution expressly authorizing Congress to vest the appointment of inferior federal officers in "the courts of law" (Art. II, Sec. 2).

[65] In recent years there have been suggestions that the decision of the hearing examiner should be final, to be reviewed by the agency itself only if the agency had assented to such review on an application for review made to it setting forth substantial reasons therefor. The hearing examiners as a group have not yet, however, succeeded in creating a sufficiently favorable public image of their stature to make such a plan acceptable. An intermediate step would be to place the decision in the hands of a board of examiners (perhaps three in number) of whom the hearing examiner would be one. In hearings of the kind here involved, the adjudicator's presence at the hearing, with its opportunity for the observation of the witnesses, is of little importance.

hearings on suspension or revocation of licenses before the various enforcement (chiefly licensing) agencies found in that state, while nominally preserving the adjudicatory power of the prosecuting agency, has in substance in the ordinary case greatly impaired if not destroyed it. In one of the most comprehensive official evaluations of administrative adjudication in a state thus far made (that of New York, completed in 1942), although the combination of functions was, in general, approved, a recommendation for complete separation was made (but not acted upon by the legislature) in the case of the state labor relations board.[66]

13. UNION OF ADJUDICATORY FUNCTION WITH THAT OF LEGISLATION

The criticism that the administrative agency, in an enforcement proceeding before it, improperly combines the functions of prosecutor and of judge is commonplace. Much less frequent is the criticism, perhaps equally valid, that it often combines the function of legislator and judge.

We shall not here discuss, since it is beyond our theme, whether it is wise to entrust the power of promulgating regulations to the officer who is to enforce the regulation; whether the very fact that enforcement is to be in his hands may not cause him to draft regulations with less precision and with more concern for his own ease in administering them than might be the case were his responsibility purely legislative. But one may ask whether it is sound to vest the power of adjudication in the hands of those who have promulgated the legislation under which the adjudication arises. When an administrative agency promulgates regulations and then sits in judgment in matters arising out of the enforcement of those regulations, it is natural to expect that it will construe those regulations in a doubtful case as it intended them to be construed when it promulgated them, even if such intent would not be drawn from the language of the regulations by a neutral mind.

With respect to so-called regulatory commissions, dealing with a single industry or industry group, still another factor inimical to judicial impartiality may enter. It is considered proper that the members of such a commission should meet with the representatives of the industry on an informal basis, so that they may better become acquainted with the problems connected with the regulation of the industry. But such habit of informal conference may imperceptibly carry over to matters in which the commission is to sit not as a regulatory but as an adjudicatory agency. In the 1958 congressional investigation of the exertion of improper influence on members of regulatory commissions, substantial evidence of this improper practice was adduced.

[66] Benjamin, Administrative Adjudication in the State of New York, 48 (1942).

15

Proceedings Against Private Parties
Other Than Enforcement Proceedings

1. TAXATION. 2. CONDEMNATION. 3. RATE REGULATION. 4. DISMISSAL OR DEMOTION OF PUBLIC EMPLOYEE.

The enforcement proceeding under a regulatory statute, though the most controversial type of administrative proceeding against the private party, is by no means the only one, nor the one involving the greatest number of adjudications. The area of administrative adjudication against the private party that affects the greatest number of people is the area of tax determination. The growing condemnation of private property for military or other large public projects affects increasing numbers of people. The imposition, on a corporation (or individual) operating a public utility, of a reduction in rates, or an increase in service, represents another type of agency proceeding against a private party, which, while entailing far fewer actual adjudications than does the assessment of taxes, obviously affects vast numbers of people. Finally, by no means to exhaust the list, the dismissal or demotion of a public employee enjoying the right to continued employment is, though perhaps not commonly so regarded, in effect a governmental proceeding against a private party.[1]

In the present chapter these several representative types of proceeding will be briefly reviewed, chiefly in order to ascertain the respects in which they differ from the enforcement proceeding of which an account was given in the preceding chapter. The reader may assume, unless the contrary is indicated, that that account applies also, in its essentials, to the proceedings considered in the present chapter.

[1] Examples of other proceedings in this category are these: in municipal proceedings, the imposition of special assessments on property benefited by public improvements; and in the federal field, determinations made under the various crop control acts, fixing for each individual grower the maximum acreage ("allotment") on which he may grow a given crop.

1. TAXATION

The pervasiveness and impersonality of the taxing process and the routine and uncontested character of the determinations involved in all but a very small proportion of cases tend to mask the fact that it is, as to many types of tax, in effect a massive proceeding against private parties, involving, as to each party proceeded against, an individual determination of the amount for which he is liable.

Viewed then as a procedure for determination of the individual tax, the tax proceeding presents at several points a striking contrast to the enforcement proceeding. The notice to the taxpayer ordinarily takes the form of a notice that a given amount of tax, or a given valuation, has been tentatively fixed, and will become final unless protest is made. Such notice need not, in the case of property taxes, be given to each taxpayer individually, though in some local tax procedures, notice of an increase in valuation is not infrequently so given, So far as the requirements of due process are concerned, however, a public posting pursuant to statute is sufficient.

The procedure provided for protest by the taxpayer varies greatly. Formal hearing with a record of evidence is the exception.

In not a few forms of tax the tax collector does not require the aid of the courts to enforce collection. In real property taxes, the tax, upon the assessment becoming final, is a lien upon the property, and if it remains unpaid for a period fixed by statute the property (or the lien) may be sold by the authorities. With respect to taxes on income, sales, gross receipts, franchises, inheritances, and the like, judicial proceedings for collection are indeed commonly provided by statute. That this is not, however, indispensable, and that the tax collector may, consistent with due process, be empowered to seize and sell the property of the delinquent without the aid of any judicial decree, is evidenced by the practice followed by the federal government, the internal revenue authorities having from the beginning of the government been vested with such power. Similar powers are vested in some state taxing authorities.[2]

This summary procedure for the collection of federal taxes is the more striking in that there is provided, as to some of those taxes, no opportunity for the taxpayer to seek before payment a review of even the legal questions involved.[3] Only after he has paid may he invoke the

[2] Under some taxing statutes the administrative certificate that a tax is due, when filed with a court clerk, has the same effect as a money judgment for the amount stated to be due, and may be enforced in the same manner. Cf. New York Labor Law, Sec. 523, Subd. 2, regarding unemployment insurance tax.

[3] Mention has already been made (p. 187, note 6) of the statutory prohibition of injunction proceedings to restrain collection of a federal tax. Shortly after the federal courts were authorized to grant declaratory judgments, attempts were made to obtain a declaration that a particular tax was unconstitutional. Congress thereupon

aid of the courts by way of a suit for refund. This drastic procedure functioned without serious complaint for well over the first century of the existence of the federal government, during which federal taxation, with minor exceptions, took the form of excise taxes only. When, following the constitutional amendment of 1913, the income tax, more complex and more fruitful of disagreements between tax gatherer and taxpayer than the traditional types of federal tax, first became a permanent part of our tax structure, no change was made in the established assessment or collection procedure. But the injustice of requiring payment without contest of large sums as to which there was real dispute soon became apparent; and Congress in 1924 provided opportunity for judicial contest before payment. The tax meanwhile remains unpaid (though liability for interest on the amount ultimately determined to be due is of course incurred).[4] This procedure has been applied also to taxes payable under the gift tax and estate tax laws. The collection of other federal taxes, however, still follows the traditional procedure; payment first, and contest afterward, through action for refund.

It is difficult to reconcile on any strictly logical basis the approval which the Supreme Court has lent to the summary method for the collection of federal taxes with its insistence, in enforcement proceedings, that, except in emergencies, due process requires that opportunity be provided for contest before an order is enforced. The explanation is to be found in history rather than in logic. The summary collection of taxes was an established feature of our legal system long before the concept of "due process" as a constitutionally guaranteed right of the individual and the recognition of an opportunity to be heard as an essential element of that right had taken root in our law; and the Court has been averse to unsettling so old an institution. It is further to be said, of course, that the prompt collection of the revenue is indispensable to the functioning of government; and that any wholesale withholding of taxes pending determination of all objections to their payment might interfere with its ordinary operations. On the other hand, it is hardly realistic to suppose that a tax fairly administered and carrying penalties for wrongful delay in payment would be subject to wholesale contest, particularly if provision were made for immediate payment of such portion as was concededly due.

In real estate taxation, a form of taxation affecting almost as many people as does income taxation, the valuation of each parcel, and the amount of tax payable as a result, are characteristically made known to

---

forbade the use of the declaratory judgment action for this purpose. A federal court may now "declare rights" "except with respect to federal taxes." 28 U.S. Code, Sec. 2201.

[4] The commissioner is empowered, however, to demand payment (or a bond to secure payment) in advance of contest if he "believes that the assessment or collection of a deficiency will be jeopardized by delay. . . ." 26 U.S. Code, Sec. 273(a).

the taxpayer by some form of public posting. The taxpayer is afforded an opportunity, before payment becomes due, to protest the assessment and to offer evidence in support of his contention that it should be reduced; and the Supreme Court has held that the constitution guarantee of due process so requires—a doctrine difficult to reconcile with the Court's approval of enforced payment before hearing in the case of federal taxes. There appears to be no requirement, however, that an opportunity be afforded the protesting taxpayer to interrogate the officials responsible for the initial assessment as to the basis of the figure arrived at by them.[5] Here again, the exigencies of tax collection have moved the courts to approve a more summary method of procedure than is countenanced in enforcement proceedings.

But perhaps the most notable departure in the field of taxation from the doctrines applicable in enforcement proceedings relates to the scope of the judicial review of tax determinations, whether exercised in a statutory proceeding to review an assessment or in an action for refund after payment. In this field the courts, in the absence of controlling statute to the contrary, undertake in not a few jurisdictions to review not only the rules of law administratively applied, but also the determinations of fact administratively made. There appears to be no foundation in principle for the departure of the courts in this field from their general reluctance to review determinations of fact made by administrative tribunals. The explanation is again to be found rather in the development of the law on this subject at a period anterior to the development of the modern doctrine of limited judicial review of facts administratively adjudicated—the doctrine that review will limit itself ordinarily to a determination that there was some substantial basis in the record for the determination made.

In the field of federal taxes is found an unusual tribunal—one devoted exclusively to the judicial review of administrative tax determinations.[6] This tribunal, known as the United States Tax Court, was created by Congress in 1924 (known until 1942, however, as the Board of Tax Appeals). An appeal by the taxpayer from a determination of tax due (known as the "determination of a deficiency") made by the Commissioner of Internal Revenue under the income, gift, or estate tax statues is the only proceeding that can come before it. It is composed of sixteen judges, who either on appointment are or soon become well versed in the manifold intricacies and technicalities of these statues, which frame a legal landscape quite apart from the rest of the world of the law. Nevertheless, a determination of these expert judges may be upset on appeal (taken either by the taxpayer or the tax authorities) by any of the eleven regional

[5] Nickey v. Mississippi, 292 U.S. 393, 396 (1934).
[6] Similar courts are found in New Jersey and Oregon.

courts of appeal, the judges of which may know little of this technical field; and the final word is spoken, when the Supreme Court sees fit to entertain a further appeal, by that court, not a few of the members of which are likewise, because of their unfamiliarity with it, little alert to the "invisible boomerangs" with which, as one of the most experienced members of Court has warned his associates, the atmosphere of this technical field is filled.

It is doubtless indispensable that the Supreme Court should have the power to pass on a tax case in which constitutional questions may be involved; but it is difficult to see any reason either for entrusting to it or for burdening it with a case involving purely special technical questions of statutory construction on which a more expert judicial tribunal has already passed. Needless to say, in this view the jurisdiction of the regional courts of appeals in the field is even more indefensible; for though the members of those courts may have more frequent opportunity than have the members of the Supreme Court to become familiar with the technicalities of income, gift, and estate taxation, their dispersion among eleven uncoordinated tribunals more than offsets this slight advantage. If it be thought that there should be opportunity for a further review of the determinations of the Tax Court, a specialized appellate court, appointment to which might perhaps be made by the Supreme Court from among the members of the Tax Court of long experience or from among judges of courts of appeals who have displayed a special competence in this field, would be a logical arrangement.[7] The point is not to be lost sight of that the essential function of the court is to interpret a statute (for the facts are seldom in dispute in important cases) and that an interpretation which encounters the strong disapproval of the tax bar or the business or financial community may, if Congress sees fit, readily be corrected, even retroactively, by a statutory amendment.

The review by the Tax Court of the determinations of the Internal Revenue Service (which has an internal adjudicatory procedure of an informal kind) has been referred to in the foregoing as a form of judicial review—this not withstanding that the statute creating the court expressly

[7] See Griswold, The Need for a New Court of Tax Appeal, 57 Harv. Law Rev. 1153 (1944); Pope, A Court of Tax Appeals: A Call for Re-examination, 39 Amer. Bar Assn. Jour. 275 (1953). For a critical evaluation of the Supreme Court's role in tax cases, see Lowndes, Federal Taxation and the Supreme Court, in Kurland (ed.), Supreme Court Review–1960 (1960). In the field of customs duties, Congress has in fact provided for a specialized appellate court. An application for review of an appraisement of imported merchandise made by a collector of customs or for remission of additional duties imposed by him is heard by the Customs Court (which is thus analogous to the Tax Court). Appeals from the Customs Court, however, instead of going to a Court of Appeals, go to the Court of Customs and Patent Appeals. The Supreme Court may, on application, grant a review of a determination of that court, but it rarely does.

declares it to be a part of the executive branch.[8] This statutory declaration doubtless makes clear the intent of Congress that the body of statutory law applicable to the federal judiciary shall not apply to the Tax Court. Doubtless it also makes clear that in the view of Congress the fifteen-year term of the members of the court does not violate the constitutional requirement that members of the judicial branch shall hold office during good behavior. These matters aside, it is difficult if not impossible to discover any difference between the Tax Court and a similar special court which might be created by assigning thereto, for fixed terms, a like number of federal district judges. A better illustration could hardly be found of the thesis that once an "administrative tribunal" is completely divorced from all functions other than that of adjudication, the distinction between it and a judicial tribunal loses any basic significance.

The field of state taxation abounds in federal constitutional questions twofold in character. On the one hand, a state tax is often attacked on the ground that the particular class of persons or objects affected is defined arbitrarily, resulting in a denial of equal protection of the laws. Again, a state tax may be alleged to impose an undue burden on interstate commerce—a ground on which scores of state taxes have, over the years, been invalidated by the Supreme Court. Although Congress early prohibited the federal courts from enjoining the collection of a federal tax, it imposed on them no such prohibition as to state taxes; and the proceedings in a federal court to enjoin the collection of a state tax, on the ground of its repugnance to the Constitution, was for some years an established feature of our jurisprudence. In 1937, however, as already noted, Congress withdrew from the federal courts jurisdiction in such a proceeding in any case where a prompt determination of the federal question could be had in the state courts (and thence to the Supreme Court). The federal court injunction against a state tax has consequently become virtually obsolete.

2. CONDEMNATION

One of the most drastic of governmental actions against the private party is that of the appropriation of his property—normally real property —for public use. Needless to say, monetary compensation, in an amount determined by either judicial or administrative proceedings, is always made; but it is equally obvious that forcible expulsion from one's home,

[8] 26 U.S. Code, Sec. 1100. The Customs Court is by contrast by statute termed a "court of the United States," along with the Supreme Court and the other federal courts. 28 U.S. Code, Sec. 451. Needless to say, the legal questions which come before it are not to be compared in complexity and importance with those entrusted to the Tax Court.

or even from business premises, often inflicts injury of a type which a monetary award, even if generously computed—which it by no means always is—does not fully compensate.[9]

The power of determining that a particular parcel of land is required for a public purpose is vested in a number of agencies in the federal government, and normally in but a small number of state agencies. In counties and municipalities it is ordinarily vested in the legislative body. In special governmental units—such as school, water, or irrigation districts—it is typically vested in the small board, usually elective, which administers such unit.

The determination that the taking of a particular parcel of land is necessary for the purported public purpose is often made without any opportunity having been afforded the owner or owners of the land in question to present evidence or argument in opposition to such determination; and this is equally true whether the ownership of the land is in one or many, and whether the authority making the determination is the legislative authority itself, or an administrative agency to which the power of determination has been delegated. The constitutional requirement of due process does not, it is established, necessitate such an opportunity. Moreover, the determination having been made, the courts, under established doctrines, will ordinarily decline to review it unless specifically empowered by statute to do so. In determining that one rather than another possible piece of land is the most suitable for the public purpose in view, the element of discretion involved is so great that the courts have been reluctant to intervene in the absence of specific statutes; and such statutory authorization is the exception rather than the rule.

Statutes delegating the power of appropriating privately owned land, or easements thereon, to public utility corporations (particularly to railroad and telephone companies) are also common. The choice of the particular land affected is, however, commonly made by legislative or administrative authority in advance, the utility corporation having only the power of appropriating the land so designated. Under some statutes the land to be taken is determined by a judicial proceeding instituted by the utility corporation, the several owners whose property is affected being made respondents in such proceeding.

The proceeding for determination of the amount of the monetary compensation to be paid for the property appropriated by a governmental agency is under some statutes instituted in the courts (jury trial being indeed sometimes provided), and under others before a special

---

[9] In point of fact, many condemnation statutes fail to provide any compensation for the loss necessarily incurred in moving one's household or business establishment, limiting total compensation to the value which the premises would have had had they been vacant.

administrative tribunal, the members of which are commonly called commissioners. The judicial review provided in the latter case is ordinarily limited, as to the finding of the value of the property condemned, by doctrines analogous to the substantial evidence rule.

3. RATE REGULATION

The regulation of the rates charged by persons engaged in public callings has a long history in English and colonial law, with both legislative and administrative fixation of rates resorted to. American regulation of the modern type may be said to have begun, however, with the movement for the regulation of railroad rates and grain elevator rates in the last quarter of the nineteenth century. The earliest regulations of railroad rates took the form of legislative enactments; and chiefly from this circumstance the function of fixing rates has often been referred to by the courts as legislative. Under modern statutes, however, a rate is ordinarily fixed in the first instance by the utility itself, and rate regulation characteristically takes the form, on the one hand, of permission accorded to the utility by an administrative agency to change an existing rate or service and, on the other, of an order by the agency to the utility directing it to make such a change.

Under such a regime, since the agency is bound by standards laid down in the statute, and its determination is subject, as we shall see, to a measure of judical review, its function can hardly be regarded as purely legislative[10] Its task is not to formulate policy but to determine, on the basis of evidence submitted to it, what is essentially a question of fact—usually the relation of the rate to the cost of the service rendered—and to apply to the facts thus found, established legal standards of reasonableness. So regarded, a proceding for the fixing of a rate may, at any rate from the procedural standpoint, be treated as a form of adjudication.

For the present purpose, discussion must be confined to the proceeding in which the utility is proceeded against by the regulatory agency, the objective being ordinarily to effect a reduction in an existing rate, or an increase in service.

The statute empowering the Interstate Commerce Commission to change rates charged by rail carriers is typical of the statutes in this field and is indeed historically the model for many of the state statutes. It

---

[10] It has been said that since there is no one rate which is reasonable, but only an upper and lower limit of reasonableness, the choice of a rate between those limits is legislative, not adjudicative. Rosenberry, Administrative Law and the Constitution, 25 Am. Pol. Sci. Rev. 37 (1931). However, judicial proceedings abound in instances in which the court, or the jury, is required to make an analogous choice of a definite figure within a zone of reasonableness.

provides that if the commission concludes, after a hearing (upon complaint made to it, or upon its own initiative) ". . . that any individual or joint rate, fare or charge whatsoever . . . or that any individual or joint classification, regulation or practice whatsoever . . . is or will be unjust or unreasonable or unjustly discriminatory or unduly preferential or prejudicial, or otherwise in violation of any of the provisions of this part" of the act, it may "determine and prescribe what will be the just and reasonable individual or joint rate, fare or charge . . . to be thereafter observed in such cases, or the maximum or minimum or maximum and minimum to be charged, and what individual or joint classification, regulation or practice will be just, fair and reasonable, to be thereafter followed. . . ."[11]

In making these determinations (as well as others which the act empowers it to make) it is required to "give due consideration, among other factors, to the effect of rates on the movement of traffic by the carrier . . .; to the need in the public interest of adequate and efficient railway transportation service at the lowest cost consistent with the furnishing of such service; and to the need of revenues sufficient to enable the carriers, under honest, economical and efficient management, to provide such service."

The courts in the early days of rate regulation sought to avoid the burden of passing on the reasonableness of rate determinations made by administrative agencies, finding refuge in some cases in the contention already noted that the function of rate fixing was a legislative one and, therefore, not subject to judicial review; the legislative investment of the power to fix rates in an administrative agency was, they said, a delegation of legislative power. Other courts made use of the term quasijudicial, using the qualifying adjective as the alleged reason why such determinations were not judicially reviewable. In more recent years, however, the courts have uniformly accepted the view that the order of an administrative agency fixing the rates chargeable by a public utility is reviewable by the courts, at least to the extent of ascertaining whether the proper legal criteria were employed by the agency in arriving at the rate and whether, applying those criteria, there is any substantial evidence in the record to sustain the determination made. At one time the Supreme Court appeared to be prepared to lay down the rule that such a review might not in all cases satisfy the constitutional requirement of due process; that where the utility made a showing that the rates prescribed by the regulatory body were confiscatory and, hence, an unconstitutional taking of its property, it was as a matter of constitutional due process entitled to an independent review of the facts by a judicial tribunal;[12] but in later

[11] 49 U.S. Code, Sec. 15 (1).
[12] Ohio Valley Water Co. v. Ben Avon Borough, 253 U.S. 287 (1920).

cases it has appeared to retreat from this view.[13] Some state courts, however, adhere to it.[14]

Judicial review in this field has until recent years dealt largely with the question of the method to be employed by the regulatory agency in arriving at the rate base—i.e., the valuation of the property used by the utility in rendering the service for which the rate is to be fixed. After an earlier sweeping disclaimer of power to inquire into the reasonableness of utility rates fixed by state legislative action, the Supreme Court in 1886 announced that a rate which did not yield the utility a fair return on its investment worked a deprivation of property without due process of law, in violation of the guarantees against such deprivation, whether by state or federal action, afforded by the Constitution; and that it was consequently the duty of the courts—including especially the federal courts—to set aside such a confiscatory rate.[15] This imposed upon the courts the necessity of determining the value of the property used by the utility, or at any rate of insuring that the agency which had set the rate had made such a determination and had used proper methods in doing so. Since the governing statutes uniformly failed to prescribe the methods to be employed in determining value, there resulted a series of litigations, extending over half a century, many of them finding their termination only in the Supreme Court, in which the methods of valuation developed by the various state utility regulatory bodies, and by the Interstate Commerce Commission with respect to the railroads, were brought before the courts for review, with resultant condemnation and modification in many cases. There are few chapters in American legal history which illustrate so forcefully, and in so melancholy a fashion, the weaknesses of a procedure by which basic questions of economic policy underlying governmental regulation are left to be determined by piecemeal decision, in particular cases, by the courts, instead of being comprehensively and consistently laid down at the outset by the legislature or under its authority.

Now that the question of methods of valuation has at length, albeit by so unsatisfactory and needlessly wasteful a process, been set more or

[13] Federal Power Commission v. Hope Gas Co., 320 U.S. 591 (1944); New York v. U.S., 331 U.S. 284 (1947).

[14] Some state courts in recent years, instead of adhering to the traditional practice of confining their review of the facts to a scrutiny of the record made before the regulatory body, have permitted additional evidence to be introduced before them. This they have done by permitting the utility, instead of appealing from the rate-making order, to institute an action to enjoin its application, taking the position that where a statute providing for such appeal is silent on the point, the right to an action for an injunction continues unaffected. Cf. Staten Island Edison Corp. v. Maltbie, 296 N.Y. 374 (1947).

[15] Railroad Commission Cases, 116 U.S. 307 (1886).

less at rest, the judicial review of utility rates fixed by administrative proceedings has dwindled somewhat in importance.

Much of the criticism which both the courts and regulatory bodies have suffered, occasioned by the unsatisfactory character of rate regulation proceedings, is to be charged to the difficulties inherent in a *prospective* rate determination, rather than to the methods of necessity resorted to to cope with those difficulties. It is worth considering whether the whole concept of the attempted determination *in advance* of a rate which will yield only a reasonable return to the utility should not be abandoned as impracticable.[16]

4. DISMISSAL OR DEMOTION OF PUBLIC EMPLOYEE

At first sight it might seem that a proceeding by a governmental agency against one of its own employees—whether looking to his dismissal or demotion or the imposition of some other penalty—is hardly to be regarded as one of an agency proceeding against a private party, since the employee is himself a part of the government personnel. In this situation, however, the issue concerns the rights of the employee as a private party —rights not merely to a continuance of his compensation, but, increasingly, to what may be regarded as almost a vested right in the pension allowance to which he may become entitled on retirement for age or disability.

From the standpoint of protection against unjust dismissal there are, broadly speaking, two distinct categories of public civilian personnel— those whose selection was made by the appointing authority in the exercise of its sole discretion (subject perhaps to the satisfaction of minimum qualifications by the appointee), and those who received their appointment by some form of competition (even if only competition in early filing of application for employment) under a statute requiring the appointing authority to appoint from among those successful in the competition. In general, the first category of public personnel is freely removable by the appointing authority, without accountability to any other authority, administrative or judicial. To this there are, however, several exceptions, the most notable being the appointive judiciary, whose virtual irremovability was discussed in an earlier chapter. Another important exception is found in many administrative boards, particularly those vested with judicial functions. Here irremovability during the term for which appointed, except for cause, is frequently provided in the statutes. Such statutes have been construed as giving the courts the power to intervene where the removal has been made without cause being alleged, or where the cause alleged is on its face irrelevant to the official duties of the person removed; but the courts have refused, in general, to

[16] For a suggested method of retrospective rate determination see Note, 28 N.Y.U. Law Rev. 418, 428–429 (1953).

intervene where the allegation is merely that the facts alleged as constituting the cause for removal did not in truth exist.

Another notable exception to the generalization that personnel selected
in the discretion of the appointing authority may be removed in the discretion of that authority is to be found in the statutes governing the
teaching staffs of the public schools in certain areas and the instructional
staffs of certain publicly supported institutions of higher learning. Though
appointed at discretion, members of these staffs may be removed, under
the statutes in question, commonly known as tenure laws, only on particular grounds stated in the statute. Characteristically the governing
statutory provisions, in addition to specifying the causes on which dismissal may be based, require the filing of written charges and their proof
at a hearing in which the teacher proceeded against enjoys the right of
cross-examination of witnesses and of representation by counsel. Upon
the record of the hearing thus had, the dismissed teacher may ordinarily
obtain a judicial review of the question whether the evidence produced
against him was relevant to the statutory ground on which the dismissal
was made, and if so, whether it was substantial in character.

Where employees are recruited by a process of open competition, and
the governing statute or regulation requires that appointment be made
from among those ranking highest, appointment is commonly regarded
as giving the person appointed a species of right to retention in employment (at least after the termination of a probationary period.) The extent
of the legal protection against arbitrary removal actually provided to the
competitively appointed employee varies greatly, however, from state to
state, and within the same state. Teachers appointed by competitive procedures generally enjoy the benefits of tenure statutes of the character
already discussed. Among other local employees, members of the police
and fire forces tend to enjoy a more complete statutory protection than
do other employees, the statutes frequently following the same lines as do
the teachers' tenure statutes; and cognate protection is afforded in some
states to similar personnel in state employ. In the federal service, the
special protection afforded to hearing examiners by the Administrative
Procedure Act has already been mentioned. As to employees outside these
special services, typical provisions, whether embodied in statute or regulation, merely require that the employee shall be informed of the ground of
his intended dismissal and given an opportunity to make an explanation.
An unjust dismissal following compliance with a requirement of this kind
is, except in the rarest cases—as where the ground stated for dismissal is
wholly irrelevant—beyond correction by the courts. Increasingly, however, statutes and regulations in this field are being amended to provide
for formal hearing before dismissal, and for appeal from the administrative authority which ordered the dismissal to the central personnel agency
of the governmental unit involved (that agency being commonly also the

agency in charge of examinations for entrance to the service, the so-called civil service commission or department). Where such provisions is made, the field opened for judicial review of the proceedings tends to be correspondingly increased; but in the absence of specific provisions the courts, in their review of the facts, will confine themselves to the minimal task of ascertaining whether there was any basis in the evidence for the conclusion reached.

On several occasions attempts have been made to secure from the courts the establishment of the principle that a statute or regulation governing dismissal which does not entitle the employee to be informed of the specific allegations against him or which fails to provide a hearing at which he may confront the witnesses against him and cross-examine them is repugnant to the constitutional requirement of due process of law. The courts have, however, with substantial unanimity, refused to accept this contention, taking the view that the employee's claim to retention is not of that category of rights which falls within the constitutional guarantee. The position of the Supreme Court on this question is still uncertain. On an appeal from a ruling of a federal court of appeals, upholding the dismissal of a federal employee on charges of disloyalty to the government of the United States, under the procedure, set up by executive order in 1949, which denied the employee the opportunity of confrontation and cross-examination,[17] the eight justices of the Supreme Court who heard the appeal were evenly divided.[18] No case raising this issue has been reviewed by the Court since this 1951 decision.[19] The changes in the membership of the Court in the interval make it by no means certain that, should a case arise, the procedure in question will be upheld.[20]

[17] Under this procedure, a board of inquiry received in confidence the evidence of disloyalty and gave the suspected employee an opportunity to contest the substance of the charge but not the specific evidence (which was not disclosed to him). A procedure for appeal to a reviewing board was also provided; but the appellate proceedings likewise gave the employee no opportunity to ascertain the specific evidence against him. The Executive Order which established this "loyalty board" procedure authorized dismissal where "reasonable grounds exist for belief" that the employee is disloyal. In 1951 an amendment made "reasonable doubt as to loyalty" a sufficient ground for dismissal.

[18] Bailey v. Richardson, 341 U.S. 918 (1951). Justice Clark did not participate, as he had been Attorney General at the time the regulations were promulgated. Where the Court is equally divided on an appeal, the determination of the lower court stands.

[19] Two cases, involving the dismissal not of government employees but of employees of government contractors, in obedience to government security requirements, have been disposed of by the Court without reaching any constitutional question. Greene v. McElroy, 360 U.S. 474 (1959); Cafeteria Workers Union v. McElroy, 367 U.S. 886 (1961).

[20] See McKay, The Right of Confrontation, Washington U. Law Quart., April 1959, p. 122.

16

Permissions and Grants

1. PERMITS.   2. OCCUPATIONAL   LICENSES.   3. FRANCHISES.   4. DIS-
PENSATIONS.   5. GRANTS.

The permits, franchises, dispensations, grants, and benefits provided
for by federal, state, and local enactments exhibit a multiplicity and un-
ending variety of which the average citizen, whose experience is limited
to but a small number of them, has little conception. With this diversity
we are not here, however, concerned. From the present standpoint only
one line of differentiation is of interest—whether or not, in passing upon
applications for such permissions or grants a formal adjudicatory process
is involved. The manner in which the courts act as a check on the wrongful denial of an application made without such formal adjudication has
been discussed at a previous point. In this chapter are considered those
situations in which the person seeking a permission or grant is entitled,
before denial of his application becomes final, to a formal adjudication.

At an earlier page it was noted that the courts do not interfere with
administrative action (or inaction) where an element of discretion has
been entrusted by statute to the administrative officer merely because
such discretion may in the opinion of the court have been unwisely exercised. Only if the administrator has acted in a fashion so arbitrary as to
be inconsistent with the honest exercise of discretion and thus to constitute an abuse of discretion will the courts, so they have declared, interfere.
Consequently, judicial control in this field plays on the whole a less important role than in other areas of administrative adjudication; for in
many varieties of permissions and grants much latitude is given to the
discretion of the responsible administrative official.

It would be little to the purpose, even were space available, to review
or even to catalog the numerous types of permission or grant in the
allowance of which formal adjudicatory procedures are or should be
employed. In what follows, it is proposed to consider a few of the more

important types and to inquire to what extent the discretion of the administrative agencies in respect to them is controlled or supervised by the courts.

1. PERMITS

The first type of permission that calls for examination is the permission to do a particular act, a "permit." This we encounter chiefly in the economic field. Here a type of permit of great interest is that which certain kinds of public utilities and banks are required to obtain from the regulatory agency before entering into certain types of contract, particularly those relating to mergers.[1] A requirement imposed upon all employers, inaugurated during the second world war, and continued in force, under successive statutes, until 1952, was that for permission to raise wages or salaries of employees. But of wider interest than these is perhaps the permit which an American citizen requires for travel abroad, and the permission to enter the United States, required by an alien.

Passports

When the United States is at war, or during the existence of any national emergency declared by the President, no citizen may leave the country (unless his destination is a country excepted by the President) without a passport.[2] This requirement was imposed (under previous statutes) in 1918, and has since been in force virtually continuously, as to all but a few countries of destination.

The statutes authorize the Secretary of State and certain designated officials abroad acting under his authority to issue passports "under such rules as the President shall designate and prescribe." The statute thus imposes no limitation on the discretion of the officials empowered to issue passports, nor do the regulations promulgated by the President; and it was for many years the practice, in the occasional case in which a passport application was denied, to make no formal disclosure to the applicant of the reason for such denial and to refuse all requests for such disclosure, the Department of State taking the position that the discretion entrusted to it was plenary, and that the citizen had no right to challenge that discretion and, hence, no right to a disclosure of the basis for its exercise. In 1952, however, a three-judge federal court, on the application

---

[1] A plan for the reorganization of the capital and debt structure of a railroad carrier which has got into financial difficulties, developed in the first instance through a judicial proceeding, requires the approval of the Interstate Commerce Commission before it may be approved by the court, perhaps the only instance in which the concurrent action of a judicial and an administrative tribunal is required. 11 U.S. Code, Sec. 205.

[2] 8 U.S. Code, Sec. 1185(b).

of a citizen whose passport had been revoked, rather than refused, set aside the revocation on the ground that the department's refusal to disclose the reason for its action and to afford the citizen an opportunity to present proof in opposition was unwarranted by the statute. Had the statute expressly authorized such refusal, declared the court, it would have been repugnant to the requirement of due process of law.[3]

Following this decision (from which no appeal was taken by the government), the State Department instituted a formal hearing procedure, with departmental appellate machinery, which is available to anyone whose application for passport has been rejected (or whose passport it is proposed to revoke).

In cases subsequent to the establishment of this adjudicatory procedure, the Supreme Court has extended the requirement of due process in passport matters beyond the merely procedural, holding that the right to travel abroad is a constitutional one, and that the courts have power to pass on whether, in rejecting a request for a passport, the Department of State has abused its discretion by acting arbitrarily.[4] Thus has been abandoned the historic position of the executive that, since considerations of foreign policy may be involved in the refusal of a passport, the matter is solely one for executive discretion. Moreover, in these decisions the Court has laid down the principle that the executive can in no case have an absolute discretion to encroach on the individual's constitutional rights and that Congress would be without power to confer such absolute discretion—a principle whose far-reaching significance needs no emphasis.

Permission to enter the United States

Turning from the passport to the opposite side of the shield, the permission to an alien to enter the United States,[5] we find two separate sets of administrative agencies at work—the United States consul abroad, whose approval (in the form of a visa endorsed on the prospective entrant's foreign passport) is ordinarily prerequisite, and the immigration inspectors at the port of entry.

The procedure at the consulate makes no provision whatever for formal hearing to the person denied a visa. In the case of a person desiring to enter as an immigrant the quota statutes make such a procedure obviously inapplicable; and even in the case of a person seeking to enter as a visitor the practical difficulties in instituting such a procedure, as has

[3] Bauer v. Acheson, 106 F. Supp. 445 (1952).

[4] Kent v. Dulles, 357 U.S. 116 (1958); Dayton v. Dulles, 357 U.S. 144 (1958).

[5] Other aspects of this important subject, of which space does not permit discussion, are the renewal, to one admitted as a visitor, of permission to remain in the United States for a further period, and the grant of permission to a temporary visitor to leave the country, the statute authorizing the denial of such permission during a declared state of war emergency.

been proposed, are great. A less secretive attitude on the part of the Department of State would, however, furnish greater assurance that the discretion entrusted to it in this field is being wisely exercised.

The procedure at the port of entry, by contrast, provides that when an entrant has been denied admission by the inspector charged with the initial examination, he is afforded a formal hearing before a so-called special inquiry officer—that is to say, an immigration inspector designated for the purpose. At such hearing "which shall be kept separate and apart from the public, the alien may have one friend or relative present." The inquisitorial procedure at such hearings has been adversely criticized by observers. Criticized also was the use, until recent years, of the regular inspection personnel as hearing officers, in defiance of the principle, adopted by Congress in the Administrative Procedure Act of 1946, that adjudicatory personnel should perform no other functions—an anomaly made possible by a specific statutory exception. Eventually, however, while no separate position of hearing examiner, such as is found in other federal adjudicatory agencies, was created, the responsibility for conducting hearings was confined to a group of inspectors who have no other duties; and such is now the situation.

From an adverse decision of the special inquiry officer, appeal lies to the Attorney General—in practice, to the Commissioner of Immigration and Naturalization.

Since 1952, however, the right to a hearing may be denied to an alien whose exclusion is ordered on the ground that he is a subversive alien "if the Attorney General is satisfied that the alien is excludable on the basis of information of a confidential nature, the disclosure of which would be prejudicial to public interest, safety or security. . . ." The constitutionality of this provision has not been passed upon by the Supreme Court; however, in upholding the denial of a hearing in the cognate case of a German national excluded after the cessation of hostilities but while the state of war still existed, the majority opinion of the Court declared categorically: "Admission of aliens to the United States is a privilege granted to an alien only in such terms as Congress may prescribe. . . . Whatever the procedure authorized by Congress, it is due process as far as the alien is concerned."[6] The harsh doctrine of this emphatic statement, which reaffirms earlier pronouncements, is predicated on the premise that the physical presence of the immigrant within our boundaries at the immigration inspection station confers on him no greater rights than were he abroad.[7]

[6] U.S. ex rel. Knauff v. Shaughnessy, 338 U.S. 537, 542–544 (1950), decided by a vote of 4 to 3. The provision referred to is in 8 U.S. Code, Sec. 1225(c).

[7] The alien long resident in this country who goes abroad for a visit and returns after a short period is in no better position in this respect than is the alien who has never entered the country. Shaughnessy v. United States, ex rel. Mezei, 345 U.S. 206

Where a hearing has been accorded the excluded alien, judicial review is, in accordance with these views, more restricted than in an alien deportation proceeding. The tendency has been for the courts, without even applying the "substantial evidence" test, to uphold the exclusion order unless there is "error so flagrant as to convince the courts of the essential unfairness of the trial."[8]

Though these holdings apparently remain in force, the Supreme Court in 1956 opened the way to a substantial enlargement of the judicial review available to an excluded alien by ruling that he could institute an action for a declaratory judgment, with its opportunity for an independent evaluation of the evidence by the court, rather than a mere review of the determination of the immigration authorities.[9] As a practical matter it is not, however, likely that the run of excluded aliens will have the resources to avail themselves of this remedy.

Occasionally, an American consul is asked for a visa by one who alleges that he is a United States citizen but has no United States passport (as may well be the case if, for example, the applicant was born abroad of American parents and has never been in this country). Formerly, by statute of 1940, such a person, if denied a visa as a citizen, was permitted, while still abroad, to institute an action here for a declaratory judgment, and to enter the country provisionally, pending the determination of the action; but in 1952, Congress withdrew this privilege. He can now bring such an action only after he has presented himself at one of our ports of entry and has been excluded.[10]

2. OCCUPATIONAL LICENSES

The issuance of the innumerable occupational licenses called for by federal, state, or local enactments is ordinarily a routine procedure not involving any formal adjudication. If, however, the license is denied on the basis of alleged information in the possession of the licensing agency, which is not disclosed to the applicant, the question of a denial of due process of law arises. There have up to this time been few significant

---

(1953). However, as to a resident-alien seaman temporarily absent upon a voyage to foreign ports, exclusion is in effect a deportation, and a hearing must be accorded. Kwong Hai Chew v. Colding, 344 U.S. 590 (1953).

[8] Vajtauer v. Commissioner, 273 U.S. 103, 106 (1927).

[9] Brownell v. Tom We Shung, 352 U.S. 180 (1956).

[10] The present provision is 8 U.S. Code, Sec. 1503. It also authorizes a consul to issue to a person claiming American citizenship, upon a showing that the claim is made in good faith, a "certificate of identity," which renders easier than it would otherwise be the bearer's task of convincing the immigration authorities of his citizenship. This provision is applicable, however, only to a person who at some time prior to his application for a certificate has been physically present in the United States, or to a person under sixteen born aboard of an American citizen.

judicial proceedings raising this question. In the most important of them, what was involved was the "clearance" required by an American seaman, in possession of the usual papers, before he is permitted to ship. The granting of the clearance is entrusted to the Coast Guard, which is authorized to deny it for security reasons. It has been held that the seaman is entitled to a hearing before denial of clearance.[11]

3. FRANCHISES

The term franchise, as applied to the grant by a public body of permission to operate a business, has ordinarily been applied chiefly to transportation enterprises and cognate utilities requiring a right of way. However, the monopilistic feature of such grants—the fact that the grant does not issue as a matter of right to anyone satisfying prescribed requirements, the granting authority being permitted to take into consideration the injury to the public interest from competition—is found in a number of other fields to which the term franchise is not ordinarily applied. An obvious illustration is afforded by the field of banking, in which the grant of permission to open a new institution is typically dependent upon the determination of the granting authority that additional facilities are needed. The grant of permission to open a retail package liquor store is ordinarily similarly discretionary. In these and other fields which might be mentioned, the term "franchise" would doubtless be more accurate than the loose terms "license," "certificate," or "charter" generally employed.

The grant of important franchises was in this country in earlier times a function of the legislature rather than of the executive. The early banks operated under legislative franchises (or "charters"). The railroads and canals of the nineteenth century were until toward its close for the most part constructed under charters granted by state legislatures and Congress, while local utilities were commonly granted franchises by municipal councils and the like—a practice which still survives. Outside the municipalities, however, administrative bodies have now in most cases been set up to grant monopolistic franchises of various types. The statutes exhibit great diversity both as to the nature of the formal proceeding, if any, preceding action on the application for franchise, and as to the extent to which such action is subject to judicial review. In view of the large element of discretion necessarily involved in such a grant, the complete denial of judicial review, which is seemingly contemplated in some statutes, is in this field presumably consistent with due process.

A proceeding in this field in which a strict adjudicatory procedure is

[11] Parker v. Lester, 227 F. 2d 708 (9th Circ. 1955). The government did not seek a review of the decision of the Court of Appeals, and the Coast Guard then instituted a hearing procedure, the operation of which has in turn been criticized as wanting in due process.

employed, with judicial review specifically provided for, is the proceeding before the Federal Communications Commission for passing on an application for a franchise (inaccurately styled by the statute a "license") for a broadcasting station. In a considerable proportion of these proceedings there are before the commission two or more competitive applications; and the proceeding then assumes also the character of a controversy between private parties, with formal submission of proof as to the financial ability and competence of the several applicants and the comparative merits of the contemplated stations they propose to construct. Despite the adjudicatory framework of the proceeding, a large element of discretion necessarily enters into the determination to be made, since the commission is empowered to grant a license only "if public convenience, interest or necessity will be served. . . ."[12]

The statute provides for an appeal from the determination of the commission to the United States Court of Appeals for the District of Columbia (at which even persons not parties to the original proceeding, "who would be aggrieved or whose interests would be adversely affected by a modification or reversal of the decision of the Commission" may intervene). In this review by the court, "findings of fact by the Commission, if supported by substantial evidence, shall be conclusive unless it shall clearly appear that the findings of the Commission are arbitrary or capricious." Although it is only "findings of fact" that the quoted words thus purport to subject to rejection by the court, the effect of the statute is necessarily to vest the court with power to review also in some measure the discretion exercised by the commission.[13]

It is of interest to compare these provisions with those governing the grant of a charter, so called, to a federal savings and loan association. Here similarly, the granting authority (the Federal Home Loan Bank Board) is not to issue the charter "unless in the judgment of the Board a necessity exists for such an institution in the community to be served, nor unless there is a reasonable probability of its usefulness and success, nor unless the same can be established without undue injury to properly conducted local thrift and home-financing institutions."[14] No provision is made by the statute for hearing, for intervention by interested parties, or

[12] 47 U.S. Code, Sec. 319(a).

[13] Under the Radio Act of 1927, the Court of Appeals of the District of Columbia was expressly authorized, on appeal from the decisions of the then Radio Commission, to "alter or revise the decision appealed from and enter such judgment as to it may seem just." The Supreme Court held that this provision made the court "a superior and revising agency" in the administrative field, and that consequently its decision was not a "judicial" judgment, which the Supreme Court can review. Federal Radio Commission v. General Electric Co., 281 U.S. 464, 467 (1930). Following this decision the language of the statute was amended and given its present form.

[14] 12 U.S. Code, Sec. 1464(e).

for judicial review. In the absence of such specific statutory provision, judicial review of the action of the board in refusing to grant a charter is in effect unobtainable. The Administrative Procedure Act of 1946, it will be recalled, while laying down the general principle that every order of an administrative agency is judicially reviewable at the instance of the party aggrieved, excepts from its application agency action which is "by law committed to agency discretion."

The contrast between these two statutes illustrates at once the impossibility of any useful general statement regarding the extent either of formal adjudicatory procedure or of judicial review in the field of franchises and the seeming want of any consistent principle by which the legislator has been guided.

Perhaps unique among statutory provisions authorizing the administrative grant of franchises are those applicable to international air transportation. Although the power to grant a "certificate of convenience and necessity" for an international route is vested (as in the case of a domestic route) in the Civil Aeronautics Board, the further approval of the President is required; and though the board proceeds by formal hearing and findings of fact, no such requirement is imposed on the President. Moreover, although the board's actions are expressly subject to comprehensive judicial review, the President's action is expressly excepted from judicial review. The provision for presidential approval might be thought to have only perfunctory significance; but experience under it has been to the contrary.[15]

Patents

A United States patent may be defined for the present purpose as the privilege of invoking the aid of a court to prevent another during a seventeen-year period from using, manufacturing, or selling the subject matter of the patent (and to obtain damages for such use, manufacture, or sale).

The initial stage of the proceeding in the Patent Office for obtaining a patent consists, following the application, of an exchange of communications between the applicant and the examiner. If the examiner rejects the application, or if his allowance of the "claims" asserted by the applicant is too restricted to be acceptable to the applicant, the applicant may appeal to a board of examiners within the Patent Office (known as the Board of Appeals). From a rejection by this board, a further appeal lies to the Court of Customs and Patent Appeals, which as its name indicates is a tribunal independent of the Patent Office. (From its determinations, in turn, request for further review may be made to the Supreme Court; but in fact such petition is seldom if ever made or granted.)

The statute provides, however, an entirely different alternative pro-

[15] 49 U.S. Code, Secs. 601, 646(a); and see Civil Aeronautics Board v. Waterman Steamship Corp., 333 U.S. 103 (1948).

cedure for procuring review of the rejection of the applicant's claims by the Board of Appeals. The applicant may, instead of appealing on the record already made in the Patent Office to the Court of Customs and Patent Appeals, institute in the United States District Court for the District of Columbia an action against the Commissioner of Patents to compel him to issue the patent sought.[16] From an adverse decision by this court, appeal lies to the Court of Appeals for the District of Columbia (and, though unknown in practice, a review, on permission granted, by the Supreme Court). No reason is apparent for thus permitting the applicant to ignore the specialized appellate procedure provided and to resort instead to a single judge in a court having no special relation to the subject matter, none of whose score of judges may indeed have had any previous contact with it.

4. DISPENSATIONS

An increasingly important group of permissions are those which confer upon the recipient the privilege of doing something which the law forbids or the privilege of exemption from doing something which the law requires. The increased complexity of regulatory legislation has brought with it the necessity for increased provision for exemption from the requirements of the statutes in cases of hardship or in other circumstances which render the statutory requirement inapplicable.[17] One not familiar with the matter is little likely to appreciate how numerous are the statutes which make provision for their own suspension in particular cases by administrative action.

Selective service: exemption and deferment

In one aspect, the procedure whereby one is compelled to enter the armed forces may be regarded as a form of proceeding against the individual. Looked at more realistically, however, the vast machinery of the Selective Service System has for its chief function the granting to registrants of deferments or exemptions from service.

The genesis of the present selective service statute is to be found in the

[16] 35 U.S. Code, Sec. 63.

[17] An interesting example of such a provision is that which permits the Securities and Exchange Commission to issue a so-called acceleration order. The statute prohibits the public offering of a security for sale in interstate commerce or through the mails until twenty days after a registration statement, or the latest amendment thereto, has been filed. The commission is empowered, however, to determine with respect to an amendment, "having due regard to the public interest and the protection of investors" that it shall become "effective" earlier. 15 U.S. Code Sec. 77h(a). Should the commission refuse to grant such acceleration order (often of extreme importance to the underwriters, who have made all plans for the opening of subscriptions on the effective date of the original registration statement), the right of judicial review granted by the statute with respect to all orders of the commission is in fact without value, owing to shortness of time.

statute of 1917.[18] The concepts of classification and deferment and of enforcement machinery introduced by that statute have persisted, though with some modification in detail, in the succeeding statutes.[19]

The initial process, in the local board, of passing on the registrant's claim for deferment or exemption is, as is well known, informal, no provision existing for formal hearing. Should the registrant appeal to the appeal board there is again no hearing;[20] although the appeal board is empowered to examine the case *de novo*, it does so only on the basis of the file forwarded by the local board. In certain cases, a further appeal to the President is permitted.

No judicial review of the determination of any of these authorities is provided for by the statute, which declares the classification made by the Selective Service authorities to be "final." In this absence of statutory provision, the courts have rejected all attempts to invoke direct judicial review except by way of the habeas corpus proceeding—available only if the registrant has submitted to induction and is thus either actually or constructively under restraint by the military. In such a proceeding, the scope of the inquiry which the court will permit itself is limited by the established doctrines in this field. It will of course inquire whether the registrant was lawfully within the jurisdiction of the local selective service board, and whether it afforded him all the rights of presentation of proof and of appeal permitted by the statute and regulations. With respect to the findings of fact implicit in the rejection of his claim for deferment or exemption (implicit because neither the local nor the appeal board is required to make explicit findings of fact), the court will inquire only whether the board has abused its discretion by making a finding contrary to all the substantial evidence given by the registrant—a review even more restricted than that to which administrative findings of fact are subjected under the "substantial evidence" rule.

If the registrant, having been accepted for induction, fails to report for induction, or having reported, refuses to submit to induction, he commits a criminal offense. On his being prosecuted for that offense he frequently sets up the defense that his classification is invalid, the selective service authorities having allegedly disregarded the law. Whether the trial court may in view of the silence of the statute entertain this defense and inquire

---

[18] 40 Stat. 76.

[19] 54 Stat. 885 (1940) and 62 Stat. 604 (1948), now in 50 U.S. Code Appendix, Secs. 451–470.

[20] Where, however, the registrant declares that he is a conscientious objector (who may be classified for non-combat service) the statute provides for reference of the claim to the Department of Justice, which is, after appropriate inquiry, required to "hold a hearing with respect to the character and good faith of the objections of the person concerned. . . ." 50 U.S. Code Appendix, Sec. 456(j). The department then makes a recommendation (non-binding) to the Appeals Board. As to the nature of the hearing required, see United States v. Nugent, 346 U.S. 1 (1953).

into the validity of the classification[21] is a question on which the members of the Supreme Court have divided, the majority holding that it may. Hence, where the claim of the defendant in a criminal case is that he is exempt from service (as on the ground that he is a minister of religion), such defense must be examined on appeal and the conviction set aside where the court fails to find in the record any "proof that is incompatible with registrant's proof of exemption," so that the rejection of his claim for exemption is wholly without support in the evidence.[22]

5. GRANTS

One of the earliest forms of governmental grant in our history is the land grant, originally made at the pleasure of the Crown and subsequently of the legislatures. The regularization of the system of land grants, so as to confer a right to a grant upon any one satisfying statutory requirements, may be said to have come in with the nineteenth century. A substantial amount of federal public land is still available for grant, as is indeed some state land; but the administrative adjudication of land claims by public land officials, once characteristic of this field and attaining at times considerable volume, is now of only minor significance. Today the characteristic public grant is a monetary payment, whether by way of a pension, allotment, or allowance, or by way of an insurance benefit, or by way of a subsidy. The vast subsidy schemes found in our federal legislation, particularly in the statutes affecting agriculture and shipping are of too technical and complex a character to admit of discussion here.

Pension and allotment payments

The magnitude of the number of persons receiving allotment and pension payments from federal, state, or local funds is perhaps not commonly appreciated. In the federal sphere are found old age and survivors' benefits under the social security law, allotments to dependents of servicemen, and pensions to veterans and to retired federal employees and officials. In

---

[21] The Administrative Procedure Act provides that the action of an administrative agency is subject to judicial review in criminal proceedings for its enforcement; but the Selective Service Act expressly excepts operations under it from the Administrative Procedure Act (except as to matters of public information). 50 U.S. Code Appendix, Sec. 463(a).

[22] Estep v. United States, 327 U.S. 114 (1946); Cox v. United States, 332 U.S. 442 (1947); Dickinson v. United States, 346 U.S. 389 (1953). In the Estep case, by holding that the statute was not intended to preclude judicial review, the majority avoided passing on the question whether a statute which did expressly preclude such review would be constitutional. Two members of the majority, however, declared it would not be, while a dissenting member declared it would be (and that the existing statute was indeed intended by Congress to preclude judicial review).

both state and local governments, systems for pensioning retired employees are increasingly common.

In public pension systems characteristically no provision is found for the formal adjudication of disputed claims; but the rejected claimant may invoke judicial aid through the usual forms of action. Under the regulations governing veterans' pensions, however, a procedure for formal appeal within the Veterans' Administration is provided, but judicial review is expressly prohibited.[23] In the field of old age (and survivors') insurance benefits under the Social Security Act—a field in which the number of claimants will no doubt in time exceed those in any other category—Congress has on the other hand provided not only for a formal adjudicatory procedure, on appeal from an initial rejection of a claim, within the agency itself, but for a judicial review of the agency decision, subject to the usual limitations as to findings of fact.[24] In this statute, moreover, Congress has departed from the pattern, so often employed since 1914, of entrusting judicial review to the regional courts of appeals—a pattern which, since further review by the Supreme Court is rarely granted by that court, makes the first court review in effect the final one; instead, the statute provides that the claimant may proceed "by civil action" in a federal district court, and that the judgment of that court may be further reviewed "in the same manner as a judgment in other civil actions."

The wide diversity of the schemes provided by Congress for the adjudication of claims under these statutes—a diversity paralleled in cognate state statutes—suggests the need, particularly in view of the likelihood of expansion in this field, for a restudy of the matter.

[23] 38 U.S. Code, Sec. 705.
[24] 42 U.S. Code, Sec. 405.

17

The Adjudication of Private Disputes

1. VARIETIES OF ADMINISTRATIVE ADJUDICATION OF PRIVATE DISPUTES.
2. WORKMEN'S COMPENSATION PROCEEDINGS. 3. ADJUDICATION WITH-
OUT ORAL TESTIMONY. 4. THE AGENCY AS COMPLAINANT IN DISPUTES
BETWEEN PRIVATE PARTIES. 5. CLAIMS AGAINST GOVERNMENT.

When administrative tribunals are under discussion, the unstated premise is likely to be that they are engaged in adjudicating between government and private parties. The extent to which they are also engaged in adjudicating disputes between private parties is lost sight of.

1. VARIETIES OF ADMINISTRATIVE ADJUDICATION OF PRIVATE DISPUTES

Despite the tendency thus to assign a minor place in the field of administrative adjudication to the private dispute or claim, it is probably true that quantitatively this category of the business of administrative tribunals looms larger in the total picture than does adjudication between government and private party. This is due, needless to say, to the vast number of claims of injured or diseased workmen against their employers, or their employers' insurers; for compensation claims are almost everywhere adjudicated by administrative rather than judicial tribunals. But workmen's compensation claims furnish by no means the sole example of private claims administratively determined. Under the Interstate Commerce Act, a claim by a shipper against a carrier for the recovery of an alleged overcharge may be determined by the Interstate Commerce Commission, and similar jurisdiction, in their respective fields, is exercised by the Federal Communications Commission and the Federal Power Commission. Similarly, the Secretary of Agriculture may adjudicate a claim by a fruit or vegetable grower against a commission merchant, broker, or dealer in these commodities, and similar powers are vested in the agriculture departments of some of our states. In the Patent Office "interference proceeding," the issue is which of two or more applicants for patent covering the same

489

subject matter first conceived such subject matter and reduced it to practice (such priority, rather than priority in date of filing of application, being determinative of the right to the patent). Under the federal residential rent control legislation of the second world war (and under successor legislation in some of the states) disputes between landlord and tenant as to their rights under the law were adjudicated solely by administrative tribunals; and in a few places legislation of this type is still in force.[1] The Federal Maritime Board is vested with jurisdiction of claims of shippers against operators of ships classified as common carriers for damages for refusal to accept a tendered shipment (a type of claim which in one 1961 case resulted in an award by the board of approximately a quarter of a million dollars).

Moreover, although not so empowered by law, administrative agencies not infrequently adjudicate informally private claims asserted against persons subject to their jurisdiction. Thus an official empowered to grant licenses to employment agencies, and to suspend or revoke such licenses for cause, may assume to adjudicate a claim of overcharge asserted by a client of an employment agency against such agency, such claim having reached the official, however, not as a claim for restitution, over which he has no legal jurisdiction, but in the form of a complaint of wrongful conduct justifying suspension or revocation of license. Though without statutory power to order a reimbursement of an overcharge which he finds to have been made, his power to confront the employment agency with the alternative of a suspension of license if the reimbursement is not made is, as a practical matter, even more effective than would be a statutory power to order reimbursement. This form of extralegal administrative adjudication of private disputes prevails on an extensive scale.

In addition, there are not a few administrative proceedings which, though in form between the administrative agency and the private party are in substance, in whole or in part, a controversy between private parties. That this may be so in the case of applications for licenses in the nature of franchises was pointed out in the preceding chapter.

In a proceeding before the National Labor Relations Board for an alleged labor practice condemned by the governing statute, although the formal complaint is issued by the board (and will not be issued, as already pointed out, if the board's staff concludes on informal inquiry that no ground for proceeding exists), the proceeding is in fact initiated by a complaint made to the board by the employer, employee, or union allegedly aggrieved by the practice in question; and in the absence of such complaint no action may be taken by the board. A similar situation exists with respect to many of the proceedings instituted by the Federal Trade Commission to

---

[1] A novel feature of some of these laws was the provision that a judicial proceeding for the eviction of the tenant might not be instituted unless the landlord first obtained the permission of the administrative agency.

compel the cessation of allegedly unfair methods of competition, although that commission, unlike the Labor Relations Board, is authorized by the statute to institute such proceedings on its own initiative and frequently does so.

In principle, the field of administrative adjudication of private disputes and claims presents as a whole little of interest which has not already been touched upon in connection with other types of administrative adjudication. Particular types of proceeding in this field exhibit, however, special features warranting brief mention.

A doctrine related to this type of proceeding, but affecting the courts rather than the administrative tribunals, has in recent years developed in disconcerting fashion. The administrative jurisdiction in private disputes created by statute in some cases parallels the existing jurisdiction of the courts, without, however, necessarily being coextensive with it, the jurisdiction of the court and its power to grant relief being often the more comprehensive. In this situation, under the so-called primary jurisdiction doctrine developed by the courts, they will not take jurisdiction unless the complainant has first proceeded in the administrative tribunal and exhausted the relief he can obtain there.[2] This doctrine, whatever its basic soundness, may lead to needless delay and waste motion when applied with relentless thoroughness, as it has been by the federal courts (some state courts declining to take so inflexible a position).

Thus, to take a simple example, the Civil Aeronautics Board is empowered to determine that certain practices are repugnant to the Civil Aeronautics Act and to order them discontinued. However, the same practices may be equally repugnant to the antitrust laws (which govern all areas of business, air transport included), enforcement of which is in the hands of the courts; and the courts may, in addition to ordering the discontinuance of unlawful practices, award punitive damages to the person injured thereby. Nevertheless, that person may be required first to obtain from the Civil Aeronautics Board an order declaring the practices unlawful and prohibiting their further use, and then to institute an action in the courts for damages.[3] These indefensible results of the primary jurisdiction doctrine stem not from any statutory commandment but from the pronouncements of the courts—particularly the Supreme Court. How reconcile this extreme reluctance of the Court to authorize the exercise by the courts of a remedial jurisdiction expressly conferred upon them with its readiness to assert for itself in the constitutional field a power supported by no express textual foundation?

[2] The doctrine applicable to the federal courts was first announced by the Supreme Court in 1907 (Texas & Pacific R. Co. v. Abilene Cotton Oil Co., 204 U.S. 426). It is only in more recent years, however, with the growth of federal administrative adjudication, that it has attained prominence.

[3] S.S.W. Inc. v. Air Transport Assn., 191 F. 2d 658 (1951); certiorari denied 343 U.S. 955 (1951).

2. WORKMEN'S COMPENSATION PROCEEDINGS

In almost every state, under the state workmen's compensation law, the claim of the injured workman for compensation for the cost of medical care, loss of wages, and disability occasioned by accident or disease arising out of his employment (or, if death occurs, the claim of his next of kin) is adjudicated not by the regular judicial tribunals, but by special tribunals organized as part of the executive branch.[4] The same is true of the systems created by Congress, covering longshoremen and harbor workers as well as federal employees. The volume of claims so adjudicated (aside from the enormous number which call for no adjudication, not being disputed by the employer or his insurer) perhaps exceeds that of any class of civil claims judicially adjudicated. Since the workmen's compensation tribunal deals with only a single category of dispute, standardized forms may to a considerable extent take the place of pleadings.[5] In the reception of evidence, there being no jury, minor importance is attached to some of the strict rules of evidence developed under the regime of jury trial—a phenomenon observable even in judicial tribunals where no jury is present; but some of the basic restrictions are observed, as is the principle of oral testimony as opposed to deposition. In many respects, the procedure followed may be likened to that followed in a court of minor civil jurisdiction when disposing of a monetary claim of no great amount without a jury. The absence of a jury, it may be remarked, gives to any adjudicatory proceeding a flexibility which is impossible to attain where the cumbersome jury apparatus must be employed; and it is worthy of reflection to what extent the claimed superiority of administrative over judicial tribunals in respect of expedition and flexibility in this and in certain other types of proceeding may be due in large measure to the absence of a jury, which would normally be necessary, under present constitutional provisions, in a judicial tribunal sitting in the same type of proceeding.

It is notable, however, that when a claim for workmen's compensation involves a large amount (as in an accident causing death or claimed total permanent disability), or involves a question of law the decision of which is important to the insurance carrier (as in certain cases involving disability resulting from disease allegedly contracted in the course of the claimant's work), and the issues are vigorously contested, the procedure of the compensation tribunal is likely to assume a formality and strictness approximating, if indeed not quite equaling, that of a

---

[4] In New Mexico, the 1957 statute substituting administrative for judicial determination of workmen's compensation claims was held unconstitutional as a delegation of judicial power to the executive, contrary to the intent of the state constitution. State ex rel. Hovey Concrete Products Co. v. Mechem, 316 P. 2d 1069 (1957).

[5] The use of standardized forms for this purpose is, however, by no means confined to administrative tribunals; such use is found also in certain courts as, for example, those dealing with decedent's estates, and in small claims courts.

court in which a claim of equal importance might be litigated.

In the discussion of judicial proceedings mention was made of the desirability of providing the court with expert opinion not paid for by either party. In the administrative tribunals engaged in adjudicating workmen's compensation claims, such provision is frequently found. At least in the larger tribunals of this kind, the testimony of the agency's own medical staff as to the extent and probable duration of the disability of the claimant, and its causal relation to the alleged accident or to the alleged disease-producing conditions of employment, is frequently the essential, if not the sole, testimony forming the basis of the determination. Here again we are in the presence of an arrangement no more appropriate, inherently, to an administrative than to a judicial tribunal, but one which through inertia, legislative as well as judicial, our civil judicial tribunals have for the most part thus far failed to install.

In the larger states the hearing of a workmen's compensation claim is usually before a hearing officer whose determination is subject to confirmation by a board of plural membership. In the smaller states, an individual member of the board ordinarily hears the claim, his determination being similarly subject to confirmation by the board as a whole. In either case, the board, in deciding whether to confirm, modify, or disaffirm the recommended award may take into consideration not only the papers and evidence before the hearing officer, but such additional evidence as it may see fit to take itself—a procedure which, as we have seen, is not, under present practice, in most states, open to an appellate court.

In a few states, a claimant dissatisfied with an award made by the workmen's compensation tribunal may insist upon a jury trial of his claim de novo. Except in these few states, the award so made is final unless set aside by a court as being erroneous in law. In no state is the court empowered to review the determination of fact implied in the award if there is any substantial basis therefor in the evidence; and in some states the statute categorically declares such finding of fact to be final. Even so categorical a statutory declaration, however, has not prevented the courts (which are in every state given power to correct, on appeal, errors of law made by the workmen's compensation tribunal) from setting aside awards on the ground that the tribunal's finding of fact could have been arrived at only by one having an erroneous view of the law.

Workmen's compensation laws are a relatively recent arrival on the American juristic scene. The earliest laws were enacted at the end of the first decade of this century, and a few of the state statutes are not yet a quarter of a century old. The federal act covering federal employees was enacted in 1916, and that covering longshoremen and harbor employees in 1927.[6]

[6] Most employees of interstate railroads are not covered by any compensation system. The injured employee brings action in a state or federal court. He enjoys, however, the protection of the extremely favorable rules embodied in the Em-

These laws introduced several distinct novelties, and in appraising their results, it is essential to keep these several features distinct. In the first place, they made an industrial injury compensable regardless of whether it was due to the negligence of the employer, the injured employee, a fellow employee, or a stranger, regardless indeed of whether any negligence was discernible anywhere—a complete revolution in legal doctrine. In the second place, they set up a definite schedule of compensation for particular injuries and particular disabilities in place of the largely discretionary rules of measure of damage which the courts had developed over the years. Finally, except in a few states, they substituted non-jury trial before a tribunal organized under the administrative branch for jury trial in a court.

It will be evident that no comparison of the results accomplished by the administrative compensation tribunal with those formerly accomplished by the courts in this field can be made without taking into consideration that the principal issues which were formerly adjudicated by the courts in this class of cases either do not exist at all in the compensation proceeding —as with the issue of negligence—or exist only in very much less troublesome form—as with the issue of damages. Had these changes been made in the underlying legal doctrine, had jury trial been abolished, had the courts been furnished with the requisite auxiliary personnel for disposing of the vast mass of uncontested claims and with impartial expert assistance in passing on vexing medical questions, they could, it may well be contended, have discharged the task quite as well as have the administrative tribunals. It was in fact the greater ease of accomplishing the shift from jury to non-jury trial without encountering constitutional obstacles and without alarming public opinion, rather than any inherent superiority in operation, that was largely responsible for the choice of the administrative tribunal in this field. Indeed, question has in recent years been raised whether, at least in point of economy, the system of administrative adjudication of workmen's compensation claims has justified the expectations of its proponents.[7]

There is a tendency among the advocates of the administrative tribunal

ployer's Liability Act (applicable only to interstate railroads) enacted by Congress in 1908. Nor is there any compensation system covering seamen; the doctrines of admiralty law, supplemented by statute, are more favorable to the injured seaman than were the doctrines of the common law to the employee on land. The failure of the railway workers' and seamen's labor organizations to seek compensation legislation is generally attributed to the fact that because of these favorable doctrines and of the absence, in an action for damages, of the limitations on amount always found in compensation systems, these employees see no advantage in the latter. See also p. 264, note 36.

[7] As to the administrative costs of workmen's compensation proceedings, see Conard, Workmen's Compensation: Is It More Efficient Than Employers' Liability? 38 Amer. Bar Assn. Jour. 1011 (1952). But see Gellhorn and Lauer, The Administration of the New York Workmen's Compensation Law, 37 N.Y.U. Law Rev. 564, 604 (1962).

in this type of proceeding to stress the freedom of that tribunal from the shackles placed on the judicial tribunal by the rules of evidence. This emphasis greatly exaggerates the part played by those rules, in non-jury trials at least, in delaying or frustrating the proceedings. On the other hand, it ignores the fact that the orderly presentation of evidence and the exclusion of irrelevancy and worthless hearsay make for expedition and for sound decision—a fact of which some administrative adjudicators have shown inadequate appreciation—and that the needless inflation of the record by testimony without probative value imposes an additional burden upon a party taking an appeal, a burden much more lightly borne, needless to say, by an appellant insurer than by the injured workman taking an appeal. In so far as rules of evidence may be a hindrance rather than an aid, they may of course as readily be modified by the legislature for the judicial as for the administrative tribunal.

3. ADJUDICATION WITHOUT ORAL TESTIMONY

In the adjudication of workmen's compensation claims, evidence is characteristically given, as in a judicial proceeding, by oral testimony (with the right of cross-examination) unless the presence of the witness is impracticable. In several other varieties of administrative adjudication of private disputes, however, no hearing is provided for, the decision being based on written statements of the parties. Thus by statute enacted in 1930 Congress has empowered the Secretary of Agriculture to adjudicate certain private claims of less than $500, if he deems it proper, on the basis solely of "depositions or verified statements of fact."

However, the order made by the Secretary in such a proceeding (known as a "reparation order") is given on judicial review only the effect of prima facie evidence of the facts found by the Secretary in making it.[8] In another far more extensive system of federal administrative adjudication of private disputes—disputes involving moreover in many cases sums considerably in excess of $500—findings of fact based only on written statements of the parties, unsworn, were given finality, unless appeal was taken and allowed. This was the system of adjudication of disputes between landlord and tenant as to their rights under the residential rent control regulations promulgated during World War II and continued for certain areas for some years thereafter. Successor state statutes

---

[8] However, the person against whom the "reparation order" is made is in every case one licensed by the Secretary of Agriculture (being a commission merchant, dealer, or broker in perishable agricultural commodities); and non-compliance with the order is, aside from the complainant's right to collect the amount awarded through the courts, ground for suspension of license. It should be noted that the complainant's claim in these proceedings is not based on rights created by the statute (7 U.S. Code, Ch. 20A); it is based on fraud, breach of contract, or breach of agency, all of which give ground for judicial redress independently of statute.

followed the same system of adjudication—so complete a departure from traditional procedure that by the very novelty of the design, carrying with it no resemblance to customary institutions, it oddly enough gained acceptance more readily than would have some mere modification of our familiar procedure.[9]

4. THE AGENCY AS COMPLAINANT IN DISPUTES BETWEEN PRIVATE PARTIES

In a proceeding before the National Labor Relations Board, the complainant is in form the agency itself, as it would be in an enforcement proceeding. Realistically, however, as already pointed out, the proceeding is rather to be regarded as one for the adjudication of a private dispute. So viewed, the proceeding presents a striking contrast between the role of the board and the role of a court in a proceeding between private parties. Like a judicial tribunal the board is powerless to initiate proceedings of its own motion; it must wait until a complaint is laid before it by a private party seeking redress. Once such a complaint is received, however, the role of the complainant is exhausted. The entire conduct of the proceeding is henceforth in the hands of the board (or rather in those of the essentially independent agency, termed the Office of the General Counsel of the Board), instead of, as in a judicial proceeding, continuing in the hands of the plaintiff.

Aside from the psychological disadvantage at which the respondent is placed by this form of complaint, with its implication of a measure of adverse prejudgment at the very outset of the proceeding, he finds himself pitted against the resources of a government agency. The supposed rationale in thus furnishing the aid of the government to one of the two parties to a dispute is no doubt that the conduct complained of is a social as well as an individual injury—a view equally applicable, however, to innumerable types of wrongful conduct redressed by the courts; and also perhaps that the complainant would normally be a wage earner of small means and the respondent an employer with ample resources—a supposition by no means correct, since the complainant has often been a labor union with adequate funds, and indeed, since 1947, an employer.[10]

Viewing the matter as a whole, it is difficult to see why the adjudication

[9] During and following World War I rent control statutes were enacted in several states; but disputes between landlord and tenant arising under such statutes were adjudicated by the courts.

[10] If the complainant is a powerful union, and the person complained of is a small employer, the representation of the complainant by the government is in effect a topsy-turvy form of legal aid. The same is true if the complainant is a powerful corporation; and the respondent, a weak union. The inequity is heightened, where the complaint is eventually dismissed, by the fact that the respondent does not, as in a judicial proceeding, recover costs from the complainant.

of complaints under the National Labor Relations Act should not follow substantially the same course as a judicial adjudication, with the pleadings and presentation of evidence entirely in the hands of the parties. If legal assistance to either of the parties is a proper public responsibility, it could be provided in those cases where the need was demonstrated.

The pattern furnished by the National Labor Relations Act has in general been followed by the several state labor relations acts which have been enacted to provide for the relatively minor areas of employment deemed not to be even indirectly related to interstate or foreign commerce.

As already indicated, not a few of the proceedings instituted by the Federal Trade Commission to restrain unfair methods of competition may also be regarded as in substance disputes between private parties.[11]

5. CLAIMS AGAINST GOVERNMENT

A claim against a government, arising either out of a contract or out of an injury to person or property committed by governmental personnel, may be regarded an analogous to a claim of one private party against another; and in large measure such claims are indeed adjudicated by the courts in the ordinary manner. There is, however, in addition in the federal government, and also in the state and local governments, a considerable amount of administrative adjudication of such claims—adjudication as opposed to mere settlement by agreement with the claimant.[12]

Such adjudication occurs chiefly in connection with claims of contractors for compensation for extra work, or for changes ordered while the contract was in course of execution, or for compensation for damage suffered by the contractor owing to a discontinuance or reduction of the work originally contracted for. Moreover, in many federal contracts for wartime procurement (and latterly, even for postwar defense procurement) there is found provision for "renegotiation," whereby the price fixed by the contract may be determined to be excessive and, hence, subject to reduction by the government, such determination first becoming possible after experience as to the cost of production has been accumulated.

The governing statutes and contract provisions vary with respect to the degree of finality to be accorded to the determinations of the contracting agency in these matters, so as to preclude judicial review. There has been a definite tendency in federal contracts to attempt to procure an advance assent by the contractor to the subsequent determinations of the contract-

[11] Insofar as the particular "unfair method of competition" may also be a violation of the antitrust laws, the person aggrieved may also seek redress by suit in the federal courts.

[12] See Sass, A Government Lawyer Looks at the Contract Appeals System, 8 Cath. U. Law Rev. 23 (1959).

ing agency, involving, in effect, a waiver of any right to review by the courts that the contractor might otherwise have. This tendency reached its extreme expression in a widely used form of contract purporting to give virtually absolute finality to the determination of the administrative officer; and this language was upheld by the Supreme Court. Congress thereafter prohibited the inclusion in any government contract of a provision purporting to make final, and thus put beyond judicial review, the administrative determination on a question of fact "if not supported by substantial evidence," or on a question of law.[13]

An interesting and quite exceptional administrative tribunal for the adjudication of claims against the government is the Indian Claims Commission, created by act of 1946.[14] The three-member temporary commission is empowered to hear and determine claims against the United States in behalf of any Indian tribe, board, or other identifiable group, including "claims which would result if the treaties, contracts and agreements between the claimant and the United States were revised on the ground of fraud, duress, unconscionable consideration, mutual or unilateral mistake, whether of law or fact, or any other ground cognizable by a court of equity," and also "claims based upon fair and honorable dealings that are not recognized by any existing rule of law or equity." Unlike the Court of Claims, in which the claimant bears the sole burden of establishing his claim, the commission is provided with an investigating staff.

The statute provides for appeal from the determination of the commission to the Court of Claims and for further review on questions of law by the Supreme Court by its permission. On questions of fact the scope of review by the Court of Claims is governed by the usual limitations applicable to judicial review of findings of fact made by administrative tribunals.[15]

---

[13] Act of May 11, 1954; now 41 U.S. Code, Sec. 342. The case upholding the form of contract which the statute now forbids was United States v. Wunderlich, 342 U.S. 98 (1951).

[14] 25 U.S. Code, Secs. 70 ff.

[15] In 1954 there was constituted, as successor to certain departmental agencies, an independent agency known as the Foreign Claims Settlement Commission. Its chief function is to adjudicate claims of American citizens arising out of the nationalization or other taking of property by certain foreign governments which have made agreements with the United States for the settlement of such claims (principally, Yugoslavia, Poland, and Czechoslovakia). It is provided by statute that the determinations made by the commission "shall be final and conclusive on all questions of law and fact and not subject to review . . . by any court by mandamus or otherwise." See 22 U.S. Code, Secs. 1621–1642 and 50 U.S. Code Appendix, Secs. 2001 ff. In 1962, several additional classes of cognate claims were placed in the jurisdiction of the commission. Public Law 87–846; 76 Stat. 1107.

18

The Personnel of Administrative Tribunals

1. AGENCY HEADS. 2. AGENCY HEADS DE FACTO. 3. SUBORDINATE AD-
JUDICATING PERSONNEL. 4. ATTORNEYS AND AGENTS IN PROCEEDINGS
BEFORE ADMINISTRATIVE TRIBUNALS.

That the effectiveness of a tribunal is determined not only by its
doctrine and procedures, but at least equally by its personnel, is obviously
just as true of administrative as of judicial tribunals. Indeed, in view of
the concentration in many administrative agencies of both prosecuting
and adjudicating powers, and of the importance of some of the matters
adjudicated, the need for an exceptionally high type of intelligence and
character may be greater than among the minor judiciary.

Clearly, under the existing structure of administrative adjudication the
problem has two quite distinct aspects, concerned with the individual or
board composing the tribunal in which is reposed the power of adjudication, and on the other with the subordinate personnel whose recommendation may precede final adjudication by the tribunal itself. Quite
generally, these two categories of adjudicatory personnel come from different worlds of public life.

1. AGENCY HEADS

No single general description will fit all types of agency head. In the
states and cities a distinct line of cleavage can usually be traced between
the type of individual found on the various occupational license boards
and those holding top rank in other administrative agencies. The former
are likely to be without pronounced connection with party politics; while
the latter are quite generally persons who have been politically active. In
the selection of the members of principal federal regulatory bodies having
adjudicatory powers, though there are frequent exceptions, the practice
has been to restrict selection to those who have been politically service-

able, even if not active. In neither the state nor the federal sphere, generally speaking, has there been any disposition to regard a person selected for membership on an administrative tribunal as embarking on a possibly lifelong career, as in the case of many judicial tribunals. In a certain proportion of cases, however, an outstanding member has succeeded, despite the brief terms of office often found in this field, in establishing a more or less permanent tenure.

It is an interesting aspect of our political thinking that though in the case of the state judiciary proposals for replacing popular election by appointment evoke much opposition, appointment as the method of selection of the state administrative judiciary, if so it may be called, is taken for granted.

In the discussion of the selection of judges, it was pointed out that there exists no defined standard of experience or learning against which a prospective nomination or appointment may be tested. Even more strikingly is this so in the case of the members of the administrative tribunals. Since neither a legal nor any other variety of special education is ordinarily considered requisite for membership, the way is open for the appointment of anyone whom the exigencies of politics may suggest. This is not to say that men well-qualified by experience have not frequently been selected; but, equally, there have been appointments of men whose political services so clearly constituted their sole claim to office that a comparable appointment to judicial office would doubtless have provoked an outcry.

Indeed, in view of the perennial lament over the political factor in the selection of judges, it is not a little remarkable that so little is heard of the part that politics thus plays in the selection of the members of our administrative tribunals, the more important of which, as we have seen, exercise powers much greater than those possessed by many of our judicial tribunals. The term of office is ordinarily short—six years being typical.[1] Nor has the shortness of the term been tempered, as in the case of some of the state judiciary, by the tradition of automatic reappointment.[2] On the contrary, that an overturn of the party in power will be followed, when the new administration takes office, by an attempt to "gain control" of the membership of at least some of these agencies as soon as sufficient vacancies occur or can be effected, is accepted as in the nature of things.[3]

[1] Among the federal boards, the usual term is five years. Terms of six and of seven years are also found.

[2] On the contrary, there is said to have developed, as to the federal agencies, a policy *against* reappointment. Landis, The Administrative Process, 47 Amer. Bar Assn. Jour. 138 (1961),

[3] The statutes governing the federal multimember boards under discussion (and similar provisions are generally found in cognate state statutes) typically provide that a member may be removed only for inefficiency, neglect of duty, or malfeasance

In connection with some of the federal agencies exercising judicial power, still another factor has been present—the desire of the Administration to use those tribunals as the means of elaborating, according to its own views, the statutes they are called upon to enforce. In the case of such an agency as the Federal Trade Commission, the existence of prosecuting functions has confused the issue; but in the case of the purely judicial Labor Relations Board the situation is transparently clear. There has been a frank recognition that the statute, despite its revision in 1947, is so vague that the board (subject to approval by the courts) largely makes the law. Hence the contest between labor and management over the content of the law, which should properly be confined to Congress, is carried on also to the process of selection of members to fill the vacancies in the board. Were all administrative tribunals relieved of prosecuting, administrative, and rule-making functions, so that their judicial function alone remained to be discharged by those appointed to them, the incongruity of the present-day political pressures in selection would more clearly appear and reform would be speeded.

The membership of administrative tribunals has thus characteristically been selected from without the agency, rather than by promotion from within (although in recent years, in the federal agencies, such promotion has become increasingly frequent). Deaths and resignations tend to reduce the average term of office to something substantially below the already short statutory term. Since reappointment is by no means the rule, it is not safe to assume that the members of an administrative tribunal are predominantly of long experience. The point is of importance in connection with the emphasis so often placed on the supposedly specialized knowledge and experience possessed by administrative tribunals.

Boards with power to revoke occupational licenses

The foregoing discussion, as already indicated, is not applicable, generally speaking, to the members of the numerous occupational licensing boards found in our states and cities. They are likely to owe their appointment not to political connections but rather to their prominence in one or another of the professional or occupational organizations, which often

---

in office. Some of the statutes use the phrase "upon notice and hearing"; others do not. No federal agency member appears to have been removed upon notice and hearing. An attempted removal by the President of a member of the Federal Trade Commission (where the governing statute does not require notice and hearing), without any allegation by the President that any of the grounds for removal specified by the statute existed, was held ineffectual by the courts. Humphrey v. United States, 295 U.S. 602 (1935). The reason assigned by President Roosevelt for his action (as stated in his purported order of removal) was that Commissioner Humphrey's views of public policy differed from his own. He seemingly regarded statutory limitations on the President's power of removal as unconstitutional, a view which the Court rejected as inapplicable to "quasi-judicial" offices.

play an extralegal role in this field. On the licensing boards affecting the major professions the members are likely to be of high caliber; in those dealing with less exacting occupations, they tend to be of an indifferent quality, too often but dubiously worthy of the responsibilities with which they have been entrusted.

Superficially, the entrusting of occupational license revocation in effect to the membership of the licensed occupation is attractive; but it must be recognized that, unless the quality of that membership be high, such an arrangement peculiarly lends itself to abuse and oppression. It is to be noted that the power of revoking the license of the lawyer is vested not in a board composed of lawyers, but in the courts; and it may well be questioned whether the tribunal, whether judicial or administrative, in which is vested license revocation power might not well, in the case of many occupations, exhibit a higher level of competence and trustworthiness were its members not so closely associated with the occupation. The whole question of the personnel of these numerous tribunals (as well as of their procedure) is one that has received inadequate attention.

2. AGENCY HEADS DE FACTO

At a previous page it was pointed out that where the adjudicatory function is vested in an administrative department in which it is overshadowed by the much more important operational activities of the department, the head of the department, though nominally assuming final responsibility for all adjudications, is in practice compelled to delegate that responsibility to a high-level subordinate, such as an assistant secretary or solicitor. Such is the situation in the Agriculture,[4] Post Office, and Treasury departments, and in all but the most exceptional immigration cases, in the Department of Justice. In the selection of these officials also, as is well known, considerations of party patronage commonly play a part; but the official is likely to have a solid professional background and a professional outlook, and to contemplate, if not a public career, at any rate a tenure of probably substantial duration. The officials on this level on the whole present a satisfactory picture. The anonymity of their labors however, reduces the likelihood of attracting men of first-rate ability to the task.

3. SUBORDINATE ADJUDICATING PERSONNEL

The range of qualifications and of quality possessed by the hundreds of officials engaged in the work of administrative adjudication on the sub-

---

[4] See Flavin, the Functions of the Judicial Officer, United States Department of Agriculture, 26 Geo. Wash. Law Rev. 277 (1958).

ordinate level in the variegated federal, state, and local administrative agencies is far too great to permit of any generalized statement. In its survey in 1938 the Attorney General's committee found a great diversity in the previous employments followed and the types of work previously done by the federal personnel in this category as well as in their educational or professional preparation. Since the enactment of the Administrative Procedure Act in 1946, subjecting the appointment of hearing examiners to the civil service law, most appointments have been of lawyers, usually of some experience. A criticism made by those professionally concerned is that an undue proportion of the adjudicating personnel in some agencies tends to be drawn from the lawyers already in the service of the agency in non-adjudicatory work, including the work of prosecuting complaints before the hearing examiners; and that the result is a prepossession in favor of the agency's point of view, inimical to adjudicatory objectivity.

In compensation, too, a wide range is found. Particularly in some of the smaller state and local agencies are to be found subordinate adjudicators receiving very modest salaries. In the federal service, the salary scale enjoyed by an examiner is hardly likely to attract or retain an adjudicator of the highest caliber.

Ideally a subordinate adjudicator should be well-qualified educationally and, where necessary, professionally, and should be mature and experienced—his experience, in part at least, having been outside the government service. The salary should be substantial. He should be selected by a method likely to find and appoint the best-qualified man. Only at scattered points are these desiderata met.

It would be a mistake to assume, however, that the setting of high qualifications and adequate salary rates will necessarily cause a sufficient number of candidates of quality to present themselves. To accomplish this, something additional is necessary—the assurance that the occupant of the post will enjoy prestige and professional respect. The scheme of the Administrative Procedure Act contains two features which militate seriously against this—the name given to the office and the machinery of selection, promotion, etc. The nondescript title of "examiner" fails to convey, except to those familiar with the matter, the importance and authority of the office. The terms "referee" or "special master" and "commissioner" employed for cognate officers in the judicial branch, are distinctly more attractive in this respect, and perhaps furnish useful suggestions (the terms "referee" and "deputy commissioner" being indeed occasionally found even in administrative adjudication).

The agency designated by the Administrative Procedure Act to control selection, salary increase, and promotion—the Civil Service Commission—is associated in the public mind with mass methods of selection for routine posts at the lower, indeed the lowest, levels. True it is that it is responsible for the preparation of eligible lists for a considerable number of scientific and technical posts of some importance; but this aspect of its work is not the one that contributes much to the general public's impression of the process. It is significant that in the endeavor to build up a career corps of quality, the State Departnment has resisted, and successfully, attempts to transfer to the Civil Service Commission responsibility for recruitment, parallel as the commission's methods are, in preparing lists for posts, to those of the State Department itself. The selection of adjudicating personnel similarly calls for a separate organ of recruitment as independent of the agencies involved as is the Civil Service Commission, but operating in a setting of greater individualization, and headed by a board of exceptional distinction, in which would sit members drawn from the judiciary as well as from those expert in the professions which may be concerned.[5]

There is still another factor of importance in attracting a high grade of ability into this field—the inherent interest of the work itself. An important factor in the appeal which judicial office often makes to able lawyers is the great diversity of the subject matter with which the judge's work deals. By contrast, the able hearing officer, confined to proceedings before a single agency, in some cases under a single statute of limited scope, often finds his work, after a time, monotonously repetitious. The organization of the federal hearing officers as an independent corps, along the lines mentioned at an earlier point, would greatly facilitate the occasional shifting of one or another of its members to another agency, and thus do much to counteract that intellectual stagnation which is too often the product of a narrowly bureaucratic way of life. Membership in such a corps would, moreover, carry with it more prestige than can be expected to attach to the post of subordinate in an administrative agency.

In the states, too, even in those in which the volume of administrative adjudication is as yet small, a similar development could not but improve the quality of administrative justice. Up to the present time, only California has, as already noted, moved on this direction.

It would seem to go without saying that the selection of hearing examiners should be completely nonpartisan, under a merit system (though not necessarily one administered by the civil service agency responsible

---

[5] In a bill embodying a comprehensive program for the improvement of federal administrative adjudication, sponsored by the American Bar Association, it was proposed that the appointment of hearing examiners be made by the director of a new agency to be established—an Office of Administrative Practice. 43 Amer. Bar Assn. Jour. 425 (1957). Oddly, although the association is committed to the establishment of nonpartisan boards to compile lists of persons qualified for judicial office, appointments to be made only from among such persons, no corresponding board was provided for in this proposal.

for the selection of employees generally), and that they should have tenure during good behavior. Yet this is far from being everywhere the case. Political selection, with consequent turnover when an election changes the party in power, is by no means unknown.[6]

4. ATTORNEYS AND AGENTS IN PROCEEDINGS BEFORE ADMINISTRATIVE TRIBUNALS

The extent to which parties in administrative proceedings are represented by counsel varies greatly from one to another type of proceeding. Such representation, needless to say, is almost invariable in important regulatory or rate-making proceedings. At the other extreme is the workmen's compensation proceeding, in which many appear without counsel.

But it is not only lawyers who represent parties in administrative proceedings. In not a few agencies, representation by non-lawyers is by no means uncommon; and in the case of some agencies, mere membership at the bar does not entitle one to represent a party before the agency. Thus, the Patent Office requires that one prosecuting an application for patent on behalf of another shall, whether or not a member of the bar, have "sufficient basic training in scientific and technical matters," proof of which is to be furnished in part by passing an examination.

The small body of statutory provisions governing the rights of the parties to an administrative proceeding, and of judicial decision interpreting those provisions, is in many cases well within the competence of a person not possessed of a legal education. The proposition has been strongly urged that only members of the bar should be permitted to appear before administrative agencies in adversary proceedings, in which a record is to be made which will subsequently be subject to judicial review. Representation of a party in such a proceeding, it is contended, requires a knowledge of the same elements of procedure as are present in judicial proceedings—the preparation of pleadings, motions, depositions, and affidavits, and the examination and cross-examination of witnesses within a framework of rules of evidence, albeit those rules may be less rigorous than are applied in judicial proceedings. Again, it is pointed out that both before the institution of the administrative proceeding, and during its continunace, the question of the desirability at that stage of a possible recourse to a judicial tribunal may arise. Moreover, however narrow and sharply limited the legal question arising under a particular

[6] Even in New York, where the merit system has long been firmly established in state employment generally, the hearing examiners in workmen's compensation cases (known as referees) "are in most instances chosen because of their political connections . . . and their survival in office is largely dependent upon their party's electoral success." Gellhorn and Lauer, The Administration of the New York Workmen's Compensation Law, 37 N.Y.U. Law Rev. 203, 223 (1962).

statute may seem to be, there are points at which it may, unknown to the layman, impinge on larger principles of law. For all those reasons, it is contended, representation of parties in adversary administrative proceedings should be the exclusive prerogative of the bar.[7]

There is undoubtedly much force in these contentions. On the other hand, a layman is quite capable of mastering in short order the elements of practice and procedure in question; nor does it require a comprehensive legal background to appreciate some of the more obvious legal problems involved. Moreover, just as the client may lack assurance that the layman is fully equipped on the purely legal side, he may equally lack assurance that the lawyer is completely at home in the technical matters of railroading, broadcasting, and the like. Indeed in the field of taxation, there are undoubtedly many non-lawyers, particularly among accountants, whose technical equipment surpasses that of many lawyers. The truth of the matter seems to be that in a number of administrative tribunals no proper standards of admission to practice have been formulated; that were such standards formulated and applied, there are many lawyers who would, unless equipped by special study or experience not directly related to legal doctrine, fail to qualify, and that there are many laymen who would qualify. In the field of taxation, where the drawing of the line of division between the accountant and the lawyer has long been a source of difficulty, there would seem to be room for a special profession, possessing qualifications which neither the lawyer nor the accountant as such possesses, but which a member of either profession could acquire with relatively little difficulty. Cognate situations are to be found in other specialized administrative fields. The matter is one not to be satisfactorily disposed of by generalization. Instead, there is needed for each of the agencies affected a formulation of specific standards of admission to representation appropriate to it.

[7] For a typical presentation of this point of view see vom Baur, Adversary Administrative Proceedings: The Problem of Laymen as Trial Counsel, 37 Amer. Bar Assn. Jour. 147 (1951). In Bennett, Non-Lawyers and the Practice of Law before State and Federal Agencies, 46 Amer. Bar Assn. Jour. 705 (1960), the interesting question is discussed of the possible violation, by a layman admitted to practice before a federal administrative tribunal, of the law of the state in which he has his office, prohibiting the practice of law by laymen. In Speery v. Florida, 373 U.S. 379 (1963) the Supreme Court held that a state may not enjoin, as unlawful practice of law, the representation by a patent agent of an applicant for a patent before the U.S. Patent Office.

PART III MILITARY TRIBUNALS AND THEIR CONTROL BY THE COURTS

The courts and the administrative tribunals comprise ordinarily the whole of the machinery of adjudication to which the civilian must respond. For a member of the armed forces (and in certain cases for the civilian connected with the armed forces as well) there is a third system of adjudication to which he is subject—the system of courts-martial.

In a few instances in our history, military tribunals have been constituted in particular areas of our country by the executive, who has assumed to vest them with jurisdiction over the civilian population. This has occurred, on the one hand, under state authority, in time of civil disorder when the state militia has been charged with responsibility for restoring order, and on the other hand in time of war, in areas deemed by the President, as commander in chief, to require such treatment for reasons of military security. Moreover, in time of war additional military tribunals have come into existence, to deal with persons charged with aiding the enemy or with spying or with offenses against the laws of war. Finally, when enemy territory has been occupied and military government set up, courts have ben constituted by the military government to exercise jurisdiction of greater or less extent over the inhabitants of the occupied territory and, it may also be, of American civilians in the territory.

Each of these varieties of American military adjudication calls for separate discussion.

19

Courts-Martial: Proceedings Against Members of the Armed Forces

1. DEVELOPMENT. 2. PERSONS SUBJECT TO JURISDICTION. 3. OF-
FENSES AGAINST CRIMINAL LAW. 4. OFFENSES AND PENALTIES. 5.
COURT STRUCTURE. 6. CHOICE OF COURT. 7. INVESTIGATION PRECE-
DENT TO GENERAL COURT-MARTIAL. 8. GENERAL COURT-MARTIAL:
COMPOSITION AND PROCEDURE. 9. INFERIOR COURTS-MARTIAL: COM-
POSITION AND PROCEDURE. 10. RIGHTS OF THE SUSPECT OR ACCUSED.
11. INDEPENDENCE OF MEMBERS OF COURT. 12. REVIEW WITHIN THE
MILITARY ORGANIZATION. 13. REVIEW BY COURT OF MILITARY APPEALS.
14. INTERVENTION BY THE FEDERAL COURTS.

By federal statute, a number of acts are, if committed by a member
of the armed forces (or, in certain circumstances, by a civilian connected
therewith) made punishable by a variety of penalties (including the death
penalty) to be imposed and executed by the personnel of the armed forces
themselves.[1] The acts thus punishable are of two quite distinct categories.
In one category are purely military offenses ranging from the trivial (such
as overstaying a leave for a few hours) to the capital (such as running
away in the presence of the enemy); in the other are offenses having no
military aspect, being denounced also by the civilian criminal law.

In dealing with the first category—that of purely military offenses—the
court-martial system is in large part a system for the imposition of relatively minor penalties for breaches of discipline; and from this standpoint
it engages our interest but little more than do the systems of disciplinary

[1] The federal statutes assume to regulate courts-martial in the National Guard
even when not in the federal service. The provisions are, however, meagre. 32 U.S.
Code, Secs. 326 ff. A few of the states have comprehensive statutes. Cf. New York
Military Law, Art. VII, adopted in 1953. In 1961 the commissioners on uniform
laws recommended a uniform statute, which in effect reproduces, so far as applicable,
the federal Uniform Code of Military Justice. Ohio has adopted this act. See 9
Uniform Laws Annotated.

penalties found in the police and fire departments of our municipalities and in other large public personnel organizations (and indeed in some private organizations). In what follows, therefore, attention will be given chiefly to those aspects of the court-martial system in which it deals with offenses of a more serious character—grave derelictions of duty, on the one hand, and, on the other, offenses against person and property of the kind cognizable in civilian life by the criminal courts.

The number of adults subject to the military jurisdiction is greater than is subject to the criminal jurisdiction of any but the largest states; and if account is taken of the fact that the military personnel is chiefly male and chiefly in the age groups having high crime rates, military justice may be regarded as having a still greater importance.[2]

1. DEVELOPMENT

The system for the punishment of offenses committed by members of the armed forces has an ancient lineage as a system for dealing with small professional armies. In this century, however (as during the Civil War), it has been called upon to adapt itself to far-reaching changes in its application. Originating as a system of disciplinary punishments for a small professional army, it has been adapted to extend over a force of millions of men and women drawn from civilian life.

The power of Congress in this field stems from the express language of the Constitution, which empowers it "to make rules for the government and regulation of the land and naval forces," a power which includes the provision for trial and punishment of offenses by members of those forces in the traditional manner, i.e., by tribunals distinct from those for the trial of civilian offenses. The specific constitutional guarantees of the rights of the accused (except the prohibitions of double jeopardy, excessive fines, and cruel and unusual punishments) are qualified by words seemingly making them inapplicable to court-martial proceedings.[3] However, Con-

[2] Karlen and Pepper, The Scope of Military Justice, 43 Jour. Crim. Law, Criminology, and Police Sci. 285 (1952) is a detailed examination of the quantitative importance of military justice.

[3] The right to indictment by grand jury is expressly made inapplicable to "cases arising in the land and naval forces"; the privilege against self-incrimination is given "in any criminal case"; and the rights to jury trial, to confrontation, to compulsory process for obtaining witnesses, and to the assistance of counsel are given "in all criminal prosecutions." In Wade v. Hunter, 336 U.S. 684 (1949), in rejecting the contention of one convicted by court-martial that he had been subjected to double jeopardy, the Supreme Court apparently assumed that the constitutional prohibition against double jeopardy, which is not specifically limited by the Constitution to "criminal cases" or "criminal prosecutions," is applicable to court-martial proceedings. The right to be exempt from compulsory self-incrimination and the rights to counsel and to confrontation are fully respected in court-martial proceedings; and, perhaps as a consequence, no reported cases involving the application to those proceedings of the constitutional guarantees have reached the Court. The Court of Military Appeals has held that in a general court-martial the accused has a right to a

gress has by statute provided that the accused in a court-martial proceeding shall enjoy all those rights other than indictment by grand jury and trial by jury; so that the Supreme Court has not been called upon to define with precision the extent to which those rights are constitutional as well as statutory. Moreover, the pervasive constitutional prohibition against deprivation of life, liberty, or property "without due process of law" does control Congress in the formulation of the system of military justice and the military in their administration of the system.

On the basis of the system developed in the British army in the seventeenth and eighteenth centuries, and employed in the Continental army during the Revolution, Congress in 1789 adopted, and in 1806 revised, a code of military justice (known as the "Articles of War," but applicable in peacetime as well) for the Army, and in 1800 a cognate one for the Navy. These two statutes, despite the vicissitudes and demands of the Civil War and the two world wars, remained with little change till 1948 when the Articles of War were revised in important respects. In 1950 a new statute, based largely on the recently revised Articles of War, replaced the two existing statutes, placing military justice in all the armed forces (including the Coast Guard when in war service) under a single statute. This statute, which became effective May 1, 1951, is termed the "Uniform Code of Military Justice."[4]

Though the basic statutes thus remained static over this period of a century and a half, the system in operation saw numerous changes effected by administrative action, made possible because the statutes placed in the hands of the President extensive discretion in their amplification, in addition to such power as he might enjoy, in the absence of express statutory authorization, by virtue of his constitutional position of commander in chief.

Several changes affecting only the Army were made in the years immediately following World War 1. The administration of military justice during that war, particularly by the Army, had created much dissatisfaction in the ranks, drawn as they were from civilian life. The changes made were in the direction of providing in serious cases a review of the conviction and sentence by a departmental board unconnected with the line of command.

Despite these changes, the second world war, involving larger forces and a much longer period of service, evoked a new wave of dissatisfaction,

---

public trial. United States v. Brown, 7 U.S.C.M.A. 251 (1956). The court did not find it necessary, however, to hold that the right was constitutional, basing its holding instead on the concept of due process in military justice, which in its view is required in all court-martial proceedings to carry out the intent of the Uniform Code of Military Justice. See, generally, the chapter by Chief Justice Warren on "The Bill of Rights and the Military" in Cahn (ed.), The Great Rights (1963).

[4] 10 U.S. Code, Ch. 47, Secs. 801–940.

particularly among civilian lawyers who had, as members of the armed forces, had firsthand contact with the administration of military justice. The result was first the 1948 revision of the Articles of War and then the present statute, which (in addition to substituting a uniform code for the separate codes previously in force for the Army and Navy) made statutory many of the changes previously made administratively (chiefly in the Army) and introduced for the first time an appellate court, with civilian judges, totally independent of the armed forces.

In the following account of the system now operating under the Uniform Code of Military Justice, no attempt is made to set forth the minutiae of procedure, as prescribed by the code itself and by the voluminous *Manual for Courts-Martial* promulgated by the President under its authority. Rather is the purpose chiefly to examine the extent to which the system affords protection to the rights of the accused, particularly in more serious cases, and to draw attention to those features in which the system contrasts most strongly with the criminal justice administered in our civilian courts.

2. PERSONS SUBJECT TO JURISDICTION

An offense condemned by the Code is punishable, under its provisions, not only when committed by a member of the armed forces but also when committed, in time of war, by a person serving or accompanying armed forces in the field and, even in peacetime, when committed outside the United States by persons "serving with, employed by or accompanying the armed forces" (the latter phrase having been construed by the Army to apply to the dependents of military personnel abroad accompanying them by military authorization).[5] By a series of decisions in 1957–1960, however, the Supreme Court declared Congress to be powerless to subject any civilian to court-martial jurisdiction in peacetime.[6]

The problem of punishing one who is no longer in the military service for an offense committed while in the service, particularly if the offense was committed abroad, presents constitutional difficulties, and has not yet been resolved. A novel statutory provision, enacted in 1950 as part of the Uniform Code of Military Justice, assumed to subject to court-martial jurisdiction a person who had terminated his connection with armed service, if there was charged against him an offense allegedly committtted while in service, for which a sentence of confinement for more than five years could be imposed and which could not under existing law be tried

[5] Art. 2, Subd. (10) and (11). Court-martial jurisdiction of offenses committed by military prisoners and by prisoners of war is also provided for.

[6] As to persons employed by the armed forces see McElroy v. Guagliardo, 361 U.S. 281 (1960); as to persons "accompanying" the armed forces, see Kinsella v. Singleton, 361 U.S. 234 (1960).

in the courts of the United States or of any state territory.[7] This provision was, however, held unconstitutional by the Supreme Court, the Court refusing to recognize the power of Congress to treat a person no longer in any way connected with the military service as still subject to court-martial jurisdiction in any form.[8] Congress could doubtless provide for the prosecution, under the regular criminal procedure, of a person no longer in the military service, for an offense committed while in the service, even if committed abroad;[9] but it has not done so.

3. OFFENSES AGAINST CRIMINAL LAW

It has already been mentioned that the Code provides for the punishment not only of military offenses, but of offenses having no connection whatever with military affairs—offenses not involving any other member of the armed forces, not committed in a military area, not affecting military property, and in nowise different from offenses committed by civilians.

It might be supposed that the reason for thus duplicating, so far as domestic territory is concerned, the existing criminal statutes is that military personnel are not subject to them. But such is not the case. Congress might doubtless have exempted the armed forces from the application of civilian statutes; but it has never done so. The person subject to the Code remains fully subject to the laws of the state in which he may be and to the federal statutes as well. Thus a person subject to the Code may by a single act violate both the Code and the criminal statutes.

Where an offense of this dual character has been committed, unless the offender has already been held to answer by the military authorities, or has been convicted, the practice is, in time of peace, to deliver him to the civil authorities if requested, reserving to the services only the imposition of purely military penalties, such as reduction in rank, administrative reprimand, etc. In time of war, however, the military ordinarily asserts exclusive jurisdiction; and there is no process by which the civil authorities, should they wish to do so, can compel his surrender to them.

That there is no inherent necessity, even in time of war, for the trial by court-martial of non-military offenses against the criminal law in our own territory is clear from the experience of other countries, in which the trial

---

[7] Art. 3A. The need for such a provision was brought to public attention in 1950 by a case in which a murder allegedly perpetrated by members of the United States armed forces in Italy, but not discovered till after their separation from the service, could not be charged against them under the existing statutes governing military justice. Neither could they be proceeded against in the federal criminal courts, there being no applicable statute. An attempt by the Italian government to procure their extradition to Italy for trial proved unsuccessful.

[8] Toth v. Quarles, 350 U.S. 11 (1955).

[9] See p. 19 regarding existing federal statutes making punishable acts committed abroad.

of such offenses is remitted to the regular courts.[10] In the controversy which has raged (and has still by no means died out) over the propriety of the appointment of the personnel of a court-martial (including the defense counsel) by their superior in command—a matter shortly to be discussed—the compromise proposal has been made that the existing system be retained for purely military offenses, but that offenders against the criminal law be handed over to separate tribunals, whether military, civilian, or mixed.

When members of our armed forces are stationed within the borders of another friendly nation, it is not customary, under international practice, for that nation to assert the jurisdiction of its criminal courts over them; the host nation looks to us to punish violations of law by any member of our forces. During the world wars arrangements with the United Kingdom regularizing this practice were made by agreement, and subsequently by express legislation by Parliament. However, under an agreement now in force between the nations signatory to the North Atlantic Treaty of 1949, of which the United States is one, "the authorities of the receiving state shall have jurisdiction over the members of a force or civilian component and their dependents with respect to offenses committed within the territory of the receiving State and punishable by "the law of that State."[11] Cognate arrangements have been made with respect to our military forces in Japan.[12]

[10] In Great Britain, although the statute gives courts-martial jurisdiction over offenses against the criminal law, such jurisdiction is seldom asserted even in time of war. Jurisdiction over murder, manslaughter, and rape is limited to "places out of his Majesty's dominions" and is seemingly restricted even there. No exception is made for time of war. 8 Halsbury's Laws of England, 641–642 (1933). A similar exception as to murder or rape committed within a state or the District of Columbia was made by the former statute which was replaced by the Uniform Code of Military Justice (Articles of War, Art. 92, Act of June 4, 1920, 41 Stat. 805). This exception applied, however, only in time of peace. The reason for its omission in the Uniform Code is not clear. In France and Germany, following World War I, such offenses were tried by the regular courts with the addition of military members. Rheinstein, "Military Justice," in Puttkammer (ed.), War and the Law, 158, 159 (1944). In 1957, the jurisdiction of courts-martial of non-military offenses committed by members of the armed forces of West Germany was withdrawn and placed exclusively in the hands of the civilian courts.

[11] Agreement between the Parties to the North Atlantic Treaty Regarding the Status of their Forces, Art VII, Sec. 1(b), ratified by the Senate July 15, 1953. In ratifying, the Senate expressed its "sense" that "where there is danger that the accused will not be protected because of the absence or denial of constitutional rights he would enjoy in the United States, the commanding officer shall request the authorities of the receiving state to waive jurisdiction . . . and if such authorities refuse to waive jurisdiction, the commanding officer shall request the Department of State to press such request through diplomatic channels. . . ." Dept of State Publication 5307 (1954). See Levie, The NATO Status of Forces Agreement: Legal Safeguards for American Servicemen, 44 Amer. Bar Assn. Jour. 322 (1958) and Snee and Pye, Status of Forces Agreements and Criminal Jurisdiction (1957).

[12] The cognate provisions contained in the "administrative agreement" made with Japan pursuant to the security treaty were attacked as unconstitutional, but were sustained by the Supreme Court. Wilson v. Gerard, 354 U.S. 524 (1957).

4. OFFENSES AND PENALTIES

In addition to defining specific offenses against discipline and crimes against person or property the Code provides that "all disorders and neglects to the prejudice of good order and discipline in the armed forces, all conduct of a nature to bring discredit upon the armed forces, and crimes and offenses not capital, of which persons subject to this code may be guilty . . . shall be punished. . . ."[13] The Code, following military tradition, thus rejects the basic principle of the civilian criminal law that no act is punishable unless specifically defined as such in advance of its commission. The extent to which this feature of the Code actually works injustice is difficult to assess. Its apparent repugnance to principle is in reality much reduced by a specific listing of offenses under this article, in connection with the prescription of maximum punishments therefor by the President.[14] Nowhere, however, is there any specific provision prohibiting punishment under this article for an act not so listed; and in practice it is not so limited.

The list of penalties, it may be added, enumerates and apparently therefore is intended to include as "disorders and neglects to the prejudice of good order and discipline" or as "conduct of a nature to bring discredit on the armed forces," acts not in the course of duty which are hardly regarded as criminal offenses in civilian life—such as "failing to pay a just debt under such circumstances as to bring discredit upon the military service," or "loaning money . . . at a usurious or unconscionable rate of interest to another in the military service."

Except as to a few offenses for which it imposes the death penalty, the Code itself prescribes no specific punishments for the several offenses, instead authorizing the President to prescribe maximum punishments. The maximum punishments so prescribed by him include dishonorable and bad conduct discharges (with forfeiture of all pay and allowances), forfeiture of pay, total or partial, and confinement at hard labor, fine, reduction in grade, and reprimand. The maximum periods of confinement at hard labor (for which may be substituted proportionately longer periods of hard labor without confinement or of restriction to limits) range from three days (for each day of absence without leave) to twenty years (for aggravated arson or for assault with intent to commit robbery or rape). For several offenses (such as desertion and disobedience of orders) the Code permits the imposition of the death penalty if the offense is committed in

---

[13] Moreover, "conduct unbecoming an officer and a gentlemen" is made an offense for "any officer, cadet or midshipman."

[14] Manual for Courts-Martial, United States 225–226 (1951). This volume (665 pages) prescribes in detail the procedure of courts-martial. The Court of Military Appeals has in a few cases criticized the instructions for members of courts-martial contained in this manual.

time of war; and the maximum terms of imprisonment applicable to such offenses are also suspended in time of war.

5. COURT STRUCTURE

Unlike civilian courts, courts-martial under our system have no continuing existence. A separate court is appointed (or as the phrase is, "convened") for each and every trial (though in the larger military and naval establishments a particular officer or panel of officers may be designated to hold court regularly for the trial of routine offenses). The power to "convene the court" is in fact, as will shortly appear, the power to name the jury.

There are three grades of court, known, respectively, as summary, special, and general courts-martial, the grade of the court corresponding not, as in civilian systems, to the gravity of the offenses of which it has jurisdiction, but to the severity of the penalties it may impose. In this aspect both the summary and the special courts may be deemed inferior courts, inasmuch as the penalty which even the special court may impose may not exceed confinement for six months, and forfeiture of not over two-thirds pay for not over six months; while the penalty imposable by the summary court, which has jurisdiction only over enlisted men, is limited to a maximum of one month's confinement and forfeiture of two-thirds of a month's pay. The general court is thus the only one by which serious charges are ordinarily tried.

The power to convene the lowest grade of court-martial—the summary court—is vested in a considerable number of officers. The power to convene the intermediate grade of court-martial—the special court—is vested in a much smaller category of officers; while the power to convene a court of the highest grade—the general court-martial—is entrusted only to officers of high command.[15]

6. CHOICE OF COURT

Ordinarily the immediate commander of the person suspected of having committed an offense is the first one to take official action. He may dismiss the charges, if charges have been preferred to him by another, or may without further formality, if he sees fit, impose a penalty consisting of

[15] A summary court may be ordered by any commanding officer, even by the commander of a detachment. A special court may be ordered only by the commander of a specified larger unit or establishment, while the power to convene a general court is restricted to commanders of still larger specified units or establishments. The power to convene a general court is vested also in the President and the secretaries of the departments of Army, Navy, Air, and Treasury (the latter with respect to the Coast Guard).

withholding of privileges or restriction to specified limits, or other minor penalties.[16] Should he, however, after investigation, consider that the facts if established would warrant more serious punishment, he must forward charges to the officer exercising summary court-martial jurisdiction over the command of which the accused is a member. That officer, after making such further investigation as he deems proper, may either dismiss the charges, order trial by summary court-martial, or may forward the charges, with recommendations, to a superior officer empowered to convene the appropriate court-martial. That officer may in turn dismiss the charges or convene either a general or a special court-martial (or, if he regards a general court-martial as called for, but is not himself empowered to convene one, may in turn forward the charges to an officer who is so empowered). Before a general court-martial may be convened, however, a formal investigation of the charges must have been made (the nature of which will shortly be discussed), and the officer convening it must have referred the charge to his staff judge advocate or legal officer for consideration and advice, and must himself find that the charge is warranted by evidence indicated in the report of the investigation required to have been made.

The discretion thus vested in a commanding officer empowered to convene only a summary court, to convene such a court instead of forwarding the charges to higher authority, is a great one. By convening a summary court, he irrevocably limits the punishment which may be inflicted for the offense to the maximum punishment which a summary court may impose; for the Code prohibits any subsequent prosecution for the same offense. Equally crucial is the discretion vested in the officer empowered either to convene a special court-martial or to forward the charges to a higher authority competent to convene a general court-martial, and the discretion, vested in an officer empowered to convene a general court-martial, to convene a special court instead.

As already suggested, the summary court-martial is, in effect, because of the minor character of the penalties it usually imposes, characteristically a disciplinary tribunal, and the special court-martial largely so. It is only by a general court-martial that serious offenses are ordinarily tried, and it is that court that first invites our attention.

7. INVESTIGATION PRECEDENT TO GENERAL COURT-MARTIAL

A summary or a special court-martial may be convened on the basis of sworn charges preferred by any person subject to the Code; a general

[16] He may, if he sees fit, offer the accused the election of refusing such punishment and risking trial by court-martial, which, if it finds the accused guilty, may impose more serious punishment.

court-martial, however, may be convened, as already noted, only after a formal preliminary proceeding, which the Code describes as a "thorough investigation," on notice to the accused, who has the right to be represented by counsel, to cross-examine witnesses against him if they are available, to present anything he may desire in his own behalf, and to demand the examination of additional witnesses.

In many cases, needless to say, an investigation has already been conducted prior to the formulation of the charges. If the accused was present at such investigation and was afforded the same opportunities for representation, cross-examination, and presentation of evidence on his own behalf as are required in the formal investigation to be conducted after charges have been framed, such formal examination may be dispensed with; but the accused, after being informed of the charge, may demand further investigation at which he may recall witnesses for further examination and offer new evidence in his own behalf.

Both in the formal investigation and in the informal interrogation which may precede it, the accused (or the suspect) enjoys the privilege of refusing to incriminate himself. The sweeping character given the privilege in our military justice will be described at a later point.

The right of the accused to counsel in the investigation is fortified by the provision that he shall be represented by civilian counsel if provided by him, or military counsel of his own selection "if such counsel be reasonably available," or by counsel appointed for him—a provision identical with that applicable to the right to counsel at the trial itself.

Though seemingly well-designed, at least from the procedural standpoint, to protect the suspect against the possibility of being brought to trial on charges inadequately supported by evidence, the investigation procedure just described has been criticized as in fact tending to prejudice a fair trial of the charges by the court-martial when convened. The very fact that the charges have already been presumably thoroughly investigated (the accused having been given every opportunity to clear himself in the course of such investigation), and that only after such investigation has trial been ordered, creates in the minds of the members of the court, so it is urged, a presumption of the guilt rather than of the innocence of the accused—a presumption all the more unfounded, it is pointed out, in that the officer conducting the investigation may have been quite unequal to the task, there being no requirements that he be of special competence or experience.[17] Nevertheless, it is worth considering whether this investigative proceeding, developed in military practice without any reference to

[17] The power of a commanding officer hostile to a member of his command to influence the members of the court-martial appointed by him has long been the target of attack. See below, p. 525. To the extent that this criticism has validity, it applies with still greater force to the power of the commanding officer to influence the officer making the investigation.

the experience of civilian justice, does not have lessons for our criminal procedure.

It will be apparent that this proceeding has no analogue in our civilian criminal justice. It is not like the preliminary examination before a magistrate, for its purpose is not to determine whether the accused shall be held in custody; the commanding officer has power to order the accused held in arrest or confinement without any preliminary procedure. It has some resemblance to a grand jury investigation; but in that proceeding the accused has no slightest participation. Moreover, the investigation is conducted after the chages have been tentatively framed; and it embraces not only the truth of the matter set forth in the charges, but their form and the disposition that should be made of them in the interest of justice and discipline. Nor does the officer conducting the investigation have any power of disposition; he merely prepares a report.

Before convening a general court-martial, the convening officer must refer the charges to his staff judge advocate or legal officer for consideration and advice; and he is required first to satisfy himself that the charge "is warranted by evidence indicated in the report of investigation."[18]

8. GENERAL COURT-MARTIAL: COMPOSITION AND PROCEDURE

The officer who convenes the general court-martial determines how many members, above the minimum of five prescribed by the statute, the court shall have. He appoints its members, may relieve a member of the court during the trial, and may even replace a member while the trial is in progress; however, the governing regulations enjoin upon him that neither of these changes is to be made except for controlling reasons. The accused may challenge any member of the court for cause (the fact that such member is the accuser or a witness for the prosecution or has acted as investigating officer or counsel in the case is specifically mentioned by the Code as a ground of ineligibility for membership on the court), and is in addition entitled to one peremptory challenge. The prosecution has the same right of challenge. Rulings on challenges for cause are made by the court by secret ballot of the members, a tie vote being sufficient to disqualify the member challenged.

The officer convening the court is required to appoint a prosecutor (termed "trial counsel") and a defense counsel, with equal legal qualifications. The accused has, however, the right to retain civilian counsel instead of or in addition to the counsel assigned him, or to be represented by military counsel of his own selection, if "reasonably available."

The senior member of the court is its president, so-called. His presid-

---

[18] The latter requirement is applicable also to the convening of a special court-martial.

ing function is, however, nominal. That function is in fact discharged by a separate officer, known as the law officer, appointed by the convening authority.[19] It is not the president of the court but the law officer who rules upon questions of admissibility of evidence and other legal questions which arise in the course of the trial; and at the close of the evidence he also instructs the court upon the law. The respective functions of the law officer and of the voting members of the court are thus analogous to those of the judge and the jury in a civilian court; the members of the court may, however, on the objection of any member, overrule the law officer on his disposition of a motion for a finding of not guilty—equivalent, in a criminal trial, to a motion for a directed verdict of acquittal—or on the question of the accused's present sanity, powers not possessed by the criminal jury in cognate situations. Voting on the question of overruling the law officer on either of these matters is done in closed session, viva voce, beginning with the junior in rank.

In the opinion of qualified students of military justice, the position of the law officer should be strengthened. It has been urged that he should be the presiding officer in name as well as in fact, and that his disposition of a motion for a finding of not guilty should not be subject to reversal by the court.[20] Doubtless the failure to accord him the status possessed by the judge in a criminal trial is due in part to the circumstance that he is frequently junior in rank to the senior members of the court. Were he, however, attached to an independent judicial corps, within the service but outside the line of command, this difficulty would be minimized.

All the appointees of the convening officer—the members of the court, the law officer, the trial counsel, and the assigned defense counsel—are his subordinates in the direct line of command. This is the foundation for the contention that the entire proceeding is in effect under "command control." This matter will shortly be reverted to.

The procedure of the court-martial, which in general follows that of the criminal proceeding in civilian courts, is prescribed in great detail by presidential regulation. The procedure of the civilian criminal courts of not a few jurisdictions might well profit from a similarly precise formulation.

The court deliberates and votes on its findings and on the penalty in secret. After its findings have been reached, it may, however, consult with the law officer as to the form of its findings.

The unanimous vote of all members of the court present at the time

[19] The law officer must be a member of the bar of a federal court or of the highest court of a state, and must be certified to be qualified for such duty by the chief law officer (termed the Judge Advocate General) of the armed force (Army, Navy, or Air Force) of which he is a member.

[20] Cf. McBratney, Reform of Military Justice Is Not Complete, 35 Jour Am. Judicature Soc. 81 (1951).

the vote is taken is required for conviction of an offense for which the death penalty is made mandatory by law, and for any death sentence. A three-fourths vote of the members present is required for a sentence of life imprisonment or of confinement in excess of ten years. A two-thirds vote of the members present is required for all other convictions or sentences. As stated, the Code does not prescribe the number of members of the court, but only the minimum of five. The chances of conviction would seem to vary with the size of the court. Unanimity in a court of nine, for example, is less likely than in one of five.

9. INFERIOR COURTS-MARTIAL: COMPOSITION AND PROCEDURE

The special court-martial is composed of not less than three members. Unlike the general court-martial it has no law officer, his duties being performed instead by the president of the court. The accused enjoys the same right of counsel as in a trial by general court-martial,[21] and the procedure is also similar. The members of the court may be challenged as in the case of a general court-martial.

In a summary court-martial, which is held by a single officer, there is no provision for counsel. However, the officer holding the court is enjoined by the governing regulations to give the accused every assistance in bringing out evidence favorable to him. Moreover, he is required to inform the accused of the charge against him, the name of his accuser, and the names of the witnesses who will probably be called. He is also to advise the accused of his right to cross-examine the witnesses called against him, or to have the court ask them any questions he desires to have answered, of his right to call any witnesses or produce any evidence on his own behalf, and of his right to testify or remain silent—the latter privilege being again explained to the accused before the trial is brought to a conclusion.[22]

10. RIGHTS OF THE SUSPECT OR ACCUSED

At several points in the foregoing there were noted provisions of the Code intended to afford protection to the suspect or the accused. These are not, however, the only provisions of this character.

[21] Counsel are not required, however, as in general court-martial proceedings, to be lawyers.

[22] It has been proposed that summary courts-martial be abolished in favor of non-judicial punishment, and special courts-martial be stripped of their power to adjudge punitive charges. Bills in Congress to this end have thus far failed to reach the floor. See Burns and Rapson, Sounding the Knell of Drumhead Justice, 48 Amer. Bar Assn. Jour. 843 (1962).

Objection to summary trial

An accused may object to being tried by summary court-martial, in which event trial by a special or general court-martial will be ordered. Either of these tribunals, however, it will be noted, has power to impose more severe punishment than has the summary court-martial.

Right to counsel

The provisions for furnishing counsel to the accused in the investigation preceding a trial by general court-martial and in the trial before either a general or special court-martial have already been noted.

The Code requires that in a trial by general court-martial any person appointed as either prosecutor or defense counsel shall be a member of the bar (or if a judge advocate, or, in the Navy or Coast Guard, a law specialist, shall be in the alternative a graduate of an accredited law school). Regrettably, this requirement does not apply to either prosecutor or defense counsel appointed to act in a trial by special court-martial. Doubtless a mandatory requirement, however desirable, would often encounter serious practical difficulties; but the Code could well add the requirement with suitable provision for dispensing with it where imperative.

In connection with the provision of counsel in court-martial proceedings, it must be taken into account that the legal knowledge called for is confined within fairly definite limits. Much of the equipment of the lawyer, whether in substantive or in procedural matters, is quite unlikely to be drawn upon. It would indeed be possible to provide for a suitable number of officers a training course of not undue length, covering the substantive criminal law, the rules of evidence, and the procedure of courts-martial. From officers thus trained counsel could be drawn, where fully trained lawyers are not available, for special courts-martial.

There is no requirement that the counsel appointed to represent the accused in the investigation which precedes trial by general court-martial shall be appointed to defend him at the trial. This has been regarded by some as a serious defect, particularly in view of the short period sometimes allowed, under service conditions, between the order convening the court and appointing counsel, and the trial itself, giving the defense counsel less time to acquaint himself with the facts than is normally the case in civilian justice. The lack of facilities afforded the defense counsel, both in the investigation proceeding and at the trial, for independent investigation of the facts has also been criticized.

Finally, it is pointed out that the defense counsel is a subordinate in the line of command to the officer convening the court, and may be torn between his duty to the accused and his fear of displeasing his superior. Unquestionably, a corps of defense counsel, wholly outside the line of command and responsible only to the Judge Advocate General of the service, would do more than any procedural device whatever to safeguard the accused against unjust conviction or sentence.

Whatever the weaknesses of the system of assigned counsel in court-martial proceedings, however, it is undoubtedly the fact that the accused, even where the offense charged is not of the gravest, is more certain to have some legal assistance than an indigent defendant has ordinarily had in the typical civilian criminal proceeding.

Privilege against self-incrimination

Perhaps chief of the constitutional rights of the accused in a criminal proceeding which Congress has carried over into the court-martial proceeding is the privilege against self-incrimination. Indeed, the principle, long applied to the proceedings before the court-martial itself, has been extended by the Code to an area in which it is not applied in civilian justice—that of the interrogation of the suspect by the officer charged with investigating the crime. The constitutional privilege against self-incrimination extends only to testimony which is compellable under oath; it has no relation to the mere interrogation of a witness or suspect by an officer who has no power to compel a response. Accordingly, the civilian interrogator is under no obligation to inform the person interrogated, before putting questions to him, that he is under no obligation to give incriminating answers; for he is under no legal obligation to answer any questions whatever.[23] The refusal of a member of the armed services, however, to respond to the questions put to him by an officer detailed to investigate a suspected offense would constitute a punishable breach of discipline. It is for this reason, doubtless, that the framers of the Code introduced into it a rule previously unknown in the armed services—the rule that the person interrogating or requesting a statement from an accused or a person suspected of an offense shall first inform him of the nature of the accusation and advise him "that he does not have to make any statement regarding the offense of which he is accused or suspected," and that any statement made by him may be used as evidence against him in a trial by court-martial. Moreover, no statement obtained from any person in violation of these provisions may be received in evidence against him in a trial by court-martial. That the Court of Military Appeals is of a mind to insist upon the rigorous enforcement of this provision is made clear by its early reversal of a conviction for murder,

[23] However, some courts have regarded interrogation of a suspect by police or prosecutor, without informing him that he is not required to answer, as a form of coercion which may tend to make inadmissible in evidence any admissions thus obtained.

because of the reception at the trial of testimony of an investigating officer that, in informal interrogation directly after the commission of the crime (a time when, as is well known, confession is often spontaneously made by the perpetrator), the accused had admitted his guilt, without, however, having first been informed that he did not have to make any statement.[24]

Whatever may be thought of the rationale of the privilege against self-incrimination in civilian justice—and in previous pages much of the accepted rationale of the privilege has been drawn into question—the indiscriminate extension of the principle to the field of military justice, exemplified by the provisions just reviewed, is somewhat wanting in logic. The court-martial system, as already pointed out, deals not merely with criminal offenses, but with offenses that are little more than breaches of discipline. If the punishments meted out for such disciplinary breaches are more severe than would be penalties for similar breaches of discipline in civilian organizations, the difference is to be accounted for by the greater necessity for iron discipline in the military than in the civilian sphere, rather than by any real difference in the nature of the offense involved. There would seem no reason for extending to administrative inquiries into breaches of discipline the principle that the suspect may remain mute—a principle unknown in civilian administration. If the privilege against self-incrimination has any place at all in the system of military justice, it should be restricted to cases where the offense involved is criminal in its nature and not merely disciplinary.

The privilege against self-incrimination is conferred by the Code also on any witness before a court-martial or in any auxiliary proceeding. In this, the Code continues long-standing statutory provisions.

Convening of court-martial by officer other than accuser

It has already been pointed out that the presumptive thoroughness of the preliminary investigation which precedes the convening of a general court-martial has been thought by some to be prejudicial to the accused, as creating in the minds of the judges, their oaths and the law to the contrary notwithstanding, a presumption of guilt. Manifestly, to the extent that there may be substance in this view, the danger is aggravated when the investigation has been conducted, and the charges preferred, by the very superior officer who has convened the court and selected its members; yet prior to the reform of the Articles of War in 1948, this was not infrequently the situation. The new principle, carried over into the Code, is that when any commander who would normally convene the court-martial is the accuser, he must (except in the case of a summary

[24] United States v. Wilson and Harvey, 8 C.M.R. 48 (1952). One of the three judges dissented.

court-martial) refer the charges to a superior officer who will convene the court (or designate another officer to do so). It has been pointed out that this provision does not prevent a commanding officer, who desires to cause a member of his command to be tried and yet wishes to retain in his own hands the selection of the court and of counsel, from causing the charges to be made by one of his subordinates.

Enlisted men as members of general or special courts-martial trying enlisted man

The application to military justice of the notion that a man is to be tried by his peers would presumably require that the members of the court be of the same rank or grade as the accused. Needless to say, in view of the origin of courts-martial as instruments for the maintenance of military discipline, and the persistence of their disciplinary function as their chief function, the contrary principle in fact governs. No member of the court, if it can be avoided, is to be junior in rank or grade to the accused; and in practice a majority at least of the members are of superior rank. In the trial of an enlisted person (for to speak only of an enlisted man is no longer accurate), the membership of the court was until recent years composed exclusively of officers. The radical innovation then introduced, one to which its proponents attach considerable importance, is the right of an accused enlisted person to request that enlisted persons serve on the court by which he is to be tried.[25] Upon such a request, the convening authority must appoint, from among enlisted persons not in the same unit as the accused, at least one-third of the members of the court "unless eligible enlisted personnel cannot be obtained on account of physical conditions or military exigencies." The extent to which this privilege has in fact been availed of by accused enlisted personnel, and its effect where employed, are as yet unclear.

Confrontation

The right of the accused to be confronted by the witnesses against him is recognized by the Code. Detailed provision is, however, made by the Code and by the supplementary regulations for the use of depositions by the prosecution under safeguards similar to those found in criminal proceedings.

Right to be furnished a copy of the record

An accused tried by general or special court-martial is entitled to be given a copy of the record of the proceedings as soon as authenticated. The record of a general court-martial trial (like the record of a special

---

[25] Provision for the membership of enlisted personnel was first made for the Army (by the act of 1948). The Code extended the provision to all the armed forces.

court-martial where a bad conduct discharge is adjudged) under present regulations contains a verbatim transcript of all proceedings in the open sessions of the court. In other trials, only a summary of the proceedings need be made.[26]

This provision for freely furnishing a copy of the record to the accused is in striking contrast to the practice of our civilian criminal courts, where a copy of the record is never furnished to a party as a matter of routine. Even the indigent defendant obtains a copy of the record at public expense only on special application therefor.

11. INDEPENDENCE OF MEMBERS OF COURT

From the standpoint of the protection of the accused, whatever the procedural safeguards prescribed, it is of at least equal importance that he have assurance that the members of the court are impartial. In particular he should have assurance that they (and his military defense counsel as well) are independent of the officer responsible for bringing him to trial.

The problem of the independence of the members of the court was prominently before the committees of Congress which framed the Code. Responsible civilian critics of the then existing system condemned "command control" of the court-martial. This "control" stems from the power to appoint the members of the court, a power which can be abused, it is alleged, by a commanding officer hostile to the accused, and against which the right of the accused to challenge for cause affords no real protection. These critics advocated stripping the commanding personnel of this power and vesting it in an independent legal and judicial corps of officers not in the line of command.[27] At the other extreme were defenders of the then existing system, almost exclusively military men with command experience, who insisted that any diminution of the commanding officer's power to select the membership of the court would be injurious if not fatal to discipline—a contention which, whatever its validity with respect to offenses purely disciplinary, would seem to have only limited application to offenses unrelated to military duty. The congressional com-

[26] In a general court-martial trial it contains also a verbatim transcript of any consultation between the court and the law officer in closed sessions with respect to the form of the findings.

[27] Shortly after the end of World War II, the Secretary of War and the Secretary of the Navy each appointed a board of distinguished civilians to make recommendations for improvement of the court-martial system. The War Department report (often referred to as the Vanderbilt Report) recommended the appointment of courts by the Judge Advocate's Department instead of by the commanding officer, all members of the Judge Advocate's Department in turn to be free from any control by the commanding officer in matters of promotions, assignments, leaves, and fitness reports. The American Bar Association and a number of veteran and bar organizations endorsed these recommendations.

mittees which framed the Code retained the principle of command appointment of the court, but sought to mitigate in two ways its possible adverse effect upon an accused to whom the commanding officer might be hostile—by enlarging the opportunity for the convicted man to procure a review of his conviction and sentence, a matter shortly to be considered, and by prohibiting command influence.

The Code forbids any "attempt to coerce, or by any unauthorized means, influence the action of a court-martial . . . or any member thereof in reaching the findings or sentence in any case," and forbids any commanding officer to "censure, reprimand or admonish such court or any member, law officer or counsel thereof, with respect to the findings or sentence adjudged by the court, or with respect to any other exercise of its or his functions in the conduct of the proceeding," and it makes it an offense, punishable by court-martial, to fail to comply with any of its provisions regulating the conduct of proceedings. The difficulty of detecting violations of these provisions is obvious; and there is difference of opinion as to their efficacy.

But the intangible factor which no regulation, however artfully drawn, is likely to reach is the power possessed by a commanding officer to influence either favorably or adversely the service careers of officers subordinate to him, including the law officer, the prosecuting and assigned defense counsel, and some at least of those whom he appoints to serve on the court-martial. This power stems from his duty to make (or to make endorsements upon) periodical reports on the qualities of these officers, since such reports become a part of the permanent personnel file of the officer reported on and have substantial weight in determining his promotion. Aware of this fact, a law officer or a member of a court-martial or of counsel must possess exceptional rectitude and courage to resist being influenced by what he may know are the commander's wishes or hopes with respect to the outcome of the trial.[28]

Hence despite assurances that the provisions of the Code have put an end to the possibility of "command control," proposals to free the personnel of courts-martial of all connection with the command continue to be pressed on Congress.

In this connection the question suggests itself whether, at least in peacetime, the conditions which originally gave rise to the institution of a court appointed ad hoc for each offense have not ceased to exist, and

---

[28] A pointed illustration is furnished in a 1953 decision of the Court of Military Appeals, vacating a conviction because of command influence. The convening officer had conducted a conference with the members of the court immediately before the trial, at which he read a letter to him from higher headquarters in which, among other things, it was stated that it was proper to recognize an officer's proper performance of his court-martial duties by notation on his efficiency report. United States v. Littrice, 3 U.S.C.M.A. 487 (1953). See also United States v. Kennedy, 8 U.S.C.M.A. 251 (1957). But compare United States v. Danzen, 12 U.S.C.M.A. 350 (1961).

whether it would not be better to establish, certainly for the graver offenses (except where impracticable due to special service conditions), a standing system of courts, staffed presumably by members of the Judge Advocate's department, and wholly independent of officers exercising command.[29] A first step in this direction has been taken by the Department of the Army. For each army area there has been appointed a member of the Judge Advocate's corps, responsible only to the Judge Advocate General of the Army, and thus wholly independent of the general commanding the forces in the area, to serve as law officer in all court-martial trials in that area.[30]

12. REVIEW WITHIN THE MILITARY ORGANIZATION

In our account of the procedure in civilian criminal proceedings, it was pointed out that in all but a trifling proportion of cases, a conviction by a jury is final; rarely will the presiding judge set it aside as unfounded in law, and in few cases, relatively, is an appeal taken by the convicted defendant. In the absence of appeal, no provision exists for a scrutiny of the evidence; and even if appeal be taken, a reappraisal of the evidence apart from possible error of law is not as such a part of the duty of the appellate court. Moreover, no provision exists, except by appeal, for a reappraisal of the sentence imposed; and even on appeal the appellate court is without power in many jurisdictions, if it affirms the conviction, to revise the sentence.

In striking contrast to the virtual finality thus accorded in civilian criminal procedure to the verdict of guilty and to the sentence, our military justice subjects the findings and sentence of every court-martial to automatic independent review, and in many cases not merely by one, but by two or three successive authorities—a review directed solely to mitigating the court-martial's findings of guilt or its sentence; for a finding of not guilty may not be set aside nor a sentence increased. It is not a little remarkable that the contrast to civilian criminal justice offered by this feature of our military justice (which, though elaborated and reinforced by the Code, is particularly in the Army of long standing) should have attracted so little comment.[31]

[29] An intermediate suggestion is that the court be appointed ad hoc, but by a member of the Judge Advocate's Department (who is also to function in the same manner as the law officer under the present Code), from a panel of names furnished him by the convening officer. See Morgan, The Background of the Uniform Code of Military Justice, 6 Vand. Law Rev. 168, 177 (1953).

[30] See Mummey and Meager, Judges in Uniform, 44 Jour. Amer. Judicature Soc. 46 (1960); Wiener, The Army's Field Judiciary System, 46 Amer. Bar Assn. Jour. 1178 (1960).

[31] Pointing out that virtually all the cases tried by summary court-martial and many of those tried by special court-martial are "on the police court level," an observer comments: "Even for these cases, however, the new Code and the *Manual* provide for an *automatic* and fact reweighing type of review, the like of which in

Every sentence of a court-martial, as well as the findings on which it is based, must pass before the convening officer for approval, disapproval, or modification; and he is enjoined by the Code to "approve only such findings of guilty, and the sentence or such part or amount of the sentence, as he finds correct in law and fact and as he in his discretion determines should be approved," a burden of responsibility far exceeding that of the civilian appellate court in a criminal case. Moreover, the Code requires that, in the case of a general court-martial proceeding, the convening officer shall, before passing on the record, refer it to his staff legal officer, who shall submit to him a written opinion thereon; so the record is in effect passed upon twice at this stage.[32]

Nevertheless, the review up to this point, though given in every case, is made by officers in, or attached to, the line command, and as such, whether rightly or wrongly, fails to command the same confidence in its judicial impartiality as does the review by an independent tribunal on appeal, available to the defendant in a criminal proceeding.

Whether there is available such a review by an independent tribunal depends, under the somewhat complex machinery for subsequent review created by the Code and by the supplementary executive orders and departmental regulations, upon the gravity of the sentence. If the sentence, as approved by the convening officer, affects (1) a general or flag officer or extends to (2) death, (3) dismissal (of an officer, cadet, or midshipman), (4) dishonorable or bad conduct discharge, or (5) confinement for one year or more, it is reviewed by one of the so-called boards of review, established in the offices of the Judge Advocates General of the several services (and elsewhere if deemed necessary). It is urged, by civilians with experience in military justice, that these limitations are much too restrictive, and that the right to have independent review should be greatly enlarged.

A board of review is composed of not less than three members of the bar, either officers or civilians,[33] appointed by a Judge Advocate General. It is enjoined by the Code to "affirm only such findings of guilty, and the sentence or such part or amount of the sentence, as it finds correct in fact and determines on the basis of the entire record, should be approved." Moreover: "In considering the record it shall have authority to weigh

---

civilian police court procedure would be revolutionary indeed." Ward, UCMJ—Does It Work, 6 Vand. Law Rev. 186, 208 (1953).

[32] A cognate provision governs the review by a commanding officer exercising general court-martial authority of the sentence of a special court-martial which includes a bad conduct discharge.

[33] The introduction of civilians into the boards of review represents the first participation of civilians in the process of military justice. In Great Britain, however, the tradition is that the offices corresponding to that of Judge Advocate General shall be held by civilians.

the evidence; judge the credibility of witnesses, and determine controverted questions of fact, recognizing that the trial court saw and heard the witnesses"—a charter of appellate power far broader than granted any American appellate court in a criminal case.

The accused has the right to representation before a board of review by his own civilian counsel; if he retains none, he is represented before the board, if he so requests, by an officer of the Judge Advocate General's office having a standing designation as appellate defense counsel (a public defender on the appellate level, as it were). If the government is represented by counsel before the board of review, the accused is also to be so represented, even without request on his part. The great liberality of these provisions as contrasted with the provision of appellate counsel hitherto made in civilian criminal proceedings needs no emphasis.

That the system of review thus provided by the Code is in practice by no means perfunctory is clearly indicated by the substantial number of modifications and disapprovals of court-martial findings and sentences by convening officers and boards of review.

13. REVIEW BY COURT OF MILITARY APPEALS

A board of review, as just described, may be regarded as in the nature of an appellate court; but the appointment of its members by the Judge Advocate General, and his power of supervision though not of direction over it, undoubtedly deprive it of the wholly impartial status, in the public mind, which a completely independent tribunal would enjoy. Such a status is, however, possessed by an entirely new tribunal created by Congress in 1950, as part of the reforms embodied in the Code—the Court of Military Appeals, a bench of three civilian judges appointed for fifteen-year terms by the President with the advice and consent of the Senate. To this court go only cases already passed upon by a board of review. Cases in which the sentence affects a general or flag officer, or extends to death, go to the court automatically; in other cases the accused must petition the court to grant a review, which is to be granted only "on good cause shown." In addition, the Judge Advocate General may forward a case to the court for review.

The review by the court extends only to matters of law; and the court, like other reviewing authorities, is to act only if "the error materially prejudices the substantial rights of the accused." It has been urged that the court be given the right to review findings of fact as well—a change which would doubtless necessarily carry with it an enlargement of the court and its sitting in divisions.

The court has, through the numerous opinions handed down by it, clarified a number of important legal questions under the Code and in the field of military justice generally. It is developing an authoritative body of doctrine in this field which should materially improve the administration of military justice; and since there exists in this field no such ancient and somewhat petrified complex of rules and practices as is found in civilian criminal justice, it may well chart new directions which civilian justice can with profit explore.

It should be noted that while the introduction of civilian members into the boards of review, and still more the creation of a civilian court of appeals, represents a distinct novelty in the American system of military justice, civilian judges as members of the court-martial itself, at least in time of peace, have been a familiar feature of several Continental systems of military justice.

The failure of Congress to give the judges of the Court of Military Appeals tenure during good behavior has been adversely criticized by some, who see in it another manifestation of the desire of the executive to retain a measure of influence in even the highest tribunal of military justice. While in theory there is much to be said for life tenure, it is hardly to be doubted that a tradition of virtually automatic reappointment of a sitting judge will develop in this court.

The Court of Military Appeals is the only civilian judicial tribunal created by federal statute whose determinations are under no circumstances reviewable by the Supreme Court.[34]—an exception which would seem to manifest the intention of Congress to keep the administration of military justice quite separate from the federal courts.

14. INTERVENTION BY THE FEDERAL COURTS

But the federal courts, including the Supreme Court, which have for many years past played a role in this field, continue to do so. This they do through the habeas corpus proceeding. Detention by the military does not in this respect differ from detention by the civilian authorities. Equally in both cases its legality may be inquired into by the courts.

By long-standing doctrine (which continues to be characterized by the courts as unalterable, despite material alterations they have themselves made) the only inquiry which the court may make in a habeas corpus proceeding instituted by a person held in custody by the military for an offense under the Code is the jurisdiction of the tribunal. The petitioner may allege that he is not in any event subject to the Code; or, admitting that

[34] The fact that the court is not a "constitutional" but a "legislative" court offers no obstacle to the provision by Congress of such a review; whether, however, the initial court-martial proceeding which is reviewed by the Court of Military Appeals can be regarded as one of the cases or controversies enumerated by the Constitution as falling within the "judicial power of the United States," so as to be reviewable by the Supreme Court, is a more difficult question.

he is subject to the Code, he may allege illegality in the proceedings against him affecting the jurisdiction of the court-martial.

If his claim is that he is not subject to the Code, the federal court will inquire into the merits of his claim at any stage of the procceding or subsequent imprisonment. If, however, he admits that he is subject to the Code, there is no illegality in his initial detention by the military; the illegal detention can arise only if he is subsequently imprisoned under an illegal sentence by the court-martial. Moreover, the Code declares that the sentence of a court-martial, following its approval, review, or affirmance, "shall be final and conclusive"; and this has been held by the courts to mean that the accused should be required to exhaust all possible opportunities for challenging the legality of his conviction within the court-martial system before applying to the civilian courts. Unless the accused has done so, those courts will accordingly refuse to inquire into the legality of the sentence.

The want of jurisdiction of the court-martial may be due to the fact that the offense charged is not within the cognizance of a court-martial, or that the court-martial was not constituted according to law. Even though the court had jurisdiction, the legality of the sentence may be inquired into by the court if it is claimed that the punishment imposed exceeded the limits prescribed by the Code.

Under accepted concepts, once a tribunal acquires jurisdiction, it can lose that jurisdiction only by some event external to itself—the withdrawal of jurisdiction by the legislative power, the withdrawal of the proceeding by the party who instituted it, or the like. It cannot lose jurisdiction by any error on its own part in its conduct of the proceeding. Yet the federal courts, with the approval of the Supreme Court, in a seeming attempt to preserve the verbal façade of the habeas corpus proceeding unimpaired while altering its inner structure, have declared, as already noted in connection with civilian criminal proceedings, that a court vested with unquestioned jurisdiction at the institution of a proceeding may lose that jurisdiction if during the course of the proceeding it deprives the accused of basic constitutional rights; and that the accused may, therefore, after exhausting his remedies within the military justice system, seek redress by way of a habeas corpus proceeding in the federal courts. Thus, those courts have inquired whether there was a complete lack of evidence supporting the conviction, whether the accused was provided with counsel, or was coerced into pleading guilty, and whether the trial as a whole was vitiated by unfairness.[35]

---

[35] An occasional additional participation of the courts in the field of military justice arises through the institution, by military personnel dismissed (or deprived of pay or other monetary perquisites) by the court-martial sentence, of actions for recovery of pay lost, on the claim that the court-martial was without jurisdiction.

One might have expected that, in creating the civilian Court of Military Appeals, Congress would restrict the defendant's right, after conviction or sentence had been affirmed by that court, to seek further review by way of habeas corpus proceedings in the federal district court; but it did not do so, and such proceedings are still instituted, though infrequently. The "inverted pyramid" appellate structure, characteristic of the system for review of federal administrative determinations, is thus now found in the field of military justice as well, with ultimate decision sometimes in the court of appeals of the particular circuit in which the military prisoner happens to be confined.[36] Assuming that the military convict really needs rights of review additional to the generous ones already provided, the protracted habeas corpus procedure, with the possibility of four successive proceedings (district court, court of appeals, application to the Supreme Court to grant review, review by that Court), is, as a review procedure, just as indefensible here as in the case of the state prisoner seeking federal review of his conviction.

[36] The final disposition of the habeas corpus application of a military prisoner by a district court, or by a court of appeals, may lead to disconcerting results not found in connection with federal civilian convictions (where a motion to set aside the sentence, made in the court where the conviction was had, has replaced the habeas corpus proceeding). In a case in which two codefendants were convicted by court-martial and sentenced to life imprisonment, their convictions and sentences being upheld on appeal by the Court of Military Appeals, it happened that they were sent to different military prisons to serve their sentences. Both instituted habeas corpus proceedings, each in the district in which he was imprisoned, each setting up the same claim of technical error in his sentencing. In the case of one, the court of appeals upheld the sentence, and it was subsequently upheld by the Supreme Court. Meanwhile, in the case of the other, imprisoned in a prison situated in a different circuit, the court of appeals vacated the sentence and ordered his release. The government did not appeal. When the Supreme Court's ruling in the companion case was subsequently announced, it was too late to reincarcerate him. Jackson v. Taylor, 353 U.S. 569 (1957); and De Costa v. Madigan, 223 F2d 906 (1955).

20

Military Tribunals Exercising Jurisdiction Over Civilians in Domestic Territory

1. MILITARY COMMISSIONS IN TIME OF WAR. 2. MILITARY COMMISSIONS IN TIME OF DOMESTIC VIOLENCE.

On a few occasions in our history the executive has assumed to create (in no case with express statutory authority) military tribunals exercising jurisdiction over civilians. The basis for this assumption has been either a state of war—the tribunals being created under authority of the President—or a state of grave disorder, the tribunals acting under gubernatorial authority.

The occasion in question have been few. There is not even the meagerest legislation on the subject; and the judicial discussion of it is so slight and, in general, so belated as to be of theoretical rather than practical value. Hence it would hardly be to the purpose to attempt a statement of established principles; in truth none is possible. More useful will be a brief review of the circumstances under which military tribunals have existed on domestic territory.

1. MILITARY COMMISSIONS IN TIME OF WAR

The Civil War furnished the first occasion in our history for the use of military commisssions to try civilians outside the zone of actual military operations. By proclamation of September 24, 1862, President Lincoln directed the creation of military tribunals wherever necessary for the trial of persons charged by the military with interfering with the draft or with discouraging volunteer enlistment. Neither of these acts was condemned as unlawful by any statute; the President assumed to have the power to declare them to be offenses against martial law though he did not make use of that term. He thus in effect declared that by reason of

533

the emergency martial law existed, even outside the zones of combat, concurrently with the statute law of the country. Under the purported authority of this proclamation, many citizens were in fact arrested, tried, convicted, and sentenced by military commissions, so called, composed of officers designated by the military commander and proceeding according to the then existing practice of courts-martial. The constitutional guarantees of indictment by grand jury and trial by jury, before a court whose judges hold office during good behavior, were all disregarded. The defendant's recourse to the federal courts by way of habeas corpus proceedings had, as already mentioned in a previous chapter, been cut off by the effective suspension of the writ of habeas corpus; no recourse by way of appeal to the civil courts from the judgment of conviction was possible because, under the statutes defining the appellate jurisdiction of the federal courts, and in particular of the Supreme Court, that jurisdiction did not extend to appeals from the judgments of military commissions.[1]

In March 1863, the situation was ameliorated by the act already referred to,[2] which permitted appeal to the courts against detention by a prisoner by the military after the federal grand jury had adjourned without indicting him. In 1866 a case reached the Supreme Court in which this act had been invoked by one Milligan, in custody under a sentence of imprisonment following conviction by a military commission in Indiana. The Court unanimously found him entitled to release.[3] A narrow majority of the Court declared (though the declaration was not necessary to the disposition of the case) that the entire procedure had been unconstitutional and that military jurisdiction "can never be applied to citizens in states which have upheld the authority of the government, and where the courts are open and their process unobstructed"—a statement which would exclude even the power of Congress to authorize such jurisdiction. The minority, refusing to go so far, asserted that such military jurisdiction could at any rate not be established without the express authority of statute.

[1] Ex parte Vallandigham, 1 Wallace 243 (1864). Inasmuch as there was no statutory provision for appeal to the Supreme Court from the judgment of a military commission, the petitioner in this case applied to the Court for a writ of certiorari to be directed to the Judge Advocate General of the Army of the United States, to send up to the Court for review the proceedings of the military commission which had sentenced him. The Court declared itself without power to issue the writ.

[2] See p. 302.

[3] Ex parte Milligan, 4 Wallace 2 (1866). The case came to the Court on questions certified to it by the lower court, the judges of which were equally divided. On April 10, 1866, the Court, without opinion, instructed the lower court that Milligan was entitled to his release under the 1863 statute (see preceding note). This disposition, made unanimously, rendered unnecessary, and indeed irrelevant, any discussion of constitutional issues that might have required consideration had not the statute disposed of the case. Nevertheless, some eight months later, lengthy majority and minority opinions, summarized in the text above, were issued. Though thus pure dictum, the majority opinion is regularly cited as if it were authoritative doctrine.

Notwithstanding the pronouncement of the majority in the Milligan case, proposals were made in Congress during World War I, but unsuccessfully, to set up military commissions to try all persons accused of "sabotage, sedition or propaganda against the United States."[4] During World War II no such proposals were made.

During that war, however, there occurred, in the territory of Hawaii, a total displacement of the civilian territorial courts by military commissions, as part of a complete supersession of the civil government of the territory by a military government, to which reference has been made in an earlier chapter. In their stead were created multimember "military commissions" and single-member "provost courts," the members in both cases being officers appointed by the military commander, most of them without any legal training or experience. These courts imposed sentences of imprisonment as well as fines. After a short period, the territorial courts were permitted to open with restricted powers "as agents of the Military Governor"; but they were to proceed without grand jury indictment or jury trial. The military tribunals continued to function in cases involving breach of military regulations. A writ of habeas corpus issued by the United States District Court for the territory (which, not being part of the territorial government, was not affected by the governor's proclamation of martial law, and remained open) was ignored by the military commander.[5]

In contrast to the action taken by the President during the Civil War, these acts were done under the purported authority of Congress. The organic act creating the territory authorized the imposition of "martial law" by the governor when there was "imminent danger of invasion."

The suspension of the local courts, together with the military's defiance of the federal court, made it impossible for a case challenging the legality of the military commissions to reach the Supreme Court until 1945. When the Court, after the war, decided the case, it did not reaffirm its pronouncement of 1866 that military tribunals exercising jurisdiction over the citizen could never constitutionally be instituted where the courts were open. Instead, it disposed of the matter not on constitutional grounds but on the ground that the statute in authorizing the imposition of "martial law" was not intended "to authorize the supplanting of courts by military tribunals."[6]

At least one member of the Court, however, would have declared it unconstitutional for Congress to authorize the suspension of the civil

---

[4] Swisher, American Constitutionl Development, 615–618 (1943).

[5] The judge then held the commander in contempt of court and imposed a fine upon him—a proceeding which the commander likewise ignored. The matter was never carried to a higher court. See Anthony, Martial Law, Military Government and the Writ of Habeas Corpus in Hawaii, 31 Cal. Law Rev. 447 (1943), and 35 Amer. Bar Assn. Jour. 365 (1949) and 36 id. 825 (1950).

[6] Duncan v. Kahanomoku, 327 U.S. 304 (1946). Two members of the court dissented.

courts even in the face of threatened invasion. In his view, only if the civil courts were "utterly incapable of trying criminals or of dispensing justice in their usual manner" could the constitutional guarantee of jury trial, or the other constitutional provisions for the protection of the accused, be dispensed with.

It will be noted that neither in the Civil War nor in World War II was a case testing the legality of the military jurisdiction decided by the Supreme Court till after that jurisdiction had ceased to be exercised. It is unlikely that in any cognate future emergency a decision of the Court will be obtained more promptly, the more so in that the Court itself has evidenced no disposition to speed, or even to welcome, such a case. The inferior federal courts are obviously in an even more unfavorable position physchologically to challenge the executive's assertion of military power; and indeed where they have attempted to do so, as they have on both the occasions referred to, their mandates have been flouted by the military, acting with the sanction of the President.

It would seem that in view of the relative impotence of the courts in this field, Congress, which has undoubted power to do so, ought to add to our permanent law a precise formulation of the conditions under which military tribunals with jurisdiction over civilians may be brought into existence by the President. Included in such a statute might well be the provision that before invoking military jurisdiction the President must find—and must state in his announcement of military jurisdiction that he has so found—that the courts are unable to discharge their normal functions. It is to be remembered that there is inherently no greater difficulty in the enforcement of military regulations by the civilian courts than in the enforcement of any other regulation made by the executive, the military being indeed only an agency of the executive, precisely as are civilian administrative agencies. It has already been noted that in connection with the military regulations designed for the surveillance, and subsequently the relocation, of the Japanese population on the Pacific Coast during World War II, Congress did in fact provide for such enforcement through criminal prosecution in the courts.

2. MILITARY COMMISSIONS IN TIME OF DOMESTIC VIOLENCE

In a previous chapter mention was made of the assumption of the power of preventive arrest by military commanders of state militia forces called out by the governor to preserve order in areas affected by labor disputes, and of the refusal of the courts, in most cases, to intervene or subsequently to condemn this assumption of power. On a few of these occasions the military commander has gone further and, without assuming to order the closing of the civilian courts, has set up military commissions to try violations of the regulations promulgated by him for the preservation of order—such as regulations prohibiting the carrying of firearms. In only one of these episodes—that which occurred in the Paint Creek region of West Virginia in 1912–1913—were any severe sentences imposed by these tribunals, but in that case the legality of the military commission was upheld by the West Virginia courts. The pardon granted by the governor was doubtless the reason that the question was never carried to the Supreme Court. In the other states involved a similar result ensued.[7]

It is to be noted that the military, in the cases in question, could not, even assuming they would have preferred to do so, have resorted to the courts; for the regulations whose violation was charged were not cognizable by the courts, having been promulgated without any statutory authority. Were the statutes, however, to vest in the governor the power, upon his finding that a state of disorder beyond the control of the local authorities impended in any area, to promulgate appropriate regulations affecting that area during the period of the emergency (or better still, to put into effect an emergency code of regulations preformulated by the legislature), the courts could take jurisdiction in the ordinary way of violations of such regulations, thus destroying at least in part the purported justification for the military jurisdiction.

[7] The cases are reviewed in Rankin, When Civil Law Fails (1939). See also Fairman, The Law of Martial Rule (2nd ed. 1942).

21

Tribunals for Offenses Against the Laws of War

1. AMERICAN WAR CRIMES TRIBUNALS. 2. AMERICAN PARTICIPATION IN INTERNATIONAL WAR CRIMES TRIBUNALS. 3. AMERICAN WAR CRIMES TRIBUNALS CONSTITUTED PURSUANT TO INTERNATIONAL AGREEMENT.

By practice already well established prior to the Constitution, all persons (including nationals) charged in time of war with spying and aiding the enemy were tried by military tribunals. This has continued to be the practice of the American military service; and Congress has given it statutory recognition by subjecting to military justice "any person who in time of war is found lurking as a spy or acting as a spy," and "any person who (1) aids or attempts to aid, the enemy with arms, ammunition, supplies, money, or any other thing; or (2) without proper authority, knowingly harbors or protects or gives intelligence to or communicates or corresponds with or holds any intercourse with the enemy either directly or indirectly." Moreover, by another statutory provision, recognition is given to the power of the military "to try any person who by the law of war is subject to trial by a military tribunal."[1] The Supreme Court has held that by these provisions, Congress, in the exercise of its constitutional power to define and punish "offenses against the law of nations," has adopted the traditional concept of the "laws of war," so as to authorize the President as commander in chief, and all other military commanders within the limits of their authority, to convene military tribunals to try offenses against the laws of war.[2]

Though a court-martial may be convened to try these offenses, it is customary to employ instead a tribunal termed a military commission (or,

---

[1] This provision, as well as those quoted above, is found in the Uniform Code of Military Justice, 50 U.S. Code, Ch. 22.

[2] Ex parte Quirin, 317 U.S. 1, 30 (1942).

for minor offenses, a provost court). The proceedings of such a tribunal, though conducted ordinarily in conformity with established court-martial procedure, are not subject to the rigid statutory restrictions applicable to court-martial proceedings.

1. AMERICAN WAR CRIMES TRIBUNALS

Though military commissions of this character were used in both the Mexican and the Civil War, their employment raised no legal questions. Shortly after the Civil War had ended, however, an extraordinary use was made of the military jurisdiction over spies. It was invoked to subject those charged with responsibility for the assassination of President Lincoln to a military instead of a civilian trial. They were charged with conspiring with the leaders of the Confederacy to commit the murder. The alleged conspiracy was of course an offense against the criminal laws. It was not so prosecuted, however. Instead, it was treated as an attack by enemy agents, in violation of the laws of war, on the commander in chief, in pursuance of a conspiracy to assassinate also, among others, General Grant.

During the trial before the military commission constituted for the purpose by the Army, counsel for the accused challenged the jurdisiction of the tribunal; but the commission condemned several of the defendants to death, the remainder to confinement in military prisons. Counsel for one of those condemned to death attempted to test in the courts the jurisdiction of the commission by applying for a writ of habeas corpus; but the privilege of the writ had been suspended by the President, and the attempt failed. An application for the writ made some time later, after the suspension of the writ had been terminated, on behalf of one of the defendants serving a sentence of imprisonment was rejected by the court. No appeal appears to have been taken. The legality of this unique proceeding, the subject of much controversy, was thus in effect never passed upon by the higher courts.[3]

In both world wars, the military jurisdiction over spies and offenders against the laws of war was in a number of cases employed in the traditional manner in the actual course of military operations. In the second world war, however, it was in addition employed in several unusual cases in which the defendants sought in the courts to question the jurisdiction of the military.

Early in the war, there were apprehended in this country (and thus

---

[3] In the habeas corpus case referred to (Ex parte Mudd, Fed. Case No. 9899, 1868), if any opinion was written, it cannot be found. An elaborate opinion advising that the alleged conspirators were properly triable before a military commission for an offense against the law of war, rather than before a civilian court as accessories to murder, was rendered to President Johnson by Attorney General Speed; and this opinion is recited in Johnson's order for the creation of the military commission.

"within the lines") several members of the (German) enemy armed forces, who, on landing here by submarine, had discarded their uniforms, their alleged purpose being to spy upon our forces and installations and to commit sabotage. By order of the President as commander in chief a military commission was constituted to try them for acts contrary to the laws of war. Habeas corpus proceedings were instituted on their behalf in the federal court, their contention being that they were not subject to military jurisdiction, having been apprehended not in a zone of active military operations, but in an area in which the civil authorities and courts were freely functioning. This contention was rejected by the Supreme Court.[4] The fact that the defendants were apprehended and were to be tried in places within the control of the civilian rather than the military authorities was held to be without significance. All were executed under sentence of the military commission.

The case was notable both for its support of the military jurisdiction, and for its declaration (despite language in a proclamation issued by the President as commander in chief, purporting to deny to any enemy entering our coasts all access to the civil courts) that anyone held on American soil by a military tribunal had the right to challenge in the courts the legality of his detention.

After the war the power of the courts to inquire into the existence of jurisdiction in a military tribunal of this character was again asserted in the celebrated case of the Japanese general Yamashita, condemned to death by a military commission constituted after the cessation of hostilities by the American commander in the Philippines. The charge on which the defendant was convicted was that he had, in violation of the laws of war, while in command of the Japanese troops in the Philippines during the war, failed to take proper measures to prevent his troops from outraging the civil population. The American officers assigned to Yamashita as counsel applied to the Philippine courts for a writ of habeas corpus, their principal contention being that the specific acts charged did not constitute an offense against the laws of war and that the military commission was accordingly without jurisdiction. The Philippine courts took jurisdiction of the application, but rejected the defendant's contentions. The Philippines were at that time still an American possession, and appeal was accordingly taken to the Supreme Court of the United States, which unanimously affirmed the conclusion of the Philippine court as to its own power to hear the application; as to the jurisdiction of the military commission, the Court divided, a majority, however, sustaining that jurisdiction.[5] (The two dissenting members of the Court were further of the opinion that in habeas

---

[4] Ex parte Quirin, 317 U.S. 1 (1942).
[5] In re Yamashita, 327 U.S. 1 (1946).

corpus proceedings instituted by one convicted by a military commission, the Court should also inquire whether the accused had been accorded due process of law. Their own view was that he had not been.)

The right of one brought before a military tribunal on a charge of violation of the law of war to challenge in the courts the jurisdiction of that tribunal came before the Supreme Court in still another case. That case arose in connection with the conviction, by an American military commission in the Chinese theater, of a group of German nationals who had been connected with German forces cooperating with the Japanese in that theater, and who were charged with having, in violation of the law of war, continued hostilities after the German surrender. One of them applied for and obtained, in the courts of the District of Columbia, a writ of habeas corpus directed to the Secretary of War, as the superior of the commandant of the U.S. military prison abroad in which the petitioner was confined. Had the Supreme Court not vacated this writ, the jurisdiction of the military commission which tried the petitioner would have been litigated, his contention being that the acts charged were not violations of the law of war. A divided Court held, however, that the writ had been erroneously issued, in that an enemy alien not within our borders has no right of access to our courts. The dissenting justices strongly criticized the holding on the ground that it made the rights of the enemy alien petitioner depend on the locale in which he was (perhaps unlawfully) held in custody, a circumstance in their opinion immaterial.[6]

2. AMERICAN PARTICIPATION IN INTERNATIONAL WAR CRIMES TRIBUNALS

In addition to military commissions thus set up exclusively under American authority, in World War II there were created after the cessation of hostilities international tribunals for the trial of war crimes, through the joint action of the allied governments. Although these tribunals were in no sense part of the American legal system, a brief reference to them is perhaps relevant.

Pursuant to the so-called London Agreement of August 8, 1945, between the United States, France, the United Kingdom, and the U.S.S.R., for the prosecution and punishment of major war criminals "whose offenses have no particular geographical location," the International Military Tribunal (sitting at Nuremberg) was constituted by the act of the four-power Control Council for Germany. The act of the council creating this

---

[6] Johnson v. Eisentrager, 339 U.S. 763 (1950). The Yamashita case (see preceding note) was distinguished on the ground that the Philippines, where that case arose, were at that time still a United States possession.

tribunal declared the following to be crimes against peace, war crimes, and crimes against humanity, respectively:

(a) Crimes against peace. Namely, planning, preparation, initiation, or waging of a war of aggression or a war in violation of international treaties, agreements, or assurances, or participation in a common plan or conspiracy for the accomplishment of any of the foregoing.

(b) War crimes. Namely, violations of the laws or customs of war. Such violations shall include, but not be limited to, murder, ill treatment, or deportation to slave labor or for any other purpose of civilian population of or in occupied territories, murder or ill treatment of prisoners of war or persons on the seas, killing of hostages, plunder of public or private property, wanton destruction of cities . . . not justified by military necessity.

(c) Crimes against humanity. Namely, murder, extermination, enslavement, deportation, and other inhumane acts committed against any civilian population before or during the war or persecutions on political, racial, or religious grounds in execution of or in connection with any crime within the jurisdiction of the Tribunal, whether or not in violation of the domestic law of the country where perpetrated.[7]

None of the defendants condemned by this tribunal sought the intervention of any American court.

In Japan also, an international tribunal was created. Despite the international character of this tribunal, composed of judges appointed by each of ten allied powers, it was mistakenly believed by many to be an American tribunal, owing to the fact that the entire military command in Japan was, by agreement with our allies, in the hands of the American commander, and the occupation forces were exclusively American. An attempt by some of the defendants condemned by this tribunal to procure from the Supreme Court a review of the legality of their conviction was defeated by the holding of the Court that the tribunal was not an American but an international one and that consequently "the courts of the United States have no power or authority to review, to affirm, set aside or annul the judgments and sentences imposed."[8]

The controversial question whether the acts charged as war crimes before these international tribunals (and before the American tribunals next to be considered, set up pursuant to international agreement) were indeed crimes under concepts of international law then existing is outside the province of this volume.[9]

---

[7] 13 Dept. of State Bull., 222, 224 (1945).

[8] Hirota v. MacArthur, 338 U.S. 197 (1948). Only seven members of the Court voted; one dissented (but did not state his views). The Court could have refused jurisdiction instead on the ground adopted by it some months later, that an enemy alien abroad had no right of access to our courts. An extended account of the proceedings of the International Military Tribunal of the Far East, including a statement of the grounds for its claimed jurisdiction, is given in Robinson, Surprise Attack: Crime at Pearl Harbor and Now, 46 Amer. Bar Assn. Jour. 973, 1085 (1960).

[9] See Appleman, Military Tribunals and International Crimes (1954).

3. AMERICAN WAR CRIMES TRIBUNALS CONSTITUTED PURSUANT TO INTERNATIONAL AGREEMENT

In Germany, subsequent to the creation of the International Military Tribunal at Nuremberg, the four-power military Control Council decided that "in order to establish a uniform legal basis in Germany for the prosecution of war criminals and other similar offenders other than those dealt with by the International Military Tribunal" the offenses already enumerated, declared in the act authorizing that tribunal to be crimes against peace, war crimes, and crimes against humanity, should be regarded as such crimes also in other prosecutions; and it decreed that the tribunal by which persons charges with such offenses should be tried, and the rules of procedure to be followed, should be determined for each zone by its commander.[10]

Accordingly, several tribunals were constituted by the commander of the American Zone, to try the so-called subsequent cases of "major" war crimes. These courts were composed chiefly of judges of American state courts, appointed by the President in his capacity as commander in chief. The cases tried before them involved about 180 defendants. Of these about a third filed petitions in the Supreme Court of the United States, seeking a review of the legality of their sentences. These petitions were in every case denied without hearing (four of the justices being of opinion, however, that the question of jurisdiction was substantial enough to merit a hearing). No opinion was written; so it is impossible to say with assurance whether the ground of denial was a lack of jurisdiction in the federal courts because of the international authorization (albeit the American operation) of the military tribunals involved, or because of a lack of jurisdiction in the Supreme Court as distinguished from the inferior federal courts, or because of the view (first expressly announced in 1950, as has been seen, in a case in which application had been made to a district court by an alien held abroad under conviction by a purely American military commission) that the federal courts have no jurisdiction to issue the writ of habeas corpus on behalf of an enemy alien held abroad.[11]

One of the defendants, instead of applying to the Supreme Court, applied to the United States District Court for the District of Columbia and, repulsed by that court, appealed to the Court of Appeals. That court sustained the lower court, on the express ground that the military tribunal, despite its exclusively American control and personnel, was an international, not an American, tribunal.[12] The Supreme Court, in denying a request that it review this holding,[13] refrained, as is customary in

[10] 15 Dept. of State Bull., 862 (1946).
[11] The first of these cases decided was Milch v. U.S., 332 U.S. 789 (1947). A list of cases is given in 339 U.S. 768. For further details see Fairman, Some New Problems of the Constitution Following the Flag, 1 Stanford Law Rev. 587 (1949) from which some of the facts given in the text regarding these proceedings are drawn.

such circumstances, from any statement of its reasons. It was not long after, however, that the Court announced its holding, already noted, that non-resident enemy aliens have no right of access to the courts of the United States.

There were also constituted by the commander of the American Zone additional tribunals for the trial of "conventional" war crimes; and these tried cases involving some 1,600 defendants. Some 60 applications for review of the proceedings of these tribunals were filed in the Supreme Court of the United States. All were denied, without a statement of the grounds therefor.

In Japan, also, pursuant to agreement of the allied powers in the Far East, courts were constituted by the American command to try persons charged with war crimes. These courts, sitting at Yokohama, tried several thousand cases, none of which appears to have reached any United States court.[14]

The proceedings to punish war crimes before the American military tribunals in Germany and Japan constitute in the aggregate far the most extensive application of military justice ever undertaken. An objective analysis and evaluation of these proceedings, necessarily involving some examination of the thousands of trial records of these tribunals and of the processing of their findings and sentences by the reviewing machinery created for the purpose, still remains to be done.

[12] Flick v. Johnson, 174 F. 2d. 983 (1949).
[13] 338 U.S. 876 (1949).
[14] For an account of these proceedings see Spurlock, The Yokohama War Crimes Trials, 36 Amer. Bar Assn. Jour. 387 (1950).

22

Tribunals Constituted by Military Government in Occupied Territory

Upon the occupation of enemy territory by a victorious force, the former civil government of that territory in theory disappears, all governmental power being now vested in the commander of the occupying force. Nevertheless, the existing machinery of civil government, including the courts (as well as the laws), may be and traditionally has been kept more or less intact by the occupying power and employed by it, the military government thus confining itself chiefly to the promulgation of regulations to insure the security of the occupying forces;[1] and the military tribunals constituted to punish violations of such regulations, or other offenses against the law of war, are essentially the same as those discussed in the preceding chapter.

The civil government apparatus of the defeated enemy may, however, be found to be so disorganized that the occupation authorities may deem it desirable to supersede it to a greater or less extent by military government machinery; and tribunals may under these circumstances be constituted by the military government with extensive criminal and civil jurisdiction.

In most of the dozen or more occupations of enemy territory by American forces which have marked our history, the military government constituted has been of the limited character first described. However, during the Mexican War, the Civil War, and the Spanish-American War, military government of the more comprehensive kind was employed;[2] and during World War II, as is well known, our military government, first in

---

[1] This is the procedure prescribed by the Convention with respect to the Laws and Customs of War on Land, adopted by the First Hague Peace Conference (1899) and revised at the Second Conference (1907). 10 Encyc. Soc. Sci. 458 (1933).

[2] The military control of Puerto Rico and the jurisdiction of military government tribunals over the civilian population continued even after the annexation of the island by treaty, and until the organic act creating a civil government went into effect. Santiago v. Nogueras, 214 U.S. 260 (1909).

Italy and then in Germany, took on an unprecedentedly wide scope. The military government courts constituted in these various occupations are hardly to be regarded as part of the American system of judicature. Nevertheless, some of them present features of interest to us.

During the Civil War, military government on a wide scale was instituted in the territory of the seceded states. In some instances military governors independent of the field commanders were appointed by the President (as the military governors of Tennessee, North Carolina, and Arkansas); in others the field commanders of the Union forces set up systems of military government in the areas occupied by their troops. In Louisiana, a so-called provisional court was constituted by direct order of the President, who also appointed the judges. Subsequently Congress intervened. The territory of the seceded states was placed under military government, the commander of each of the five military districts set up being expressly authorized to create military tribunals to try offenses.[3]

In World War II in the occupation of German territory by American forces, a radical departure was made from the traditional pattern of military jurisdiction. On the ground apparently (for no official statement on the point was made) that the German judicial system, after more than a decade of totalitarian rule, was incapable of administering criminal justice according to law, a system of American military courts, known as military government courts, was constituted to try all offenses, including those against German law. Following the German surrender and the establishment of the American zone of occupation, the military government similarly established military government courts throughout the zone. These courts were given complete civil as well as criminal jurisdiction, all the German courts having been suspended. In 1948 these courts were reorganized, a process of replacement of their military members by American civilians initiated, and an appellate court constituted. A procedure compounded of the procedure of American civilian courts, American courts-martial, and German courts was formulated and eventually indeed codified and promulgated. In 1949 responsibility for the government of the American zone of occupation was transferred to a civilian, bearing the title of United States High Commissioner for Germany, the military commander being under orders to take necessary measures, on the request of the High Commissioner, for the maintenance of law and order. Thus, although the government was no longer termed "military government," it continued to be a government prescribed by the occupying

---

[3] For the tribunals constituted before the cessation of hostilities, see Carpenter, Military Government in Southern Territory, 1861–1865, 1 Amer. Hist. Assn. Annual Rept. for 1890, 467 (1891). The constitutionality of the tribunals created by the military government act of Mar. 2, 1867, was challenged before the Supreme Court, but no decision was reached, Congress having withdrawn the case from the Court's jurisdiction. See p. 325.

power, and it depended upon the continuing military occupation of the territory.

This entire episode, unique in the history of modern judicature, presents many interesting aspects. However, the life of these military government courts was short. Following the making of the peace contract with the new government of Western Germany, and the re-establishment of the German judicial system, their jurisdiction was restricted to civilian dependents of military personnel present in the American zone under military authorization; and shortly afterward they ceased to exist. Hence, detailed discussion of this purely transient phase of American judicature must be foregone.[4] One point, however, warrants mention.

In the earlier American occupations of enemy territory, the jurisdiction of the military government tribunals extended solely over the population of that territory; all American occupying personnel, including civilians attached to the military forces, responded solely to the court-martial jurisdiction of the army. In the occupation of Germany, however, the presence of large numbers of American civilians not attached to the military forces presented a new problem. Although at that time the constitutionality of the statute providing that the dependents of American military personnel accompanying them abroad were subject to court-martial jurisdiction had not yet been questioned, our military government adopted the policy of trying them by the military government courts set up for the conquered population. The curious result ensued in the occupied territory that while the members of the armed forces and civilians attached thereto (and indeed prisoners of war in the custody of the armed forces in that territory) were entitled to trial by court-martial, with all the statutory safeguards applicable to such trial (and since 1951 the right of appeal to the Court of Military Appeals in grave cases), the dependents of military personnel in the occupied territory had no right to such trial, but were subject to trial by military government courts subject to no statutory restrictions whatever. On the other hand, trial by court-martial would have meant trial by army officers exclusively, while trial by the military government courts was trial by civilian judges, all of them experienced lawyers, not a few of them judges of long experience in high state courts.

That military government courts have jurisdiction over the dependents of members of the armed forces, and that consequently the right to trial by jury and the related constitutional rights of the accused are not possessed by an American citizen arraigned before such a court, has been affirmed

---

[4] See Nobleman, American Military Government Courts in Germany, Annals Amer. Acad. Pol. and Soc. Sci. (1950); Clark and Goodman, American Justice in Occupied Germany, 36 Jour. Amer. Bar Assn. 443 (1950). For the courts established both in Germany and Italy before the cessation of hostilities, see Campbell, Some Legal Problems Arising Out of the Establishment of the Allied Military Courts in Italy, 1 Int. Law Rev. 192 (1947).

by the Supreme Court,[5] over the dissent, however, of one member, who without going so far as to say that such jurisdiction over American citizens was in itself unconstitutional, declared that the power of the President, even in his character of commander in chief, did not extend so far as to warrant the creation by him of such jurisdiction, without specific statutory authorization.

[5] Madsen v. Kinsella, 343 U.S. 341 (1952). In 1958, after the Supreme Court had rendered the first of its decisions holding unconstitutional the statutory provisions conferring on courts-martial jurisdiction of civilians in peacetime (see p. 511), the defendant in this case sought leave from the Court to file a petition for reargument; but leave was denied, no opinion being written (356 U.S. 925). In its opinions holding court-martial jurisdiction of civilians unconstitutional, the Court had drawn a distinction between the military occupation of a conquered territory (the condition prevailing during the existence of the military government courts) and the peacetime stationing of our troops abroad.

1. AWARD OF DAMAGES FOR REFUSAL TO PROCEED WITH AGREED ARBI-
TRATION. 2. ACTION BROUGHT IN BREACH OF AGREEMENT TO
ARBITRATE. 3. JUDICIAL COMPULSION TO PROCEED WITH AGREED
ARBITRATION. 4. PROCEDURE. 5. FORM OF REDRESS. 6. JUDICIAL
ENFORCEMENT OF AWARD. 7. NON-ARBITRABLE DISPUTES. 8. GROWTH
OF COMMERCIAL ARBITRATION. 9. LABOR ARBITRATION.

Over a considerable area of American business life, and in many isolated instances outside the field of business, controversies between private parties (including in that term employer and labor organizations) are adjudicated not by tribunals constituted by government, before which one party may summon the other willy-nilly, but by non-governmental tribunals constituted or accepted by agreement of both parties.

Voluntary arbitration is often spoken of as if the arbitration proceeding were a proceeding for enforcing one's legal rights—essentially the same in purpose as the proceeding before a judicial or administrative tribunal, but with less delay, expense, and publicity. But the fact is far otherwise. An agreement to submit a dispute to arbitration involves essentially an abandonment of the attempt to enforce legal rights, and a reliance instead upon the sense of fair play of the individual or individuals chosen to arbitrate the dispute. This is not to say that the arbitrator, if there appears to him to be a conflict between the strict legal rights of the parties and the essential merits of the dispute, will give no consideration to the legal rights involved: he probably will, and if he is a lawyer he almost certainly will. But in most jurisdictions he is under no obligation, legal or moral, to do so.

549

The voluntary arbitration of disputes by persons chosen by the disputants is of course as old as human society; and a regular system for the arbitration of commercial disputes has always taken root wherever a closely knit mercantile community has developed. Especially is the practice of arbitration of disputes likely to become routine among the merchants engaged in dealing in a particular class of commodities, among whom, indeed, a formal organization is very likely to be closely connected with their arbitration machinery. Such an organization, and its arbitration machinery, may indeed attain such proportions as to withdraw from the courts a considerable class of disputes—as in the case of the various securities and commodities exchanges in this country, disputes between members of a given exchange seldom reaching the courts.

Frequently, in these and other cognate situations, the accepted procedures are participated in by the parties, and the awards announced by the arbitrators are honored, quite regardless of whether any legal compulsion is possible; the sense of honor of the parties, or their desire to conserve their standing in the mercantile or professional community or, it may even be, to retain their indispensable membership in the mercantile or professional exchange or association, suffices without any legal sanction.

The present chapter concerns itself, by contrast, with voluntary arbitration in a more restricted sense—voluntary in the sense that the parties have voluntarily agreed to arbitrate, and to be bound by the resulting award; but involuntary in that if at some later point one of the parties either declines to proceed with the arbitration or, the arbitration having proceeded to an award, declines to honor the award, the courts may be invoked to come to the aid of the aggrieved party. The extent to which the courts will in either case do so is the essential question to be considered.

1. AWARD OF DAMAGES FOR REFUSAL TO PROCEED WITH AGREED ARBITRATION

If parties have agreed to submit an existing dispute to arbitration, but one of the parties thereafter refuses to proceed (as by refusing to nominate an arbitrator as required by the agreement, or the arbitrators having been named, by refusing to submit his evidence to them, or at any point before an award has been made by announcing his refusal to proceed) he is, under traditional doctrines, liable in damages to the other party as for any breach of contract. The difficulty, however, of establishing any substantial damage makes this remedy of theoretical rather than practical value; and except in jurisdictions which have developed the more effective remedy, shortly to be discussed, of compelling the arbitration to proceed, a party to an arbitration agreement of this character may in effect thus dishonor it with impunity.

Even this remedy of damages, be it noted, is available under traditional doctrines only where the dispute agreed to be submitted to the arbitrators is already in existence when the agreement is made. A provision in a contract to submit to arbitration disputes which may thereafter arise under the contract was traditionally held not to be enforceable even to the extent of an award of damages for refusal to proceed. The curious rationale of this doctrine is that an agreement in advance to submit any future dispute to arbitration attempts to bind the parties not to resort to the courts, and is in consequence contrary to public policy.

By statutes enacted in some fifteen states, beginning with the New York statute of 1920, and by a statute enacted in 1926 applicable to the federal courts, an agreement to arbitrate future disputes is now in the courts of those jurisdictions on the same footing as an agreement to submit an existing dispute to arbitration; and as will shortly appear, these statutes have provided, in the case of either type of agreement, new and effective remedies.[1] Even in the absence of statute, the state courts have increasingly abandoned the doctrine that a contract to arbitrate future disputes is void.

2. ACTION BROUGHT IN BREACH OF AGREEMENT TO ARBITRATE

Where an agreement has been entered into, in proper form, to arbitrate an existing dispute, and one of the parties to the agreement, in disregard thereof, institutes action on the dispute, the courts will on application stay the prosecution of the action, or, in a proper case, dismiss it. Where traditional doctrines in this field still hold sway, the courts in a number of jurisdictions will not, however, lend their aid in this way to an agreement to arbitrate a future dispute; but under all the modern statutes referred to, an agreement to arbitrate a dispute that may arise in the future receives the same enforcement in this respect as does one relating to an existing dispute.

3. JUDICIAL COMPULSION TO PROCEED WITH AGREED ARBITRATION

Conformably to traditional doctrines, the courts long refused to compel a party to choose his arbitrator as required by an arbitration agreement (even where the agreement concerned an existing dispute), and refused to enjoin him from withdrawing from participation in the arbitration proceeding. The rationale of this latter refusal, stemming from a dictum of

---

[1] Modern statutes are now found in Arizona, California, Connecticut, Florida, Hawaii, Illinois, Louisiana, Massachusetts, Michigan, Minnesota, New Hampshire, New Jersey, New York, Ohio, Oregon, Pennsylvania, Rhode Island, Washington, Wisconsin and Wyoming.

Lord Coke in the first decade of the seventeenth century, was founded on the seemingly irrelevant principle that one may at any time revoke the authority of one's agent; but despite the precariousness of its reasoning, the doctrine until recent decades commanded almost unanimous obedience from our courts and is still applied in a number of states.

By contrast, the modern arbitration statutes provide effective measures for insuring that the arbitration shall proceed as agreed, notwithstanding the recalcitrance of one of the parties; and some state courts have reached similar results more or less completely without the aid of modern statutes. If the agreement provides, as is common, that both sides shall each choose an arbitrator (who shall jointly choose a third) and one party fails within the time agreed to make his nomination, the court will order him to do so within a specified time, on pain of having the court appoint one instead. If the two arbitrators fail to appoint the third (often referred to as the umpire) the court will on application do so, and will similarly where necessary fix a date for the hearing before the arbitrators. Any other obstruction of the proceedings by one of the parties may similarly be removed by the court.

Jurisdiction of recalcitrant

Unless the party allegedly recalcitrant is within the jurisdiction of the court in such fashion that notice of an application to the court may be served upon him or it in a manner similar to that required for service of a summons in an action in personam, the court must be able to find (consistently with the principles of prior consent to jurisdiction discussed in connection with civil proceedings generally) that by the terms of the arbitration agreement he consented to the jurisdiction, so that notice of the application to the court may then be given by one or another of the conventional methods for the service of process outside the jurisdiction (personal service, mail, etc.). Not always does an arbitration agreement express in unambiguous terms the consent of the absent party to the jurisdiction of the court; and troublesome questions have consequently arisen in the construction of agreements in this respect.

When the court to which application is made for aid in compelling the recalcitrant to proceed decides that, despite the failure to serve notice within the jurisdiction and the failure of the respondent to appear in opposition to the application, it nevertheless has jurisdiction, it orders the arbitration to proceed in the respondent's absence. Should an attempt subsequently be made to enforce the resulting award in another jurisdiction (most likely the respondent's own jurisdiction), the court in that jurisdiction may be required to pass anew on the question whether the court which ordered the arbitration to proceed did indeed have jurisdiction of the respondent. In short, the problem here is substantially identical with that presented to a court asked to enforce a judgment rendered in another jurisdiction; for an arbitration award, as will shortly appear, is, for enforcement purposes, convertible into a judgment of the court. Presumably, the difficult questions of due process and full faith and credit which have been presented to the Supreme Court in connection with judgments in civil proceedings emanating from courts whose jurisdiction is attacked, will in due course be presented to it in connection with judgments confirming arbitration awards, for such cases have in recent years made their appearance in other courts. With the current increase of arbitration provisions in contracts arising out of foreign trade, there will presumably be a corresponding increase also in cognate questions of the jurisdiction of our courts, under the terms of particular arbitration agreements, to compel arbitration here against foreign parties; and of foreign courts, to compel arbitration abroad against American parties. The continuing efforts of international trade organizations to extend the use of standard forms of arbitration clause in contracts of international trade will doubtless greatly assist in the solution of these jurisdictional problems.

Issues presented on application to compel arbitration

The court's jurisdiction of the recalcitrant party being assumed, he may raise other objections which, unless overruled, will preclude action by the court. Thus it may be contended that the agreement to arbitrate was not in fact made, or was not made by properly authorized persons, or in the manner required by the statute (which typically calls for a writing, and in some instances, with certain formalities). It may be contended that there has in fact been no refusal to proceed, or that the adverse party's appointment of his arbitrators, or the selection of the third arbitrator by the two appointed by the parties, was not in accordance with the agreement. On issues of fact presented by such contentions the statutes typically give the parties the right to jury trial. A final contention may be that the dispute whose arbitration the petitioner seeks to compel is not of the kind contemplated by the agreement, or if it is, is not of the kind that the statute embraces—a point shortly to be discussed.

4. PROCEDURE

There may be a single arbitrator, or a board, depending on the agreement. The three-man board, one member chosen by each of the two parties, the two so chosen in turn selecting the third, long a standard type of arbitration tribunal in commercial arbitrations not conducted by trade associations, is giving way to a completely impartial tribunal, whether of three or one. In the account of arbitral procedure which follows, it will be assumed, for simplicity, that there is a single arbitrator.

The arbitrator himself determines the procedure he shall follow, subject, however, to any rules of procedure that may have been adopted by the parties by previous agreement. Arbitration clauses in standard forms of contract employed in particular trades usually provide that arbitration proceedings shall be conducted according to the rules of the trade organization. A code of procedure fomulated by the American Arbitration Association is frequently adopted by the arbitration agreement.

None of the provisional remedies or the pretrial procedures found in civil litigation—in particular, the examination before trial—is an accepted feature of arbitral procedure. Such procedures are found if at all only where the parties have expressly stipulated for them. Under some statutes, however, the party initiating the arbitration may in an appropriate case proceed against the property of the other party as if the dispute were to be adjudicated by judicial instead of arbitral proceedings.[2]

That the parties may, in the absence of express provision in the agreement or the adopted rules, be represented by attorney is now the prevailing view of the courts, and is in some states expressly provided. Earlier views to the contrary have been generally abandoned, experience having shown that in arbitral as in judicial proceedings a party may be so wanting in the ability to order and present the evidence on his side that to deny him the assistance of counsel is to deny him justice—particularly if the other party, perhaps a corporation, is represented by an officer experienced in such proceedings (who may indeed be a member of the bar, though appearing in the ostensible character of a business executive).

The modern (and some of the older) statutes require the courts to compel the attendance of witnesses and the production of papers before the arbitrator, where his request therefor, by subpoena, is not complied with voluntarily.

The arbitrator may, unlike the judge or juror, rely on his own special knowledge of the customs of the trade, or of other specialized matters involved; it is not necessary, as it is in a judicial proceeding, to introduce evidence on such matters (or, in the alternative, an agreed statement of fact.) Nor is the arbitrator bound by the exclusionary rules of evidence applied in a judicial trial; he may receive any evidence he deems relevant. The wide discretion allowed the arbitrator in this respect has on occasion been abused to such an extent that the court has been constrained, on its aid being subsequently invoked to enforce the resulting award, to declare the arbitrator guilty of misconduct.

Under traditional American (as contrasted with English) doctrine, the

[2] Thus under the federal act (Sec. 9), if the dispute arises out of a claim cognizable in admiralty, the claimant may, despite the arbitration agreement, institute a proceeding in court for the purpose of seizing the vessel or other property, and the arbitration then proceeds, the court retaining jurisdiction to enter its decree upon the award.

arbitrator is not required, as is the judge, to apply (or indeed even to ascertain) legal doctrines governing the rights of the parties; he may be guided merely by his intuitive sense of justice. In general, arbitration statutes have accepted and confirmed this traditional doctrine. In a few states, however, the statute has in effect imposed upon the arbitrator the obligation to apply the settled law. This it has done by permitting the court, upon being applied to for aid in enforcing the arbitrator's award, to set aside or modify it if repugnant to law; and in at least one state the arbitrator's award is in effect a report to the court, to be acted upon by the court in the light of the applicable law[3]

5. FORM OF REDRESS

There is no requirement, either traditional or statutory, that the arbitration agreement specify the form of redress to be awarded by the arbitrators; and even agreements submitting an existing dispute to arbitration seldom do so. The arbitrator thus has a freer hand in shaping the form of the redress he will grant than does a court in a like controversy, restricted as it is both by the form of redress requested by the plaintiff in his initial pleading, and by traditional and statutory limitations on the forms of redress it may grant. Thus, in a dispute arising out of the discharge of an employee, the court may under traditional doctrine be powerless to order his reinstatement, but may only award damages, payable in a lump sum. By contrast the arbitrator may order the employee's reinstatement, or may order the payment of damages in weekly installments until the employee secures other employment, or may combine the several possible forms of redress in part, or in the alternative, in any way that seems to him just. Even a court enjoying equitable jurisdiction hardly possesses so wide a discretion in shaping the remedy as does the arbitrator; and the aid of such a court is not available, as has been seen, in the ordinary run of disputes.

6. JUDICIAL ENFORCEMENT OF AWARD

If an award is not complied with, application is made to the court to compel compliance. An award of a sum of money is readily converted by the court into a money judgment. Other types of award require other forms of judgment; and a court may thus find itself in the position of granting, in enforcement of an arbitration award, a form of redress which (as in the case just suggested) it would have declared itself incapable of

[3] The state is Massachusetts. In Illinois the arbitrator may state his award in the form of a conclusion of fact for the opinion of the court on questions of law, the court thereupon making the final award.

granting in a judicial proceeding arising out of the same facts; and if the appropriate redress be a judgment in personam, it will be enforceable by contempt proceedings.[4]

In connection with an application to the court for enforcement of an award, there may, as already pointed out, arise difficult questions of the jurisdiction of the court to grant judicial redress against the non-complier—questions which may be renewed should the attempt be made to enforce the judgment in another jurisdiction.

The jurisdiction of the court being assumed, various kinds of objection to the enforcement of the award may be urged; but not all may be within the power of the court to consider. On this vital point, there is much divergence between one jurisdiction and another, depending on whether the arbitration was had under traditional doctrine or under statutory authority, and if under statutory authority, on the particular provisions of the governing statute.

Under all statutes, the court will refuse to lend its aid if it appears that the dispute passed upon by the arbitrators is not of the character contemplated by the statute—a point shortly to be considered. Moreover, the statutes generally give as grounds for refusing to confirm the award that the award was procured by fraud, corruption, or other unfair means, that there was evident partiality in the arbitrators or either of them, that they refused to postpone the hearing, upon sufficient cause shown, or refused to hear material evidence, or exceeded their powers or so imperfectly executed them that a final and definite award upon the subject matter submitted to them was not made.

Some statutes, however, as already noted, go much beyond this and require the court to refuse enforcement where the award is contrary to law. In states where the statute does not so require, however, the courts have consistently refused to review the arbitrator's award, even when concerned solely with what would, in a judicial proceeding, be regarded as purely a question of law—such as the meaning of the language of a contract.

A further ground for refusing to enforce an award which has been taken by some courts is that the award is contrary to public policy. This doctrine has been invoked particularly in cases in which the arbitrator, after assessing against a party a sum calculated to compensate the other party for the damage suffered, adds an additional sum as a penalty or punishment—a result traditionally abhorred by our law in civil disputes (though authorized by statute in certain special cases).

---

[4] In at least one case, a recalcitrant employer who had been ordered by the arbitration award, subsequently converted into a judgment, to reinstate a discharged employe was ordered jailed by the court until he purged himself of his contempt of the court by complying with the judgment.

7. NON-ARBITRABLE DISPUTES

At several points in the foregoing, reference was made to the necessity for a determination by the court whether the dispute agreed to be arbitrated may not be of such a nature that the court must refuse its aid in enforcing the agreement to arbitrate.

Only one arbitration statute—the federal—limits the subject matter of the dispute to which an enforceable arbitration agreement may relate. The arbitration of disputes arising out of a "maritime transaction" or a transaction involving interstate or foreign commerce,[5] but none other, may be compelled by the federal courts. Moreover, an agreement to arbitrate even such a dispute may be enforced by a federal court only if that court would have had jurisdiction of an action arising out of such dispute.[6]

A number of the state statutes, in varying language, exclude from their application any dispute which could not be the subject of an action; and the same as just seen is in effect true of the federal statute. Under such statutes, where parties who desire to contract with one another are unable to agree upon the terms of their contract, their inability to agree does not constitute an arbitrable dispute, since such inability to agree cannot in the nature of the case be the subject of an action. Hence, an agreement between two such parties that a third party shall make their agreement for them is held by some courts not to be enforceable under such statutes, either by way of compelling the hearings before the third party to proceed, or by way of enforcing the award made by the third party. This doctrine obviously places grave limitations on the power of the courts to enforce the award of an arbitrator chosen to fix the terms of an employer-union contract, when direct negotiations between the parties have become deadlocked.

For similar reasons, some courts have held that compliance with provisions in contracts that price or value shall at some future time be fixed by appraisers cannot be compelled under such statutes. In some states, however, the statute is expressly made applicable to such agreements.

A type of dispute which, though not expressly excluded by the statutes, the courts have in several cases declared not subject to arbitration, is one

[5] Disputes arising out of commerce within the District of Columbia or a territory are also included.

[6] The act expressly provides that it shall not apply "to contracts of employment" (9 U.S. Code, Sec. 1). However, Congress in 1947 conferred on the federal courts jurisdiction of "suits for violation of contracts between an employer and a labor organization representing employes" in industries affecting interstate or foreign commerce (see p. 185); and the Supreme Court has held that this enactment in effect repeals the prohibition contained in the arbitration statute, so that the federal courts may enforce arbitration provisions in collective bargaining contracts. Textile Workers Union v. Lincoln Mills, 353 U.S. 448 (1957). An arbitration provision in a contract between a single employee and his employer is presumably still unenforceable in the federal courts.

concerning the custody of children. In a judicial proceeding involving the custody of a child, the court, it is said, does not sit merely as an umpire between the disputants; it sits also, and indeed primarily, as a guardian, on behalf of the state, of the welfare of the child. Thus, once it has assumed jurisdiction of such a dispute in the course of a judicial proceeding the court will not permit it, as in other civil cases, to be settled by agreement of the contending parties on any terms they see fit; it will scrutinize the agreement to insure that the welfare of the child is fully protected. Such being the function of the court in such a controversy, it cannot be assumed, the courts have said, that it was the intention of the statute to permit the disputants to displace the court as the agent of the state and appoint a private party of their own choosing to act for the state in safeguarding the interests of the child.

8. GROWTH OF COMMERCIAL ARBITRATION

The role of trade associations and exchanges in imposing upon their members arbitral rather than judicial adjudication of intermember disputes has already been mentioned. The formation of such associations in trades formerly unorganized continues apace, and with it a corresponding substitution of arbitral for judicial processes in such disputes.

The trade association tends to promote arbitration also, however, in quite a different field—that of disputes between members and non-members, or more realistically between members and their customers. This it does by furnishing its members with a standard form of contract, to be used by them in their dealings with their customers, in which is included a provision for arbitration of all disputes which may arise under the contract. Needless to say, such a provision often passes unnoticed— particularly when appearing at the foot of a sales memorandum, or among a multitude of other provisions in such an instrument as a warehouse receipt. The courts, nevertheless, generally hold such a provision binding on the customer, and will refuse jurisdiction should he seek judicial redress for an alleged breach of the contract.[7]

The justice of holding the customer to have waived his right to judicial redress by the mere acceptance of a standard form memorandum issued to him by a seller presumably thoroughly familiar with its provisions may well be questioned.[8] Particularly, however, may a question be raised where

---

[7] Indeed, in a few cases, the customer has been held to an arbitration clause, of which he alleges he was not aware, contained not in the sales memorandum issued to him, but in a standard form of sales agreement stated in that memorandum to be a "part" thereof. Cf. Brookside Mills, Inc. v. Avon Converting Co., 191 F. 2d 905 (1951); Level Export Corp. v. Wolz, Aiken & Co., 305 N.Y. 82 (1953). These cases represent, however, the exception rather than the rule.

[8] Conceivably, there is a case for legislation requiring that in contract memoranda prepared and issued unilaterally, arbitration clauses appear separately from all other

the effect of the inconspicuous provision is not merely to substitute arbitral for judicial procedures, but to subject the recipient to the jurisdiction of an arbitration proceeding likely to be weighted against him. Such a result is probable where the provision recites that the arbitration is to be had pursuant to the rules of the trade association responsible for the standard form of contract, of which association the seller is presumably a member. The arbitration rules of the association when examined are more than likely to provide for participation of the association in the selection of the arbitrators (if it does not indeed provide that the association's own arbitration committee shall be the arbitrator), and to require the tribunal to take cognizance of the usages of the trade—in contrast to the rule applied by the courts that trade usages are binding, in the absence of proof of knowledge, only on those in the trade.

Even where the dispute to be arbitrated is between members of the trade, the problem of insuring an impartial tribunal is sometimes a difficult one. The arbitrators are, typically, members of the trade; indeed the fact that they are, and are thus familiar with the usages and the technology of the trade, is admittedly one of the chief advantages which the arbitral tribunal possesses over the judicial. But members of the trade are likely to have had past dealings with one or the other of the parties; more important, there is always the possibility or even the probability of future dealings with either party. Under these circumstances that disputant whose goodwill in the trade is more to be valued than the other's is likely to be the beneficiary of a partiality, however subconscious, on the part of the arbitrators.

The extent to which arbitration has supplanted litigation in commercial disputes cannot readily be determined, though various estimates, constructed on somewhat precarious premises, have been made.[9] The chief reasons advanced for the preference shown by the business com-

---

provisions, in characters of a prescribed minimum size, etc. There is precedent for such legislation in statutes fixing such requirements for automatic renewal clauses in residential leases, etc.

[9] Aside from the impossibility of gathering complete data, there is the difficulty of distinguishing true arbitrations of disputes from the process, carried on in many trade organizations, of referring to a disinterested member of the trade differences between buyer and seller as to the commercial grade in which a particular lot of merchandise falls. The third party acts here not as an arbitrator, but rather as a grader, a type of expert provided by the government in connection with the marketing of certain agricultural commodities. The magnitude of the arbitration process in certain industries is indicated by the operations under the "Inter-Company Arbitration Agreement," to which some hundreds of the country's insurance companies have subscribed since its formulation in 1955. Under this agreement the signatory companies agree to arbitrate claims against each other arising out of insurance losses. In 1957, nearly fifteen thousand claims were disposed of through the extensive arbitration machinery set up under this agreement. See Demer, 270 Insurance Companies Arbitrate Inter-Company Claims, 42 Jour. Amer. Judicature Soc. 92 (1958).

munity for the arbitral tribunal are economy, expertness, privacy, speed, and finality.[10] All these advantages are undoubtedly present. It is worth considering to what extent they are inherent in the arbitral as compared to the judicial process, and to what extent they reflect the failure of the judicial process to adjust itself to the needs of modern business.

The economy of arbitration proceedings to the parties is associated in part with the absence of lawyers, and in part with the finality of the award—a point to be reverted to. The growing tendency to employ lawyers in commercial arbitration has tended to reduce its advantage in cost. Speed is, again, not inherently greater in arbitration, but rather the reflection of the inefficient organization of the courts, which under a proper procedure and organization should be capable of functioning as swiftly as does an arbitral tribunal. Expertness equal to that possible in an arbitral tribunal would be attainable in the courts only through the use of expert referees—a procedure often suggested but nowhere yet adopted. Privacy also is readily attainable in judicial proceedings, through appropriate changes in court rules, as the existing judicial practice in certain classes of proceedings amply demonstrates; the dominant fetish of the full publicity of all judicial proceedings against the wishes of the parties calls for re-examination.

The finality of an award in arbitration (assuming it is not followed by a court contest over the enforcement of the award) cannot be equaled by a judgment rendered by a court; for from the latter an appeal is always possible. Only if the parties stipulated in advance that the judgment of the court of first instance should be final could the judicial compete with the arbitral proceeding in finality. Under such circumstances it could indeed surpass the arbitral proceeding in finality, since in its judgment are merged also all those legal questions which in an arbitral proceeding may be used as a basis for judicial intervention to delay or nullify the award.

There is, however, a certain unreality about a comparison of arbitral and judicial proceedings on the purely procedural level. Such a comparison necessarily omits from consideration the difference in the attitude of the parties in the two types of proceeding. Virtually every commercial dispute which reaches the courts could have been disposed of by arbitration had the parties desired it.[11] The fact that it has reached a judicial tribunal usually evidences that one, or it may be both, of the parties are

[10] In the small claims division of the New York City Civil Court, the parties are urged, in order to avoid lengthy waits in court for their cases to be reached, to agree to arbitration forthwith by one of a panel of unpaid arbitrators, members of the bar of extended experience, who have volunteered for this service. In a majority of cases, the parties elect arbitration.

[11] A trustee or other fiduciary may, however, be without power to submit to arbitration a claim on behalf of or against the fund with the care of which he is entrusted.

in an intransigent mood, rejecting that spirit of conciliation which so often conduces to speed and finality in arbitration proceedings. In short, in the commercial field litigation is, to a far greater extent than arbitration, concerned with the bitter-end residue rather than the staple of business disagreements. It would perhaps be fair to say that each method is best adapted to the type of commercial dispute that characteristically comes before it.[12]

9. LABOR ARBITRATION

The use of the arbitrator, so called, in labor-management disputes occurs in two quite different settings. The one is akin to commercial arbitration—the adjudication of disputes arising out of a contract between a union and an employer. The other setting is virtually unknown to commercial arbitration. Here there is no contract between the parties, but only a common desire on their part to arrive at a contract, coupled with an inability to reach an agreement on its terms, resulting, finally, in their empowering a third party—miscalled an arbitrator—to fix the terms of their future contract for them. Such an "arbitrator" is, as pointed out in an earlier connection, not a judge, but a legislator. Consideration of his role thus falls outside the scope of this volume.

Even in the first setting, the situation confronting the labor arbitrator is ordinarily quite different from that encountered in commercial arbitration. The commercial transaction out of which a dispute has arisen has characteristically been completed or terminated before the arbitration begins; and even if the arbitration concerns something still to be done, it can ordinarily be accomplished with a minimum of contact between the parties. In a labor arbitration, by contrast, the contract between the parties is ordinarily still subsisting, and may indeed have many months to run, during all of which time the parties must continue in daily collaboration in the employer's business. The particular dispute before the arbitrator may concern only one employee (as in the cases of alleged wrongful discharge which bulk so large in labor arbitration) or working conditions affecting only a small group of employees. In this setting there develops a tendency for the labor arbitrator to regard himself as not merely or perhaps even primarily an impersonal judge of facts, and to think of his task rather as that of conciliation, or at any rate as being a compound of adjudication and conciliation, the dictates of justice in the particular case being qualified by the larger consideration of the need

[12] Still another class of disputes in which one of the parties is likely to reject arbitration arises out of situations in which the facts are not in dispute, but there is disagreement as to the legal result of the facts. A party who believes that the law is entirely on his side will see no reason for submitting the controversy to an arbitrator's intuitive sense of justice.

for conserving an atmosphere in which collaboration can proceed. That such a conception of the arbitrator's role can in the long run only impair the value of the arbitration process is the prevailing, though not the unanimous, view of those in the field.

As is well known, the questions of construction and application of their contract which may arise between union and management in the day-to-day operation of a vast industrial enterprise are so numerous, and call for such speedy resolution, that resort to the courts, while theoretically possible, would be quite out of the question as a practical matter. In such a situation resort has been had to a standing arbitrator, who thus becomes in effect a part of the administrative machinery of the industry.[13]

In the field of labor arbitration there has presented itself, in a different context, a difficulty in securing impartial arbitrators akin to that already noticed in connection with commercial arbitration. The difficulty here is that each arbitral award is capable of being regarded as a victory for either labor or management; as such it tends to affect the favor in which the arbitrator is held by those union officials and those management executives in whose hands rests the choice or veto in the selection of arbitrators in this field. The professional labor arbitrator—and there are many such, depending for the whole or a substantial part of their income on their services in labor arbitrations—is thus under a strong temptation to consider how his decision will affect his standing with one or the other group—a consideration the impropriety of which needs no emphasis. It might be thought that in this situation the arbitrator would from self-interest, if from no higher motive, resolve on complete and impersonal impartiality as least likely to alienate either side. Some of those familiar with the field, however, relate that such is by no means the invariable result; and suggestions have been heard that the professional labor arbitrator should in effect be abolished, by the acceptance on all hands of the principle that the employment of any arbitrator (other than as standing arbitrator) in more than a given number of labor arbitrations in a given period be considered improper. Others contest these views, asserting that any arbitrator who allows considerations of self-interest to affect his decisions soon disqualifies himself quite effectively.

[13] Under the Railway Labor Act (45 U.S. Code, Secs. 151 ff.) there was established in 1934 an elaborate machinery for arbitration of disputes between railway management and labor "growing out of grievances or out of the interpretation or application of agreements concerning rates of pay, rules or working conditions." Awards are enforceable by the federal courts. This system of what is in effect compulsory arbitration of disputes was created by statute following the failure of an earlier voluntary system. Kroner, Minor Disputes Under the Railway Labor Act: A Critical Appraisal, 47, N.Y.U. Law Rev. 41 (1962). In disputes as to the making of a new agreement, the act does not provide for arbitration, but only for mediation.

Appendix A. *Selected References*

The following list is selective only.

Developments subsequent to the publication of the works listed may be traced in the *Annual Survey of American Law,* published since 1942.

The *Encyclopedia of Social Sciences* (1930–1934) has several score articles which in the aggregate touch on substantially every phase of the American legal system. (Lists of these articles are given in vol. 15, pp. 548 ff., captioned Administration of Justice, Crime, Jurisprudence, and Legal Relations.) For a definitive review of the decisions of the Supreme Court, the best source is Corwin (ed.), *The Constitution of the United States of America. Analysis and Interpretation* (1953). For state constitutions, see *Index-Digest of State Constitutions* (2nd Ed., 1959).

PART I. THE COURTS

American Bar Association (Section of Judicial Administration), *The Improvement of the Administration of Justice, a Handbook,* 4th ed. (1961).

Aumann, *The Instrumentalities of Justice* (1956).

Berman, *The Nature and Functions of Law* (1958).

Kinnane, *Anglo-American Law,* 2nd ed. (1952).

Klein, *Judicial Administration and the Legal Profession* (1963).

(A voluminous classified bibliography, invaluable in searching the periodical literature and the innumerable pamphlet publications in this field.)

Murphy and Pritchett, *Court, Judges and Politics* (1960).

Paulsen, *Legal Institutions Today and Tomorrow* (1959).

Shartel, *Our Legal System and How it Operates* (1951).

Vanderbilt (ed.), *Minimum Standards of Judicial Administration* (1949). This work is unique in bringing together detailed data regarding a number of aspects of judicial organization and procedure in all the states.

Willoughby, *Principles of Judicial Administration* (1929).

1. THE DUAL JUDICIAL POWER

Harris, *The Judicial Power of the United States* (1940).

Hart and Wechsler, *The Federal Courts and the Federal System* (1953).

Wagner, *The Federal States and their Judiciary* (1959).

2. CRIMINAL PROCEEDINGS: BASIC ASPECTS

Allen, "The Supreme Court, Federalism and State Systems of Criminal Justice," 8 University of Chicago *Law School Record* 3, (1958).

Beaney, *The Right to Counsel in American Courts* (1955).

Fellman. *The Defendant's Rights* (1958).
Mayers, *Shall We Amend the Fifth Amendment?* (1959).
McGuire, *The Evidence of Guilt* (1959).

The most complete review of the history and rationale of the privilege against self-incrimination is in Wigmore, *A Treatise on the Anglo-American System of Evidence,* (McNaughton, rev. 1961) Secs. 2263 ff.

A series of ten pamphlets, *Problems in Criminal Law and its Administration,* Paulsen (ed.) issued by the Joint Committee on Continuing Legal Education of the American Law Institute and the The American Bar Association in 1961–1962, deals with a number of basic problems.

3. CRIMINAL PROCEEDINGS: INVESTIGATION

Inbau and Reid, *Criminal Interrogation and Confession* (1962).
Moley, *Politics and Criminal Prosecution* (1929).
National Commission on Law Observance and Enforcement, *Reports* (1931), No. 11, *Lawlessness in Law Enforcement;* No. 14, *Police.*
Orfield, *Criminal Procedure from Arrest to Appeal* (1947).
Ottenberg, *The Federal Investigators* (1962).
Puttkammer, *Administration of Criminal Law* (1953).
Smith, *Arrest, Search and Seizure* (1959).
Sowle (ed.), *Police Power and Individual Freedom* (1962).
U. S. Commission on Civil Rights, *Report* (1961), Book 5, *Justice;* and *The Fifty States Report* (1961).
Varon, *Searches, Seizures and Immunities* (1961).

Surveys of crime and of local police methods and administration have been published in several states.

4. CRIMINAL PROCEEDINGS: PROSECUTION

American Bar Association Commission on Organized Crime, *Organized Crime and Law Enforcement* (1952).
American Law Institute, *Code of Criminal Procedure* (1928–1931).
Dession, *Criminal Law Administration and Public Order* (1948). (Contains much material excerpted works not readily available.)
Donnelly, Goldstein and Schwartz, *Criminal Law* (1962).
Law and Contemporary Problems, Vol. 23 (1959).
Moreland, *Modern Criminal Procedure* (1959).
National Commission on Law Observance and Enforcement, *Reports* (1931), No. 4, *Prosecution;* No. 8, *Criminal Procedure.*
Orfield, *Criminal Appeals in America* (1939).
———, *Criminal Procedure from Arrest to Appeal* (1947).
Pound, *Criminal Justice in America* (1930).
Puttkammer, *Administration of Criminal Law* (1953).
Tappan, *Crime, Justice and Correction* (1960).

7. CIVIL PROCEEDINGS: PROCEDURE

Blume, *American Civil Procedure* (1955).
Frank, *Courts on Trial* (1949).
Joiner, *Civil Justice and the Jury* (1962).
Karlen, *Appellate Courts in the United States and England* (1963).
———, *Primer of Procedure* (1952).
Millar, *Civil Procedure of the Trial Court: Historical Perspective* (1952).
Pound, *Appellate Procedure in Civil Cases* (1948).

9. THE COURTS AS A CHECK ON INVESTIGATION

Barth, *Government by Investigation* (1956).
Beck, *Contempt of Congress* (1960).
Eberling, *Congressional Investigations* (1928).
Taylor, *Grand Inquest* (1955).

10. THE COURTS AS A CHECK ON LEGISLATION

Black, *The People and the Court* (1960).
Cahn (ed.), *Supreme Court and Supreme Law* (1954).
————, *The Great Rights* (1963). (Four lectures by justices of the Supreme Court:
 Black, Brennan, Douglas, and Warren)
Crosskey, *Politics and the Constitution in the History of the United States* (1953).
Freund, *The Supreme Court of the United States* (1961).
Frank, *The Marble Palace* (1958).
Hand, *The Bill of Rights* (1958).
Haines, *The Role of the Supreme Court in American Government and Politics* (1944–
 1957).
Hook, *The Paradoxes of Freedom* (1962).
Mason, *The Supreme Court: Palladium of Freedom* (1962).
McCloskey, *The American Supreme Court* (1960).
Mendelson, *The Constitution and the Supreme Court* (1959).
Pritchett, *Congress versus the Supreme Court, 1957–1960* (1961).
Rostow, *The Sovereign Prerogative* (1962).
Warren, *The Supreme Court in United States History*, rev. ed. (1935).

11. THE COURTS AS MOLDERS OF THE LAW

Association of American Law Schools, *Essays in Anglo-American Legal History*
 (1907).
Aumann, *The Changing American Legal System: Some Selected Phases* (1940).
Cardozo, *The Nature of the Judicial Process* (1921).
————, *The Growth of the Law* (1924).
Gray, *The Nature and Sources of Law,* 2nd ed. (1921).
Hurst, *The Growth of American Law: The Law Makers* (1950).
————, *Law and the Social Process in United States History* (1960).
Kempin, *Legal History: Law and Social Change* (1963).
Law: A Century of Progress, 1835–1935 (1937).
Levi, *An Introduction to Legal Reasoning* (1949).
Plucknett, *A Concise History of the Common Law,* (3rd ed. (1940).
Zelemyer, *The Process of Legal Reasoning* (1963).

12. COURT ORGANIZATION AND THE ADMINISTRATION OF JUSTICE

American Bar Association (Section of Judicial Administration), *The Improvement of
 the Administration of Justice, a Handbook,* 4th ed. (1961).
Elliott, *Improving Our Courts* (1959).
Vanderbilt (ed.), *Minimum Standards of Judicial Administration* (1949).

13. THE PERSONNEL OF THE COURTS: JUDGES, JURORS, AND LAWYERS

Association of American Law Schools, *Select Readings on the Legal Profession* (1962).
Bruce, *The American Judge* (1924).
Blaustein and Porter, *The American Lawyer* (1954).
Council of State Governments, *The Book of the States* (published biennially).

Drinker, *Legal Ethics* (1953).
Haynes, *The Selection and Tenure of Judges* (1944).
Moley, *Politics and Criminal Prosecution* (1929).
Pound, *The Lawyer from Antiquity to Modern Times* (1953).
Warren, *A History of the American Bar* (1911).

Part II. ADMINISTRATIVE TRIBUNALS AND THEIR SUPERVISION BY THE COURTS

Attorney General's Committee on Administrative Procedure, *Report* and *Monographs* (1941).
Attorney General's Manual on the Administrative Procedure Act (1947).
Chamberlain, Dowling, and Hayes, *The Judicial Function in Federal Administrative Agencies* (1942).
Cushman, *The Independent Regulatory Commissions* (1941).
Davis, *Administrative Law Treatise* (1958).
Gellhorn, *Federal Administrative Proceedings* (1941).
Pound, *Administrative Law: Its Growth, Procedure and Significance* (1942).
President's Committee on Administrative Management, *Report* (1937).
Schwartz, *American Administrative Law* (1950).
———, *Le droit administratif américain* (1952). (These two monographs, written primarily for British and French readers respectively, contain much valuable comparative material.)
United States Commission on the Organization of the Executive Branch, *Task Force Report on Legal Services and Procedure* (1955).

16. PERMISSIONS AND GRANTS

Gellhorn, *Individual Freedom and Governmental Restraints* (1956).
Gordon and Rosenfield, *Immigration Law and Procedure* (1959).
Konvitz, *Civil Rights in Immigration* (1953).
Lowenstein (ed.), *The Alien and the Immigration Law* (1957).

17. THE ADJUDICATION OF PRIVATE DISPUTES

Dodd, *The Administration of Workmen's Compensation* (1936).
Gellhorn and Lauer, "The Administration of the New York Workmen's Compensation Law," 27 *N.Y.U. Law Review* 3, 203, 564 (1962).

Part III. MILITARY TRIBUNALS AND THEIR CONTROL BY THE COURTS

Walker, *Military Law* (1954).

19. COURTS-MARTIAL: PROCEEDINGS AGAINST MEMBERS OF THE ARMED FORCES

Aycock and Wurfel, *Military Law under the Uniform Code* (1955).
Everett, *Military Justice in the Armed Forces of the United States* (1956).
Manual for United States Courts-Martial (1951).
Snedeker, *Military Justice under the Uniform Code* (1953).
"Symposium on Military Justice," *Vanderbilt Law Review* (1953).

20. MILITARY TRIBUNALS EXERCISING JURISDICTION OVER CIVILIANS IN DOMESTIC TERRITORY

Fairman, *The Law of Martial Rule* (1942).
Rankin, *When Civil Law Fails* (1939).

22. TRIBUNALS CONSTITUTED BY MILITARY GOVERNMENTS IN OCCUPIED TERRITORY

von Glahn, *Occupation of Enemy Territory* (1958).

PART IV. VOLUNTARY ARBITRATION TRIBUNALS AND THEIR CONTROL BY THE COURTS

"Commercial Arbitration," *Law and Contemporary Problems* (1952).
Domke, *Commercial Arbitration* (to be published 1964).
Kellor, *American Arbitration, Its History, Functions and Achievements* (1948).
McKelvey (ed.), *Arbitration and the Law* (1959).
Sturges, *Cases on Arbitration Law* (1953).

Appendix B. *Bibliography*

N.B.—Following are the titles of all works listed in the Selected References on pp. 563 ff, or cited in the footnotes. Articles in periodicals or in collections are not listed; the names of their authors are included in the Index.

American Bar Association, Commission on Organized Crime, *Organized Crime and Law Enforcement*, Grosby Press, 1952.

American Bar Association, Section of Judicial Administration, *The Improvement of the Administration of Justice, a Handbook*, 4th ed., 1961.

American Civil Liberties Union, Ill. Div., *Secret Detention by the Chicago Police*, The Free Press, 1959.

American Law Institute, *Study of the Division of Jurisdiction between State and Federal Courts* (Tentative Draft No. 1), 1963.

American Law Institute, *Code of Criminal Precedure*, 1928–1931.

Annual Survey of American Law, New York University Law School, 1942–

Appleman, John A., *Military Tribunals and International Crimes*, Bobbs-Merrill Co., 1954.

Association of American Law Schools, *Select Essays in Anglo-American Legal History*, 3 vols., Little, Brown & Co., 1907.

Association of American Law Schools, *Select Readings on the Legal Profession*, West Publishing Co., 1962.

Attorney General's Committee on Administrative Procedure, *Report* (77th Cong. 1st Sess., Doc. No. 8), 1941

Attorney General's Manual on the Administrative Procedure Act, Government Printing Office, 1947.

Aumann, Francis A., *The Changing American Legal System: Some Selected Phases*, Ohio State University Press, 1940.

———., *The Instrumentalities of Justice*, Ohio State University Press, 1956.

Aycock, William B. and Wurfel, S. W., *Military Law under the Uniform Code*, University of North Carolina Press, 1955.

Barth, Alan, *Government by Investigation*, Viking Press, 1955.

Beaney, William N., *The Right to Counsel in American Courts*, University of Michigan Press, 1955

Beck, Bertram M., *5 States*, Amer. Law Institute, 1951.

Beck, Carl, *Contempt of Congress*, Hauser Press, 1960.

Benjamin, Robert M., *Administrative Adjudication in the State of New York*, 1942 6 vols.

Berman, Harold J., *The Nature and Functions of Law*, Foundation Press, 1958.

Black, Charles L., Jr., *The People and the Court: Judicial Review in a Democracy*, The Macmillian Company, 1960.

568

Blaustein, Albert P., and Porter, Chas. O., *The American Lawyer,* University of Chicago Press, 1954.

Blume, William W., *American Civil Procedure,* Prentice-Hall, Inc., 1955.

Book of the States, see Council of State Governments.

Borchard, Edward M., and Lutz, E. R., *Convicting the Innocent,* Yale University Press, 1932.

Brownell, Emery A., *Legal Aid in the United States,* Lawyers Co-operative Publishing Co., 1951. (Supplement, 1961.)

Bruce, Andrew A., *The American Judge,* The Macmillan Company, 1924.

Cahn, Edmond (ed.), *Supreme Court and Supreme Law,* University of Indiana Press, 1954.

———, *The Great Rights,* The Macmillan Company, 1963.

California Judicial Council, *Tenth Biennial Report,* 1944.

Cardozo, Benjamin N., *The Growth of the Law,* Yale University Press, 1924.

———, *The Nature of the Judicial Process,* Yale University Press, 1921.

Carr, Robert K., *Federal Protection of Civil Rights: Quest for a Sword,* Cornell University Press, 1947.

Chamberlain, Joseph P., Dowling, Noel T., and Hays, Paul R., *The Judicial Function in Federal Administrative Agencies,* Commonwealth Fund, 1942.

"Commercial Arbitration," *Law and Contemporary Problems,* vol. 17, nos. 3, 4, Duke University Law School, 1952.

Conway, Margaret M., *A Single Court of Patent Appeals—A Legislative History,* Study No. 20, Senate Committee on Judiciary, Subcommittee on Patents, 85th Cong., 2d Sess., 1959.

Corwin, Edward S. (ed.) *The Constitution of the United States of America. Analysis and Interpretation,* Government Printing Office, 1953.

Council of State Governments, *The Book of the States,* (published biennially).

Crosskey, William W., *Politics and the Constitution in the History of the United States,* University of Chicago Press, 1953, 2 vols.

Cushman, Robert E., *The Independent Regulatory Commissions,* Oxford University Press, 1941.

Dash, Samuel, Schwartz, Richard F., and Knowlton, Robert E., *The Eavesdroppers,* Rutgers University Press, 1959.

Davis, Kenneth C., *Administrative Law Treatise,* West Publishing Co., 1958, 2 vols.

de Tocqueville, Alexis, *Democracy in America,* ed. Phillips Bradley, Alfred A. Knopf, 1945.

Dession, George H., *Criminal Law Administration and Public Order,* Michie Casebook Corporation, 1948.

Documents Illustrative of the Formation of the Union, Government Printing Office, 1927.

Dodd, Walter F., *Administration of Workmen's Compensation,* The Commonwealth Fund, 1936.

Domke, Martin, *Commercial Arbitration,* Prentice-Hall, Inc., (to be published 1964).

Donnelly, Richard C., Goldstein, Joseph, and Schwartz, Richard D., *Criminal Law,* The Free Press, 1962.

Drinker, Henry, *Legal Ethics,* Columbia University Press, 1953.

Eberling, Ernest J., *Congressional Investigations,* Columbia University Press, 1928.

Elliot, Jonathan (ed.), *The debates in the several state conventions on the adoption of the federal constitution . . . together with the journal of the federal convention etc.* J. B. Lippincott & Co., 1836.

Elliott, Shelden D., *Improving Our Courts,* Oceana Publications, Inc., 1959.

Emmerich, Herbert, *Essays in Federal Reorganization,* University of Alabama Press, 1950.

Everett, Robinson O., *Military Justice in the Armed Forces of the United States,* Military Service Publishing Co., 1956.

Fairman, Charles, *The Law of Martial Rule,* 2nd ed., Callaghan & Co., 1942.

Fellman, David, *The Defendant's Rights,* Rhinehart, 1958.

Frank, Jerome, *Courts on Trial,* Princeton University Press, 1949.

Frank, Jerome and Barbara, *Not Guilty,* Doubleday, 1957.

Frank, John P., *Marble Palace,* Alfred A. Knopf, 1958.

Freund, Paul A., *The Supreme Court of the United States,* World Book Publishing Co., 1961.

Gardner, Erle S., *The Court of Last Resort,* Coward-McCann, Inc., 1952.

Gellhorn, Walter, *Federal Administrative Proceedings,* The Johns Hopkins Press, 1941.

———, *Individual Freedom and Governmental Restraints,* Louisiana State University Press, 1956.

Goodnow, Frank J., *Politics and Administration,* The Macmillan Company, 1900.

Gordon, Charles, and Rosenfield, Harry, *Immigration Law and Procedure,* Banks & Co. 1959.

Gray, John C., *The Nature and Sources of Law,* 2nd ed., The Macmillan Company, 1921.

Haines, Charles G., *The American Doctrine of Judicial Supremacy,* 2nd ed., University of California Press, 1932.

———, *The Role of the Supreme Court in American Government and Politics,* University of California Press, 1944, 1957, 2 vols.

Hand, Learned, *The Bill of Rights,* Harvard University Press, 1958.

Harris, Robert J., *The Judicial Power of the United States,* Louisiana State University Press, 1940.

Hart, Henry M., and Wechsler, Herbert, *The Federal Courts and the Federal System,* Foundation Press, 1953.

Haynes, Evan, *The Selection and Tenure of Judges,* National Conference of Judicial Councils, 1944.

Henderson, Gerald C., *The Federal Trade Commission,* Yale University Press, 1924.

Hilkey, Charles J., *Legal Development in Colonial Massachusetts, 1630–1686,* Columbia University Press, 1910.

Holdsworth, William S., *A History of English Law,* Little Brown & Co., 12 v., 1903-1938.

Hook, Sidney, *The Paradoxes of Freedom,* University of California Press, 1962.

Howell, Thomas B., *A Complete Collection of State Trials,* Hansard, 21 v., 1816.

Hurst, James W., *Law and the Social Process in United States History,* University of Michigan Law School, 1960.

———, *The Growth of American Law: The Law Makers,* Little, Brown & Co., 1950.

Inbau, Fred E., *Self-Incrimination: What Can an Accused Person Be Compelled to Do?* Chas. S. Thomas, 1950.

Inbau, Fred, and Reid, John E., *Criminal Interrogation and Confessions,* Williams & Wilkins Co., 1962.

Index-Digest of State Constitutions, Legislative Drafting Research Fund of Columbia University, 2d ed., 1959.

Joiner, Charles W., *Civil Justice and the Jury,* Prentice-Hall, Inc., 1962.

Karlen, Delmar, *Appellate Courts in the United States and England*, New York University Press, 1963.

————, *Primer of Procedure*, Campus Publishing Co., 1952.

Kellor, Frances, *American Arbitration, Its History, Functions and Achievements*, Harper & Row, 1948.

Kempin, Frederick G., Jr., *Legal History: Law and Social Change*. Prentice-Hall, Inc., 1963.

Kinnane, Charles H., *Anglo-American Law*, 2nd ed., Bobbs-Merrill Co., 1952.

Klein, Fannie J., *Judicial Administration and the Legal Profession*, Oceana Publications, 1963.

Konvitz, Milton R., *Civil Rights in Immigration*, Cornell University Press, 1953.

Kurland, Philip B. (ed.), *The Supreme Court Review, 1960,* University of Chicago Press, 1960.

Law: A Century of Progress, 1835–1935, New York University Press, 1937, 3 vols.

Levi, Edward H., *An Introduction to Legal Reasoning*, University of Chicago Press, 1949.

Lindman, Frank T., and McIntyre, Donald M., Jr. (ed.), *The Mentally Disabled and the Law*, University of Chicago Press, 1961.

Lowenstein, Edith (ed.), *The Alien and the Immigration Law: A Study of 1446 Cases*, Common Council for American Unity, 1957.

Manual for Courts-Martial, United States 1951.

Mason, Alpheus T., *The Supreme Court: Palladium of Freedom*, University of Michigan Press, 1962.

Maurer, David W., *The Big Con*, Bobbs-Merrill Co., 1940.

Mayers, Lewis, *Shall We Amend the Fifth Amendment?* Harper & Row, 1959.

McCloskey, Robert G., *The American Supreme Court*, University of Chicago Press, 1960.

McGuire, John M., *The Evidence of Guilt*, Little, Brown & Co., 1959.

McKelvey, Jean (ed.), *Arbitration and the Law*, Bureau of National Affairs, 1959.

McWhinney, Edward, *Judicial Review in the English-speaking World*, 2nd ed., University of Toronto Press, 1960.

Mendelson, Wallace, *The Constitution and the Supreme Court*, Dodd, Mead & Co., 1959.

Mental Illness and Due Process: Report of Special Committee to Study Commitment Procedure, Association of the Bar of the City of New York, Cornell University Press, 1962.

Millar, Robert M., *Civil Procedure of the Trial Court: Historical Perspective*, Law Center of New York University, 1952.

Moley, Raymond, *Politics and Criminal Prosecution*, Minton, Balch & Co., 1929.

Moreland, Ray, *Modern Criminal Procedure*, Bobbs-Merrill Co., 1959.

Murphy, Walter F., and Pritchett, C. H., *Courts, Judges and Politics*, Random House, 1962.

National Commission on Law Observance and Enforcement, *Reports*, Government Printing Office, 1931, 6 vols.

National Council on Crime and Delinquency, *Procedure and Evidence in the Juvenile Court*, 1962.

Orfield, Lester B., *Criminal Appeals in America*, Little, Brown & Co., 1939.

————, *Criminal Procedure from Arrest to Appeal*, New York University Press, 1947.

Ottenberg, Miriam, *The Federal Investigators*, Prentice-Hall, Inc., 1962.

Paulsen, Monrad G., *Legal Institutions Today and Tomorrow*, Columbia University Press., 1959.

Paulsen, Monrad G. (ed.), *Problems in Criminal Law and its Administration* [10 pamphlets], Joint Committee on Continuing Legal Education of the American Law Institute and the American Bar Association, 1961–1962.

Plucknett, Theodore F. T., *A Concise History of the Common Law,* 3rd ed., Butterworth & Co., 1940.

Pound, Roscoe, *Administrative Law: Its Growth, Procedure and Significance,* University of Pittsburgh Press, 1942.

———, *Appellate Procedure in Civil Cases,* Little, Brown & Co., 1948.

———, *Criminal Justice in America,* Henry Holt, 1930.

———, *The Lawyer from Antiquity to Modern Times,* West Publishing Co., 1953.

President's Committee on Administrative Management, *Report,* 1937.

Pritchett, C. Herman, *Congress versus the Supreme Court, 1957–1960,* University of Minnesota Press, 1961.

Puttkamer, Ernst W., *Administration of Criminal Law,* University of Chicago Press, 1953.

Puttkamer, Ernst W., (ed.), *War and the Law,* University of Chicago Press, 1944.

Rankin, Robert S., *When Civil Law Fails,* Duke University Press, 1939.

Rosenheim, Margaret K. (ed.), *Justice for the Child,* The Free Press, 1962.

Rostow, Eugene V., *The Sovereign Prerogative,* Yale University Press, 1962.

Russell, Bertrand, *Portraits from Memory,* Simon & Schuster, 1956.

Schwartz, Bernard, *American Administrative Law,* Sir Isaac Pitman & Sons, Ltd., 1950.

———, *Le droit administratif américain: notions générales,* Recueil Sirey, 1952.

Select Essays in Anglo-American Legal History, see Association of American Law Schools.

Shartel, Burke, *Our Legal System and How It Operates,* University of Michigan Press, 1951.

Smith, Bruce, *Police Systems in the United States,* 2nd rev. ed., Harper & Row, 1960.

Smith, Howard M., *Arrest, Search and Seizure,* Charles C. Thomas, 1959.

Smith, Reginald H., *Legal Service Offices for Persons of Moderate Means* [A report to the American Bar Association], 1947.

Snedeker, James, *Military Justice under the Uniform Code,* Little, Brown & Co., 1953.

Snee, Joseph M., and Pye, A. Kenneth, *Status of Force Agreements and Criminal Jurisdiction,* Oceana Publications, Inc., 1957.

Sowle, Claude R. (ed.), *Police Power and Individual Freedom: The Quest for Balance,* Aldine Publishing Co., 1962.

Story, Joseph, *Commentaries on the Constitution of the United States,* Hilliard, Gray & Co., 1833.

Sturges, Wesley A., *Cases on Arbitration Law,* Matthew Bender & Co., 1953.

Sunderland, Edson R., *Study of Justices of the Peace and Other Minor Courts,* University of Michigan Legal Research Institute, 1948.

Sutherland, Edwin H. (ed.), *The Professional Thief,* University of Chicago Press, 1937.

Sutherland, Edwin H., *White Collar Crime,* Holt, Rinehart & Winston, 1961.

Swisher, Carl B., *American Constitutional Development,* Houghton Mifflin Company, 1943.

"Symposium on Military Justice," *Vanderbilt Law Review,* vol. 6, no. 2, 1953.

Tappan, Paul W., *Crime, Justice and Correction,* McGraw-Hill Book Company, 1960.

Taylor, Telford, *Grand Inquest,* Simon & Schuster, 1955.

ten Broeck, Jacobus, Barnhart, Edwin N., and Matson, Floyd W., *Prejudice, War and the Constitution,* University of California Press, 1954.

Towle, Dorothy S. (ed.), *Records of the Vice-Admiralty Court of Rhode Island, 1716–1752,* American Historical Association, 1936.

Ubbelohde, Carl, *The Vice-Admiralty Courts and the American Revolution,* University of North Carolina Press, 1960.

U.S. Commission on Civil Rights, *Report,* Government Printing Office, 1961.

——, *The Fifty States Report,* Government Printing Office, 1961.

U.S. Commission on the Organization of the Executive Branch of the Government, *The Independent Regulatory Commissions,* 1949.

U.S. Commission on the Organization of the Executive Branch, *Legal Services and Procedure,* 1955.

——, *Task Force Report on Legal Services and Procedure,* 1955.

U.S. Federal Bureau of Investigation, *Crime Reports for the United States, 1962,* Government Printing Office, 1963.

Vanderbilt, Arthur T., *Minimum Standards of Judicial Administration,* Law Center of New York University, 1949.

Varon, Joseph A., *Searches, Seizures and Immunities,* Bobbs-Merrill Co., 1961.

von Glahn, Gerhard, *The Occupation of Enemy Territory,* University of Minnesota Press, 1957.

von Mehren, Arthur T., *The Civil Law System,* Prentice-Hall, Inc., 1957.

Wagner, Wienczyslaw, *The Federal States and Their Judiciary: A Comparative Study,* Humanities Press, 1959.

Walker, Daniel (ed.), *Military Law,* Prentice-Hall, Inc., 1954.

Warren, Charles, *A History of the American Bar,* Little, Brown & Co., 1911.

——, *The Supreme Court in United States History,* rev. ed., Little, Brown & Co., 1935, 2 vols.

Warren, George (ed.), *The Federal Administrative Procedure Act and the Administrative Agencies,* New York University School of Law, 1947.

Wigmore, John H., *A Treatise on the Anglo-American System of Evidence,* 3rd ed., Little, Brown & Co., 1940, 10 vols. (Vol. 8, McNaughton rev., 1961).

Willoughby, William F., *Principles of Judicial Administration,* Brookings Institution, 1929.

Wright, Benjamin F., *The Growth of American Constitutional Law,* Houghton Mifflin Company, 1942.

Zelermyer, William, *The Process of Legal Reasoning,* Prentice-Hall, Inc., 1963.

Appendix C. *Selected Provisions of the Constitution of the United States of America*

Section 2. The House of Representatives . . . shall have the sole Power of Impeachment.

Section 3. The Senate shall have the sole Power to try all Impeachments. When sitting for that Purpose, they shall be on Oath or Affirmation. When the President of the United States is tried, the Chief Justice shall preside: And no Person shall be convicted without the Concurrence of two thirds of the Members present.

Judgment in Cases of Impeachment shall not extend further than to removal from Office, and disqualification to hold and enjoy any Office of honor, Trust or Profit under the United States: but the Party convicted shall nevertheless be liable and subject to Indictment, Trial, Judgment and Punishment, according to Law.

Section 8. The Congress shall have Power . . .

To constitute Tribunals inferior to the supreme Court;

To define and punish Piracies and Felonies committed on the high Seas, and Offenses against the Law of Nations; . . .

To make Rules for the Government and Regulation of the land and naval Forces;

Section 9. The Privilege of the Writ of Habeas Corpus shall not be suspended, unless when in Cases of Rebellion or Invasion the public Safety may require it.

No Bill of Attainder or ex post facto Law shall be passed.

Section 10. No State . . . shall pass any Bill of Attainder, ex post facto Law. . . .

ARTICLE II

Section 2. The President . . . shall have Power to grant Reprieves and Pardons for Offenses against the United States, except in cases of Impeachment. He . . . shall nominate, and by and with the Advice and Consent of the Senate, shall appoint . . . Judges of the supreme Court, and all other Officers of the United States, whose Appointments are not herein otherwise provided for, and which shall be established by Law: but the Congress may by Law vest the Appointment of such inferior Officers, as they may think proper, in the President alone, in the Courts of Law or in the Heads of Departments.

Section 4. The President, Vice President and all civil Officers of the United

States, shall be removed from Office on Impeachment for, and Conviction of, Treason, Bribery, or other high Crimes and Misdemeanors.

ARTICLE III

Section 1. The judicial Power of the United States, shall be vested in one supreme Court, and in such inferior Courts as the Congress may from time to time ordain and establish. The judges, both of the supreme and inferior Courts, shall hold their Offices during good Behaviour, and shall, at stated Times, receive for their Services, a Compensation, which shall not be diminished during their Continuance in Office.

Section 2. The judicial Power shall extend to all Cases, in Law and Equity, arising under this Constitution, the Laws of the United States, and Treaties made, or which shall be made, under their Authority;—to all Cases affecting Ambassadors, other public Ministers and Consuls;—to all Cases of admiralty and maritime Jurisdiction;—to Controversies to which the United States shall be a Party;—to Controversies between two or more States;—between a State and Citizens of another State;—between Citizens of different States;—between Citizens of the same State Claiming Lands under Grants of different States, and between a State, or the Citizens thereof, and foreign States, Citizens or Subjects.

In all Cases affecting Ambassadors, other public Ministers and Consuls, and those in which a State shall be Party, the supreme Court shall have original Jurisdiction. In all the other cases before mentioned, the supreme Court shall have appellate Jurisdiction, both as to Law and Fact, with such Exceptions, and under such Regulations as the Congress shall make.

The Trial of all Crimes, except in Cases of Impeachment, shall be by Jury; and such Trial shall be held in the State where the said Crimes shall have been committed; but when not committed within any State, the Trial shall be at such Place or Places as the Congress may by Law have directed.

Section 3. Treason against the United States, shall consist only in levying War against them, or in adhering to their Enemies, giving them Aid and Comfort. No Person shall be convicted of Treason unless on the Testimony of two Witnesses to the same overt Act, or on Confession in open in Court.

ARTICLE IV

Section 1. Full Faith and Credit shall be given in each State to the public Acts, Records, and judicial Proceedings of every other State. And the Congress may by general Laws prescribe the Manner in which such Acts, Records and Proceedings shall be proved, and the Effect thereof.

Section 2. The Citizens of each State shall be entitled to all Privileges and Immunities of Citizens in the several States.

A Person charged in any State with Treason, Felony, or other Crime, who shall flee from Justice, and be found in another State, shall on Demand of the executive Authority of the State from which he fled, be delivered up, to be removed to the State having Jurisdiction of the Crime.

ARTICLE VI

This Constitution, and the laws of the United States which shall be made in Pursuance therof; and all Treaties made, or which shall be made, under the Authority of the United States, shall be the supreme Law of the Land; and the Judges in every State shall be bound thereby, any Thing in the Constitution or Laws of any State to the Contrary notwithstanding.

[AMENDMENT IV]

The right of the people to be secure in their persons, houses, papers, and effects, against unreasonable searches and seizures, shall not be violated, and no Warrants shall issue, but upon probable cause, supported by Oath or affirmation, and particularly describing the place to be searched, and the persons or things to be seized.

[AMENDMENT V]

No person shall be held to answer for a capital, or otherwise infamous crime, unless on a presentment or indictment of a Grand Jury, except in cases arising in the land or naval forces, or in the Militia, when in actual service in time of War or public danger; nor shall any person be subject for the same offence to be twice put in jeopardy of life or limb, nor shall be compelled in any criminal case to be a witness against himself, nor be deprived of life, liberty, or property, without due process of law; nor shall private property be taken for public use, without just compensation.

[AMENDMENT VI]

In all criminal prosecutions, the accused shall enjoy the right to a speedy and public trial, by an impartial jury of the State and district wherein the crime shall have been committed, which district shall have been previously ascertained by law, and to be informed of the nature and cause of the accusation; to be confronted with the witnesses against him; to have compulsory process for obtaining Witnesses in his favor, and to have the Assistance of Counsel for his defence.

[AMENDMENT VII]

In Suits at common law, where the value in controversy shall exceed twenty dollars, the right of trial by jury shall be preserved, and no fact tried by a jury, shall be otherwise re-examined in any Court of the United States, than according to the rules of the common law.

[AMENDMENT VII]

Excessive bail shall not be required, nor excessive fines imposed, nor cruel and unusual punishments inflicted.

[AMENDMENT XI]

The Judicial power of the United States shall not be construed to extend to any suit in law or equity commenced or prosecuted against one of the United States by Citizens of another State, or by Citizens or Subjects of any Foreign State.

[AMENDMENT XIV]

Section 1. All persons born or naturalized in the United States, and subject to the jurisdiction thereof, are citizens of the United States and of the State wherein they reside. No State shall make or enforce any law which shall abridge the privileges or immunities of citizens of the United States; nor shall any State deprive any person of life, liberty, or property, without due process of law; nor deny to any person within its jurisdiction the equal protection of the laws.

Section 5. The Congress shall have power to enforce, by appropriate legislation, the provisions of this article.

Index of Cases

Abbate v. United States, 359 U.S. 187 (1959), 20

Abel v. United States, 367 U.S. 217 (1960), 60

Adair v. United States, 208 U.S. 161 (1908), 330

Adamson v. California, 322 U.S. 46 (1947), 16, 17, 121

Adkins v. Children's Hospital, 261 U.S. 525 (1923), 330

Alabama Public Service Commission v. Southern Railway Co., 341 U.S. 341 (1951), 199

Alcorta v. Texas, 355 U.S. 28 (1958), 109

American Insur. Co. v. Canter, 1 Pet. 511 (1828), 397

Anderson v. Dunn, 6 Wheaton 204, (1821), 307

Armstrong v. Board of Education, 323 F. 2d 333 (1963), 376

Ashcraft v. Tennessee, 327 U.S. 274 (1946), 106

Bailey v. Richardson, 341 U.S. 918 (1951), 476

Baiz, In re, 135 U.S. 403 (1890), 193

Baker v. Carr, 369 U.S. 186 (1962), 334

Balzac v. Porto Rico, 258 U.S. 298 (1922), 114

Baltimore Radio Show, Inc. v. State, 67 A. 2d 397 (1949); cert. denied 338 U.S. 912 (1949), 96

Barkus v. Illinois, 359 U.S. 121 (1959), 20

Bartlett v. Kane, 16 Howard 263 (1853), 430

Barsky v. Board of Regents, 346 U.S. 442 (1954), 442

Bauer v. Acheson, 106 F. Supp. 445 (1952), 479

Benanti v. United States, 355 U.S. 96 (1957), 61

Boyd v. United States, 116 U.S. 616 (1886), 34

Bridges v. California, 314 U.S. 252 (1941), 41

Bridges v. Wixon, 326 U.S. 135 (1945), 437

Brimson v. Interstate Commerce Commission, 154 U.S. 447 (1894), 306

Brinegar v. United States, 338 U.S. 160 (1949), 59

Brookside Mills Inc. v. Avon Converting Co., 191 F. 2d 905 (1951), 558

Brown v. Board of Education, 347 U.S. 483 (1954), 334

Brown v. Mississippi, 297 U.S. 278 (1936), 49

Brown v. Walker, 161 U.S. 591, 596 (1896), 70

Brownell v. Tom We Shung, 352 U.S. 180 (1956), 481

Buchalter v. New York, 319 U.S. 427 (1943), 17

Cafeteria Workers Union v. McElroy, 367 U.S. 886 (1961), 476

Chicago R. Co. v. Whitton, 13 Wallace 270 (1871), 200

Chisholm v. Georgia, 2 Dall. 419 (1793), 195

Civil Aeronautics Board v. Waterman Steamship Corp., 333 U.S. 103 (1948), 484

Claflin v. Houseman, 93 U.S. 130 (1876), 197

Coe v. Coe, 334 U.S. 378 (1948), 247

Cohen v. Hurley, 366 U.S. 117 (1961), 407

Cohens v. Virginia, 6 Wheaton 264 (1821), 320

Colting v. Kansas City Stock Yards, 183 U.S. 79 (1901), 441

Craig v. Harney, 331 U.S. 367 (1947), 41, 381

577

Crooker v. California, 357 U.S. 458 (1958), 47

Counselman v. Hitchcock, 142 U. S. 547 (1892), 35, 330

Cox v. United States, 332 U.S. 442 (1947), 487

Daniel Ball, The, 10 Wallace 557 (1871), 190

Dartmouth College v. Woodward, 4 Wheaton 518 (1819), 331, 413

Dayton v. Dulles, 357 U.S. 144 (1958), 479

Debs, In re, 158 U.S. 564 (1895), 40

De Costa v. Madigan, 223 F. 2d 906 (1955), 532

Dickinson v. United States, 346 U.S. 389 (1953), 487

District of Columbia v. Clawans, 300 U.S. 617 (1937), 143

Dobson v. Commissioner, 320 U.S. 489 (1943), 444

Douglas v. California, 372 U.S. 355 (1963), 133

Draper v. Washington, 372 U.S. 487 (1963), 133

Dred Scott v. Sandford, 19 Howard 393 (1857), 325

Duncan v. Kahanomoku, 327 U.S. 304 (1946), 535

Endo, Ex parte, 323 U.S. 283 (1944), 304

Engle v. Vitale, 370 U.S. 421 (1962), 333

Erie R. Co. v. Tompkins, 304 U.S. 64 (1938), 353, 357

Eskridge v. Washington State Board, 357 U.S. 214 (1958), 366

Estep v. United States, 327 U.S. 114 (1946), 487

Faubus et al. v. United States et al., 254 F. 2d 797 (1958), cert. denied 358 U.S. 829 (1958), 168

Fay v. New York, 332 U.S. 261 (1947), 119, 404

Federal Power Commission v. Hope Gas Co., 320 U.S. 591 (1944), 473

Federal Radio Commission v. General Electric Co., 281 U.S. 464 (1930), 483

Ferguson v. Georgia, 366 U.S. 570 (1961), 33

Fisher v. Pace, 336 U.S. 155 (1949), 40

Fletcher v. Peck, 6 Cranch 87 (1810), 320

Flick v. Johnson, 174 F. 2d 983 (1949), cert. denied, 338 U.S. 876 (1949), 544

Fong Yue Ting v. United States, 149 U.S. 698 (1893), 425

Frank v. Mangum, 237 U.S. 309 (1915), 16, 117

Frank v. Maryland, 359 U.S. 360 (1959), 61

Frothingham v. Mellon, 262 U.S. 447 (1923), 188

Gallegos v. Nebraska, 342 U.S. 55 (1951), 52

Garland, Ex parte, 4 Wallace 333 (1867), 325

Genesee Chief, The, 12 Howard 443 (1851), 190

Georgia v. Pennsylvania R. Co. et al., 324 U.S. 439 (1945), 195

Georgia v. Tennessee Copper Co., 206 U.S. 230 (1907), 195

Gideon v. Wainwright, 372 U.S. 335 (1963), 28

Glidden Co. v. Zdanok, 370 U.S. 530 (1962), 397

Gong Lum v. Rice, 275 U.S. 78 (1927), 335

Gordon v. U.S. 2 Wallace 561 (1865), 325

Great Northern Ry. v. Sunburst Oil Co., 287 U.S. 358 (1932), 353

Griffin v. Illinois, 351 U.S. 12 (1956), 17, 133

Green v. United States, 355 U.S. 184 (1957), 92

Green v. United States, 356 U.S. 165 (1958), 40

Greene v. McElroy, 360 U.S. 474 (1959), 476

Groban, In re, 352 U.S. 330 (1957), 306

Haddock v. Haddock, 201 U.S. 562 (1906), 214, 353

Hamilton v. Alabama, 368 U.S. 52 (1961), 90

Hayburn's Case, 2 Dallas 409 (1792), 323

Hernandez v. Texas, 347 U.S. 475 (1954), 118

Hirota v. MacArthur, 338 U.S. 197 1948), 542

Humphrey v. United States, 295 U.S. 602 (1935), 501

Hurtado v. California, 110 U.S. 516 (1884), 15, 88

Hylton v. United States, 3 Dallas 171 (1796), 323

Insurance Co. v. Morse, 20 Wallace 445 (1875), 202

International Milling Co. v. Columbia T. Co., 292 U.S. 511 (1934), 210

International Shoe Co. v. Washington, 326 U.S. 310 (1945), 213

Irvin v. Dowd, 366 U.S. 717 (1961), 95, 116

Jackson v. Taylor, 353 U.S. 569 (1957), 532

Johnson v. Eisentrager, 339 U.S. 763 (1950), 541

Johnnson v. Zerbst, 304 U.S. 458 (1938), 28

Kasper v. Brittain, 245 F. 2d 92 (6th Circ. 1957), cert. denied 355 U.S. 834 (1957), 167

Kawakita v. United States, 343 U.S. 717 (1952), 130

Kent v. Dulles, 357 U.S. 116 (1958), 479

Ker v. California, 374 U.S. 23 (1963), 57

Kilbourn v. Thompson, 103 U.S. 168 (1881), 308

Kingsley Books v. Brown, 354 U.S. 436 (1957), 265

Kinsella v. Singleton, 361 U.S. 234 (1960), 511

Korematsu v. U.S., 323 U.S. 214 (1944), 304, 305

Kwong Hai Chew v. Colding, 344 U.S. 590 (1953), 480

Level Export Corp. v. Wolz, Aiken & Co., 305 N.Y. 82 (1953), 558

Leyra v. Denno, 347 U.S. 556 (1954), 49, 106

Louisiana ex rel. Francis v. Resweber, 329 U.S. 459 (1947), 125

Louisville, Cincinnati and Charleston R. Co. v. Letson, 2 Howard 497 (1844), 201

Louisville Land Bank v. Radford, 295 U.S. 555 (1935), 330

Lumbermen's Casualty Co. v. Elbert, 348 U.S. 48 (1954), 202

Lung's Case, 1 Conn. 428 (1815), 345

Luther v. Borden, 7 Howard 1 (1848), 298

Madsen v. Kinsella, 343 U.S. 341 (1952); 356 U.S. 925 (1958), 548

Mallory v. United States, 354 U.S. 449 (1957), 53

Manley v. Georgia, 279 U.S. 1 (1929), 102

Mahnich v. Southern S. S. Co., 321 U.S. 96 (1944), 349

Mapp v. Ohio, 367 U.S. 643 (1961), 17, 60

Marbury v. Madison, 1 Cranch 137 (1803), 323

Martin v. Hunter, 1 Wheaton 304, (1816), 320

Massachusetts v. Mellon, 262 U.S. 447 (1923), 195

McCardle, Ex parte, 7 Wallace 506 (1869), 325

McCarthy v. Arndstein, 266 U.S. 34 (1924), 35

McCarthy v. Clancy, 110 Conn. 482 (1930), 74

McCollum v. Board of Education, 333 U.S. 203 (1948), 333

McComb v. Jacksonville Paper Co., 336 U.S. 187 (1949), 182

McDonald, In re, Fed. Cases No. 8, 751 (1861), 302

McElroy v. Guagliardo, 361 U.S. 281 (1960), 511

McGee v. International Life Insurance Co., 355 U.S. 220 (1957), 213

McGrain v. Daugherty, 273 U.S. 135 (1927), 307

McNabb v. United States, 318 U.S. 332 (1943), 51, 365

Merryman, Ex parte, Fed. Cases No. 9, 487 (1961), 302

Milch v. U.S., 332 U.S. 789 (1947), 543

Milligan, Ex parte, 4 Wallace 2 (1866) 302, 534

Mineo v. Eureka Security Fire Insurance Co., 125 A. 2d 612 (1956), 12

Monaco v. Mississippi, 292 U.S. 313 (1934), 196

Mondou v. N.Y.N.H. & H.R. Co. 223 U.S. 1 (1912), 197

Monroe v. Pape, 365 U.S. 167 (1961), 296

Moore v. Dempsey, 261 U.S. 86 (1923), 117

Moore v. New York, 333 U.S. 565 (1948), 404

Morgan v. United States, 304 U.S. 1 (1938), 439

Moses Taylor, The, 4 Wallace 411 (1867), 200

Mudd, Ex parte, Fed. Cas. 9,899 (1868), 539

National Labor Relations Board v. Jones & Laughlin Steel Corp., 301 U.S. 1 (1937), 430

Nat. Mut. Ins. Co. v. Tidewater Transfer Co., 337 U.S. 582 (1949), 200

Neal v. Delaware, 103 U.S. 370 (1881), 15

New Jersey v. Wilson, 7 Cranch 164 (1812), 320

New York v. United States, 331 U.S. 234 (1947), 473

Ng Fung Ho v. White, 259 U.S. 276 (1922), 447

Nickey v. Mississippi, 292 U.S. 393 (1934), 467

Norris v. Alabama, 294 U.S. 587 (1935), 118

Oceanic Steam Nav. Co. v. Stranahan, 214 U.S. 320 (1909), 430

Office Employes Internat. Union v. Nat. Labor Relations Bd., 353 U.S. 313 (1957), 433

Ohio Valley Water Co. v. Ben Avon Borough, 253 U.S. 287 (1920), 472

Olmstead v. United States, 277 U.S. 438 (1928), 62

Order of Travelers v. Wolfe, 331 U.S. 586 (1947), 245

Osborn v. Bank of U.S., 9 Wheaton 738 (1824), 320

Palko v. Connecticut, 302 U.S. 319 (1937), 17, 65, 131

Parker v. Lester, 227 F. 2d 708 (1955), 482

Pennekamp v. Florida, 328 U.S. 331 (1946), 41

Pennoyer v. Neff, 95 U.S. 714 (1878), 207

People v. De Biasi, 7 N.Y. 2d 544 (1960), 47

People v. Defore, 242 N.Y. 13, 21 (1926), 59

People v. Mendes, 3 N.Y. 2d 120 (1957), 101

People v. Savvides, 1 N.Y. 2d 554 (1956), 109

Pickelsimer v. Wainwright, 375 U.S. 2 (1963), 366

Plessy v. Ferguson, 163 U.S. 537 (1896), 335

Pollock v. Farmers' Loan & Trust Co., 158 U.S. 601 (1895), 187

Powell v. Alabama, 287 U.S. 45 (1932), 28

Powers Mercantile Co. v. Olson, 7 F. Supp. 865 (1934), 299

Quirin, Ex parte, 317 U.S. 1 (1942), 538, 540

Quinn v. United States, 349 U.S. 155 (1955), 309

Railroad Commission Cases, 116 U.S. 307 (1886), 473

Ramspeck v. Federal Trial Examiners Conference, 345 U.S. 128 (1953), 461

Rea v. United States, 350 U.S. 214 (1956), 364

Regan v. New York, 349 U.S. 58 (1955), 35

Rideau v. Alabama, 373 U.S. 165 (1963), 95

Doherty & Co. v. Goodman, 294 U.S. 623 (1935), 212

Robinson, Ex parte, 19 Wallace 505 (1874), 39

Sacher v. U.S., 343 U.S. 1 (1952), 40

St. Joseph Stock Yards Co. v. U.S., 298 U.S. 38 (1936), 442

Santa Clara County v. Southern Pac. R. Co., 118 U.S. 394 (1886), 332

Santiago v. Nogueras, 214 U.S. 260 (1909), 545

Schwartz v. Texas, 344 U.S. 199 (1952), 61

Shaughnessy v. Pedreiro, 348 U.S. 48 (1955), 449

Shaughnessy v. United States, ex rel. Mezei, 345 U.S. 206 (1953), 480

Shepherd v. Florida, 341 U.S. 50 (1951), 117

Sheppard v. Ohio, 352 U.S. 910 (1956), 116

Simpson v. United States, 355 U.S. 7 (1957), 312

Skidmore v. B. & O. R. Co. 167 F. 2d 54 (1948), 269

Skiriotes v. Florida, 313 U.S. 69 (1941), 20

Snyder v. Massachusetts 291, U.S. 97 (1934), 16

Speery v. Florida, 373 U.S. 379 (1963), 506

Springer v. Philippine Islands, 277 U.S. 189 (1928), 418

S.S.W. Inc. v. Air Transport Assn., 191 F. 2d 658 (1951); cert. denied 343 U.S. 955 (1951), 491

Standard Oil Co. v. United States, 337 U.S. 293 (1949), 165

State ex. rel. Hovey Concrete Products Co. v. Mechem, 316 P. 2d 1069 (1957), 492

State v. Tickle, 77 S.E. 2d 632 (1953), 19
Staten Island Edison Corp. v. Maltbie, 296 N.Y. 374 (1947), 473
Sterling v. Constantin, 287 U.S. 378 (1932), 299
Stroble v. California, 343 U.S. 181 (1952), 116
Sutton v. Lieb, 342 U.S. 402 (1952), 202
Sweeney v. Woodall, 344 U.S. 86 (1952), 85
Sweezy v. Wyman, 354 U.S. 234 (1957), 310
Swift v. Tyson, 16 Peters 1 (1842), 357

Testa v. Katt, 330 U.S. 386 (1947), 197
Texas & Pacific R. Co. v. Abilene Cotton Oil Co., 204 U.S. 426 (1907), 491
Textile Workers Union v. Lincoln Mills, 335 U.S. 446 (1957), 186, 351, 557
Tot v. United States, 319 U.S. 463 (1943), 103
Toth v. Quarles, 350 U.S. 11 (1955), 512
Tumey v. Ohio, 273 U.S. 510 (1927), 16
Twining v. New Jersey, 211 U.S. 78 (1908), 16, 121

United States v. Accardo, 298 F. 2d 133 (1962), 115
United States v. Brown, 7 U.S.C.M.A. 251 (1956), 510
United Brick and Clay Workers v. Deena Artware, Inc., 198 F. 2d 637 (1952), 446
United States v. Danzen, 12 U.S.C.M.A. 350 (1961), 526
United States v. Germany, 216 F. Supp. 54 (1963), 32
United States v. Kennedy, 8 U.S.C.M.A. 251 (1957), 526
United States v. Littrice, 3 U.S.C.M.A. 487 (1953), 526
United States v. Nugent, 346 U.S. 1 (1953), 486
United States v. Rabinowitz, 339 U.S. 56 (1950), 60
United States v. Sharpnack, 355 U.S. 286 (1958), 19
United States v. United Mine Workers, 330 U.S. 258 (1947), 165

United States v. Williams, 341 U.S. 58 (1951), 292
United States v. Wilson and Harvey, 8 C.M.R. 48 (1952), 523
United States v. Wunderlich, 342 U.S. 98 (1951), 498
United States ex rel Knauff v. Shaughnessy, 338 U.S. 537 (1950), 480
Upshaw v. United States, 335 U.S. 410 (1948), 365

Vajtauer v. Commissioner, 273 U.S. 103 (1927), 481
Vallandigham, Ex parte, 1 Wallace 243 (1864), 302, 534

Wade v. Hunter, 336 U.S. 684 (1949), 509
Wadley So. Ry. Co. v. Georgia, 235 U.S. 651 (1915), 441
Watkins v. United States, 354 U.S. 178 (1957), 312
Weeks v. United States, 232 U.S. 383 (1914), 59, 61, 364
Weiss v. United States, 308 U.S. 321 (1939), 61
Wheat v. Wheat, 318 S.W. 2d 793 (1958), 214
Wheatley v. State, 114 Ga. 175 (1901), 348
White v. Maryland, 373 U.S. 274 (1963), 81
Williams v. North Carolina, 317 U.S. 287 (1942), 172, 214, 353
Williams v. United States, 341 U.S. 97 (1951), 292
Wilson v. United States, 162 U.S. 613 (1896), 64
Winberry v. Salisbury, 5 N.J. 240, 74 A. 2d 406 (1950), 228
Wolf v. Colorado, 338 U.S. 25 (1949), 60, 365

Yakus v. United States, 321 U.S. 414 (1944), 291
Yamashita, In re, 327 U.S. 1 (1946), 540
Youngstown Steel Co. v. Sawyer, 343 U.S. 579 (1952), 290

Zorach v. Clauson, 343 U.S. 306 (1952), 333

General Index

Accomplice, testimony of, 37
Accounting, action for, 153
Acquittal, significance of, 123
Accused, right of to testify in own behalf, 75
Accusatorial method, 102
Administrative agencies, investigation by, 71
Administrative court, proposal for, 451
Administrative Procedure Act, 432, 434, 436
Administrative process defined, 421
Administrative regulations, judicial determination of validity, 290
Administrative tribunals, 417-506
Admiralty cases: appellate review in, 278; concurrent jurisdiction of law courts in, 190; special doctrines of, 243; two-stage trial in, 255
Admiralty Court: British, 217; criminal jurisdiction of, 343; development of, 188; expert adviser in, 259
Admiralty courts: colonial, 4; criminal jurisdiction of, 113, 343
Admiralty jurisdiction, delimitation of, 188
Admissibility in evidence of objects unlawfully seized, 59
Adoption of child, jurisdiction of, 222
Adversary system, 99
Advisory opinion on constitutionality, 314
Affidavit, in application for injunction, 237
Affirmative defense, 241
Agricultural Adjustment Act, invalidation of, 326
Agricultural products, licensing of dealers in, 423
Agriculture Department as adjudicator, 419
Alaska, judicial selection in, 384, 391
Alien: failure to comply with deportation order, 441; permission to enter, 479
Alimony, out-of-state enforcement of order for, 171
Ambassadors, cases affecting, 192
Amer, P., cited, 397
American Arbitration Association, rules of procedure, 554
American Bar Association: hearing examiner corps proposal, 462; judicial nominating board proposal, 392; office of administrative practice proposal, 504
American Law Institute, 363
Andrews, C., cited, 189
Annulment of marriage, 172
Anthony, G., cited, 535
Antitrust laws: consent judgment in action under, 271; conviction under as evidence in civil suit, 12; jurisdiction

of civil suits under, 186; venue in suits under, 223; uncertainty of meaning of, 11
Appearance in action, effect of, 213
Appellate courts: delay in decision by, 381; organization of, 374; power to review sentence, 130
Appellate review: in civil cases, 271; of criminal conviction, 130; of juvenile court orders, 148
Arbitration award, conversion into judgment, 211
Arbitration tribunals, 549 ff.
Ares, C., cited, 549
Arizona, arbitration statute, 551
Arkansas, use of troops to enforce court order in, 168
Army, independent judge advocate as court-martial law officer, 527
Arraignment, 90
Arrest: before formal accusation, 80; of defendant in civil action, 235; of judgment-debtor, 160; without warrant, power of officer to make, 53
Arrest of judgment, 124
Arrest of vessel, 233
Articles of Confederation: judicial structure under, 12; provision for disputes between states, 144
Articles of War, 510
Assimilative Crimes Act, 19
Attachment, 216
Attaint of judgment, 273
Attorney General (U.S.): action to enforce voting rights, 183, 293; intervention in proceedings to enforce court order, 168; participation in selection of judges, 396; powers of, in federal law-enforcement, 43, 44, to detain spies and saboteurs, 305; review of deportation orders by, 450; role in promotion of federal judges, 401
Attorney General (state): control over local prosecutor, 45, 453; subpoena power of, 73
Attorney General's Committee on Administrative Procedure, cited, 459; survey of personnel by, 503
Auby, J., cited, 460
Aumann, F., cited, 318, 347

Bad check law, 143
Bail, necessity for, 48
Bankruptcy Act, 175
Bankruptcy discharge as defense in state court, 245
Bankruptcy proceeding: appointment of receiver and trustee in, 239; jury trial in, 263; stages in, 234; state law in, 245
Barrett, E., cited, 54, 77, 365
Beck, B., cited, 128
Bell, R., cited, 284

Benefits: ineligibility for as penalty, 428; judicial check on award of, 294
Benjamin, R., cited, 428, 438, 463
Bickel, A., cited, 273, 351
Bill of particulars, 271
Bill of Rights, not restrictive of states, 13
Bill of Rights (English), 113, 316, 341
Bills of Lading Act, 359
Binding over, 48
Bipartisan courts: federal, 400; state, 391
Black, Justice, cited, 17, 40
Blumrosen, A., cited, 296
Board of Appeals of Patent Office, 484
Board of Immigration Appeals, 439, 450
Board of review for court-martial, 129, 528
Body execution, 160
Books and papers: pretrial inspection by adverse party, 253; seizure under search warrant, 60
Berchard, E., cited, 131
Boundary dispute between states, 185, 194
Boycott, suit to enjoin, 186
Brandeis, Justice, cited, 442
Breach of promise of marriage, action for, 205
Brennan, Justice, cited, 17, 265
Broadcasting: of court proceedings, 116; pretrial, as contempt of court, 96
Broadcasting station, licensing proceeding, 483
Brownell, E., cited, 31
Bullitt, W., cited, 321
Burden of proof: civil cases, 258; criminal cases, 107, 149
Burns, A., cited, 520
Butler Amendment, 326

California: adoption of Field substantive code by, 361; arbitration statute, 551; code for administrative adjudication, 434; commission on complaints against judges, 393; conciliation in marital matrimonial actions in, 173; discretion in sentencing in, 127; grand jury in, 88; hearing examiner corps, 462; judicial selection in, 384; police detention in, 54; sentencing procedure in, 128; separate jury trial on sentence, 130
Campbell, T., cited, 547
Canada: patent jurisdiction in, 373; pretrial disclosure of prosecution evidence, 93
Canal Zone, local law in, 356
Cardozo, Justice, cited, 47, 65
Career judiciary, 380
Carr, R., cited, 292
Case law, 347
Caution to suspect under interrogation, 522
Cease and desist order, 182, 428
Certificate of authority to do business, 210
Certification of questions to appellate court, 274

Challenge to the array, 118
Chancellor, English, 217
Chancery Court, English, special doctrines of, 342
Change of venue, 94, 117
Charge to jury, 121, 266
Charter as franchise, 482
Chattel, judgment awarding possession of, 161
Cheatham, E., cited, 283
Chicago, police detention in, 51
Chief Justice of the United States, to preside at trial of impeachment of President, 150
Children, neglected or abandoned, jurisdiction of juvenile courts, 149
Chinese exclusion legislation, deportation provisions, 425
Citizen as including corporation in diversity case, 201
Citizen complaint tribunal as check on police abuses, 50
Citizenship, definition of by 14th Amendment, 199, 207
Civil Aeronautics Board: judicial review of orders of, 450; powers, 426, 454, 484; primary jurisdiction of, 491
Civil contempt proceeding, 217
Civil law vs. common law, 342
Civil proceeding: disobedience of order or judgment as contempt, 41, 165; jurisdiction, 184 ff.; procedure, 225 ff.
Civil rights, penalties for deprivation of, 292, 296
Civil Service Commission, supervision of hearing examiner corps by, 461, 462
Civil War, military commissions in, 533, 546
Civilians serving with or accompanying armed forces: jurisdiction of courts-martial, 511; of military government courts, 547
Claims against government, adjudication of, 497
Clark, W., cited, 547
Class action, 230
Class discrimination in jury selection, 119
Clayton Act, 426
Closing statement to jury, 120
Coast Guard, application of code of military justice to, 510
Codification of law, 360
Cohen, I., cited, 69
Cole, K., cited, 398
Collateral attack on conviction, 134
Colorado, photographing and broadcasting of trials in, 116
Comity in enforcement of judgments, 156
Command control of court-martial, 519, 525
Commerce Court, 449
Commerce Department, denial of export license by, 429
Commercial arbitration, 558
Commercial law, development of, 346

Commissioner of Immigration, adjudication by, 450
Commissioner to try issues, 260
Commodity Exchanges Act, 426
Commissioners of Uniform Laws, 358
Common law, genesis of, 341
Commutation of sentence, 138
Complaint, as criminal accusation, 188; in civil proceeding, 240
Compurgation, 112
Conard, A., cited, 494
Condemnation, 469
Conference of Commissioners of Uniform Laws, 358
Conference of State Chief Justices, 336, 360
Conference on Administrative Procedure, 457
Confession: coerced, 49, 106; obtained during unlawful detention, 59
Confidential communications, protection against disclosure, 437
Conflict of laws, 244
Confrontation, right to: in criminal proceeding, 13; in court-martial, 524; in employee dismissal proceedings, 476
Congress: contempt of by refusal of committee witness to answer, 311; power over federal court organization, 368; power to punish disobedience of subpoena, 306; regulation of state criminal procedure by, 29
Congressional investigation, witness' privilege in, 308, 310
Connecticut: abandonment of grand jury in, 88; appeal by prosecution in, 131; appointment of prosecutor in, 313; arbitration statute, 551; inquiry by justices of the peace, 74; new trial ordered by legislature, 347
Conscientious objector, procedure for, 486
Consent judgment, 271
Consent to jurisdiction of state, 208
Conservatory remedies, 235
Constitution: as creating private rights of action, 186; initial lack of protection of state criminal defendant, 136
Constitutional Convention, opposition to federal courts in, 7
Constitutional guarantees: applicability to courts-martial, 509; in criminal proceedings, 13, 17
Constitutional provisions for court organization, 367
Consuls, actions involving, 193
Contempt: civil, 165; criminal, 38; of Congress by committee witness refusing to answer question, 113
Continental Congress, review of decisions in prize cases by, 5
Contingent fee, 284
Contract, judgment directing performance of, 164
Contracts clause of Constitution, 331
Control Council for Germany, 541

Controversies between citizens of different states, 8, 199 ff.
Controversies between states, 194; adjudication of under Articles of Confederation, 5
Copyright, jurisdiction of suit to enjoin infringement of, 186
Coroner, 62
Coram nobis, writ of, 124
Corporate affairs, mandatory judgments in, 365
Corporation: as citizen in diversity case, 201; criminal prosecution of, 11; judicial dissolution of, 177; service of process on, 232
Corpus Juris Civilis, 342
Correspondence with foreign government punishable, 19
Costliness: of civil litigation, 282; of criminal defense, 31; of judicial review of administrative adjudication, 443
Costs: imposition of as remedy for delay, 280; recoverable by prevailing party, 285
Council of State Governments, proposal on Supreme Court, 336
Council of the North, 112
Counsel: furnished to indigent defendant at trial, 29; on appeal, 133; incompetence of as ground for vacating conviction, 30; prior consultation with witness, 102; right to: at arraignment, 90, at police interrogation, 46, 47, at preliminary examination, 81, at trial, 28, in administrative adjudicatory proceeding, 435, in general court-martial, 517, 518, 521, in grand jury hearing, 70
Counterclaim, interposition of, 242
County, financial resources of as affecting criminal justice, 45
County court, 369
Court of Chancery, 218 ff.
Court of Claims, 195, 217
Court of Common Pleas, 218
Court of Criminal Appeal (England), power to take additional evidence, 133
Court of Customs and Patent Appeals, 468, 484
Court of Indian Offenses, 19
Court of King's Bench, 131, 217, 342
Court of Military Appeals, 529
Court officers, misbehavior as contempt, 38
Courtroom, size of as affecting trial, 168
Courts: as check on executive, 289, on investigations, 307, on legislation, 314; as molders of law, 338; organization of as related to administration of justice, 367; personnel, 379; power to make rules of procedure, 227
Courts of appeals, review of administrative adjudications by, 449
Courts of law vs. courts of equity, 217
Courts-martial, 508 ff.
Crimes at common law, 21

Criminal contempt proceeding, 38

Criminal procedure, 76 ff.; constitutional framework, 12; role of courts in molding, 363

Criminal proceeding: investigation, 42; prosecution, 76

Criminal record of defendant: cross-examination as to, 107; as cause for waiving jury trial, 115

Cross-examination: in criminal trial, 105; in employee dismissal proceeding, 476

Crosskey, W., cited, 323, 324, 328

Cruel and unusual punishment, prohibition of, 125

Curia Regis, judicial powers of, 149

Cushman, R., cited, 318

Custody of minor, proceeding to determine, 161

Customs, penalties for undervaluation, 424

Customs Court, 468, 469; as constitutional court, 397

Dash, S., cited, 62

Davis, K., cited, 290, 458

Death penalty, 125

Debts, as subject to garnishment, 154

Decedent's estate, distribution of, 153, 174

Decision: following non-jury trial, 260; in administrative adjudication, 438

Declaration of rights in state constitutions, 317

Declaratory judgment action, 164; against public officer, 292; by alien denied admission, 481; in tax matters, 465

Declaratory order in administrative adjudication, 439

Default judgment, 215, 270

Defendant (criminal): cross-examination of on criminal record, 107; failure to take stand, comment on by judge, 121; not compelled to take stand at trial, 106; prospective, exemption from questioning by grand jury, 33, 71

Defense Production Act, 426, 429

Delay: in civil proceedings, 280; in criminal appeals, 134

Demer, R., cited, 559

Demurrer to the evidence, 124

Denaturalization as penalty for crime, 125

Dependent, proceeding to compel support of, 179

Deportation, varieties of, 418

Deportation order: power of adjudicating agency to enforce, 439; review of, 447

Deportation proceeding: development of, 425; issue of citizenship in, 447; need for counsel in, 435

Deposition of witness: in criminal trial, 94; outside jurisdiction, 253

Desegregation of schools, as obligation to authorities, 292

Desegregation suits, government participation in, 168

Dession, G., cited, 69

Detention: of persons suspected of engaging in espionage or sabotage, 305; without arrest, 53; wrongful, remedy for, 162

Detention Review Board, 305

De Tocqueville, A., cited, 334

Dickinson, J., cited, 442

Dimock, E., cited, 31

Diplomatic representatives, immunity from process, 193

Directed verdict of acquittal, 121, 123, 124

Directors, action against, 268

Discovery and inspection, 251

Dismissal of indictment or information, 90

Dismissal of prosecution at instance of prosecutor, 97

Dismissal of public employee, 474

Dissolution of corporation, 176

District of Columbia: as state for diversity jurisdiction, 201; Court of General Sessions, 217; federal judges in, 397; local law in, 356

Diversity of citizenship cases, jurisdiction of, 8, 199 ff.

Divisible divorce, 172, 215

Divorce action, 171; between citizens of different states, 204; jurisdiction of, 214; possible federal jurisdiction of, 249; service by publication in, 235; undefended, investigation of by public officer, 270

Divorce decree, recognition of by sister state, 316

Doing business by corporation, effect of, 210

Domesday Book, 112

Domestic corporation, jurisdiction of, 207

Domicile, significance of, 207

Dorr Rebellion, 298

Double appeal as causing delay, 281

Double jeopardy, 91, 124; in court-martial proceeding, 509; prosecution by both state and federal government as constituting, 20

"Due process of law": early use of phrase, 14; in state criminal proceedings, what constitutes, 16

Due process clause: application to civil procedure, 229, to criminal procedure, 14 ff.; effect on state jurisdiction, 9, 206; vagueness of, 315

Duress as causing confession, 106

Dying declarations, admissibility of, 104

Eavesdropping, electronic, 62; on telephone conversation, 61

Ecclesiastical courts, 217; jurisdiction of decedents' estates, 222; special doctrines of, 343

Ejectment, action in, 160, 220

Elections in private association, judicial intervention in, 177

Electronic eavesdropping, 62
Eleventh Amendment, 195, 320
Elliot's Debates, cited, 322
Emergency Court of Appeals, 291
Emergency Price Control Act of 1942, 291
Emmerich, H., cited, 453
Employer-labor union contract, federal jurisdiction of suits under, 185
Employment agencies, adjudication of claims against, 490
Enemy aliens: prohibition of suits by, 229; seizure of property of, 297
England: civil jury trial in, 263; costs in, 287
Enforcement proceedings, administrative, 422 ff.
Enlisted personnel, eligibility to court-martial membership, 524
"Equal protection of the laws," 14, 333
Equitable vs. legal remedies, 217
Equity court, 217
Equity judgment, appellate review of, 278
Escaped prisoner, extradition of, 85
Espionage, detention of person suspected of engaging in, 305
Evidence: failure to disclose, 168; improperly obtained, exclusion of, 37; permissible types of, 143; in administrative proceeding, 42; in workmen's compensation proceeding, 495
Excessive verdict, setting aside of, 268
Exchanges, arbitration between members of, 550
Exclusion of evidence improperly obtained, 37, 364
Exclusionary rules of evidence, importance of, 77; in administrative proceedings, 407
Execution of money judgment: against person of judgment-debtor, 160; against property of judgment-debtor, 154
Exhaustion of administrative review as prerequisite to judicial review, 443
Ex parte divorce, 215; validity, 257
Ex parte proceeding, 215
Ex parte restraining order, 238
Expert referee as aid to jury trial, 264
Expert testimony, 109, 258; costliness of, 31, 285
Expertness in administrative adjudication, 456
Expulsion of member of private association, 178
Extradition, 81
Extraordinary remedies, 226

Fair Labor Standards Act: enforcement of by injunction, 182; held constitutional, 327; jurisdiction of state courts under, 197; subpoena powers of administrator, 72
Fairman, C., cited, 299, 537, 543
False arrest, action for, 295
Federal Bureau of Investigation, 44

Federal Communications Commission: antimonopoly powers, 426; as regulatory agency, 420; judicial review of orders, 450, 483; jurisdiction of private claims, 489
Federal courts: concurrent jurisdiction of with state courts, 8, 196; criminal procedure in, 74; discharge of state prisoner by in habeas corpus proceeding, 97; examination of prospective jurors in, 120; exclusive jurisdiction of, 9, 184, 192; intervention in state criminal proceedings, 21; judges, 397; jurisdiction in divorce actions, 204, 249; state statute denying access to, 202
Federal criminal proceedings, constitutional guarantees in, 13
Federal employees, workmen's compensation for, 493
Federal enclaves, jurisdiction of offenses in, 18
Federal habeas corpus for state prisoner, 131
Federal Home Loan Bank Board, 483
Federal Maritime Board, 490
Federal law, application of in state courts, 245
Federal offenses, prosecution of in state courts, 27
Federal Power Commission: antimonopoly powers, 426; as regulatory agency, 420; judicial review of orders, 450; jurisdiction of private claims, 489
Federal property, crimes on, 18
Federal question, 3, 272; as a source of delay in appellate process, 134
Federal Reserve Board: antimonopoly powers, 426; judicial review of orders, 450
Federal review of state convictions, 135
Federal rules of civil procedure, 227
Federal rules of criminal procedure, 80; plea of guilty under, 26; provision for expenses of indigent's counsel, 42
Federal Trade Commission: as referee in antitrust suit, 269; complaint to, 490; creation, 426; delay in proceedings before, 457; functions of, 455; investigation by, 72; lack of contempt power, 39; of regulatory functions, 420; penalty for noncompliance with order of, 440; proceeding as dispute between private parties, 497; reasons for establishment, 453; removal of member, 501; review of orders of, 449
Federal troops, use of in domestic disorder, 300
Federalist, cited, 191, 199, 317
Felony as synonymous with infamous crime, 88; distinguished from misdemeanor, 23
Fiduciaries, supervision of, 174
Field Code, 226, 360
Fifth Amendment: due process clause of, 14, 315; self-incrimination clause of, 33, 34

Fine, as compensation to person injured, 12

Fire-fighting authorities, power to destroy property, 297

Fire marshal, 63

Fires, investigation of, 63

Flavin, T., cited, 502

Florida: arbitration statute, 551; Spanish law in, 339

Foreclosure, 158

Foreign Claims Settlement Commission, 498

Foreign corporation, jurisdiction of, 209

Foreign insurance corporation, jurisdiction of state of insured's residence, 213

Foreign law, application of in American courts, 245

Foreign money judgment, enforcement of in U.S., 157

Foreign state, suit against, 19

Forfeiture of property, 177, 296

Fourteenth Amendment: as ground for voiding economic regulations, 321; as not guaranteeing jury trial in the states, 114; as restriction on states, 331; citizenship defined by, 199, 207

Fraenkel, O., cited, 291

France, offenses by members of armed forces, 513

Franchises, 482

Frank, J., cited, 131, 269

Frankel, J., cited, 394

Frankfurter, F., cited, 39

Frankfurter, Justice, cited, 165, 442

Freedom of the press, relation to publicizing of court proceedings, 96, 116

Friendly, H., cited, 355

Fugitive from justice, federal statute punishing, 83

Full faith and credit clause: as applied to conflict of laws, 244; as compelling recognition of sister-state judgment, 206; as to judgments in personam, 157; in Articles of Confederation, 205; in out-of-state enforcement of injunctions and mandatory judgments, 169

Gambling, federal regulation of, 24

Gardner, E., cited, 131

Garnishment, 154

Gellhorn, W., cited, 427, 494, 505

General Counsel of National Labor Relations Board, 496

General verdict, 123, 266, 273

Georgia: defendant not permitted to take stand in, 33; overruling of precedents in, 248

Gerhart, E., cited, 181

German spies, trial of, 540

Germany: military government tribunals in, 546; offenses by members of armed forces of, 513

Getty, G., cited, 31

Goldfarb, R., cited, 116

Goldstein, A., cited, 77

Good behavior, security for, 145

Goodman, T., cited, 547

Goodnow, F., cited, 418

Governor: immunity from judicial control, 82, 183, 297; power, in domestic disorder, 299, in pardon and commutation of sentence, 138, in selection of judges, 383, over local prosecutor, 44

Government contractors: claims by, 497; dismissal of employees by, 416

Grand jury, 67, 88; exclusion of Negroes from, 15; selection of, 406

Grand jury minutes, inspection of, 92

Grand jury witness: compulsory return from out-of-state, 68; privilege against self-incrimination, 70

Great Britain: court-martial jurisdiction, 513; legal aid in civil cases, 284

Griswold, E., cited, 468

Habeas corpus proceeding: as remedy for unlawful detention, 56; by one threatened with extradition, 84; constitutional necessity for, 295; discharge of defendant before trial by, 135; federal, for state prisoner, 136; to determine custody of minor, 161; to procure release from mental institution, 162

Habeas corpus writ: liability of judge refusing to issue, 295; suspension of: in Civil War, 302, 534, in domestic disorder, 299, in Hawaii, 303, 533

Haines, C., cited, 313, 322

Hand, L., cited, 336

Hamilton, Alexander, cited, 199, 317

Harbor employees, workmen's compensation for, 493

Harlan, Justice, cited, 336

Harper, F., cited, 273

Harrington, C., cited, 31

Hawaii: arbitration statute, 551; judicial selection in, 384; martial law in, 308, 535

Hazardous Substances Act, 167

Hazeltine, H., cited, 344

Health authorities, power to destroy property, 297

Health, Education and Welfare Department as adjudicator, 419

Hearing examiner (federal): restrictions on, 432; selection, 461, 503

Hearsay evidence, 37; in administrative proceeding, 437

Hector, L., cited, 420

Henderson, G., cited, 452

High Commission, Court of, 112

High misdemeanor, 23

High seas, jurisdiction of felonies committed on, 19, 20

Hilkey, C., cited, 12

Holmes, Justice, cited, 418

Holtzoff, A., cited, 121

Holdsworth, W., cited, 40

Homestead exemption, 154

Hook, S., cited, 336

Hoover Commission, 460, 461

House of Commons, impeachment by, 149
House of Lords: judicial function of, 149, 342; refusal to reverse holdings, 352
Howrey, E., cited, 456
Hughes, Chief Justice, cited, 448

Illinois: arbitration statute, 551, 555; examination of prospective jurors in, 120
Immunity from prosecution: grant of by administrative agency, 73; legislative investigations, 309; statutes, 36; waiver of, 71
Impeachment proceedings, 149
Inadequate verdict, setting aside of, 268
Inbau, F., cited, 50
Income tax law of 1892, 187
Income tax statutes, records required by, 73
Incompetence of witness, 104
Incompetency, adjudication of, 173
Indemnity: for wrongful conviction, 140; to person wrongfully detained on suspicion of espionage or sabotage, 305
Indeterminate sentence, 127
Indian Claims Commission, 498
Indian reservations, crimes on, 19
Indiana, discretion in sentencing in, 127
Indictment: copy of furnished to accused, 93; necessity for, 88; waiver of, 89
Indigent defendant: provision of trial counsel for, 29; right to appellate review, 133; to counsel in preliminary examination, 81; waiver of grand jury action by, 89
Infamous crime, 88
Infant, supervision of estate of or transaction with, 175
Information, as criminal accusation, 86
Informer, entitled to share in penalty, 153
Injunction, 162; against federal official, 187; against unconstitutional statute, 198; enforcement outside jurisdiction, 211; in labor dispute, jury trial in contempt proceeding for violation of, 167; temporary (or preliminary), 236
Inquest by coroner, 62
Inquisitorial method, 102
In rem proceeding for forfeiture of property used illegally, 177
Insanity, plea of, 90
Insolvent, supervision of estate of, 153, 175
Insolvency laws, 175
Inspection of grand jury minutes, 92
Inspection of premises, necessity of warrant, 61
Insurance claims: arbitration in, 559; controversy between claimants, 203
Insurrection, use of troops to suppress, 298
Instructions to jury, 121, 266; appellate review of, 132, 276

Interference proceeding, 489
Internal Revenue Service, review of determinations of, 468
International Military Tribunal in Germany, 541; in Japan, 542
Interpleader proceeding, 203
Interstate commerce: states not to burden, 315; vs. commerce among the states, 328
Interstate Commerce Commission: anti-monopoly powers, 426; approval of railroad reorganization by, 176, 498; as regulatory agency, 517; jurisdiction of shippers' claims, 420, 489; penalty for noncompliance with orders of, 440; rate regulation by, 471; review of orders by district courts, 449
Investigation: by administrative agencies, 71; by judicial officer, 73; precedent to general court-martial, 516
Iowa, judicial selection in, 384, 391

Jackson, Andrew, refusal to honor writ of habeas corpus, 301
Jackson, Justice, cited, 117, 165, 304
Janewicz, J., cited, 382
Japan, status of forces agreement with, 513
Japanese ancestry, relocation of persons of, 306, 536
Jenner bill, 327
Jeopardy assessment, 466
Judge: disposition of current cases as prerequisite to payment of salary, 281; examination of prospective jurors by, 120; improper conduct of, 216; popular election of, 79; power to question witnesses, 101; to comment on evidence, 121; role in sentencing, 128
Judges, federal. See Federal judges
Judges, state. See State judges
Judgment-creditor, 153
Judgment-creditor's action, 155
Judgment-debtor, arrest of, 160
Judicial Committee of Privy Council, 344
Judicial councils, 79, 372
Judicial notice, 143
Judicial review of administrative adjudication: availability, 440; mechanism, 448; scope, 444
Judicial review of legislation, 313 ff.
Judiciary Act of 1789, 7, 79, 188, 319, 322
Juge d'instruction, 66, 74
Jurisdiction: in civil proceedings, 84 ff.; of crimes, 18; of party to arbitration agreement, 552
Juror, right to question witness, 101
Jury: as related to development of rules of evidence, 103; influence of on procedure, 226; power to fix penalty, 126, 129; selection, 119, 403
Jury trial in civil cases, 261 ff.
Jury trial: in criminal contempt proceeding, 40, 113, 237; in petty offenses, 143;

origin and development, 111; waiver of, in contracts, 261; in criminal cases, 114

Justice Department: advice on mergers given by, 183; as adjudicator, 419; role in school desegregation litigation, 167; subpoena power in antitrust investigations, 72

Justice of the peace: as coroner, 63; development of office of, 141; holding of preliminary examination by, 81

Juvenile courts, 373

Juvenile offenders, proceedings against, 146

Karlen, D., cited, 509

Kent, James, 346

Kidnaping as federal offense, 20

Knowlton, R., cited, 62

Knox, J., cited, 181

Kroner, J., cited, 562

Labor arbitration, 561

Labor dispute injunction, 163, 237; federal, 201; jury trial for violation of, 167

Labor disputes, proposed adjudication of, 181

Labor Management Relations Act, 163, 232

Labor-Management Reporting and Disclosure Act, 167, 178

Labor organizations: enforceability of contracts, 181; federal jurisdiction of action for breach of contract with employer, 185; regulation of elections in, 178; service of process on, 232

Lacey, F., cited, 54

Laches, 119

LaFollette Amendment, 326

Landis, J., cited, 39, 420, 500

Landrum-Griffin Act, 178

Lauer, L., cited, 494, 505

Law guardian for juvenile offender, N. Y. law providing for, 148

Law officer in court-martial, 519; as independent judge-advocate in Army court-martial, 527

Law of nations, jurisdiction of offenses against, 18

Law of the forum, 243

"Law of the land," in early state constitutions, 14

Law revision, governmental agencies for, 355

Law vs. equity, 279

Lawyers, 407; in arbitration proceedings, 560

Laws of war, trial of offenses against, 538

Laymen, admission to practice before administrative tribunals, 505

Lee, L., cited, 395

Legal vs. equitable remedies, 217 ff.

Legislative apportionment, judicial review of, 334

Legislature as court, 345; power to authorize investigations, 308

Letters rogatory, 254

Levie, H., cited, 513

Lewis, A., cited, 400

Libel and slander, judgment ordering retraction of, 165

License revocation by administrative agencies, 423

Lien: enforcement of, 158; of judgment, 153

Liliburne, trial of, 113

Lincoln, President: creation of military commissions by, 534; on Supreme Court, 435; suspension of habeas corpus by, 302; trial of alleged conspirators in assassination of, 529

Lindbergh law, 125

Lindeman, F., cited, 173

Line-up, 50

Liquor licensing, 427

Local courts, 370

London Agreement, 541

Longshoremen, workmen's compensation for, 473

Lottery, denial of mail to, 424

Louisiana: arbitration statute, 551; civil procedure, 225; decree of specific performance in, 164; grand jury in, 88; jury, in civil cases, 269, in criminal cases, 123; privilege against self-incrimination of public officials, 71; Spanish and French law in, 339

Lowndes, C., cited, 468

Loyalty board procedure, 476

Lump-sum award in personal injury claims, 259, 282

Magistrate, discretion in sentence for petty offense, 145

Magna Carta, 113

Malpractice actions, 258

Mandamus proceeding, 165, 221

Mandatory judgment, 164; administrative order analogous to, 428; enforcement of outside jurisdiction, 168

Manual for Courts-Martial, 514

Maritime cases, jurisdiction of, 188

Marshall, Chief Justice, 325

Marshals, federal, enforcement of law by, 168

Martial law in domestic disorder, 298

Maryland: judicial selection in, 384; waiver of jury in, 115

Massachusetts: arbitration statute, 551, 555; as source of legal doctrine, 351; life tenure of judges in, 383

Material witness, arrest of, 552

Matrimonial actions, 170, 213

Maurer, D., cited, 115

Mayers, L., cited, 35, 65, 249, 256

McBratney, W., cited, 519

McIntyre, D., cited, 173

McKay, R., cited, 476

McWhinney, E., cited, 313

Meagher, T., cited, 527
Mears, T., cited, 189
Medical examiner, 63
Medical issues, proof on, 259
Mental competency of criminal defendant, 100
Mental institution, release from, 162
Mergers, advice of Department of Justice on, 183
Mexican War, military government tribunals in, 546
Michigan: arbitration statute, 551; one-man grand jury, 75
Middle-class defendant, appeal costs as a burden on, 133
Migratory divorce, 249
Military commissions: in domestic violence, 536; in war, 533
Military government tribunals, 546
Militia: power of President to use to enforce federal law, 168; use of in domestic disorder, 297
Miner, J., cited, 256
Minnesota, arbitration statute, 551
Minor, judgment awarding custody of, 161
Misdemeanor, distinguished from felony, 23
Mississippi, use of troops to enforce court order in, 168
Missouri, judicial selection board in, 391
Model Judicial Article, 368
Model State Administrative Procedure Act, 434
Money judgment: action for, 152; collection of, 156 ff.
Morgan, E., cited, 529
Montgomery, R., cited, 269
Morris, Gouverneur, 322
Motor vehicle operation in state as giving jurisdiction of non-resident, 211
Motor vehicle operator licensing, 427
Mueller, G., cited, 47
Multi-judge trial court, 265
Mummey, R., cited, 527
Murphy, Justice, cited, 404

Narcotics seller: as federal offender, 21; ineligible to probation, 126
National Commission on Law Observance, cited, 457
National Guard, courts-martial in, 508
National Industrial Recovery Act, invalidation of, 326
National Labor Relations Act, 426, 428, 430; held constitutional, 327
National Labor Relations Board: adjudicatory character, 419, 454; as complainant in private dispute, 490, 496; exclusion of cases by, 433; General Counsel, 454; judicial review of orders, 450; labor-management contest over appointments to, 501
NATO status of forces agreement, 513

Navigable waters of the U.S., definition of, 190
Nebraska: judicial selection in, 384, 391; special majority required to declare statute void, 318
Negotiable Instruments Act, 359, 360
Negroes: exclusion from jury, 15, 118; voting rights, 183
New Deal, invalidation of statutes of, 326
New Hampshire: arbitration statute, 551; judicial tenure in, 383
New Jersey: arbitration statute, 551; assignment of counsel to indigent defendants, 31; integration of courts, 372; lay members of highest court in, 381; power of appellate court to take additional testimony, 133; rule-making power, 228; school segregation in, 335; tax court, 467
New Mexico: defeat of judicial board selection proposal in, 391; workmen's compensation adjudication in, 492
New Orleans, Spanish and French law in, 339
New trial on ground of newly discovered evidence, 124, 271
New York: arbitration statute, 551; as source of legal doctrine, 351; code of civil procedure, 226, of criminal procedure, 79, of military justice, 508; Court of Errors, 345; grant of immunity by administrative agency, 309; guardian law for juvenile offender in, 148; legislators as members of appellate court, 320; privilege against self-incrimination of public officials, 71; reception of English law in, 340; removal of governor for acts antedating office, 154; right to counsel at police interrogation, 47; school segregation in, 335; separate jury trial on capital sentence, 130; youthful offender law, 148
New York (city): arbitration in small claims court, 560; bail experiment in, 48
Nobleman, E., cited, 547
Nolo contendere, plea of, 91
Nonpartisan selection of judges, 389
Non-resident defendant: jurisdiction of, 209, 211 ff.; service of process on, 231
Norris-LaGuardia Act, 163; hearing on injunction, 237; on temparary restraining order, 238; jury trial on charge of violating injunction, 167
North Dakota, special majority required to declare statute void, 318
Not guilty verdict, significance of, 123
Notice pleading, 240

Oath, sanctity of, 155
Obscene matter, denial of mail delivery to sender, 424
Occupational licenses, 481; revocation as penalty for crime, 125

Occupational license boards: appointment of members of, 501; power to revoke license, 423, 428; official notice, 437

Official referee, 280

Ohio: arbitration statute, 551; code of military justice, 508; special majority required to declare statute void, 318

Oklahoma, court of criminal appeals, 377

Ombudsman, 290

"One-man grand jury," 74

Oral testimony, 104; absence of in certain administrative proceedings, 495

Ordeal, trial by, 112

Oregon: arbitration statute, 551; tax court, 467

Orfield, L., cited, 93

Pardon, 138

Parole, 139

Parole board, 128, 139

Partnership, dissolution of by court, 176

Partition of property held jointly, 176

Passport, grant of, 478

Patent, proceeding for, 484

Patent infringement action: jurisdiction of, 186; two-stage trial in, 255

Patent Office, as judge of priority of invention, 418, 489

Peck, D., cited, 385

Pedigree, English inquiry procedure, 256

Penalty, civil action for, 125, 153, 186

Pennsylvania: arbitration, 221, 551; separte jury trial on capital sentence, 130; special body to note unconstitutional legislation, 317

Pension proceeding, 487

Pepper, L., cited, 509

Peremptory challenge to juror, 120

Permit, proceeding to obtain, 478

Person non sui juris, supervision of estate of, 174

Personal injury claims: administrative vs. judicial adjudication, 492 ff.; delay by parties in, 282; medical issues in, 258; proposed special courts for, 373; substitution of compensation for negligence as basis, 410; workmen's compensation for, 492

Personal judgment, 177

Personal property, 222

Personnel: of administrative tribunals, 499; of courts, 379

Petitions of grace, 217

Petty offense: defined, 22; prosecution of, 140

Piracy, jurisdiction of, 18

Plea of guilty: importance of, 24; not permitted, 90; to lesser offense than charged, 25

Pleading procedure, 243

Police: local organization of, 44; power of courts to discipline, 296; questioning of persons in custody by, 45 ff.; relation of to prosecutor, 42

Police (state), investigative function of, 44

Pope, W., cited, 468

Postal service, investigative agency in, 43

Post-conviction proceeding, 134

Postmaster General: lack of regulatory power, 454; refusal of mail delivery by, 429

Pound, R., cited, 90

Precedent, role of, 347

Preliminary examination, 32, 63, 80; as prerequisite to information, 87; disclosure of prosecution's evidence in, 93; requirement of prompt production of suspect for, 52

Preliminary injunction, 236

President: exemption from court proceedings, 290; power as commander-in-chief, 301; to approve international air route, 484, to enforce law and court orders, 168, to prescribe regulations in domestic disorder, 300; powers under code of military justice, 511

President's Committee on Administrative Management, cited, 459

Presumptions, in criminal trial, 107, 153

Pretrial examination of issues, 256

Pretrial publicity, 95

Preventive arrest, 298

Primary jurisdiction doctrine, 491

Private associations, judicial control of, 177

Privilege against self-incrimination, 32, 43; in court-martial, 522; in grand jury investigation, 69; in investigation by administrative agency, 73; in preliminary examination, 64

Privileges and immunities clause, as giving right to sue, 229

Privy Council: adjudication of boundary disputes between colonies, 194; as check on colonial courts, 13, 344; veto of colonial statutes by, 344

Prize cases, adjudication under Articles of Confederation, 5

Probate courts, 222

Probate of will, 173

Probation, 126

Professional juror, 404

Prosecutor: influence in sentencing, 127; investigative function, 44; power to file information, 87; questioning of persons in custody, 45; relation to police, 42; selection, 411; state control of, 44

Prostitution as criminal offense, 142

Provisional remedies, 235

Public defender, 30

Public employee, dismissal or demotion, 473

Public housing, judicial check on allocation of, 294

Public ministers, cases affecting, 192

Public officer: civil proceeding against, 291; waiver of immunity by, 71

Public trial, 110; absence of in juvenile delinquency proceeding, 147
Public utility corporation, condemnation by, 470
Publication: contempt by, 40; of evidence before trial, 95; service of process by, 233
Publicity during criminal trial, 115
Puerto Rico: jury trial, 114, 261; local law, 356; tenure of federal judge, 397
Putzel, C., cited, 292

Questioning of persons in custody, 45
"Quickie divorce" states; reason for resorting to, 249; residence requirement in, 207

Racial segregation, prohibited by Fourteenth Amendment, 333
Radio broadcast of criminal trial, 111
Railroad, jurisdiction of suit against, 210
Railroad reorganization, approval by Interstate Commerce Commission, 178
Railway Labor Act, 562
Randolph, plan for constitution, 199
Rankin, A., cited, 48
Rankin, R., cited, 299, 537
Rapson, I., cited, 520
Rate regulation as adjudication, 471
Real estate: lien of judgment on, 153; jurisdiction of suits affecting, 208; specific performance of contract for sale of, 164
Reasonable doubt, 110
Recall of judges, 394
Receiver: in partnership dissolution or in bankruptcy, 239; to collect income of judgment-debtor's property, 155
Recess appointments, 402
Reciprocal state legislation: for compulsory attendance of witnesses, 68; for enforcement of support, 179; for extradition of criminals, 84
Redlich, N., cited, 308
Reed, Justice, cited, 365
Referee (federal), to register voter discriminated against, 293
Referee to try issues, 260
Regional appellate courts, 374
Regulatory agency, defined, 419
Religion, freedom of protected against states by Fourteenth Amendment, 333
Removal of judge: federal, 400; state, 392; of member of administrative tribunal, 500
Removal to federal court: action against federal officers, 205; case arising under federal statute, 198; criminal case, 96
Rent-control laws, 490
Rent-control proceedings, absence of oral testimony in, 495
Reparation order, 420, 495
Replevin, 160, 220
Res judicata, 246
Residence in state, test of, 199, 207

Restatements of the law, 362
Retroactivity of rules of criminal procedure promulgated by courts, 366
Revised Statutes of United States, 362
Rheinstein, M., cited, 513
Rhode Island: arbitration statute, 551; Dorr Rebellion, 298; life tenure of judges in, 383
Rich, S., cited, 389
Roberts, Justice, cited, 349
Robinson, J., cited, 542
Roman law: contributions to English law, 342, to procedural rules, 226
Roosevelt, President: authorization of military area control, 303; proposal to enlarge Supreme Court, 326; removal of Commissioner Humphrey, 50
Rosenberry, M., cited, 471
Rostow, E., cited, 305, 409
Rules of decision act, 356
Rules of evidence, 103, 235, 495
Runaway grand jury, 69

Sabotage, detention of person suspected of engaging in, 305
Sales Act, 359
Sass, F., cited, 497
Satisfaction (satisfaction-piece), 153
Schlesinger, A., cited, 344
School desegregation decision, 334, 335; enforcement of judgment, 167; institution of suit by federal officials, 183
Scotland, Roman law in, 342
Schwartz, B., cited, 461
Schwartz, R., cited, 62
Seaman, clearance required by, 482
Searches: constitutional restrictions upon, 57; in connection with arrest, 60
Search warrant, 58 ff.
Secretary of Agriculture: adjudicatory powers, 426; judicial review of orders, 450; jurisdiction of private claims, 489; reparation order by, 495
Secretary of Labor: power to declare government contractor ineligible, 435; suit by to void labor organization election, 178
Secured debt, obtaining payment of, 158
Securities Act, 426; jurisdiction of state courts under, 198
Securities and Exchange Commission, 426; acceleration order by, 485; judicial review of orders, 450; role in corporate reorganization proceeding, 176
Segregation, racial, prohibited by Fourteenth Amendment, 333
Seizures, constitutional limitations upon, 57
Selective Service System, 485
Self-incrimination privilege. See Privilege against self-incrimination
Sentence, 125; commutation of, 138
Separation, action for, 173, 213
Separation of church and state, required by Fourteenth Amendment, 333

Service of process, 231
Severance of issues for trial, 254
Sherman Antitrust Act, 350
Skoler, D., cited, 382
Small Business Administration, 244
Small claims court: arbitration in, 560; evidence in, 235; use of forms, 492
Smith, B., cited, 44
Smith, R., cited, 283
Standing: to challenge constitutionality of statute, 396; to sue, 230, 293
Star Chamber, Court of, 112
Social Security Act, 488
Sovereignty of state, 206
Special court-martial, 520
Special master, 260
Special pleading, 242
Special verdict: in civil case, 268, 273; in criminal case, 123
Specialized courts: trial courts, 372; appellate courts, 377
Specific performance of contract, judgment directing, 216
Speedy trial, constitutional guarantee of, 98
Spanish-American War, military government tribunals in, 546
Spurlock, P., cited, 544
Star Chamber, 78
Stare decisis, 348
Stark, F., cited, 45
State, Department of, as adjudicator, 419
State Judges, selection, etc., 381 ff.
State judicial review of legislation, 316
State law, application of in federal court, 245
State supervision of local police, 296
Status of forces agreement, 513
Stay of execution, 279
Stockholder's action, 204, 230; notice to stockholders of proposed consent judgment, 271
Story, Joseph, 346; cited, 14
Struck jury, 119
Sturz, H., cited, 48
Subpoena: of Federal Trade Commission, penalty for disobedience, 72; of investigative agency, 63, 73, 306 ff.
Subpoena power, as to citizens abroad, 68
Substituted service of process, 209
Subversive Activities Control Board, 426, 450
Summary court-martial, 520, 521
Summary judgment, 250
Summary proceeding for punishment of petty offenses, extension of, 143
Summing-up, 120
Sunderland, E., cited, 395
Supplementary proceedings, 155
Support: action for by ex-wife, 247; of dependent, proceeding to compel, 179
Suppression of evidence, 100, 109
Supremacy clause of Constitution, 319

Supreme Court: absence of divisional organization, 376; adjudication of disputes between states by, 196; appellate jurisdiction, proposal to define by constitutional provision, 327; as arbiter of state jurisdiction, 206; authorized to make rules of procedure, civil, 227, criminal, 80; created by Congress, 6; historic role of, 327; independent determination of voluntariness of confession by, 49; jurisdiction, 6; justices, 401; overruling of precedents by, 349; permission required for review by, 274; recess appointments to, 402; regulation of state criminal procedure by, 16 ff., 332, 363 ff.; size, proposal to enlarge, 326, to fix by constitutional provision, 326; withdrawal of appellate jurisdiction of, 325
Surprise, 92, 257
Suspect: rights of, 33, 45, 71; in court-martial, 520
Suspension of sentence, 126
Sutherland, E., cited, 12, 115
Swisher, C., cited, 535

Taft-Hartley Act, 163, 186, 232, 350, 557
Taney, Chief Justice, 302
Tax officials, power to compel testimony and production of records, 72
Taxes, federal injunction against, 187, 198
Taxpayer, standing to challenge governmental disbursement, 187, 314
Taxpayer's action, 230, 293
Technicality in criminal procedure, 77
Telephone conversation, unauthorized interception of, 61
Television broadcast of criminal trial, 111
Temporary injunction, 236
Ten Broeck, J., cited, 305
Tenure: of judges, federal, 400, of Court of Military Appeals, 530, state, 382; of members of administrative tribunals, 500
Texas: action for unjust discharge in, 159; as sovereign state, 206; court of criminal appeals, 377; Spanish law in, 339; special verdict in, 270
Third degree, 47
Three-judge federal court, 187, 198
Traffic violations, plea of guilty without personal appearance, 140
Treason: challenges allowed in trial, 120; death penalty for, 125
Treasury Department: as adjudicator, 419; investigative agencies in, 44
Treaty, as giving right to sue, 230
Trial by battle and by ordeal, 112
Trial courts: defined, 368; organization, 368
Trial de novo: in civil cases, 272; in petty offenses, 145; in workmen's compensation cases, 493

Trustee: in bankruptcy, 239; in corporate reorganization, 239; payment of money misappropriated by, 154
Two-stage trial, 254

Ubbelohde, C., cited, 189
Unanimity: requirement of for verdict in civil cases, 267, in court-martial, 519, in criminal trials, 127
Unconstitutional laws, list of, 327
Uniform Code of Military Justice, 510
Uniform Commercial Code, 359
Uniform Criminal Extradition Act, 84
Uniform laws, commissioners of, 358
Uniform Reciprocal Enforcement of Support Act, 179
Uniformity of state law, 356
Unincorporated association, service of process on, 232
Union Pacific Railroad Company, 210
U.S. as party, 193
U.S. attorney, 44
U.S. Commision on Civil Rights, cited, 47
U.S. Code, 362
U.S. commissioner, 53, 81
U.S. High Commissioner for Germany, 546
U.S. Tax Court, 467
Unlawful arrest, liability of officer making, 56
Unlawful detention: habeas corpus as remedy for, 56; use of by police and prosecutor, 51
Unreasonable searches and seizures, constitutional prohibition of, 57
Unsecured debt, action for payment, 153
Utility rates, federal injunction against, 198

Vagrancy as criminal offense, 54
Vanderbilt Report, 207
Vehicle, search of, 59
Veniremen, 118
Venue, 223; change of, 94
Verdict: appellate review of judgment entered on, 273; direction of, 121, 267; form of, 123, 266; vote required for, 123, 267; setting aside of by judge, 123, 267
Vermont: appeal by prosecution in, 131; judge's term of office in, 383; special body to note unconstitutional legislation, 317
Vessel: "arrest of," 233; bringing in diseased immigrant, penalty, 424; search of, 59
Veterans' Administration, 488
Virgin Islands, local law, 356, 363
Voluntary arbitration tribunals, 549 ff.
Voir dire, 119
Vom Baur, T., cited, 506
Von Mehren, A., cited, 380
Voting rights: of Negroes, 1957 statute protecting, 183; racial discrimination in, 293

Wages, garnishment of, 154
Wages and Hours Law: enforcement of by injunction, 182; investigation under, 72; jurisdiction of state courts under, 197
Wagner Act, 426
Waite, J., cited, 47, 52, 77, 365
Waiver: of immunity by grand jury witness, 71; of indictment, 89; of jury trial, 114, 261; of preliminary examination, 66
Walsh-Healy Act, 428
War, judicial check on power of executive during, 301
War crimes tribunals, American, 539, 543; international, 541
War Relocation Authority, 303
Ward, C., cited, 528
Warehouse Act, 426
Warehouse Receipts Act, 359
Warren, Chief Justice, cited, 35, 509
Warren, C., cited, 21
Washington, arbitration statute, 551
"Watchdog" grand jury, 69
Wayward minors, proceedings against, 148
Wechsler, H., cited, 336
Weinstein, J., cited, 256
Wellington, H., cited, 351
West Virginia, military commission in, 537
Whipping as punishment, 125
White slave trade as federal offense, 30
Wiener, F., cited, 376, 527
Wigmore, J., cited, 35, 36, 65
Will: jurisdiction of controversies relating to, 208; probate of, 173
Winters, G., cited, 65
Wiretapping, 61
Wisconsin, arbitration statute, 551
Witness: arrest of, 55; effect of trial setting on, 110; outside jurisdiction, deposition of, 94, 253; obligation to testify, 68; power of administrative tribunal to compel appearance and answer, 435; refusal to answer as criminal offense, 39; unreliability of testimony of, 99
Witnesses: confrontation of, 104; disclosure of identity of by prosecutor, 93
Wool Labelling Act, blacklist under, 429
Workmen's compensation proceedings, 492; absence of jury in, 263; instalment award in, 159
Wormuth, F., cited, 389
Wright, B., cited, 321
Wrongful conviction, indemnity for, 140
Wyoming, arbitration statute, 551
Wyzanski, C., cited, 373

Youthful offenders' federal procedure in sentencing, 128; New York law regarding, 148; proceedings against, 146

Zal, F., cited, 261